microsoft® office powerpoint®
A Professional Approach

POWERPOINT 2007

Pat R. Graves

Amie Mayhall

McGraw-Hill
Higher Education

Boston   Burr Ridge, IL   Dubuque, IA   New York   San Francisco   St. Louis
Bangkok   Bogotá   Caracas   Kuala Lumpur   Lisbon   London   Madrid   Mexico City
Milan   Montreal   New Delhi   Santiago   Seoul   Singapore   Sydney   Taipei   Toronto

 McGraw-Hill
Higher Education

MICROSOFT® OFFICE POWERPOINT® 2007: A PROFESSIONAL APPROACH
Published by McGraw-Hill, a business unit of The McGraw-Hill Companies, Inc., 1221 Avenue of
the Americas, New York, NY, 10020. Copyright © 2008 by The McGraw-Hill Companies, Inc. All
rights reserved. No part of this publication may be reproduced or distributed in any form or by
any means, or stored in a database or retrieval system, without the prior written consent of The
McGraw-Hill Companies, Inc., including, but not limited to, in any network or other electronic
storage or transmission, or broadcast for distance learning.

Some ancillaries, including electronic and print components, may not be available to customers
outside the United States.

This book is printed on acid-free paper.

2 3 4 5 6 7 8 9 0 BAN/BAN 0 9

ISBN   978-0-07-351918-0 (student edition)
MHID   0-07-351918-9 (student edition)
ISBN   978-0-07-329461-2 (annotated instructor edition)
MHID   0-07-329461-6 (annotated instructor edition)

Vice President/Editor in Chief: *Elizabeth Haefele*
Vice President/Director of Marketing: *John E. Biernat*
Publisher: *Linda Schreiber*
Associate sponsoring editor: *Janna Martin*
Developmental editor I: *Alaina Grayson*
Marketing manager: *Sarah Wood*
Lead media producer: *Damian Moshak*
Media producer: *Marc Mattson*
Director, Editing/Design/Production: *Jess Ann Kosic*
Senior project manager: *Rick Hecker*
Senior production supervisor: *Janean A. Utley*
Designer: *Marianna Kinigakis*
Senior photo research coordinator: *Jeremy Cheshareck*
Media project manager: *Mark A. S. Dierker*
Cover design: *Asylum Studios*
Interior design: *JoAnne Schopler, Graphic Visions*
Typeface: *10.5/13 New Aster*
Compositor: *Aptara*
Printer: *R. R. Donnelley*

Library of Congress Cataloging-in-Publication Data

Graves, Pat R.
  Microsoft Office PowerPoint 2007 : a professional approach / Pat. R. Graves.
    p. cm.
  Includes index.
  ISBN-13: 978-0-07-351918-0 (student edition : alk. paper)
  ISBN-10: 0-07-351918-9 (student edition : alk. paper)
  ISBN-13: 978-0-07-329461-2 (annotated instructor edition : alk. paper)
  ISBN-10: 0-07-329461-6 (annotated instructor edition : alk. paper)
    1. Presentation graphics software. 2. Microsoft PowerPoint (Computer file) I. Title.
T385.G737445 2008
005.5'8–dc22

                                                                    2007014889

www.mhhe.com

contents

POWERPOINT

Unit 1 Basic Skills

Unit 2 Presentation Illustration

Unit 3 Visual Impact

Unit 4 Development and Distribution

Approved Courseware

What Does This Logo Mean?

The logo means this courseware has been approved by the Microsoft® Office Certification Program to be among the finest available for learning *Microsoft® Office PowerPoint® 2007*. It also means that if you complete and fully understand this courseware, you will be prepared to take an exam certifying your proficiency in this application.

What Is a Microsoft Office Specialist?

A Microsoft Office Specialist is an individual who has passed exams that certify his or her skills in one or more of the Microsoft Office desktop applications such as Microsoft Word, Microsoft Excel, Microsoft PowerPoint, Microsoft Outlook, or Microsoft Access. The Microsoft Office Specialist Program is the only program in the world approved by Microsoft for testing proficiency in Microsoft Office desktop applications. This testing program can be a valuable asset in any job search or career advancement.

More Information

To learn more about becoming a Microsoft Office Specialist, visit www.microsoft.com/officespecialist.

The availability of Microsoft Office certification exams varies by application, application version, and language. Visit the site listed above for exam availability.

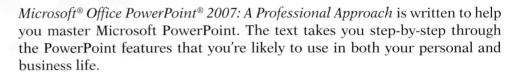

Microsoft® Office PowerPoint® 2007: A Professional Approach is written to help you master Microsoft PowerPoint. The text takes you step-by-step through the PowerPoint features that you're likely to use in both your personal and business life.

Case Study

Learning about the features of PowerPoint is one thing, but applying what you learn is another. That's why a Case Study runs through the text. The Case Study offers the opportunity to learn PowerPoint in a realistic business context. Take the time to read the Case Study about Good 4 *U*, a fictional business located in New York City. All the documents for this course involve Good 4 *U*.

Organization of the Text

The text includes four units. Each unit is divided into smaller lessons. The 14 lessons are each self-contained, but they build on previously learned procedures. This building block approach, together with the Case Study and the features listed next, enables you to maximize the learning process.

Features of the Text

- Objectives are listed for each lesson.
- Required skills for the Microsoft Certification Exam are listed for each lesson.
- The estimated time required to complete each lesson up to the Lesson Applications section is stated.
- Within a lesson, each heading corresponds to an objective.
- Easy-to-follow exercises emphasize learning by doing.
- Key terms are italicized and defined as they are encountered.
- Extensive graphics display screen contents.
- Toolbar buttons and keyboard keys are shown in the text when used.
- Large toolbar buttons in the margins provide easy-to-see references.
- Lessons contain important Notes, useful Tips, and helpful Reviews.
- A Lesson Summary reviews the important concepts taught in the lesson.
- A Command Summary lists the commands taught in the lesson.
- Concepts Review includes true/false, short answer, and critical thinking questions that focus on lesson content.
- Skills Review provides skill reinforcement for each lesson.
- Lesson Applications ask you to apply your skills in a more challenging way.
- On Your Own exercises let you apply your skills creatively.
- Unit Applications give you the opportunity to use the skills you learn throughout a unit.
- An Appendix of Microsoft's certification standards, a Glossary, and an Index are included.

Microsoft Office Certification Program

The Microsoft Office certification program offers certification for each application, and an overall Office Specialist option once enough exams have been passed. This certification can be a valuable asset in any job search. For more information about this Microsoft program, go to www.microsoft.com/officespecialist. For a complete listing of the skills for the PowerPoint 2007 certification exam and a correlation to the lessons in the text, see the Appendix: Microsoft Office Certification.

Professional Approach Web Site

Visit the Professional Approach Web site at www.mhhe.com/pas07 to access a wealth of additional materials.

Conventions Used in the Text

This text uses a number of conventions to help you learn the program and save your work.

- Text to be keyed appears either in **red** or as a separate figure.
- Filenames appear in **boldface.**
- Options that you choose from tabs and dialog boxes, but that aren't buttons, appear in green; for example, "Choose Print from the Office menu."
- You're asked to save each document with your initials followed by the exercise name. For example, and exercise might end with this instruction: "Save the document as *[your initials]*5-12" Documents are saved in folders for each lesson.

If You Are Unfamiliar with Windows

If you're unfamiliar with Windows, review the "Windows Tutorial" available on the Professional Approach Web site at www.mhhe.com/pas07 before beginning Lesson 1. This tutorial provides a basic overview of Microsoft's operating system and shows you how to use the mouse. You might also want to review "File Management" to get more comfortable with files and folders.

Screen Differences

As you practice each concept, illustrations of the screens help you follow the instructions. Don't worry if your screen is different from the illustration. These differences are due to variations in system and computer configurations.

installation requirements

You'll need Microsoft PowerPoint 2007 to work through this textbook. PowerPoint needs to be installed on the computer's hard drive or on a network. Use the following checklists to evaluate installation requirements.

Hardware

- Computer with 500MHz or higher processor and at least 256MB of RAM.
- CD-ROM drive and other external media (3.5-inch high-density floppy, ZIP, etc.).
- 1.5GB or more of hard disk space for a "Student" Office installation.
- 1024 × 768 or higher-resolution video monitor.
- Printer (laser or ink-jet recommended).
- Mouse.
- Modem or other Internet connection.

Software

- PowerPoint 2007 (from Microsoft Office Systems 2007).
- Windows XP with Service Pack 2 or later, or Windows Vista or later operating system.
- Browser and Internet access.

Installing New Features

FEATURE	USE	HOW TO INSTALL/USE
Student data files	Build a new document based on a template.	Copy template files to C:\Users\\UserName\ AppData\Roaming\Microsoft\Templates for files to appear on the My Templates tab of the New dialog box.
Clip Art additional	Use clip art related to the case.	Copy image files to any usable folder.
Templates (Spreadsheet Solutions)	Build a new document based on template.	Part of typical installation; files are in C:\Program Files\Microsoft Office 11\Templates\1033.
Internet functionality	Use online help, use online Template Gallery, use additional research tools, view Web pages.	Specific to classroom.
Language tools	Use thesaurus and translation tools in the Research task pane.	Part of a typical installation for Office 2007 Professional. Install if/when prompted at first use. May require installation CD.

FEATURE	USE	HOW TO INSTALL/USE
Visual Basic Editor	View, edit, and save macros.	Part of a typical installation for Office 2007 Professional. Install if/when prompted. May require installation CD.
Digital Signature	Create a digital signature.	Part of a typical installation for Office 2007 Professional. Listed under Microsoft Office Button, Prepare. Create a digital ID on first use.
Goal Seek	Perform what-if analysis.	Part of a typical installation for Office 2007 Professional.
Solver	Perform what-if analysis.	Choose Microsoft Office Button, Excel Options, Add-Ins. Choose Analysis ToolPak and then Solver Add-in. Click OK.
Microsoft Query	Import a database file.	Part of a typical installation for Office 2007 Professional. Install if/when prompted. May require installation CD.
Notepad or WordPad	Open text files.	Part of typical Vista installation.
XPS/PDF Add-in	Save files in XPS or PDF format.	

If you are not familiar with Windows, review this "Windows Tutorial" carefully. You will learn how to

- Use a mouse.
- Start Windows.
- Use the taskbar, menus, Ribbon, dialog boxes, and other important aspects of Windows.

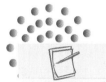

NOTE

All examples in this tutorial refer specifically to Windows Vista. If you are using any other version of Windows, your screen might differ slightly from the images shown in this tutorial. However, because most basic features are common to all versions of Windows, this tutorial should be helpful to you no matter which version of Windows you use.

If you are familiar with Windows but need help navigating Windows files and folders, refer to the section "File Management." There you will find information on how Windows stores information and how to use Windows Explorer, a tool for managing files and folders.

Computers differ in the ways they can be set up. In most cases, when you turn on your computer, Windows loads automatically and the Windows log-on screen appears. When you see the Windows log-on screen, you need to log on and key a password. In order to log on, you need to know how to use the mouse, a device attached to your computer.

Using the Mouse

A *mouse* is a pointing device that is typically attached to your computer. Optical versions, which are not attached, are also available. The mouse is your access to the computer screen, allowing you to accomplish specific tasks. It operates through a pointer, a screen object you use to point to objects on the computer screen. The normal shape for the mouse cursor is an arrow. To move the pointer arrow on the screen, you roll the mouse on any flat object, or on a mouse pad, which has a smooth surface designed for easy mouse rolling. Although you can use the keyboard with Windows, you will probably find yourself using the mouse most of the time.

To use the mouse to point to an object on the computer screen:

1. Turn on the computer (if it is not on already). Windows loads, and the log-on screen appears. The screen includes a log-on name and picture assigned to you by your instructor.

To log on, you need to move the mouse pointer to the log-on name that was assigned. The pointer on the computer screen mirrors the actions made by the mouse when you roll it. Place your hand over the mouse and roll it to the left. The pointer on the screen moves to the left.

2. Roll the mouse to the right, and watch the pointer on the screen move to the right.
3. Practice rolling the mouse in all directions.
4. Roll your mouse to the edge of the pad, and then lift it up and place it back in the middle of the pad. Try it now to see how it works. When you feel that you can control the mouse position on the screen, roll the mouse to the name you have been assigned.

To log on, you will need to click the name to select it. Mouse clicks are covered in the next section; instructions for logging onto Windows Vista are covered in succeeding sections.

Clicks and Double-Clicks

A mouse typically has two buttons at the front (the edge of the mouse where the cord attaches)—one on the left (primary) and one on the right (secondary). A mouse might also have a center button or a wheel.

Single-click actions with the mouse are used to position the pointer at a specific screen location. To perform a single click:

1. Roll the mouse around on the mouse pad until the pointer on the screen is over an object on the screen. Remember that the direction in which you move the mouse on the pad represents the pointer's movement on the screen.

2. Press and release the left mouse button once. Pressing and releasing the mouse button is referred to as a *click*. The computer tells you that the action has been performed when the object you click is *highlighted* (typically, the color of the selected object changes) to indicate to you that it has been *selected*. In Windows, you often need to select an object before you can perform an action. For example, you usually need to select an object before you can copy it.

Pressing and releasing the mouse button twice is referred to as a *double-click*. When you double-click an object on the screen, it is selected—the object is highlighted—and an action is performed. For example:

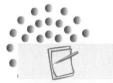

- When you double-click a folder, it is highlighted and opens to a window showing the items the folder contains.

- When you double-click a word in a text file, it is selected for a future action. In a text file, the pointer becomes an I-beam for selecting text in the document.

Selecting and Dragging

You can also select a larger object such as a picture or a block of text by using the mouse.

1. Position the pointer on one side of the object, and hold down the left mouse button.

2. Roll the mouse until the pointer reaches the other side of the object.

3. Release the mouse button. The selected object is highlighted.

Drag and Drop—Moving an Object Using the Mouse

You can use the mouse to move an object on the screen to another screen location. In this operation, you select an object and drag the mouse to move the selected object, such as an icon. The operation is known as *drag and drop*.

1. Using the mouse, move the pointer over the object you want to drag.
2. Perform a single-click action by pressing the left mouse button but keep it pressed down. The selected object will be highlighted.
3. With the left mouse button still depressed, roll the mouse until the pointer and selected object are placed at the desired new location.
4. Release the mouse button to drop the object. The object is now positioned at the new location.

Using the Right Mouse Button

Pressing and quickly releasing the right mouse button is referred to as a *right-click*. Although the right mouse button is used less frequently, using it can be a real time-saver. When you right-click an icon, a *shortcut menu* appears with a list of commands. The list of commands displayed varies for each icon or object.

As you progress in this tutorial, you will become familiar with the terms in Table 1, describing the actions you can take with a mouse.

TABLE 1 Mouse Terms

TERM	DESCRIPTION
Point	Roll the mouse until the tip of the pointer is touching the desired object on the computer screen.
Click	Quickly press and release the left mouse button. Single-clicking selects objects.
Double-click	Quickly press and release the left mouse button twice. Double-clicking selects an object and performs an action such as opening a folder.
Drag	Point to an object on screen, hold down the left mouse button, and roll the mouse until the pointer is in position. Then release the mouse button (drag and drop).
Right-click	Quickly press and release the right mouse button. A shortcut menu appears.
Select	When working in Windows, you must first select an object in order to work with it. Many objects are selected with a single click. However, depending on the size and type of object to be selected, you may need to roll the mouse to include an entire area: Holding down the left mouse button, roll the mouse so that the pointer moves from one side of an object to another. Then release the mouse button.

Pointer Shapes

As you perform actions on screen using the mouse, the mouse pointer changes its shape, depending on where it is located and what operation you are performing. Table 2 shows the most common types of mouse pointers.

TABLE 2 Frequently Used Mouse Pointers

SHAPE	NAME	DESCRIPTION
	Pointer	Used to point to objects.
	I-Beam	Used in typing, inserting, and selecting text. When the I-beam is moved to a selected location, it turns into a blinking bar.
	Two-pointed arrow	Used to change the size of objects or windows.
	Four-pointed arrow	Used to move objects.
	Busy	Indicates the computer is processing a command. While the busy or working in background pointer is displayed, it is best
	Working in background	to wait rather than try to continue working. Note: Some of the working in background actions will not allow you to perform other procedures until processing is completed.
	Hand	Used to select a *link* in Windows' Help or other programs.

Starting Windows: The Log-on Screen

The Windows Vista log-on screen allows several people to use the same computer at different times. Each person is assigned a user account that determines which files and folders you can access and your personal preferences, such as your desktop background. Each person's files are hidden from the others using the computer. However, users may share selected files using the Public folder. The log-on screen lists each user allocated to the computer by name.

If the administrator has added your name to a given computer, the log-on screen will include your name. If the computers are not assigned to specific individuals, you may find a box for Guest or for a generic user. If your computer is on a network, your instructor might need to provide you with special start-up instructions.

After you have logged on to Windows Vista, the desktop is the first screen you will see. It is your on-screen work area. All the elements you need to start working with Windows appear on the desktop.

1. If you have not already turned on the computer, do so now to begin the Windows Vista loading process. The Windows log-on screen appears.

NOTE

On some computers, the log-on screen does not appear automatically. You might have to press the following keys, all at once, and then quickly release them: Ctrl + Alt + Delete .

2. Click your name to select it. The Password box appears with an I-beam in position ready for you to type your password.

3. Type your password.

4. Click the arrow icon to the right of the box. If you have entered the password correctly, the Windows desktop appears. If you made an error, the Password box returns for you to type the correct password.

The Windows Desktop

The Desktop includes the Start button, taskbar, and sidebar. You may also see icons on the desktop that represent folders, programs, or other objects. You can add and delete icons from the desktop as well as change the desktop background. The Start button is your entry into Vista functions.

Figure 1
Windows Vista
Desktop

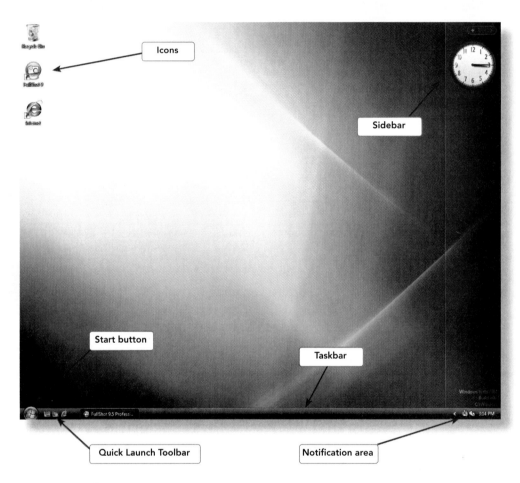

Using the Start Menu

Click the taskbar Start button to open the Start menu. You can also press the Windows logo key on the keyboard to open the Start menu. Use the Start menu to launch programs, adjust computer settings, search for files and folders, and turn off the computer. If this is a computer assigned to you for log-on, your Start menu may contain items that differ from those of another user assigned to the same computer. To open and learn about the Start menu, first click the Start button on the Windows taskbar. The Start menu appears.

Figure 2
Start menu

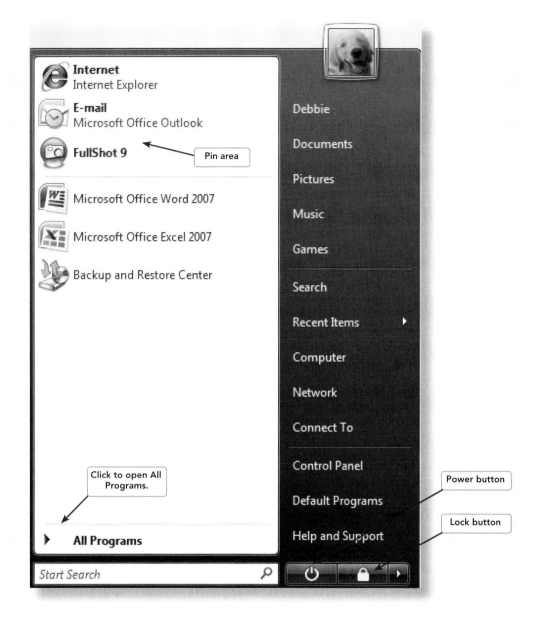

The left pane consists of three sections divided by separator lines. The top section, called the *pin area*, lists programs that are always available for you to click. These can include your Internet browser, e-mail program, your word processor, and so forth. You can remove programs you do not want listed, rearrange them, and add those you prefer.

Below the separator line are shortcuts to programs you use most often, placed there automatically by Windows. You can remove programs you do not want listed, rearrange them, but not add any manually.

All Programs displays a list of programs on your computer and is used to launch programs not listed on the Start menu.

Below the left pane is the *Search box* which is used to locate programs and files on your computer.

The right pane is also divided into three sections. It is used to select folders, files, and commands and to change settings. Use the icons at the bottom of the right pane to save your session, lock the computer, restart, switch users, and shut down.

Table 3 describes the typical components of the Start menu.

TABLE 3 Typical Components of the Start Menu

COMMAND	USE
Left Pane	
Pin area	Lists programs that are always available. You can add and delete items to the pin area.
Internet	Connects to the default browser.
E-mail	Connects to the chosen e-mail service.
Below the First Separator Line	
Programs	Lists programs that you use most often. You can add to and rearrange the programs listed.
Below the Second Separator Line	
All Programs	Click to display a list of programs in alphabetical order and a list of folders. Click to open a program.
Start Search	Use to search programs and folders. Key text and results appear.
Right Pane	
Personal folder	Opens the User folder.
Documents	Opens the Documents folder.
Pictures	Opens the Pictures folder.
Music	Opens the Music folder.
Games	Opens the Games folder.
Search	Opens the Search Results window. Advanced Search options are available.
Recent Items	Opens a list of the most recent documents you have opened and saved.
Computer	Opens a window where you can access disk drives and other hardware devices.
Network	Opens the Network window where you can access computers and other devices on your network.
Connect To	Opens a window where you can connect to a different network.
Control Panel	Opens the Control Panel.
Default Programs	Opens the Default Programs window where you can define default programs and settings.
Help and Support	Opens the Windows Help and Support window. Help offers instructions on how to perform tasks in the Windows environment.
Power button	Turns off the computer.
Lock button	Locks the computer, or click the arrow beside the Lock button to display a menu for switching users, logging off, restarting, or shutting down the computer.

Using the All Programs Command

Most programs on your computer can be started from the All Programs command on the Start menu. This is the easiest way to open a program not listed directly on the Start menu.

1. To open the All Programs menu, click the Start button. The Start menu appears.

2. Click All Programs or the triangle to the left near the bottom of the left pane. The All Programs menu appears, listing the programs installed on your computer. Every computer has a different list of programs. Notice that some menu entries have an icon to the left of the name and others display a folder. Click a folder, and a list of programs stored in that folder appears. Click a program to open it. Point to a program to see a short description of the program.

Figure 3
All Programs
window

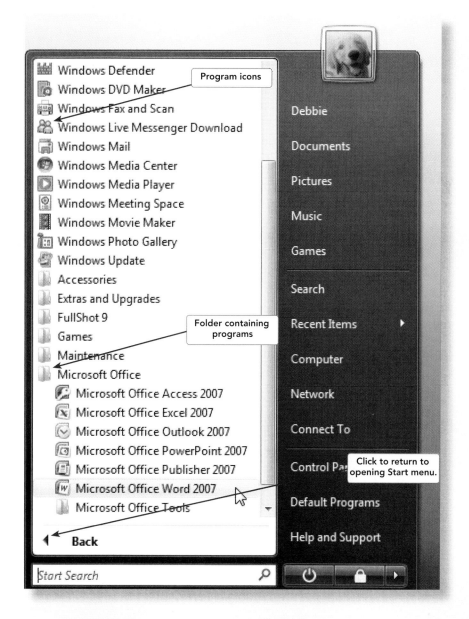

3. Click Microsoft Office to open a list of programs in the Microsoft Office folder. Click Microsoft Office Word 2007. (See Figure 3.) In a few seconds, the program you selected loads and the Word window appears. Notice that a button for the program appears on the taskbar. Leave Word open for the present.

Customizing the Start Menu

Both the Start menu and the desktop can be customized. You can add shortcuts to the desktop if you prefer, and you can add and delete items from the Start menu. However, if your computer is used by others, the administrator may limit some customization functions.

To add a program to the pin area of the Start menu:

1. Select the program you want to add to the pin list from the All Programs menu, and right-click it. A shortcut menu appears.
2. Click Pin To Start Menu on the shortcut menu. The program will be added to the pin list in the left pane above the first separator line.

To remove a program from the pin area of the Start menu:

1. Select the program you want to remove from the pin list, and right-click. A shortcut menu appears.
2. Click Unpin From Start Menu. The program will be removed from the pin list.

To change the order in which programs are listed in the pin area:

1. Point to the program icon.
2. Drag the icon to the desired position.

Using the Taskbar

The taskbar at the bottom of your screen is one of the most important features in Windows Vista. The taskbar is divided into several segments, each dedicated to a different use. It shows programs that are running, and you can use the taskbar to switch between open programs and between open documents within a program. If your computer has the Aero interface, a thumbnail preview appears when you move the mouse over a button on the taskbar.

Figure 4
The Desktop with the taskbar and the Word window

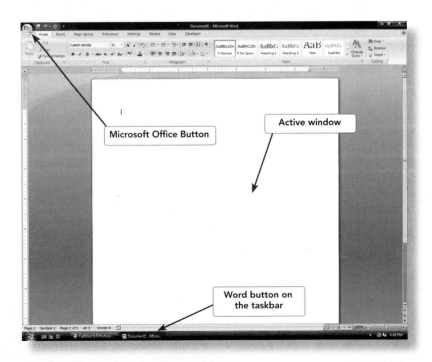

Windows displays a button on the taskbar for each opened program and document. Notice that there is a button for Word, showing the Word icon and the name of the program. Point to the Word button to view a thumbnail of the document window. Since the taskbar can become crowded, Windows combines access to documents or programs under single buttons. The button shows the name of the program (Microsoft Office Word) and the number of items in the group (9). The shape of the arrow varies, depending on what the button contains. Clicking the button opens the menu of available items.

Figure 5
Button contents for
Word documents

List of open documents in Word

Taskbar button to open Word program

Taskbar Notification Area

TIP

If you are not sure of what an item is or does, pointing to it without clicking displays a ScreenTip with a short description.

The *notification area* is on the right side of the taskbar, where the current time is usually displayed. Along with displaying the time, tiny icons notify you as to the status of your browser connection, virus protection, and so forth. It is also known as the *system tray*. In the interest of removing clutter, the notification area hides most of the icons. Clicking the Show Hidden Icons button ◄ "hides" or "unhides" the icons in the notification area. Click the left-pointing arrow next to the icons to expand the notification area. Click the right-pointing arrow to hide the notification area.

The Active Window

The window in which you are working is called the *active window*. The title bar for the active window is highlighted, and its taskbar button is also highlighted. The program window for Microsoft Word that you opened earlier should still be open. To examine additional features of the taskbar, open a second program, Microsoft Excel, a spreadsheet program in Microsoft Office.

1. If Word is not open, click the Start button and then click All Programs, Microsoft Office, Microsoft Office Word 2007 from the Start menu. The Word window displays.

2. Click the Start button and then click All Programs, Microsoft Office, Microsoft Office Excel 2007 from the Start menu. The Excel window displays. Notice how the Excel window covers the Word window, indicating that the window containing Excel is now active. Notice, too, that a new button for Excel has been added to the taskbar.

Figure 6
Excel (the active
window) covering
the Word window

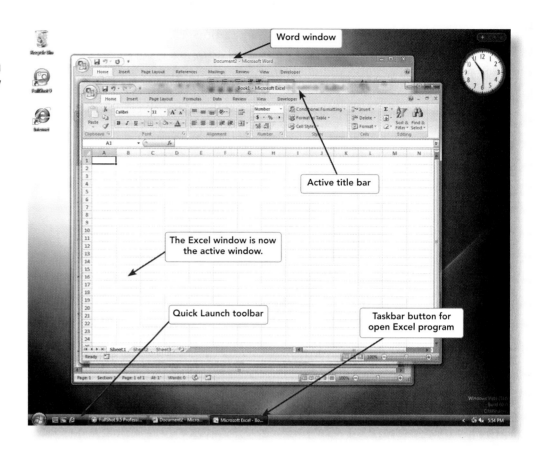

Figure 6
Excel (the active
window) covering
the Word window

3. Click the button on the taskbar for Word, the first program you opened. Word reappears in front of Excel. Notice the change in the appearance of the title bar for each program.

4. Click the button on the taskbar for Excel. Notice that you switch back to Excel.

5. Click the button on the taskbar to return to Word.

6. Locate the Quick Launch toolbar to the right of the Start button, and point to the Switch between windows button .

7. Click the Switch between windows button, and notice the desktop view.

8. Click the Excel window.

Changing the Size of the Taskbar

You can change the size of the taskbar using your mouse if your toolbar is crowded. It is usually not necessary, because of the multiple document style buttons and other hide/unhide arrows on the taskbar. Before you can change the size of the taskbar, it may be necessary for you to unlock it. To unlock the taskbar, right-click an open area of the taskbar and click Lock the Taskbar to remove the checkmark. A checkmark is a toggle command. Click to turn it off, and click a second time to turn it on.

1. Move the pointer to the top edge of the taskbar until it changes from a pointer to a two-pointed arrow . Using the two-pointed arrow, you can change the size of the taskbar.

2. With the pointer displayed as a two-pointed arrow, hold down the left mouse button and move the arrow up until the taskbar enlarges upward.

3. Move the pointer to the top edge of the taskbar once again until the two-pointed arrow displays. Hold down the left mouse button, and move the arrow down to the bottom of the screen. The taskbar is restored to its original size.

Using Menus

Windows uses a system of menus that contain a choice of options for working with programs and documents. Most Windows programs use a similar menu structure. These operations are either mouse or keyboard driven. They are called commands because they "command" the computer to perform functions needed to complete the task you, the user, initiate at the menu level.

Executing a Command from a Menu

In Windows, a program may display a *menu bar*, a row of descriptive menu names at the top, just below the title bar. You open a menu by clicking the menu name listed in the menu bar. When a menu is opened, a list of command options appears. To execute a particular command from an open menu, press the left mouse button and then drag down and release the chosen option (click and drag). You can also click the command once the menu is open.

Keyboard Menu Commands

For people who prefer to use the keyboard to a mouse, Windows has provided keyboard commands for many menu items. You can use the keyboard to open menus and choose menu options.

Some menu items include not only the name of the command but a combination of keyboard keys. For example, under the File menu in WordPad, the Save command contains the notation Ctrl+S to its right. This means that you can also execute the command by pressing the Ctrl key together with the S key to save a document.

Figure 7
Title and menu bars with the File menu Open

Command name

Command with three dots opens a dialog box.

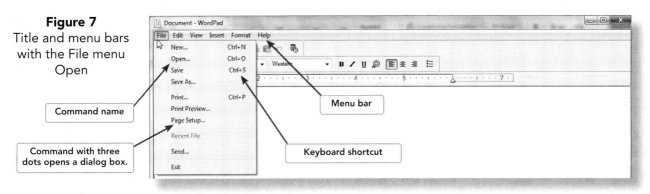

Menu bar

Keyboard shortcut

Other Menu Symbols

Three dots following a menu option indicate that a dialog box is displayed when that menu option is chosen. (Dialog boxes, discussed later, are small windows requesting and receiving input from a user.) Some commands also display a check box. Click an empty check box to select the option. A checkmark will appear in the square and indicates the option is selected. To turn off the option, click the check box to remove the checkmark. Commands that appear gray or dimmed are currently not available.

Perform the following steps for keyboard command practice:

1. Open the Start menu, click All Programs, and click the Accessories folder. Click WordPad. The WordPad program opens, and a button appears on the Windows taskbar.

2. Click File in the menu bar. The File menu displays. Click File to close the menu.

3. Press Alt, and notice that the items in the menu bar display underlined letters (File, Edit). The underlined letters are a shortcut to open a menu. Press the letter "f" to open the File menu. Release Alt, and click outside the menu in a blank area to close the menu.

4. Press Alt+V, the keyboard shortcut for the View menu. The View menu displays.

5. Notice the four check boxes. All are selected. Click the Options command. The Options dialog box opens.

6. Click Cancel to close the dialog box.

7. Click File in the menu bar. Click Exit. Click Don't Save if prompted to save the document.

Displaying a Shortcut Menu

When the mouse pointer is on an object or an area of the Windows desktop and you right-click, a shortcut menu appears. A shortcut menu typically contains commands that are useful in working with the object or area of the desktop to which you are currently pointing.

1. Position the mouse pointer on a blank area of the desktop, and right-click. A shortcut menu appears with commands that relate to the desktop, including view and sort options.

2. Click outside the shortcut menu to close it.

3. Right-click the time in the bottom right corner of the taskbar. A shortcut menu appears.

4. Click Adjust Date/Time on the shortcut menu. The Date/Time Properties dialog box appears. You can use this dialog box to adjust your computer's date and time.

Figure 8
The Time shortcut menu

5. Click Cancel.

6. Right-click an icon on the desktop to display its shortcut menu, and then close the shortcut menu.

Using the Ribbon

Microsoft Office 2007 applications include a Microsoft Office Button, a Quick Access Toolbar, and a Ribbon. The *Microsoft Office Button* displays the Office menu which lists the commands to create, open, save, and print a document. The *Quick Access Toolbar* contains frequently used commands and is positioned to the right of the Microsoft Office Button. The *Ribbon* consists of seven tabs by default, and each tab contains a group of related commands. The number of commands for each tab varies. A command can be one of several formats. The most popular formats include buttons and drop-down lists.

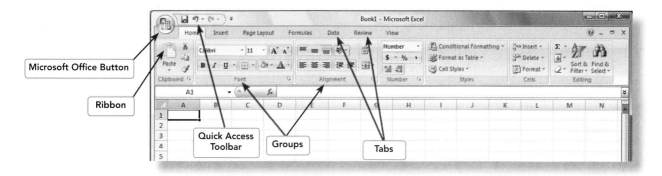

1. Activate the Excel program.

2. Point to and click the Microsoft Office Button. Notice the commands and icons in the menu.

3. Click a blank area of the window to close the menu.

4. Locate the Quick Access Toolbar beside the Microsoft Office Button. Point to each button in the Quick Access Toolbar to identify it. Notice that a keyboard shortcut displays beside each button.

5. Click the Page Layout tab. Notice the change in the groups and commands.

6. Click the Home tab.

Using Dialog Boxes

Windows programs make frequent use of dialog boxes. A *dialog box* is a window that requests input from you related to a command you have chosen. All Windows programs use a common dialog box structure.

1. Click the Excel program button on the taskbar to make Excel the active window if necessary.

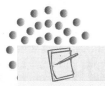

NOTE

A keyboard shortcut is available for the print dialog box: Press Ctrl + P to open the Print dialog box.

2. Click the Microsoft Office Button. The File menu displays.

3. Click Print to display the Print dialog box.

4. The Print dialog box contains several types of dialog box options.

Figure 10
Print dialog box

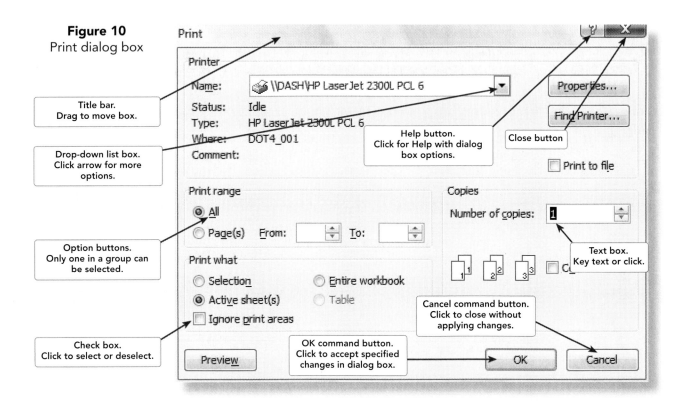

Title bar.
Drag to move box.

Drop-down list box.
Click arrow for more
options.

Option buttons.
Only one in a group can
be selected.

Check box.
Click to select or deselect.

Help button.
Click for Help with dialog
box options.

Close button

Text box.
Key text or click.

Cancel command button.
Click to close without
applying changes.

OK command button.
Click to accept specified
changes in dialog box.

5. To close the Print dialog box, click Cancel, located in the lower right corner of the dialog box. The Print dialog box closes without applying any changes.

Another type of dialog box uses tabs to display related options. Only one tab can display at a time. The Word Font dialog box offers many options for choosing character formatting.

1. Make Word the active window.
2. Click the Home tab, and click the small arrow that appears on the right of the Font group [Font]. The Font dialog box displays.

Figure 11
Font dialog box

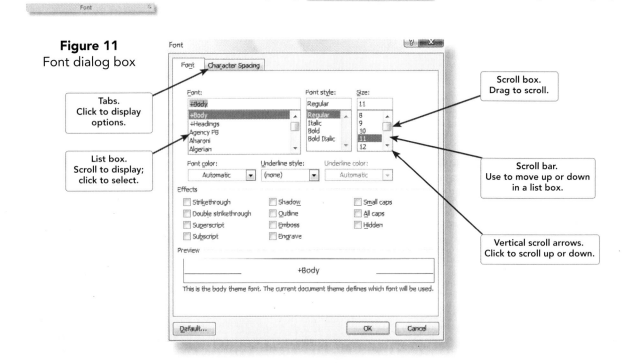

Tabs.
Click to display
options.

List box.
Scroll to display;
click to select.

Scroll box.
Drag to scroll.

Scroll bar.
Use to move up or down
in a list box.

Vertical scroll arrows.
Click to scroll up or down.

The scroll boxes are used to specify a font by name, its style, and its size. When you select a paragraph in a Word document, you can select its typographic features using this dialog box. The Font list box at the top left displays a list of all the typefaces installed on your computer. By clicking the name of the font, you select it for your paragraph.

The vertical scroll bar on the right side of a list box or a window indicates that there is more content to view. To view the hidden content, click the downward-pointing arrow or the upward-pointing vertical scroll arrow. You can also drag the scroll box on the scroll bar up or down to view all the content. The Character Spacing tab at the top of the Font dialog box displays additional character formatting options. Click the Character Spacing tab to view its contents, and then return to the Font tab.

Use the Font dialog box to style a paragraph as follows:

1. Type a very short paragraph in your Word document.
2. Position the I-beam at the beginning of the text, and hold down the left mouse button.
3. Drag the mouse to the end of the paragraph. The paragraph will change color, showing that it has been selected.
4. Open the Font dialog box by pressing Ctrl+D.
5. In the Font list box, click Verdana. You may need to scroll down to locate it.
6. In the Font style box, click Bold.
7. In the Size box, click 12.
8. If you wish to change the color of your paragraph, move your pointer to the Font color drop-down list box and click the down-facing arrow. A color pallet appears. Point to the color you wish to use, and click.
9. When you have completed your selections, click OK at the bottom of the Font dialog box and look at the paragraph you have styled. If you wish, you can try other font formats, while your paragraph is selected.

Changing the Size of a Window

You can change the size of any window using either the mouse or the sizing buttons. Sizing buttons are the small buttons on the right side of the title bar that allow you to minimize or maximize the window (see Figure 12). This can be especially useful when you would like to display several open windows on your desktop and see them simultaneously.

NOTE

Notice that the window occupies the entire desktop, and the Maximize button has changed to a Restore Down button. This type of function is known as a toggle: When a button representing one state (Maximize) is clicked, an action is performed, the button toggles to the alternate state, and the other button (Restore Down) appears. A number of actions in Windows operate this way.

1. Make Excel the active window, if it is not already. Click the Maximize button on the Excel title bar if the Excel window does not fill the entire desktop.

Figure 12
Sizing buttons

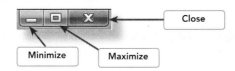

Table 4 describes these buttons. To practice changing the size of a window, follow these steps:

TABLE 4 Sizing Buttons

BUTTON	USE
Minimize	Reduces the window to a button on the taskbar.
Maximize	Enlarges the window to fill the entire desktop (appears only when a window is reduced).
Restore Down	Returns the window to its previous size and desktop position (appears only when a window is maximized).

NOTE

You can double-click a window title bar to maximize or restore the window or right-click the program button on the taskbar and choose minimize, maximize, restore, or close.

2. Click the Restore Down button on the Excel title bar. The Excel window reduces in size, and the Word window appears behind it. The Restore Down button has now changed to a Maximize button. Notice that the highlighted title bar of the Excel window indicates it is the active window.

3. Click the Minimize button. The Excel window disappears, and its button appears on the taskbar.

How to Display Two Program Windows Simultaneously

1. Open the Start menu, and click All Programs to open Excel and Word if they are not already open from an earlier section of the tutorial.

2. Click the Excel button on the taskbar to move its window to the front of the screen.

3. Click the Restore Down button if the Excel window is maximized.

4. Move the pointer to the right border of the Excel window. The pointer changes to a horizontal two-pointed arrow.

5. With the two-pointed arrow displayed , drag the border to the left to make the window narrower.

TIP

Sometimes the borders of a window can move off the computer screen. If you are having trouble with one border of a window, try another border or drag the entire window onto the screen by using the title bar.

Figure 13
Sizing a window

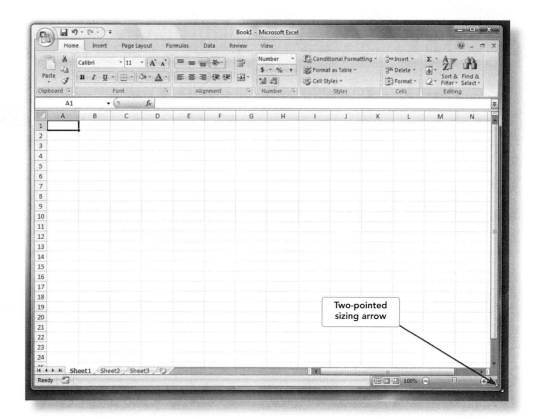

Two-pointed
sizing arrow

NOTE

You can place the pointer on any part of the window border to change its size. To change both the height and width of the window, move the pointer to the bottom right corner of the window. The double-pointed arrow changes its orientation to a 45-degree angle (see Figure 13). Dragging this arrow resizes a window vertically and horizontally.

NOTE

The taskbar contains options to Show Windows Stacked, Cascade Windows, and Show the Desktop.

6. Click the title bar or any part of the Word window behind the Excel window. The Word window becomes the active window. The Excel window is still open, but it is now behind the Word window.

7. Click the Maximize button if the Word window does not fill the entire desktop.

8. Click the Minimize button on the title bar of the Word window. The Excel window becomes the active window.

9. Make the Word window the active window by clicking the Word button on the taskbar.

10. Click the Restore Down button on the Word window. The Word window reduces in size. The Excel window might be partially visible behind the Word window. You can drag the two reduced windows so that parts of both can be seen simultaneously.

11. Right-click the taskbar, and click Show Windows Side by Side. The windows display vertically.

12. Press the Alt key, and hold it down while pressing Tab. You can switch to the previous window by pressing this shortcut, or you can continue to press Tab to switch to an open window on the desktop.

13. Click the Show Desktop button located on the Quick Launch toolbar to see the desktop. The Word and Excel programs are minimized.

14. Click the Show Desktop button again to restore the programs.

15. Click the Close buttons on the title bars of each of the two program windows to close them and to show the desktop.

Using the Documents Command

Windows lets you open a recently used document by using the Recent Items command on the Start menu. This command allows you to open one of up to fifteen documents previously saved on your computer.

1. Click the Start button on the taskbar to display the Start menu.
2. Click Recent Items. The Recent Items submenu appears, showing you up to the last fifteen documents that were saved.
3. Click a document. The program in which the document was created opens, and the document displays. For example, if the document you chose is a Word document, Word opens and the document appears in a Word program window.
4. Click the program window's Close button. The program window closes, and the desktop is clear once again.

Changing the Desktop

The Control Panel lets you change the way Windows looks and works. Because your computer in school is used by other students, you should be very careful when changing settings. Others might expect Windows to look and work the standard way. Having Windows look or work in a nonstandard way could easily confuse other users. (Table 5 describes how to access other settings.)

To change the appearance of your computer, follow these steps. Talk to your instructor first, however, before changing any settings on your computer.

1. Click the Start button on the taskbar.
2. Click Control Panel on the right pane. The Control Panel window displays.
3. Click the Appearance and Personalization link. The Appearance and Personalization window displays.
4. Click Personalization and click Window Color and Appearance.
5. Click Default and click OK.
6. Close the Appearance and Personalization window.

TABLE 5 Settings Options

OPTION	USE
Control Panel	Displays the Control Panel window, which lets you change background color, add or remove programs, change the date and time, and change other settings for your hardware and software. The items listed below are accessed from the Control Panel.
Network and Internet	Includes options to view the network status, connect to a network, set up file sharing, change Internet options, and so on.
Hardware and Sound	Includes options to add a printer, change default settings for AutoPlay, sound, mouse settings, keyboard, and so on.
Appearance and Personalization	Includes options to change the desktop background, adjust screen resolution, customize the Start menu and icons on the taskbar, and change sidebar properties.

Using the Search Command

If you do not know where a file or folder is located, you can use the Search command on the Start menu to help you find and open it.

1. Click the Start button on the taskbar. Notice the blinking insertion point in the Start Search box. You can start typing the name of a program, folder, or file immediately.
2. Click Search in the right pane of the Start menu. The Search Results dialog box appears.
3. Click Document in the Show Only section.

Figure 14
Search Results
dialog box

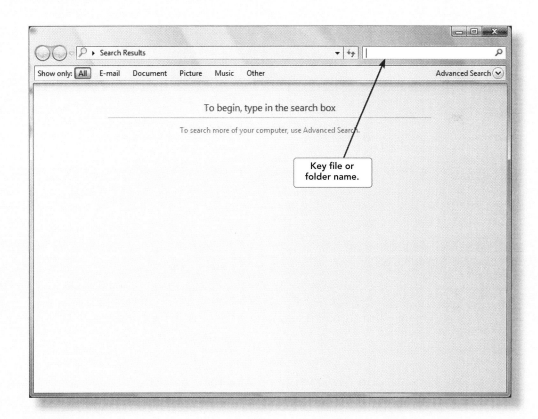

4. Type the name of the file or folder you want to find in the Search box. View the search results.

   To search for files by date, size, type, or other attributes, click Advanced Search.

1. Click the arrow to the left of the Search Results text box to specify where you want Windows to search. The default location is the C drive.
2. Click Search to start the search. Any matches for the file are shown in the right pane of the dialog box.
3. Double-click any found item to open the program and view the file or folder Windows has located.
4. When you are finished with your search, close all open windows and clear your desktop.

Using the Run Command

Windows allows you to start a program by using the Run command and typing the program name. This command is often employed to run a "setup" or "install" program that installs a new program on your computer. It is best to use this command after you have become more familiar with Windows Vista.

1. Click the Start button on the taskbar.
2. Click All Programs, and click the Accessories folder.
3. Click Run.

Figure 15
Run dialog box

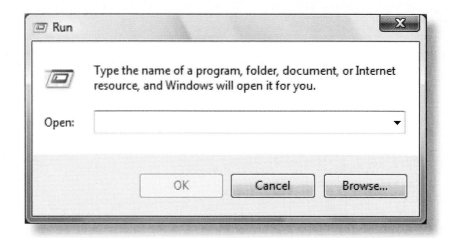

4. If you know the name of a program you want to run, type the name in the Open text box. Often you will need to click Browse to open a drop-down list of the disk drives, folders, and files available to you.
5. Click Cancel to close the Run dialog box.
6. Open the Start menu, and locate the Start Search box.
7. Key run, and notice that the Start menu displays the Run program.
8. Click the program name, and the Run dialog box displays.
9. Close the Run dialog box.

Deleting Files Using the Recycle Bin

The *Recycle Bin* is the trash can icon on your desktop. To delete a file:

NOTE

As a protection against deleting a file unintentionally, any file you have placed in the Recycle Bin can be undeleted and used again.

1. Click its icon, and drag it to the Recycle Bin.
2. Double-click the Recycle Bin icon. A window opens listing files you have deleted.
3. To undelete a file, merely drag it out of the Recycle Bin window and place it on the desktop or right-click the file and click Restore.
4. To empty the Recycle Bin and permanently delete files, click Empty Recycle Bin in the Recycle Bin dialog box, or right-click the Recycle Bin icon. The shortcut menu appears.
5. Click Empty Recycle Bin.

Exiting Windows

You should always exit any open programs and Windows before turning off the computer. This is the best way to be sure your work is saved. Windows also performs other "housekeeping" routines that ensure everything is ready for you when you next turn on your computer. Failure to shut down properly will often force Windows to perform time-consuming system checks the next time it is loaded. You can either log off the computer to make it available for another user, or shut it down entirely.

To Log Off

1. Click the Start button on the taskbar.
2. Click the arrow to the right of the Lock this computer button , and click Log Off.

To Shut Down

To exit Windows, use the Lock this computer command on the Start menu. This command has several shut-down options.

- *Restart:* Restarts the computer without shutting off the power. This is sometimes necessary when you add new software.
- *Shut down:* Closes all open programs and makes it safe to turn off the computer. Some computers will turn off the power automatically.
- *Sleep:* Puts the computer in a low-activity state. It appears to be turned off but will restart when the mouse is moved. Press the computer power button to resume work.

1. Click the Start button on the taskbar.
2. Click the arrow beside the Lock this computer button.
3. Click the Shut Down option.
4. Windows prompts you to save changes in any open documents. It then prepares the computer to be shut down.

There is more to learning a presentation graphics program like Microsoft Office PowerPoint 2007 than simply keying text on colored backgrounds and calling the result a presentation. You need to know how to use PowerPoint in a real-world situation. That's why all the lessons in this text relate to everyday business tasks. The text will show you how to create well-organized presentations that are designed effectively, too.

As you work through the lessons, imagine yourself working as an intern for Good 4 *U*, a fictional New York restaurant.

Good 4 *U* Restaurant

The Good 4 *U* restaurant has been in business for only a little more than three years, but it's been a success from the time it served its first veggie burger. The restaurant, which features healthy food and has as its theme the "everyday active life," seems to have found an award-winning recipe for success. (Figure CS-1 shows the interior of the largest dining room in the restaurant. It features plants and a wide expanse of windows looking out over Central Park South, a tree-lined avenue on the south side of New York's Central Park.)

Figure CS-1 Interior of Good 4 *U* restaurant and a sampling of the fresh food prepared daily

The food at Good 4 *U* is all low-fat. The menu features lots of vegetables (all organic, of course) as well as fish and chicken. The restaurant doesn't serve alcohol, instead offering fruit juices and sparkling water. Good 4 *U*'s theme of the "everyday active life" is reflected on the restaurant's walls with running, tennis, and bicycling memorabilia. This theme reflects the interests of the two co-owners: Julie Wolfe, who led the New York Flash to two Women's Professional Basketball Association championships in her 10 years with the team, and Gus Irvinelli, who is an avid tennis player and was selected for the U.S. amateur team. Even the chef, Michele Jenkins, leads an everyday active life—she rides her bicycle 10 miles a day in and around Central Park.

Two years ago, Roy Olafsen was a marketing manager for a large hotel chain. He was overweight and out of shape. In the same week that his doctor told him to eat better and exercise regularly, Roy received a job offer from Good 4 *U*. "It was too good to pass up," he said. "It was my chance to combine work and a healthy lifestyle." As you work through the text, you'll discover that Good 4 *U* is often involved in health-oriented as well as athletic events.

In your work as an intern at Good 4 *U* restaurant, you will meet many of the people who work at Good 4 *U* and will interact with the four key people shown in Figure CS-2. You will be doing most of your work for Roy Olafsen, the marketing manager.

All the presentations you will use and create in this course relate to the Good 4 *U* restaurant. As you work with the presentations in the text, note the following things:

- The types of presentations needed in a small business to carry on day-to-day business.
- The design of presentations. Real businesses must often focus on designing eye-catching, informative presentations for customers. The business's success often depends on developing attractive and compelling presentations that sell its services to customers.

Figure CS-2 Key employees

Julie Wolfe
Co-Owner

Gus Irvinelli
Co-Owner

Michele Jenkins
Head Chef

Roy Olafsen
Marketing Manager

As you use this text and become more experienced with Microsoft Office PowerPoint 2007, you will also gain experience in creating, editing, and designing the sort of presentations generated in a real-life business environment.

In your first meeting with Roy Olafsen, he gave you the following tips for designing presentations. These guidelines can be applied to any presentation.

Tips for Designing Presentations

- Prepare a distinctive title slide. Make sure the title identifies the presentation content.

- Maintain a consistent color scheme throughout the presentation for a sense of unity.

- Keep the background simple, and modify it to help create a unique theme for your presentation.

- Choose colors carefully so all text can be seen clearly. You must have a high contrast between background colors and text colors for easy reading.

- Write lists with parallel wording and be concise. Limit bulleted text to no more than seven words on a line and no more than seven lines on a slide.

- Avoid small text. Body text on slides, such as for bulleted lists, should be no smaller than 24 points. Text for annotations may be slightly smaller, but not less than 20 points. Establish a hierarchy for text sizes based on text importance and then use those sizes consistently.

- Think and design visually to express your message. Use graphics such as boxes, lines, circles, and other shapes to highlight text or to create SmartArt graphics that show process diagrams and relationships. Illustrate with pictures and clip art images.

- Select all images carefully to make your presentation content more understandable. They should not detract from the message. Avoid the temptation to "jazz up" a slide show with too much clip art.

- Keep charts simple. The most effective charts are pie charts with three or four slices and column charts with three or four columns. Label charts carefully for easy interpretation.

- Provide some form of handout so your audience can keep track of the presentation or make notes while you are talking.

- Include multimedia elements of animation, transitions, sound, and movies if these elements strengthen your message, engage your audience, aid understanding, or make your presentation more compelling.

- Your final slide should provide a recommendation or summary to help you conclude your presentation effectively.

unit 1

BASIC SKILLS

PPT1.1

Lesson 1

Getting Started in PowerPoint

OBJECTIVES

MCAS OBJECTIVES

In this lesson:
PP07 4.3.6
PP07 4.4.2
See Appendix

After completing this lesson, you will be able to:

1. Explore PowerPoint.

2. View a presentation.

3. Add text using placeholders.

4. Name and save a presentation.

5. Prepare presentation supplements.

6. End your work session.

Estimated Time: 2 hours

PowerPoint is an easy-to-use presentation graphics program you can use to create professional-quality presentations. PowerPoint can be used in a variety of settings by people in many different career fields. For example, a day care worker may develop a presentation showing parents pictures of their children in all of the year's activities, or a minister may utilize PowerPoint to display notes on the sermon or song lyrics for the congregation. An instructor may use it for notes for a lecture to help students keep focused and their notes organized, or a hotelier may develop a presentation to help market the hotel at conferences and meetings. PowerPoint is also an effective tool for creating flyers and other printed products because of its versatile drawing and layout tools.

This lesson begins with an overview of many PowerPoint features and will help you become accustomed to the application window.

Exploring PowerPoint

If you are already familiar with other Microsoft Office 2007 programs, you'll feel right at home with PowerPoint. Although a number of new features appear in the PowerPoint window shown in Figure 1-1, it's easy to recognize similarities to Microsoft Word and Microsoft Excel.

TABLE 1-1 Main Parts of the PowerPoint Window

Part of Window	Purpose
Title bar	Contains the name of the presentation.
Quick Access toolbar	Located by default at the top of the PowerPoint window and provides quick access to commands that you use frequently.
Microsoft Office Button	Located in the upper left-hand corner and contains commands to open, save, print, and share your PowerPoint file with others.
Ribbon	Consists of task-oriented tabs with commands organized in groups.
Tabs	Task-oriented collections of commands. In addition to the standard tabs, there are other tabs which appear only when they are useful for the type of task you are currently performing.
Groups	Logical sets of related commands and options.
Command buttons	Buttons designed to perform a function or display a gallery of options.
Slide pane	The area where you create, edit, and display presentation slides.
Notes pane	The area where you can add presentation notes for the presenter.
Slides and Outline pane	The area that can display either an outline of the presentation's text or *thumbnails*—miniature pictures—of the presentation's slides. You choose either Outline or Slides by clicking the appropriate tab. (If this pane is not displayed, click the Normal view button.)
Scroll bars	Used with the pointer to move a slide or outline text right or left and up or down. You can also use the vertical scroll bar to move from slide to slide.
Status bar	Displays information about the presentation you are working on.
View buttons	Buttons used to switch between Normal view, Slide Sorter view, and Slide Show view.

Figure 1-1
Main features in
PowerPoint's Normal
view

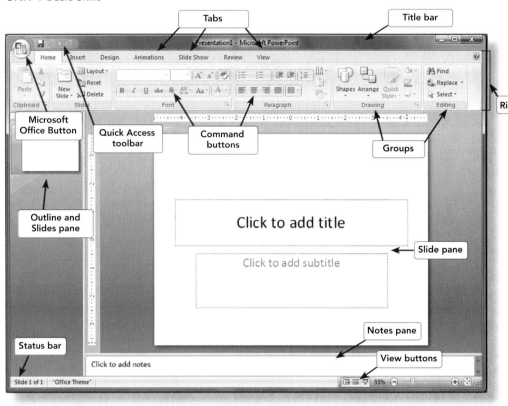

Figure 1-1
Main features in
PowerPoint's Normal
view

Exercise 1-1   IDENTIFY PARTS OF THE POWERPOINT WINDOW

The first step to becoming familiar with PowerPoint is to identify the parts of the window. The *Ribbon* contains seven task-oriented tabs: Home, Insert, Design, Animations, Slide Show, Review, and View. Commands are organized in logical groups with command buttons and other controls. ScreenTips will help you identify command buttons and other objects. A *ScreenTip* is the box displaying an object's name and sometimes a brief description that appears under a command button or other object when you point to it. Within the Ribbon groups are drop-down galleries that easily present formatting options, graphics choices, layouts, and more.

Figure 1-2
ScreenTip over the
Microsoft Office
Button

1. Using Figure 1-1 as a guide, move your pointer over items in the PowerPoint window to identify them by name using ScreenTips similar to Figure 1-2.

Exercise 1-2   USE THE QUICK ACCESS TOOLBAR

The *Quick Access toolbar* is a customizable toolbar containing a set of common commands that function independently of the tab that is currently displayed. This toolbar's default location is above the Ribbon. It can be moved under the Ribbon, but this location requires more space.

1. Click the drop-down arrow at the end of the Quick Access toolbar.

2. Choose Show Below the Ribbon.

3. Click the drop-down arrow again and choose Show Above the Ribbon to return to the default position.

Exercise 1-3   OPEN AN EXISTING PRESENTATION

When you first open PowerPoint, a new blank presentation automatically appears, ready for you to add text and graphics. However, in this exercise you open an existing PowerPoint presentation. The presentation was created for this lesson to give you an overview of many PowerPoint features.

1. Point to the Microsoft Office Button and click the left mouse button to open a menu.

2. Choose Open.

3. In the Open dialog box, navigate to the appropriate drive and folder for your student files according to your instructor's directions.

4. When you locate the student files, click the arrow next to the Views button (see Figure 1-3) in the Open dialog box to display a menu of view options.

Figure 1-3
Folders listed in the
Open dialog box

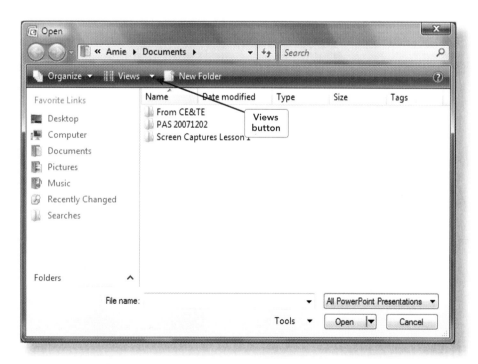

NOTE

Your instructor will advise you where to locate the files for this course. For more information about working with files, folders, and directories in Windows, refer to "File Management" at the Professional Approach Online Learning Center at **www.mhhe.com/pas07**.

5. Choose Small Icons to list all files by name.

6. Click the Views button  again and choose Details to see the type of file and the date when it was last modified.

7. Locate the file **ThreeYr1** (use the scroll bar if you need to) and click once to select the file.

8. Click Open. (You can also double-click the file's name to open it.) PowerPoint opens the file in Normal view.

NOTE

The presentations you create in this course relate to the case study at the front of this text about Good 4 U, a fictional restaurant.

Exercise 1-4 WORK WITH RIBBONS, TABS, GROUPS, AND COMMAND BUTTONS

PowerPoint organizes command buttons in a logical way. On the Ribbon, the tabs reflect tasks or activities you commonly perform and provide easy access to the commands. Within each tab, the commands are divided into related groups of buttons and other controls.

Live Preview is a feature that allows you to see exactly what your changes will look like before clicking or selecting an effect. Sometimes the available effects are presented in a *gallery* that displays thumbnails of different options you can choose.

1. Click the Insert tab on the Ribbon.

2. Identify each of the groups located on the Insert tab: Tables, Illustrations, Links, Text, and Media Clips.

3. These groups each contain command buttons that either provide options through dialog boxes or through galleries of options.

Exercise 1-5 USE MICROSOFT OFFICE POWERPOINT HELP

Microsoft Office provides a *Help* feature that is an excellent reference tool for reinforcing skills presented in a lesson and for finding more information on any PowerPoint feature. Each program in Microsoft Office has a separate Help window.

F1 for help or ? icon top right

1. Click Microsoft Office PowerPoint Help button located on the upper-right of the Ribbon or you can press F1. The Help window will appear on top of your open PowerPoint presentation.

2. Key **Ribbon** in the search box located on the help window, and then press ⌈Enter⌋.

3. Scroll through the list of options that display and select Use the Ribbon.

4. Read and scroll through the entire Help window.

5. When you have finished, click the Close button ▭×▭ in the upper-right corner of the Help window to close it and return to PowerPoint.

Viewing a Presentation

PowerPoint provides multiple views for working with your presentations. Using these various views, you can work in outline format, rearrange slides in *Slide Sorter view*, or work on an individual slide in the Slide pane of Normal view.

Exercise 1-6 USE NORMAL AND SLIDE SORTER VIEWS

The Normal view is the best for entering text directly on a slide and planning the design of your presentation. *Normal view* is the default view when you open PowerPoint. The *Slide Sorter view* presents a window of *slide thumbnails*, which are miniature versions of the slides. To rearrange slides, you can click on a thumbnail then hold down the left mouse button while you *drag* it to a new position. Slide Sorter view makes it easy to apply special slide-show effects.

1. From the View tab, in the Presentation Views group, choose the Slide Sorter button ▦ .

2. Click and drag slide 7 to place it before slide 6. You will be able to tell where your slide is when dragging by the vertical line that appears.

3. From the View tab, in the Presentation Views group, choose the Normal button ▤ to return to Normal view.

Exercise 1-7 USE THE SLIDES AND OUTLINE PANE

In Normal view, the *Slides and Outline pane* is at the left of the Slide pane. It provides some alternative ways to work with your presentation. The Outline tab shows only slide titles and listed text with *bullets*, small circular shapes, in front of each listing. The Outline tab allows you to enter just your text content as an outline without modifying the design or adding graphics to

Figure 1-4
Working with the
Slides and Outline
pane

Outline and Slides tabs

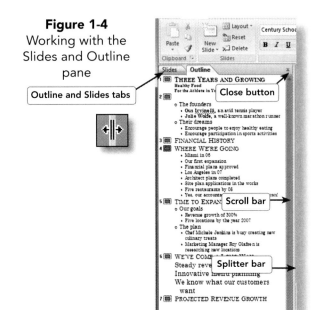

your slide. The Slides tab provides thumbnails similar to the slide sorter view.

1. Click the Outline tab at the top of the Slides and Outline pane. The Outline pane displays the presentation's text in an outline format.

2. Point to the right border of the Slides and Outline pane. When the splitter appears, drag the border about an inch to the right. This increases the size of the Slides and Outline pane.

3. Scroll in the outline text until you see the text for slide 4.

4. Working in the Outline tab, change each of the years (06, 07, and 08) to **2007, 2008,** and **2009.** The first line, for example, should read **Miami in 2007.** Notice that as you work, your changes are reflected in the Slide pane.

NOTE

When you have several bulleted lists, you can key them all in outline format if that's the way you like to work.

5. Click in front of Miami, then from the Home tab, in the Paragraph group, choose the Decrease List Level button to promote the item by moving it to the left. Apply this same treatment to Los Angeles in 2008 and Five Restaurants by 2009. This distinguishes the main items in the list from the more detailed items under them.

6. Click the Close button on the Slides and Outline pane to hide it. The Slide pane expands to fill the space.

7. From the View tab, in the Presentation Views group, choose the Normal view button. The Slides and Outline pane is displayed again.

8. Click the Slides tab at the top of the Slides and Outline pane. The Slides and Outline pane becomes smaller and the size of the Slide pane increases.

Exercise 1-8   MOVE FROM SLIDE TO SLIDE

PowerPoint provides several ways to move from slide to slide in a presentation:

- Use the pointer to drag the scroll box.

- Use the pointer to click the Previous slide or Next slide buttons.

- Use the PageUp and PageDown keys on the keyboard.

Figure 1-5
Moving from slide
to slide

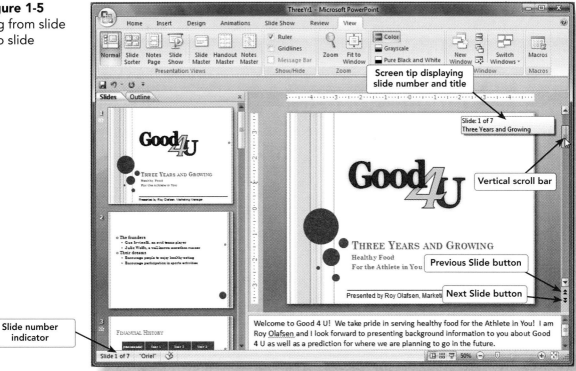

Slide number
indicator

1. Drag the vertical scroll box on the Slide pane to the bottom of the scroll bar. Notice the box that displays slide numbers and slide titles as you drag. When you release the mouse button at the bottom of the scroll bar, slide 7 appears in your window. Notice slide 7 has a highlighted border around it in the Slide pane. This identifies it as the current slide.

2. Drag the scroll box up to display slide 6. Notice that Slide 6 of 7 is indicated on the left side of the status bar.

3. Click the Previous Slide button 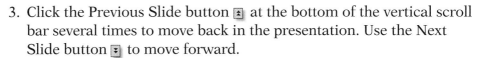 at the bottom of the vertical scroll bar several times to move back in the presentation. Use the Next Slide button ⬇ to move forward.

4. As an alternative to clicking the Next Slide button ⬇ and the Previous Slide button ⬆, press `PageDown` and `PageUp` on your keyboard several times. Use this method to move to slide 2. Check the status bar for the slide number.

Exercise 1-9   USE THE ZOOM AND FIT TO WINDOW

PowerPoint provides two different ways to *zoom* and *fit to window*. Zoom is a great tool for magnifying your slide so you can see small details for precise alignment and corrections. The fit to window command will change from the current zoom settings to fit in the window that is open.

- From the View tab, in the Zoom group, choose the Zoom or Fit to Window command buttons.

- Use the Zoom slider and Fit to Window buttons on the right end of the status bar.

1. From the View tab, in the Zoom group, click the Zoom button .

2. On the Zoom dialog box, click the radial button beside **200%** and click OK. You can use the zoom feature in normal or slide sorter view to change the percentage of what you are viewing.

TIP

You can also click and drag the Zoom slider toward the minus to zoom out and toward the plus to zoom in.

3. On the right end of the status bar is a Zoom slider. Click the Zoom out button (a minus) 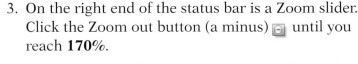 until you reach **170%**.

4. From the View tab, in the Zoom group, choose the Fit to Window button 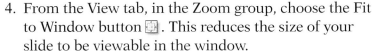 . This reduces the size of your slide to be viewable in the window.

Exercise 1-10 RUN A SLIDE SHOW

A *slide show* displays slides sequentially in full-screen size. One way to start a slide show is to click the Slide Show command button. After you begin running a slide show, PowerPoint provides navigation tools to move from slide to slide. You may start a slide show from any slide by moving to the slide you wish to start on and clicking the Slide Show command button.

TIP

As an alternative to clicking the left mouse button, you can press the Spacebar to move forward. Also, you can press N which means "next" to move forward and P which means "previous" to move backward. You can also use the right and left arrow keys or PageDown and PageUp to move forward and backward.

1. Move to slide 1 if it is not currently displayed. Click the Slide Show button located on the status bar to the left of the Zoom slider. The first slide in the presentation fills the screen.

2. Click the left mouse button to move to slide 2. The left mouse button is one of many ways to move forward in a slide presentation.

3. Press N on the keyboard to move to the next slide, slide 3.

Exercise 1-11 OBSERVE ANIMATION EFFECTS

Animation effects are the special visual or sound effects used as objects are displayed on the screen or removed from view. *Transition effects* are the effects seen in the process of changing between slides.

1. Press Ⓝ again to move to slide 4, which is titled "Where We're Going."

2. Using the left mouse button, click anywhere to see a sample of a PowerPoint text animation. Click twice more to see the remaining text on this slide.

3. Press Ⓝ again to move to slide 5. Notice the Box Out transition effect between slides 4 and 5.

4. Click the left mouse button two times to bring in the text from slide 5.

5. Press Ⓝ to move to slide 6. Press Ⓝ three more times to bring in the text for slide 6. Notice the Entrance and Emphasis effects placed on this text. If your sound is on, you should also hear sound effects with each text item.

6. Press Ⓝ to move to slide 7 and Ⓝ again to finish the presentation.

7. Press Esc or ⊟ (minus) to end the slide show.

Adding Text Using Placeholders

Adding and editing text in PowerPoint is very similar to editing text in a word processing program. You click an *I-beam* to position the *insertion point* where you want to key new text. An I-beam is a pointer in the shape of an uppercase "I." An insertion point is a vertical blinking bar indicating where the text you key will be placed. You can also drag the I-beam to select existing text. The keys Enter, Delete, and Backspace work the same way as in a word processing program.

It is important to understand that you *activate* a placeholder when you click the I-beam in it, making it ready to accept text.

Exercise 1-12   KEY PLACEHOLDER TEXT

Text on the slide is contained in text *placeholders.* Placeholders are used for *title text* (the text that usually appears at the top of a slide), *body text* (text in the body of a slide), and other objects, such as pictures. Placeholders help keep design layout and formatting consistent within a presentation.

Body text often contains *bullets* (small dots, squares, or other symbols) to indicate the beginning of each item in a list; therefore, this text is sometimes called bulleted text. Bullets can be decorative, also, for an attention-getting effect.

1. Move to slide 2, click in the Title Text Placeholder to activate the placeholder. Notice the box that surrounds the text. The border is made up of tiny dashed lines, and sizing handles indicates that the text box is activated and in edit mode, meaning you can edit and insert text.

2. Key the text **Where We Came From.**

3. Click anywhere on the line of text that begins "Gus Irvinelli."

4. Without clicking, move the pointer outside the border to the right and then back inside.

5. Drag the I-beam across the text "an avid" to select it as shown in Figure 1-6. (Click to the left of "an avid," hold down the left mouse button, drag the I-beam across the two words, and then release the mouse button.)

Figure 1-6
Selecting text to edit it

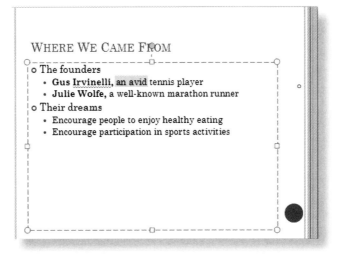

6. Key **a professional** to replace the selected text. (You don't need to delete selected text before keying new text.)

7. Click the I-beam to place the insertion point to the right of the words "healthy eating," near the bottom of the slide.

8. To insert a new line, press Enter. Notice that a new dimmed bullet appears at the beginning of the new line.

9. Key **Make their financial investment grow** on the new blank bullet line.

10. Click a blank part of the slide area to deactivate the text box. To make sure you are clicking a blank area, click when the pointer is a simple arrow, not an I-beam or a four-pointed arrow.

Exercise 1-13   CHANGE AND RESET PLACEHOLDER LAYOUT

Placeholders can be moved, resized, and rearranged on your slide. The layout feature of PowerPoint can be used to choose different layouts or reset the placeholder back to the original.

1. Still working on slide 2, click in the title placeholder to activate it.

2. Move your pointer to the outer border of the title placeholder.

3. When your pointer turns to a four-pointed arrow ⊕ (see Figure 1-7), click and drag the title placeholder to the bottom of the slide.

Figure 1-7
Selecting a
placeholder

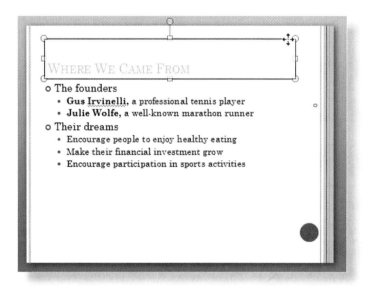

 4. From the Home tab, in the Slides group, click the Layout command button 🔲, and choose the Title and Content Layout to reposition the placeholders to their original position.

Naming and Saving a Presentation

In PowerPoint, presentations are saved as files. When you create a new presentation or make changes to an existing one, you must save the presentation to make your changes permanent. Until your changes are saved, they can be lost if there's a power failure or a computer problem.

The first step in saving a document is to give it a *filename*. Filenames can be up to 255 characters long.

Throughout the exercises in this book, your document filenames will consist of two parts:

• The number of the exercise, such as **1-15**.

• **Your initials**, which might be your initials or an identifier your instructor asks you to use, such as **rst**.

When you're working with an existing file, choosing the Save command (or clicking the Save button 🖫 on the Quick Access toolbar) replaces the file with the file on which you're working. After saving, the old version of the file no longer exists and the new version contains all your changes.

You can give an existing presentation a new name by using the Save As command. The original presentation remains unchanged and a second presentation with a new name is saved as well.

Exercise 1-14   CREATE A FOLDER FOR SAVING YOUR FILES

NOTE

Your instructor will advise you of the proper drive or folder to use when creating your lesson folders.

Before saving a file, you need to decide where you want to save it: in a folder on your fixed disk drive, on a jump drive, floppy disk or other removable medium, or on a network drive.

When you save a file, it's a good idea to create separate folders for specific categories to help keep your work organized. For example, you might want to create folders for different projects or different customers. In this course, you will follow these steps to create a new folder for each lesson's work before you begin the lesson.

NOTE

Even though you clicked Cancel to close the Save As dialog box, your new folder has been created. You could have saved your presentation before closing the Save As dialog box, but you will do that in the next exercise instead.

1. Click the Microsoft Office Button 🌀, choose Save As then PowerPoint Presentation. The Save As dialog box appears.

2. Using the list box at the top or links on the left, follow your instructor's directions to navigate to the location where you should create your folder. If you will be using a jump drive or other media, put it in your computer's drive now.

3. Click the Create New Folder button 🖿 New Folder on the Save As dialog box toolbar as shown in Figure 1-8.

Figure 1-8
Creating a new folder in the Save As dialog box

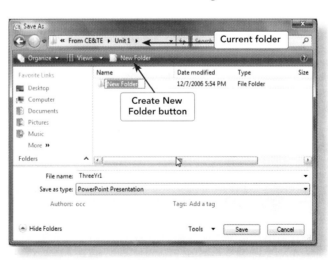

4. With the words New Folder selected, key **Lesson 1** and click off of the folder. A yellow folder icon with the name "Lesson 1" appears.

5. Click Cancel to close the Save As dialog box.

Exercise 1-15   NAME AND SAVE A PRESENTATION

To name files, you can use uppercase letters, lowercase letters, or a combination of both. Filenames can also include spaces. For example, you can use "Good 4 U Sales Report" as a filename.

1. Click the Microsoft Office Button ☺, choose Save As to reopen the Save As dialog box.

2. Navigate to the drive and folder where you created your new Lesson 1 folder.

3. Double-click the Lesson 1 folder to open it.

4. In the File name text box, key **[1-15your initials]**.

5. Click Save. Your document is saved and named for future use. Notice that the title bar displays the new filename.

Preparing Presentation Supplements

Although the primary way of viewing a presentation is usually as a slide show, you can also print PowerPoint slides, just as you print Word documents or Excel worksheets. PowerPoint provides a variety of print options, including printing each slide on a separate page or printing several slides on the same page. You should utilize the PowerPoint Print Preview option when preparing to print.

Throughout this course, to conserve paper and speed up printing, you usually print a *handout* instead of full-size slides. A handout contains several scaled-down slide images on each page (one, two, three, four, six, or nine to a page) and is often given to an audience during a presentation.

Exercise 1-16   PREVIEW A PRESENTATION

The PowerPoint *Print Preview* feature lets you see what your printed pages will look like before you actually print them. You can view preview pages in black and white, grayscale, or color.

1. Click the Microsoft Office Button ☺.

2. Point to the arrow next to Print.

3. Click Print Preview. The Preview window opens, showing you how the printed slide will appear on paper. The Print Preview Ribbon (see Figure 1-9) is displayed at the top of the window.

Figure 1-9
Print Preview Ribbon

TABLE 1-2 Print Preview Ribbon Buttons

Toolbar Button	Name	Purpose
	Print	Open the Print dialog box.
	Options	Choose from a variety of options and preview them before printing.
	Print what	Choose between printing slides, handouts, notes pages, or an outline.
	Orientation	Switch the pages between portrait (vertical) and landscape (horizontal) layouts.
	Zoom	Change the magnification in the Preview window.
	Fit to window	Zoom the presentation so that the slide fills the window.
	Next page	Display the next page to be printed.
	Previous page	Display the previous page to be printed.
	Close Print Preview	Close the Print Preview window and return to Normal view.

4. From the Print Preview tab, in the Preview group, click the Next Page button 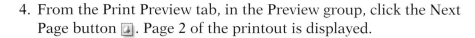. Page 2 of the printout is displayed.

5. Move your pointer to the middle of the slide. Notice that the pointer is in the shape of a magnifying glass ⬚.

6. Click the magnifying glass pointer in the center of the slide. The display is magnified.

7. Click again. The display returns to its regular size.

8. Click the Close the Print Preview window button ⬚.

Exercise 1-17 PRINT A SLIDE, NOTES PAGE, OUTLINE, AND HANDOUT

You can start the printing process in one of the following ways:

- Click the Microsoft Office Button ⬚, point to the arrow next to Print, and choose Print Preview. From the Print Preview Ribbon, in the Print group, click the Print button ⬚.

- Click the Microsoft Office Button, and choose Print.

- Press Ctrl + P.

- From the Quick Access toolbar, click the Quick Print button ⊞ .

The first method opens the Print Preview window, which you learned in Exercise 1-16. The next two methods open the Print dialog box, where you can choose printing options. The last method, Quick Print ⊞ , should be used with caution. You must first customize the Quick Access Toolbar to make the button available. This feature prints a presentation with the most recently used print options and does not open the print options dialog box. Usually this will result in printing your entire presentation with one slide on a page.

Printing an outline view is a nice feature if you want to print text only and avoid the slide thumbnails. Printing notes pages allows the speaker to record notes and print them along with an image of the slide. Printing several slides on a single page is a handy way to review your work and to create audience handouts. It's also a convenient way to print class assignments. You can create handouts in the Print Preview window or in the Print dialog box.

1. To print the first slide in your presentation, display slide 1, click the Microsoft Office Button ⊙, and then choose Print. The Print dialog box displays PowerPoint's default settings and indicates the designated printer as shown in Figure 1-10.

Figure 1-10
Print dialog box

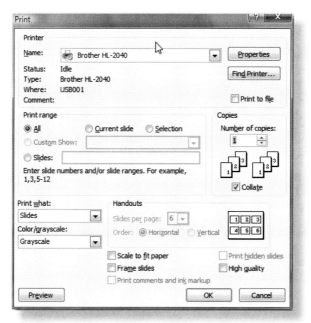

NOTE

The information below the Name box applies to the selected printer. For example, "Status" indicates if the printer is idle or currently printing other documents.

2. At the top of the Print dialog box, click the down arrow in the Name box. This is where you choose another printer, if one is available. Follow your instructor's directions to choose an appropriate printer from the list.

3. In the Print range option box, choose Current Slide.

TIP

You can create a presentation that uses overhead transparencies by printing your slides on transparency film. Before printing, insert transparency sheets directly into your printer (choosing the correct type of transparency for a laser or ink-jet printer).

TIP

If two slides are not displayed in the Print Preview screen, click the Print button, and under Print range, choose All. In the Print what drop-down list, choose Handouts. Then, under the Handouts heading, choose 2 from the drop-down list. Last of all, click Preview to return to Print Preview. This reverses the action where you chose Current Slide.

4. From the Print what drop-down list box, choose Slides.

5. Click OK to start printing.

6. Click the Microsoft Office Button, point to the arrow next to Print, and choose Print Preview. From the Print Preview tab, in the Page Setup group, click the arrow next to the Print what list box and then choose Handouts (2 Slides per page). Two slides are displayed on the preview page. This is what would print if you chose to print at this point.

7. Still working in the Page Setup group, click the Orientation button and choose Landscape.

8. Open the Print what list box and then choose Outline View (this provides text only).

9. Open the Print what list box and then choose Notes Pages (this provides a snapshot of the slide as well as speaker notes).

10. Open the Print what list box again and choose Handouts (9 Slides per page). Now the entire presentation is displayed on one page.

11. From the Print Preview tab, in the Preview group, click the Close Print Preview button.

Exercise 1-18   CHOOSE PRINT OPTIONS

NOTE

Because the Pure Black and White option simplifies your presentation graphics, it can sometimes speed up printing time.

TIP

To print consecutive slides, you can use a hyphen. For example, key 2-4 to print slides 2 through 4. To print a combination of slides, you can key the range 1,3, 5-9, 12 to print slides 1, 3, 5 through 9, and 12.

In addition to the options covered previously, there are two options for printing in black and white. The *Grayscale* option converts the presentation colors to shades of gray. The *Pure Black and White* option converts all colors to either black or white, eliminating shades of gray. Multiple copies can be printed, too, and the *Collate* option will print the slides in sequence.

The Print dialog box is divided into several areas: Printer, Print range, Copies, Print what, and Handouts. Each area presents choices that let you print exactly what you want in a variety of layouts.

1. Still working in **1-15your initials**, click the Microsoft Office Button and choose Print to open the Print dialog box.

2. Under Print range, click Slides and key **1,2** in the text box to print only slides 1 and 2.

3. Under Copies, in the Number of copies box, key **2**. The Collate check box is selected by default to print the slide show from beginning to end two times.

4. From the Print what drop-down list box, choose Notes Pages.

5. If you have a black-and-white printer, choose Grayscale from the Color/grayscale list box. If you have a color printer, you can choose Color from the list box but the grayscale will conserve your colored ink/toner.

6. Click the Scale to fit paper check box to expand items to the full width of the page.

7. Click OK.

8. Open the Print dialog box again and set the following options:

   - For Print range, choose All to print all slides.

   - For Number of copies, key **1**.

   - In the Print what list box, choose Handouts.

   - Under Handouts, choose 3 Slides per page.

   - From the Color/grayscale list box, choose Pure Black and White.

   - Click the Frame slides check box if it is not already checked.

9. Click OK to print the presentation handout and close the Print dialog box.

10. Click the Microsoft Office Button , and choose Save As.

11. In the File name text box, key **[1-18your initials]**.

12. Click Save. Your document is saved and named for future use. Notice that the title bar displays the new filename.

NOTE

You are still on landscape orientation since you set that in a previous exercise.

Ending Your Work Session

After you finish working on a presentation and save it, you can close it and open another file or you can exit the program.

To close a presentation and exit PowerPoint, you can:

- Click the Microsoft Office Button and choose Close or Exit PowerPoint.

- Use keyboard shortcuts. Ctrl+W closes a presentation and Alt+F4 exits PowerPoint.

- Use the Close button in the upper-right corner of the window.

Exercise 1-19 CLOSE A PRESENTATION AND EXIT POWERPOINT

1. Click the Microsoft Office Button.

2. Choose Close to exit the presentation.

3. Click the Close button in the upper-right corner of the window to exit PowerPoint.

Lesson 1 Summary

- Microsoft PowerPoint is a powerful graphics program used to create professional-quality presentations for a variety of settings.

- Identify items in the PowerPoint window by pointing to them and waiting for their ScreenTips to appear.

- PowerPoint command buttons are arranged in groups that can be accessed by clicking tabs on the Ribbon.

- The Quick Access toolbar contains a set of commands independent of the tab that is currently displayed. The toolbar includes commonly used commands such as save, undo, redo, and print.

- PowerPoint Help window is a great place to look for additional information on a topic or steps to completing a task.

- Key and edit text on a slide in the same way as you would in a word processing program.

- Use the Slide Show button to run a slide show. A slide show always starts with the slide that is currently selected.

- To print handouts that contain more than one slide on a page, use the Print dialog box or Print Preview window to select from the Print what options.

- Printing options provide a variety of ways to print your presentation: as slides, handouts, notes pages, and outline view.

LESSON 1		Command Summary	
Feature	**Button**	**Ribbon**	**Keyboard**
Open a presentation		Microsoft Office Button, Open	Ctrl + O
Display Slides and Outline pane		View tab, Presentation Views group, Normal	
Zoom		View tab, Zoom group, Zoom	
Help		Help button	F1
Normal view		View tab, Presentation Views group, Normal	
Slide Sorter view		View tab, Presentation Views group, Slide Sorter	
Next Slide			PageDown
Previous Slide			PageUp
Slide Show		View tab, Presentation Views group, Slide Show	F5
Save		Microsoft Office Button, Save; Quick Access toolbar, Save button	Ctrl + S
Save with a different name		Microsoft Office Button, Save As	
Next Slide (Slide Show view)		Right-click, Next	N , PageDown
Previous Slide (Slide Show view)		Right-click, Previous	P , PageUp , Backspace
End a slide show		Right-click, End Show	Esc or −
Layout		Home tab, Slides group, Layout	
Print Preview		Microsoft Office Button, Print arrow, Print Preview	
Print		Microsoft Office Button, Print; Quick Access toolbar, Quick Print button	Ctrl + P
Close a presentation		Microsoft Office Button, Close	Ctrl + W or Ctrl + F4
Exit PowerPoint	X Exit PowerPoint	Microsoft Office Button, Exit PowerPoint	Alt + F4

Concepts Review

True/False Questions

Each of the following statements is either true or false. Select your choice by indicating T or F.

T F   1. When you start PowerPoint, it automatically displays a blank presentation.

T F   2. Editing text in PowerPoint is similar to editing text in a word processing program.

T (F)   3. ScreenTips identify command buttons by name only.

(T) F   4. In the Slides and Outline pane, you can display either slide thumbnails or outline text, but not both at the same time.

(T) F   5. You can edit text in Normal view or in the Outline tab.

(T) F   6. You can display multiple slides as thumbnails in Slide Sorter view.

T (F)   7. When viewing a slide show, pressing the plus sign moves to the next slide.

T (F)   8. If you choose the Quick Print button ⬚ on the Quick Access toolbar, you can choose exactly which items to print.

Short Answer Questions

Write the correct answer in the space provided.

1. Where on the PowerPoint window are the View buttons located?

   Bottom right corner

2. What are the names of the three View buttons?

   Normal, Slide Show, Slide Sorter

3. If the Slides and Outline pane is not displayed, what button can you click to make it appear?

   Normal

4. What shape is the pointer when you move it over a text box?

   I beam

5. How would you save a copy of your presentation under a different filename?

   Save as

6. Name all the ways to use the keyboard for moving to the previous slide during a slide show.

N, space bar, up down arrow, p up down

7. Which keys can you press to stop a slide show?

esc. or — sign

8. What is the maximum number of slides you can print on a handout page?

Nine

Critical Thinking

Answer these questions on a separate page. There are no right or wrong answers. Support your answers with examples from your own experience, if possible.

1. In this lesson you learned how to display slide thumbnails in the Slides and Outline pane and also in Slide Sorter view. Which way do you prefer to view thumbnails and why? What advantages and disadvantages do you think there are for each option?

2. You can produce slide shows, printouts, 35 mm slides, overhead transparencies, and other presentation media with PowerPoint. Why might you choose one medium over another? What factors would influence your decision?

Skills Review

Exercise 1-20

Open a file, identify parts of the PowerPoint window, key and edit text, and save as a new file.

1. Open a presentation by following these steps:
   a. Click the Microsoft Office Button .
   b. Choose Open.
   c. Choose the appropriate drive and folder, according to your instructor's directions.
   d. Double-click the file **Answers**.
2. Click anywhere on the text "Click to add subtitle" and key **your name**.
3. Select the two question marks in the text "Exercise 1-??" by dragging the I-beam across them. Key **20**.
4. To move to slide 2, click the Next Slide button at the bottom of the vertical scroll bar.

5. Key the answers to the questions on slide 2 by following these steps:

   a. Click to position the insertion point after the word "Answer:" and press [Spacebar].

   b. Key the **answer**.

   c. Click after each of the words "Answer" and key the **answers to the next three questions**. Explore PowerPoint and remember to use your ScreenTips to help you answer the questions.

6. Save the presentation as **[1-20your initials]** in your Lesson 1 folder by following these steps:

   a. Click the Microsoft Office Button, choose Save As to open the Save As dialog box.

   b. Choose your Lesson 1 folder from the appropriate drive and folder, following your instructor's directions.

   c. Key the filename **[1-20your initials]** in the File name text box.

   d. Click Save.

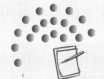

Exercise 1-21

NOTE

Before making the changes indicated in Figure 1-11, refer to "Proofreaders' Marks" at the Professional Approach Online Learning Center at **www.mhhe.com/pas07**. Proofreaders' marks are special notations used to mark up a printed draft with changes to be made before final printing. Some proofreaders' marks might be confusing if you are unfamiliar with them. For example, a handwritten "=" indicates that a hyphen is to be inserted.

Edit text on a slide, save a presentation, run a slide show, preview and print a presentation, and end your work session.

1. Open the file **GoodFood**.

2. Notice on the status bar and by viewing the thumbnails in the Slides and Outline pane that this is a three-slide presentation (slide 1 of 3 now appears). Move to slide 3 by dragging the vertical scroll box.

3. Make corrections to the slide's text as shown in Figure 1-11.

Figure 1-11

```
Just Sweet Enough

     Carob Pecan Yogurt Cream Pie
                                            s                 a
This light and fluffy desert has an all-natural grahm cracker crust,

great flavor, and very little sugar.

     Key Lime Soufflé
      intense                      chef
The striking lime flavor is Michelle's secret. Made from organic key

limes, sweetened with white grape juice, and thickened with organic egg

whites.
```

TIP

If you are trying to insert text, but the text to the right of your insertion point is disappearing, click your Insert button once on your keyboard. This will take PowerPoint out of Overtype mode.

4. Move to slide 2, and notice that two items show the name of a dish and two items show the descriptions. The descriptions should be indented to distinguish them from the name of each dish; therefore, place your insertion point before each description and press Tab to indent those lines.

5. Run the presentation as a slide show by following these steps:

   a. Display slide 1. Click the Slide Show button 🖳 on the status bar.

   b. After slide 1 appears, click the left mouse button to advance to the next slide.

   c. Click the left mouse button three more times to return to Normal view.

6. Save the presentation as **[1-21your initials]** in your Lesson 1 folder.

7. Print slides 1 and 3 only by following these steps:

   a. Click the Microsoft Office Button 🔘.

   b. Choose Print to open the Print dialog box.

   c. In the Print range area, click Slides and key **1,3** in the text box.

   d. From the Print what drop-down list, choose Slides. Choose Grayscale, and click OK.

8. Close the presentation by clicking the Close button 🗙 in the upper-right corner of the PowerPoint window.

Exercise 1-22

Work with views, edit text, run a slide show, save a presentation, preview and print a presentation, and close a presentation.

1. Open the file **DressCd1**.

2. View the presentation's text in outline format by following these steps:

   a. If the Slides and Outline pane is not displayed, click the Normal view button 🖼.

   b. Click the Outline tab.

   c. Point to the Outline pane's right vertical border.

   d. When you see the splitter bar ⬌, drag it to the right to the center of the screen to see the text on these slides. Move the splitter bar back to its original position.

3. Click the Slide Sorter view button 🖼 to view the presentation in Slide Sorter view.

4. Double-click slide 1 in Slide Sorter view to change back to Normal view.

5. Create a subtitle on slide 1 by following these steps:

   a. Click the text placeholder containing the text "Click to add subtitle."

   b. Key **your name**.

   c. Press Enter to start a new line; then key **today's date**.

6. Run a slide show and navigate within the show by following these steps:

   a. Click the Slide Show button 🖳 on the status bar.

   b. Advance through the slides by pressing (PageDown) several times.

7. Save the presentation as **[1-22your initials]**.

8. Preview the presentation before printing by following these steps:

   a. Click the Microsoft Office Button 🔘, point to the arrow beside Print, and choose Print Preview.

   b. In the Print what drop-down list, choose Handouts (4 slides per page).

   c. In the Options drop-down list box, point to Color/Grayscale and then choose Grayscale.

   d. In the Options drop-down list box, be sure there is a check beside Frame Slides. If it is not checked, click Frame Slides.

   e. Click the Print button 🖨.

   f. Click OK.

9. Click Close Print Preview 🗙 to close the Print Preview window and then close the presentation.

Exercise 1-23

Key text on a slide, save the file, and print.

1. Open the file **SpEvent1**.

2. Display slide 2.

3. Insert a new line of bulleted text by following these steps:

   a. Click the I-beam to the right of the word "team" at the end of the line "National In-Line Skate demo team."

   b. Press (Enter) to start a new line with an automatic bullet.

   c. Key **Autograph session with Marsha Miles**.

4. Edit the text you keyed by following these steps:

   a. Click the I-beam between the words "with" and "Marsha" to position the insertion point.

   b. Key **aerobic video star** and insert any necessary spaces.

5. Save the presentation as **[1-23your initials]** in your Lesson 1 folder.

6. Print the slides full size by following these steps:

   a. Click the Microsoft Office Button 🔘.

   b. Choose Print to open the Print dialog box.

   c. In the Print what drop-down list box, choose Slides.

   d. In the Color/Grayscale drop-down list box, choose Grayscale.

   e. Click Preview.

   f. Click the Next Page button 🔽 to preview slide 2.

   g. Click the Print button 🖨 and then click OK.

   h. Click the Close Print Preview button 🗙 to close the Preview window.

7. Close the presentation by clicking the Close button 🗙.

Lesson Applications

Exercise 1-24

Edit text, change presentation views, save, print, and close a presentation.

1. Open the file **Party1**.

2. Using the Slide pane, make the changes to slides 2 and 3 as shown in Figure 1-12.

Figure 1-12

Slide 2

    Entertainment

    • Audition bands
        ○ Charlie's Dingbats
        ○ The Electrolytes
        ○ ~~Wired Rabbits~~ Pure Power

    • Contact Marsha Miles
                                    dance-style   ?
        ○ Is she willing to lead aerobics
        ○ Is she available New Year's Eve?

Slide 3

    Menu

    • Michele needs suggestions by November 1
            tasting   5
    • Staff party to be held December 2

    • Menu printing deadline is December 10

3. Save the presentation as **[1-24your initials]**.

4. View each slide in the presentation as a slide show.

5. Preview the presentation as handouts, three slides per page, grayscale, framed, and then print it.

6. Close print preview and then close the presentation.

Exercise 1-25

Edit text, run a slide show, save, print, and close a presentation.

1. Open the file **JulyFun1**.

2. Move to slide 2. Working in the Slide pane, change "am" in the first and second bullets to **a.m.**, and change the date in the last bullet to **June 25**.

3. Click the Outline tab and drag the Outline pane's right border to make it wider.

4. Working on slide 3 in the outline area, change the age in the second bullet from "21" to **18**. Save the presentation as **[1-25your initials]**.

5. Click the Slides tab and display slide 1. Run a slide show of the presentation, clicking to display each new slide and text animation.

6. Preview and then print the presentation as handouts, six slides per page, grayscale, framed.

7. Close the presentation.

Exercise 1-26

Edit text, change presentation views, save, print, and close a presentation.

1. Open the file **DressCd2**.

2. On slide 1, key the word **Personnel** to the left of "Training" so the title reads "Personnel Training Session."

3. Locate the last line of text on slide 2 (which begins "Under no circumstances"). Position the insertion point at the end of that line and key **while on the job**.

4. Locate the last line of text on slide 3. Position the insertion point between "Good 4 U" and "test" and key **proficiency** (the phrase should read "Good 4 U proficiency test").

5. Click the Outline tab and make the Outline pane wide enough to work comfortably. Scroll down to display the outline text for slide 4.

6. Working on slide 4 in the Outline pane, delete the periods at the ends of the two sentences that begin "Guests."

7. Below the third bullet, change "Shirts are" to **T-shirts will be**.

8. Save the presentation as **[1-26your initials]**.

9. Preview and then print the presentation as handouts, four slides per page, grayscale, framed.

10. Close the presentation.

Exercise 1-27 ◆ Challenge Yourself

Edit text, print a slide and handouts, and close a presentation.

1. Open the file **RacePrep**.

2. Using whichever view you choose, edit slide 2 and slide 3 as shown in Figure 1-13.

Figure 1-13

Slide 2

```
Entertainment
                                        on
  • The Electrolytes will be here for marathon eve, injecting
       charging up the runners
    mental energy for all

  • Julie will again lead her famous pre-marathon "Pump-you-up"
    chant
```

Slide 3

```
Pre Marathon
Carbo Loading Menu

  • Marathon Angel
       mountain                    pasta served
    o  A huge pile of angel hair with fat-free tomato sauce
       and sprinkled with tiny bite-sized meat balls

  • Bagel Bonanza
    o  Bagels brushed with a mixture of olive oil, garlic,
       and delicate herbs
```

3. Save the presentation in your Lesson 1 folder as **[1-27your initials]**.

4. View the presentation in Slide Sorter view.

5. Run the presentation as a slide show, beginning with slide 1.

6. Preview and then print all slides in grayscale, framed.

7. Print the presentation as handouts, three slides per page, grayscale, framed.

8. Close print preview and then close the presentation.

On Your Own

In these exercises you work on your own, as you would in a real-life work environment. Use the skills you've learned to accomplish the task—and be creative.

Exercise 1-28

Open the file **SpEvent1**. Change slide 2 so that its title is Summer Events. Edit the slide's bullets by changing the events to be for June and July, describing activities relating to summer sports such as swimming, softball, sand volleyball, or others. Save the presentation as **[1-28your initials]**. Preview and then print the presentation as handouts, two slides per page.

Exercise 1-29

Open the file **GoodFood**. On slide 2, replace the text describing the pasta dishes with pasta creations from your imagination. On slide 3, replace the text describing the desserts with your own combination of sweet delights. Be sure the desserts you describe use healthy ingredients.

Save the presentation as **[1-29your initials]**. Preview and then print the presentation as handouts, three slides per page.

Exercise 1-30

Open the file **Fruitjuices**. On slide 2, promote each of the list levels that begin with the word variations. After the word variations under each type of juice, key your own creation of combinations of juices that could create new juice titles. Get creative with your juice combinations since the Good 4U restaurant described in the case study at the beginning of this text prides itself in serving healthy food and drinks. Save the presentation as **[1-30your initials]**. Preview and then print the presentation as handouts, landscape orientation, two slides per page.

Developing Presentation Text

OBJECTIVES

After completing this lesson, you will be able to:

1. Create a new blank presentation.
2. Use the font group commands.
3. Adjust text placeholders.
4. Work with bullets and numbering.
5. Work with text boxes.

Estimated Time: 1¾ hours

MCAS OBJECTIVES

In this lesson:
PP07 1.1.1
PP07 1.5
PP07 2.1.1
PP07 2.1.2
PP07 2.1.3
PP07 2.1.4
PP07 2.2.3
PP07 2.2.5
PP07 2.2.6
See Appendix

You can add interest to a PowerPoint presentation by varying the appearance of text—that includes changing the font, text style, bullet shape, or position of text. You can change text appearance before or after you key it. Always strive for readability and continuity within your presentation.

In this lesson you will learn how to change text attributes such as color, font, font style, and font size. You will also work with bullets and numbering for easy-to-read lists and use different ways of indenting your text. You will change the indent settings, set tab stops, adjust line spacing, and manipulate text in other ways. Several keystrokes you will use to quickly move around on slides or within your presentation are shown in Table 2-1.

Creating a New Blank Presentation

To create a new blank presentation, you can begin with either:

- A *design theme*, which adds uniform colors and design background to each slide in the presentation.

- A blank presentation (simple text on a plain background), to which you can later apply a design template.

You build each slide by choosing a slide layout and keying slide text.

Exercise 2-1 START A NEW BLANK PRESENTATION

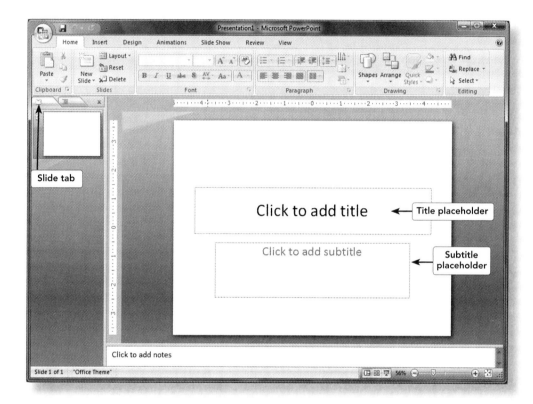

NOTE

If PowerPoint is already open and a blank title slide is not displayed, click the Microsoft Office Button and choose New. Choose Blank Presentation and click Create.

One way to create a presentation is to start with a blank slide, focusing first on content, and then adding color and other design elements later.

1. Start PowerPoint. A blank title slide appears, ready for your text input, as shown in Figure 2-1.

Figure 2-1
Title slide

2. Click the title placeholder to activate it and key **For the Pleasure of Your Company**.

3. Click the subtitle placeholder and key **Plan Your Next Event with Good 4 U**.

NOTE

The documents you create in this course relate to the case study in the front of this text about Good 4 U, a fictional restaurant business.

4. Position the insertion point after the word "Event" in the subtitle; then press Shift + Enter. The subtitle is now split into two lines. Delete the space before "with" on the second line of the subtitle.

5. Split the title text into two lines so that "Your Company" appears on the second line.

TABLE 2-1 Using the Keyboard to Navigate on a Slide and in a Presentation

Keystrokes	Result
Ctrl + Enter	Selects and activates the next text placeholder on a slide. If the last placeholder (subtitle or body text) is selected or activated, pressing Ctrl + Enter inserts a new slide after the current slide. Pressing Ctrl + Enter never selects other objects on a slide (including text boxes) that are not placeholders.
Esc	Deactivates the currently activated text placeholder or text box and selects the entire text box instead. If a text box is selected but not activated, pressing Esc deselects the text box.
Tab	If a text placeholder or text box is activated, inserts a tab character at the insertion point; if not activated, selects the next object on the slide. If the insertion point is between a bullet and the first text character on a line, pressing Tab demotes the bulleted text. Pressing Tab repeatedly when no objects are activated cycles through all the objects on a slide but never moves to another slide.
Shift + Tab	If a text box or text placeholder is not activated, selects the previous object on a slide. If the insertion point is between a bullet and the first text character on the line, promotes the bulleted text.
Esc, Tab	Moves to the next object on a slide, regardless of whether a text box is activated. It never inserts a new slide.
Shift + Enter	If a text box or text placeholder is activated, inserts a new line (but not a new paragraph) at the insertion point.
Enter	If a text box or text placeholder is activated, inserts a new paragraph, including a bullet if in a body text placeholder. If a text box or text placeholder is selected but not activated, selects all the text in the object.
Ctrl + M	Inserts a new slide after the current slide.

Exercise 2-2   ADD NEW SLIDES AND USE SLIDE LAYOUTS

To add a new slide after the current slide in a presentation, you can do one of the following:

- From the Home tab, in the Slides group, click the New Slide button ▣.

- Press Ctrl + M.

- When a placeholder is selected, press Ctrl + Enter one or more times until a new slide appears.

When a new slide first appears on your PowerPoint window, you don't need to activate a placeholder to start keying text. When no placeholder is selected, as long as your slide pane is active, the text you key automatically goes into the title text placeholder. Knowing this can speed up the process of developing a presentation.

1. From the Home tab, in the Slides group, click the top of the New Slide button ▣. A new slide appears, containing a title text placeholder and a body text placeholder.

2. Key **Excellent Service**. The text appears automatically in the title placeholder.

Figure 2-2
Keying text on a slide

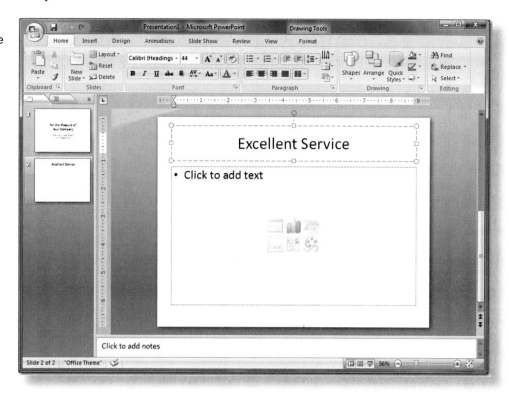

3. Press Ctrl + Enter or click the body text placeholder to activate it and key the following text, pressing Enter at the end of each bulleted line:

- We put your employees and guests at ease
- We make your company look good
- We adhere to promised schedules
- We provide a professional and courteous staff
- We guarantee customer satisfaction

TIP

When you insert a new slide in a presentation, it uses the same layout as the previous slide (unless the previous slide was the title slide). You learn how to change slide layouts later in this lesson.

4. Press Ctrl + M to create a new text slide.

5. Key **A Delightful Menu** as the title and then key the following body text:

- High-quality, healthy food
- Variety to appeal to a broad range of tastes

6. From the Home tab, in the Slides group, click the down arrow on the New Slide button 🔲 to see thumbnail *slide layouts* with their names, as shown in Figure 2-3. Layouts contain placeholders for slide content such as titles, bulleted lists, charts, and shapes that you will learn about in other lessons.

PowerPoint 2007

Figure 2-3
Inserting a new slide
by using the slide
layouts

TIP

PowerPoint's *AutoCorrect* feature automatically corrects common spelling and other errors as you key text. It can be turned on or off, and you can customize it so it will find errors that you frequently make.

7. Click the Title and Content slide layout.

8. Key **High-Energy Fun** as the title and then key the following body text:

   • **Athletic decor**

   • **Sports promotions**

9. Notice that PowerPoint's AutoCorrect feature automatically adds the accent mark to the word "décor."

10. Press Ctrl+M to insert another slide; then key **A Healthy Atmosphere** as the title and key the following body text:

    • **Smoke-free**

    • **Alcohol optional**

    • **We sell none**

    • **We'll gladly serve your own**

11. Move to slide 4 ("High-Energy Fun") and from the Home tab, in the Slides group, click the down arrow on the New Slide button ☐. Click the Two Content slide layout.

12. Key **Events That Are Good 4 U** as the title and then key the following bulleted text in the left body text placeholder:

    • **High-energy meetings**

    • **Productive lunches**

    • **Company celebrations**

    • **Celebrity promotions**

13. Key the following bulleted text in the right body text placeholder:

    - **Entertaining customers**
    - **Demonstrating products**

14. Notice how each slide is numbered in the Slides and Outline pane.

15. Create a new folder for Lesson 2 and save the presentation **[2-2your initials]** in your new Lesson 2 folder.

16. Close the presentation.

Using the Font Group Commands

One way to change the appearance of text in your presentation is by changing the font. A font is a set of characters with a specific design. You can change the *font face* (such as Times New Roman or Arial) and the *font size*. Fonts are measured in *points* (there are 72 points to an inch) indicating how tall a font is.

It is useful to understand that different fonts can take up different amounts of horizontal space, even though they are the same size. For example, a word formatted as 20-point Arial will be wider than a word formatted as 20-point Garamond, as shown in Figure 2-4.

Figure 2-4
Comparing fonts

20 point Arial:	**Formatting**
20 point Garamond:	Formatting

Another way to change the appearance of text is by applying text attributes. For example, you can apply a text style (such as bold or italic) and effect (such as underline or shadow). You use the Font group commands, shown in Figure 2-5 and described in Table 2-2, to change selected text.

Figure 2-5
The Font group on the Home tab

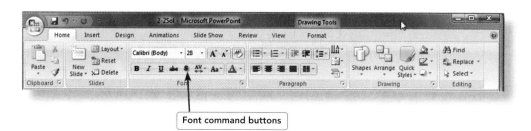

Font command buttons

TABLE 2-2 The Font Group Formatting Command Buttons

Button		Purpose
Century Gothic (B ▼)	Font	Enables you to choose a font face for selected text or for text to be keyed at the insertion point.
36 ▼	Font Size	Enables you to choose a font size for selected text or for text to be keyed at the insertion point.
A˄	Increase Font Size	Increases the size of selected text by one font size.
A˅	Decrease Font Size	Decreases the size of selected text by one font size.
Aa	Clear All Formatting	Removes all formatting from the selected text.
B	Bold	Applies the bold attribute to text.
I	Italic	Applies the italic attribute to text.
U	Underline	Applies the underline attribute to text.
S	Shadow	Applies a text shadow.
abc	Strikethrough	Draws a line through selected text.
AV↔	Character Spacing	Increases or decreases the space between characters.
Aa ▼	Change Case	Applies different capitalizations such as uppercase, lowercase, or sentence case.
A ▼	Font Color	Changes text color.

Exercise 2-3   CHANGE THE FONT FACE AND FONT SIZE

One convenient way to apply text formatting is to first key the text, focusing on content, and then select the text and apply formatting, such as by changing the size or font. Keep in mind that no more than two or three fonts should be used in a presentation. Also remember that the font size should be large enough for easy reading when the presentation is displayed on a large projection screen.

Another thing to be aware of is the type of font you choose. The font drop-down list displays all the fonts available for your computer. On the left side of each font is a symbol indicating the font type. *Truetype* fonts have the following symbol: ⊤. If you plan to show your presentation on a different computer or print it with a different printer, it is best to choose a Truetype font.

The Increase Font Size ⒜ and Decrease Font Size ⒜ buttons change the size of all the text in a selected placeholder by one font size increment as shown in the font size box on the formatting toolbar. If several sizes of text are used

in the placeholder, each size is changed proportionately. For example, if a text placeholder contains both 24-point text and 20-point text, clicking the Increase Font Size button A will change to the point sizes 28 and 24 at the same time.

Many of the buttons used to format text are toggle buttons. A *toggle button* switches between on and off when you click it. The Shadow button s is an example of a toggle button: click it once to apply a shadow, once again to remove it. Other examples of toggle buttons are Bold B, Italic I, and Underline U.

Figure 2-6
Font drop-down list

1. Open the file **Health1**.

2. Examine the Font group and locate the command buttons listed in Table 2-2.

3. On slide 1, click the title placeholder to activate it and key **Heart**.

4. Select the word you just keyed.

5. In the Font group, click the down arrow next to the Font box. A drop-down list of available fonts appears, as shown in Figure 2-6.

6. From the drop-down list, choose Arial Black. As you can see, text formatting in PowerPoint is similar to text formatting in a word processing program.

Figure 2-7
Font size drop-down list

7. With "Heart" still selected, click the down arrow next to the Font Size box, as shown in Figure 2-7. Choose 66. The text size increases to 66 points.

8. Click the Decrease Font Size button A. The font size decreases by one size increment. Notice the number "60" displayed in the Font Size box.

9. Click the Increase Font Size button A twice. The font size increases by two size increments, to 72 points (the equivalent of 1 inch tall).

NOTE

Theme colors are preselected groups of colors that provide variations suitable for many presentation needs. However, font colors or other graphic colors may need more emphasis than using the Theme colors will provide.

Exercise 2-4   APPLY BOLD, ITALIC, COLOR, AND SHADOW

Sometimes it's convenient to apply text formatting as you key. This is particularly true with bold, italic, and underline if you use the following keyboard shortcuts:

- Ctrl + B for bold

- Ctrl + I for italic

- Ctrl + U for underline
- Ctrl + S for shadow

TIP

A shadow can help to make the shapes of characters more distinctive. Be sure you always have a high contrast in color between your text colors and your background colors (light on dark or dark on light) for easy reading. Apply a shadow when it helps to make your text stand out from the background color and apply the same type of shadow in a similar way for unity of design in your presentation.

1. Position the insertion point to the right of "Heart" and press Spacebar. Click the Bold button B (or press Ctrl + B) and then the Italic button I (or press Ctrl + I) to turn on these attributes.

2. Key **Smart!** The word is formatted as bold italic as you key. Notice that this word is also 72-point Arial, like the previous word.

3. Double-click the word "Heart" to select it then press Ctrl + B to make it bold.

4. Select the word "Heart."

5. From the Home tab, in the Font group, locate the Font Color button. Click its down arrow to open the Font Color menu showing Theme colors and Standard colors, as shown in Figure 2-8.

6. Drag your pointer over the row of standard colors and you will see the live preview of that color before it is applied. Click the red box and the color is applied.

Figure 2-8
Font color menu

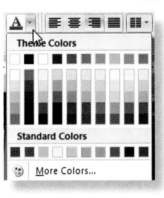

7. Click in the word "Smart" to deselect "Heart." "Heart" is now red.

8. Select both of the two words in your title placeholder. From the Home tab, in the Font group, click the Shadow button S. Now the text appears to "float" above the slide background with a soft shadow behind it.

Exercise 2-5   CHANGE THE CASE OF SELECTED TEXT

If you find that you keyed text in uppercase and want to change it, you don't have to re-key it. By using the Change Case button, as shown in Figure 2-9, you can change any text to Sentence case, lowercase, UPPERCASE, Capitalize Each Word, or tOGGLE cASE. You can also cycle through uppercase, lowercase, and either title case or sentence case (depending on what is selected) by selecting text and pressing Shift + F3 one or more times.

Figure 2-9
Change Case dialog box

1. Move to slide 3.

2. Use the I-beam pointer to select the title "walk to good health," which has no letters capitalized.

3. From the Home tab, in the Font group, click the down arrow on the Change Case button . Choose Capitalize Each Word. This option causes each word to begin with a capital letter.

4. Select the word "To" in the title. Press Shift + F3 two times to change it to lowercase.

5. Select the first item in the body text placeholder by clicking its bullet. This text was keyed with Caps Lock accidentally turned on.

6. From the Home tab, in the Font group, click the Change Case button and choose tOGGLE cASE. This option reverses the current case, changing uppercase letters to lowercase, and lowercase letters to uppercase.

7. Select the two bulleted items under "Walking" (beginning with "reduces" and "lowers") by dragging your I-beam across all the words.

8. From Home tab, in the Font group, click the Change Case button and choose Sentence case. Now only the first word in each item is capitalized.

Exercise 2-6   CHANGE LINE SPACING WITHIN PARAGRAPHS

You can control *line spacing* by adding more space between the lines in a paragraph or by adding more space between paragraphs. Increased line spacing can make your text layout easier to read and enhance the overall design of a slide.

To change spacing between lines within a paragraph, you can use the Line Spacing button to change the space between lines within a paragraph by increments of 0.5 lines.

Figure 2-10
Line spacing sizes

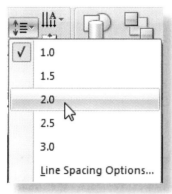

1. Move to slide 2. Click within the first bulleted item, which is considered a paragraph in the placeholder.

2. From the Home tab, in the Paragraph group, click the Line Spacing button and a drop-down list of sizes appear, as shown in Figure 2-10.

3. Click 2.0 and the line spacing of the first paragraph increases.

4. Usually you will want to change the line spacing for an entire text placeholder. Select the placeholder.

5. From the Home tab, in the Paragraph group, click the Line Spacing button , and change the line spacing to 1.5 lines.

Exercise 2-7   CHANGE LINE SPACING BETWEEN PARAGRAPHS

The default paragraph line spacing measurement is single. Using the Paragraph dialog box, you can add space by inserting points for before or after paragraphs to expand the space between them. In PowerPoint, each bulleted item in a list is treated as a paragraph.

1. Still working on slide 2, click within the second bulleted item (a paragraph) then in the Paragraph group, click the Dialog Box Launcher to open the Paragraph dialog box, as shown in Figure 2-11.

Figure 2-11
Paragraph dialog box

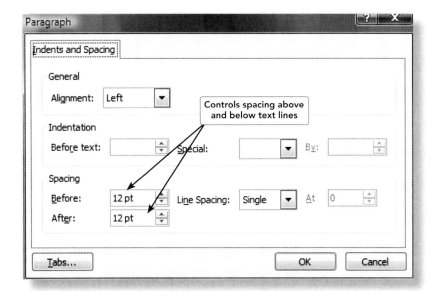

2. In the Spacing section, change the Before setting by clicking the spin-box up arrow twice to 18 points. Click OK.

3. To make all paragraph spacing uniform, select the entire text placeholder and open the Paragraph dialog box. Change the Before spacing to 12 points and the After spacing to 12 points. Change the Line spacing setting to Single. Click OK. The text is now evenly spaced in the placeholder.

4. Save the presentation as [**2-7your initials**] in your Lesson 2 folder but do not print it. Leave the presentation open for the next exercise.

Exercise 2-8   USE THE FONT DIALOG BOX TO MAKE MULTIPLE CHANGES

The Font dialog box is a convenient place to apply several font attributes all at one time. In addition to choosing a font, font style, and font size, this dialog box enables you to choose various effects, such as underline or shadow, and a font color.

1. Go to slide 1 and select the words "Diet and Exercise" in the subtitle. Notice that handles appear around the entire subtitle placeholder, but the colored area showing selection appears only around the text. This has happened because the placeholder is much bigger than the three words that are keyed in it.

2. Right-click the selected text to display the shortcut menu. Choose Font to open the Font dialog box, as shown in Figure 2-12.

TIP

Underlining is not the best way to emphasize text. Underlining can cut through the bottom of letters (the descenders) causing the text to be more difficult to read. And because underlining is used so much for hyperlinks on the Internet, underlining seems to have the connotation of a hyperlink. So emphasize your text in different ways, such as by using a larger font size, more dramatic color, or bold.

3. Choose the following options in the Font dialog box:

   • From the Latin text font list box, choose Arial.

   • From the Font style list box, choose Bold Italic.

   • From the Size list box, key **48**.

   • For Underline style, choose Wavy heavy line.

   • For Underline color, choose Dark red.

   • Notice the additional options available in this dialog box.

Figure 2-12
Font dialog box

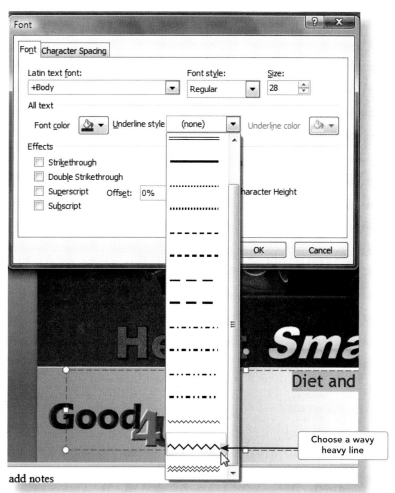

4. Click OK to close this dialog box.

5. Select the word "Heart" and then from the Home tab, in the Font group, click the Underline button to turn on underlining. Click the Underline button again to turn off this attribute.

NOTE

You can change text attributes in the Outline tab in the same way as in the Slide tab.

6. With the word "Heart" still selected, change the size to 80 points.

7. Save the presentation as **[2-8your initials]** in your Lesson 2 folder.

8. Preview and then print the title slide only, grayscale, framed.

Adjusting Text Placeholders

You can change formatting features for an entire placeholder by first selecting the placeholder and then choosing the formatting. For example, you can change the text size, color, or font.

You can select placeholders several ways:

- Click the border of an active placeholder with the four-pointed arrow ⊕.

- Press Esc while a placeholder is active (when the insertion point is in the text).

- Press Tab to select the next placeholder on a slide (only when a text box or text placeholder is not active).

You can deselect placeholders several ways:

- Press Esc to deselect a placeholder or other object. (Press Esc twice if a text placeholder or text box is active.)

- Click an area of the slide where there is no object.

Exercise 2-9   SELECT A TEXT PLACEHOLDER

Selecting and applying formatting to an entire placeholder can save time in editing.

1. On slide 3, click anywhere in the title text to make the placeholder active. Notice that the placeholder is outlined with small dashes to create a border showing the size of the rectangle. Circles are positioned on the corners and squares are positioned at the midpoint of all four sides, as shown in Figure 2-13. When the placeholder looks like this, the insertion point is active (an I-beam) and you are ready to edit the text within the placeholder.

Figure 2-13
Selecting a text
placeholder

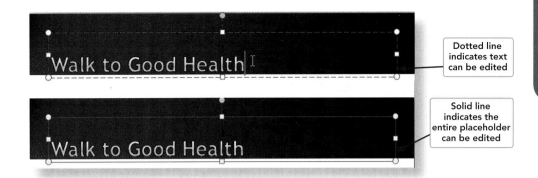

Dotted line
indicates text
can be edited

Solid line
indicates the
entire placeholder
can be edited

2. Point to any place on the dotted line border but not on a circle or square. When you see the four-pointed arrow ⊕ , click the border. Notice that the insertion point is no longer active and the border's appearance has changed slightly—it is now made up of a solid line instead of a dashed line. This indicates that the placeholder is selected. You can make changes to all of the text within it, the fill color of the placeholder, the size of the placeholder, or the position of the placeholder.

3. Press Tab. Now the body text placeholder is selected.

4. Press Esc to deselect the body text placeholder. Now nothing on the slide is selected.

5. Still working on slide 3, click inside the title placeholder text and then press Esc. This is another way to select an active placeholder.

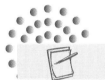

NOTE

Pressing Tab cycles through all objects on a slide, not just text placeholders. If a slide contains a graphic object, Tab selects that as well.

6. Click the Increase Font Size button A five times. The font size increases to 60 points.

7. Click the Decrease Font Size button A two times until the font size is 48 points.

8. Press Tab to select the body text placeholder. Notice the 23+ in the Font Size box. This indicates that there is more than one font size in the placeholder, and the smallest size is 23 points.

9. Click any text in the first bullet. Notice that its font size is 26 points. Notice also that when you click text inside a placeholder, its border is no longer selected. (The dashed line returns to the border showing that you are editing the text.)

TIP

Another way to increase or decrease font size is to press Ctrl + Shift + > or Ctrl + Shift + <.

10. Click the first sub-bullet text, which is 23 points.

11. Press Esc to reselect the entire placeholder.

12. Click the Increase Font Size button A twice so that 28+ appears in the Font Size box.

13. From the Home tab, in the Font group, click the down arrow on the Font Color button and choose Standard color dark blue (the color sample second from the right), making all the body text on this slide dark blue.

14. Still working in the Font group, click the Shadow button ⓢ to test that effect. Now all the text has a shadow, but with the colors being used, the text looks blurred. Remove the Shadow by clicking the Shadow button ⓢ again.

15. Leave the presentation open for the next exercise.

Exercise 2-10   CHANGE TEXT HORIZONTAL ALIGNMENT

Bulleted items, titles, and subtitles are all considered paragraphs in PowerPoint. Just as in a word processing program, when you press ⌨Enter, a new paragraph begins. You can align paragraphs with either the left or right placeholder borders, center them within the placeholder, or justify long paragraphs so that both margins are even. However, the last alignment option should be reserved for longer documents such as reports when you want a formal appearance. Fully justified text is not appropriate for presentation slides.

You can change text alignment for all the text in a placeholder or for just one line, depending on what is selected.

1. Move to slide 5 and select the body text placeholder.

2. Position the insertion point in the first line, "Earn Good 4 U discounts."

3. From the Home tab, in the Paragraph group, click the Align Right button ≡. The text in the first line aligns on the right.

4. Click the Align Left button ≣ and the paragraph aligns on the left.

5. Select the placeholder border and click the Center button ≡. Both lines are centered horizontally within the placeholder. Because the lines are centered, remove the bullets by clicking on the Bullet list button ⊞▾.

6. Make the text bold.

7. Leave the presentation open for the next exercise.

Exercise 2-11   RESIZE A PLACEHOLDER

At times you will want to change the way text is positioned on a slide. For example, you might want to make a text placeholder narrower or wider to control how text wraps to a new line, or you might want to move all the text up or down on a slide. You can change the size and position of text placeholders in several ways:

- Drag a *sizing handle* to change the size and shape of a text placeholder. Sizing handles are the four small circles on the corners and the squares on the border of a selected text placeholder or other object.

- Drag the placeholder border to move the text to a new position.

- Change placeholder size and position settings by using the Format Shape dialog box.

To change the size or shape of a placeholder, you must first select it, displaying the border as a solid line with sizing handles. It is important to make sure that you're dragging a sizing handle when you want to change a placeholder's size.

By dragging a corner sizing handle, you can change both the height and width of a placeholder at the same time.

1. Display slide 5 and select the body text placeholder. Notice the small white circles and squares on the border. These are the sizing handles, as shown in Figure 2-14.

2. Position the pointer over the bottom center sizing handle.

3. When the pointer changes to a two-pointed vertical arrow , hold down your left mouse button and drag the bottom border up until it is just below the second line of text.

4. As you drag, the border moves and the pointer turns into a crosshair ⊞. When you release the mouse, the border adjusts to the new position.

Figure 2-14
Resizing a
placeholder

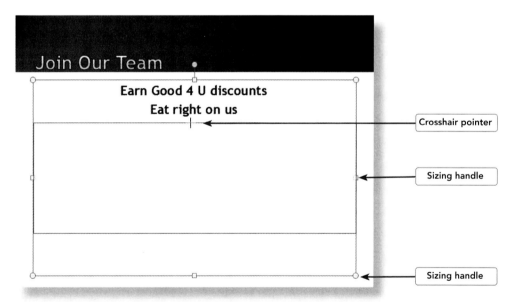

5. Position your pointer over the lower-left-corner sizing handle; then drag it toward the center of the text. Both the height and width of the placeholder change.

6. Click the Undo button once to restore the placeholder to its previous size.

7. Leave the presentation open for the next exercise.

Exercise 2-12   MOVE A PLACEHOLDER

As with changing the size of a placeholder, to change a placeholder's position you must first select it. Drag any part of the placeholder border except the sizing handles when you want to change its position.

TIP

To fine-tune the position of an object, hold down Alt while dragging or press the arrow keys to "nudge" an object. Press Ctrl + arrow keys to nudge an object in very small increments.

1. Select the body text placeholder on slide 5.

2. Position the pointer over the placeholder border anywhere except on a sizing handle. The pointer changes to the four-pointed arrow ⊕.

3. Drag the four-pointed arrow ⊕ down until the placeholder appears vertically centered on the white area of the slide, as shown in Figure 2-15.

Figure 2-15
Moving a placeholder

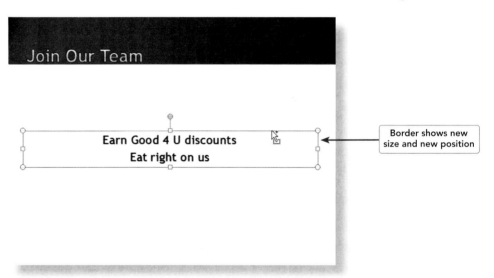

Border shows new size and new position

4. Deselect the placeholder. The text is now attractively placed on the slide.

5. Move to slide 1 and save the presentation as **[2-12your initials]** but do not print it.

6. Leave the presentation open for the next exercise.

Working with Bullets and Numbering

When you work with body text placeholders, each line automatically starts with a bullet. However, you can turn bullets off when the slide would look better without them. You can remove bullets, add new ones, change the shape and color of bullets, and create your own bullets from pictures. The Bullets and Numbering buttons are both found in the Paragraph group.

Exercise 2-13 REMOVE BULLETS

As you have learned in previous exercises, the Bullets button can turn bullets off and on. Depending on how your text is selected, you can affect a single bullet or all the bulleted lines in a body placeholder when you use the Bullets button. The Bullets button is another example of a toggle button.

1. Display slide 2. Click within the body text to activate the placeholder. Press [Esc] to select the entire placeholder.

2. From the Home tab, in the Paragraph group, click the Bullets button. This turns bullets off for the entire placeholder and moves the text to the left.

3. Click the Bullets button again to reapply the bullets.

4. Click within the first bulleted item, "Exercise regularly," and click the Bullets button to turn off the bullet.

5. Click the Bullets button again to reapply the bullet.

Exercise 2-14 PROMOTE AND DEMOTE BULLETED TEXT

As you create bulleted items, a new bullet is inserted when you press [Enter] to start a new line. When you want to expand on a slide's main points, you can insert indented bulleted text below a main point. This supplemental text is sometimes referred to as a sub-bullet or a level 2 bullet. PowerPoint body text placeholders can have up to five levels of indented text, but you will usually want to limit your slides to two levels.

To *demote* body text, you increase its indent level by moving it to the right. To *promote* body text, you decrease its indent level by moving it to the left. These changes can be made by moving the insertion point before the text and pressing [Tab] to demote (increase indent) or [Shift]+[Tab] to promote (decrease indent) or by using the Increase List Level or Decrease List Level buttons found on the Home tab, in the Paragraph group.

1. With slide 2 displayed, move your insertion point after "regularly" then press [Enter] to create a new bulleted line.

2. Press [Tab] to indent to the second-level bullet and key **Walk 30 minutes daily** then press [Enter].

3. Notice that the text is now indented automatically to the second-level bullet.

4. Key **Alternate aerobic and weight training** then press [Enter].

5. To return to the first-level bullet, press [Shift]+[Tab].

6. Key **Get sufficient rest**.

7. Leave the presentation open for the next exercise.

NOTE

If you press [Tab] when the insertion point is within the text placeholder, you insert a tab character instead of demoting text.

Exercise 2-15 CHANGE THE COLOR AND SHAPE OF A BULLET

The Bullets gallery provides just a few choices to change the shape of a bullet. The Bullets dialog box provides many more choices to change the bullet shape by choosing a character from another font. Fonts that contain potential bullet characters include Symbol, Wingdings, and Webdings. Another source of bullet characters is the Geometric Shapes subset available for most other fonts.

1. Working on slide 2, select the body text placeholder.

2. From the Home tab, in the Paragraph group, click the down arrow on the Bullets button 📇 to see the gallery options, as shown in Figure 2-16.

3. Click the checkmark bullet option.

Figure 2-16
Bullets and
Numbering gallery

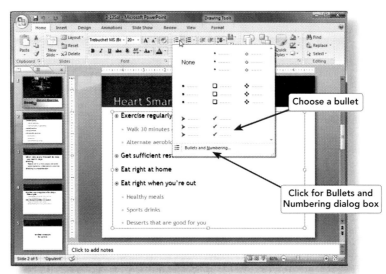

4. With the body text placeholder still selected, click the Bullets button again and then choose Bullets and Numbering at the bottom.

5. In the Bullets and Numbering dialog box, as shown in Figure 2-17, click the Bulleted tab.

Figure 2-17
Bullets and
Numbering dialog
box

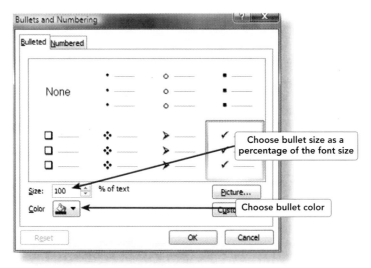

6. In the Color box, choose a Standard red.

7. In the Size box, click the down arrow several times until 80 is displayed. Click OK. All bullets on slide 2 are now red checks, sized at 80 percent of the font size.

8. Select the first line of bulleted text then press ⌈Ctrl⌉ while you use your I-beam pointer to select the text of the remaining three level-one bulleted text lines.

9. From the Home tab, in the Paragraph group, click the Bullets button down arrow then choose Bullets and Numbering.

10. Click Customize to open the Symbol dialog box, shown in Figure 2-18.

11. In the Font drop-down list (upper-left corner of the dialog box), scroll to the top and choose Monotype Corsiva if it is not displayed.

12. In the Subset drop-down list (upper-right corner), choose Geometric Shapes (near the bottom of the list). Several characters suitable for bullets appear in the dialog box grid.

Figure 2-18
Symbol dialog box

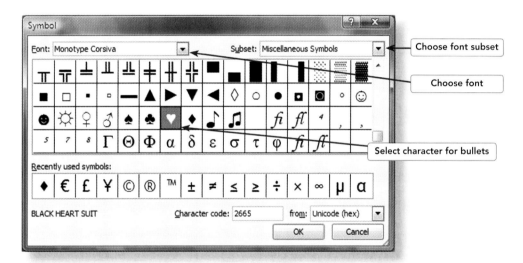

13. Click the heart bullet to select it; then click OK. The Symbol dialog box closes, and the Bullets and Numbering dialog box reappears.

14. Change the Size to 110% and leave the Color on a Standard red. Click OK. The selected three bullets on the slide change to red hearts. While the percentage you use is related to the size of the font for that bulleted item, symbols vary in size. So you may need to try more than one adjustment before you accept a size that is pleasing to you.

15. Leave your presentation open for the next exercise.

Exercise 2-16 CREATE A BULLET FROM A PICTURE

A picture bullet can add a unique or creative accent to your presentation. A picture bullet is made from a graphic file and can be a company logo, a special picture, or any image you create with a graphics program or capture with a scanner or digital camera.

1. Display slide 3 and select the text of the first two bullets (but not the sub-bullets).

2. From the Home tab, in the Paragraph group, click the Bullets button down arrow then choose Bullets and Numbering.

3. Click the Picture to open the Picture Bullet dialog box. The Picture Bullet dialog box displays a variety of colorful bullets. You can choose from one of these bullets or you can import a picture file of your own.

4. Key the search text **walking**. Click the check box to include content from Office Online then click Go.

5. Look through the images to find a simple one that would represent a person walking for exercise, as shown in Figure 2-19.

6. Click the picture of a person walking to select it and then click OK. The bullets are replaced with picture bullets, but they are too small.

Figure 2-19
Inserting a picture bullet

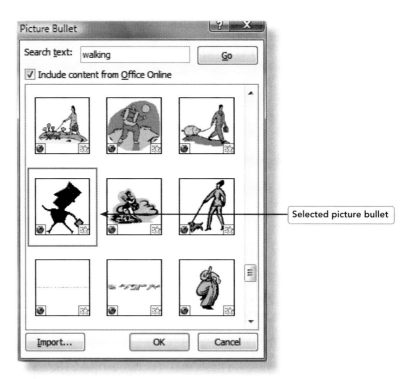

7. With the two bullet items still selected, reopen the Bullets and Numbering dialog box. In the Size box, change the size to 200%. Click OK.

PowerPoint 2007

NOTE

If the AutoFit Options button ⊞ appears near the placeholder, click it and choose AutoFit Text to Placeholder.

8. Using the steps outlined above, change the bullet for the last bulleted item ("Walking is a mood elevator") to the picture of the walker and size it to match the other bullets.

9. Leave your presentation open for the next exercise.

Exercise 2-17 CREATE NUMBERED PARAGRAPHS

Instead of using bullet characters, you can number listed items. A numbered list is useful to indicate the order in which steps should be taken or to indicate the importance of the items in a list.

Using the Numbered tab in the Bullets and Numbering dialog box, you can apply a variety of numbering styles, including numbers, letters, and Roman numerals. You can also create a numbered list automatically while you key body text.

1. Display slide 5 and select the body text placeholder.

2. From the Home tab, in the Paragraph group, click the Align Text Left button ▤.

3. Select all the text in the placeholder and delete it.

4. With the placeholder activated, key **1.** and press Tab. Key **Walk with us**.

5. Press Enter. The second line is automatically numbered "2."

6. Key **Eat with us** and press Enter.

7. Key **Do what's Good 4 U**. The slide now has three items, automatically numbered 1 through 3.

8. Your text may have resized to be smaller because earlier you made this placeholder just tall enough for two text lines. Press Esc to select the placeholder, then use the bottom sizing handle to drag down and increase the placeholder size to see all three items.

9. From the Home tab, in the Paragraph group, click the down arrow on the Numbers button ▤ to see several different numbering styles. Then click Bullets and Numbering to open the Bullets and Numbering dialog box and click the Numbered tab.

10. Click the first numbered option. In the Color box, choose Red and change the size to 100% of text. Click OK.

TIP

You can control the numbering style that is applied automatically by keying your first item with the style you want, such as 1. or A.

11. Move to slide 1 and save the presentation as **[2-17your initials]** in your Lesson 2 folder.

12. Preview and then print the presentation as handouts, six slides per page, grayscale, framed. Leave the presentation open for the next exercise.

Exercise 2-18 USE THE RULER TO ADJUST PARAGRAPH INDENTS

A text placeholder will have one of three types of paragraph indents that affect all text in a placeholder. These paragraph indents are:

- *Normal indent*—where all the lines of the paragraph are indented the same amount from the left margin.

- *Hanging indent*—where the first line of the paragraph extends farther to the left than the rest of the paragraph.

- *First-line indent*—where only the first line of the paragraph is indented.

These paragraph indents are controlled by the Paragraph dialog box shown in Figure 2-20 that is accessed through the Paragraph Dialog Box Launcher.

Figure 2-20
Paragraph Indent
dialog box

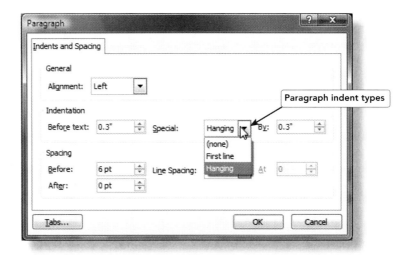

You can also set indents by using the ruler. If the ruler is displayed, you can see and manipulate *indent markers* when you activate a text object for editing. Indent markers are the two small triangles and the small rectangle that appear on the left side of the ruler.

At times you might want to change the distance between the bullets and text in a text placeholder. For example, when you use a large bullet (as you did in Exercise 2-16), the space that it requires may cause the text that follows it to word-wrap unevenly. You can easily adjust this spacing by dragging the indent markers. The following steps will guide you through this process.

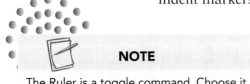

NOTE

The Ruler is a toggle command. Choose it once to display the rulers; choose it again to hide them.

1. Display slide 3. Notice how the text does not align correctly and the square second-level bullets are not indented enough.

2. From the View tab, in the Show/Hide group, click to select the Ruler. The vertical and horizontal rulers appear, as shown in Figure 2-21.

Figure 2-21
Horizontal and
vertical rulers

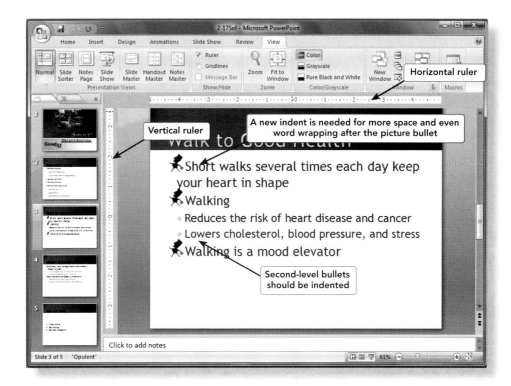

NOTE

You must have an insertion point somewhere inside a text box to change settings on the ruler. The appearance of the ruler reflects whether the entire placeholder is selected or the insertion point is active within the placeholder. If text is already in the placeholder, it must be selected for any ruler changes to apply to the text.

3. Click anywhere within the placeholder as if you were planning to edit some text. Notice the indent markers that appear on the horizontal ruler. Also notice that the white portion of the ruler indicates the width of the text placeholder.

4. Select all of the text in the placeholder.

5. Point to the first-line indent marker on the ruler (triangle at the top of the horizontal ruler, shown in Figure 2-22) and drag it to the right, to the 1-inch mark. The first line of each bulleted item beginning with the picture bullet is now indented the same way.

Figure 2-22
Indent markers

6. Drag the small rectangle (below the triangle on the bottom of the ruler) to the 1-inch mark on the ruler. Notice that both triangles move when you drag the rectangle.

7. Drag the left indent marker (triangle at the bottom of the ruler) to the right to the 2-inch mark on the ruler and the text will word-wrap with even alignment after the picture bullet.

8. Select the text in the lines beginning with square bullets. Drag the first-line indent marker to the 2.5-inch mark on the ruler. Drag the left indent marker to the 3-inch mark on the ruler. Now the text has much better alignment.

9. Save the presentation as **[2-18your initials]** in your Lesson 2 folder but do not print it. Leave the presentation open for the next exercise.

Working with Text Boxes

Until now, you have worked with text placeholders that automatically appear when you insert a new slide. Sometimes you'll want to use *text boxes* so you can put text outside the text placeholders or create free-form text boxes on a blank slide.

You create text boxes by clicking the Text Box button found on the Insert tab, in the Text group, and then dragging the pointer to define the width of the text box. You can also just click the pointer, and the text box adjusts its width to the size of your text. You can change the size and position of text boxes the same way you change text placeholders.

NOTE

You can also click and drag the text tool pointer to create a text box in a specific width. The text you key will wrap within the box if it does not fit on one text line. You can use the resizing handles to increase or decrease the text box width. You can practice making other text boxes on this slide and then click Undo as needed to return to just the first text box.

Exercise 2-19   CREATE A TEXT BOX

When you use the Text Box button to create a single line of text, you are free to place that text anywhere on a slide, change its color and font, and rotate it. This type of text is sometimes called floating text.

1. Display slide 5.

2. From the Insert tab, shown in Figure 2-23, in the Text group, click the Text Box button.

Figure 2-23
Insert tab

3. Place the pointer below the "G" in "Good 4 U" and click. A small text box containing an insertion point appears, as shown in Figure 2-24.

Figure 2-24
Creating floating text

1. **Walk with us**
2. **Eat with us**
3. **Do what's Good 4 U**

4. Key **Join Our Team Today!** Notice how the text box widens as you key text.

5. Leave the presentation open for the next exercise.

Exercise 2-20 CHANGE THE FONT AND FONT COLOR

You can select the text box and change the font and font color using the same methods as you did with text placeholders.

1. Click the text box border to select it. Change the text to 44-point, bold, shadowed.

Figure 2-25
Placement for floating text

2. With the text box selected, choose an attractive script font such as Monotype Corsiva or Script MT Bold.

3. Using the Font color button, change the text color to red.

4. Using the four-pointed arrow [✣], move the floating text box to the bottom-right corner of the slide. See Figure 2-25 for placement.

Exercise 2-21 ROTATE AND CHANGE TEXT DIRECTION

You can *rotate* almost any PowerPoint object—including text boxes, placeholders, and clip art—by dragging the green rotation handle that appears at the top of a selected object. You can also control rotation of text boxes and placeholders by using the Format Shape dialog box.

To *constrain* the rotation of an object to 15-degree increments, hold down [Shift] while rotating.

When text is in a rotated position, it can be awkward to edit. Fortunately, when you select a rotated text box for editing, it conveniently returns to a horizontal position while you revise the text.

TIP

You can key a precise angle of rotation measurement on the 3-D Rotation tab of the Format Shape dialog box in the Z area.

1. On slide 5, click "Join Our Team Today!" and drag the text box up slightly so that you will have enough space to angle it on the slide.

Figure 2-26
Rotating a text box

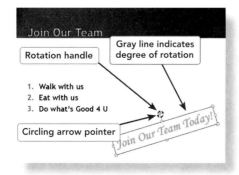

2. Point to the green rotation handle at the top of the text box and drag it to the left. Notice the circling arrow pointer that appears while you drag.

3. Position the text box as shown in Figure 2-26.

4. With the "Join Our Team Today!" text box selected, press Ctrl+C to copy.

5. Move to slide 4 and press Ctrl+V to paste.

6. Rotate the copied text box to make it straight again, then change the text to read **Offered Daily!** The text box should resize itself to fit this text.

7. With the text box selected, from the Home tab, in the Paragraph group, click Text Direction 📄 then choose Rotate All Text 270° to make the text read from the bottom up.

8. Reposition this rotated text on the right of the slide.

9. Save the presentation as **[2-21your initials]** in your Lesson 2 folder but do not print it. Leave the presentation open for the next exercise.

Exercise 2-22 WRAP TEXT AND CHANGE ALIGNMENT

When you drag the pointer to define the width of a text box, *word wrapping* is automatically turned on. As you key, your insertion point automatically jumps to a new line when it gets to the right side of the box. The height of the box automatically adjusts to accommodate additional text lines.

1. Move to slide 2, "Heart Smart Living."

2. From the Insert tab, in the Text group, click the Text Box button 📄.

3. Position your pointer to the right of "Exercise regularly"; then drag to the right to create a rectangle that is about 2 inches wide (use the ruler as a guide).

4. In the text box, key **Be consistent wherever you are!**

5. Click the text box border to select it; then increase the font size to 28 points, bold, and red; and then right-align the text. Resize the text box if necessary to match Figure 2-27 and position the text box as shown.

Figure 2-27
Text wrapped in a
text box

6. Save the presentation as **[2-22your initials]** in your Lesson 2 folder and print a handout page with six slides per page, grayscale, and framed.

Lesson 2

- Creating a presentation by starting with a blank presentation lets you concentrate on textual content. Anytime during the process, you can choose a design and color theme.

- Keyboard shortcuts are a big time-saver when creating a presentation. For example, Ctrl+Enter moves to the next text placeholder and Ctrl+M inserts a new slide.

- When you add a new slide, you can choose a slide layout. Slide layouts can be either text layouts or content layouts containing different arrangements of placeholders.

- After a slide is added, you can change the layout of the current slide or of a group of selected slide thumbnails.

- Before keying text in a placeholder, activate it by clicking inside it.

- Using the Outline pane is a quick way to enter slide titles and bulleted text.

- A font is a set of characters with a specific design, for example, Arial or Times New Roman.

- Font size (the height of a font) is measured in points, with 72 points to an inch. Fonts of the same size can vary in width, some taking up more horizontal space than others.

- Many formatting buttons are toggle buttons, meaning that the same button is clicked to turn an effect on and clicked again to turn it off.

- Change text attributes and effects such as bold, italic, and text color by first selecting the text and then clicking the appropriate buttons on the Home tab in the Font group. Or, apply formatting before you key text.

- The Font dialog box, accessible through the Font dialog box launcher, enables you to apply multiple formatting styles and effects all at one time.

- When a text placeholder is selected, formatting that you apply affects all the text in the placeholder.

- Text in placeholders can be aligned with the left or right side of the placeholder, centered, or justified.

- Body text placeholders are preformatted to have bulleted paragraphs. Bullets for selected paragraphs or placeholders are turned on or off by clicking the Bullets button .

- Use the Bullets and Numbering dialog box to change the shape, size, and color of bullets or numbers.

- Graphic files can be used as picture bullets.

- Paragraph indents can be adjusted in text placeholders and text boxes by dragging indent markers on the ruler when a text object is selected.

- To display the ruler for a text object, from the View tab, in the Show/Hide group, choose Ruler, and then activate the text object as if to edit the text.

- Bulleted text always uses a hanging indent. Changing the distance between the first-line indent marker (top triangle) and the left indent marker (bottom triangle) on the ruler controls the amount of space between a bullet and its text.

- Indent and tab settings apply only to the selected text object and all the text in the text box. To create more than one type of indent or tab setting, you must create a new text object.
- Line spacing and the amount of space between paragraphs are controlled using the Line Spacing button 🔧 and dialog box. Line and paragraph spacing can be applied to one or more paragraphs in a text object, or to the entire object.
- Text boxes enable you to place text anywhere on a slide. From the Insert tab, in the Text group, click the Text Box button 🅰, then click anywhere on a slide or draw a box and then start keying text.
- Text in a text box can be formatted by using standard text-formatting tools. Change the width of a text box to control how the text will word-wrap.
- When you select a text box on a slide, a green rotation handle appears slightly above the top-center sizing handle. Drag the rotation handle left or right to rotate the object.

LESSON 2		Command Summary	
Feature	**Button**	**Menu**	**Keyboard**
Create new presentation	📄	Microsoft Office Button, New	Ctrl+N
Insert new slide	🖼	Home tab, Slides group, New Slide	Ctrl+M
Activate placeholder			Ctrl+Enter
Deactivate placeholder			Esc
Insert line break			Shift+Enter
Move to next placeholder			Ctrl+Enter
Decrease List Level	📋		Shift+Tab or Alt+Shift+←
Increase List Level	📋		Tab
Decrease Font Size	A˅	Home tab, Font group, Decrease Font Size	Ctrl+Shift+<
Increase Font Size	A˄	Home tab, Font group, Increase Font Size	Ctrl+Shift+>
Bold	**B**	Home tab, Font group, Bold	Ctrl+B
Italic	*I*	Home tab, Font group, Italic	Ctrl+I
Underline	U	Home tab, Font group, Underline	Ctrl+U

continues

LESSON 2		Command Summary _continued_	
Feature	**Button**	**Menu**	**Keyboard**
Shadow	S	Home tab, Font group, Shadow	
Font Color	A	Home tab, Font group, Font Color	
Apply a font	Century Gothic (t	Home tab, Font group, Font	Ctrl + Shift + F
Change font size	36	Home tab, Font group, Font Size	Ctrl + Shift + P
Change case	Aa	Home tab, Font group, Change Case	Shift + F3
Align Text Left		Home tab, Paragraph group, Align Text Left	Ctrl + L
Center		Home tab, Paragraph group, Center	Ctrl + E
Align Text Right		Home tab, Paragraph group, Align Text Right	Ctrl + R
Justify		Home tab, Paragraph group, Justify	Ctrl + J
Turn bullets on or off		Home tab, Paragraph group, Bullets	
Turn numbering on or off		Home tab, Paragraph group, Numbering	
Change paragraph spacing		Home tab, Paragraph group, Line Spacing	
Text Box	A	Insert Tab, Text group, Text Box	
Change text box options		Drawing Tools Format tab	

Concepts Review

True/False Questions

Each of the following statements is either true or false. Select your choice by indicating T or F.

Ⓣ F   1. You can add text to a new presentation by using a blank presentation.

T Ⓕ   2. You can add a new slide by pressing Ctrl+Y.

T Ⓕ   3. You can display slide thumbnails and the Outline pane at the same time.

T Ⓕ   4. You can use Ctrl+Enter both to activate the next slide placeholder and to insert a new slide.

Ⓣ F   5. You can change selected text from uppercase to lowercase by using the Shift+F3 keyboard shortcut.

T Ⓕ   6. Sentence case capitalizes the initial letter of all words in a paragraph.

T Ⓕ   7. You can drag a sizing handle to reposition a placeholder.

Ⓣ F   8. To move a text box, the pointer must remain on the border and not touch a sizing handle.

Short Answer Questions

Write the correct answer in the space provided.

1. Name two ways to insert a new slide.

_____

2. Which key do you press to insert another bullet at the same level?

_____

3. Which command buttons change font size?

_____

4. What must you do before you can change an attribute for existing text?

_____

5. How do you change the distance between bullets and text?

_____

6. What is the difference between line spacing and paragraph spacing?

_____

7. How do you create a text box that adjusts its width to the width of the text you key?

_____

8. How can you rotate a text box in 15-degree increments?

_____

Critical Thinking

Answer these questions on a separate page. There are no right or wrong answers. Support your answers with examples from your own experience, if possible.

1. Explain how font faces can affect a presentation. Can you use too many fonts in a presentation? Explain your answer.

2. Under what circumstances might you choose to use a text box instead of a text placeholder?

Skills Review

Exercise 2-23

Create a new presentation, add new slides, and insert a new slide with a different layout.

1. Start PowerPoint.

2. Complete the title slide by following these steps:

   a. Key **Healthy Eating** as the first line of the title (you don't have to click the text "Click to add title" to begin keying the title slide text).

   b. Press Enter to start a new title line.

   c. Key **for Young Athletes** to complete the title.

   d. Press Ctrl + Enter.

   e. Key the subtitle **A Good 4 U Seminar.**

3. Add a new slide with the **Title and Content** layout by following these steps:

   a. Press Ctrl + M.

   b. Key **Basic Food Groups** as the title.

   c. Key the following bulleted text:

   - Fats, oils, and sweets
   - Dairy products
   - Meat, poultry, fish, eggs, beans, and nuts
   - Fruits and vegetables
   - Rice, bread, and pasta

4. From the Home tab, in the Slides group, click the top of the New Slide button 🔲 to insert a third slide.

5. Key **Elements of a Healthy Diet** as the title of the slide and the following bulleted text:

   • **Choose a variety of foods**

   • **Eat moderate amounts**

   • **Choose low-fat foods**

   • **Choose fresh, unprocessed foods**

   • **Avoid candy and junk foods**

6. Move to slide 1 and save the presentation as **[2-23your initials]** in your Lesson 2 folder.

7. Preview and then print the presentation as handouts, three slides per page, grayscale, framed. Close the presentation.

Exercise 2-24

Change font size, apply text attributes to selected text, and change the case of selected text.

1. Open the file **ComWalk**.

2. On slide 1, change font size and color and apply bold and shadow effects for the title by following these steps:

   a. Select the title text "Power Walking" by dragging the I-beam pointer across the text.

   b. From the Home tab, in the Font group, change the Font Size to 36 points.

   c. From the Home tab, in the Font group, click the Font Color button 🔲 drop-down list and choose **red**.

   d. Still working in the Font group, click the Bold button 🔲 and the Shadow button 🔲.

3. On slide 3, increase the font size for the title by following these steps:

   a. Move to slide 3 and select the title text.

   b. From the Home tab, in the Font group, click the Increase Font Size button 🔲 several times until 36 appears in the Font Size box.

4. On slide 5, use the Font dialog box to change the title text formatting by following these steps:

   a. Select the title text.

   b. From the Home tab, in the Font group, click the Font dialog box launcher 🔲.

   c. Choose the font style Bold and change the font color to red.

   d. In the Size box, choose 36 points.

   e. Click OK.

5. Change the case of text on slide 5 by following these steps:

    a. Select the last bulleted item by clicking its bullet.

    b. From Home tab, in the Font group, click the Change Case button [Aa].

    c. Choose tOGGLE cASE.

6. Using step 4 above as a guide, change the title text formatting on slides 2, 3, 4, and 6 to match slide 5. On slide 6, if necessary, resize the placeholder slightly on the right side so that the title fits on one line.

7. Move to slide 1 and save the presentation as **[2-24your initials]** in your Lesson 2 folder.

8. Preview and then print the presentation as handouts, six slides per page, grayscale, framed. Close the presentation.

Exercise 2-25

Adjust indents using the ruler.

1. Open the file **EmpAward**.

2. Move to slide 2.

3. Create first-line indents by following these steps:

    a. Click within the text box to activate the ruler.

    b. Select the bulleted text.

    c. From the Home tab, in the Paragraph group, click the Bullet button [≡] to remove the bullets from the body text placeholder.

    d. If the ruler is not displayed, click the View tab, in the Show/Hide group, and choose Ruler.

    e. Drag the first-line indent marker (top triangle) to the right, to the 1-inch mark on the ruler.

    f. Drag the small rectangle to the left, to the zero point on the ruler.

4. Move to slide 3 and change the spacing before the bullets by following these steps:

    a. Select all of the text in the body text placeholder.

    b. Drag the left indent marker (bottom triangle) to the right one tick mark, to the 0.5-inch position on the ruler.

5. Move to slide 4 and select all the text. Increase the space between the bullets and text by one tick mark on the ruler. Resize the placeholder on the right so the text does not word-wrap. Move the oval shapes that emphasize the words "week" and "paid" up and slightly to the right.

6. Move to slide 6 and modify the line spacing by following these steps:

    a. Select both paragraphs (the quotation and hobbies).

    b. From the Home tab, in the Paragraph group, choose the Dialog Box Launcher and change the Before paragraph spacing to 0. Now the text will fit better on the slide.

7. Save the presentation as **[2-25your initials]** in your Lesson 2 folder.

8. Print the presentation as handouts, six slides per page, grayscale, framed. Close the presentation.

Exercise 2-26

Change text box settings and page setup options.

1. Open the file **Upgrade1**.

2. On the title slide, make these changes:

   a. Title placeholder—Change to 66 points, shadow, and Pink, Accent 2 color.

   b. Subtitle placeholder—Change to 40 points and left alignment. Resize the placeholder to fit the text and then position the placeholder on the lower right of the slide.

3. On slide 2, make the following changes to the body text placeholder:

   a. Remove the bullet and make the first line of the paragraph indent to the 1.5-inch mark on the ruler.

   b. Move the placeholder slightly to the right so the left paragraph edge aligns with the word "Why" in the slide title.

4. On slide 3, from the Insert tab, in the Text group, click the text box button ▣ and create three text boxes under each of the pictures to identify the equipment categories. For all three text boxes, use the font Corbel, 24 points, bold, and the Orange, Accent 1 color.

   Kitchen Equipment
   Tableware
   Computer Equipment

5. Center align the text in each text box and then center the text boxes below each of the three pictures as shown in Figure 2-28.

Figure 2-28
Text box alignment

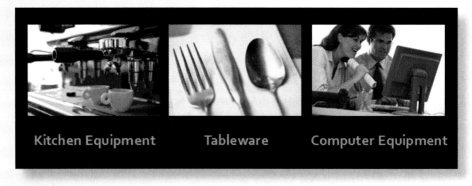

6. Move to slide 6, move the picture of the computer up and to the right, even with the rainbow colored line under the slide title.

7. Save the presentation as **[2-26your initials]** in your Lesson 2 folder.

8. Preview and then print the presentation as handouts, six slides per page, grayscale, landscape, framed. Close the presentation.

Lesson Applications

Exercise 2-27

Create a new blank presentation and add slides using different slide layouts.

1. Start a blank presentation.

2. Create a title slide with the text First in Food Safety as the title and Good 4 U Employee Training as the subtitle.

3. Using the text in Figure 2-29, create three slides. For slides 2 and 3, use the Title and Content layout. For slide 4, use the Two Content layout and key the first three bulleted items in the left placeholder and the last three bulleted items in the right placeholder.

Figure 2-29

```
         Our Food Safety Programs
            • Food handler training
Slide 2     • Management inspections
            • Safety supervisors on-site
            • Reports to USDA

         Safe Food-Handling Practices
            • Wear gloves, hair nets, and beard nets
Slide 3     • Wash hands before and after handling food
            • Wear clean uniforms
            • No smoking

         Food Procurement
            • Know your suppliers
            • Prefer local growers
Slide 4     • Prefer organic food
            • Insist on freshness
            • Insist on cleanliness
            • Test for pesticides
```

4. Check both body text placeholders for extra blank lines and remove them if necessary.

5. Move to slide 1 and save the presentation as **[2-27your initials]** in your Lesson 2 folder.

6. Preview and then print the presentation as handouts, four slides per page, grayscale, framed, landscape. Close the presentation.

Exercise 2-28

Work with indents, tabs, line spacing, and page setup options.

1. Open the file **Inventory**.

2. Move to slide 2, and apply the following formatting changes:

   • Change the first-level bullet to a large solid square from the Wingdings 2 font.

   • Use the ruler to increase the space between the bullet and text for even word-wrapping of the text.

   • Change the paragraph after spacing to 12 points.

3. On slide 3, make the following changes to the body text placeholder:

   • Change the bullets to a numbered list, formatting the numbering at 100% of text size.

   • Reduce the width of the text placeholder to approximately 7 inches, making the line endings more even.

   • Change the paragraph after spacing to 12 points.

4. On slide 4, select the three first-level bulleted items and make these changes:

   • Change the bullets to a numbered list, formatting the numbering at 100% of text size.

   • Change the indent on the second-level bullets so the bullet is indented 1.25 inches and the text is indented 1.5 inches.

   • Select the second-level bullet on item 1, item 2, and the second-level bullet on item 3 then change the paragraph after spacing to 12 points.

5. On slide 5, do the following:

   • Remove the bullets.

   • Press [Tab] after Miami and Tucson so the dates are aligned.

   • Change the line spacing to 2.

   • Adjust the size of the placeholder to fit the text.

   • Center the placeholder horizontally so you have even spacing on both sides of the text.

6. On slide 6, do the following:

   • Increase the size of the placeholder on the right so no lines word wrap.

   • Change the line spacing to 2.

7. Save the presentation as **[2-28your initials]** in your Lesson 2 folder.

8. Print as handouts, six slides per page, grayscale, landscape, framed. Close the presentation.

Exercise 2-29

Add slides, promote and demote text, insert a text box, and move bullets and slides.

1. Open the file **Marketing**.

2. On slide 1, increase the size of the title to 60 points and move the placeholder to the left slightly so the text aligns evenly with the picture on the left.

3. Select the subtitle placeholder then make the text right aligned and bold.

4. On slide 2, key the title **Our Products** and make it bold.

5. Still working on slide 2, move the picture to the left of the slide. Make a text box and key the following items. Press [Enter] after each item.

   - Merchandise

   - Food services

   - Honeys and confections

   - T-shirts

   - Caps

6. Select the text box and change the font size to 28 and the paragraph line spacing to 1.5.

7. Add bullets to the list and then customize them to choose Arrow Bullets in a blue color that works well with your design theme colors.

8. Resize the text box as needed so the lines do not word wrap.

9. Align the bulleted list beside the picture as shown in Figure 2-30.

Figure 2-30

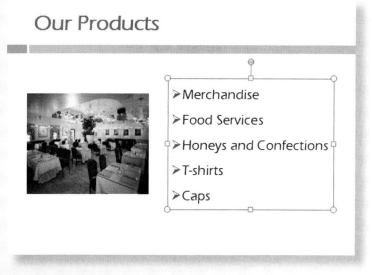

10. Move to slide 1 and save the presentation as **[2-29your initials]** in your Lesson 2 folder.

11. Preview and then print the presentation as handouts, two slides per page, grayscale, landscape, framed. Close the presentation.

Exercise 2-30 ◆ Challenge Yourself

Work with indents, line spacing, and text box settings.

1. Open the file **Party2**.

2. On slide 2, remove all the bullets and hanging indents from both body text placeholders. Make the text in the left placeholder bold, resize the placeholder and move it under the slide title so it is aligned on the left.

3. Resize the "Directions" text placeholder and position it as shown in Figure 2-31 aligned on the left.

Figure 2-31
Slide 2

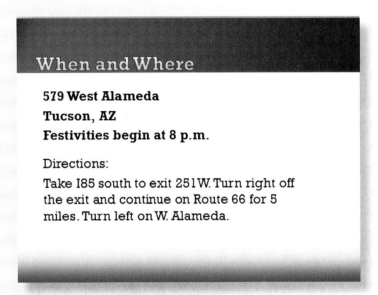

4. Move to slide 4 and create text boxes to key the text below. Center align all the text and use a black font. Use 20 points for the text and 24 points for the heading in each section. Add spacing of 12 points after the heading in each section. Refer to Figure 2-32.

Figure 2-32
Slide 5

TIP

A quick way to create these boxes is to make the first one, adjust all formatting settings, then select the text box, and press Ctrl+D three times to duplicate that text box for the other shapes. Then reposition and edit each one.

5. Save the presentation as **[2-30your initials]** in your Lesson 2 folder.

6. Preview and then print the presentation as handouts, four slides per page, grayscale, landscape, scale to fit paper, framed. Close the presentation.

On Your Own

In these exercises you work on your own, as you would in a real-life work environment. Use the skills you've learned to accomplish the task—and be creative.

Exercise 2-31

Locate a recipe for a food dish that you enjoy. Organize the recipe steps to make it easy to teach someone to make it. Put the steps into an outline with at least four main points suitable for slide titles. Create the outline by using any method that is comfortable for you (index cards, Word, PowerPoint, etc.). From the outline, create a PowerPoint presentation with a title slide. Save the presentation as **[2-31your initials]**. Preview and then print the presentation as an outline and as handouts.

Exercise 2-32

Assume you are on a planning committee for a student organization or for your employer that has the responsibility to plan a holiday banquet. Create a slide show to guide discussion at your first meeting as your group starts planning this project. Identify all the tasks that must be accomplished before the event, and plan for the various courses of the meal, such as salad, main dish, side items, and dessert. Using the skills that you have learned up to this point, format the text attractively. Save the presentation as **[2-32your initials]**. Preview and then print the presentation as handouts.

Exercise 2-33

Imagine that you work at a car dealership where the computer system needs to be replaced. Research computer systems online, and create a presentation for your boss recommending what brand and options would be appropriate. Be sure to include a slide describing the costs and a slide with the benefits of choosing this system. Provide the URL addresses for the sites where you found the information. Create at least six slides using different slide layouts. Save the presentation as **[2-33your initials]**. Preview and then print the presentation as an outline and as handouts.

Lesson 3

Revising Presentation Text

OBJECTIVES

After completing this lesson, you will be able to:

1. Select, rearrange, and delete slides.

2. Use the clipboard.

3. Check spelling and word usage.

4. Insert headers and footers.

5. Apply a consistent background and color theme.

6. Add movement effects.

Estimated Time: 1¹/₂ hours

MCAS OBJECTIVES

In this lesson:
PP07 1.2.1
PP07 1.3
PP07 1.4.2
PP07 1.5
PP07 2.2.1
PP07 2.2.4
PP07 2.3.2

See Appendix

When using PowerPoint, it is important to review your presentation to ensure that it flows logically, is free of errors in spelling and grammar, and is consistent in its visual representation. Many PowerPoint tools will help with this important task.

Selecting, Rearranging, and Deleting Slides

Just as you frequently rearrange paragraphs or sentences in a word processing document, you will often need to rearrange or delete slides in a PowerPoint presentation. You can change the arrangement of slides by dragging them to a new position in the Slides tab, in the Outline tab, or in Slide Sorter view.

You can delete selected slide thumbnails by pressing Delete on your keyboard.

Exercise 3-1 SELECT MULTIPLE SLIDES

If you select multiple slides, you can move them to a new position all at one time. You can also delete several selected slides at one time. In addition, you can apply transitions, animations, and other effects to a group of selected slides.

There are two ways to select multiple slides:

Figure 3-1
Selecting contiguous slides

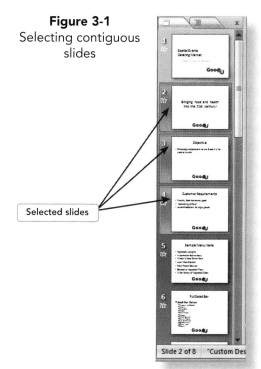

Selected slides

- To select *contiguous slides* (slides that follow one after another), click the first slide in the selection and then hold down Shift while you click the last slide in the selection.

- To select *noncontiguous slides* (slides that do not follow one after another), click the first slide and then hold down Ctrl while you click each slide you want to add to the selection, one at a time.

1. Open the file **SpEventCatering**.

2. In the Slides and Outline pane, click the Slides tab to display slide thumbnails if they are not already displayed.

3. Without clicking, point to each thumbnail one at a time and notice that a ScreenTip appears displaying the title of the slide.

4. Click the thumbnail for slide 2 ("Bringing Food and Health . . .") to select it.

5. Hold down Shift and click the slide 4 thumbnail ("Customer Requirements"). Release Shift.

   Slides 2, 3, and 4 are all selected, as indicated by the heavy borders around their thumbnails, as shown in Figure 3-1. This is a contiguous selection.

6. With Shift released, click slide 3. Now it is the only slide selected.

7. Hold down Ctrl and click slide 1. Slide 1 and slide 3 are both selected. This is a noncontiguous selection.

Figure 3-2
Selecting noncontiguous slides

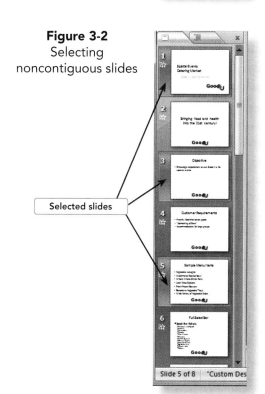

Selected slides

8. While holding down Ctrl, click slide 5. Now three noncontiguous slides are selected, as shown in Figure 3-2. You can add as many slides as you want to the selection if you hold down Ctrl while clicking a slide thumbnail.

Exercise 3-2   REARRANGE SLIDE ORDER

The Slides tab is a convenient place to rearrange slides. You simply drag selected slide thumbnails to a new position. *Slide Sorter View* enables you to see more thumbnails at one time and is convenient if your presentation contains a large number of slides. You select slides in Slide Sorter view in the same way as in the Slides tab.

1. Click the Slide Sorter View button .

2. Click the slide 2 thumbnail to select it.

Figure 3-3
Moving a slide in the
Slide Sorter View

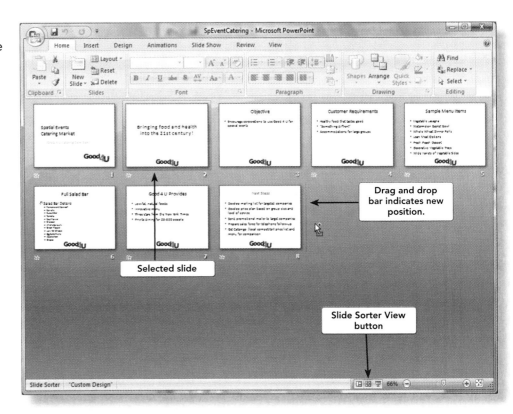

NOTE

While you are dragging, be sure not to release the left mouse button until it is pointing where you want the selection to go. Otherwise, you might either cancel the selection or drop the slides in the wrong place.

3. Position the pointer within the selected slide's border, press the left mouse button, and drag the pointer after the eighth slide, as shown in Figure 3-3. Notice the drag-and-drop bar (the vertical line) as you drag. The vertical line indicates where the slide will go.

4. Release the mouse button. Slide 2, titled "Bringing Food and Health . . . ," becomes slide 8.

5. Using Ctrl, make a noncontiguous selection of slides 3 ("Customer Requirements") and 6 ("Good 4 U Provides").

6. Point to either slide in the selection and drag the selection after the first slide. Both slides move to the new position.

7. Check to make sure your slides are in the following order. If not, rearrange your slides to agree.

   Slide 1: Special Events Catering Market (This slide has a spelling error that you will correct later.)

   Slide 2: Customer Requirements

   Slide 3: Good 4 U Provides

   Slide 4: Objective

   Slide 5: Sample Menu Items

   Slide 6: Full Salad Bar

   Slide 7: Next Steps

   Slide 8: Bringing Food and Health into the 21st Century!

8. Double-click slide 1 to display it in Normal view.

Exercise 3-3   DELETE SLIDES

When you want to delete slides, you first select them (in the Slides tab or in Slide Sorter view) the same way you select slides you want to move. You delete them by pressing Delete on your keyboard or clicking the Delete button  on the Home tab, in the Slides group.

REVIEW

To advance through a slide show, click the left mouse button, press the Spacebar, press PageDown, or press N.

1. Working in Normal view, display the Slides tab if it is not already showing.

2. Click the slide 4 thumbnail to select it. The slide 4 title should be "Objective."

3. Press Delete on your keyboard. Slide 4 is deleted and the new slide 4 becomes selected.

4. Move to slide 1 and click the Slide Show button to start a slide show.

5. Advance through the slides (using any method), reading the text and observing the built-in animation effects.

6. Create a new folder for Lesson 3. Save the presentation as **[3-3your initials]** in the Lesson 3 folder. Do not print the presentation at this point, and do not close it.

Using the Clipboard

The *Cut, Copy,* and *Paste* commands are almost universally available in computer programs. When you cut selected text or a selected object, it is removed from the presentation and placed on the *Clipboard,* a temporary storage space. When you copy text or an object, it remains in its original place and a copy is placed on the Clipboard. When you paste a Clipboard item, a copy of the item is placed at the location of the insertion point and the item remains on the Clipboard to use again if needed.

Each item you cut or copy is stored on the Clipboard, which can hold up to 24 items at a time. Clipboard items can be viewed and managed by using the Clipboard task pane. When working with the Office Clipboard, it is important to understand that unlike the Cut command, Delete does not save items to the clipboard.

The following cut, copy, and paste keyboard shortcuts are big time-savers when you do extensive editing:

- Ctrl + C   Copy

- Ctrl + X   Cut

- Ctrl + V   Paste the most recent item stored on the clipboard.

Exercise 3-4   USE CUT, COPY, AND PASTE TO REARRANGE SLIDES

In the previous objective, you learned how to rearrange slides by dragging their thumbnails. This exercise presents another way to arrange slides by using the clipboard. From the Home tab, in the Clipboard group, you can open the Clipboard task pane by clicking the Dialog Box Launcher ⬒.

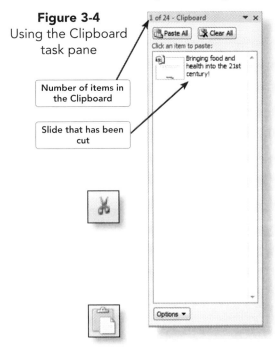

Figure 3-4
Using the Clipboard task pane

Number of items in the Clipboard

Slide that has been cut

1. With the **[3-3your initials]** presentation open, from the Home tab, in the Clipboard group, click the Dialog Box Launcher ⬒ to display the Clipboard task pane, as shown in Figure 3-4.

2. On the Slides tab, click the thumbnail of slide 7 ("Bringing Food and Health into the 21st Century!").

3. From the Home tab, in the Clipboard group, click the Cut button ✄. This removes the slide and stores it on the clipboard.

4. Select the thumbnail for slide 1 ("Spatial Events Catering Market"). Later you will change the spelling of the first word.

5. From the Home tab, in the Clipboard group, click the Paste button ▣. The cut slide (on the clipboard) is inserted (or pasted) after slide 1. This accomplishes the same thing as if you moved the slide by dragging its thumbnail.

6. Select the slide 1 thumbnail ("Spatial Events Catering Market"). From the Home tab, in the Clipboard group, click the Copy button ⬜. Notice that two slides are stored on the Clipboard task pane.

7. Move to slide 7 ("Next Steps"). From the Home tab, in the Clipboard group, click the Paste button ⬜ to paste ("Spatial Events Catering Market"). A copy of the slide is inserted at the end of the presentation to use for making a concluding comment.

8. Move to slide 8, the pasted slide.

9. Delete the subtitle text and key the following text in its place on four lines:

   Catering Market Slogan:
   Make Your Event Special
   Call Good 4 U at
   800-555-1234

10. Move to slide 1 and save the presentation as **[3-4your initials]**. Keep the presentation open for the next exercise.

REVIEW

If the Outline tab and Slides tab are not visible, click the Normal view button ⬜.

Exercise 3-5 USE CUT, COPY, AND PASTE TO REARRANGE TEXT

Figure 3-5
Text and slides stored on the Office Clipboard

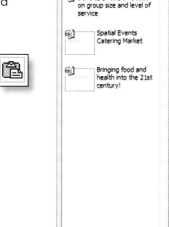

Just as you cut, copy, and paste slides, you can cut, copy, and paste text, and store it on the Office Clipboard. The Paste Options button ⬜ appears near a pasted item if the item's *source* formatting is different from the formatting of similar elements in its *destination* presentation. A clipboard item's source is the presentation or other document from which it was cut or copied. Its destination is the presentation or other document in which it is pasted.

1. Display slide 7 ("Next Steps").

2. Activate the body text placeholder; then click the second bullet to select all its text.

3. Press Ctrl+X to cut the text from the slide. It appears on the Clipboard task pane. Notice the difference between text and slides on the Clipboard, as shown in Figure 3-5.

4. Click in front of the text in the first bulleted item.

5. Click the first item on the Clipboard task pane ("Develop price plan . . .") to insert that text as the first bulleted item.

6. Move to slide 6 ("Full Salad Bar").

7. Select the title text "Full Salad Bar," and press Ctrl+C to copy the text from the slide.

8. Move to slide 5, and click after the text "Wide Variety of Vegetable Sides," press Enter to create a new bullet, and press Ctrl+V. Notice that a Paste Options button 📋 appears each time you paste.

9. Click the Paste Options button 📋 that appears underneath the new bulleted item, and choose Keep Source Formatting from the drop-down list. Notice that the new bulleted item font size does not match that of the other bullets.

10. Click the Paste Options button 📋 again. This time choose Use Destination Theme, as shown in Figure 3-6. The bullet design changes to match the size of the other bulleted items.

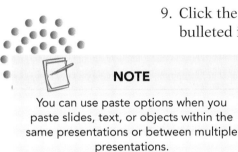

NOTE

You can use paste options when you paste slides, text, or objects within the same presentations or between multiple presentations.

Figure 3-6
Viewing the Paste Options button

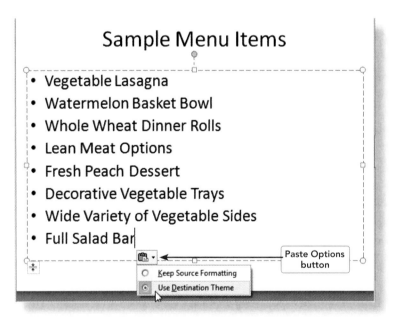

Exercise 3-6   CLEAR THE CLIPBOARD TASK PANE

The Clipboard task pane is a quick way to see a series of items that have been cut or copied to the Clipboard. The advantage of using the Clipboard to paste items is that you can have several items on the Clipboard and then choose which ones you want to paste instead of having to paste immediately after copying or cutting. If you have copied a lot of items, however, you may want to clear the Clipboard task pane.

The Clipboard Options button [Options ▼] allows you to control the settings of the Clipboard task pane.

1. If the Clipboard task pane is not open, from the Home tab, in the Clipboard group, click the Clipboard Dialog Box Launcher 🖾.

2. Click the Clipboard Options button [Options ▼] at the bottom of the task pane, as shown in Figure 3-7.

3. Choose Show Office Clipboard Automatically to enable the Clipboard to automatically pop up when you use the cut, copy, or paste commands.

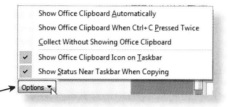

Figure 3-7
Viewing the clipboard task pane options

4. At the top of the Clipboard task pane, click the Clear All button [Options ▼] on to clear all of the contents held in the Clipboard.

5. Click Close ⊠ on the Clipboard task pane.

Exercise 3-7   USE UNDO AND REDO

The *Undo* button 🔄 on the Quick Access toolbar reverses the last action you took. You can undo a series of editing actions, including keying or deleting text, promoting or demoting items, or deleting slides. By using Undo more than once, you can undo multiple actions. The *Redo* button 🔄 found beside the Undo button 🔄 reapplies editing commands in the order you undid them.

In PowerPoint, unlike Word, Undo and Redo are cleared when you save a presentation. In other words, you cannot undo or redo actions performed before saving a presentation. Therefore, in PowerPoint, don't save unless you are sure you won't want to undo an action.

TIP

By default, PowerPoint can undo the last 20 actions. You can increase or decrease this number by choosing the Microsoft Office Button, PowerPoint Options, Advanced tab, and changing the Maximum number of undos. Increasing the number uses up more RAM memory on your computer.

1. Move to slide 7 ("Next Steps"). Click at the end of the second bulleted line and press [Enter].

2. Click the Undo button 🔄. Notice the new bullet is removed and your insertion point is back at the end of the first line.

3. Click the Redo button 🔄. The bullet is back and ready to accept text beside it.

4. On the new bulleted line, type the text below:

   Fully develop a menu choices plan

TIP

It's fairly common to make unintentional deletions and unintentional text moves. The ⟨Ctrl⟩+⟨Z⟩ key combination is very handy to use when the unexpected happens.

5. Press ⟨Ctrl⟩+⟨Z⟩, the keyboard shortcut for Undo. Part of your text will go away.

6. Press ⟨Ctrl⟩+⟨Y⟩, the keyboard shortcut for Redo. The text that was taken away in step 5 is now back on your screen.

7. In the Slides and Outline pane, click on slide 6, and press ⟨Delete⟩ on your keyboard. Notice the slide is deleted.

8. Press ⟨Ctrl⟩+⟨Z⟩ to undo this deletion and put the slide back into place.

Exercise 3-8   USE FORMAT PAINTER

If you use Word or Excel, you may be familiar with the *Format Painter* tool. This tool makes it easy to copy the formatting, for example, the font size, color, and font face, from one object to another object on the same slide or within a presentation.

When you copy the format of an object, many default settings associated with that object are copied as well.

1. On slide 6, select the title "Full Salad Bar."

2. From the Home tab, in the Clipboard group, click the Format Painter button ✅. The Format Painter picks up the font formatting of this title.

3. Click within the word "cucumber" on the same slide. The text appears with the same formatting as the title. Click the Undo button ↩.

4. Select the title "Full Salad Bar" once again and double-click the Format Painter button ✅. Double-clicking keeps the Format Painter active, so you can copy the formatting to more than one object.

5. Move to slide 7, and click on "Next" in the title. Notice when you just click a word, it changes only that single word.

6. Click "Steps" to format it the same way.

7. Click the Format Painter button ✅ again or press ⟨Esc⟩ to restore the standard pointer.

Checking Spelling and Word Usage

PowerPoint provides many tools to edit and revise text, and improve the overall appearance of a presentation:

- *Spelling Checker*, which corrects spelling by comparing words to an internal dictionary file.

- *Research*, which allows you to search through reference materials such as dictionaries, encyclopedias, and translation services to find the information you need.

- *Thesaurus*, which offers new words with similar meanings to the word you are looking up.

- *Find* and *Replace*, which allows you to find a certain word or phrase and replace it with a different word or phrase.

Exercise 3-9 CHECK SPELLING

The *Spelling Checker* in PowerPoint works much the same as it does in other Microsoft Office applications. It flags misspelled words with a red wavy underline as you key text. It can also check an entire presentation at once. The Spelling Checker is an excellent proofreading tool, but it should be used in combination with your own careful proofreading and editing.

1. In slide 1, a word in the subtitle has a red wavy underline indicating a spelling error. Right-click the word. Choose the correct spelling ("Committee") from the short-cut menu and click to accept it.

2. Notice the spelling of "Spatial" in the title. This is an example of a word that is correctly spelled but incorrectly used. The Spelling Checker can't help you with this kind of mistake. Change the spelling to **Special**. Do this on slide 8 also.

3. Move to slide 1 and run the Spelling Checker for the entire presentation. From the Review tab, in the Proofing Group, click the Spelling button 🗸 or press F7.

4. PowerPoint highlights "diffrent," the first word it doesn't find in its dictionary. It displays the word in the Spelling dialog box and suggests a corrected spelling, as shown in Figure 3-8.

Figure 3-8
Using the spelling checker

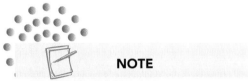

NOTE

If the Spelling dialog box is hiding a misspelled word, move the dialog box to a different position by dragging its title bar.

5. Click Change to apply the correct spelling of "different."

6. When the spelling checker locates "Privite," click Change on the correct spelling of "Private."

7. At the next spelling error "Caterngo," click Ignore because this is the correct spelling of the company name.

8. Click OK when the spelling check is complete.

Figure 3-9
Research task pane
with definitions

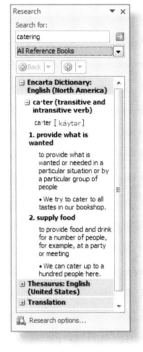

Exercise 3-10   USE RESEARCH

Research is a handy reference tool to look up many facets of a word. For example, when you research the word "catering," you find information about the definition of the word from the dictionary, synonyms in the thesaurus, and an area where you can translate this word into another language.

1. From the Review tab, in the Proofing group, click the Research button.

2. On the Research task pane in the Search for box, type **catering** and press [Enter].

3. Look in the definition area and notice that the context for the word "catering" is definition number 2, as shown in Figure 3-9.

4. On the Thesaurus task pane, click the Close button.

Exercise 3-11   USE THE THESAURUS

The *Thesaurus* is used to find words with similar meanings. This tool is extremely helpful when the same word becomes repetitious and you would like to use a similar word, or if you are looking for a more appropriate word with a similar meaning.

1. On slide 6, put your insertion point on the word "Full." From the Review tab, in the Proofing group, click the Thesaurus button. On the Research task pane, the word "full" is automatically placed in the Search for box, a search has already been performed, and the results displayed, as shown in Figure 3-10.

Figure 3-10
Search word
highlighted and
Thesaurus task pane

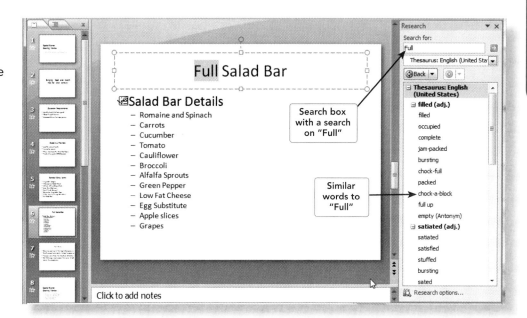

TIP

If you click on any word in the Thesaurus
list, you will see another list of words that
are related to that word.

2. Scroll down until you find the word "extensive."
Click the down arrow beside extensive, and choose
Insert. Notice that the word "Full" is replaced by
the word "Extensive," and the slide now reads
"Extensive Salad Bar."

3. Click the Thesaurus task pane Close button 🗙 .

Exercise 3-12   USE FIND AND REPLACE

When you create presentations—especially long presentations—you often
need to review or change text. In PowerPoint, you can do this quickly by
using the Find and Replace commands.

The *Find* command locates specified text in a presentation. The *Replace*
command finds the text and replaces it with a specified alternative.

1. Move to slide 1. From the Home tab, in the Editing group, click the
Find button 🔍 (or press Ctrl + F) to open the Find dialog box.

2. In the Find what text box, key **full**, as shown in Figure 3-11.

Figure 3-11
Find dialog box with
text selected

• Fresh Peach Dess
• Decorative Veget
• Wide Variety of V
• Full Salad Bar

PowerPoint 2007

3. Click the Find Next button and PowerPoint locates and selects the text. This could be used if you were looking for a particular word in the presentation.

4. Click the Close button ⊠ to close the Find dialog box.

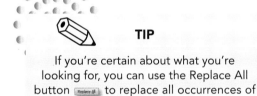

5. Move back to slide 1. From the Home tab, in the Editing group, click the Replace button Replace (or press Ctrl+H) to open the Replace dialog box.

6. In the Find what text box, key **Full** if it is not displayed already. In the Replace with text box, key **Extensive** as shown in Figure 3-12.

7. Check Match case and Find whole words only, to ensure that you find only the text "Full" and not words that contain these letters (such as "fuller" or "fullest").

Figure 3-12
Replace dialog box

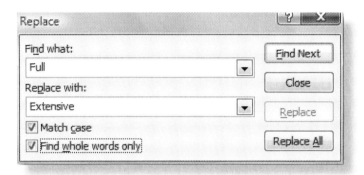

TIP

If you're certain about what you're looking for, you can use the Replace All button Replace All to replace all occurrences of text in one step.

8. Click the Find Next button and PowerPoint finds the first occurrence of "Full." Click the Replace button Replace . Click the Find Next button Find Next once again. A dialog box appears to tell you the search is completed. Click OK.

9. Click the Close button ⊠ to close the Replace dialog box.

10. Return to slide 1 and save the presentation as **[3-12your initials]** in your Lesson 3 folder. Leave the presentation open for the next exercise.

Inserting Headers and Footers

You can add identifying information to your presentation, such as header or footer text, the date, or a slide or page number. See Table 3-1. A *header* is text that appears at the top of each notes page or handouts page. A *footer* is text that appears at the bottom of each slide, notes page, or handouts page. Header and footer text appears in special header and footer placeholders.

As is true in Word and Excel, the Header and Footer button ▦ is on the Insert tab in the Text group. In PowerPoint, this command opens the Header and Footer dialog box, which has two tabs: the Slide tab and the Notes and Handouts tab.

TABLE 3-1 Adding Identifying Information to Presentations

Information	Description
Date and Time	Current date and time—can be updated automatically or keyed
Header	Descriptive text printed at the top of the page on notes and handouts pages only
Page Number	Number placed in the lower-right corner of notes and handouts pages by default
Slide Number	Number placed on slides, usually in the lower-right corner
Footer	Descriptive text printed at the bottom of slides, notes pages, and handouts pages

Exercise 3-13   ADD SLIDE DATE, PAGE NUMBER, AND FOOTER

Using the Slide tab in the Header and Footer dialog box, you can add information to the footer of all slides in a presentation by clicking Apply to All, or you can add footer information to only the current slide by clicking Apply.

1. Working on the presentation **[3-12your initials]**, from the Insert tab, in the Text group, click the Header and Footer button 🖻. Notice the two tabs in the Header and Footer dialog box, one for adding information to slides and one for adding information to notes and handouts, as shown in Figure 3-13. Click the Slide tab.

Figure 3-13
Header and Footer
dialog box, Slide tab

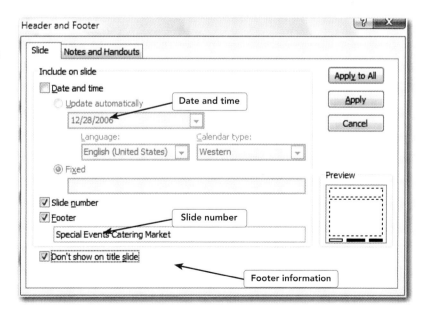

2. In the Preview box, notice the positions for the elements you can place on a slide. As you enable each element by selecting its check box, PowerPoint indicates where the element will print with a bold outline.

3. Click the Slide number check box to select it.

4. Click the check box labeled Don't show on title slide. When this box is checked, footer and page number information does not appear on the slides using the title slide layout.

5. Clear the Date and Time check box so there is no check.

6. Click the Footer check box and key **Special Events Catering Market**.

7. Click Apply to All. The presentation now has footer information including slide numbers at the bottom of each slide except the title slide.

8. Move to slide 1 and click the Slide Show button 🖳 on the Status bar to view the presentation. Notice the footer information and slide number at the bottom of the slide.

Exercise 3-14 ADD HANDOUT DATE, PAGE NUMBER, AND HEADER

Using the Notes and Handouts tab, you can insert both header and footer information on notes pages and handouts that are usually printed.

1. From the Insert tab, in the Text group, click the Header and Footer button 🗐. On the Header and Footer dialog box, click the Notes and Handouts tab as shown in Figure 3-14.

2. Under the Date and time option, click Update automatically to add today's date. Each time you print the presentation handout, it will include the current date. You can choose different date and time formats from the drop-down list.

Figure 3-14
Header and Footer
dialog box, Notes
and Handouts tab

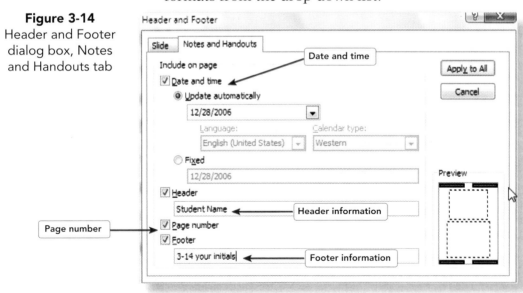

3. Make sure Header is checked and key **Your Name** in the header text box. The header is printed in the upper-left corner of a notes or handouts page.

4. Make sure the Page number option is checked. Page numbers are printed at the bottom right of the page.

5. Make sure the Footer check box is selected. Then key the filename **[3-14your initials]** in its text box.

6. Click Apply to All to add this information to all handouts pages you print (but not to individual slides).

7. Save the presentation as **[3-14your initials]** in your Lesson 3 folder.

Applying a Consistent Background and Color Theme

When you create a new blank presentation, the presentation contains no special formatting, colors, or graphics. Sometimes it's convenient to work without design elements so that you can focus all your attention on the presentation's text. Before the presentation is completed, however, you will usually want to apply a *design theme* to add visual interest. You can apply a design theme or change to a different one at any time while you are developing your presentation.

Exercise 3-15   SELECT A DESIGN THEME

The presentation that you have been working on in this lesson contains no theme. To select a design theme, from the Design tab, in the Themes group, click a design theme. The process to change a design theme is the same as to apply it for the first time.

1. From the Design tab, in the Themes group, click the More button 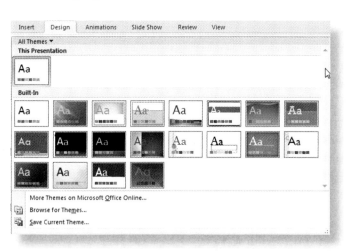 to display the theme choices shown as thumbnails.

Figure 3-15
Applying a design theme

2. Use the vertical scroll bar in the All Themes window to view the many design thumbnails. The window is divided by "This Presentation" and "Built-In." Links are available for "More Themes on Microsoft Office Online," "Browse for Themes," and "Save Current Theme," as shown in Figure 3-15.

3. Point to one of the design theme thumbnails. Notice the live preview working as you point to one of the design themes; PowerPoint automatically previews what that design theme will look like applied to your presentation. A ScreenTip also appears to indicate the name of the theme you are previewing or choosing.

4. Point to several design themes to sample what your presentation will look like with them applied.

5. Right-click any design theme thumbnail. Notice that you can apply the slide design to matching slides, all slides, or selected slides.

6. Click Apply to All Slides. The design theme that you selected is applied to all the slides in your presentation.

7. Locate the Flow design theme in the list of design theme thumbnails and click it. By clicking on the design theme, it automatically changes all slides in the presentation. (If Flow is not available on your computer, use a different theme.)

8. Notice that each thumbnail on the Slides tab shows the new theme design. Note also that the name of the template appears at the left on the status bar below the slide.

9. Move to slide 1 and view the presentation as a slide show; then return to slide 1 in Normal view.

Exercise 3-16   CHANGE THEME COLORS

You can apply different built-in colors to the current design theme by changing the *theme colors*. To display the built-in theme colors, from the Design tab, in the Themes group, click the Colors button ▣.

NOTE

You can choose to apply to selected slides, matching slides, or all slides on each of the theme elements including designs, colors, fonts, and effects.

1. From the Design tab, in the Themes group, click the Colors button ▣. Several choices for theme colors are available, as shown in Figure 3-16.

2. Point to any theme color set to see a live preview of what it will look like applied to your presentation.

Figure 3-16
Theme Colors drop-down list

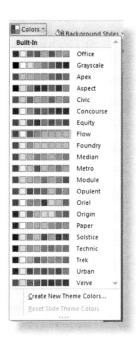

3. Click any theme color to apply it to your presentation.

4. Click the Aspect theme color to apply it to your presentation.

5. View the presentation as a slide show; then return to Normal view.

6. Move to slide 8.

7. From the Design tab, in the Themes group, click the Colors button.

8. Right-click on the Office theme color and choose Apply to Selected Slides. Notice that the color of only slide 8 changes to make this closing slide look a little different from the other slides.

Exercise 3-17   CHANGE THEME FONTS

You can apply different built-in fonts to the current design theme by changing the *theme font*. To display the built-in theme fonts, from the Design tab, in the Themes group, click the Fonts button .

Figure 3-17
Theme Font drop-down list

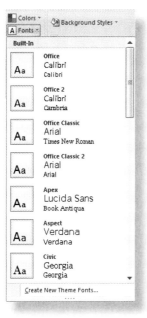

1. From the Design tab, in the Themes group, click the Fonts button. Several choices for theme fonts are available, as shown in Figure 3-17.

2. Point to any theme font to see a live preview of what it will look like applied to your presentation. A ScreenTip will pop up showing the name of the theme font.

3. Click any theme font to apply it to your presentation.

4. Click the Oriel Theme Font (Century Schoolbook) to apply it to your presentation.

5. View the presentation as a slide show; then return to Normal view.

Exercise 3-18   CHANGE THEME EFFECTS

You can apply different built-in effects to the current design theme by changing the *theme effects*. To display the built-in theme effects, from the Design tab, in the Themes group, click the Effects button.

Figure 3-18
Theme Effect drop-down list

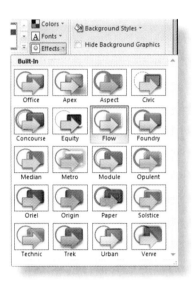

1. From the Design tab, in the Themes group, click the Effects button ⊡ . Several choices for theme effects are available, as shown in Figure 3-18.

2. Click any theme effects to apply it to your presentation. Right now you may not see any changes because these effects are most noticeable when applied to graphics you will use in later lessons.

3. Click the Metro theme effects to apply it to your presentation.

4. View the presentation as a slide show; then return to Normal view.

Exercise 3-19   CREATE NEW THEME FONTS

Although many built-in theme fonts are available, it is sometimes better to choose your own. You can accomplish this by creating new theme fonts.

1. From the Design tab, in the Themes group, click the Fonts button 🅰 .

2. Click Create New Theme Fonts at the bottom of the Font Theme drop-down list.

3. Click the drop-down arrow under Heading font, and choose Gloucester MT Extra Condensed, as shown in Figure 3-19.

4. Click the drop-down arrow under Body font, and choose Goudy Old Style.

5. In the Name box, key **Special Event Presentation Font Theme**.

Figure 3-19
Create New Theme Fonts dialog box

6. Click Save. Notice the change in the fonts of your presentation.

7. Save the presentation as **[3-19your initials]** in your Lesson 3 folder.

Adding Movement Effects

A *slide transition* is an effect that appears between two slides as they change during a slide show. You can choose to make one slide blend into the next in a checkerboard pattern, a fade pattern, or choose from many other effects. Transitions can have an effect like turning pages of a book. Movement can be applied to all slides in a presentation to control how they enter and exit the screen.

Exercise 3-20 APPLY SLIDE TRANSITIONS

Transitions can be applied to individual slides, to a group of slides, or to an entire slide show. To apply transitions, from the Animations tab, in Transition to This Slide group, click the More button ⬛ to display transition options. Click on the transition that you would like to apply.

1. Move to slide 1 and from the Animations tab, in the Transition to This Slide group, click the More button ⬛ to view all of the transition options shown as thumbnails.

Figure 3-20
Choosing the Box Out transition

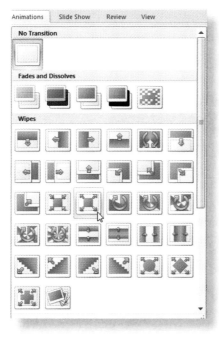

2. Point to several transitions and notice that the live preview shows you how this transition effect will look applied to your slide.

3. Choose Box Out from the list of transitions, as shown in Figure 3-20. This applies the transition to slide 1 only.

4. From the Animations tab, in the Transitions to This Slide group, click the Apply to All button ⬛ . This applies the transition to all slides in the presentation.

5. View the presentation as a slide show, and notice the Box Out transition between slides.

Exercise 3-21 ADJUST SOUNDS AND SPEEDS

Transitions also have the option to include sounds during the transition, and you can adjust the speed at which the transition occurs.

1. Move to slide 1. From the Animations tab, in the Transitions to This Slide group, click the drop-down arrow in the Transition Speed list box.

2. Choose Medium to slow the speed of the transition a little. This applies only to slide 1.

3. From the Animations tab, in the Transitions to This Slide group, click the Apply to All button . This applies the transition speed to all slides in the presentation.

4. Click the drop-down arrow in the Transition Sounds list box, and point to several sounds to listen to the possibilities for transition sounds.

5. Move to slide 1 and choose Applause from the Transition Sounds list box to apply the applause sound.

TIP

Try not to apply transition effects randomly. You might choose one transition for most of your presentation and then select one or two other effects to better emphasize the slide content as it appears. Be careful about using sounds, too, because they may detract from your presentation unless specifically suited to your content.

6. Still working in the Transitions to this Slide group, for Advance slide select On mouse click if it is not already checked.

7. View the presentation as a slide show to hear this sound as slide 1 appears.

8. Save the presentation as **[3-21your initials]** in your Lesson 3 folder.

9. Print the presentation as handouts, grayscale, framed, three slides per page.

Lesson 3 Summary

- To change the order of slides in a presentation, use either the Slides and Outline pane or the Slide Sorter view. Select the slides you want to move; then drag them to a new location. You can also delete selected slides.

- The Clipboard can store up to 24 items that you cut or copy from a presentation. The items can be text, entire slides, or other objects. Insert a Clipboard item at the current location in your presentation by clicking the item.

- Text can be moved or copied by using the Cut, Copy, and Paste commands. Slides can also be rearranged by using these commands.

- The Paste Options button ▣ enables you to choose between a pasted item's source formatting and its destination formatting. The source is the slide or placeholder from which the item was cut or copied, and the destination is the location where it will be pasted.

- PowerPoint enables you to undo—and if you change your mind—redo multiple editing actions. The default number of available undos is 20. When you save a presentation, the list of undos is cleared.

- The Format Painter button ◪ enables you to copy formatting from one object to another. This is a great time-saver if you applied several effects to an object and want to duplicate the effects.

- Double-clicking the Format Painter button ✒ keeps it active, so that multiple objects can receive the copied format. Click the Format Painter button ✒ again to turn it off.
- Right-clicking a word flagged with a red wavy line provides a shortcut list of suggested spelling corrections. You can spell check an entire presentation at one time by using the Spelling dialog box.
- Use the Research task pane to research items in the dictionary, thesaurus, and translator all at once.
- Use the Thesaurus task pane to find words with similar meanings.
- The Find command and the Replace command search your entire presentation for specified text. The Replace feature enables you to automatically make changes to matching text it finds.
- Headers and Footers can appear at the top and bottom of notes and handouts pages. Footers can also appear at the bottom of slides. They are commonly used to provide page numbers, dates, and other identifying information common to an entire presentation.
- Design Themes are a great way to add color, design, fonts, and effects all at once.
- There are several built-in Theme Colors, Theme Fonts, and Theme Effects. You can access these from the Design tab, in the Theme group.
- Design themes, Theme Colors, Theme Fonts, and Theme Effects can be applied to individual slides, to a group of selected slides, or to an entire presentation.
- Slide transitions add visual interest to slide shows. They can be applied to individual slides, a group of slides, or an entire slide presentation.
- Transition sounds and speed can be adjusted to add interest in a presentation.

LESSON 3		Command Summary	
Feature	**Button**	**Ribbon**	**Keyboard**
Select contiguous slides			Shift +click left mouse button
Select noncontiguous slides			Ctrl +click left mouse button
Delete selected slides	🗑	Home, Slides group, Delete	Delete
Cut selected object or text	✂	Home, Clipboard group, Cut	Ctrl + X
Copy selected object or text	📄	Home, Clipboard group, Copy	Ctrl + C
Paste (insert) cut or copied object or text	📋	Home, Clipboard group, Paste	Ctrl + V

continues

LESSON 3		Command Summary *continued*	
Feature	**Button**	**Ribbon**	**Keyboard**
Paste options			
Display Clipboard task pane		Home, Clipboard group, Dialog Box Launcher	
Clear the Clipboard task pane	Clear All	Clipboard task pane, Clear All	
Copy formatting of an object		Home, Clipboard group, Format Painter	
Undo		Quick Access toolbar, Undo	Ctrl + Z
Redo		Quick Access toolbar, Redo	Ctrl + Y
Spelling checker	ABC	Review, Proofing group, Spelling	F7
Research definitions		Review, Proofing group, Research	
Thesaurus		Review, Proofing group, Thesaurus	
Find		Home, Editing group, Find	Ctrl + F
Replace	Replace	Home, Editing group, Replace	Ctrl + H
Header and footer		Insert, Text group, Header and Footer	
Apply Design Theme		Design, Themes group, Design Theme	
Choose Theme Colors		Design, Themes group, Colors	
Choose Theme Fonts	A	Design, Themes group, Fonts	
Choose Theme Effects		Design, Themes group, Effects	
Slide transition		Animation, Transition to This Slide group	

Concepts Review

True/False Questions

Each of the following statements is either true or false. Select your choice by indicating T or F.

T (F) 1. The only way to change the order of slides is to drag them to a new position in Slide Sorter view.

(T) F 2. The Clipboard can store up to 24 items that you cut or copy from a presentation.

(T) F 3. The keyboard shortcut for undoing a task is Ctrl+Z.

(T) F 4. You can use the Format Painter tool to copy formatting from one slide to another.

T (F) 5. You can put headers on slides, but not on handouts.

T (F) 6. You can activate the Spelling Checker by pressing F1. *help*

T (F) 7. The Find command is located on the Review tab. *on home tab*

(T) F 8. Slide transitions appear when you move from one slide to the next while presenting a slide show.

Short Answer Questions

Write the correct answer in the space provided.

1. How do you select two noncontiguous slides at the same time?

   Control

2. How do you change the color theme of just one slide in a presentation?

   Apply to selected Slide

3. Name two ways to copy a selection of text.

   Ctrl C or Click copy

4. What is the default number of actions that you can undo using the Undo feature in PowerPoint?

   20

5. How do you use the Thesaurus?

   Review tab, proofing group click word

6. When you use the Header and Footer dialog box to add slide numbers to a presentation, where do the numbers usually appear on the slides?

bottom right

7. How would you apply a transition to all of the slides in a presentation?

Apply to all (Anim trans. to slide g

8. What feature can you use to copy the formatting of selected text to new text?

format painter

Critical Thinking

Answer these questions on a separate page. There are no right or wrong answers. Support your answers with examples from your own experience, if possible.

1. PowerPoint enables the user to choose a different design theme, color, font, effect, transition, and animation for each slide. How can these effects be applied consistently and why is it important to portray consistency throughout the presentation?

2. You can use headers and footers to identify your slides, handouts, and notes pages. What information is most important to include? Why?

Skills Review

Exercise 3-22

Add text, rearrange slides, and delete slides.

1. Open the file **Resort**.
2. On slide 1, replace "Student Name" with **your name**.
3. On slide 2, change the title "Customer Requirements" to **Vacationer's Expectations**.
4. On slide 3, insert a new bullet line after the first bullet point and key **Our name associated with gourmet dining**.
5. On slide 4, insert the following text into the blank body text placeholder: Key **Miami Beach** and press Enter; key **Palm Springs** and press Enter; and key **Niagara Falls**.
6. Reverse the position of slides 2 and 3 by following these steps:

    a. Click the Slides tab on the Slides and Outline pane.

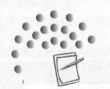

NOTE

If the Slides and Outline pane is not displayed, click the Normal view button to display it.

    b. Position your pointer on the right border of the Slides tab and drag the Splitter bar to the right to enlarge the slide thumbnails.

    c. Click the slide 3 thumbnail to select it.

    d. Drag slide 3 up until the drag-and-drop bar (the horizontal line) is between slides 1 and 2.

    e. Release your mouse button.

7. Reverse the position of slides 5 and 6.

8. Select slide 7 ("Key Benefits") and press ⌈Delete⌋ on your keyboard.

9. Move to slide 1 and save the presentation as **[3-22your initials]** in your Lesson 3 folder.

10. Preview and then print the presentation as handouts, nine slides per page, grayscale, framed.

11. Close the presentation.

Exercise 3-23

Rearrange slides, use cut and paste, and check spelling.

1. Open the file **EatGuide**.

2. Move to slide 3 ("Basic Food Groups") and cut the text "Use Sparingly" by using the following steps:

    a. Click the I-beam pointer before "Use" and drag to select "Sparingly."

    b. From the Home tab, in the Clipboard group, click the Cut button ⌈✁⌋.

3. Move to slide 7, and paste the copied text by following these steps:

    a. Click the I-beam pointer in the body text placeholder after "Sweets."

    b. Press ⌈Enter⌋ two times.

    c. From the Home tab, in the Clipboard group, click the Paste button ⌈📋⌋.

4. Promote "Use Sparingly" so it is even with the word "Examples."

5. In the Slide pane, drag slide 10 below slide 3.

6. Check spelling in the presentation by following these steps:

    a. Move to slide 1.

    b. From the Review tab, in the Proofing group, click the Spelling button ⌈✓⌋.

    c. Make corrections if needed, and click OK when the Spelling Checker has completed checking the document.

7. Move to slide 1 and save the presentation as **[3-23your initials]** in your Lesson 3 folder.

8. Preview and then print the presentation as handouts, four slides per page, landscape, grayscale, framed. Close the presentation.

Exercise 3-24

Apply a design theme, use the Undo command, and change the theme color.

1. Start a new presentation.
2. Apply a design theme by following these steps:
   a. From the Design tab, in the Themes group, click the More button ⊡ to show more design themes.
   b. Click on the Verve design theme to apply it to the presentation.
3. On the first slide, key **Smart Diet Options** for the presentation title. Key **Choosing Low-Fat Foods** for the subtitle.
4. Insert a new slide with the Two Content layout.
5. Key the title for slide 2 (on two lines) and bulleted text for slide 2 shown in Figure 3-21, demoting the bulleted text below "Under 30%" and "Over 30%" as shown.
6. Insert a new slide with the Two Content layout. Key the title for slide 3 (on two lines) and bulleted text for slide 3 shown in Figure 3-21, demoting the bulleted text below "Under 30%" and "Over 30%" as shown.

Figure 3-21
Content for slide 2 and 3

```
Calories from Fat:

Bread, Cereal, Rice, Pasta

• Under 30%              • Over 30%
     o Bagels                 o Muffins
     o Corn tortillas         o Biscuits
     o Pita bread             o Taco shells
```
Slide 2

```
Calories from Fat:

Vegetables

• Under 30%              • Over 30%
     o Raw                    o French fries
     o Steamed                o Hash browns
     o Vegetable juice        o Onion rings
```
Slide 3

7. View the presentation as a slide show starting on slide 1. Return to Normal view when you're finished.
8. Apply a different design theme by following these steps:
   a. From the Design tab, in the Themes group, click the More button ⊡ to view the design theme options.
   b. Click on the Concourse design theme to apply it to the presentation.
   c. Scroll through the presentation to view the applied design.
9. Change the presentation's theme colors by following these steps:
   a. From the Design tab, in the Themes group, click the Colors button ▦ to display the built-in theme colors.
   b. Click Opulent to apply to the color theme to your presentation.

10. Click the Undo button 🔄 to compare the new theme colors with the previous ones.

11. Click the Redo button 🔄 to reapply the color change.

12. Check spelling in the presentation.

13. Create a handout header and footer; include the date and your name as the header, and the page number and text **[3-24your initials]** as the footer by following these steps:

    a. From the Insert tab, in the Text group, click the Header and Footer button 🔲 .

    b. Click the Notes and Handouts tab.

    c. Check Date and Time and then select the Update Automatically option.

    d. Check the Footer box and key **[3-24your initials]** in the Footer text box.

    e. Make sure Page number is checked.

    f . Click Apply to All.

14. Move to slide 1 and save the presentation as **[3-24your initials]** in your Lesson 3 folder.

15. Preview and then print the presentation as handouts, three slides per page, grayscale, framed. Close the presentation.

Exercise 3-25

Add headers and footers to a presentation, change the theme color, and apply a slide transition.

1. Open the file **Takeout**.

2. On slide 1, replace "Student Name" with your name.

3. Add a transition effect by following these steps:

    a. From the Animations tab, in the Transition to This Slide group, click the More button 🔽.

    b. From the list of slide transitions, in the category of Fades and Dissolves, select Dissolve.

    c. Click the arrow to open the Transition Sound drop-down list and choose Cash Register for the sound.

    d. Click the arrow to open the Transition Speed drop-down list and choose Medium for the speed.

    e. From the Animations tab, in the Transition to This Slide group, click the Apply to All button 🔲 .

4. Add a footer and slide numbers by following these steps:

    a. From the Insert tab, in the Text group, click the Header and Footer button 🔲 .

    b. Click the Slide tab.

    c. Check Slide number.

    d. Check Footer and key your name as a footer.

       e. Click Don't show on title slide so that the footer and slide number do not print on slide 1.

       f. Click Apply to All.

5. Scroll through the presentation to check the footer and slide numbers. Notice that with this theme the footer shows at the top of the slide.

6. Create a handout header and footer; include the date and your name as the header, and the page number and text **[3-25your initials]** as the footer.

7. Save the presentation as **[3-25your initials]** in your Lesson 3 folder.

8. View all slides as a slide show.

9. Print all the slides as handouts, six slides per page, grayscale, framed. Close the presentation.

Lesson Applications

Exercise 3-26

Rearrange slides, cut and paste text, and check spelling.

1. Open the file **SafeFd1**.

2. On slide 4, cut the bulleted items in column 2 and paste them at the bottom of column 1. Ignore the Paste Options button 📋 that appears because the text is formatted correctly.

3. Change the layout of slide 4 to the Title and Content layout.

4. Edit text in slide 4 and demote bullets as shown in Figure 3-22.

Figure 3-22
Completed slide

5. Add a new slide 5 using the Title and Content layout, containing the text shown in Figure 3-23.

Figure 3-23
Slide 5 Content

```
Inspections
• Training inspections
  o Scheduled
  o Cooperative
• Internal evaluation inspections
• USDA inspections
```

6. Check spelling in the presentation.

7. Move to slide 1 and save the presentation as **[3-26your initials]** in your Lesson 3 folder.

8. View the presentation as a slide show.

9. Preview and then print the presentation as handouts, four slides per page, grayscale, framed. Close the presentation.

Exercise 3-27

Delete and reorder slides, check spelling, find and replace text, and add a header and footer.

1. Open the file **Premium**.

2. On slide 1, change the subtitle text to the following:

   Item 1: Water bottle
   Item 2: Visor
   Item 3: Knee pads

3. Make a noncontiguous selection that includes the thumbnails for slides 2 ("Introduction"), 7 ("Real Life"), and 8 ("What This Means").

4. Delete the selected slides.

5. Click the Replace button [Replace] and replace each occurrence of the word "Topic" with the word "Item." Use the Match case and Find whole words only options so that you replace only "Topic" and not "Topics" or "topic."

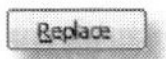

6. Edit slides 2 ("Topics of Discussion") through 6 ("Next Steps") so they contain only the text shown in Figure 3-24.

Figure 3-24
Content for slide 2 through 6

Slide 2
```
Topics of Discussion ——— Title
• Introduce new premium items to give away
at special events
• All premium items will contain the Good 4 U logo
```

Slide 3
```
Item 1: Water Bottle ——— Title
• Made of durable plastic
• Excellent for outdoor sports and indoor workouts
```

Slide 4
```
Item 3: Knee Pads ——— Title
• Made of durable vinyl/foam
• Essential protection for skaters
```

Slide 5
```
Item 2: Visor ——— Title
• Made of white cotton blend
• Adjustable, one size fits all
• Ideal for tennis, running, walking
```

Slide 6
```
Next Steps ——— Title
• Create designs
• Produce prototype items
• Analyze production costs
```

7. Reverse the order of slide 5 ("Item 3: Visor") and slide 4 ("Item 2: Knee Pads").

8. Check spelling in the presentation.

9. View the presentation as a slide show.

10. Add your name to the handout header and the filename **[3-27your initials]** to the handout footer, and set the date and time to update automatically.

11. Move to slide 1 and save the presentation as **[3-27your initials]** in your Lesson 3 folder.

12. Preview and then print the presentation as handouts, six slides per page, grayscale, framed.

Exercise 3-28

Check spelling, add a header and footer, apply a design theme, change the theme colors, and add transitions.

1. Create a new presentation, using the text shown in Figure 3-25.

Figure 3-25
Presentation content

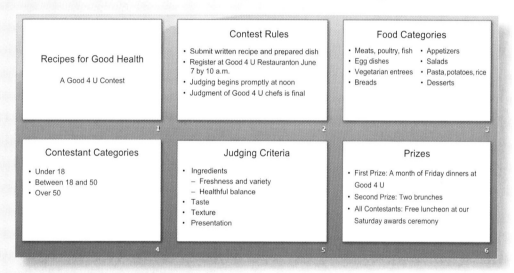

2. Apply the design theme Foundry.

3. Apply the color theme Median.

4. Check spelling in the presentation.

5. Add the Wedge slide transition to all slides.

6. Add slide numbers to all slides.

7. Create a handout header and footer; include the date and your name as the header, and the page number and text **[3-28your initials]** as the footer.

8. Move to slide 1 and save the presentation as **[3-28your initials]** in your Lesson 3 folder.

9. Preview and then print slide 3 in full size in grayscale or in color if available.

10. Preview and then print the entire presentation as handouts, six slides per page, grayscale, framed. Close the presentation.

Exercise 3-29 ◆ Challenge Yourself

Rearrange and delete slides, cut and paste text, check spelling, add a handout header/footer, change a design theme, change a color theme, add transition effects.

1. Open the file **CookCon1**.

2. On slide 1, key the subtitle **Rules, Judging, and Prizes**.

3. Add a new slide using the Title and Content layout after the title slide, using the text shown in Figure 3-26.

Figure 3-26
Slide content

```
Contest Rules
• Submit an original written recipe and dish
    o Good 4 U Restaurant, Saturday, June 7
    o 10 a.m. to noon
• Judging is from noon to 2 p.m.
• Judges' decisions are final
• Anyone may enter except Good 4 U employees and their
  families
```

4. Change slide 5 ("Ingredients to Use") to a Two Content layout; then cut the body text from slide 3 and paste it in the second column of slide 5.

5. Change the title of slide 5 to **Recipe Ingredients**. Insert a new line at the top of the first column. Key **Use** on the new line and demote all the text below it. Insert **Avoid** at the top of the second column and demote all the text below it.

6. Delete slide 3 ("Ingredients to Avoid"); then rearrange the remaining slides where needed so that they appear in the following order:

    Slide 1: Recipe Contest   Slide 4: Awards

    Slide 2: Contest Rules   Slide 5: Judging Criteria

    Slide 3: Recipe Ingredients

7. Change the design theme to Equity and the color theme to Apex.

8. Check spelling in the presentation.

9. Review the presentation as a slide show.

10. Add the Newsflash transition with Medium speed to all slides in the presentation.

11. Create a handout header and footer; include the date updated automatically and your name as the header, and the page number and text **[3-29your initials]** as the footer.

12. Move to slide 1 and save the presentation as **[3-29your initials]** in your Lesson 3 folder.

13. Preview and then print the presentation as handouts, six slides per page, grayscale, framed. Close the presentation.

On Your Own

In these exercises you work on your own, as you would in a real-life work environment. Use the skills you've learned to accomplish the task—and be creative.

Exercise 3-30

Imagine that you are organizing a drawing for your local community college to raise money for an internship banquet and updated technology for the business department. Local businesses have donated interesting products, and business students will sell tickets for a drawing to determine who will receive the products. Decide how you might organize such an event and prepare a slide show to promote it. Rearrange slides and copy and paste text as necessary to get them in a logical order. Apply a design theme of your choice to the first and last slides in your presentation and apply a different but complementary design theme to the other slides. Add a handout footer with your name and the file name in it. Check spelling in the presentation. Save the presentation as **[3-30your initials]**. Preview and then print the presentation as handouts.

Exercise 3-31

Create a presentation describing briefly a personal hobby that you have, i.e., scrapbooking, building guitars, quilting, riding motorcycles. Create at least six slides using a design theme, theme color, theme effects, and slide transitions. Copy and paste as necessary to put the text in a logical sequence. Rearrange or delete slides as necessary to finalize your presentation. Check spelling in the presentation. Add page numbers to the slides. Save the presentation as **[3-31your initials]**. Preview and then print the presentation as handouts.

Exercise 3-32

Choose a children's story, for example, a Dr. Seuss classic, Berenstain Bears, or Frog and Toad's adventures. Create a presentation that includes a title slide with the subject title being the title of the book and the author's name for the subtitle. After the title slide, insert multiple slides describing the major points of the story. Rearrange slides and copy and paste text as necessary to get them in a logical order. Choose a design theme and theme color that conveys the mood of the book. Add transition effects. Add page numbers to the slide. Check the spelling in the presentation. Save the presentation as **[3-32your initials]**. Preview and then print the presentation as handouts.

Unit 1 Applications

Unit Application 1-1

Copy and delete slides, edit slide text, check spelling, add header and footer information to handouts and slides, modify bullet color, use the format painter, and choose print options.

1. Open the file **ThreeYr2**.

2. Use Slide Sorter view to move slide 2 ("Projected Revenue Growth") after slide 7.

3. Delete the newly numbered slide 2 ("Presenting Good 4 U").

4. Move slide 4 ("Financial History") after slide 5.

5. On slide 2, add the title Who We Are and delete the text "Their dreams" and the subtext below it.

6. Move to slide 3, which contains blank placeholders, and add the title What We Want and key these bulleted items:

   - To encourage healthy eating
   - To promote participation in sports activities
   - To expand our market base

7. Change the bullets on slide 3 to a new color that matches the theme color in the presentation.

8. Move to slide 8. Change the bullets on slide 8 to the square bullets used throughout the presentation using Format Painter.

9. Check spelling in the presentation (assume that all proper names are spelled correctly).

10. View the presentation as a slide show, starting on slide 1.

11. Create a header and footer for handouts that includes today's date as a fixed date, your name as the header, and the filename **[U1-1your initials]** as the footer.

12. Using the Header and Footer dialog box, add a slide number to all slides, including slide 1.

13. Move to the first slide and save the file as **[U1-1your initials]** in a new folder for Unit 1 Applications.

14. Preview and then print the presentation as handouts, four slides per page with landscape orientation, pure black and white, framed.

15. Close the presentation.

Unit Application 1-2

Rearrange slides, edit text, change bullet color, find and replace text, check spelling and style, add slide transitions, add slide numbers, and add handout headers and footers.

1. Open the file **NewFood1**.

2. Find the word "desert" and replace it with **dessert**.

3. On slide 5 ("Just Sweet Enough"), delete the sentence that begins "The striking lime flavor."

4. On slide 3 (the first "Pasta Delights" slide), change the title to **Salad Delights**.

5. Select all the bulleted text on slide 3 and delete it, leaving a blank body text placeholder. In the placeholder, key the text shown in Figure U1-1.

Figure U1-1

- Julie's Spin*a*ch Salad

- Grilled Chicken Salad
    Michelle's
- ~~Michael's~~ Cobb Salad

- Wild Rice and Smoked Turkey Salad
    Southwestern
- ~~Corn, Black Bean, and Mango~~ Salad

6. Change the color of the bullets in slide 3 to a new color that matches the current theme color.

7. Move slide 2 with the subtitle text "A New Dining Event" to the end of the presentation. (It will become slide 6.)

8. Move the new slide 5 ("Appetizer Specials") after slide 1 so that it becomes slide 2. Increase the size of the body text placeholder slightly so the size of the text will match the other body text placeholders.

9. Check spelling in the presentation.

10. Use the Thesaurus to replace the word "Event" on slide 6. Choose "experience" to replace it from the Thesaurus window. Use cut and paste and insert words as needed to get the text on slide 6 to read **A New Experience in Dining**.

11. Add the Shape Diamond slide transition to all slides.

12. Add a Drum Roll transition sound to only the first slide.

13. Add slide numbers to all slides except the title slide layouts. Add a handout header that contains your name, add a handout footer that contains the filename **[U1-2your initials]**, with the page number and current date.

14. Save the presentation as **[U1-2your initials]** in your Unit 1 Applications folder.

15. Preview and then print the entire presentation as handouts, six slides per page, grayscale, framed.

16. Print slide 2 of the presentation in full size, grayscale, framed.

17. Close the presentation.

Unit Application 1-3

Create slides, change theme colors, change slide layout, apply text formatting, change text alignment, replace text, and change bullets.

1. Open the presentation **PowerWalk**.

2. Change the theme color to Metro.

3. On slide 1, change the slide title font to Arial Black and take the title off ALL CAPS.

4. Make the subtitle stand out more:

   - Make "Good 4 U" bold.
   - Increase the font size of "4" by one font size increment.
   - Move the placeholder up slightly so all text fits in the green area.
   - Right-align the subtitle text.

5. Working in either the Slide tab or the Outline tab, create slides 2 through 4 using the text shown in Figure U1-2. Use the Title and Content layout.

Figure U1-2

```
Slide 2  ┌Objectives
         │   • Encourage morning power walkers to breakfast at G4U
         └   • Make G4U a social center for power walkers
         ┌Strategies
         │   • Guided walks
Slide 3  │   • Seminars
         │   • G4U merchandise
         └   • Advertising
         ┌Cost/Benefits Analysis
         │   • Costs
         │       _ Walk guides' salaries
         │       _ Seminar leaders' salaries
         │       _ Merchandise costs
         │       _ Advertising costs
Slide 4  │   • Benefits
         │       _ Increase breakfasts served
         │       _ Increase repeat business
         │       _ Increase merchandise sales
         └       _ Increase general sales
```

6. On slide 1, copy the text Good 4 U. Use the Replace command to change all instances of "G4U" to Good 4 U.

7. On slide 2, change the title text font to Arial Black and increase the size by one increment.

8. Double-click the Format Painter then apply this new formatting to the title on slides 3 and 4.

9. On slide 4, make the following changes:

   - Change the slide layout to Comparison.
   - Move the "Benefits" bullet and all its second-level bullets into the right column by cutting and pasting the text.
   - Cut "Costs" and "Benefits" and put them into their respective comparison heading boxes.
   - Increase the size of "Costs" to 32 points and make it bold. Use the Format Painter to give "Benefits" the same treatment.
   - Change the color of bullets on this slide to Pink, Accent 2. and make them 80 percent of the text size.

10. Check spelling in the presentation.

11. View the presentation as a slide show.

12. Create a handout header and footer; include the date and your name as the header, and the page number and text **[U1-3your initials]** as the footer.

13. Move to slide 1 and save the presentation as **[U1-3your initials]** in your Unit 1 Applications folder.

14. Preview and then print the presentation as handouts, landscape orientation, four slides per page, grayscale, framed.

15. Close the presentation.

Unit Application 1-4 ◆ Using the Internet

Research a topic, create a presentation, use cut and paste, rearrange slides, apply a design theme, change theme color, change theme font, add slide and handout header/footer, check spelling, modify bullets, add a text box, and add transition effects.

Use the Internet to research a self-help topic. Choose something that interests you, such as weight loss, anti-aging, body toning, exercise, quit smoking, spirituality, personality improvement, etc. The following is a list of suggested information to gather:

- Background on the topic.

- Who might be interested in this topic.

- Main points to begin the process of self-help in this area.

- Any other information that you think would be useful for a presentation.

- Be sure to cite where you found the information.

Use the material you researched to prepare an informative presentation on your subject. Be sure to include at least five slides in the presentation. Choose any design theme, a new theme color, a new theme font, and new theme effects. Format the presentation attractively. Add a transition to all slides in the presentation.

Use cut and paste and rearrange slides as necessary to get presentation information into a logical sequence.

Change bullets in the presentation to a new shape and color. Add at least one text box within the presentation.

In the slide footer, include the text **Prepared by** followed by your name. Include the slide number on all slides but not the date. In the handout footer, include the text **[U1-4your initials]**. In the handout header, key **Presented to** and then identify to whom you would be giving this presentation (instructor or class). Include in the handout the date you would be delivering the presentation as a fixed date.

Check spelling in the presentation and save it with the filename **[U1-4your initials]** in your Unit 1 Applications folder. Practice delivering the presentation. Preview and then print the presentation handouts, choosing an appropriate number of slides per page, grayscale, framed. Close the presentation.

unit 2

PRESENTATION ILLUSTRATION

PPT2.4

Working with Graphics

OBJECTIVES

After completing this lesson, you will be able to:

1. Work with shapes.

2. Insert clip art images.

3. Insert and enhance pictures.

4. Create WordArt.

5. Create a photo album.

Estimated Time: 2 hours

MCAS OBJECTIVES

In this lesson:
PP07 2.2.2
PP07 2.2.7
PP07 3.3.1
PP07 3.3.2
PP07 3.3.3
PP07 3.3.4
PP07 3.4.1
PP07 3.4.2
PP07 3.5.1
PP07 3.5.2
PP07 3.5.3
See Appendix

An effective presentation slide show consists of more than text alone. Although text may carry most of the information, you can use several types of objects to help communicate your message or draw attention to key points. For example, you can add shapes, free-floating text objects, clip art images, and photographs to help illustrate your presentation.

After you add an object to a slide, you can change its size, position, and appearance. In this lesson, you will concentrate on some basic drawing skills and begin to explore some of the many special effects made possible in PowerPoint 2007.

Working with Shapes

PowerPoint provides a variety of tools you can use to create original drawings. These tools are available in three tabs: Home, Insert, and Drawing Tools Format. In this lesson, you learn basic drawing skills. In later lessons, you learn how to enhance simple shapes and create more complex drawings.

When drawing shapes, the ruler can help you to judge size and positioning. When the ruler is displayed, it appears in two parts: the horizontal measurement is across the top of the slide and the vertical measurement is on the left. By default, the ruler measures in inches; the center of the slide (vertically and horizontally) appears as zero. A dotted line on each ruler indicates the horizontal and vertical position of your pointer.

TABLE 4-1 Tools for Basic Drawing

Button	Name	Purpose
	Select	Selects an object. This tool is automatically in effect when no other tool is in use.
	Picture	Inserts a bitmap or photo image from a file.
	Clip Art	Inserts a clip art object, which could be drawings, sounds, movies, or stock photography.
	Photo Album	Creates a presentation made of pictures with each one on a separate slide.
	Shapes	Opens the Shapes gallery, which contains predefined shapes you can draw.
	Line	Draws a straight line.
	Arrow	Draws an arrow.
	Rectangle	Draws a rectangle or square.
	Oval	Draws an oval or circle.
	Text Box	Inserts text anywhere on a slide.
	WordArt	Creates a Microsoft WordArt object on a slide.
	Shape Fill	Fills a shape with colors, patterns, or textures.
	Shape Outline	Changes the color of a shape's outline or the color of a line.
	Shape Effects	Adds a visual effect such as shadow, glow, or bevel.

Exercise 4-1 DRAW SHAPES—RECTANGLES, OVALS, AND LINES

In this exercise, you practice drawing several *shapes* on a blank slide. To draw a shape, click the appropriate drawing tool button (such as the Line, Rectangle, or Oval); then drag the *Crosshair pointer* on your slide until the shape is the size you want.

You can draw multiple shapes with the same drawing tool by using the *Lock Drawing Mode* option. This keeps the button activated, so you can draw as many of the same shapes as you want without the need to reclick the button. This feature is deactivated when you click another button.

If you don't like an object that you created, you can easily remove it from your slide. Simply select the object by clicking it, and then press Delete on your keyboard.

As you draw with different tools, the ones you have used appear at the top of the list in a Recently Used Shapes category of the Shapes gallery; however, each tool is also shown in a related group when you access the entire Shapes gallery.

NOTE

Three of the slides in this presentation were created by using the Blank slide layout. The Blank slide layout contains no text placeholders. The text that appears on the slides is placed in text boxes as shown in Lesson 2.

NOTE

The green handle just above the rectangle is a *rotation handle*. It can be used to rotate a shape in the same way it was used to rotate a text box in the previous lesson.

1. Open the presentation file **Opening1**.

2. Insert a new slide after slide 2 and use the Blank layout. You will use this slide to practice drawing.

3. If the rulers are not showing, right-click on the blank slide and choose Ruler from the short-cut menu.

4. While watching the horizontal ruler at the top of the slide, move your pointer back and forth, observing the dotted line on the ruler indicating the pointer's position. While moving your pointer up and down, observe the dotted line on the vertical ruler. From the Home tab, in the Drawing group, click the Shapes button 🔲 then click the Rectangle button 🔲. The pointer changes to a crosshair pointer ⊞.

5. Notice that zero is placed at the midpoint of the slide on both the vertical ruler and the horizontal ruler. Move the crosshair pointer ⊞ to the 3-inch mark on the horizontal ruler to the left of the zero and to the 2-inch mark on the vertical ruler above the zero.

6. Click and hold the left mouse button. Drag diagonally down and to the right until you reach the 2-inch mark below the zero on the vertical ruler and the 3-inch mark to the right of the zero on the horizontal ruler. Release your mouse button. A blue rectangle with a white outline appears. See Figure 4-1 to compare the size and placement of the completed rectangle.

Figure 4-1
Drawing a shape on a slide

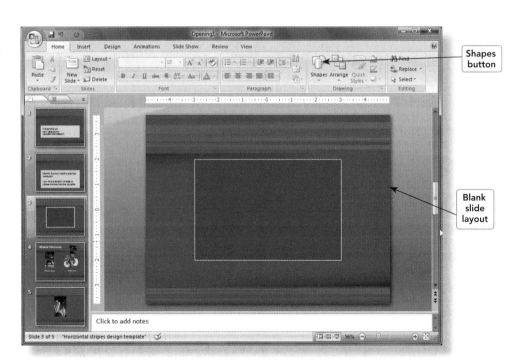

7. From the Home tab, in the Drawing group, click the Shapes button 🔳 , and then choose the Oval button ⬭ .

8. Draw a small oval (approximately one-inch wide) on the inside of the rectangle that you previously drew, using the same method that you used to draw the rectangle.

9. From the Home tab, in the Drawing group, click the Shapes button 🔳 , and then right-click the Line button ◱ and choose Lock Drawing Mode. Drag your pointer diagonally to draw a line from the left corner of the rectangle to the outline of the oval.

10. Because the drawing mode is locked, notice that the pointer is still the crosshair pointer ⊞ showing that the Line button ◱ is still selected. Draw three more lines from each corner of the rectangle to the outline of the oval.

11. Your screen should look similar to the back of an envelope with a seal, as shown in Figure 4-2.

Figure 4-2
Drawing an oval
and lines

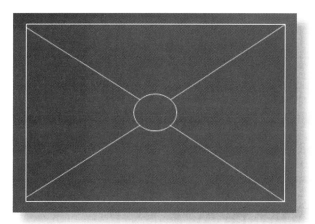

12. Click the Line button ◱ again to deactivate it.

13. Hold ⟨Shift⟩ down while you click to select all four lines and the oval then press ⟨Delete⟩ to remove them all at once. The slide should now contain one rectangle only.

Exercise 4-2 DRAW HORIZONTAL CONSTRAINED LINES

You use ⟨Shift⟩ to *constrain* a shape as you draw it on a slide. For lines, constraining enables you to make perfectly straight horizontal or vertical lines. If you try to angle a constrained line, lines are limited to angles in increments of 45 degrees.

When using ⟨Shift⟩ to constrain a shape, it's important to release your mouse button before releasing ⟨Shift⟩. Otherwise, you might accidentally move the pointer when ⟨Shift⟩ is no longer in effect, resulting in a shape that is no longer constrained.

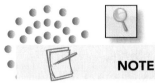

NOTE

Depending on the settings of your computer and the size of your screen, you may need to use a different percent so you can focus on the rectangle and not the entire slide.

REVIEW

To insert a footer on one slide only, move to the slide before opening the Header and Footer dialog box; then click Apply instead of Apply to All.

NOTE

The documents you create in this course relate to the case study about Good 4 U, a fictional restaurant business described at the beginning of this text.

Figure 4-3
Drawing horizontal lines

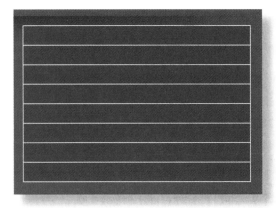

1. Still working on slide 3, from the View tab, in the Zoom group, click the Zoom button. On the Zoom dialog box, key **150** percent and click OK. Scroll as needed to display the rectangle. Zooming in on the area will make it easier to see what you're doing when you work on detailed objects.

2. From the Home tab, in the Drawing group, right-click the Line button then choose Lock Drawing Mode. You're going to draw several constrained lines without needing to reclick the Line button each time you draw.

3. Position the crosshair pointer ⊞ on the left side of the rectangle on the vertical ruler's zero marker, hold down Shift, and drag straight across to the right side of the rectangle. (As you drag, notice that the line remains straight, even if you move the pointer up or down a little.)

4. Release the mouse button first, and then release Shift.

5. With the Line button still activated, position the crosshair pointer ⊞ at the left end of the rectangle again about a half inch above where you drew the last line. Hold down Shift and drag to the right edge of the rectangle. Release the mouse button, and then release Shift. Continue this process until the rectangle is full of horizontal lines a half inch apart, as shown in Figure 4-3.

6. Press Esc to release the locked drawing mode.

7. From the View tab, in the Zoom group, click Fit to Window to display the entire slide.

8. Insert a footer only on slide 3 that contains Your Name, a comma, and the text **[4-2your initials]**. (Do not include the date.)

9. Create a new folder for Lesson 4. Save the presentation as **[4-2your initials]** in the new Lesson 4 folder. Print only slide 3, full size, grayscale, and framed. Keep the presentation open for the next exercise.

Exercise 4-3 ADD CONNECTOR LINES

Sometimes two or more shapes need to be connected with a line; therefore, PowerPoint provides a variety of *connector lines* for this purpose. These lines are either straight connectors, elbow connectors (with 90-degree angles between connected shapes), or curved connector lines. Some lines have arrowheads on one or both ends to show a relationship or movement between the shapes when creating a diagram.

1. Insert a new slide after slide 3 using the Blank layout.

2. On the new slide 4, from the Home tab, in the Drawing group, click the Shapes button 🔲 and then choose the Rounded Rectangle button 🔲. Notice that a ScreenTip will appear that labels each drawing tool button.

3. Position the crosshair pointer ⊞ on the left of your slide then click and drag to create a rectangle as shown in Figure 4-4.

4. Repeat this process to create a similar rectangle on the right of the slide.

5. Now select the Elbow Connector button 🔲. Point to the left rectangle and you will see a red square appear on all four sides of this rectangle. These are *connection sites* where the line and rectangle can be joined.

6. Click the red square at the bottom. This step connects the beginning portion of your line.

7. Now drag the line to the right until you connect to the red square on the left side of the second rectangle.

8. Notice that the connector line has two yellow diamond shapes. These are *adjustment handles* that enable you to change the horizontal or the vertical portions of the line. Adjust the line as shown in Figure 4-4.

Figure 4-4
Elbow connector lines

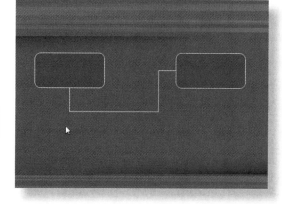

9. With the connector line still selected, press Delete to remove the connector line.

10. Now add a different connector line. Click the Curved Double-Arrow Connector button 🔄 and repeat the process of connecting the bottom of the left rectangle with the left side of the rectangle on the right.

Figure 4-5
Double-arrow
connector lines

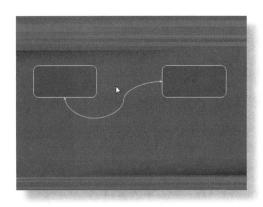

11. Notice how the adjustment handles affect the curve of the line as you move them horizontally or vertically. Adjust the line as shown in Figure 4-5.

Exercise 4-4   CREATE SQUARES AND CIRCLES

When you constrain other shapes, such as rectangles or ovals, they grow at an equal rate horizontally and vertically as you draw, creating symmetrical objects such as squares and circles.

NOTE

Your square might look more like a rectangle if your monitor's horizontal size and vertical size are not perfectly synchronized. Your square will print correctly, even if it is distorted on your screen.

1. Insert a new slide after slide 4 using the Blank layout.

2. On the new slide 5, from the Home tab, in the Drawing group, click the Shapes button 🔲 and then choose the Rectangle button 🔲.

3. Position the crosshair pointer ⊞. on the left of your slide.

4. Press and hold Shift then drag diagonally down and to the right, ending near the center of the slide. Release the mouse button first, and then release Shift. See Figure 4-6 for the approximate size and placement of the completed square.

Figure 4-6
Drawing a circle and
a square

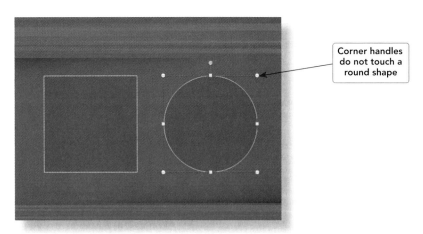

Corner handles
do not touch a
round shape

5. From the Home tab, in the Drawing group, click the Shapes button 🔲 and choose the Oval button 🔲.

6. Position your pointer to the right of the square.

7. While pressing ⎡Shift⎤, drag diagonally down and to the right to create a circle the same size as the square. Your screen should resemble Figure 4-6. Both the square and the circle in this example have a Height and Width measurement of 3.5 inches.

8. Notice that with a circular shape, the corner handles do not touch the shape.

9. Save the presentation as **[4-4your initials]** in your Lesson 4 folder, but do not print it. Leave it open for the next exercise.

Exercise 4-5   RESIZE AND MOVE SHAPES

A shape that you draw is resized in the same way that you resize a text placeholder: Select it, and then drag one of its sizing handles. Holding down ⎡Shift⎤ and/or ⎡Ctrl⎤ while dragging a sizing handle has the following effects on an object:

- ⎡Shift⎤ preserves a shape's *proportions*, meaning that its height grows or shrinks at the same rate as its width, preventing shapes from becoming too tall and skinny or too short and wide.

- ⎡Ctrl⎤ causes a shape to grow or shrink from the center of the shape, rather than from the edge that's being dragged.

- ⎡Ctrl⎤+⎡Shift⎤ together cause a shape to grow or shrink proportionately from its center.

You reposition a shape by dragging it with the four-pointed arrow ✛. Point anywhere in the shape and when you see the four-pointed arrow, drag the shape to another place on your slide.

NOTE

These techniques also apply to resizing and moving clip art and photo images, too.

1. Still working on slide 5, select the circle by clicking anywhere inside it, and then point to its bottom center sizing handle. Your pointer changes to a two-pointed vertical arrow ↕.

2. Drag the handle down. As you drag, the pointer changes to a crosshair ✛. The circle has changed into an oval and is now larger.

3. Drag the bottom-left corner handle diagonally up and to the left. The oval is now wider and flattened, taking on an entirely new shape.

4. Click the Undo button ↶ twice to restore the circle to its original size and shape.

5. Point to the circle's lower-left corner sizing handle. While holding down ⎡Shift⎤, drag diagonally out from the circle's center, making it larger. (Don't worry if the circle overlaps the rectangle.) The circle retains its original shape. Press ⎡Ctrl⎤+⎡Z⎤ to Undo this action and revert the circle to the original size.

6. While holding down both ⌃Ctrl and ⇧Shift, drag the lower-left corner sizing handle toward the center of the circle. The circle becomes smaller, shrinking evenly from all edges. With this technique, all expanding and contracting of the size occurs from the shape's center, as shown in Figure 4-7.

Figure 4-7
Resizing a shape
from its center

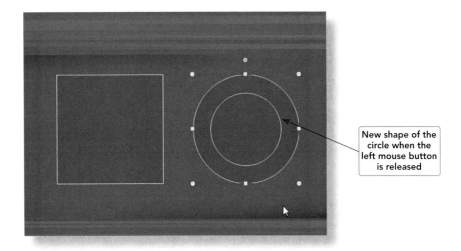

New shape of the
circle when the
left mouse button
is released

7. Select the circle and press ⌫Delete to remove it.

8. Select the square shape and then from the the Drawing Tools Format tab, in the Size group, key **4.5** in both the Height and Width boxes.

9. Point in the square so you see the four-pointed arrow ✥ then drag the square to the middle of the slide

10. To control precise sizing and positioning, click the Dialog Box Launcher in the Size group.

TIP

If you like working with the ruler measurements, you can precisely size and position objects without the need to open the Size and Position dialog box, but keep in mind that the rulers measure distances from the center of the slide. So, if you point to the two-inch mark at the right of the zero mark on the horizontal ruler, you need to do some math to figure out how far you are from either edge of the slide. The Position tab on the Size and Position dialog box lets you choose to measure either from the center of the slide or from its top left corner.

11. On the Size tab in the Size and Position dialog box, click the Lock aspect ratio option to keep the vertical and horizontal sizing in the same ratio as a shape (or other object) is resized. This can be very important when working with photographs.

12. Click the Position tab then change the Horizontal position of the square to be 2.75 inches from the top left corner and the Vertical position to be 1.75 inches down from the top left corner.

13. Click the Close button ⊠.

14. Save the presentation as **[4-5your initials]** in your Lesson 4 folder, but do not print it. Leave it open for the next exercise.

Exercise 4-6 USE ADJUSTMENT HANDLES TO MODIFY SHAPES

The rectangles, ovals, and lines that you have created are very simple shapes. Many additional shapes are available, as shown in Figure 4-8.

Shape tools are arranged in nine different categories, as shown in Figure 4-8. You resize all of these shapes in the same way, and many shapes include one or more adjustment handles which enable you to change the shape dimensions after it is drawn.

Figure 4-8
Additional shapes in the Shapes gallery

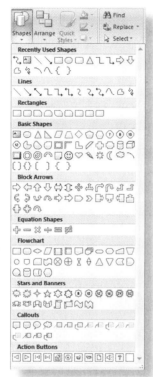

1. You no longer need slides 3 and 4 where you practiced making shapes. From the Slides and Outline pane, select each of these slide thumbnails and press Delete to remove them.

2. Now working on slide 3, from the Home tab, in the Drawing group, click the Shapes button 📷 to display the Shapes gallery.

3. In the Stars and Banners category, point to the various shape buttons and read their ScreenTips to see what each one is called.

4. Right-click the 5-Point Star button ☆ and choose Lock Drawing Mode. Draw several stars in different sizes positioned randomly on the slide with some stars overlapping. Place stars on the rectangle and on the blank area of the slide.

5. Press Esc to exit the locked drawing mode.

6. Select one of the stars and drag its yellow diamond-shaped adjustment handle ◆ toward the center to make the points more narrow, as shown in Figure 4-9.

7. Press Ctrl+Z several times until there is only a square left on the slide.

TIP

Use Shift to create a symmetrical Shape in the same way that you use Shift when you draw a circle or square.

Figure 4-9
Dragging an adjustment handle

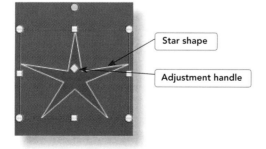

Star shape

Adjustment handle

8. From the Home tab, in the Drawing group, click the Shapes button and in the Basic Shapes category, click the Sun button . Draw a sun, about two inches in diameter, in the upper right corner of the slide.

9. Drag the adjustment handle toward the center of the Sun shape to make the center circle smaller and the points longer.

Exercise 4-7   PLACE TEXT IN A SHAPE AND ROTATE

You can easily transform a shape into an attention-getting background for text. Simply select the shape and key the text (or paste it from the clipboard). You can format and edit the text in the same way as in a text placeholder. The text in a shape is centered by default.

1. Select the Sun shape on slide 3 and press Delete.

2. From the Home tab, in the Drawing group, click the Shapes button to display the Shapes gallery.

3. In the Stars and Banners category, choose the 16-Point Star button then click and drag to draw this shape in the upper right of the slide. It should slightly overlap the large square.

4. Key **Grand Opening**. The text automatically appears in the center of the star in the same color as the star's outline. Notice the dashed-line border similar to a text placeholder border.

5. Click the star's outline anywhere between two sizing handles to select it.

6. From the Home tab, in the Font group, change the size from 18 points to 28 points and apply bold. The text becomes too large for the star.

7. Drag the center sizing handle on the left side to make the star wide enough to contain the text without word wrapping. Part of the star shape will be over the square shape.

Figure 4-10
Inserting text in a shape

8. Drag the top-center sizing handle down to flatten the star, as shown in Figure 4-10.

9. Click on the green rotation handle and drag it slightly to the left to rotate the star.

10. Drag the star down until it overlaps the lower-right corner of the square, as shown in Figure 4-11.

Figure 4-11
Rotating a shape
with text

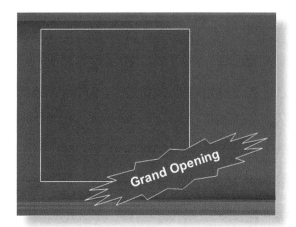

11. Compare slide 3 with Figure 4-11 and make any necessary adjustments.

12. Create a handout header and footer: Include the date and your name as the header, and the page number and text **[4-7your initials]** as the footer.

13. Move to slide 1 and save the presentation as **[4-7your initials]** in your Lesson 4 folder.

Inserting Clip Art Images

Included with Microsoft Office is a collection of ready-to-use images known as clip art, also called *clips*, that you can insert on PowerPoint slides. The *clip art* collection includes *vector drawings*—images made up of lines, curves, and shapes that are usually filled with solid colors. It also includes *bitmap pictures*—photographs made up of tiny colored dots that are made from scanned photographs or a digital camera. These photographs can be accessed from the Insert Clip Art task pane.

You can insert clip art and picture images into a PowerPoint presentation in two ways:

- Search for Clip Art. On the Insert tab, in the Illustrations group, click the Clip Art button 🖼 to display the Clip Art task pane where you can search for appropriate images from Microsoft's Clip Organizer collection. Also, if your slide uses a layout that includes a content placeholder, double-click the Clip Art button 🖼 to display the Clip Art task pane.

- Insert Picture from File. On the Insert tab, in the Illustrations group, click the Picture button 🖼 to insert picture files stored on a hard drive, removable drive, or network drive. This method is useful for inserting your own images that you have stored on your computer and that are not part of the Microsoft Clip Organizer collection.

Exercise 4-8 FIND CLIP ART THEN MODIFY A SEARCH

Each clip art image that Microsoft provides has *keywords* associated with it that describe the subject matter of the picture. You use keywords to find the art you need for your presentation.

Clip art images (and other media such as photographs, sound, and movie files) are organized into collections and media types. You can choose to search all collections and types or to select a particular type. If you know that you want a photograph only, be sure to select that type of media only to make the search more efficient.

If you search for a keyword and don't find any images, or you don't find one you like, you can modify your search and try again.

1. If you have Internet access, but are not connected, make a connection now (unless your instructor tells you otherwise).

2. Move to slide 2, and then from the Insert tab, in the Illustrations group, click the Clip Art button. The Clip Art task pane, as shown in Figure 4-12, is displayed on the right.

Figure 4-12
Clip Art task pane

3. In the Clip Art task pane, click the Search in list box arrow. Be sure that Everywhere is checked. All categories in the Microsoft Clip Organizer will be searched and, if you are connected to the Internet, Microsoft Office Online will be searched, too.

4. Close the list box by clicking anywhere on your screen.

5. Click the Results should be list box arrow. In this list box, you can choose to search all media types or limit your search to specific types. These options are helpful if you have a large number of media files stored on your computer, or you are searching on the Internet. Check only the Clip Art category and remove all other checks.

6. In the Search for text box at the top of the Clip Art task pane, key **food** and then click Go. The Results box shows thumbnails (miniature images) of clips that match the search word, as shown in Figure 4-13.

Figure 4-13
Search results

Online icon

NOTE

Clips from the Microsoft Office Online collection have an online icon  in the lower left corner of the image thumbnail. When you do a search from all categories, some clips will have a musical note, indicating that they are sound files. Some clips will have an animation icon ⊞ displayed in the lower right corner, indicating that they are movies.

7. Use the scroll bar to review some of the thumbnails.

8. In the Search for box, key **bananas** and then click Go. Thumbnails of pictures with bananas should appear in your Results box. If you do not find a picture you like, modify the search using a different keyword.

Exercise 4-9 PREVIEW AND INSERT CLIP ART IMAGES

You can preview images in a larger format, so you can see more detail before choosing one of them.

1. Without clicking, point to a clip art thumbnail in the task pane. As your pointer is over an image, a ScreenTip showing keywords, image dimensions, size, and file format appears. A gray bar with a downward pointing triangle appears on the right side of the thumbnail that changes to blue when you point to it.

2. Choose a picture you would like to insert.

3. Click the gray bar beside the picture you have chosen to display a menu of options. You can also display this menu by right-clicking a thumbnail.

4. Choose Preview/Properties. In addition to displaying an enlarged picture, this dialog box also shows you the filename and more detailed information about the image, as shown in Figure 4-14.

Figure 4-14
Preview/Properties
dialog box

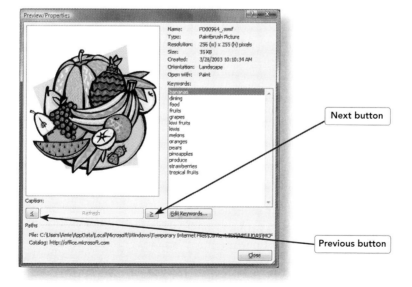

TIP

You can also drag the image directly from the task pane onto your slide or select Insert from the bar that appears next to the thumbnail.

5. Click the Next button ⊡ below the picture. The next picture in the search results pane is displayed.

6. Click the Next button ⊡ several times more; then click the Previous button ⊡. When you find a picture of health-conscious food that you like, such as the one in Figure 4-14 or Figure 4-15, click Close. Notice that the last picture you previewed has a blue selection box around it.

7. With your left mouse button, click the thumbnail for the image you chose. The clip art image is inserted on the current slide.

Figure 4-15
Positioning of clip art

8. Drag the image above the text box and resize it as necessary for a pleasing appearance. The image in Figure 4-15 was increased in size and centered on the top edge of the text box. If you used a different image, then decide how to position it attractively on the slide.

9. Move to slide 1, and search for another image that would be appropriate for Miami Beach. Search for a palm tree and choose the Photograph media option in the Results should be box.

10. When you find a photograph of a palm tree that you like, insert it on slide 1. Close the Clip Art task pane.

Exercise 4-10   REARRANGE, DELETE, COPY, PASTE, AND DUPLICATE CLIP ART IMAGES

When developing a presentation you might insert an image on one slide and later decide to move it to a different slide. You can rearrange, delete, copy, paste, and duplicate clip art images.

1. Still working on slide 1, click on the photograph to select it. When you see the four-pointed arrow ⊕, drag the photograph down to center it vertically on the right edge of the text box.

2. Move to slide 4. This slide has four clip art images that have been previously inserted. On the left, select the sunset beach scene on the top and notice that it has a green rotation handle at the top. Practice dragging this handle to rotate the image.

3. Press [Delete] to remove the sunset beach scene from this slide.

4. On the right, select the palm tree image on the top and press [Ctrl]+[C] to copy it then [Delete] to remove it from this slide. The image is still in your clipboard, however.

5. Move to side 1 press [Ctrl]+[V] to insert the palm tree on the first slide.

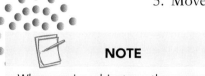

NOTE

When moving objects on the screen that need precise positioning, you can use the directional arrow keys on the keyboard to *nudge* the image gradually.

6. When this image first appears, the size is 1.84 inches for both the height and width. From the Picture Tools Format tab, in the Size group, change both height and width to 1.5 inches.

7. Drag the palm tree to the upper left of the slide, aligning the bottom of the image with the darkest blue color on the background and the left edge of the image even with the left of the slide as shown in Figure 4-16.

Figure 4-16
Duplicated clip art images

8. Press [Ctrl]+[D] to *duplicate* this image. Move the second image over so it aligns with the bottom of the first image and the branches almost touch.

NOTE

Using the duplicate command is faster than using copy/paste when you want a second image on the same slide. Copy/ paste works best when you want to copy an image from one slide and paste it on another slide.

9. With the second image selected, press [Ctrl]+[D]. Because the positioning information from your first duplication is remembered by PowerPoint, this image should go into the same alignment.

10. Repeat this process of pressing [Ctrl]+[D] five more times to create a row of palm trees across the top of the slide as shown in Figure 4-16.

11. Update your footer text to **[4-10your initials]**. Save the presentation as **[4-10your initials]**, but do not print it. Keep the file open for the next exercise.

Exercise 4-11   GROUP AND UNGROUP IMAGES AND TEXT

When you *group* objects, you combine two or more shapes or images so they behave as one. If you then move one object of the group, all the other objects move with it. Grouping assures that objects meant to stay together don't accidentally get moved individually or deleted. When you apply formatting to a group, all the objects in the group receive the same formatting. If you need to work on the objects separately, then you can *ungroup* them. *Regrouping* can combine the objects again.

1. Move to slide 4. Press [Shift] while you click on both the beach scene image and the text below it. Now selection handles appear on both images.

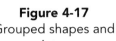

2. From the Picture Tools Format tab, in the Arrange group, click Group 🔲 then select Group. Now the clip art image and the text are combined as one object.

3. Resize the group by stretching the corner sizing handle on the top right to make the image about as large as the palm tree on the right.

4. By resizing the group, the text has moved and is not in the best position. From the Picture Tools Format tab, in the Arrange group, click the Group button 🔲, then choose Ungroup. Now you can move the image and text separately.

5. Arrange the beach scene image on the left so the bottom aligns evenly with the palm tree on the right. Move the beach scene text to be centered under the image and aligned with the palm tree text. You may need to resize the beach scene text box.

6. Now select the beach scene text and the image. From the Picture Tools Format tab, in the Arrange group, click the Group button 🔲 and choose Regroup.

7. Select the palm tree image and the palm tree text and group them.

8. Move to slide 5. Select the picture of Miami buildings and press [Ctrl]+[C].

9. Move to slide 3 and press [Ctrl]+[V]. Position the picture to be in the center of the square shape.

Figure 4-17
Grouped shapes and picture

10. Resize the left and right sides of the square shape to change it to a rectangle that evenly frames the picture.

11. Select the 16-Point Star shape. From the Drawing Tools Format tab, in the Arrange group, click Bring to Front button 🔲 so the star is on top of the picture and rectangle as shown in Figure 4-17.

12. With the star selected, press ⟨Shift⟩ while you click on the picture and the rectangle to select all three objects.

13. From the Drawing Tools Format tab, in the Arrange group, click the Group button 🔲, and choose Group.

14. Update the handout footer text to **[4-11your initials]**. Save the presentation as **[4-11your initials]**, but do not print it. Keep the file open for the next exercise.

Inserting and Enhancing a Picture

More than any other graphic element, pictures can add a sense of realism to a presentation. Microsoft's online collection offers an abundance of photo images, which are referred to as *stock photography,* that you can search for just as you search for clip art images. Pictures that you take with a digital camera also can be inserted. Or pictures that are already printed can be turned into an appropriate digital format by scanning.

Once the picture is inserted into PowerPoint, you have many options for improving its appearance, as shown by the picture tools in Figure 4-18 and Table 4-2. In the next exercises you will learn to crop to remove unwanted details, adjust brightness and contrast, and apply many different styles and special effects.

Figure 4-18
Picture tools format
Ribbon

TABLE 4-2 Format—Picture Tools

Button	Name	Purpose
☀	Brightness	Increases or decreases a picture's overall lightness.
◐	Contrast	Increases or decreases the difference between the lightest and darkest areas of a picture.
🖼	Recolor	Enables you to change the color mode (grayscale, sepia, washout, or black-and-white) and color variations of a picture.
🖼	Compress Pictures	Strips unnecessary information from a picture file to make a presentation file size smaller.
🖼	Change Pictures	Changes to a different picture in the same size and format as a selected picture.
🖼	Reset Picture	Restores a picture's original attributes if changes were made by using the Picture Adjustment tools.
🖼	Picture Styles	Provides a gallery of preset effects to quickly add interest.

continues

TABLE 4-2 Format—Picture Tools *continued*

Button	Name	Purpose
	Picture Shape	Enables you to change the rectangular appearance of a picture into a shape.
	Picture Border	Places an outline around a picture in different colors, weight, or line styles.
	Picture Effects	Provides the effects of shadow, reflection, glow, soft edges, bevel, or 3-D rotation.
	Bring to Front	Adjusts stacking order of pictures and other objects.
	Send to Back	Adjusts stacking order of pictures and other objects.
	Selection Pane	Used to select individual pictures and other objects and to change the visibility or order.
	Align	Used to make multiple objects evenly spaced.
	Group	Fastens multiple objects together to act as one object.
	Rotate	Used to angle pictures and other objects.
	Crop	Enables you to cut away the edges of a picture.
	Height	The vertical size dimension.
	Width	The horizontal size dimension.

Exercise 4-12   INSERT STOCK PHOTOGRAPHY

To search for a photograph image, use the same steps as you did for searching for clip art images except choose Photographs instead of Clip Art under the Results should be heading.

1. Move to slide 5 and delete the photo displayed on the slide.

2. From the Insert tab, in the Illustrations group, click the Clip Art button 🖼 so the Clip Art task pane is displayed on the right.

3. In the Clip Art task pane, the Search in list box should say All collections.

4. In the Clip Art task pane, in the Results should be list box check only the Photograph category and remove other checks.

5. In the Search for text box at the top of the Clip Art task pane, key **Miami** and then click Go. The Results box shows thumbnails (miniature images) of clips that match the search word.

6. Double-click the Miami night image. Drag the corner sizing handle to increase the picture height to about 4 inches. Notice that the width automatically adjusts to keep the image in proportion.

Figure 4-19
Picture inserted from search

7. Position the image as shown on Figure 4-19.

8. Close the Clip Art task pane. Keep the presentation open for the next exercise.

Exercise 4-13 CROP A PICTURE

When a picture is selected and you click the Picture Tools Format tab, many options become available to you for adjusting the picture or applying picture styles and effects. You can also *crop* (trim) parts of a picture, just as you might do with a page from a magazine by using a pair of scissors to reduce its size or remove unwanted details around the edge.

When you click the cropping tool, a picture's sizing handles change to *cropping handles*—short black markers that you drag to trim a picture.

TIP

Try holding down Alt as you crop. This enables you to make very fine adjustments.

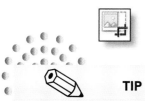

TIP

If you crop too far, use the cropping tool to drag the handle in the opposite direction to restore that part of the picture, or click the Undo button.

1. On slide 5, select the night scene picture. The colors of the lighted buildings and water reflections can be featured more if the picture is trimmed across the top and bottom.

2. From the Picture Tools Format tab, in the Size group, click the Crop button. The cropping handles appear around the edges of the picture and your pointer changes to a cropping tool.

3. Position the cropping tool on the top center handle and drag the handle down until the cropping line is positioned a little closer to the top of the tallest building, as shown in Figure 4-20.

Figure 4-20
Cropping a picture

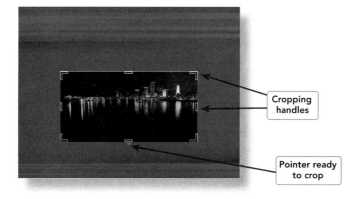

Cropping handles

Pointer ready to crop

4. Repeat this process to crop from the bottom to make the bottom edge of the picture just below where the reflections end.

5. Click on a blank area of the slide to turn off the crop function.

6. Update the handout footer text to **[4-13your initials]**. Save your presentation as **[4-13your initials]**, but do not print it. Keep the file open for the next exercise.

Exercise 4-14   RECOLOR A PICTURE THEN RESET COLORS

Color settings can be applied to *recolor* pictures using different color modes and light or dark variations of the presentation's theme colors. These effects might be used to create a subtle image that is placed behind other slide objects.

1. On slide 5, select the picture. From the Picture Tools Format tab, in the Adjust group, click the Recolor button . A gallery of color options will appear, as shown in Figure 4-21.

Figure 4-21
Recolor gallery

2. On the gallery, slowly drag your pointer over each of the options. A live preview showing the result of that option will be displayed on the picture before it is actually accepted.

   • In Color Mode you have options for Grayscale, Sepia, Washout, or Black and White.

   • Variations have options for Light and Dark settings.

3. Click Accent color 2 Dark to select this color change.

4. Now restore the colors to their original colors. With the picture selected, click the Recolor button and choose No Recolor.

5. Keep the presentation open for the next exercise.

Exercise 4-15   APPLY A PICTURE STYLE

Many different *picture styles* are available to display your pictures in beautiful and interesting ways. As with any of the creative techniques you are using, be careful that the styles and other treatments you apply to your pictures add to the appearance of the picture and do not distort it or diminish its effectiveness.

1. On slide 5, select the picture. From the Picture Tools Format tab, in the Picture Styles group, slowly drag your pointer over each of the Picture Styles options and the results of that option will be displayed on the picture.

Figure 4-22
Picture Styles

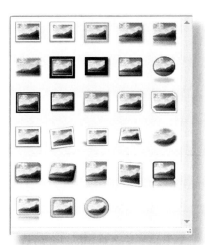

2. Click the More button ⊟ to see additional styles that are available, as shown in Figure 4-22.

3. Now click the Picture Style Double Frame, Black, as shown in Figure 4-23.

Figure 4-23
Cropped picture with
Double Frame effect

4. Update the handout footer text to **[4-15your initials]**. Save the presentation as **[4-15your initials]** in your Lesson 4 folder, but do not print it. Leave the presentation open for the next exercise.

Exercise 4-16   INSERT A PICTURE FROM FILE

When you begin to acquire a collection of digital images, you need to keep them organized in some logical way in folders on your computer that are appropriately named to identify the folders' contents. These folders might be saved in the Pictures folder that is automatically created on your computer when Microsoft Office is installed.

However, for this exercise you have a picture file stored in the same folder as all the other files for this lesson.

1. Display slide 5, then from the Home tab, in the Slides group, click the New Slide button 📄 to add a new slide with a Blank layout.

2. On slide 6, from the Insert tab, in the Illustrations group, click the Picture button 🖾.

3. In the Insert Picture dialog box, locate where your student data files for this lesson are stored and select the file **Restaurant1.jpg**. Click Insert.

PowerPoint 2007

4. With the Picture selected, click the Picture Tools Format tab. Change the Height to 5 inches and the Width will automatically change to 3.7 inches.

5. Move the picture to the left of the slide.

6. Keep your presentation open for the next exercise.

Exercise 4-17   ADJUST CONTRAST AND BRIGHTNESS

Sometimes a picture may be too dark to show needed details, or colors are washed out from too much sunshine when the picture was taken. PowerPoint's *Brightness* and *Contrast* adjustments can fix these problems. Adjusting the brightness changes the picture's overall lightness while adjusting contrast affects the difference between its lightest and darkest areas.

Figure 4-24
Brightness drop-down list

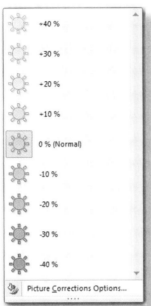

1. On slide 6, select the picture and press Ctrl+D to duplicate it. Position the second image on the right of the slide. Use it to make the color adjustments in this exercise so you can compare your changes to the original.

2. With the second picture selected, from the Picture Tools Format tab, in the Adjust group, click the Brightness button. A drop-down list appears showing adjustments in 10 percent increments, as shown in Figure 4-24, to increase or decrease the brightness of the picture.

3. Drag your pointer over the various amounts and study the effect on the picture. Click on +10% to increase the brightness.

4. Click the Contrast button. Again, a drop-down list appears showing adjustments in 10 percent increments, as shown in Figure 4-25, to increase or decrease the lightness of the picture.

Figure 4-25
Contrast drop-down list

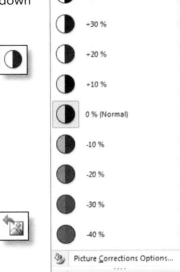

5. Drag your pointer over the various amounts and study the effect on the picture. Click on +20% to increase the contrast.

6. Now click the Reset Picture button to restore the picture's original colors and size. Change the height to 5 inches again.

7. Sometimes these 10 percent increments change a picture's colors too much, so you might need to adjust them more gradually to get good results. Click the Brightness button ⚙ then choose Picture Correction Options to open the Format Picture dialog box. Move this dialog box away from the picture so you can see the results of your changes as you make them.

8. Both the Brightness and Contrast can be adjusted by dragging the sliders to the left or right. You can also enter numbers in the spin boxes or click up or down to change in 1 percent increments.

9. This time change the Brightness to 14% and the Contrast to 24%. Click Close.

10. The picture appears a little clearer now when you compare the one changed on the right with the original version on the left, as shown in Figure 4-26.

Figure 4-26
Image-adjusted picture

11. Update the handout footer text to **[4-17your initials]**. Save the presentation as **[4-17your initials]** in your Lesson 4 folder, but do not print it. Leave the presentation open for the next exercise.

Exercise 4-18   CHANGE A PICTURE SHAPE

Any picture that is inserted on a slide can be made to fill a shape for an unusual and creative treatment.

1. On slide 6, from the Home tab, in the Slides group, click the New Slide button 🖻 to add a new slide with a Blank layout.

2. On slide 7, insert another picture from your Clip Art task pane. If the search from earlier in the lesson is not displayed, then search again for Miami photograph images.

3. Click the image that shows a beach and buildings. It has an unusual appearance because the image is angled.

4. With this image selected, from the Picture Tools Format tab, in the Picture Styles group, click the Picture Shape button ⬚. Try several of these shapes by clicking on the buttons in any of the categories. The image becomes the fill for that particular shape.

5. In the Basic Shapes category, select the Heart shape.

6. Continue to the next exercise.

Exercise 4-19   ADD A BORDER TO A PICTURE

The line that surrounds pictures is referred to as a Picture Border. This line can be shown in different colors and *line weights* (thicknesses) or in different styles (solid lines or dashes) to create a border around a picture just as you have used an outline on other shapes.

1. With the heart-shaped picture selected, from the Picture Tools Format tab, in the Picture Styles group, click the Picture Border button ⬚. As you drag your pointer over these colors, you can see how the color will look if selected.

Figure 4-27
Picture in a shape
with a border

2. From the colors that appear, in the Standard Colors group, click the Red color.

3. Click the Picture Border ⬚ again and click Weight. Choose 3 pt for a thicker red line, as shown in Figure 4-27.

4. Continue to the next exercise.

Exercise 4-20   APPLY PICTURE EFFECTS

Special effects can be applied to pictures as well as other shapes you create. To apply these effects to pictures, you will use the Picture Effects button on the Picture Tools Format tab. Many different customized settings are possible. Picture effects are available in seven categories:

- *Preset*—a collection of images with several different settings already applied.

- *Shadow*—displays a shadow behind the picture that can be adjusted in different ways to change direction, thickness, and blurring effect.

- *Reflection*—causes a portion of the image to be displayed below the image as though reflecting in a mirror or on water.

- *Glow*—adds a soft color around the picture edges that makes the picture stand out from the background.

- *Soft Edges*—changes a picture's normal hard edges to a soft, feathered appearance that gradually fades into the background color.

- *Bevel*—makes the picture looked dimensional with several different options available such as a raised button.

- *3-D Rotation*—enables the picture to be angled in different ways with perspective settings that change the illusion of depth.

1. On slide 7, select the heart-shaped picture. From the Picture Tools Format tab, in the Picture Styles group, click Picture Effects 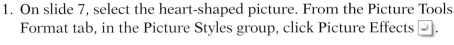.

Figure 4-28
Picture Effects categories

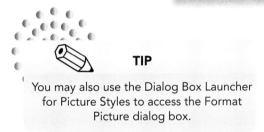

2. The drop-down list of effect categories appears, as shown in Figure 4-28. Each of these categories has several variations that you can see on your image as you drag your pointer over the effect thumbnail.

3. From the Shadow category, in the Outer subcategory, click the shadow named Offset Diagonal Bottom Right to apply a soft shadow.

4. Adjustments can be made to how the shadow appears. Click the Picture Effects button , click Shadow and then choose the Shadow Options at the bottom of this gallery.

5. From the dialog box that appears, key these numbers for each of the following settings:

   - Transparency   20%
   - Size   100%
   - Blur   10 pt
   - Angle   40°
   - Distance   15 pt

TIP

You may also use the Dialog Box Launcher for Picture Styles to access the Format Picture dialog box.

6. Click Close to accept these settings. Your heart shape should now look like Figure 4-29.

Figure 4-29
Format Picture shadow settings and shadow effects

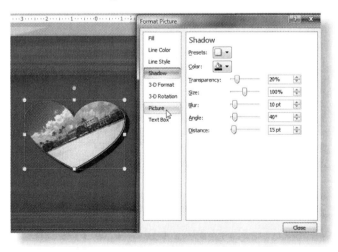

7. Update the handout footer text to **[4-20your initials]**. Save the presentation as **[4-20your initials]** in your Lesson 4 folder, but do not print it. Leave the presentation open for the next exercise.

Creating WordArt

WordArt can create special effects for decorative text that are not possible with standard text-formatting tools. You can stretch or curve text and add special shading, 3-D effects, and much more.

Exercise 4-21   CREATE AND MODIFY WORDART TEXT

In this exercise, you create a WordArt object, and then modify it by changing its shape and size. Make sure you key and proofread WordArt objects carefully.

1. Display slide 3 with the building photograph.

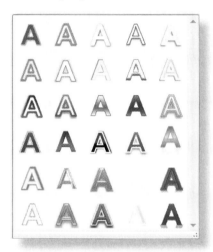

Figure 4-30
WordArt Styles gallery

2. From the Insert tab, in the Text group, click the WordArt button. The WordArt Styles gallery appears, as shown in Figure 4-30.

3. Point to the blue WordArt style that is called Fill – Accent 2, Warm Matte Bevel and click to select it. WordArt appears in the middle of your slide with sample text. At this point, you edit the text to replace the sample text, as shown in Figure 4-31, with the words you wish to display.

Figure 4-31
WordArt as it first appears

4. With the WordArt object selected key **Good For You** and delete any extra letters.

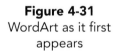

TIP

Many different styles are displayed in the WordArt gallery using the colors of your current theme. When applied, some of the styles may need color adjustments so the text is easily readable on the background color.

5. Click anywhere on the blank part of the slide to accept these changes and the bevel effect of this style becomes more evident.

6. To edit WordArt text, simply select the text and change it. In this case change the wording to **Good 4 U**.

7. Move the WordArt object to the upper left of the slide above the picture as shown in Figure 4-32.

Figure 4-32
WordArt showing positioning

8. Update the handout footer text to **[4-21your initials]**. Save the presentation as **[4-21your initials]** in your Lesson 4 folder, but do not print it. Leave the presentation open for the next exercise.

Exercise 4-22   APPLY WORDART EFFECTS

Figure 4-33
Text Effects

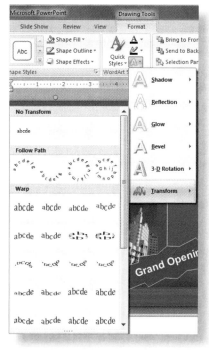

The same types of effects you have applied to pictures can be applied to WordArt. From the Drawing Tools Format tab, in the WordArt Styles group, the Text Effects are shown in Figure 4-33. In Exercise 4-20 you were introduced to these effects when applying them to a picture: Shadow, Reflection, Glow, Bevel, and 3-D Rotation. But the last category, *Transform*, is unique to WordArt because it enables you to change your text into different shapes.

1. Still working on slide 3, with the Good 4 U WordArt selected, click the Drawing Tools Format tab, in the WordArt Styles group, click the Text Effects button and choose Transform.

2. The default for WordArt text is No Transform because text will appear straight. When you drag your pointer over the various effects shown in this gallery, you will see that effect being applied to your text. The text sample on each of the buttons gives you an indication of the particular effect.

Figure 4-34
Using Transform to
apply the Deflate
Bottom Warp effect

3. From the Warp category, choose the effect Deflate Bottom that causes the text in the middle of the WordArt to become smaller.

4. Move the WordArt to the top of the picture so the letters G and U just slightly overlap with the blue rectangle as shown in Figure 4-34.

5. Keep your presentation open and continue to the next exercise.

Exercise 4-23 EDIT WORDART TEXT FILL AND TEXT OUTLINE COLORS

The *Text Fill* color of WordArt text can be changed as well as the *Text Outline* color and the weight of the outline. The outline goes around the edge of each letter. Making it thick emphasizes the outline; making it thin provides less emphasis but still makes the text look quite different than if no outline is applied.

1. Move to slide 7.

2. From the Insert tab, in the Text group, click the WordArt button 4. For the style, click the white WordArt style that is called Fill – White, Warm Matte Bevel and click to select it.

3. Key **We Love Miami Beach!** then select the text. From the Home tab, in the Font group, change the font size to 44 points.

4. Move the WordArt object above the heart, centered horizontally on the slide.

5. With the WordArt selected, from the Drawing Tools Format tab, in the WordArt Styles group, click the Text Fill button. From the Standard Colors, choose Red.

6. Now the WordArt color is almost too intense with such a bright red on the blue background. So apply a line color to tone down this effect.

7. With the WordArt selected, from the Drawing Tools Format tab, in the WordArt Styles group, click the Text Outline button.

8. Choose More Outline Colors, and then from the Colors dialog box, choose Black. Click OK.

9. Click the Text Outline button ![icon], click Weight, and choose 1 pt.

10. Now change the shadow effect so it better matches the heart shape. From the Drawing Tools Format tab, in the WordArt Styles group, click the Dialog Box Launcher button ![icon].

11. From the Format Text Effects dialog box, choose Shadow. Change to these settings: Transparency 20%, Size 100%, Blur 4 pt, Angle 45°, distance, 2 pt. Click Close.

12. From the Drawing Tools Format tab, in the WordArt Styles group, click the Text Effects button ![icon], click Transform, and from the Warp category, choose Wave 2.

13. Resize and adjust any necessary spacing so your slide resembles Figure 4-35.

Figure 4-35
Completed WordArt
object

14. Update the handout footer to show **[4-23your initials]**.

15. Save the presentation as **[4-23your initials]** in your Lesson 4 folder and print it as handouts with nine slides per page. Close the presentation.

Creating a Photo Album

A presentation consisting of mostly pictures can be created quickly using PowerPoint's *Photo Album* feature. Picture files can be inserted from different locations on your computer and will be displayed with one picture on a slide. The pictures can be displayed at full screen size or framed in different shapes. Also, text can accompany each picture at the time you create the photo album, or text can be added to the individual slides. When complete, your saved photo album can be displayed just as any other presentation.

While this feature can be important for business situations, it could also be very helpful for creating a display for open house functions, or even wedding or birthday celebrations.

Exercise 4-24 CREATE ALBUM CONTENT BY INSERTING NEW PICTURES

In your Lesson 4 student data files you have a folder named **Salads** containing five pictures for this exercise. Copy the **Salads** folder to your storage location.

1. Open PowerPoint if necessary. Start a new blank presentation.

2. From the Insert tab, in the Illustrations group, click the top of the Photo Album button 🖼. The Photo Album dialog box appears, as shown in Figure 4-36.

Figure 4-36
Photo Album dialog box

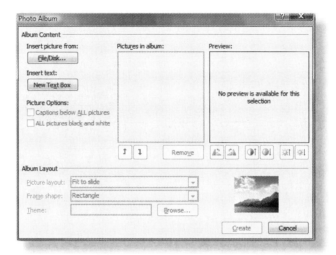

3. Click the File/Disk button ⬚ then choose the storage location where you have the **Salads** folder. Select the folder name then click Open.

4. Select all of the picture files and click Insert.

5. At the bottom of the dialog box, notice the Album Layout options. By default, the Picture layout is Fit to slide. This option will expand each picture to fill your computer's screen. Click Create.

6. Each picture appears on a separate slide and a title slide has been created.

7. Continue to the next exercise to edit the Photo Album settings.

Exercise 4-25 ADJUST PICTURE ORDER, BRIGHTNESS, AND CONTRAST

Using the Format Photo Album dialog box, pictures can easily be reordered by selecting the picture name and clicking the up or down arrows. Pictures can be rotated if their orientation needs to change and even the brightness and contrast can be adjusted. These changes can be made at the time you create the Photo Album or later by editing it.

1. From the Insert tab, in the Illustrations group, click the lower half of the Photo Album button 📷 then click Edit Photo Album.

2. Highlight picture 5, **tuna**, that has a vertical orientation. Click the up arrow twice to position it in the middle of the other four pictures.

3. Highlight picture 2, **avocado**, click twice on the Increase Contrast button 🔘.

4. Highlight picture 1, **apples**, and click once on the Increase Brightness button 🔘 and click twice on the Increase Contrast button 🔘.

5. Click Update to accept these changes.

6. Continue to the next exercise.

Exercise 4-26   CONTROL ALBUM LAYOUT

Album Layout allows you to change the Picture layout from Fit to slide to different options with one to four pictures on a slide. You can choose to display titles for each slide or change to one of seven different Frame shapes for the pictures. Using Picture Options, you can choose to place captions below all pictures.

1. From the Insert tab, in the Illustrations group, click the lower half of the Photo Album button 📷 then click Edit Photo Album.

2. For Picture Layout, change to 1 picture.

3. Now Picture Options are available. Click Captions below ALL pictures.

4. For Frame shape, select several of the available options and notice how the effect is displayed in the thumbnail area on the right. Select Simple Frame, White.

Figure 4-37
Photo Album edited options

5. Now apply a background theme that will provide soft coloring on the background behind the pictures. For the Theme, click Browse [Browse...] and choose Apex then click Select. (You may have to navigate to your themes for Office 2007.)

6. Be sure the options on your Edit Photo Album dialog box match Figure 4-37. Click Update.

7. Now the pictures appear a little smaller on the slide and have a white frame with a subtle shadow effect, as shown in Figure 4-38. The Apex theme provides a soft background that is subtle and does not detract from the pictures.

Figure 4-38
Slide with framed picture

8. Notice that the file names for each picture now appear in text boxes below each picture. This text could now be changed to a more descriptive title for each salad.

9. On slide 1, key **New Salads** for the presentation title and key **Good 4 U** for the subtitle. Change the subtitle text size to 36 points and apply bold.

10. Add a header on the handout page with **[4-26your initials]** and nothing in the footer.

11. Save the presentation as **[4-26your initials]** in your Lesson 4 folder.

12. Print a handout copy with six slides on a page in portrait orientation. For print options, choose Scale to Fit Paper so each slide appears larger on the page.

13. Close your presentation.

Lesson 4 Summary

- In addition to text placeholders, PowerPoint provides a variety of objects that you can use to enhance the visual appearance of your slides. These include shapes, text boxes, clip art, and pictures.

- PowerPoint's drawing tools enable you to create a variety of shapes including squares, circles, rectangles, ovals, and straight lines drawn at any angle.

- To draw a shape, from the Insert tab, in the Illustrations group, click the Shapes button ▣, choose a shape, and then drag diagonally on your slide to create the shape in the size you need.

- If you don't like a shape you drew, select it and press Delete to remove it from your slide, or press Ctrl+Z to undo the action.

- Press ⌜Shift⌝ while drawing a line or other shape to constrain it. Constraining a shape makes it perfectly symmetrical, for example, a circle or a square, or it can make a line perfectly straight.

- Press ⌜Ctrl⌝ while drawing a shape to make it grow in size from the center instead of from one edge.

- Change the size of a drawn object by dragging one of its sizing handles (small white circles on its border) with a two-pointed arrow ⌜⇕⌝.

- To preserve an object's proportions when resizing it, hold down ⌜Shift⌝ while dragging a corner sizing handle.

- Move a drawn object by pointing to it and when the four-pointed arrow ⌜✥⌝ appears, drag the object to a new position.

- The Shapes gallery has many predefined shapes that are organized into several categories.

- When a shape is selected, text that you key appears inside the shape.

- Use the Clip Art task pane to search for clip art and photograph images. If you are connected to the Internet, the task pane's Search command will automatically search the Microsoft Office Online collection.

- To see the file properties of a clip art image or photograph, point to a clip art thumbnail in the Clip Art task pane, and then click the vertical bar that appears on the right side of the thumbnail (or right-click the thumbnail).

- Using the Cut, Copy, and Paste commands, you can easily move or copy clip art or other images from one slide to another or from one presentation to another.

- Using the Duplicate command is the quickest way to create a copy of an object on the same slide.

- Resize a clip art image by dragging one of its sizing handles. If you want to preserve proportions, drag a corner handle. If you want to distort the proportions, drag one of the side handles.

- From the Picture Tools Format tab, in the Adjust group, use tools to change a picture's brightness, contrast, and colors.

- Clip art images (vectors, bitmaps, or scanned images) can be cropped. Cropping is trimming away edges of a picture, much like using scissors to cut out a picture from a newspaper or magazine.

- WordArt enables you to create special effects with text that are not possible with standard text-formatting tools.

- WordArt is modified by using the WordArt Styles and Text Effects to change its appearance in many different ways. These options are available on the Drawing Tools Format tab when a WordArt object is selected.

- PowerPoint's Photo Album feature can be used to quickly create a presentation consisting mostly of pictures. One or more pictures can be placed on each slide with a choice of different framing techniques.

- Once a photo album is created, it can be modified by choosing the Edit Photo Album option to rearrange pictures, request captions and add a theme. A photo album is saved as any other presentation.

LESSON 4   Command Summary

Feature	Button	Ribbon
Rectangle	☐	
Oval	○	
Line	╲	
Constrained line	Shift + ╲	
Square	Shift + ☐	
Circle	Shift + ○	
Shapes		Home tab, Drawing group, Shapes or Insert tab, Illustrations group, Shapes
Search for Clip Art and Photographs		Clip Art task pane, Search
Insert Pictures		Insert tab, Illustrations group, Picture
Adjust Picture Brightness		Picture Tools Format tab, Adjust group, Contrast
Adjust Picture Contrast		Picture Tools Format tab, Adjust group, Brightness
Adjust Picture Color		Picture Tools Format tab, Adjust group, Recolor
Change Picture Shape		Picture Tools Format tab, Picture Styles group, Picture Shape
Apply Picture Border		Picture Tools Format tab, Picture Styles group, Picture Border
Picture Effects		Picture Tools Format tab, Picture Styles group, Picture Effects
Crop a Picture		Picture Tools Format tab, Size group, Crop
Insert WordArt		Insert tab, Text group, WordArt
Apply WordArt Styles		Drawing Tools Format tab, WordArt Styles group, Quick Styles
Change WordArt Color		Drawing Tools Format tab, WordArt Styles group, Text Fill
Change WordArt Outline		Drawing Tools Format tab, WordArt Styles group, Text Outline
Apply WordArt Text Effects		Drawing Tools Format tab, WordArt Styles group, Text Effects

Concepts Review

True/False Questions

Each of the following statements is either true or false. Select your choice by indicating T or F.

T **F** 1. You can type text only in an existing placeholder.

T F 2. Use [Shift] with ☐ to create a square.

T **F** 3. Every Shape includes an adjustment handle.

T F 4. A green handle on a PowerPoint object indicates that the object can be rotated.

T **F** 5. ☆ is found in the Basic category of the Shapes gallery.

T **F** 6. When you want to change the height of an object, but not the width, press [Shift] while dragging a corner sizing handle.

T F 7. To apply a frame or shadow effect to a picture, choose a Picture Style.

T F 8. WordArt enables you to create special effects with text.

Short Answer Questions

Write the correct answer in the space provided.

1. How do you draw a perfect circle?

   Shift, draw

2. What kind of handle is the yellow diamond?

   adjustment

3. How can you make a picture have a different shape?

   Select picture. Choose Shape then shape it

4. What happens if you apply a bevel effect to a picture or shape?

5. Which task pane is used to search for a photograph?

   Clip art

6. What setting on the Format Picture dialog box will cause a shadow to appear from a particular direction?

   angle in picture format

7. How do you resize an object?

sizing handle dragging

8. How do you change the shape of a WordArt object?

Select obj, WordArt, text effects, transform'n then style

Critical Thinking

Answer these questions on a separate page. There are no right or wrong answers. Support your answers with examples from your own experience, if possible.

1. Consider the Shapes gallery and explain how three different shapes could help you to illustrate or draw attention to a concept you need to explain.

2. Describe how Picture Styles can enhance the appearance of a photograph.

Skills Review

Exercise 4-27

Create shapes, key text in a shape, and use the Format Shape dialog box.

1. Open the file **Seminar1**. Move to slide 3.
2. Use the drawing tools to create the shapes shown in Figure 4-39. First, create the wide rectangle that appears on top of the triangle by following these steps:

Figure 4-39
Drawing shapes

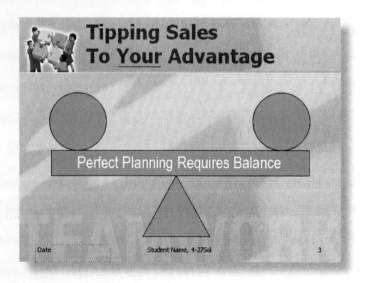

a. From the Insert tab, in the Illustrations group, click the Shapes button 🔳 then the Rectangle button ▢.

b. Position the crosshair pointer ⊞ on the left of the slide.

c. Drag the pointer diagonally down and to the right, creating a wide rectangle, like the one shown in Figure 4-39. Release the mouse button. (Don't worry about the exact size or position. You size and place it in the next step.)

3. Precisely size and position the rectangle by following these steps:

a. Select the rectangle, and from the Drawing Tools Format tab, in the Size group, click the Dialog Box Launcher.

b. In the Height text box change the size to **0.75** inches and in the Width text box change the size to **8** inches.

c. Click the Position tab. Key **1** inches in the Horizontal text box and **4** inches in the Vertical text box. Click Close.

4. Key text in the rectangle by following these steps:

a. Select the rectangle.

b. Key **Perfect Planning Requires Balance**.

c. From the Home tab, change the font to Arial Narrow, the size of the text to 36 points, the text color to white, and alignment to center.

5. Create the triangle shown in Figure 4-39 by following these steps:

a. From the Insert tab, in the Illustrations group, click the Shapes button 🔳, then from the Basic Shapes category, click the Isosceles Triangle button △.

b. Position the pointer at the bottom center of the new rectangle.

c. Drag diagonally down and to the right to create a triangle then center it under the rectangle.

6. Draw a circle by following these steps:

a. From the Insert tab, in the Illustrations group, click the Shapes button 🔳, then from the Basic Shapes category, click the Oval button ◯.

b. Position the crosshair pointer ⊞ above the left end of the rectangle, hold down [Shift], and drag diagonally to draw a circle approximately the same size as the one in Figure 4-39.

c. Hold down [Ctrl] while using the arrow keys on your keyboard to fine-tune the circle's position.

7. Select the circle then press [Ctrl]+[D] to duplicate it. Drag the second circle to the other end of the rectangle, positioning it appropriately.

8. Create a horizontal line on slide 3 by following these steps:

a. From the Insert tab, in the Illustrations group, click the Shapes button 🔳, then from the Lines category, click the Line button ◺.

b. Position the pointer below the Y in the word *Your*.

c. Hold down [Shift] and drag to the right to draw a straight line below the word. Release the mouse button first, and then release [Shift].

d. From the Drawing Tools Format tab, in the Shape Styles group, click the Dialog Box Launcher to access the Format Shape dialog box. Change the Line Width to 3 points and then on the Line Color tab change the Line color to Red, Accent 2.

e. Adjust the position of the line, if necessary.

9. Check spelling in the presentation.

10. Create a footer for slide 3: Include the slide number, date, and your name, followed by a comma and the text **[4-27your initials]**.

11. Create a handout header and footer: Include the date and your name as the header, and the page number and text **[4-27your initials]** as the footer.

12. Move to slide 1 and save the presentation as **[4-27your initials]** in your Lesson 4 folder.

13. Print slide 3 in full size, framed. Preview and print the presentation as handouts, four slides per page, grayscale, landscape, framed. Close the presentation.

Exercise 4-28

Insert a picture from a file, crop a clip art image, search for and insert a clip art image, and place text on a shape.

1. Open the file **Seminar2**.

2. On slide 1, insert the picture file **Logo1** (from your student files) by following these steps:

a. From the Insert tab, in the Illustrations group, click the Picture button.

b. Browse to find the student data files for Lesson 4, and click on **Logo1**.

c. Click Insert.

3. Now remove the white color in the image by following these steps:

a. From the Picture Tools Format tab, in the Adjust group, click the Recolor button and choose Set Transparent Color. Your pointer will change to a pen.

b. Click on the white area to make it transparent.

4. Resize the logo to make it slightly smaller.

5. Position the logo at the bottom of the slide below the white graphic shape that is on the background.

6. Move to slide 2 and, in the content placeholder, click the Clip Art button. The Clip Art task pane will appear.

a. In the Search for box, key **refrigerator**. In the Results should be box, select Clip Art and then click Go.

b. Look for an image that most closely resembles a commercial-grade refrigerator, and then insert it by clicking its thumbnail.

7. Resize the image proportionately from the center by following these steps:

a. Select the image.

b. Hold down Ctrl while dragging a corner handle.

   c. When the image is the size you want, release ⌈Ctrl⌉ first, and then release the mouse button.

8. Crop clip art by following these steps:

   a. Move to slide 3. Select the image on the right side of the slide.

   b. From the Picture Tools Format tab, in the Size group, click the Crop button 🔲 .

   c. Drag the top cropping handle down to just above the square containing the chef's hat.

   d. Drag each of the side cropping handles in, so that only the squares containing the chef's hat and the rolling pin remain.

   e. Click a blank area on the slide to deactivate the Crop button 🔲 .

   f. Increase the size of the cropped image and position it beside the list with balanced spacing above and below the image.

9. On slides 4 and 6, search for and insert clip art images appropriate to the slide text content and the overall presentation design. Crop and/or resize the images if necessary.

10. On slide 2, at the bottom, insert a text box and key **Ask for our list of wholesale appliance dealers** and change the font to 24-point Arial Narrow, italic. Position the text box on the lower left.

11. Check spelling in the presentation.

12. Create a handout header and footer: Include the date and your name as the header, and the page number and text **[4-28your initials]** as the footer.

13. Move to slide 1 and save the presentation as **[4-28your initials]** in your Lesson 4 folder.

14. Preview, and then print the presentation as handouts, six slides per page, grayscale, framed. Close the presentation.

Exercise 4-29

Insert and size a picture from a file, adjust its contrast and brightness, and create WordArt.

1. Open the file **Seminar3**.

2. Replace the title on slide 1 with a WordArt text object by following these steps:

   a. Highlight the title text and turn off bold.

   b. From the Insert tab, in the Text group, click the WordArt button and choose the Fill - Accent 2, Matte Bevel (on the last row).

   c. Delete the original placeholder with the title.

   d. Reposition the WordArt where the title placeholder was located.

3. Change the shape of a WordArt object by following these steps:

   a. Select the WordArt object.

   b. From the Drawing Tools Format tab, in the WordArt Styles group, click the Text Effects button 🔲 , then select Transform.

c. Select the Chevron Up shape and the text will increase in size when this effect is applied.

d. Hold down Ctrl and drag the bottom center sizing handle up slightly to decrease the height of the WordArt shape.

4. Add the Good 4 U logo to the title slide by following these steps:

a. Delete the subtitle placeholder.

b. From the Insert tab, in the Illustrations group, click the Picture button.

c. Navigate to the drive and directory where your Lesson 4 student data files are stored and select the file **Logo1**. Click Insert.

d. Drag the logo to the bottom of the subtitle placeholder in the center of the slide, as shown in Figure 4-40.

Figure 4-40
WordArt effect

5. Create a handout header and footer: Include the date and your name as the header, and the page number and text **[4-29your initials]** as the footer.

6. Save the presentation as **[4-29your initials]** in your Lesson 4 folder.

7. Preview, and then print the presentation as handouts, four slides per page, grayscale, landscape, framed. Close the presentation.

Exercise 4-30

Create shapes and rotate, add text, insert a picture from a file, and adjust image settings.

1. Open the file **Seminar4**. Replace the word *"Date"* on slide 1 with today's date.

2. Create a left arrow shape by following these steps:

a. Move to slide 3 and from the Insert tab, in the Illustrations group, click the Shapes button. In the Block Arrows category click Left Arrow (the second shape in the first row).

b. Position the crosshair pointer + at the top of the tallest bar in the fourth quarter of the chart, and then click and drag to create an arrow.

3. Rotate a shape by following these steps:

a. Select the arrow then drag the green rotation handle above the arrow to the left until the arrow points down at about a 45-degree angle.

b. Reposition the arrow, so it points to the top of the tallest bar, as shown in Figure 4-41.

4. Draw a text box in the space at the right of the chart. Change the font to 20-point Arial, bold, and left-align the text. Key **Los Angeles division sales expected to double in the 4th quarter**.

Figure 4-41
Adding a text box to
clarify an important
point

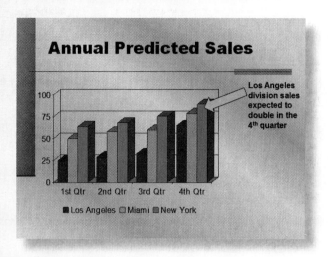

5. On slide 2, insert the **Restaurant1** picture from your student data files.

   a. Resize the picture to make it slightly smaller.

   b. From the Picture Tools Format tab, in the Adjust group, access the Picture Correction Options dialog box and adjust the Contrast and Brightness by +5 percent.

   c. From the Picture Tools Format tab, in the Picture Styles group, apply the Reflected Bevel, Black picture style.

6. On slide 4, the picture that is already positioned on this slide is very dark.

   a. Adjust the contrast and brightness to improve the image.

   b. Apply the Reflected Bevel, Black picture style to match the other picture treatment.

7. Below the picture on slide 4, insert a text box with the words **Only the finest produce!**

   a. Format the text in a size, font, and color to match slide 3 (Arial, 20 point, bold).

   b. Position the text centered below the picture.

8. On slide 5, from the Insert tab, in the Illustrations group, click the Shapes button 🔲, then in the Stars and Banners category click the 5-Point Star. Draw a star then position and size it so the star covers the gold rectangle on the right side of the horizontal line.

9. Place text in the star by following these steps:

   a. Select the star.

   b. Key **Star**, press Enter, and key **Team**. Make the text Arial Black in 32 points.

   c. Adjust the size of the star, if necessary, to fit the text.

10. Check spelling in the presentation.

11. Create a handout header and footer: include the date and your name as the header, and the page number and text **[4-30your initials]** as the footer.

12. Move to slide 1 and save the presentation as **[4-30your initials]** in your Lesson 4 folder.

13. Preview, and then print the presentation as handouts, six slides per page, grayscale, framed. Close the presentation.

Lesson Applications

Exercise 4-31

Work with lines, text effects, shapes, and clip art.

1. Open the file **Market1**.

2. On slide 1, select the title text and apply the Text Effects of Circle Bevel and Outer Offset Bottom Shadow.

3. Draw a thin horizontal rectangle below the title text that extends under the title to the right edge of the slide.

4. Delete the subtitle placeholder. Draw a rectangle, approximately three inches wide. Position it attractively on the lower right side of the slide.

5. Use the Clip Art task pane to search for a photograph image by using the search word **meeting**. Choose a picture that has a horizontal orientation and is appropriate in style, content, and color for this slide.

6. Resize and crop the picture, if necessary, to make it fit on the solid-color area on the lower right of the slide using the rectangle as a border for the picture. Select an Outer Offset Bottom Shadow effect, as shown in Figure 4-42.

Figure 4-42
Drop shadow effect

7. On slide 2, resize the body text placeholder to allow space on the right of the slide for a picture.

8. Find a similar picture to the one on slide 1 but in portrait orientation. Size and/or crop it as needed then add the same shadow effect. Position it on the right beside the bulleted list.

9. Check spelling in the presentation.

10. Create a handout header and footer: Include the date and your name as the header, and the page number and text **[4-31your initials]** as the footer.

11. Move to slide 1 and save the presentation as **[4-31your initials]** in your Lesson 4 folder.

12. Preview, and then print the presentation as handouts, six slides per page, grayscale, framed. Close the presentation.

Exercise 4-32

Insert pictures, apply effects, rotate, and insert WordArt.

1. Open the file **Orientation**.

2. On the title slide, select the clip art image, copy it, then delete it from this slide.

3. Move to slide 3 and add a slide with a blank layout to create slide 4. Paste the clip art image from slide 1 on slide 4.

4. On the title slide, increase the title text placeholder font size to 54 points. Increase the size of this placeholder so the text fits on two lines. Adjust the horizontal position so the left edge of the text aligns with the left edge of the horizontal blue shape.

5. On the title slide, in the subtitle placeholder, key **Your Name**, press Enter and key the **Current Date**.

6. Search for photograph images using the word "dining." Insert three photographs. You may need to crop them to reduce the image size to better feature one part of the picture. Adjust the size of these images for each to be 2.5 inches wide.

7. Add a Picture Style to all three of the photographs using Drop Shadow Rectangle.

8. Rotate these pictures and position them with even spacing on the left side of the slide as shown in Figure 4-43. (Your pictures may be different ones.)

Figure 4-43
Positioning of pictures

9. On slide 2, change the second bulleted item into two bulleted items and revise the wording:

    • **Company History**
    • **Company Vision**

10. Insert two new slides after slide 3; use the Title and Content slide layout. Key the text in Figure 4-44 on slides 4 and 5.

Figure 4-44
Text for slides

Slide 4

Who's Who
  • Julie Wolfe and Gus Irvinelli are the
    co-owners of the restaurant
  • Michele Jenkins is the head chef
  • Roy Olafsen is the marketing manager

Slide 5

Summary
  • Good 4 U is growing rapidly with our new franchising
    philosophy
  • Our healthy living message has worldwide appeal
  • We are relying on you, our new employees, to help us grow

11. If necessary, adjust the size of the text placeholders so the text fits within them without changing to a smaller size.

12. On slide 6, insert WordArt for the words **Welcome to Good 4 U** and make it fit on one line, left aligned. Adjust WordArt colors and effects to be appropriate for the presentation theme colors. Use the same Bookman Old Style font that is used in the slide titles.

13. Position the clip art image and the WordArt text for a pleasing arrangement.

14. Check spelling in the presentation.

15. Scroll through the presentation and check each slide to make sure the images and text are positioned appropriately.

16. Create a handout header and footer: Include the date and your name as the header, and the page number and text **[4-32your initials]** as the footer.

17. Move to slide 1 and save the presentation as **[4-32your initials]** in your Lesson 4 folder.

18. Preview, and then print the presentation as handouts, six slides per page, grayscale, framed. Close the presentation.

Exercise 4-33

Create shapes, insert and resize pictures, and insert WordArt.

1. Open the file **Investors**.

2. Using the Outline tab, insert the body text for each slide, as shown in Figure 4-45.

3. Click on the Slides tab and move to slide 1.

4. On slide 1, delete the title text and its placeholder. Create a WordArt title using the same text, **Attracting Investors**. Use the WordArt Quick Style Gradient Fill - Accent 1 in the third row, fourth column.

5. With the WordArt selected, use the Text Effect of Transform to change its shape to Deflate Bottom.

6. Resize the WordArt to stretch across the slide with a height of 2.5 inches and a width of 9.0 inches. Move it up slightly from the center of the slide. Delete the subtitle placeholder.

7. On slide 2, on the shape on the right, key **Investors are our building blocks** with a font size of 36 points and bold. Resize the shape with a height of 3 inches and a width of 3 inches so the text word-wraps on three lines. Adjust the shape's position so it is even with the bulleted list on the left.

8. On slide 3, remove the bullets from the body text placeholder and center its text. Remove the indent for the second line of text. Adjust the size of the placeholder so the text fits on three lines and move it to the bottom of the slide to make room for a picture above it.

Figure 4-45
Text for slides

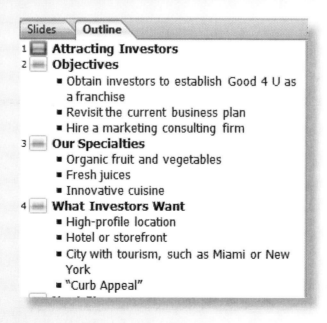

9. Search for and insert a picture of fruit and a picture of vegetables. You can use the content placeholder or the Insert tab to access the Clip Art task pane so you can look for the images. Adjust the size and image settings of the pictures, if necessary. Apply a Picture Style of Simple Frame, White.

10. On slide 4, search for a picture of New York and insert it. Resize the picture so that it fits on top of the shape on the right of the slide. The picture should be approximately four inches wide. Apply the same Picture Style of Simple Frame, White and then resize the shape so it fits evenly behind the picture.

11. On slide 5 draw a Right Arrow shape and rotate it so it points up slightly. Duplicate this arrow by pressing Ctrl+D and position the second arrow above the first one. Repeat for two more arrows. The arrows should angle up across the slide, as shown in Figure 4-46.

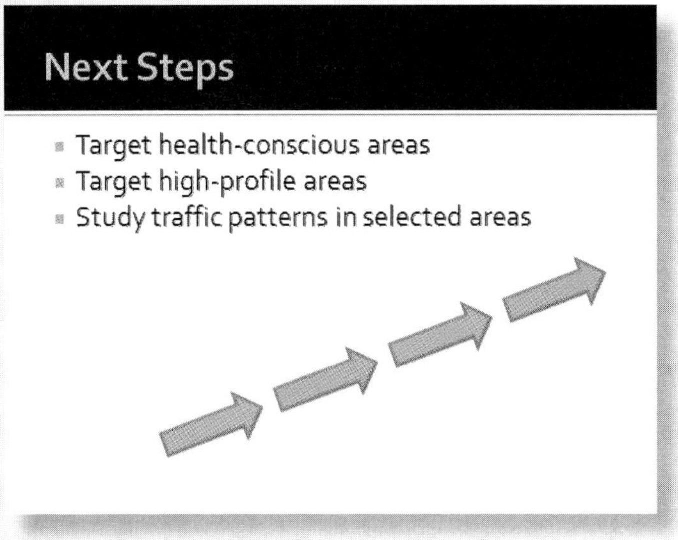

Figure 4-46
Arrow positioning

12. Review each slide, and make changes to the size and position of any objects that should be adjusted.

13. Check spelling in the presentation.

14. Create a handout header and footer: Include the date and your name as the header, and the page number and filename **[4-33your initials]** as the footer.

15. Move to slide 1 and save the presentation as **[4-33your initials]** in your Lesson 4 folder.

16. Preview, and then print the presentation as handouts, six slides per page, grayscale, framed. Close the presentation.

Exercise 4-34 ◆ Challenge Yourself

Create a photo album presentation, insert WordArt, and adjust Text Effects.

1. Start a new blank presentation.

2. From the Insert tab, in the Illustrations group, click Photo Album.

3. On the Photo Album dialog box, insert the five pictures from the **Cooking classes** folder.

4. Rearrange the picture order to put Chopping first followed by **Slicing**, **Sauce making**, **Pastry baking**, and **Bread baking**.

5. For the Album layout, choose the Picture Layout of 1 picture.

6. For Frame shape, choose Simple Frame, Black.

7. For Theme, click Browse and then choose Foundry.

8. Click Create. Once the slides appear, choose the Design tab, Colors, and choose Office theme colors.

9. On slide 1, for the title text key Cooking Classes for the slide title. For the subtitle key by Michele Jenkins, Head Chef and make it bold.

10. Insert WordArt with the text Back by Popular Demand using the Quick Style of Fill – Accent 2, Matte Bevel. Change the font size to 40 points.

11. Rotate the WordArt and position it on the upper left of the slide.

12. Insert a text box below the subtitle to show the class dates:

    October 17 and 18, 9-10:30 a.m.

    November 7 and 8, 2-3:30 p.m.

    Registration required

13. Use right alignment for the text box so it matches the title and subtitle positioning.

14. On slide 2, insert a text box and, using the font size of 18 points, key Efficient food handling methods.

15. Center this text box under the picture.

16. Press Ctrl+C to copy the text box and paste it on slide 3. Edit the text to be Fresh fruits and vegetables.

17. Repeat this process for slides 4, 5, and 6, as shown in Figure 4-47, using this text:

    | Slide 4 | Savory sauces |
    | Slide 5 | Pastry for a crowd |
    | Slide 6 | Breads like Grandma made |

Figure 4-47

18. Create a handout header and footer. Include the date and your name as the header, and the page number and filename **[4-34your initials]** as the footer.

19. Save the presentation as **[4-34your initials]**. Preview, and then print the presentation as handouts.

On Your Own

In these exercises you work on your own, as you would in a real-life work environment. Use the skills you've learned to accomplish the task—and be creative.

Exercise 4-35

Imagine that you are about to open a new retail store or restaurant. Using the content and layout of the Miami Beach presentation from this lesson as a general guide, create a presentation with at least five slides announcing the opening of your business. Use clip art, text boxes, shapes, WordArt, and, if possible, scanned photos to illustrate your presentation. Include a transition effect. Save the presentation as **[4-35your initials]**. Preview, and then print the presentation as handouts.

Exercise 4-36

Create a presentation entitled "Gift Suggestions for [*choose occasion or person*]." Select five or more suitable items from mail-order catalogs and create a separate slide describing each item, including the price and why you selected it. If you have access to a scanner, scan each item's picture from the catalog and insert it on the appropriate slide. If a scanner is not available, insert a suitable clip art image on each slide. Use your own creativity and the tools learned in this and previous lessons to add interest to the slides. Save the presentation as **[4-36your initials]**. Preview, and then print the presentation as handouts.

Exercise 4-37

Prepare a photo album presentation as a gift for a family member or friend to commemorate a special occasion when you took several pictures. If you do not have a digital camera, then you can scan printed photos. Create an appropriate theme for your presentation based on the occasion by choosing a suitable background design theme and theme colors. Add clip art, text boxes, shapes, and WordArt to illustrate your presentation like a scrapbook. Save the presentation as **[4-37your initials]**. Preview, and then print the presentation as handouts.

Creating tables

OBJECTIVES

MCAS OBJECTIVES

In this lesson:
PP07 2.1.6
PP07 3.7
PP07 3.7.1
PP07 3.7.2
PP07 3.7.3
PP07 3.7.4
See Appendix

After completing this lesson, you will be able to:

1. Create a table.

2. Draw a table.

3. Modify a table structure.

4. Align text and numbers.

5. Enhance the table.

6. Create a tabbed table.

Estimated Time: 2 hours

Tables display information organized in rows and columns. Once a table is created, you can modify its structure by adding columns or rows, plus you can merge and split cells to modify your table's design. Table content can be aligned in different ways for easy-to-read layouts. Color can be applied to highlight selected table cells or to add table borders. Working with tables in PowerPoint is similar to working with them in Word.

Creating a Table

A *table* consists of rows, columns, and cells. *Rows* consist of individual cells across the table horizontally. *Columns* consist of individual cells aligned vertically down the table. The *cell* is the intersection between the column and a row.

PowerPoint provides several convenient ways to create a table. With each method, you specify the number of columns and rows that you need.

- Insert a new slide, choose the Title and Content layout, and click the Insert Table button ▦ .

- From the Insert tab, in the Tables group, click the Table button ▦ and choose Insert Table.

- From the Insert tab, in the Tables group, click the Table button ▦ , and drag the mouse to select the correct number of rows and columns.

- Draw a table using the Draw table pen tool. To access this tool, click the Insert tab then in the Tables group, choose the Table button ▦ and then click Draw Table. Using the Pencil Pointer, click and drag to create the size of the table and then divide it into columns and rows.

- Create a tabbed table using tab settings.

When you insert a table into your presentation, your Ribbon will change to show the Table Tools Design and Layout tabs. These tabs contain many options for formatting and modifying the table you have created.

Exercise 5-1 INSERT A TABLE

When you use the Insert Table button ▦, you may define a table's dimensions by dragging down and across a grid to determine the number of rows and columns.

1. Open the file **Briefing1**. Insert a new slide after slide 1 that uses the Title Only slide layout. Key the title **Employment Levels 2006**. Resize the placeholder so the title fits on one row.

2. From the Insert tab, in the Tables group, choose the Insert Table button ▦ . A grid appears for defining the size of the table by selecting squares that represent table cells.

3. Drag your pointer down three squares and across four squares to define a 4 by 3 Table (four columns by three rows), as shown in Figure 5-1, then click your left mouse button to accept the table size.

Figure 5-1
Defining a table

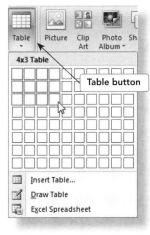

4. Point to the table's border and use the four-pointed arrow ✛ to move the table down and to the right about one-half inch.

5. Key the text shown in Figure 5-2. Use your pointer to click into the first cell of the table, and then press Tab to move from cell to cell. Entering text in a PowerPoint table is similar to entering text in a Word table.

6. Leave the presentation open for the next exercise.

Figure 5-2
Table with text

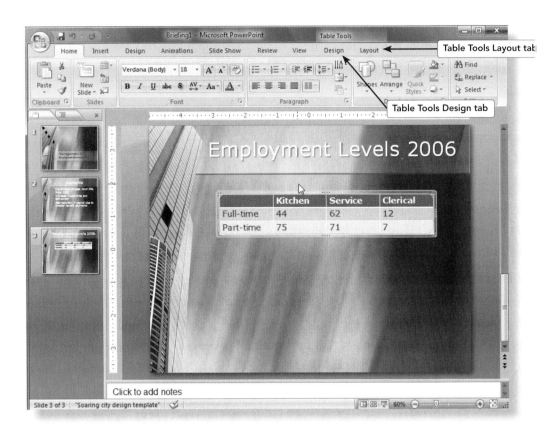

Exercise 5-2   NAVIGATE IN A TABLE

There are several ways to navigate in a table:

NOTE

When a cell is blank, pressing the left arrow key ← or the right arrow key → moves the insertion point left or right one cell. If text is in a cell, the left and right arrow keys move the insertion point one character to the left or right.

- Click the cell with the I-beam.

- Use the arrow keys ←, →, ↑, or ↓.

- Press Tab to move forward or Shift + Tab to move backward.

1. Click in the first table cell. Notice the insertion point in the cell you clicked.

2. Press Tab several times. The insertion point moves through cells from left to right. When you reach the end of a row, pressing Tab moves the insertion point to the beginning of the next row.

NOTE

If you reach the end of the table move to step three. If you accidentally press Tab at the end of the table, it will add a new row to the table. Use the Undo Button to reverse this action.

3. Press Shift + Tab several times. The insertion point moves through cells from right to left.

4. Press each arrow key several times and observe the movement of the insertion point.

5. Leave the presentation open for the next exercise.

Exercise 5-3 SELECT TABLE STYLES

A *Table Style* is a combination of formatting options, including color combinations, based on your theme colors. A table style is applied automatically to any table that you add through the Insert Table feature. Thumbnails of table styles are shown in the Table Styles gallery found on the Table Tools Design tab in the Table Styles group, as shown in Figure 5-3. When your pointer is over any thumbnail in the gallery, you will see a live preview of what your table will look like if you apply this style.

1. Right-click in any of the table cells and choose Select Table from the short-cut menu.

2. From the Table Tools Design tab, in the Table Styles group, choose the More button ☰ to open the Table Styles Gallery.

Figure 5-3
Table Tools Design tab

3. Place your pointer over several of the styles to see the ScreenTip with the name of the style and preview the effect on your table.

4. From the Best Match for Document category, choose Themed Style 1, Accent 6 by clicking on the thumbnail. Notice how this table style blends well with the background.

5. Leave the presentation open for the next exercise.

Exercise 5-4 APPLY TABLE STYLE OPTIONS

Table Style Options can be used to apply a table style to specific parts of your table.

• To emphasize the first row of the table, select the Header Row check box.

• To emphasize the last row of the table, select the Total Row check box.

• To have alternating striped rows, select the Banded Rows check box.

• To emphasize the first column of the table, select the First Column check box.

• To emphasize the last column of the table, select the Last Column check box.

• To have alternating striped columns, select the Banded Column check box.

1. With the table selected, from the Table Tools Design tab, in the Table Style Options group, click the First Column check box. Notice that the text in the first column now appears bold.

TIP

If you were comparing the number of kitchen staff versus the number of clerical staff, this formatting style would make the document easier to read. However, if you were comparing the number of full-time versus the number of part-time employees, the Banded Rows would be a better choice.

2. Click the Header Row check box to uncheck the box. Notice that the deep brown disappears and the banded rows alternate starting with the first row.

3. Click the Undo button 🔄 to reapply the Header Row formatting.

4. Click the Banded Rows check box to uncheck the box.

5. Click the Banded Columns check box to apply a check in the box.

6. Leave the presentation open for the next exercise.

Drawing a Table

The Draw Table feature in PowerPoint provides a different method of creating a table. From the Insert tab, in the Tables group, click the Table button 🔲, and choose Draw Table. Using this method allows you to control the exact size of the table using the pencil pointer to draw.

Exercise 5-5 USE PENCIL POINTER TO DRAW A TABLE

To draw a table, you first drag the *Pencil pointer* 🖊 diagonally down and across to create a rectangle the approximate size of the table's outside border. Then you draw horizontal and vertical lines within the table to divide it into columns and rows.

1. Insert a new slide after slide 3 that uses the Title Only slide layout. Key the title **Employment Levels 2007**. Resize the placeholder to fit the text on one row.

2. From the Insert tab, in the Tables group, click the Table button 🔲, and then choose Draw Table.

3. Using the pencil pointer 🖊, drag from under the left edge of the title (down and to the right) to create a rectangle that fills the available space. See Figure 5-4 for size and placement. At this point, you have a one-cell table.

Figure 5-4
Using the Pencil pointer

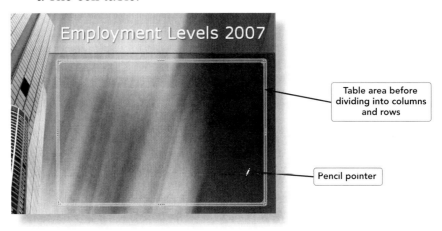

4. The Pencil pointer creates rows and columns when you draw borders within the table area. Be sure the pointer is inside the table before you start drawing so the lines you draw divide the table space. If the pointer touches the table border, a new table will be created. (If this happens, press Ctrl+Z to undo the action and try again.)

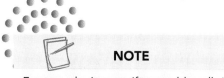

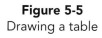

NOTE

For now, don't worry if your table cell sizes do not perfectly match Figure 5-5 or if your text wraps within the cell. You will learn how to adjust cell sizes later in the lesson.

5. With the table selected, from the Table Tools Design tab, click the Draw Table button and draw a line through the middle of the table area. Each time you draw a line, one cell is split into two cells. Because you are drawing horizontal lines now, the cells you are splitting create the table rows. Draw two more horizontal lines to create four rows in the table as shown in Figure 5-5.

6. Now, split the table with four vertical lines extending from the top of the table to create 5 columns.

7. From the Table Tools Design tab, in the Draw Borders group, click Draw Table to turn off the pencil pointer.

8. Key the table text shown in Figure 5-5. Leave the presentation open for the next exercise.

Figure 5-5
Drawing a table

Exercise 5-6 CHANGE TABLE TEXT DIRECTION

Text direction changes can affect the appearance of a table and how it fits within a given space. If the title is the only long part about the column, changing the column title text direction allows you to fit more columns in a given area. Text direction in a table can be changed in two ways:

NOTE

Some of your titles may wrap onto the next line even in the middle of words. You will fix this in a later exercise.

- From the Table Tools Layout tab (see Figure 5-6), in the Alignment group, select the Text Direction button.

- From the Home tab, in the Paragraph group, select the Text Direction button.

Figure 5-6
Table Tools Layout tab

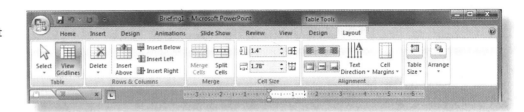

Figure 5-7
Text Direction drop-down list

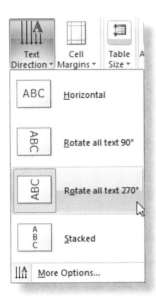

1. Click in the cell that reads Mgmt.

2. From the Table Tools Layout tab, in the Alignment group, click Text Direction button ▥.

3. From the drop-down list, choose Rotate all text 270° as shown in Figure 5-7.

4. Notice how the text reads going up in the cell. Change the text direction in the same manner for Kitchen, Service, and Clerical.

Exercise 5-7   APPLY SHADING AND BORDERS

When you first draw a table, the table cells contain no shading, allowing the slide's background to show. You can apply a shading color or other shading alternatives, such as a gradient, or picture effect to one or more cells in your table. Applying shading to a table is similar to applying shading to other PowerPoint objects. All of the shading options are available from Table Tools Design tab, in the Table Styles group, from the Shading button drop-down list. Applying shading involves two-steps:

- First, select the cells to which you want to apply the shading effect.

- Second, click the Shading button ▧ and choose the shading you wish to apply.

Table borders are the lines forming the edges of cells, columns, rows, and the outline of the table. From the Table Tools Design tab, in the Table Styles group, the Borders button ▦ drop-down list enables you to apply borders to all the cells in a selection, to just an outside border, or to just the inside borders separating one cell from another. Applying table borders is a three-step process:

- First, select the cells to which you want to apply the border effect.

- Second, select the border style, border width, and border color you want.

- Third, click the Borders button ▦ and choose an option from the drop-down list.

1. On slide 4, with the table active, select all the cells in the top row by moving your pointer to the left of row 1 until you get a solid black arrow pointing at the row. Click to select the whole row.

2. From the Table Tools Design tab, in the Table Styles group, click the Shading button 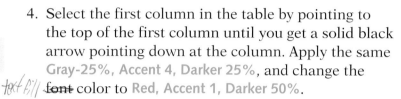 and choose Gray-25%, Accent 4, Darker 25% from the Theme Colors area.

3. Change the ~~font color~~ *txt fill* for the selected row to Gray-25%, Accent 4, Darker 90%.

REVIEW

The Font Color button is on the Home tab, in the Font group. You can also right-click to access the floating font group to make font changes.

4. Select the first column in the table by pointing to the top of the first column until you get a solid black arrow pointing down at the column. Apply the same Gray-25%, Accent 4, Darker 25%, and change the ~~font~~ *txt fill* color to Red, Accent 1, Darker 50%.

5. Select all the cells that contain numbers by clicking in the first number cell and dragging your pointer down and to the right to the last number cell.

6. From the Table Tools Design tab, in the Table Styles group, click the Shading button 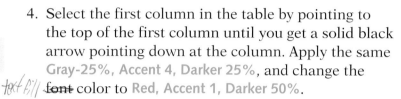 and apply a white color. With these cells still selected, change the font color to the Red, Accent 1, Darker 50% matching the first column.

7. Click outside the table to observe the effect. Now the table has an appearance that distinguishes it from the slide background. Compare your table to Figure 5-8.

Figure 5-8
Shading applied to a table

8. Select the whole table by right-clicking any cell within the table and choosing Select Table from the short-cut menu.

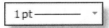

9. From the Table Tools Design tab, in the Draw Borders group, click the Pen Weight button 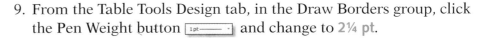 and change to 2¼ pt.

10. Still working in the Draw Borders group, click the Pen Color button ⟦⟧ , and choose Red, Accent 1.

11. Click the Borders button ⟦⟧ in the Table Styles group, and choose Top Border. Repeat this step for the Bottom Border and the Inside Horizontal Border. Click outside the table to deselect the table and notice the difference in the table with some added borders.

Exercise 5-8   CHANGE BORDER AND SHADING COLORS

Table Border and Shading styles can be changed at any point while creating your presentations.

1. Select any cell in your table. From the Table Tools Design tab, in the Draw Borders group, click Pen Style ⟦⟧ and choose the second style down (a dashed line).

2. Click the Pen Weight button ⟦⟧ and choose 1½ pt.

3. Click the Pen Color button ⟦⟧ and choose Gray-25%, Accent 4.

4. Right-click in the table and choose Select Table.

5. Click the drop-down list arrow for the Borders button ⟦⟧ , and choose Inside Borders, as shown in Figure 5-9. The inside borders of the table are now dashed lines.

TIP

You can use the pencil tool to change the color and style of a border. Set the border options in the Draw Borders group. Then, instead of clicking the Borders button ⟦⟧ , use the pencil to click the borders you want to change.

Figure 5-9
Borders button drop-down list

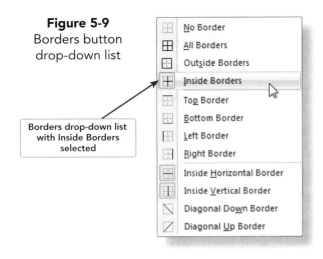

Borders drop-down list with Inside Borders selected

6. Still working on slide 4, select row 2 of the table. From the Table Tools Design tab, in the Table Styles group, click the Shading button ⟦⟧ and choose White, Text 1 to change the Shading to white for row 2.

7. Select row 3 of the table. Still working in the Table Styles group, click the Shading button ⟦⟧ and choose Gray-25%, Accent 4, Darker 25% to change the shading to gray for row 3.

8. Select row 4 of the table. Click the Shading button ⟦⟧ and choose White, Text 1 to change the Shading to white for row 4, as shown in Figure 5-10.

Figure 5-10
Completed table

Exercise 5-9   ERASE CELL BORDERS

The *Eraser* can be used to delete borders between cells.

1. Click in the last cell of the table on slide 4. Click Tab one time. Notice that PowerPoint automatically inserts another row below the last row in the table.

2. From the Table Tools Design tab, in the Draw Borders group, choose the Eraser.

3. Click each of the four borders that divide the last row of the table into five cells. Notice that as you click each border, it disappears. When all four are removed, the last row is turned into one cell.

4. Press Esc to turn off the Eraser. Click in the last row and key **Estimated Projection**. Your table may now extend past the bottom of the slide. This will be corrected later.

5. Create a new folder for Lesson 5 and save the presentation as **[5-9your initials]** in your new Lesson 5 folder.

6. Leave the presentation open for the next exercise.

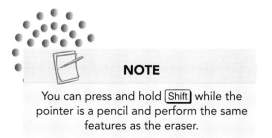

NOTE

You can press and hold Shift while the pointer is a pencil and perform the same features as the eraser.

Modifying Table Structure

When you create a table, you decide how many rows and columns the table should have. After entering some data, you might discover that you have too many columns or perhaps too few rows. Or, you might want one row or column to have more or fewer cells than the others. You can modify your table structure by inserting or deleting columns, merging a group of cells, or splitting an individual cell into two or more cells.

Exercise 5-10   INSERT AND DELETE ROWS AND COLUMNS

Columns and rows can be inserted using three methods:

- From the Table Tools Layout tab, in the Rows & Columns group, choose which option you would like to insert.

- Right-click a cell in the table and use commands on the short-cut menu.

- Insert a row at the bottom of the table by pressing [Tab] if you're in the last cell of the last table row. This is convenient if you run out of rows while you're entering data.

Columns can be inserted either to the right or the left of the column that contains the active cell. The column formatting of the active column is copied to the new column or the table style is applied. Rows can be inserted above or below the row that contains the active cell. The row formatting of the active row is copied or the table style is applied to the new row.

1. Move to slide 2, select the "Kitchen" column.

2. Right-click the selected column and click Insert and choose Insert Columns to the Left from the short-cut menu, as shown in Figure 5-11. A new column appears to the left of "Kitchen." It is the same size as the "Kitchen" column and has the formatting of the table style applied. The table is wider to accommodate the extra column.

Figure 5-11
Inserting a column through the short-cut menu

3. Click the blank cell in the upper-left corner of the table.

4. From the Table Tools Layout tab, in the Rows & Columns group, click the Insert Right button . A new column appears to the right of the selected cell, and it is the same size and formatted with the selected table style.

5. Click any cell in column B (the last column that was inserted).

6. From the Table Tools Layout tab, in the Rows & Columns group, click the Delete button ☒ then choose Delete Columns. The new column is deleted, and the table is resized. Your table should now have one blank column located to the left of the "Kitchen" column and some of your titles may be wrapped to two lines. This will be fixed later.

NOTE

If more than one column is selected when you use the Delete Columns command, all the selected columns will be deleted.

7. Still working on the Table Tools Layout tab, in the Rows & Columns group, select one cell in the second table row and click the Insert Below button ▦.

8. Click the last cell in the last row, containing the number "7." Press ⎀Tab. A new row is inserted at the bottom of the table.

9. Select cells in the blank row below the text "Full-time," right-click the selected cells, and choose Delete Rows from the short-cut menu.

10. Complete the table by keying the information shown in Figure 5-12 into the blank row and blank column.

Figure 5-12
Modified table structure

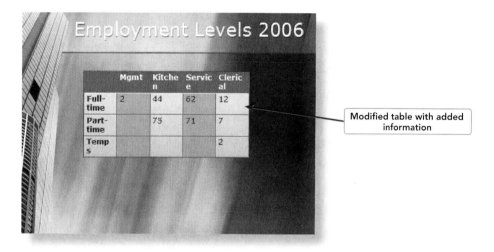

Modified table with added information

Exercise 5-11 MERGE AND SPLIT CELLS

As you discovered when drawing the table, you can split cells by drawing a line through them with the pencil pointer ✎. You can also split a cell by using the *Split Cells* button ▦ on the Table Tools Layout tab in the Merge group, or by right-clicking the cell and choosing Split Cells from the short-cut menu.

Cells can be merged together in several ways. As you learned in a previous exercise, the Eraser button ▦ removes borders between two adjacent cells to create one cell. You can merge cells by selecting two or more cells, and then from the Table Tools Layout tab, in the Merge group, click the *Merge Cells* button ▦ or by right-clicking the selected cells and choosing Merge Cells from the short-cut menu.

1. Move to slide 4. At the bottom of the table, click the cell containing the text "Estimated Projection."

2. From the Table Tools Layout tab, in the Merge group, click the Split Cells button ▦. Change the number of columns to **1** and the number of rows to **2**. The selected cell becomes two cells.

3. Click OK.

4. In the new cell, key **Revised Figures**.

5. Select the first three cells in the second row that begins "Full-time."

6. Still working on the Table Tools Layout tab, in the Merge group, click the Merge Cells button ▦. The three cells transform into one wide cell. The text and numbers from the merged cells all appear in one cell.

7. Click the Undo button ⟲ to return the merged cells to their previous state.

8. Leave the presentation open for the next exercise.

Exercise 5-12 APPLY A DIAGONAL BORDER

Borders can be placed diagonally within a cell. For example, if you are using a PowerPoint table to create a calendar, you might want to put two dates in the same square, separated by a diagonal line. Applying a diagonal border in this way does not create two separate cells, but is merely a line drawn within one cell. You can make it look like two cells by carefully placing text inside the cell.

1. Still working on slide 4, select the two rows at the bottom of the table, and then right-click and choose Merge Cells from the short-cut menu to combine the two cells into one. The text "Revised Figures" now appears on a separate line below "Estimated Projection" in one cell.

2. With the table active, move to the bottom of the table in the center at the sizing handle, and click and drag up to fit within the slide.

3. From the Table Tools Design tab, in the Draw Borders group, change the pen style to a dashed line, 1½-point, Gray-25%, Accent 4, Darker 50% gray line. Your pointer has been changed to a pencil.

4. Position the pencil tool near, but not touching, the lower-left corner of the cell in the last row. Draw a diagonal line across the cell to the upper-right corner, as shown in Figure 5-13.

Figure 5-13
Using the pencil pointer to add a diagonal border

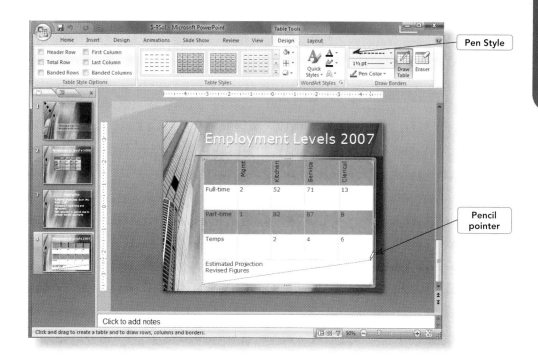

5. Press Esc to turn off the pencil pointer. Deselect the table to see the result. In a later exercise, you will apply text alignment to give this the appearance of a split cell.

Exercise 5-13 DISTRIBUTE COLUMN WIDTH AND ROW HEIGHT

If you decide to add rows or columns, or if you decide to make a column wider, the table may no longer fit on a slide. You can make a table smaller or larger by dragging its sizing handles, and you can change the height of rows and the width of columns individually by dragging cell borders. You can also choose the exact height and width of the cells by using the Cell Size group on the Table Tools Layout tab.

From the Table Tools Layout tab, in the Cell size group, use the *Distribute Columns* button ⊞ to easily adjust several columns to be the same width. The *Distribute Rows* button ⊞ works in a similar way.

1. Move to slide 2, move your pointer over the right border of the first column until the pointer changes to a two-pointed arrow ⊹.

2. Using this pointer, click and drag the column border to the right making the column wide enough so that the text "Part-time" appears on one line, as shown in Figure 5-14. The column width increases, and the adjacent column becomes smaller. Now the second column might be too narrow for the word "Kitchen."

3. Use the arrow pointer ⊞ to double-click the right border of the "Kitchen" column. Double-clicking a right border makes the column wide enough to accommodate the widest text line in the column.

4. Double-click the right border of each of the remaining columns to allow the widest text to be all on one line.

5. Position your pointer on the bottom border of the first row. When the pointer changes to ⊟ , click and drag the bottom border down, so that the row is approximately half again its original height.

Figure 5-14
Resizing column
width and row height

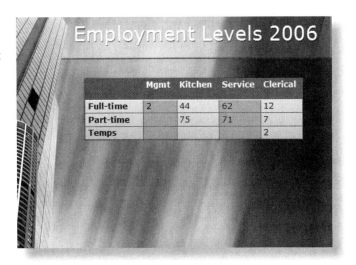

6. Move to slide 4. Select the "Mgmt," "Kitchen," "Service," and "Clerical" columns by dragging across the second, third, fourth, and fifth cells in any row (or drag the small, black, down-facing arrow ⊡ just above the top border of the four columns).

7. From the Table Tools Layout tab, in the Cell Size group, click the Distribute Columns button ⊞. The four selected columns are now all the same width.

8. Select the second through fourth cells in the first column.

9. Click the Distribute Rows button ⊞. Now the second through fourth rows are exactly the same height.

10. Select the last row of the table. From the Table Tools Layout tab, in the Cell Size group, change the height to **.7"** so the table fits better on the slide.

11. Create a handout header and footer: Include the date and your name as the header, and the page number and text **[5-13your initials]** as the footer.

12. Save the presentation as **[5-13your initials]** in your Lesson 5 folder.

Aligning Text and Numbers

Text and numbers in a table cell can be aligned vertically or horizontally. You can specify that text or numbers appear at the top, middle, or bottom of a cell, and be horizontally left-, center-, or right-aligned.

In addition, you can use *Cell Margin* settings to refine even further the position of text and numbers in a cell. A cell margin is the space between the text in a cell and its borders.

Exercise 5-14   ALIGN TEXT AND NUMBERS HORIZONTALLY

Text is aligned horizontally within cells in the same manner that you align text in other PowerPoint objects by using the alignment buttons on the Home tab, in the Paragraph group, or by right-clicking to access the floating font group.

1. On slide 2, select the cells in the first row that contain the text "Mgmt," "Kitchen," "Service," and "Clerical."

2. From the Home tab, in the Paragraph group, click the Center button 🔳. The text is horizontally centered in each cell.

3. Select all the cells that contain numbers and right-click. From the floating font group that appears, click the right-align button 🔳.

4. Move to slide 4. In the last row of the table, select the text "Revised Figures." From the Home tab, in the Paragraph group, click the right-align button 🔳. This gives the appearance that the cell is actually split instead of just having a border in it.

Exercise 5-15   CHANGE THE VERTICAL POSITION OF TEXT IN A CELL

The appearance of a table is often improved by changing the vertical alignment of text or objects within cells.

1. On slide 4, select the cells in the first row that contain the text "Mgmt," "Kitchen," "Service," and "Clerical."

2. From the Table Tools Layout tab, in the alignment group, choose the Center Vertically button 🔳. The text in the selected cells is now in the center of the cells.

3. Select all the cells in the second, third, and fourth rows.

4. Click the Align Bottom button 🔳. The text moves to the bottom edge of the cells.

Exercise 5-16 USE MARGIN SETTINGS TO ADJUST THE POSITION OF TEXT IN A CELL

Sometimes, the horizontal and vertical alignment settings do not place text precisely where you want it to be in a cell. You might be tempted to use Spacebar to indent the text, but that usually doesn't work well.

You can precisely control where text is placed in a cell by using the cell's margin settings, combined with horizontal and vertical alignment, as shown in Figure 5-15. For example, you can right-align a column of numbers and also have them appear centered in the column.

1. Move to slide 2. Select all the cells that contain numbers (blank cells in the third and fourth rows, too).

Figure 5-15
Using the Cell Text Layout dialog box to control cell margins

2. From the Table Tools Layout tab, in the Alignment group, click Cell Margins . From the drop-down list, click Custom Margins.

3. Click the Vertical alignment list box arrow to see the other settings. Choose Middle.

4. Under Internal margin, change the Right setting to 0.5" and then click OK. The numbers are still right-aligned, but some space is between the cell border and the numbers, as shown in Figure 5-16.

5. Select all the cells in the first column containing text and change the left margin to 0.2".

Figure 5-16
Table with improved alignment

Exercise 5-17 RESIZE A TABLE

To resize the entire table, drag one of the sizing handles. When you drag, make sure the pointer is one of these shapes ⬍, ↔, ⤡, and not the pointer used for changing column width ⬌ or row height ⬍.

If you hold down (Shift) while dragging a corner sizing handle, the table will resize proportionately. Whenever possible, depending on how large or small you make the table, the relative proportions of row heights and column widths are preserved.

1. Move to slide 4, and click anywhere inside the table. Notice the eight sizing handles around the border (one in each corner, and one in the middle of each side). They work just like sizing handles on other PowerPoint objects.

2. Using the diagonal two-pointed arrow ⤡, drag the lower-right corner up and to the left about ½ inch. The table becomes smaller, and the relative size of the rows and columns is preserved. Notice that your titles are wrapping onto two lines again.

TIP

Click in the table and then move your pointer to an outside border. When you get a four-pointed arrow, you may click and drag the table to position it.

3. Select the entire table and change the font size to 24 points. Resize the first row and first column as necessary to get the titles all on one row, as shown in Figure 5-17.

4. Position the table attractively on the slide by using the same method that you use to move text boxes or other objects.

Figure 5-17
Resized table

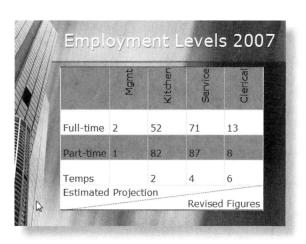

Enhancing the Table

You can enhance a table by adding one of the many three-dimensional effects available in PowerPoint 2007. Graphic images and shading effects also improve the appearance of tables.

Images can be added in open cells or across the full table; shading effects can be applied in the same manner.

Exercise 5-18   APPLY AND MODIFY A CELL BEVEL EFFECT

The *Cell Bevel* effect is a dimensional effect that can be applied to make cells look raised and rounded or pressed in, as shown in Figure 5-18. The Cell Bevel effect is found on the Table Tools Design tab, in the Table Styles group, under the Effects button .

1. On Slide 4, select the whole table. From the Table Tools Design tab, in the Table Styles group, click the Effects button ⊡. A drop-down list displays effects that can be applied to a table.

2. Choose Cell Bevel then choose Riblet. Notice the effect that is applied to the table.

3. With the table still selected, click the Effects button ⊡ and choose Cell Bevel and No Bevel. This removes the bevel effect.

4. Click the Effects Button ⊡ again, choose Cell Bevel, then choose Relaxed Inset.

Figure 5-18
Bevel effect applied to a table

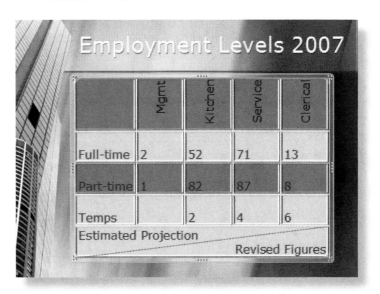

Exercise 5-19   APPLY AND MODIFY A SHADOW EFFECT

Another dimensional effect is the *Shadow* effect. You may modify where the shadow is cast, what color the shadow is, and many other aspects of the shadow. The shadow effect can be applied from the Table Tools Design tab in the Table Styles group, under the Effects Button ⊡.

1. Still working on slide 4, select the table. From the Table Tools Design tab, in the Table Styles group, click the Effects button ⊡. A drop-down list displays effects that can be applied to a table.

2. Choose Shadow and move your pointer over several of the options. Notice the effect that the shadow has on the table.

3. Without selecting a shadow, choose Shadow Options at the bottom of the drop-down list. The Format Shape dialog box appears and allows you to control every aspect of the shadow.

4. Under Presets, in the Outer group, choose Offset Diagonal Bottom Right.

5. Under Color, choose Red, Accent 1, Darker 25%.

6. Change the other settings as follows:

   • Transparency, 34%

   • Size, 100%

   • Blur, 4 pt.

   • Angle, 180°

   • Distance, 13 pt.

7. Click Close on the dialog box to return to your presentation. Notice the effect that the shadow applies to your table, as shown in Figure 5-19.

Figure 5-19
Shadow effect
applied to table

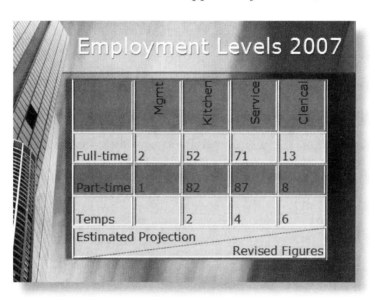

Exercise 5-20   APPLY AND MODIFY A REFLECTION EFFECT

The *Reflection* effect makes the table appear to be reflecting on a body of water or a mirror. Several preset reflection effects are available to be applied to a table. The Reflection effect is found on the Table Tools Design tab, in the Table Styles group, under the Effects button ▣.

1. Move to slide 2, and select the table.

2. From the Table Tools Design tab, in the Table Styles group, click the Effects button ▣. A drop-down list displays effects that can be applied to a table.

3. Choose Reflection and move your pointer over several of the options. Notice the effect that each reflection has on the table.

4. Choose the Half Reflection, 8 pt Offset option. The lower half of the table is reflected and the reflection is offset from the bottom of the table, as shown in Figure 5-20.

5. Leave the presentation open for the next exercise.

Figure 5-20
Reflection effect applied to a table

Exercise 5-21   INSERT A PICTURE AND APPLY GRADIENT SHADING

Pictures within a table can help viewers understand the context of the data in the table. Gradient shading on rows or columns can add interest or perhaps make text easier to read.

1. On slide 4, with the table active, click in the first cell of the table.

2. From the Table Tools Design tab, in the Table Styles group, click the Shading button ⊞ and choose Picture. A picture can be inserted in one cell, a selection of cells, or an entire table.

3. Locate your student files for Lesson 5, and double-click on **Employees** to insert the picture into the table.

4. Select the last four cells in the first row in the table. Still working on the Table Tools Design tab, in the Table Styles group, click the Shading button ⊞ and choose Gradient.

5. In the Light Variation category, choose the Linear Down pattern of gradient fill.

6. Select row three and apply the Linear Down pattern of gradient fill.

7. Select row five and apply the color Gray-25%, Accent 4, Darker 25% first, then repeat the process of applying a Linear Down pattern of gradient fill for row five.

8. Click outside the table to observe the effects. Compare your table to Figure 5-21.

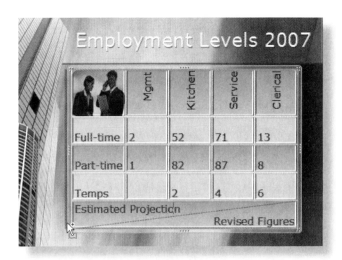

9. Update the handout footer to include the text **[5-21your initials]**.

10. Save the presentation as **[5-21your initials]** in your Lesson 5 folder. Leave it open for the next exercise.

Creating a Tabbed Table

In this lesson, you have learned several ways to create tables using PowerPoint's table tools. You can also create tables through tab settings using the *Ruler*. Sometimes information can be effectively displayed with just a very simple table.

Exercise 5-22   SET AND EDIT TABS

In PowerPoint you set tabs on the Ruler the same way you set tabs in Word, and they are left-aligned by default. However, PowerPoint's default tabs are set at one-inch intervals. To set your own tabs, click the Tab Type button (in the upper-left corner of the Slide pane, where the two rulers meet) to choose the alignment style. Then click the ruler at the location where you want to set a tab.

1. Insert a new slide after slide 4 that uses the Title Only slide layout.

2. From the View tab, in the Show/Hide group, check the box beside the Ruler if the Ruler is not displayed already.

3. Key the title **Employment Change Summary**. The title will appear on two lines.

4. Draw a text box starting an inch to the left and below the word "Employment" and extending it to the right to a similar position (approximately seven inches wide).

5. Key the following, pressing ⌨Tab where indicated: **Department** ⌨Tab **Status** ⌨Tab **2006** ⌨Tab **2007** ⌨Tab **% Change**.

6. Select the text box, apply bold, and change the font color to Brown, Accent 6.

NOTE

Tabs are set when the Tab Type symbol appears on the ruler. The tabs you set override the default tabs, and the default tabs are removed. It might take some practice before you are comfortable with tab type selection and tab placement.

7. Click anywhere within the text box to activate the text box ruler. If the ruler is still not showing, click the View tab and choose ruler in the show/hide group.

8. Click the Tab Type button at the left end of the horizontal ruler. Each time you click the button, a different tab type icon appears, enabling you to cycle through the four tab type choices, as shown in Table 5-1 and Figure 5-22.

TABLE 5-1 Types of Tabs

Tab	Purpose
⌊	Left-aligns text at the tab setting
⊥	Centers text at the tab setting
⌋	Right-aligns text at the tab setting
⊥.	Aligns decimal points at the tab setting

Figure 5-22
Types of tabs

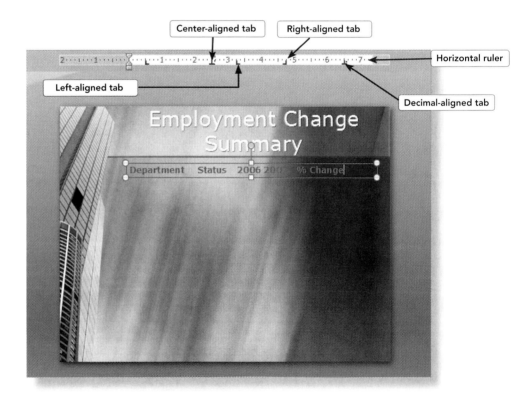

9. Click the Tab Type button one or more times until the left-aligned tab button appears. Click the ruler at the .5-inch position to set a left tab.

10. Click the Tab Type button once until the center-aligned tab button appears. Click the ruler at the 2.5-inch position. The text "Status" moves so that it is centered under the tab marker.

11. Click the Tab Type button once or more until the left-aligned tab marker appears. Click the ruler at the 3.25-inch mark to set a left tab.

12. Click the Tab Type button once or more until the right-aligned tab marker appears. Click the ruler at the 4.75-inch mark to set a right-aligned tab.

13. Click the Tab Type button once or more until the decimal-aligned tab marker appears. Click the ruler at the 6.5-inch mark to set a decimal-aligned tab.

14. Click on the first tab setting, a left-aligned tab marker, and click and drag it down and off the ruler. This removes the tab.

15. Leave the presentation open for the next exercise.

> **TIP**
>
> When setting tabs, you might want to increase the zoom setting for an enlarged view of the ruler. After tabs are set, tabbed text that you key will automatically align under the tab markers you placed on the ruler.

Exercise 5-23   CREATE A TABBED TABLE

A tabbed table is created by making a series of tabs within a text box. Since you have set the tabs, now you just need to enter text using the set tabs.

1. Working in the text box you created on slide 5, position the insertion point at the end of the text line and press [Enter] to start a new line of text.

2. Key the table text, shown in Figure 5-23, pressing [Tab] between columns and pressing [Enter] at the end of each line. The text box will increase in size as the text is keyed.

Figure 5-23
Creating a tabbed table

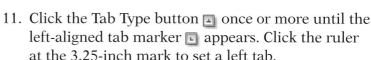
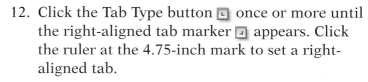

Department	Status	2006	2007	% Change
Mgmt	Full-time	2	2	0.00%
Mgmt	Part-time	0	1	100.00%
Kitchen	Full-time	44	52	18.18%
Kitchen	Part-time	75	82	9.33%
Kitchen	Temps	0	2	200.00%
Service	Full-time	62	71	14.52%
Service	Part-time	71	87	22.54%
Service	Temps	0	4	400.00%
Clerical	Full-time	12	13	8.33%
Clerical	Part-time	7	8	14.29%
Clerical	Temps	2	6	300.00%

Employment Change Summary

3. Select the entire text box by clicking its border. From the Drawing Tools Format tab, in the Shape Styles group, click the Shape Fill button ⬛ and add shape fill of Brown, Accent 6, Lighter 60%.

4. From the Drawing Tools Format tab, in the Shape Styles group, click the Shape Outline button ⬛ and add a shape outline of Brown, Accent 2.

5. Select the text in the table, and from the Home tab, in the Paragraph group, change the line spacing to 1.5.

6. Highlight the text in the text box. Drag the center-aligned tab marker from the 2.5-inch position on the ruler to 2.25 inches. The entire column moves to the left.

7. Drag the center-aligned marker down and off the ruler to remove it. The table realigns in an unattractive way that does not make sense.

8. Click the Undo button ⬛ once to restore the table's appearance.

9. Update the handout footer text to **[5-23your initials]** as the footer.

10. Save the presentation as **[5-23your initials]** in your Lesson 5 folder.

11. View the presentation as a slide show; then preview and print the presentation as handouts, six slides per page, grayscale, landscape, scale to fit paper, framed.

Lesson 5 Summary

- Tables offer a convenient way to quickly organize material on a slide. From the Insert tab, in the Table group, you can use the Insert table button ⬛ to insert a table. You can insert a table by choosing a content slide layout. You can "draw" a table directly on a slide by using the Draw Table button ⬛. Lastly, you can create a tabbed table through setting tabs.

- Before you can apply special formatting to table cells, you must first select those cells. You can select individual cells, groups of cells, or the entire table.

- Use the buttons on the Table Tools Design tab, in the Table Styles group, to apply fill effects and border effects to individual cells, a group of cells, or the entire table.

- Change the overall size of a table by dragging one of its sizing handles with a two-pointed arrow.

- Change the width of a column by dragging or double-clicking its border. Change the height of a row by dragging its border.

- Rows and columns can be easily inserted or deleted as you develop a table. Select at least one cell in the row or column where you want to insert or delete; then use buttons on the Table Tools Layout tab.

- While keying text in a table, a quick way to insert a new row at the bottom is to press Tab when you reach the last table cell.

- Occasionally, you might want one row or column to have more or fewer cells than the others. You can make this happen by merging a group of cells or splitting an individual cell into two cells.

- A diagonal line can be added to a cell to make it appear to be split into two cells. Careful placement of text within the cell completes this illusion.

- Applying and removing shading effects is similar to applying shading effects to other PowerPoint objects. Table and cell fills can be gradients, textures, or pictures.

- Before applying a border to cells or the entire table, choose the border style, border width, and border color from the Table Tools Design tab in the Draw Borders group. Then select cells and choose an option from the Borders button ▦ drop-down list or use the pencil pointer to apply it to the borders you want to change.

- Use the text alignment buttons on the Home tab in the Paragraph group to control the horizontal position of text in a cell.

- Use the Align Top ▤, Center Vertically ▤, and Align Bottom ▤ buttons on the Table Tools Layout tab in the Alignment group to control the vertical position of text within a cell.

- To fine-tune the horizontal or vertical position of text, change a cell's margin settings by using the Cell Margins button ▯ on the Table Tools Layout tab in the Alignment group.

- Add and modify 3-D effects by selecting the table and clicking the Effects button ▣ on the Table Tools Design tab.

- Click the Tab Type button ▣ on the left edge of the ruler to change the type of tab. The button cycles through four tab types: left-aligned, centered, right-aligned, and decimal.

- Create a tabbed table by using a text box and setting tabs to control how the information is indented. Remove tabs or move tabs as needed by clicking and dragging.

LESSON 5	Command Summary		
Feature	**Button**	**Ribbon**	**Keyboard**
Insert table	▦	Insert, Tables group, Table	
Navigate in a table			Tab; Shift + Tab; ↓; ↑; ←; →
Column, select		Table Tools Layout, Table group, Select, Select Column	

continues

LESSON 5		Command Summary *continued*	
Feature	**Button**	**Ribbon**	**Keyboard**
Row, select		Table Tools Layout, Table group, Select, Select Row	
Table, select		Table Tools Layout, Table group, Select, Select Table	
Apply Shading Effect to cells		Table Tools Design, Table Styles group, Shading	
Select Table Styles		Table Tools Design, Table Styles group, More	
Change Table Style		Table Tools Design, Table Style group, More	
Add Header Row		Table Tools Design, Table Style Options group	
Change Text Direction		Table Tools Layout, Alignment group, Text Direction	
Apply Border Effects		Table Tools Design, Draw Borders group	
Erase Cell Borders		Table Tools Design, Draw Table group, Eraser	
Align Table Text Vertically	or	Table Tools Layout, Alignment group	
Set Table Cell Margins		Table Tools Layout, Alignment group, Margins	
Distribute Columns Evenly		Table Tools Layout, Cell Size group, Distribute Columns	
Distribute Rows Evenly		Table Tools Layout, Cell Size group, Distribute Rows	
Insert Table Columns		Table Tools Layout, Rows & Columns group	
Insert Table Rows		Table Tools Layout, Rows & Columns group	
Delete Table Columns		Table Tools Layout, Rows & Columns group, Delete	
Draw a Table		Insert, Tables group, Table, Draw Table	
Merge Table Cells		Table Tools Layout, Merge group, Merge Cells	
Split a Table Cell		Table Tools Layout, Merge group, Split Cells	
Apply 3-D Effects		Table Tools Design, Table Styles group, Effects	

Concepts Review

True/False Questions

Each of the following statements is either true or false. Select your choice by indicating T or F.

T (F) 1. You can adjust the width of individual columns in a table, but row heights must all be the same.

(T) F 2. Effects can be used to give the table a 3-D look.

(T) F 3. You don't need to be exact when you define the size of a table because it's easy to insert rows and columns later.

T (F) 4. Borders are available in only one width.

(T) F 5. Text in a table cell can have its vertical position adjusted, independent of other cells.

T (F) 6. When you insert a new column, it is always inserted to the left of the currently selected column.

T (F) 7. Cell margins work the same way as text box margins.

(T) F 8. You can remove a tab marker by dragging it off the ruler.

Short Answer Questions

Write the correct answer in the space provided.

1. What do you call the intersection between a column and a row?

   Cell margin

2. Other than dragging down all the cells or using a button on the Ribbon, how can you select a column in a table?

   hold down arrow on outside of top cell and click

3. What tab contains the Center Vertically button?

   Align (Table tools/Layout tab)

4. What method can be used to select the entire table?

   Clicking on its border when arrow cross appears

5. What three types of 3-D effects are available to apply to the table?

   Cell bevel, Shadow, reflection

6. What are the three methods to merge cells in a table?

highligh cells right click + click on merge cells
highlight cells + Click merge in merge group

7. What is different about splitting a cell diagonally from splitting it horizontally or vertically?

8. What's the quickest way to make a group of selected columns of varying widths all the same width?

highlight all + go to layout Cells group and click on Distrip Columns

Critical Thinking

Answer these questions on a separate page. There are no right or wrong answers. Support your answers with examples from your own experience, if possible.

1. Why might you choose to put information in a table instead of in a bulleted placeholder?

2. Tables can be created in three ways: inserting, drawing, or tabbing. Why would you choose one method over another? What criteria would affect which method you use?

Skills Review

Exercise 5-24

Create a table, key text, apply table styles.

1. Open the file **CookOff** and move to slide 4, which contains the WordArt title "The Winning Fare."

2. Insert a new table by following these steps:
   a. From the Insert tab, in the Tables group, click the Table button .
   b. On the grid that appears, drag to define a (2 × 4) table two columns wide by four rows long.

3. Key text in the table by following these steps:
   a. Click the upper-left cell to select it, and then key: **Name**
   b. Press [Tab] to move to the next cell, and then key: **Recipe Description**

4. Key the text shown in Figure 5-24 for the remaining cells.

Figure 5-24
Table text

```
Amy Grand                     Hot Tomato Salsa

Juanita McLeod                Raspberry Cream Pie

William Steinberg             Roasted Chicken and Vegetables
```

5. Apply a table style from the Best Match for Document category following these steps:
   a. Select the table by right-clicking within the table and choosing Select Table from the short-cut menu.
   b. From the Table Tools Design tab, in the Table Styles group, click the More button ⊡.
   c. From the Best Match for Document category, choose Themed Style 1, Accent 1.
   d. Move the table down a little to position it better on the slide.
6. Create a slide footer for the current slide (slide 4 only) containing today's date and the text your name **[5-24your initials]**.
7. Move to slide 1 and save the presentation as **[5-24your initials]** in your Lesson 5 folder.
8. View the presentation as a slide show from slide 1.
9. Print slide 4 only. If you have a color printer, print it in color.

Exercise 5-25

Draw a table, apply border and shading options.

1. Open the file **Operate2**.
2. Insert a new slide after slide 3 that uses the Title Only layout. Key the title **Capital Equipment 2007**. From the View tab, in the Show/Hide group, click the checkbox beside Ruler if it is not checked already.
3. Draw a new table by following these steps:
   a. From the Insert tab, in the Tables group, click the Table button 🖽 and choose Draw Table.
   b. Use the Pencil pointer to draw a table from under "Capital" to under "2007" and down about 3.5 inches on the ruler.
   c. Click and drag two vertical borders to create three columns.
   d. Click and drag four horizontal borders to create five rows.
   e. Press [Esc] to turn off the Pencil pointer.

4. For the table text, key the information shown in Figure 5-25.

Figure 5-25
Table text

	Column 1	Column 2	Column 3
Row 1		Leased	Bought
Row 2	Kitchen	9,450	24,350
Row 3	Dining	14,400	18,650
Row 4	Office	10,500	25,500
Row 5	Other	8,252	16,300

5. Apply Shading effects to table cells by following these steps:
   a. Move the pointer to the outside of the table beside row 1, when you get a right-facing arrow click to select all the cells in the first row.
   b. From the Table Tools Design tab, in the Table Styles group, click the list box arrow on the Shading button.
   c. Choose Aqua, Text 2, Lighter 40%.
   d. Click the list box arrow on the Shading button again and choose Gradient.
   e. In the Variations category, choose From Center.
   f. With the first row still selected, change the font color to a deep blue, Indigo, Accent 6, Darker 50%. Apply bold to the first row.

6. Make all the columns the same width and all the rows the same height by following these steps:
   a. Select the entire table by right-clicking within the table and choosing Select Table.
   b. From the Table Tools Layout tab, in the Cell Size group, click the Distribute Columns button.
   c. From the Table Tools Layout tab, in the Cell Size group, click the Distribute Rows button.
   d. With the table still selected, change the font size of the entire table to 24 points.

7. Remove all the table's borders by following these steps:
   a. Select the entire table.
   b. From the Table Tools Design tab, in the Table Styles group, click the arrow on the Borders button and choose No Border.

8. Select all cells with numbers and the column heading cells, and make them right aligned.

9. Create a handout header and footer: Include the date and your name as the header, and the page number and text **[5-25your initials]** as the footer.

10. Move to slide 1 and save the presentation as **[5-25your initials]** in your Lesson 5 folder.

11. View the presentation as a slide show; then preview and print the presentation as handouts, four slides per page, grayscale, landscape, framed. Close the presentation.

Exercise 5-26

~~Draw a table; insert and delete rows~~ and columns; adjust column and row
width; apply formatting for text, shading, and borders.

1. Open the file **Operate3**.
2. Display slide 5, titled "Reservation Requests."
3. Draw a table on slide 5 by following these steps:
   a. From the Insert tab, in the Tables group, click the Table button ⊞ and choose Draw Table.
   b. Use the Pencil pointer to draw a table from under "Average" to under "Number" and down about 3.5 inches on the ruler.
   c. From the Table Tools Design tab, in the Draw Borders group, click the Pen Color button 🖉 and choose Light Blue, Accent 6, Darker 50%.
   d. If your pointer is not a Pencil pointer 🖉, click the Draw Table button 🖉.
   e. Within the table, draw four vertical lines (to create five columns) and three horizontal lines (to create four rows). They don't need to be the same size.
   f. Press Esc to turn off the Pencil pointer.
4. For the table's text, key the data in Figure 5-26. It's okay if the text wraps within cells; you will fix the layout in the next few steps.

Figure 5-26
Table text

	Column 1	Column 2	Column 3	Column 4	Column 5
Row 1		Brunch	Lunch	Dinner	Late Night
Row 2	Weekday	3	35	75	3
Row 3	Weekends	21	12	100	15
Row 4	Memorial Day	7	5	12	4

5. Select the table and make it bold. Make all the numbers blue.
6. If the text "Weekday" or "Weekends" wraps to a second line, make the table a little wider by dragging either the right- or left-center sizing handle. Make sure the pointer appears as ↔.
7. Insert a new row between "Weekends" and "Memorial Day" by following these steps:
   a. Right-click "Memorial Day."
   b. Choose Insert from the short-cut menu and choose Insert Above.
   c. If the table extends below the bottom of the slide, make the table smaller by dragging the bottom-center sizing handle up.

8. Insert a new column to the left of "Brunch" by following these steps:

   a. Click anywhere in the "Brunch" column.

   b. Click the Table Tools Layout tab, in the Rows & Columns group, choose Insert Left.

9. Delete a column and a row by following these steps:

   a. Select the entire "Late Night" column (which might extend beyond the right edge of the slide).

   b. Right-click the selection and choose Delete Columns from the short-cut menu.

   c. Select the "Memorial Day" row. Right-click the selection and choose Delete Rows from the short-cut menu.

10. In the second column, key **Breakfast** for the column heading. Key **5** for "Weekday" and **18** for "Weekends." Change the "Weekday" cell to **Weekdays**.

11. Key the following information in the new row:

    Holidays `Tab` **6** `Tab` **9** `Tab` **15** `Tab` **94.**

12. Move the table to a new position and change its size by following these steps:

    a. Right-click anywhere inside the table and choose Select Table from the short-cut menu.

    b. Move your pointer over the table's border until you see the four-pointed arrow ⊕. If necessary, drag the table so it is positioned on the white area of the slide so all numbers are easy to read.

    c. Make the table wider by dragging the right-center sizing handle to the right until all text and numbers are on one line. Before you drag, make sure the pointer appears as ↔.

13. Make all the columns the same width and all the rows the same height. Then adjust the first column size as needed to fit all on one line.

14. Align text horizontally by following these steps:

    a. Select the first row by clicking the first cell and dragging down to the last cell.

    b. From the Home tab, in the Paragraph group, click the Center button ☰ (or press `Ctrl`+`E`).

    c. Select all the cells that contain numbers by dragging diagonally across the cells.

    d. Click the Align Right button ☰ (or press `Ctrl`+`R`) to right-align the numbers.

15. Change cell margin settings by following these steps:

    a. Make sure all the cells that contain numbers are selected.

    b. From the Table Tools Layout tab, in the Alignment group, choose the Cell Margins button ▣ and choose Custom Margins.

    c. In the Internal margin section, key **0.5″** in the Right text box. Click OK.

16. Change the vertical alignment of text and numbers in their cells by following these steps:

    a. Select the entire table from Table Tools Layout tab, in the Table group, choose the Select button ⬚ and Select Table.

    b. Still working on the Table Tools Layout tab, in the Alignment group, click the Center Vertically button ⬚.

17. Create a handout header and footer: Include the date and your name as the header, and the page number and text **[5-26your initials]** as the footer.

18. Move to slide 1 and save the presentation as **[5-26your initials]** in your Lesson 5 folder.

19. View the presentation as a slide show; then preview and print the presentation as handouts, six slides per page, grayscale, framed. Close the presentation.

Exercise 5-27

Insert a table, merge cells, work with tabbed tables.

1. Open the file **Tucson1**.

2. Insert a new slide after slide 2 and use the Title and Content layout. Key **Appetizers** as the title.

3. Set a decimal tab at the 4.5-inch on the ruler by following these steps:

    a. Click in the body text placeholder.

    b. Click the Tab Type marker until the Decimal Tab Marker ⬚ appears.

    c. Click on the ruler at the 4.5-inch mark.

4. Key the following in the body text placeholder, pressing [Tab] before each price:

    Wild Rice Soup   [Tab]   5.25
    Dill Cucumber Salad   [Tab]   4.50
    Four Bean Salad   [Tab]   4.25

5. Insert a new slide after slide 3 and use the Title Only layout. Key **Entrees** as the title.

6. Insert a table with three columns and seven rows.

7. Merge the cells in rows three, five, and seven using the following steps:

    a. Select the cells in row three.

    b. From the Table Tools Layout tab, in the Merge group, choose the Merge Cells button ⬚.

    c. Repeat the process for row five and row seven.

TIP

You can use right tabs instead of decimal tabs to align numbers if all the numbers in the list have the same number of decimal places.

8. Key the text as shown in Figure 5-27 into your table.

Figure 5-27
Table text

	Column 1	Column 2	Column 3
Row 1	**Entrée**	**Dinner**	**Lunch**
Row 2	Chicken Fajitas	9.50	6.25
Row 3	Chunky chicken, Monterey Jack cheese, tomatoes, and olives wrapped in a flour tortilla		
Row 4	Dijon Chicken Rolls	9.95	6.50
Row 5	Rolled boneless chicken breast filled with spicy bread crumbs and dressed with a Dijon sauce		
Row 6	Thai Stir Fry	10.25	7.50
Row 7	Tasty shrimp with fresh garden vegetables served over your choice of wild or white rice		

9. Move the table down and resize as necessary the table, columns, and rows.
10. Center the text vertically in the table.
11. Create a handout header and footer: Include the date and your name as the header, and the page number and text **[5-27your initials]** as the footer.
12. Save the presentation as **[5-27your initials]** in your Lesson 5 folder.
13. Preview and then print the presentation as handouts, four slides per page, grayscale, landscape, framed. Close the presentation.

Lesson Applications

Exercise 5-28

Create a presentation with a table slide, apply table styles, arrange and format text, and change column widths and table size.

1. Open the file **Print1**.

2. Insert three slides after slide 1. Use the Title and Content layout for all three slides.

3. On slide 4, select the Table button ▦ from the content placeholder and select the correct number of columns and rows before keying the information in. Select the entire table and change the font to red. On the table, each cell in the first row should contain two lines of text.

4. Key the text in Figure 5-28.

Figure 5-28
Presentation content

Slide 2
Print Advertising 2007
- Campaigns use a variety of print media
- Each medium targets a specific market segment
- Every campaign must meet specific sales objectives

Slide 3
Coupon Redemption
- Effective measure of return on investment
- Used for promotional purposes in a variety of print media

Slide 4
Coupons Redeemed 2006

	Column 1	Column 2	Column 3	Column 4
Row 1	Newspaper Magazine	Coupons Redeemed	Average Check	Cost of One Ad
Row 2	NY Times	414	$31.50	$6,800
Row 3	NY Magazine	476	$25.00	$2,850
Row 4	NY Runner	1,063	$23.50	$975
Row 5	NY Health	125	$16.25	$650

5. On slide 4, change the Table style to Themed Style 2, Accent 4 in the Best Match for Documents category.

6. For the entire table, change all right and left cell margins to 0.2 inches. Using the pointer ⊞, double-click each column border so that each column self-adjusts to fit the widest text in the column.

7. Center the headings for the columns containing numbers.

8. Right-align all numbers.

9. Vertically center all text and numbers in the table.

10. Adjust the overall size and position of the table for attractive positioning on the slide, as shown in Figure 5-29.

Figure 5-29
Completed table slide

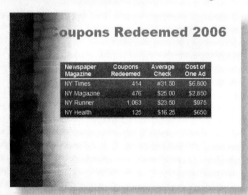

11. Create a slide footer for the current slide (slide 4) containing today's date and the text your name, **[5-28your initials]**.

12. Create a handout header and footer: Include the date and your name as the header, and the page number and text **[5-28your initials]** as the footer.

13. Save the presentation as **[5-28your initials]** in your Lesson 5 folder.

14. Print the current slide (slide 4) in full size.

15. View the presentation as a slide show; then preview and print the presentation as handouts, four slides per page, grayscale, landscape, framed. Close the presentation.

Exercise 5-29

Insert a table slide; insert rows; change row height, column width, alignment, and cell margins; and apply a 3-D effect.

1. Open the file **Ads2**.

2. On slide 1, change "Student Name" to Your Name.

3. Insert a table on a new slide after slide 1 and key the text shown in Figure 5-30.

Figure 5-30
Table text

Advertising Effectiveness

	Column 1	Column 2	Column 3
Row 1		New	Total
		Customers	Revenue
Row 2	Newspaper	28%	30%
Row 3	Radio	10%	5%
Row 4	Yellow Pages	6%	12%

4. Resize the title placeholder to fit on one line.

5. Apply the following formatting to the table's text:

- Center the text in the first row.

- Right-align all the numbers and apply a cell right margin, so that the numbers appear centered under their headings.

- Apply a 0.25-inch left margin to all the cells in the first column.

- If necessary, adjust the column width of the first row so that "Yellow Pages" is on one line.

6. Insert a row above "Yellow Pages" with the following text:

   Mailers   12%   18%

7. Make the table easy to read by adjusting the column widths, row heights, and vertical alignment of cells, as necessary. Resize and reposition the table appropriately on the slide.

8. Change the table style to Themed style 1, Accent 1.

9. Select all of the text in the table except the first row and change the font to Gray-50%, Background 2, Darker 50%.

10. Add a Convex cell bevel to the entire table.

11. Create a slide footer for the current slide (slide 2) containing today's date and your name and the text **[5-29your initials]**.

12. Create a handout header and footer: Include the date and your name as the header, and the page number and text **[5-29your initials]** as the footer.

13. Check spelling and change any words that need to be corrected.

14. Save the presentation as **[5-29your initials]** in your Lesson 5 folder.

15. Print slide 2 in full size.

16. View the presentation as a slide show; then preview and print the presentation as handouts, six slides per page, grayscale, landscape, framed. Close the presentation.

Exercise 5-30

Create a tabbed table.

1. Start a new blank presentation. Use the Concourse design theme with the Equity color theme.

2. On slide 1, key a two-line title with the text Good 4 U and Softball Schedule.

3. Key Spring/Summer 2008 for the subtitle.

4. Find a softball clip art image and insert it on the title slide in the color bar at the bottom. Duplicate the softball several times, and resize the images to look as though they are getting smaller. See Figure 5-31 for an example.

Figure 5-31
Slide 1

5. Using the Title Only layout, create slide 2 as shown in Figure 5-32. Key the table and its heading all in one text box and format the table as follows:

- Set appropriate tabs.

- Add bold to the headings.

- Change the font size to 20 points.

- Position the table appropriately on the slide.

6. Add the same softball used in slide 1 to the bottom left corner of slide 2.

Figure 5-32
Slide 2

7. Using the Title and Content layout, create slide 3 as shown in Figure 5-33.

8. Copy and paste the softball from slide 2 onto slide 3 and insert a softball image recolored to match the theme colors on the right of the slide.

Figure 5-33
Slide 3

Team Members

- Jerry Allen
- Carol Lynne
- Robert Lee
- Heidi Aaron
- Autumn Lashae
- Wyatt Charles
- Dalton Andrew
- Rowan Jacob
- Noah Riley

9. Check spelling in the presentation. The names of team members are spelled correctly; do not make any changes.

10. Create a handout header and footer: Include the date and your name as the header and the page number and filename **[5-30your initials]** as the footer.

11. Save the presentation as **[5-30your initials]** in your Lesson 5 folder.

12. Preview and then print the presentation as handouts, three slides per page, landscape, grayscale, scale to fit paper, framed. Close the presentation.

Exercise 5-31 ◆ Challenge Yourself

Edit and format a presentation including a table slide, add data, change alignment, change table colors, and merge cells.

1. Open the file **MktSum**.

2. Create a table on a new slide after slide 3 using the layout Title Only layout. Key the title Marketing Expenses 2006.

3. Draw a table using the Pencil pointer. Change the font of the first row to 28 points, brown, and bold. Center the first row vertically and horizontally within the cell. Use Figure 5-34 for as an example to create the table.

Figure 5-34
Table slide

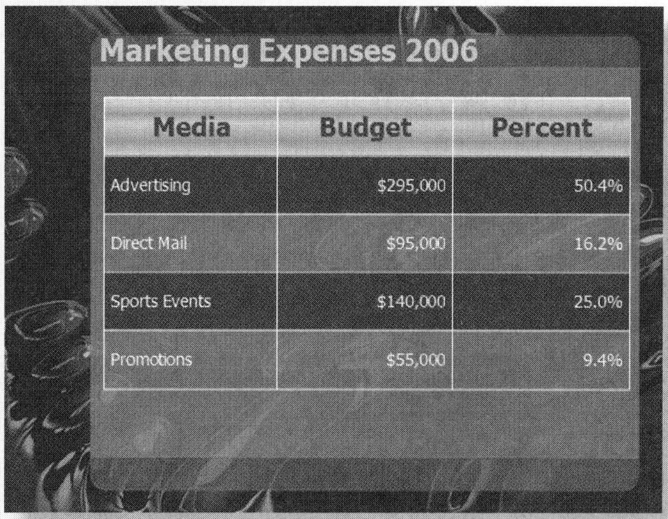

4. Use appropriate alignment techniques, fill colors, and border treatments. Use a preset gradient color for the heading row fill for a gold appearance. (This option is found under More Gradients.)

5. Distribute the columns and rows evenly.

6. Using the Title and Content layout, insert a new slide after slide 4 with the title Estimated Budget 2007. Use Figure 5-35 as an example to create the table. Choose an appropriate table style to coordinate with the theme.

7. Adjust the size of the columns, rows, and table as necessary to present an attractive table.

8. Select the table and choose the Reflection Effect of Half Reflection, 4 pt offset.

Figure 5-35
Table slide

9. Create a handout header and footer: Include the date and your name as the header, and the page number and text **[5-31your initials]** as the footer.

10. Check spelling in the presentation.

11. Save the presentation as **[5-31your initials]** in your Lesson 5 folder.

12. View the presentation as a slide show; then preview and print the presentation as handouts, six slides per page, grayscale, framed. Close the presentation.

On Your Own

In these exercises you work on your own, as you would in a real-life work environment. Use the skills you've learned to accomplish the task—and be creative.

Exercise 5-32

Use a recipe to create a series of slides describing a prepared dish. Create a title slide with the name and where the recipe came from, and, if possible, a picture of the finished dish. Add one or two slides describing in general terms what the dish contains and why it is good. Create a series of slides containing tables that present the ingredients and steps to create the recipe.

Design your own table structures to present the information in a way that you think is easy to understand using inserted tables with table styles, tables that you draw, and tabbed tables. Format your presentation attractively; picking up colors, fonts, and other style features that accent the recipe that you have chosen. Save your presentation as **[5-32your initials]**. Preview, and then print the presentation as handouts.

Exercise 5-33

Find a schedule of events from your local newspaper or other source, for example, a movie schedule, your class schedule, the TV listings, or a schedule of community or school events. Create a presentation containing a table that lists those events in a way you think is easy to understand. Create a second table listing the three events or classes you think are the most interesting in one column and a description of those events in a second column. The presentation should include a title slide, two table slides, and any other slides you think will enhance your presentation. Use your creativity to make the tables interesting and fun to view. Be sure to resize the table and cells as needed and add borders, shading, and effects to add interest. Save the presentation as **[5-33your initials]**. Preview, and then print the presentation as handouts.

Exercise 5-34

Create a single-slide presentation with a personal grocery or other shopping list in table format. (If you have a long list, use two or more slides.) Create columns based on the categories of items you need to purchase. For example, frozen meat, canned goods, refrigerated items, etc. List items that you need to buy in each section of a grocery store under the proper column heading. Format your table attractively and in keeping with your own personality (making sure it is easy to read). If you create a really thorough list, you can print copies and circle what you need to purchase each time you go to the store. Save the presentation as **[5-34your initials]**. Preview, and then print the presentation as a full-size slide(s).

Lesson 6

Creating Charts

OBJECTIVES

After completing this lesson, you will be able to:

1. Create a chart.

2. Format a column chart.

3. Use different chart types.

4. Work with pie charts.

5. Enhance chart elements.

MCAS OBJECTIVES

In this lesson:
PP07 3.6
PP07 3.6.1
PP07 3.6.2
PP07 3.6.3
PP07 3.6.4
See Appendix

Estimated Time: 1½ hours

Charts, sometimes called graphs, are diagrams that display numbers in pictorial format. Charts illustrate quantitative relationships and can help people understand the significance of numeric information more easily than when they view the same information in a table or in a list. Charts are well suited for making comparisons or examining the changes in data over time.

Creating a Chart

PowerPoint provides several ways to start a new chart. You can add a chart to an existing slide, or you can select a slide layout with a chart placeholder at the time you create a new slide. Here are two methods of inserting a chart:

- From the Insert tab, in the Illustrations group, click the Chart button .

- On a new slide with the Title and Content layout, click the Insert Chart icon in the center of the placeholder.

Microsoft Excel is opened using either method of creating charts. Microsoft Excel holds the chart data in a *worksheet* and this data is linked to Microsoft PowerPoint where the chart is displayed. If changes are made to the data in Microsoft Excel, the chart is automatically updated in Microsoft PowerPoint.

If Microsoft Excel is not installed on your computer when you start a new chart, Microsoft Graph will open with a sample *datasheet*. A datasheet provides rows and columns in which you key the numbers and labels used to create a chart. Advanced features of charting with Excel are not available with Microsoft Graph.

Exercise 6-1 CHOOSE A SLIDE LAYOUT FOR A CHART

Several slide layout choices are suitable for charts. For example, the Title and Content layout works well for one chart on a slide; the Two Content layout works well for a chart combined with text or an image.

1. Open the file **Finance1**.

2. Insert a new slide after slide 1 that uses the Title and Content slide layout, as shown in Figure 6-1. Key the slide title **Sales Forecast**. This layout contains a placeholder suitable for one chart. When you want to place more than one chart or other element on a slide, use one of the other Content layouts.

Figure 6-1
Choosing a slide
layout for a chart

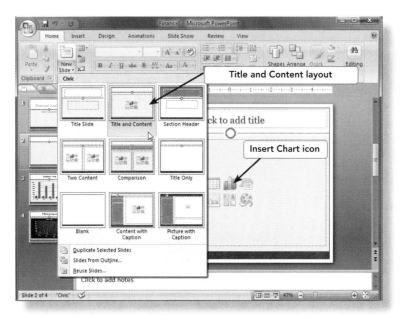

3. Click the Insert Chart icon 📊 in the center of the content placeholder.

4. Point to the options in the Insert Chart dialog box, and notice the different chart types displayed. Choose the 3-D Clustered Column Chart, and click OK. Microsoft Excel opens displaying a worksheet with sample data, and a chart is inserted into PowerPoint. Chart-related tabs appear on the Ribbon.

Exercise 6-2 EDIT THE DATA SOURCE

Each worksheet contains rows and columns. Each number or label is in a separate *cell*—the rectangle formed by the intersection of a row and a column.

As you enter data, you can monitor the results on the sample chart. You key new infor mation by overwriting the sample data or by deleting the sample data and keying your own data.

Figure 6-2
Creating a chart

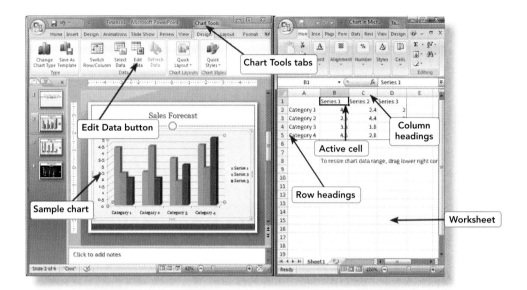

1. On the worksheet, click the words "Series 1." A heavy black border, which indicates that this is the active cell, surrounds the cell that contains "Series 1," as shown in Figure 6-2. Notice that when working on the worksheet, your pointer is a white cross , called a *cell pointer*.

2. Move around the worksheet by clicking on individual cells. Then try pressing ⌈Enter⌉, ⌈Tab⌉, ⌈Shift⌉+⌈Enter⌉, ⌈Shift⌉+⌈Tab⌉, and the arrow keys to explore other ways to navigate in a worksheet.

NOTE

If Microsoft Excel is not installed on your computer, Microsoft Graph will open a datasheet that contains gray column headings and row headings with a button-like appearance that indicate column letters and row numbers. If you like, you can move the datasheet by dragging its title bar, and you can resize it by dragging its borders.

3. Click cell B2 (the cell in column B, row 2 that contains the value 4.3) then key **10** and press ⌈Enter⌉. The chart data will automatically update in PowerPoint.

4. Click cell B2 with the value "10" which represents Category 1 of Series 1.

5. Press ⌈Delete⌉ to delete the contents of cell B2 and press ⌈Enter⌉. Notice that the first column in the chart is no longer displayed.

6. Click and drag the pointer from cell B3 to cell B5 to select the rest of the numbers in the Series 1 column.

7. Press Delete and then for Series 1 no columns are displayed in the chart. Because the Series 1 column is still included on the worksheet, however, space still remains on the chart where the columns were removed and Series 1 shows in the legend.

8. Click the box in the upper-left corner of the worksheet where the row headings meet the column headings, as shown in Figure 6-3. The entire worksheet is selected.

NOTE

If you leave gaps between columns or rows as you enter data, your chart will not display correctly.

Figure 6-3
Editing the worksheet

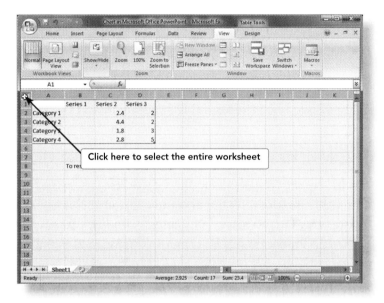

Click here to select the entire worksheet

TIP

You do not need to be concerned about number formatting in the worksheet. If any of the labels or numbers do not fit in a cell, move to the right of the column heading for the cell until you get the two-pointed arrow and double-click. This will adjust the column to fit the longest line of text.

9. Press Delete. The worksheet is now blank and ready for you to key new data. Notice that the columns in the chart are removed.

10. Click the first cell in the upper-left corner. All the cells in the worksheet are deselected.

11. Close Microsoft Excel. The worksheet is not visible. The worksheet can be closed at any point and accessed when you wish.

12. From the Chart Tools Design tab, in the Data group, choose the Edit Data button. This reopens the worksheet and you can now enter new data.

13. Key the numbers and labels shown in Figure 6-4. Be sure to put the labels in the top row and left-most column. Notice how the chart grows as you key data.

Figure 6-4
Worksheet with new data

	A	B	C	D	E
1		2008	2009	2010	
2	New York	920	1130	1450	
3	Miami	500	850	1210	
4	Los Angeles	350	760	990	
5	Row heading				

14. Notice on the chart in Microsoft PowerPoint, there is a blank area on the chart. In the sample chart, there were four categories. To fix this, row 5 must be deleted. Click on the row heading number for row 5. Right-click, and choose Delete. This will update the chart to remove the blank space where the fourth category columns were displayed before, and the remaining columns will expand to fill the chart area.

15. Leave both files open for the next exercise.

Exercise 6-3   SWITCH ROWS/COLUMN DATA

When you key data for a new chart, Microsoft Excel interprets each row of data as a *data series*. On a column chart, each data series is usually displayed in a distinct Theme color. For example, on the current chart, the 2008 worksheet column is one data series and is displayed in orange on the chart. The 2009 worksheet column is a second data series, displayed in blue on the chart, and the 2010 worksheet column is a third data series, displayed in dark red.

When creating your worksheet, you might not know whether it is best to arrange your data in rows or columns. Fortunately, you can enter the data and easily change the way it is displayed on the chart.

1. In PowerPoint, click on the slide 2 chart area to continue modifying this chart.

2. From the Chart Tools Design tab, choose the Switch Row/Column button ⊞. The chart columns are now grouped by year instead of by city. The years are displayed below each group of columns.

3. Click the Switch Row/Column button ⊞ again to group the chart columns by city. Your chart should look like the one shown in Figure 6-5.

4. Create a slide footer for the current slide (slide 2 only) containing today's date and the text your name, **[6-3your initials]**.

5. Create a new folder for lesson 6. Save the presentation as **[6-3your initials]** in your folder for Lesson 6.

6. Print the current slide (slide 2) in full size. If you have a color printer, print it in color.

Figure 6-5
Chart with new data

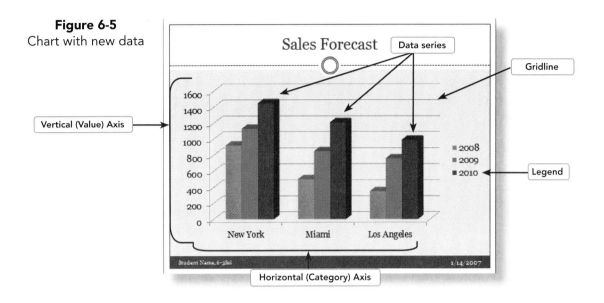

Formatting a Column Chart

You can apply a wide variety of format options to charts by changing the colors, gradients, fonts, and number formats of a chart. Some of these options are appropriate based on the particular chart type being used. In this lesson you have been working with a **3-D Clustered Column** chart.

You can alter the appearance of your chart's axes by changing text color, size, font, and number formatting. You can also change scale and tick mark settings. The *scale* indicates the values that are displayed on the value axis and the intervals between those values. *Tick marks* are small measurement marks, similar to those found on a ruler, that can show increments on the *Vertical (Value) Axis* (on the left for column charts) and the *Horizontal (Category) Axis* (on the bottom for column charts).

To make these changes, use the Format Axis dialog box, which you display in one of the following ways:

TIP

Ctrl+1 opens the Format dialog box that is appropriate for whatever chart element is currently selected.

- Click on the Chart Tools Format tab, in the Current Selection group, choose the area you want to format and click the Format Selection button ☜ .

- Right-click an axis and choose Format Axis from the shortcut menu.

Exercise 6-4   EXPLORE PARTS OF A CHART

PowerPoint provides several tools to help you navigate around the chart and ScreenTips to help you select the part of the chart on which you want to work.

1. Click on the chart to select it.

Figure 6-6
Chart elements list

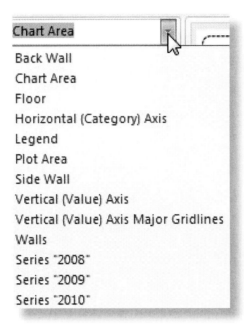

2. Move the pointer over the words "New York." The ScreenTip identifies this part of the chart as the Horizontal (Category) Axis.

3. Point to one of the horizontal gray lines (gridlines) within the chart. The ScreenTip identifies these lines as Vertical (Value) Axis Major Gridlines.

4. Move the pointer around other parts of the chart to find the Plot Area, Chart Area, and Legend Entries. Each of these areas can be formatted with fill colors, border colors, and font attributes.

5. From the Chart Tools Format tab, in the Current Selection group, the chart element that is currently selected is displayed. Click the Chart Elements list box arrow to see a list of the various chart elements as shown in Figure 6-6.

6. Choose Floor from the list to select the chart floor. Sometimes it's easier to select the chart's smaller elements this way.

7. Close the Excel worksheet, but keep the chart open for the next exercise.

Exercise 6-5   CHANGE CHART STYLES

Microsoft PowerPoint provides preset *Chart Styles* that can be applied to a chart to enhance its appearance.

1. On slide 2, click anywhere inside the chart to select it.

2. From the Chart Tools Design tab, in the Chart Styles group, click the More button .

3. Move your pointer over several of the style samples. Click the Style 4 chart style, as shown in Figure 6-7.

Figure 6-7
Chart styles drop-down gallery

4. Notice the effect that applying a style has on the selected chart. The chart still coordinates with theme colors, but has three blue colors applied.

5. Leave the presentation open for the next exercise.

Exercise 6-6 FORMAT THE VERTICAL (VALUE) AND HORIZONTAL (CATEGORY) AXES

The Vertical (Value) Axis and the Horizontal (Category) Axis can be formatted through the Format Axis dialog box to change fonts, scales, units, and more options.

1. On slide 2, point to one of the numbers on the left side of the chart. When you see the Vertical (Value) Axis ScreenTip, right-click to open the shortcut menu.

2. Using the floating font group, change the font to Arial, Bold, 18 points.

3. Right-click on the value axis again to reopen the shortcut menu and choose Format Axis. Click the Number option at the left of the dialog box, then in the Category box, choose Currency. Change the decimal places to **0** because all numbers in the worksheet are even numbers. Change the Symbol to $ English (U.S.).

4. Click Axis Options at the left of the dialog box. In the Maximum box, choose Fixed and key **1500** to set the largest number on the value axis.

5. In the Major unit box, choose Fixed and key **500** to set wider intervals between the numbers on the value axis.

6. Click Close. The chart now shows fewer horizontal gridlines, and each value is formatted as currency with a dollar sign, as shown in Figure 6-8.

Figure 6-8
Formatting the
value axis

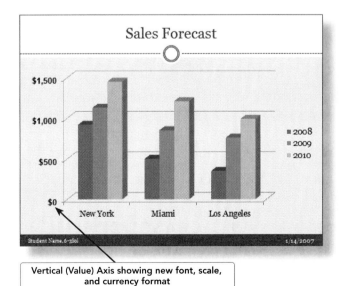

Vertical (Value) Axis showing new font, scale,
and currency format

7. Right-click the text "New York" on the horizontal (category) axis.

8. Using the floating font group, change the font to Arial, Bold, 18 points.

9. Leave the presentation open for the next exercise.

Exercise 6-7 APPLY DIFFERENT CHART LAYOUTS

Chart Layouts control the position where different chart elements appear on the chart. PowerPoint provides many different preset layouts.

1. Move to slide 3 and click anywhere within the chart area.

2. From the Chart Tools Design tab, in the Chart Styles group, click Style 2.

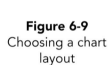

3. From the Chart Tools Design tab, in the Chart Layouts group, click the Quick Layout button.

4. Select Chart Layout 2. Notice the new position of several chart elements. Also, the vertical (value) axis is gone and it has been replaced with data labels showing the values on the columns, as shown in Figure 6-9.

Figure 6-9
Choosing a chart layout

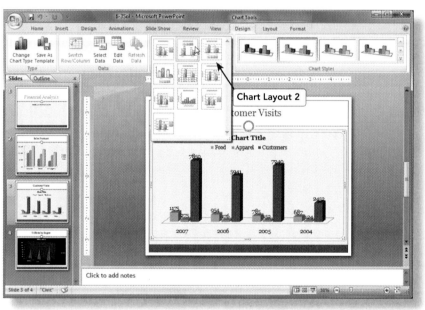

5. Select the "Chart Title" text box and press Delete to remove it.

6. Leave the presentation open for the next exercise.

Exercise 6-8 CHANGE OR REMOVE THE LEGEND

A *Legend* is a box showing the colors assigned to the data series. You can customize a chart's legend by changing the border, background colors, and font attributes.

1. Move to slide 2, and right-click the legend box.

2. Using the Floating Font group, change the font to Arial, Bold, 18 points.

3. Right-click the legend box again and choose Format Legend so you can make several changes at once. Click the Fill option at the left of the dialog box, choose Solid Fill, and select the gold accent color to change the legend background.

TIP

Choosing a fill color, even if it is the same as the background, can make it difficult to choose good grayscale settings for printing.

4. Click Legend Options at the left of the dialog box and under legend position, choose Top. Click Close. The legend appears above the chart with gold background color. Note that sizing handles surround the legend.

5. Using a right or left sizing handle, resize the legend box to make it wider so there is more space between the legend items and all three items are still visible.

6. Point to the center of the legend to select it. Drag the legend down so it fits below the top gridline and above the columns, as shown in Figure 6-10. Adjust the width of the legend if it overlaps any columns.

Figure 6-10
Legend repositioned

Exercise 6-9   APPLY OR REMOVE GRIDLINES

The chart style you used on slide 3 removed the chart gridlines. In situations where numbers are displayed within the chart, gridlines may not be needed. *Gridlines* are the thin lines that can be displayed for major and minor units on vertical or horizontal axes. They align with major and minor tick marks on the axes when those are displayed. Gridlines make quantities easier to understand.

1. Still working on slide 2, click anywhere within the chart area.

2. From the Chart Tools Layout tab, in the Axes group, choose the Gridlines button.

PowerPoint 2007

3. Choose Primary Horizontal Gridlines and Minor Gridlines. Notice that there are many horizontal gridlines now instead of only gridlines on the major units, as shown in Figure 6-11.

Figure 6-11
Gridlines options

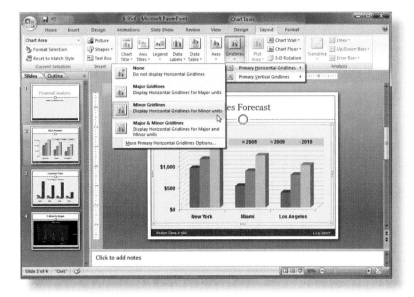

4. Update your slide footer for the current slide (slide 2 only) containing today's date and the text your name, **[6-9your initials]**.

5. Save the presentation as **[6-9your initials]** in your Lesson 6 folder.

Using Different Chart Types

In addition to the 3-D Clustered Column chart, PowerPoint offers a wide variety of chart types. Other types include bar, area, line, pie, and surface, in both two- and three-dimensional layouts. In addition, you can include more than one chart type on a single chart, such as a combination of lines and columns.

If you are working on a two-dimensional (2-D) chart, you can add a secondary axis, so that you can plot data against two different scales. For example, air temperature could be compared to wind speed, or number of customers could be compared to dollar sales. A secondary axis is also a good choice if you need to display numbers that vary greatly in magnitude. For example, sales generated by a small local brand could be compared with national sales trends.

Exercise 6-10 SWITCH TO OTHER CHART TYPES

Sometimes a different chart type can make data easier to understand. You can change chart types in the following ways:

- From the Chart Tools Design tab, in the Type group, click the Change Chart Type button to open the Change Chart Type dialog box.

- Right-click the chart area; then choose Change Chart Type from the shortcut menu.

1. Move to slide 3 and click the chart area to activate the chart. This chart compares dollar sales to number of customer visits. Because of the different types of data, the sales figures are not easy to understand.

2. Right-click the chart and choose Change Chart Type from the shortcut menu. On the Change Chart Type dialog box, chart types are organized by category, as shown in Figure 6-12.

Figure 6-12
Changing to a
different chart type

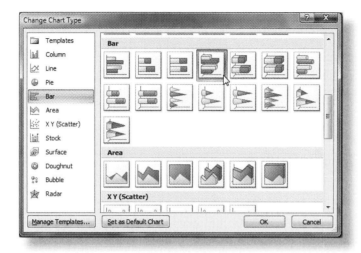

3. Click Bar at the left of the dialog box and choose the Clustered Bar in 3-D thumbnail and click OK. The chart's vertical columns change to horizontal bars.

4. Here is another way to change to a different chart type. From the Chart Tools Design tab, in the Type group, choose the Change Chart Type button [img]. The Change Chart Type dialog box opens again.

5. Click Column at the left of the dialog box and several column chart thumbnails appear. Point to different thumbnails and notice the description that appears in the ScreenTip.

6. Select the Clustered Column type in the upper left of this category. Click OK. The chart changes to a two-dimensional column chart.

7. Leave the presentation open for the next exercise.

Exercise 6-11 ADD A SECONDARY CHART AXIS

The chart on slide 3 ("Customer Visits") contains dollar values for apparel and food sales, and also unit values for number of customer visits. Plotting customer visits on a secondary axis will improve the chart by making it easier to interpret.

If you are working with a 3-D chart, you must change it to a 2-D chart (as you did in the previous exercise), before you can add a secondary axis.

1. Select the chart on slide 3.

2. From the Chart Tools Design tab, in the Chart Layouts group, change the chart layout to Layout 1 and delete the chart title text box.

3. Right-click one of the "Customers" columns and choose Format Data Series from the shortcut menu. Click Series Options at the left of the dialog box.

4. In the Plot Series On area of the dialog box, select Secondary axis. Click Close. Now the orange and blue columns have become taller, and a new scale has been added on the right, as shown in Figure 6-13. In the following exercises you will improve the appearance of this chart.

NOTE

If the Format Data Series dialog box does not contain a Plot Series On area, your current chart type does not support a secondary axis. Make sure you are working with a 2-D chart.

5. Leave the presentation open for the next exercise.

Figure 6-13
Adding a secondary axis

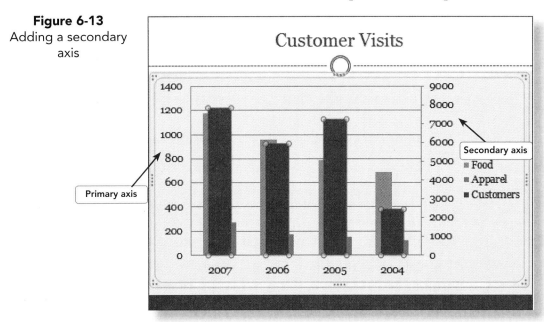

Exercise 6-12 COMBINE CHART TYPES

A good way to distinguish between different data types on a single chart is to assign different chart types. For example, with the current chart, the "Customers" data series can be shown as a line or an area, while the sales data can remain as columns, as shown in Figure 6-14.

1. Still working on slide 3 select the "Customers" data series if not already selected.

2. Right-click the data series and choose Change Series Chart Type from the shortcut menu. Click the Area category at the left of the dialog box and choose the Area chart type. Click OK.

Figure 6-14
Area and column
combination chart

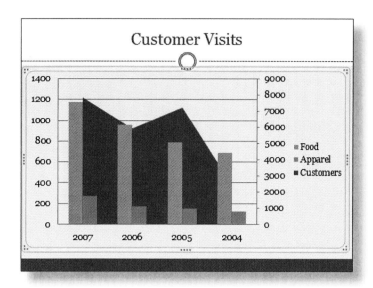

3. Click the "Customers" area to select it then right-click and choose Change Series Chart Type from the shortcut menu. Choose the Line category at the left of the dialog box and click the Line chart type. Click OK.

4. Right-click the red line representing "Customers" and choose Format Data Series from the shortcut menu.

5. Click Line Style option at the left of the dialog box, and change the Width to 3 points.

6. Choose the Line Color option at the left of the dialog box, and change the Color to Red Accent 3, Darker 50%. Click Close.

7. Leave the presentation open for the next exercise.

Exercise 6-13 FORMAT A PRIMARY AND SECONDARY AXIS

Proper formatting and labeling on a chart is always important to ensure that viewers understand the information you want to convey. This is even more important when you have both a primary and secondary axis scale on the chart.

1. On slide 3, click the chart area to select it.

2. From the Chart Tools Layout tab, in the Labels group, click the Axis Titles button and choose the Primary Vertical Axis Title and Rotated Title.

3. In the Axis Title text box located on the primary vertical axis, delete the text and key **Sales (thousands)**. The size of the text box will adjust automatically. Figure 6-15 indicates the position of the text on the chart.

4. From the Chart Tools Layout tab, in the Labels group, click the Axis Titles button 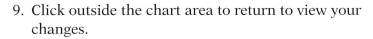 and choose the Secondary Vertical Axis Title and Rotated Title. An Axis Title text box appears beside the secondary axis scale on the left.

5. In the Axis Title text box, delete the text and key **Customer Visits (hundreds)**. Descriptive titles now appear next to both the primary and the secondary axes.

6. Right-click the Vertical (Value) Axis (the Sales numbers on the left) and choose Format Axis. Click Axis Options at the left of the dialog box; then in the Major unit text box, choose Fixed and key **500**. Under Major Tick Mark Type, choose Outside from the list box. This will insert tick marks and numbers on the axis.

7. Click Number at the left of the dialog box. In the Category list box, choose Currency. Change the Decimal places to **0**. Under symbol, choose $ English (U.S.). Click Close.

8. Right-click the Secondary Vertical (Value) Axis (the Customers numbers on the right) and choose Format Axis. Click Axis Options at the left of the dialog box, and change the value in the Major unit text box to Fixed and **1500** to reduce some of the number labels. Click Close.

9. Click outside the chart area to return to view your changes.

10. Click the Legend then right-click and choose Format Legend. For the Legend Position choose Top. Click Close. Now the chart appears more balanced with the scales evenly spaced on each side.

TIP

It is best to avoid using red and green in the same chart to distinguish between data on column and bar charts. Some individuals have difficulty distinguishing between those two colors.

Figure 6-15
Completed combination chart

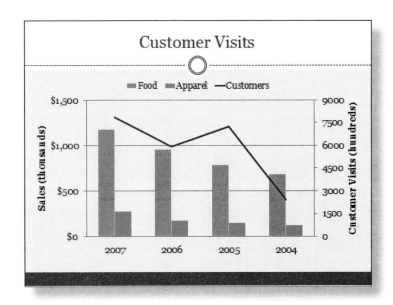

11. Create a slide footer for only slide 3 that includes the date and the text your name, **[6-13your initials]**. Save the presentation as **[6-13your initials]** in your Lesson 6 folder.

12. Print slide 3 only in full size. Leave the presentation open for the next exercise.

Working with Pie Charts

A *pie chart* is a simple, yet highly effective, presentation tool that shows individual values in relation to the sum of all the values—a pie chart makes it easy to judge "parts of a whole." Each value is displayed as a slice of the pie.

A pie chart can show only one data series. To show more than one data series, use more than one pie chart.

Exercise 6-14 CREATE A PIE CHART

In this exercise, you create a pie chart to display the breakdown of the restaurant's sales by category.

If your worksheet contains more than one series, a pie chart uses the first column of numbers. You can change to a different row or column by selecting the series you wish to use.

1. Insert a new slide after slide 3 that uses the Title Only layout. This layout provides a white background.

2. Key the title 2007 Sales Categories.

3. From the Insert tab, in the Illustrations group, click the Chart button.

4. Click the Pie category at the left of the dialog box and choose the first chart type that appears in the pie chart category called Pie. Click OK. Microsoft Excel opens and displays a sample worksheet, and in PowerPoint you will see a sample pie chart reflecting that data.

5. On the worksheet, click the box in the upper-left corner to select all the sample data, and then delete it.

Figure 6-16
Worksheet for Pie chart

	A	B	C
1		2007 Sales	
2	Food	3339	
3	Beverage	2933	
4	Apparel	1529	
5	Other	906	

6. Key the data shown in Figure 6-16.

7. Close the Excel worksheet to view the chart and leave the presentation open for the next exercise.

Exercise 6-15 ADD PIE SLICE LABELS

You can add labels to the chart's data series and edit those labels individually.

1. Click one of the pie slices to select the Chart Series data.

2. From the Chart Tools Layout tab, in the Labels group, click the Data Labels button and click More Data Label Options.

3. Click Label Options at the left of the dialog box and make several changes under the Label Contains heading:

   a. Select both Category name and Percentage.

   b. Deselect Value and Show Leader Lines.

   c. Click Close.

4. Data labels now appear on the pie slices. With the addition of the data labels, the pie is now smaller; however, the legend is no longer needed since the slices are each labeled, as shown in Figure 6-17.

NOTE

Depending on the pie chart, sometimes parts of the data labels might be hidden by the edges of the chart placeholder. In this case, you need to resize the pie by using the plot area sizing handles.

5. Right-click the legend box and choose Delete from the shortcut menu. The pie chart becomes a little larger.

6. Click any data label. All the data labels are selected. Right-click on one of the labels, and use the floating font group to change the font to Arial, 16 points, bold, and italic. Click outside the pie to turn off this selection.

7. Click the data label "Other 10%" twice to select just that label. As with columns, click once to select all labels, and click again to select just one. You can now edit the selected label's text.

8. Click within the text to display an insertion point. Delete the word "Other" (but not "10%"), and key in its place **Take-out**.

9. Click anywhere within the chart to deselect the label that now appears separated from the pie.

10. Click on the "Take-Out 10%" label two times to select just that label. Right-click and choose Format Data Label. Under the Label Position heading, choose Inside End. Click Close. Now the label is positioned on the slice.

11. Because the slide title identifies what the pie contains, the pie chart title for 2007 sales can be removed. Select this text box and press Delete. The pie will expand to fill the available space.

Figure 6-17
Pie chart with data labels

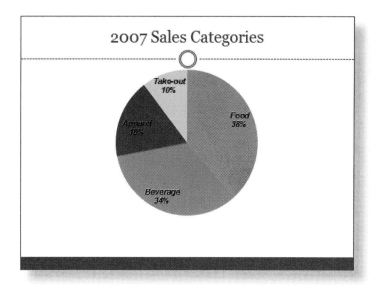

Exercise 6-16 APPLY 3-D ROTATION

You can enhance the appearance of your pie chart with additional effects, such as changing to a 3-D appearance and rotating the angle of the pie or *exploding* a slice (dragging it out from the center of the pie) for emphasis.

1. Click to select the chart. From the Chart Tools Design tab, in the Type group, click the Change Chart Type button , and select Pie in 3-D. The pie now has a perspective treatment. Click OK.

2. From the Chart Tools Layout tab, in the Background group, click the 3-D Rotation button . At the bottom of the Format Chart Area dialog box, click Default Rotation and the pie becomes more dimensional but almost flat.

3. In the Perspective box, key **0.1**°.

4. Under the Rotation heading, change the X degree to **35**° to move the "Take-out" slice to the right. Click Close.

5. Click the center of the pie once to select all the slices. Notice that each slice has selection handles where the slices join.

6. Click the "Take-out" slice so you have handles on that slice only (be careful not to select the label) and drag it slightly away from the center of the pie. This is called *exploding a slice*.

7. The labels for two slices move away from their respective slices. Select just the "Apparel 18%" label, right-click, choose Format Data Label and select the Label Position of Inside End. Click Close.

8. Select just the "Take-out 10%" label and drag it over to fit on top of the exploded slice, as shown in Figure 6-18.

Figure 6-18
Pie chart with
3-D rotation and
exploded slice

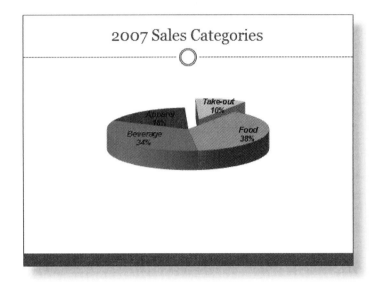

9. In Normal view, select the chart area and use the corner sizing handles to increase its size to make the pie chart larger to fill the slide.

10. Create a slide footer for slide 4 only that includes the date and the text your name, **[6-16your initials]**.

11. Save the presentation as **[6-16your initials]** in your Lesson 6 folder.

12. Print slide 4 only in full slide size. Leave the presentation open for the next exercise.

Enhancing Chart Elements

You can add many interesting effects to charts. In addition to changing colors, you can add shapes or pictures that help you make a particular point or highlight one aspect of the data. You can also annotate your charts with text to clarify or call attention to important concepts.

Exercise 6-17 ADDING SHAPES FOR EMPHASIS

Shapes can be combined with text or layered in some way to emphasize the point you need to make. For this exercise, you will combine an arrow and text.

1. Move to slide 5 ("T-Shirts by Region").

2. Because this chart reflects only one data series, the legend at the side is not needed. Select the legend and press ⌨Delete.

3. Because the slide title identifies the content of this chart, the chart title is redundant; therefore, select the chart title and press ⌨Delete.

4. From the Insert tab, in the Text group, click the Text Box button ; and click and drag above the Miami column to create a space to enter the text, change the font color to white, and key **L.A. may top Miami in 2008.**

5. Select the text inside the text box, right-click, and use the floating font group to change the text to 18-point Arial, bold, italic.

6. From the Insert tab, in the Illustrations group, click the Shapes button ; then from the Block Arrow category, click the Left Arrow shape. Draw an arrow above the Los Angeles chart shape. Change the shape fill color to a gold that coordinates with the theme and remove the shape outline. Reposition and resize the arrow and text box as needed to appear as shown in Figure 6-19.

TIP

You may want to use Zoom to enlarge the slide so you can more easily use the arrow's rotation handle.

Figure 6-19
Chart with arrow and text box

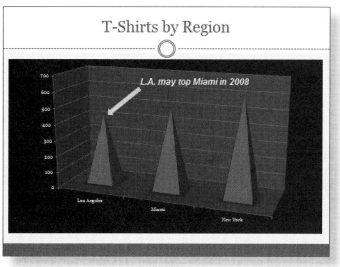

7. Create a slide footer for slide 5 that includes the date and the text your name, **[6-17your initials]**.

8. Save the presentation as **[6-17your initials]** in your Lesson 6 folder.

9. Print slide 5 in full size. If you have a color printer, print it in color. Leave the presentation open for the next exercise.

Exercise 6-18 CHANGE COLORS IN CHART AREAS

You can change the colors of individual chart areas, columns, or an entire data series. Shape fill effects, including textures and gradient fills, can be used the same way you use them for other PowerPoint shapes. You can also change the outline style of columns, bars, and other chart elements.

1. Move to slide 2 and click to select the chart. Point to one of the darkest blue columns, the 2008 series. Notice the ScreenTip that appears, identifying the data series.

2. Click any light blue column, the 2010 series. All the light blue columns are selected, as indicated by the box that is displayed around each selected column.

3. Click the light blue column for Los Angeles. Now the Los Angeles column is the only one selected. Clicking once selects all the columns in a series; clicking a second time (not double-clicking) changes the selection to just one column.

4. Click one of the darkest blue columns to select all of the 2008 series.

5. From the Chart Tools Format tab, in the Shape Styles group, click the Shape Fill button . Click a darker blue.

6. Click the darker blue column for Los Angeles, and then change to Orange, Accent 1. The Los Angeles column is now a different color from the other columns in its series. Click the Undo button 🔄 to return the column to the darker blue to match the other columns in the series.

TIP

You can change colors and fills on each part of the chart. Be sure to select the element that you would like to change before beginning to change colors or gradients, or add a picture.

7. Select the columns that contain the light blue fill color, the 2010 series. Click the Shape Fill button and choose Ice Blue, Accent 5. Click the Shape Fill button 🎨 again and choose Gradient. Under the Light Variations category, select Linear Up so the lightest color is at the top of the column.

Exercise 6-19   ADD A PICTURE FILL BEHIND CHART

A picture can help communicate the meaning of the chart by illustrating the data in some way. For instance, if you are discussing T-shirts as in this exercise, it is appropriate to have a shirt picture in the chart background.

1. Move to slide 5.

2. Change the font color of the text on both axes and in the text box to black to make it easier to read once a picture has been added.

3. With the chart active, from the Chart Tools Layout tab, in the Current Selection group, choose Chart Area from the Chart Elements drop-down list. Click the Format Selection button 🖌.

4. Choose Fill at the left of the dialog box; then choose Picture or texture fill and click File under the Insert from heading.

5. Navigate to your student files and click the file **t-shirt**. Click Insert. Click Close. The picture fills the background of your chart. You need to recolor other parts of the chart so the T-shirt is visible in the background, as shown in Figure 6-20.

6. Click the gray area behind the chart shapes, the Back and Side Walls. Right-click and choose Format Walls. Choose No Fill and click Close.

7. Right-click the Vertical (Value) Axis numbers and change the font to Arial, 18 points, and bold.

8. Right-click the Horizontal (Category) Axis labels and change the font to Arial, 18 points, and bold.

9. Adjust the position of the text box or arrow if necessary.

10. Update the slide footer for slide 5 to include the text **[6-19your initials]**.

Figure 6-20
Chart with picture background

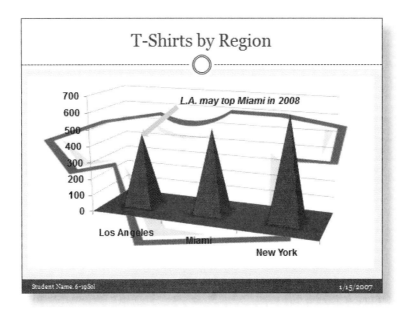

11. View the presentation as a slide show, starting with slide 1.

12. Create a handout header and footer: Include the date and your name as the header, and the page number and text **[6-19your initials]** as the footer.

13. Move to slide 1 and save the presentation as **[6-19your initials]** in your Lesson 6 folder.

14. Preview, and then print, the presentation as handouts, six slides per page, grayscale, landscape, scale to fit paper, and framed. Close the presentation.

6 Summary

- Charts are diagrams that display numbers in pictorial format. Charts illustrate quantitative relationships and can help people understand the significance of numeric information more easily than viewing the same information as a list of numbers.

- When you start a new chart, a sample worksheet appears in Microsoft Excel. A worksheet is where you key the numbers and labels used to create a chart.

- The worksheet contains rows and columns. You key each number or label in a separate *cell*—the rectangle formed by the intersection of a row and a column.

- On the worksheet, key labels are in the first row and column.

- A data series is a group of data that relates to a common object or category. Often, more than one data series is displayed on a single chart.

- Use the Switch Row/Column button ▣ to change how a data series is displayed on a chart.

- A wide variety of chart types are available including column, bar, area, line, pie, and surface with many different chart format options.

- Several Content Layouts are suitable for charts. Two Content Layouts also make it easy to combine a chart and body text on the same slide.

- Use the Chart Elements drop-down list to select specific parts of a chart or you can use ScreenTips to identify parts as you point to them.

- Special fill and border effects, including textures and gradient fills, can be used in charts the same way you use them for other PowerPoint objects.

- Use the Format Axis dialog box to modify the units, font, and number format of the value axis or secondary value axis. Modify the unit settings to specify the range of numbers displayed and increments between numbers.

- Axis titles are an important part of charts. Careful labeling ensures that your charts will be interpreted correctly.

- A legend is a box showing the colors assigned to each data series. Customize a chart's legend by changing the border, background colors, and font attributes.

- Use a secondary axis when you need to plot two dissimilar types of data on the same chart. A secondary axis is available only for a 2-D chart type.

- Proper formatting and labeling on a chart is important when your chart has both a primary and secondary axis.

- A good way to distinguish between different data types on a single chart is to assign different chart types. For example, use columns for one type of data and lines for the other type.

- A pie chart shows individual values in relation to the sum of all the values. Each value is displayed as a slice of the pie.

- A pie chart can show only one data series. To show more than one data series, use more than one pie chart.

- The plot area of a chart is the area containing the actual columns, bars, or pie slices. It can be formatted with or without a border and a fill effect.
- Exploding a pie slice (dragging it out from the center of the pie) emphasizes the slice.
- Use the Insert tab to add shapes and text boxes. Use text boxes wherever annotation is needed to clarify the chart's meaning.
- Charts can be enhanced by adding pictures, colors, and 3-D effects.

LESSON 6		Command Summary	
Feature	**Button**	**Task Path**	**Keyboard**
Insert a chart		Insert, Illustrations group, Chart	
Display worksheet		Chart Tools Design, Data group, Edit Data	
Insert axis titles		Chart Tools Layout, Labels group, Axis Titles	
Insert or remove a legend		Chart Tools Layout, Labels group, Legend	
Switch data series between columns and rows		Chart Tools Design, Data group, Switch Row/Column	
Format a chart object		Chart Tools Format, Current Selection group, Format Selection	Ctrl + 1
Change the chart type		Chart Tools Design, Type group, Change Chart Type	
Add a secondary axis		Chart Tools Format, Current Selection group, Format Selection (with Data series selected)	
Add data labels		Chart Tools Layout, Labels group, Data Labels	
Change chart style		Chart Tools Design, Chart Styles group, Chart Layout	
Apply different chart layouts		Chart Tools Design, Chart Layouts group, More	
Add/Remove gridlines		Chart Tools Layout, Axes group, Gridlines	

Concepts Review

True/False Questions

Each of the following statements is either true or false. Select your choice by indicating T or F.

T (F) 1. PowerPoint offers only one slide layout choice for slides with charts.

T (F) 2. The sample worksheet in Microsoft Excel is always blank when you create a new chart.

T (F) 3. You cannot see the chart while you are working on the worksheet.

(T) F 4. You can change the colors of columns in a chart to whatever you find appealing.

T (F) 5. The units shown on the value axis are set by PowerPoint and cannot be changed.

T (F) 6. Every chart must include a legend.

(T) F 7. You must use a two-dimensional chart if you want to include a secondary axis.

T (F) 8. Double-clicking a pie slice or column enables you to change its size.

Short Answer Questions

Write the correct answer in the space provided.

1. How can you delete all of the sample data in the worksheet at one time?

   Top left excel cell to select all then delete

2. How do you change the grouping of the data series on a chart from columns to rows?

   Switch row/column in data group

3. While working on a chart, how do you display the worksheet if it is not visible?

   Edit data in chart tools design

4. What type of number formatting do you apply to values to display dollar signs?

   Currency

5. What group found on the Chart Tools Format tab can you use to select different parts of a chart?

   current selection group

6. Which button can you click to change the color of a selected pie slice?

shape fill in styles group

7. How can you change the font size for chart labels without opening a dialog box or using the Ribbon?

right click on label & it comes up

8. On a 2-D column chart, how can you change one of the data series to be displayed as an area chart?

select click 1 time on series then right click to change series chart type

Critical Thinking

Answer these questions on a separate page. There are no right or wrong answers. Support your answers with examples from your own experience, if possible.

1. How do you decide if a chart is needed in your presentation? Do you think a presentation can have too many charts? Explain your answer.

2. Imagine that you are trying to explain to someone how you spend your waking hours during a typical day. Can you think of a chart that would break down your activities into different categories and show how much time you spend on each during the day? Describe the chart's appearance and the values that you would include.

Skills Review

Exercise 6-20

Insert a column chart.

1. Open the file **FinSum1**.
2. Create a chart by following these steps:
   a. Insert a new slide after slide 2 that uses the Title and Content layout.
   b. Key **2007 Quarterly Earnings** for the title.
   c. Click the Insert Chart icon in the center of the content placeholder.
   d. Choose a 3-D Clustered Column chart and click OK.
   e. In Microsoft Excel, click the upper-left box on the worksheet to select all the existing data and press Delete .
   f. Key the data shown in Figure 6-21.

Figure 6-21
Worksheet

	A	B	C	D	E	F
1		Q1	Q2	Q3	Q4	
2	New York	1888	2008	2116	1543	
3	Los Angeles	1743	1799	1844	1539	
4	Miami	1634	1439	1783	1469	
5						

3. Click in any cell of row 5 that was used in the sample worksheet. Right-click and then choose Delete from the shortcut menu. Choose Entire Row; then click OK. This step removes the unused row and the empty space on the chart.

4. Close Microsoft Excel.

5. Click the chart once in Normal view to select it; then use the chart's corner sizing handles to reduce the chart's height by approximately 0.5 inches and adjust the chart's position for even spacing on the slide.

6. Edit the chart by following these steps:

   a. Be sure the chart is selected; then from the Chart Tools Design tab, in the Data Group, click Edit Data 📊.

   b. Click cell E3 (Q4 for Los Angeles) to select it.

   c. Key 1849 to replace the value "1539." Press Enter.

   d. Still working on the Chart Tools Design tab, in the Data group, click the Select Data button 📊. In the Select Data Source dialog box, click the red arrow at the end of the Chart Data Range box.

   e. Click in Cell A1 and drag the pointer through E4 (the end of the data).

   f. Click the red arrow again, and click OK.

   g. Still working on the Chart Tools Design tab, in the Data group, click the Switch Row/Column button 📊.

   h. Close Microsoft Excel.

7. Create a handout header and footer: Include the date and your name as the header, and the page number and text **[6-20your initials]** as the footer.

8. Move to slide 1 and save the presentation as **[6-20your initials]** in your Lesson 6 folder.

9. View the presentation as a slide show; then preview and print it as handouts, three slides per page, grayscale, framed. Close the presentation.

Exercise 6-21

Edit and format an existing chart, change chart style, format the legend.

1. Open the file **Finance2**.

2. Edit the chart on slide 4 by following these steps:

   a. Click the chart to activate it.

   b. From the Chart Tools Design tab, in the Data group, click the Edit Data button 📊 to open Microsoft Excel.

    c. On the worksheet, click cell B3 containing the value "−2%" and key 2 to overwrite the negative value with a positive value. Press Enter.

    d. Close Microsoft Excel.

3. Change the style of the chart by following these steps:

    a. From the Chart Tools Design tab, in the Chart Styles group, choose the More button ⬇.

    b. Choose Style 25.

4. Change the font for the Horizontal (Category) Axis labels by following these steps:

    a. Click the category axis label "2007" to select the category axis.

    b. Right-click on the axis and make the following changes from the floating font group: Choose the Tahoma font, a 20 point font size, and the Brown, Background 2 font color.

5. Format the Vertical (Value) Axis by following these steps:

    a. Right-click a number on the value axis and choose Format Axis.

    b. For Major unit choose Fixed and key .05. Click Close.

    c. Right-click on the axis and make the following changes from the floating font group: Choose the Tahoma font, a 20 point font size, and the Brown, Background 2 font color.

6. Format the legend by following these steps:

    a. Right-click the legend and choose Format Legend from the shortcut menu.

    b. Under the Legend Position heading, choose Top Right and click Close.

    c. Use the floating font group to change the legend font to Tahoma at a 16 point font size.

7. Create a handout header and footer: Include the date and your name as the header, and the page number and text **[6-21your initials]** as the footer.

8. Move to slide 1 and save the presentation as **[6-21your initials]** in your Lesson 6 folder.

9. View the presentation as a slide show; then preview and print the presentation as handouts, four slides per page, grayscale, landscape, framed. Close the presentation.

Exercise 6-22

Add a chart, format chart axes, add a secondary axis, and combine chart types.

1. Open the file **Finance3**.

2. Add a slide after slide 3 with the Title and Content Layout.

3. Key the title 2007 Special Events Revenue.

4. Click the Insert Chart button 📊 in the content placeholder. In the Column category, choose the Clustered Column chart. Delete the sample data and key the information in Figure 6-22. So that you can see all of the words entered into each cell of the worksheet in Microsoft Excel,

select the cells in the worksheet; then from the Home tab, in the Cells group, click Format then choose AutoFit Column Width.

Figure 6-22
Worksheet

	A	B	C	D	E	F
1		1st Quarter	2nd Quarter	3rd Quarter	4th Quarter	
2	Special Events	71	141	118	149	
3	Total Revenue	800	1076	1149	1207	
4						

5. Once the data is keyed, click on the row 4 heading and drag down to select both rows 4 and 5. Right-click and choose Delete.

TIP

You started with a 2-D chart in this exercise since a 2-D chart is required to add a secondary axis.

6. In Microsoft PowerPoint, from the Chart Tools Design tab, in the Data group, click the Select Data button. In the Select Data Source dialog box, in the Chart data range box, change the D to an E and click OK.

7. From the Chart Tools Design tab, in the Data group, click the Switch Row/Column button.

8. Close Microsoft Excel.

9. Add a secondary axis to the chart by following these steps:

   a. Right-click one of the "Total Revenue" columns and choose Format Data series from the shortcut menu.

   b. In the Plot Series On area, click Secondary axis. Click Close.

10. Change the chart type for the "Total Revenue" columns by following these steps:

    a. Be sure the columns in this data series are still selected.

    b. From the Chart Tools Design tab, in the Type group, click Change Chart Type button.

    c. In the Line category, choose the Line chart.

    d. Click OK.

11. Change the formatting of the line for the data series by following these steps:

    a. Select the line (being careful not to select the gridlines) then right-click and choose Format Data Series from the shortcut menu.

    b. Click Line Style at the left of the dialog box and change the Width to **8 points.**

    c. Click Marker Options at the left of the dialog box and change the Marker Type to Built-In and the size to **15.**

    d. Click Marker Fill at the left of the dialog box and change to a Solid Fill then make the color Tan, Text 2. Click Close.

12. Format the secondary value axis by following these steps:

    a. Right-click one of the numbers on the right side of the chart (on the Secondary Vertical (Value) Axis) and choose Format Axis.

    b. Change the Major unit to Fixed and key **500.**

    c. Click Number at the left of the dialog box and choose Currency. For Decimal places key **0** and for Symbol choose $ English (United States). Click Close.

  d. Right-click the secondary axis again and use the floating font group to change the font to Arial.

13. Apply the following formatting to the Vertical (Value) Axis (on the left side of the chart) using the same process as for the secondary axis.

  a. Right-click the Vertical (Value) Axis and choose Format Axis.

  b. Change the Maximum to Fixed and **250** and the Major unit to Fixed and **50**.

  c. Click Number at the left of the dialog box and choose Currency. For Decimal places key **0** and for Symbol choose $ English (United States). Click Close.

  d. Right-click the vertical axis again and use the floating font group to change the font to Arial.

14. Change the formatting of the Horizontal (Category) Axis. Right-click the category axis and change the font to Arial using the floating font group.

15. Add chart titles and a legend by following these steps:

  a. Click to activate the chart.

  b. From the Chart Tools Layout tab, in the Labels group, click the Axis Titles button 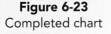.

  c. Choose Primary Vertical Axis Title and Rotated Title.

  d. Select the text that appears in the text box; delete it, and key **Special Events (thousands)**.

  e. Still working on the Chart Tools Layout tab, in the Labels group, click the Axis Titles button.

  f. Choose Secondary Vertical Axis Title and Rotated Title.

  g. Select the text that appears in the text box; delete it, and key **Total Revenue (thousands)**.

16. Right-click the legend and choose Format Legend from the shortcut menu and change the legend position to Top. Click Close.

17. Reposition the chart, so it is centered horizontally on the slide, as shown in Figure 6-23.

Figure 6-23
Completed chart

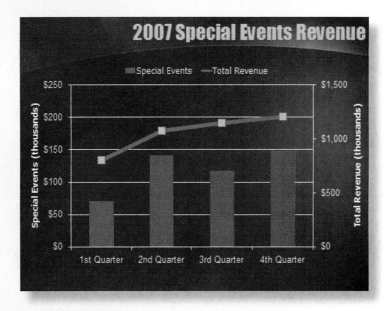

18. Create a handout header and footer: Include the date and your name as the header, and the page number and text **[6-22your initials]** as the footer.

19. Move to slide 1 and save the presentation as **[6-22your initials]** in your Lesson 6 folder.

20. View the presentation as a slide show; then preview and print the presentation as handouts, four slides per page, grayscale, landscape, framed. Close the presentation.

Exercise 6-23

Create and format a pie chart; add shapes, text boxes, and color.

1. Open the file **Apparel2**.

2. Insert a new slide after slide 2 that uses the Title and Content layout. Key the title **Apparel Mix— 2007**.

3. Create a pie chart by following these steps:

    a. Click the Insert Chart button 🔳 in the center of the content placeholder.

    b. Click the Pie category and choose the Pie in 3-D chart type. Click OK.

    c. On the worksheet, clear the sample information and key the information shown in Figure 6-24.

TIP

To use an em dash (the long straight line), key two hyphens with no space around them. Then space once after 2007 and the two hyphens will change to an em dash, a more contemporary punctuation mark. This adjustment is controlled with PowerPoint's AutoCorrect feature.

Figure 6-24
Worksheet

	A	B	C
1		Unit Sales	
2	T-Shirts	4208	
3	Bike Jerseys	1112	
4	Visors	528	
5	Knee Pads	663	
6	Elbow Pads	967	
7			

4. The sample data that you earlier deleted established a range of cells for the chart. However, not all of the current data is displayed in that range. Notice on the pie chart that no slice for Elbow Pads is included even though it is keyed on the worksheet.

5. From the Chart Tools Design tab, click Select Data. On the worksheet, notice that row 6 has not been included in the selection. Highlight all the cells for the data you entered (A1 through B6) then click OK. Now all of the items have a slice.

6. Close Microsoft Excel.

7. Format a pie slice by following these steps:

    a. Click the dark blue pie slice "T-shirts" once to select the entire pie.

    b. Click the dark blue slice again to select the individual slice.

    c. From the Chart Tools Format tab, in the Shape Styles group, click the Shape Fill button 🔳 and choose Light Blue from the Standard Colors category. This sets the color apart from the other blues.

    d. Click these slices and change to the following standard colors: Bike Jerseys, light green; Visors, yellow; Knee Pads, red; and Elbow Pads, purple.

8. Right-click the pie's legend and choose Delete from the shortcut menu.

9. Add data labels by following these steps:

   a. Activate the chart.

   b. From the Chart Tools Layout tab, in the Labels group, click the Data Labels button 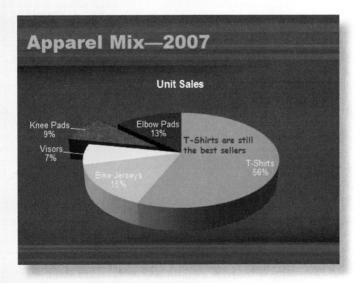 and choose More Data Label Options.

   c. In the Label Contains area, select the Category name and the Percentage check boxes and deselect the Value check box.

   d. In the Label Position area, choose Best Fit.

   e. Click Close.

10. Explode a pie slice by following these steps:

    a. Select the red "Knee Pads" slice by clicking it twice.

    b. Drag the slice slightly away from the center of the pie. The pie chart will become slightly smaller because of the additional space this requires. Therefore, increase the chart area slightly to compensate for this change.

    c. Center the chart area horizontally on the slide.

11. Insert a text box by following these steps:

    a. From the Insert tab, in the Text group, click the Text Box button.

    b. Click outside the chart area; draw the text box and key **T-Shirts are still the best sellers**.

    c. Move the text box on top of the large light blue T-shirt pie slice. Change the text box font to 18-point Comic Sans MS, bold, Dark Blue, Accent 1. Resize the box so the text fits on two lines as shown in Figure 6-25.

Figure 6-25
Exploded slice and text box

12. Create a handout header and footer: Include the date and your name as the header, and the page number and text **[6-23your initials]** as the footer.

13. Move to slide 1 and save the presentation as **[6-23your initials]** in your Lesson 6 folder.

14. View the presentation as a slide show; then preview and print the presentation as handouts, four slides per page, grayscale, framed. Close the presentation.

Lesson Applications

Exercise 6-24

Create a presentation containing a column chart and format the chart.

1. Start a new presentation using the Median design theme and the Aspect theme color.

2. Using the text in Figure 6-26, create a three-slide presentation; use the Title Slide layout for slide 1, and the Title and Content layout for slides 2 and 3. The first line of each is the title for the slide.

Figure 6-26

Slide 1 | Three Years of Phenomenal Sales

Slide 2 |
Highlights
- New York revenue still increasing
- Miami and Los Angeles meeting goals
- Revenues reach 120% of budget

Slide 3 | Sales by Region–2005 to 2007

3. Right-align the title on slide 1.

4. On slide 3, create a 3-D Clustered Column chart by using the data shown in Figure 6-27. Delete row 5.

Figure 6-27
Worksheet

	A	B	C	D	E
1		New York	Los Angeles	Miami	
2	2005	5650	4183	3843	
3	2006	8753	5892	6388	
4	2007	11332	9852	8487	
5					

5. Close Microsoft Excel.

6. Change the Vertical (Value) Axis options to have a Maximum of **12000** and a Major unit of **3000**. Change its Number formatting to $ English (U.S.) with no decimals.

7. Change to Chart Style 3.

8. For the value and category axes and legend, change the font to 16 points, not bold.

9. Move the legend to the bottom. Resize, if necessary.

10. Reposition the chart to keep spacing on both sides even. Resize if needed.

11. Create a handout header and footer: Include the date and your name as the header, and the page number and text **[6-24your initials]** as the footer.

12. Move to slide 1 and save the presentation as **[6-24your initials]** in your Lesson 6 folder.

13. View the presentation as a slide show; then preview and print it as handouts, three slides per page, grayscale, framed. Close the presentation.

Exercise 6-25

Create and format a pie chart.

1. Open the file **Expense2**.

2. Insert a new slide after slide 1 that uses the Title and Content layout. Key the title Expense Breakdown.

3. Create a 2-D pie chart on the new slide 2 by using the data from Figure 6-28.

Figure 6-28
Worksheet

	A	B
1		2007 Expenses
2	Food	2190
3	Payroll	1813
4	Depreciation	577
5	Lease	1737
6		

4. Add Percentage data labels only to the chart. Make them bold and change the font size to 32 points.

5. Increase the legend font to 20 points, bold.

6. Change the chart title size to 28 points, bold and move it to the top left of the chart area.

7. Change the chart to a Pie in 3-D.

8. Explode the "Food" slice of the pie slightly.

9. If any of the percentage labels move off the slices, then right-click, choose Format Data Label, and choose the Label Position Inside End or click and drag them onto the slices of the pie.

10. Create a handout header and footer: Include the date and your name as the header, and the page number and text **[6-25your initials]** as the footer.

11. Move to slide 1 and save the presentation as **[6-25your initials]** in your Lesson 6 folder.

12. View the presentation as a slide show; then preview and print it as handouts, six slides per page, grayscale, scaled for paper, framed. Close the presentation.

Exercise 6-26

Insert a chart; change the chart to a combination chart; format the chart text, data series, and legend; add a secondary axis; and add a shape.

1. Open the file **Earnings2** and apply the Oriel design theme using the Concourse theme color.

2. Resize and reposition the title on slide 1 so that it is right above the subtitle.

3. Insert a new slide between slides 2 and 3 that uses the Title and Content layout. Key the title Gross Income.

4. Create a clustered column chart on the new slide by using the data in Figure 6-29.

Figure 6-29

	A	B	C	D	E
1		2005	2006	2007	
2	San Francisco	1246	2033	5432	
3	Miami	2734	4630	6325	
4	Los Angeles	2871	4126	7235	
5	New York	3566	5135	7555	
6	Year Total	10417	15924	26547	
7					

5. Select all of the rows and columns in the worksheet so that all data is included in the chart.

6. Switch Row/Column.

7. Close Microsoft Excel.

8. Be sure you are using a 2-D column chart.

9. Plot the "Year Total" data series on a secondary axis. Change the chart type for the series to Line Chart. Format the line in a matching color and change the width to 10.

10. Change the font for the Vertical (Value) Axis, Horizontal (Category) Axis, the Secondary Vertical (Value) Axis, and Legend to 16-point Arial (not bold).

11. For the Vertical (Value) Axis (on the left), change the units to minimum 0 and maximum to 8,000 displayed Fixed at major units of 2,000 and change the Number formatting to Currency with no decimal places.

12. Format the Secondary Vertical (Value) Axis (on the right) with the units to minimum 0 and maximum to 30,000 displayed Fixed at major units of 5,000 and change the Number formatting to Currency with no decimal places.

13. Move the legend to the bottom of the chart.

14. Expand the width and height of the chart area.

15. Expand the width of the legend so all parts of the legend fit on one line. Apply a light blue fill to the legend area to distinguish it from the slide background.

16. Apply a gradient fill to the columns in each data series. After the first data series has been changed, you will need to reset the fill color for each series selected and then apply the gradient coloring. Choose Linear Up in the Dark Variations category so the lightest color is on top.

17. Click outside the chart area to deselect the chart.

18. Now work in the area at the top of the chart to create these graphic elements and then move them into position when complete. You might want to use Zoom to increase the size of the slide so you can work better in detail.

    a. Create a text box centered above the chart. Key **Impressive!** in the text box. Change the font to 24-point Arial.

    b. Draw a small, 5-Point Star with a yellow fill and red outline.

    c. Place the star on the top of the New York column for the year 2007.

    d. Place the text box above the columns near the star, as shown in Figure 6-30.

Figure 6-30
Completed chart

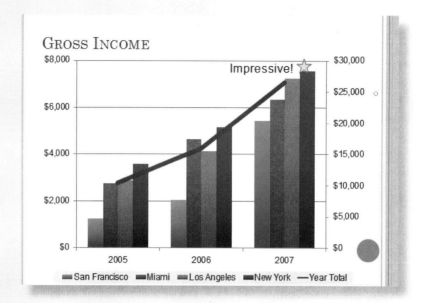

GROSS INCOME

19. Create a handout header and footer: Include the date and your name as the header, and the page number and text **[6-26your initials]** as the footer.

20. Move to slide 1 and save the presentation as **[6-26your initials]**.

21. View the presentation as a slide show; then preview and print slide 3 in grayscale.

22. Close the presentation.

Exercise 6-27 ◆ Challenge Yourself

Insert a chart; change the chart style; apply gridlines; format the chart text, data series, and legend; add a picture fill to a chart; and add a shape.

1. Open the file **Suppliers**.

2. On slide 1, key Your Name as the subtitle.

3. Insert a new slide after slide 2 that uses the Title and Content layout. For the slide title, key **Produce Cost Comparison**.

4. Create a 3-D Clustered Column chart on the new slide by using the data in Figure 6-31. On your worksheet in Microsoft Excel, select all of the cells for the chart, then from the Home tab, in the Cells group, click Format and choose AutoFit Column Width so all text is visible in the cells.

Figure 6-31
Worksheet

	A	B	C	D	E
1		Frankie's Food	Distributing by Dano	Patty's Produce	
2	Apples (20 lb)	10.99	11.84	9.85	
3	Lettuce (24 ct)	27.45	29.75	25.29	
4	Cucumbers (bushel)	19.8	20.25	19.45	
5	Tomatoes (case)	9.55	10.85	9.12	
6					
7					

5. Change the chart style to Style 7.

6. Change the Floor color to the orange that matches the slide design.

7. Select the legend and change to a Top position.

8. Deselect the chart. Draw a rectangle shape over "Patty's Produce" in the legend area then change the Fill color to None and the outline to Orange.

9. Add a text box on the right and key **Lowest Costs**. Change the Fill color to Orange and the text color to Dark red and font size to 18 points.

10. Add an arrow from the text box pointing to "Patty's Produce." Change the Fill color and the Outline color to Orange, as shown in Figure 6-32.

Figure 6-32
Completed chart

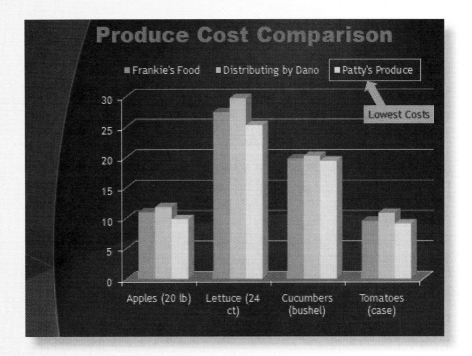

11. Insert a new slide after slide 3 using the Title and Content layout. For the slide title, key **Lead Time Comparison**.

12. Insert a Line with Markers chart and enter the data below in Figure 6-33 into the chart. Delete columns C and D and row 5.

13. Select the data from A1 through B4 so that the chart appears correctly.

Figure 6-33
Worksheet

	A	B
1		Days from Order to Delivery
2	Frankie's Food	7
3	Distributing by Dano	10
4	Patty's Produce	4
5		

14. Remove the legend. If the chart title did not automatically appear, title the chart **Days from Order to Delivery.**

15. Increase the width of the line to 8 points and make it Dark red, Accent 2. Change the Marker Options to Built-in and increase the marker size to 28 points and make it Orange.

16. Reposition the chart to fit evenly on the dark area of the slide.

17. Draw a green, 5-pointed star and place it in front of the supplier's name with the lowest lead time.

18. Change the font color of the Value and Category Axes and the chart title to Dark red, Accent 2.

19. Insert the picture **Apple** from your data files into the background of the chart.

20. Change the gridline color to orange, as shown in Figure 6-34.

Figure 6-34
Completed chart

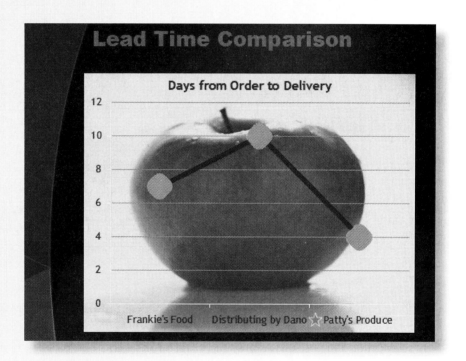

21. Create a handout header and footer: Include the date and your name as the header, and the page number and the text **[6-27your initials]** as the footer.

22. Move to slide 1 and save the presentation as **[6-27your initials]**.

23. View the presentation as a slide show; then preview and print it as handouts, four slides per page, grayscale, landscape, framed. Close the presentation.

On Your Own

In these exercises you work on your own, as you would in a real-life work environment. Use the skills you've learned to accomplish the task—and be creative.

Exercise 6-28

Obtain a list of stock quotes either online or from the *Wall Street Journal*. Create a chart listing at least five of your stock picks. Compare the prices of each stock visually through a chart. Create another chart showing the percentage change in stock value since closing the day before compared with the other stocks you have chosen. In addition, create a separate slide for each stock, giving details about the company. Format the presentation in a way that will hold a viewer's attention. Save your presentation as **[6-28your initials]**. Preview, and then print the presentation as handouts.

Exercise 6-29

Make a list of your activities during a typical weekday, including the actual time you spend on each activity. Group your activities into no more than eight categories. Make sure the times add up to 24 hours. Add a second set of times listing the amount of time you should be spending on each activity, and a third set of times listing the amount of time you would prefer to spend. (Don't be too serious about the times—make it fun.) Create a column or bar chart to represent these times, and then add three pie chart slides, one for each set of times (actual, should, prefer). Add a title slide and a conclusion slide. Use your creativity to make the charts interesting and fun to view including colors, pictures, shapes, and 3-D rotation. Save the presentation as **[6-29your initials]**. Preview, and then print the presentation as handouts.

Exercise 6-30

Research the information about your state of residence from the current census and other online resources. Prepare slides to explain the facts that you find using bulleted lists and charts. Find some statistics about diversity within your state, home ownership in your state compared to the national average, types of businesses, etc., and create at least two charts to display the statistics. Add a title slide and a conclusion slide. Format your presentation attractively, save it as **[6-30your initials]**, and then print handouts.

Lesson 7

Creating Diagrams with SmartArt Graphics

OBJECTIVES

After completing this lesson, you will be able to:

1. Choose SmartArt graphics.

2. Enhance diagrams.

3. Prepare an organization chart.

4. Create other diagrams with SmartArt.

5. Change diagram types and orientation.

Estimated Time: 1¹/₂ hours

Using diagrams is a very important way to illustrate presentation content. *Diagrams* provide a visual representation of information that can help an audience understand a presenter's message. For example, diagrams can be used to show the steps of a process or the relationship between managers and subordinates. An audience can see the process or relationship because it is portrayed with graphic shapes and connecting lines or layered in some way to show these sequences and relationships. In this lesson you will create diagrams using SmartArt, a new feature of PowerPoint that contains a wide range of predesigned diagrams that can be customized in many different ways.

Choosing SmartArt Graphics

A *SmartArt graphic* is a diagram that can be inserted on your slide and then the parts of the diagram can be filled in with identifying text. Or if you have text in a bulleted list or in text shapes, the text items can be converted to a SmartArt diagram. You will use both of these techniques in this lesson.

From the Insert tab, in the Illustration group, click the SmartArt button to see the Choose a SmartArt Graphic dialog box shown in Figure 7-1. You can display thumbnails of all possible diagrams, or you can click one of the seven categories to look at them by diagram type. On the right side of this dialog box, the diagram is displayed in a larger size with a definition below to help you decide if this is the right type of illustration for your communication needs. The white lines that you see on the sample diagram represent where your text will appear when you label each part of the diagram.

Figure 7-1
Choose a SmartArt
Graphic dialog box

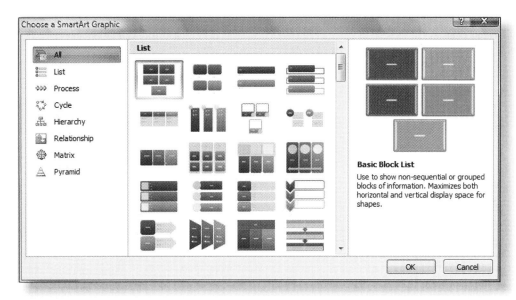

Exercise 7-1 USE DIAGRAMS FOR COMMUNICATION PURPOSES

Preparing a few bulleted lists is a simple way to create a series of slides for a presentation. However, a presentation including only bulleted lists is not very appealing to an audience from a visual standpoint and may not be the best way to communicate the meaning of your message an audience needs to understand.

NOTE

Search for SmartArt descriptions in PowerPoint's Help to find a comprehensive list of all SmartArt graphics organized by category. Each graphic is displayed with descriptions of the layout and tips for situations where each would be appropriate.

As you develop your presentation content, you should be considering your message from the viewpoint of the audience and not just thinking about what you need to say. To help your audience visualize these concepts and remember them, plan alternative ways to illustrate concepts, such as including pictures, charts, and shapes, to draw attention to key points. Also, you can choose from an extensive array of SmartArt graphics. These graphics are diagrams that are arranged in seven categories, as listed in Table 7-1.

TABLE 7-1 SmartArt Graphics Diagram Types

Diagram Type	Purpose
List	Provides an alternative to listing text in bulleted lists. List diagrams can show groupings, labeled parts, and even directional concepts through how the shapes are stacked. Several diagrams show main categories and then subtopics within those categories.

continues

TABLE 7-1 SmartArt Graphics Diagram Types *continued*

Diagram Type	Purpose
Process	Shows a sequence of events or the progression of workflow such as in a flowchart. These diagrams show connected parts of a process or even converging processes using a funnel technique. Several diagrams with arrows can portray conflict or opposing viewpoints.
Cycle	Represents a continuous series of events such as an ongoing manufacturing or employee review process. A cycle can be arranged in a circular pattern or with slices or gears to reflect interconnected parts. A radial cycle begins with a central part and then other parts extend from the center.
Hierarchy	Illustrates reporting relationships or lines of authority between employees in a company such as in an organization chart. These connections are sometimes called parent-child relationships. Hierarchy diagrams can be arranged vertically or horizontally such as in a decision tree used to show the outgrowth of options after particular choices are made.
Relationship	Shows interconnected, hierarchical, proportional, or overlapping relationships. Some of these diagrams also appear in different categories.
Matrix	Allows placement of concepts along two axes or in related quadrants. Emphasis can be on the whole or on individual parts.
Pyramid	Shows interconnected or proportional relationships building from one direction such as a foundational concept on which other concepts are built.

Exercise 7-2 USE LISTS TO SHOW GROUPS OF INFORMATION

In this exercise you will create a List diagram in two different ways:

- Start with a blank slide and key SmartArt content using a Text pane.
- Start with existing bulleted text and convert to SmartArt.

NOTE

If you added a fourth bulleted item, the shapes on the slide would become a little smaller so all shapes could be displayed.

1. Open the file **Organize**.

2. Move to slide 1. From the Home tab, in the Slides group, click the New Slide button 🖼 to insert a new slide using the Title and Content layout. On the content placeholder, click the SmartArt button 🖾 .

3. Click the List category. Click the Vertical Box List thumbnail then click OK.

4. From the SmartArt Tools Design tab, in the Create Graphic group, click the Text pane button 🔲 . A text box will appear on the left, as shown in Figure 7-2, where you can key the text after each bullet for each of the shapes in this diagram.

Figure 7-2
Entering SmartArt
text

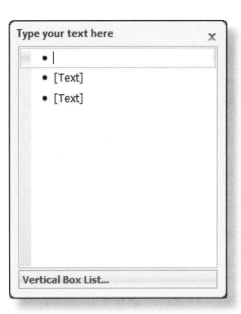

5. For the first item, key **New Procedure**.

6. Click after the second bullet and key **New Philosophy**; click after the third bullet and key **New Department**. Notice that the text you keyed as bulleted items now appears on the shapes.

7. Close the Text pane.

8. For the slide title, key **Organizational Changes** as shown in Figure 7-3. This type of list diagram will work best when you have limited information for first-level bulleted points and no subpoints in a list.

Figure 7-3
Vertical Box List
diagram

NOTE

If you already have bulleted text on a slide, then that text can be converted to a SmartArt diagram. In the following steps, you will show both the first-level and second-level text shown on slide 3.

9. In the Slides and Outline pane, click slide 3 and press Ctrl+D to duplicate the slide. Once your diagram is prepared on slide 3 and you have confirmed that all the text is appropriately displayed, you can delete slide 4 with the bulleted list. But for now, it is a good idea to leave one slide as originally prepared so it is available for comparison.

10. Now highlight all of the bulleted text on slide 3.

11. From the Home tab, in the Paragraph group, click the Convert to SmartArt Graphic button .

12. Click More SmartArt Graphics to access all categories and click the List category.

13. Click the Horizontal Bullet List thumbnail then click OK.

14. The first-level bulleted items appear in the top rectangles and the second-level bulleted items appear in the bottom rectangles with bullets. The color treatment of the first-level words is more dominant than what appears for the subpoints, as shown in Figure 7-4.

Figure 7-4
Horizontal Bullet List diagram

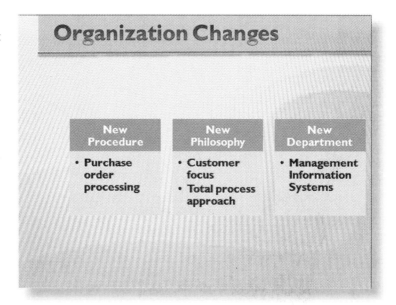

15. Now confirm that all the same text is included in the diagram on slide 3 that is in the duplicated slide 4 bulleted list.

16. When you are sure that everything matches, delete slide 4.

17. Create a new folder for Lesson 7. Create a handout header and footer. Include the date and your name as the header, and the page number and the text **[7-2your initials]** as the footer. Save the presentation as **[7-2your initials]** in your new Lesson 7 folder. Leave the presentation open for the next exercise.

Exercise 7-3   USE PROCESS DIAGRAMS TO SHOW SEQUENTIAL WORKFLOW STEPS

A *process diagram* reflects concepts or events that occur sequentially. Generally speaking, one part must be finished before the next part begins. Many variations for how these processes can be portrayed are available through SmartArt.

1. Move to slide 3. From the Home tab, in the Slides group, click the New Slide button 🖻.

2. On the slide 4 content area, click the SmartArt button 🖼 then choose the Process category.

3. Examine the different options in this category and then click the Basic Process thumbnail and click OK. A three-part diagram appears as shown in Figure 7-5. You can enter text directly in the placeholders on each diagram shape, or you can click the Text pane button ⋮ on the left to open enter text.

4. For this exercise, key directly in each of the shapes. As you key, the text will automatically word-wrap in the shape and become smaller to fit within that shape. Therefore, you need to be careful when using this method to keep the words you enter very concise.

5. Click in the first rectangle shape and key **Survey customer needs**.

6. Click in the second rectangle shape and key **Analyze survey results**.

7. Click in the third rectangle shape and key **Develop product plan**.

Figure 7-5
Basic Process
diagram

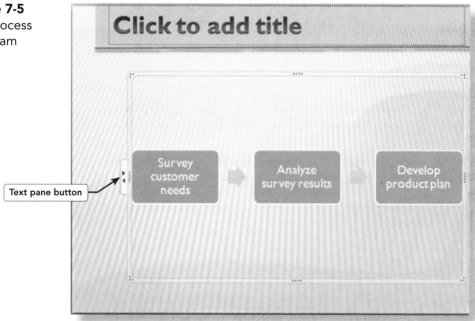

8. Because you need to include a fourth step in this process, you need to increase the size of the SmartArt area. Point to the top left corner of the SmartArt border and drag it close to the left edge of the slide.

9. Select the third shape in the diagram then click the Text pane button ⋮ to open the bulleted text dialog shape. Notice that this text is highlighted in the bulleted text dialog shape.

NOTE

When creating diagrams like this, be careful that your text does not become too small for easy reading. Later in this lesson you will make the text larger on this slide.

10. Click at the end of the word "plan" and press [Enter] then key **Introduce new products**. A fourth shape is added and text size automatically adjusted again.

11. Close the Text pane.

12. For the slide title, key the text New Development Process.

13. Update the handout footer text to **[7-3your initials]**. Save the presentation as **[7-3your initials]** in your Lesson 7 folder. Leave the presentation open for the next exercise.

Exercise 7-4   USE CYCLE DIAGRAMS TO SHOW A CONTINUING SEQUENCE

The *cycle diagram* is used to communicate a continuing sequence. In this exercise you will use the same information as you did in slide 4, but display it in a cycle. Instead of creating the diagram first, however, you will enter text using a bulleted list and then convert the list into a SmartArt graphic.

1. Insert a new slide after slide 4 and key the title New Development Cycle.

2. In the content placeholder key four bulleted items:

   Survey customer needs
   Analyze survey results
   Develop product plan
   Introduce new products

3. Select the listed text and right-click. From the pop-up menu, choose Convert to SmartArt then click the Basic Cycle thumbnail.

4. Select the four shapes. From the SmartArt Tools Format tab, in the Shape Styles group, click the Shape Fill button 🖼 and choose (Orange, Accent 1, darker 25%) to apply a darker theme fill color. Select the four arrows and apply a darker theme color (Orange, Accent 1, darker 50%), as shown in Figure 7-6.

Figure 7-6
Completed Basic
Cycle diagram

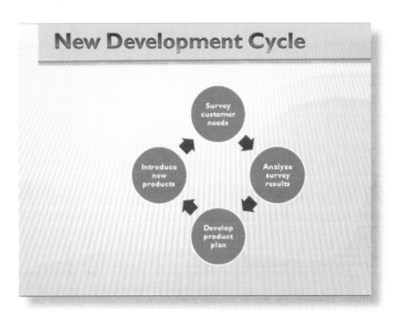

5. Update the handout footer text to **[7-4your initials]**.

6. Move to slide 1 and save the presentation as **[7-4your initials]** in your Lesson 7 folder.

7. Preview, and then print the entire presentation as handouts, six slides per page, grayscale, framed. Leave the presentation open for the next exercise.

Enhancing Diagrams

Once a SmartArt graphic is inserted on your slide, its appearance can be altered using the effects you have learned to apply to shapes. However, additional options exist for customizing these diagrams, and you will work with these design options in the next exercises.

Exercise 7-5   APPLY SHAPE QUICK STYLES

One of the quickest ways to change the appearance of shapes within a diagram is to apply *Quick Styles*. These styles include more than one preset adjustment.

1. On slide 2, select the three rectangle shapes that contain text content.

2. From the Home tab, in the Drawing group, click the Quick Styles button ▨. A gallery of preset styles appears in an array of theme colors, as shown in Figure 7-7.

Figure 7-7
Shape Quick Styles

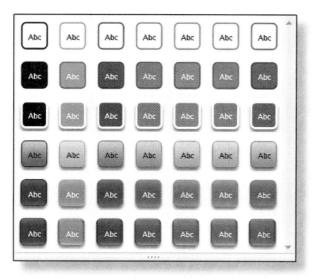

3. As you move your pointer horizontally, you will see different colors applied to the selected shapes. As you move your pointer vertically, you will see different effects such as outlines, beveling, and shadows.

4. To use a darker color and apply a shadow effect to the shapes, click on Light 1 Outline, Color Fill - Accent 2.

Exercise 7-6 ADJUST 3-D FORMAT AND ROTATION

In the previous exercises, the shapes have a *2-D* orientation—you see the shapes in dimensions of height (up/down measurement) and width (left/right measurement). Three-dimensional (*3-D*) settings add a perspective dimension to create the illusion of depth. For example, a square can look like a cube. Rotation settings enable you to tilt shapes on the screen.

1. Move to slide 4 and select the four rectangles.

2. From the Home tab, in the Drawing group, click the Shape Effects button ⬛ then choose 3-D Rotation.

3. From the gallery of options, choose Perspective Heroic Extreme Left, as shown in Figure 7-8.

Figure 7-8
3-D Rotation effects

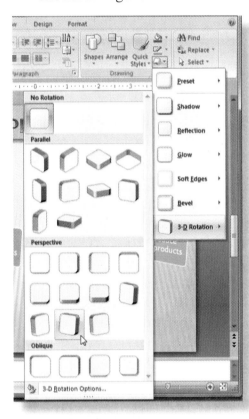

4. Now add two more shape effects to customize this diagram. With the rectangle shapes selected,

   a. click the Shape Effects button ⬛, choose Bevel, and then choose the Circle bevel.

   b. click the Shape Effects button ⬛, choose Shadow, and then from the Outer category choose Offset Diagonal Top Right.

   c. click anywhere on the slide to turn off the selection.

5. Select the three arrows and apply the same Bevel and Shadow effects that were applied to the shapes in step 4.

Exercise 7-7 ADJUST THE OVERALL SIZE AND LAYOUT OF THE DIAGRAM

Diagrams can be resized like any other PowerPoint object. However, you must always be sure the text is still readable if the size of shapes is reduced. You may need to use only a single word on small shapes if their size becomes small. In this exercise, you will experiment with a couple of sizing techniques.

1. Duplicate slide 4 then make the following changes on the slide 5 diagrams.

2. Notice that the four rectangles and connecting arrows extend across the complete slide so you don't have any extra horizontal room

unless the shapes become smaller. Resize the SmartArt area by dragging the right side about a half inch to the left. The text on the shapes becomes slightly smaller.

3. Resize the top and bottom of the SmartArt area so it is just large enough to contain the shapes.

4. Drag this diagram up to fit directly under the slide title.

5. With the diagram selected, press ⌨Ctrl+⌨D to duplicate the diagram. Position the second diagram evenly below the first one. Duplicating is a quick way to make a second diagram because you can simply edit the text on each shape for new wording without having to reset the Shape Effects.

6. On the second diagram, expand its space then change the position of the shapes, as shown in Figure 7-9. Follow these steps:

   a. Resize the bottom border of the duplicated SmartArt area to increase the size of available space for positioning shapes.

   b. Select the first rectangle and drag it to the upper left. Notice that the arrow between this rectangle and the second one automatically repositions itself.

   c. Select the second rectangle and move it to the left.

   d. Select the third rectangle and move it to the left and down slightly. Be careful that you allow enough space for the arrow.

   e. Select the fourth rectangle and move it to the left and down slightly.

   f. Adjust rectangle positioning by nudging (using the arrow keys) so the arrows remain approximately the same size.

7. Now you are still portraying the four-step process because of the connecting arrows that show the direction. But with only one diagram in this arrangement, you would have enough room on the slide for a picture or some other graphic element to accompany the diagram.

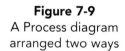
Figure 7-9
A Process diagram arranged two ways

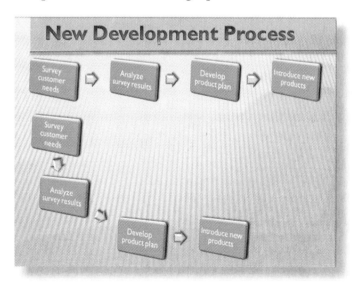

8. Update the handout footer text to **[7-7your initials]**.

9. Move to slide 1 and save the presentation as **[7-7your initials]** in your Lesson 7 folder. Leave the presentation open for the next exercise.

Exercise 7-8   ADD SHAPES

In Exercise 7-3, you added a shape so you already have some experience in modifying SmartArt. The different diagrams add shapes in different places, so the shape you have selected when you add another shape is important because the new shape is normally connected to the selected one in some way.

1. Move to slide 6 and create a new slide with the Title and Content layout. Key **Adding SmartArt Shapes** as the slide title. Click the SmartArt button in the content placeholder.

2. From the List category, choose the Stacked List then click OK.

3. Now edit the text on each shape as follows:

   a. In the circle on the left, key **One**, then for the related text key **First item** and **Second item**.

   b. In the circle on the right, key **Two**, then for the related text key **First item** and **Second item**.

   c. Notice that the text will automatically resize and word-wrap for each shape.

4. Now under the left circle labeled "One," click the "First item" text to select that shape. From the SmartArt Tools Design tab, in the Create Graphic group, click the bottom part of the Add Shape button then choose Add Shape After. A new shape appears below the first item and the diagram has been resized. Key **New item** in this shape.

5. Now select the left circle labeled "One." Click the bottom part of the Add Shape then choose Add Shape After. This time a second circle with a related rectangle shape is added, as shown in Figure 7-10.

6. In the added circle, key **New**; in the related shape, key **New item**.

7. Notice that you have the options of before and after as well as above and below when you are adding shapes, so it is very important that you choose where you want the shape to go.

8. Also, you can rearrange the order of the shapes in a diagram. Select the circle labeled "New." From the SmartArt Tools Design tab, in the Create Graphic group, click the Right to Left button and the diagram is displayed from right to left. Click the button again to display the diagram from left to right.

Figure 7-10
Adding SmartArt
shapes

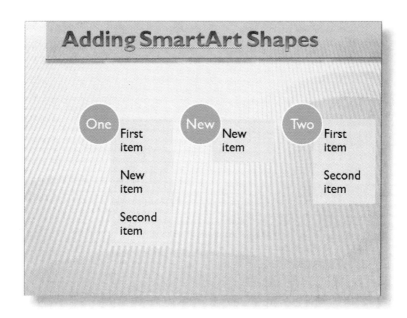

Figure 7-10
Adding SmartArt
shapes

Exercise 7-9   CHANGE COLORS AND RESET THE GRAPHIC

You have already used Quick Styles to change a diagram's appearance. Many more options are available from the SmartArt Tools Design tab, in the SmartArt Styles group, as shown in Figure 7-11.

1. On slide 7 select the SmartArt diagram. From the SmartArt Tools Design tab, in the SmartArt Styles group, click the More button ▾ to see the complete gallery of SmartArt Styles arranged in two categories, Best Match for Document and 3-D. As you point to these thumbnails you will see that effect applied to your diagram.

Figure 7-11
SmartArt Styles

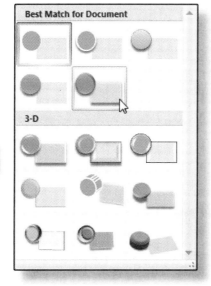

2. Click the Intense Effect thumbnail and this effect is automatically applied.

3. With your SmartArt diagram selected, from the SmartArt Tools Design tab, in the SmartArt Styles group, click the Change Colors button. Colors are arranged in eight categories: Primary Theme Colors, Colorful, and six Accent colors. The current color is selected, as shown in Figure 7-12.

Figure 7-12
Change colors for a
SmartArt diagram

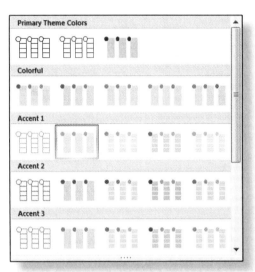

4. Point to different thumbnails in this gallery of colors and consider the changes on your slide. Notice that colors change as you go down the list between the various accent colors in the presentation's design theme. Then as you go across different line and shading treatments are used.

5. Select the Gradient Loop – Accent 5 color.

6. If you are not pleased with your change, it is always easy to remove it. From the SmartArt Tools Design tab, in the Reset group, click the Reset Graphic button and the original style of your diagram is restored.

7. Update the handout footer text to **[7-9your initials]**.

8. Move to slide 1 and save the presentation as **[7-9your initials]** in your Lesson 7 folder. Leave the presentation open for the next exercise.

NOTE

As you work with diagrams, you will find the keyboard shortcuts listed in Table 7-2 helpful because they provide a quick way to move between shapes, select shapes, or select the text within the shapes.

TABLE 7-2 Using the Keyboard to Navigate in SmartArt Graphics

Key	Result
F2	Toggles the current shape between being selected and activated.
Esc	Deactivates a selected shape.
Enter	Activated shape: Inserts a new text line.
← or →	Selected shape: Nudges the position of the shape left or right.
↑ or ↓	Selected shape: Nudges the position of the shape up or down.
Tab	Selected shape: Moves to the next shape. Activated shape: Inserts a tab character at the insertion point.
Shift + Tab	Selected shape: Moves to the previous shape. Activated shape: Inserts a tab character at the insertion point.

Preparing an Organization Chart

Organization charts are most commonly used to show a hierarchy such as the lines of authority or reporting relationships in a business. You start an organization chart in the same way as other SmartArt graphics, but it is important to consider superior and subordinate relationships.

Exercise 7-10 CREATE AN ORGANIZATION CHART

When you start a new organization chart, you begin with a default arrangement of five rectangular shapes. Each shape is positioned on a *level* in the chart, which indicates its position in the hierarchy. The top shape indicates the highest level with a direct line down to the second level (such as the president of a company and the managers who report to the president). The shape that branches from the central line reflects a supporting position (such as an assistant to the president).

1. Insert a new slide after slide 7 that uses the Title and Content layout. Key the title **New Management Structure**.

2. In the content placeholder click the SmartArt button 🖼.

3. Choose the Hierarchy category then click the Organization Chart thumbnail and click OK. A chart with five shapes appears with text placeholders that show text in a large size. The text size will become smaller as you key text.

4. Move your pointer to the top shape in the chart and click inside the text placeholder. Notice the dashed outline that indicates the shape is activated.

5. Key **Julie Wolfe &** then press Enter and key **Gus Irvinelli** to position the names on two lines. You will later format this text to fit on one line.

6. Press Enter to start a new line and key **Co-owners**.

7. Press Esc to deactivate text editing. The shape now has a solid outline.

8. Press Tab to move to the first lower-level shape.

9. Key the following three items on three lines:

    Administration
    Michael Peters
    Administration Mgr

10. The text becomes smaller to fit in the shape. Press F2 to deactivate text editing.

11. Press ⌷Tab⌷ to move to the second shape on the lower level. Key the following items on three lines:

Sales & Marketing
Roy Olafsen
Marketing Mgr

12. Press ⌷F2⌷ then press ⌷Tab⌷ to move to the third shape and key the following items on three lines:

Operations
Michele Jenkins
Head Chef

13. Press ⌷F2⌷ then press ⌷Tab⌷ to move to the shape that branches from the central line and press ⌷Delete⌷.

14. Click outside the SmartArt area to deactivate the organization chart, as shown in Figure 7-13.

Figure 7-13
Organization chart

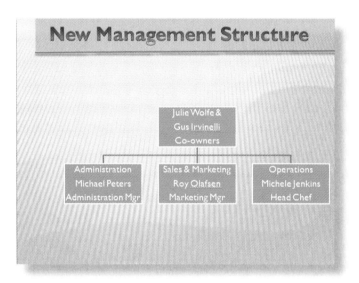

15. Update the handout footer text to **[7-10your initials]**.

16. Save the presentation as **[7-10your initials]** in your Lesson 7 folder. Leave the presentation open for the next exercise.

Exercise 7-11   INSERT SUBORDINATE SHAPES

The organization of many companies changes frequently. You might need to promote, demote, or move organization chart shapes as the reporting structure changes or becomes more complex.

To expand your organization chart as shown in Figure 7-14, you can insert additional shapes of the following types:

- *Subordinate shapes* —shapes that are connected to a superior shape (a shape on a higher level).

- *Coworker shapes*—shapes that are connected to the same superior shape as another shape.

- *Assistant shapes*—shapes that are usually placed below a superior shape and above subordinate shapes.

Figure 7-14
Structure of an
organization chart

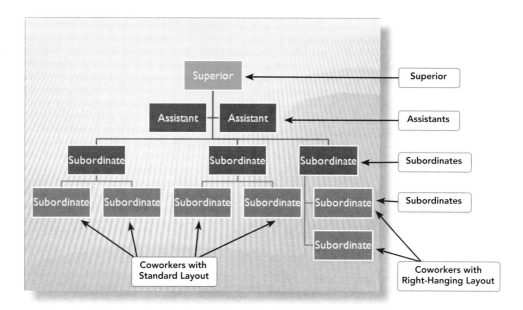

To add *subordinate shapes*, first select the shape that will be their superior; then from the SmartArtTools Design tab, in the Create Graphic group, click the Add Shape button .

1. Still working on slide 8, select the first shape on the second level, with the name "Michael Peters."

Figure 7-15
Adding organization
chart shapes

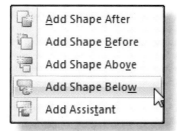

2. From the SmartArt Tools Design tab, in the Create Graphic group, click the lower half of the Add Shape button then from the pop-up list select Add Shape Below. A shape appears below the selected shape with a connecting line and now the new shape is selected.

3. Click the lower half of the Add Shape button , then from the pop-up list select Add Shape Before, as shown in Figure 7-15. Now two shapes show a reporting relationship to Michael Peters. They are currently shown with a Right-Hanging Layout. All the shapes automatically become smaller, so the chart will fit on the slide.

NOTE

Both Add Shape After and Add Shape Before insert new shapes at different levels. Add Shape Above inserts a new shape in the level above, which would be a superior position. Add Shape Below inserts a new shape in the level below, which would be a subordinate position. Add Assistant inserts a new shape between levels.

4. Repeat this process to add one shape under Roy Olafsen and three shapes under Michele Jenkins. Once again the shapes are resized to fit, but the text is now too small to read. This will be corrected later.

Exercise 7-12   ADD ASSISTANT AND COWORKER SHAPES

Assistant shapes are used for positions that provide administrative assistance or other support. They are inserted below a selected shape, but above the next-lower level.

Coworker shapes are inserted at the same level as the selected shape and report to the same superior as the selected shape.

1. On slide 8, select the level 1 shape.

2. From the SmartArt Tools Design tab, in the Create Graphic group, click the Add Shape button ▣ and choose Add Assistant. A new shape is inserted between levels 1 and 2.

3. Select the shape below Michael Peters to add another shape at the same level. From the SmartArt Tools Design tab, in the Create Graphic group, click the Add Shape button ▣ and choose Add Shape Before. A new shape is inserted at the same level—this represents a coworker.

4. Repeat step 3 to add one shape under Roy Olafsen.

5. Now increase the slide size so you can more easily see the text. From the View tab, in the Zoom group, click the Zoom button 🔍 and choose 200% then click OK.

6. On the enlarged slide, scroll to locate the assistant shape below the level 1 shape. Key **Troy Scott**, press Enter, then key **Assistant** so this text fits on two text lines.

7. In the three shapes under Michael Peters, key the following employee information on two text lines in each shape. After the text is entered, press F2 or Esc to deactivate the shape and then press Tab to move to the next shape.

MIS	Billing	HR
Chuck Warden	Sarah Conners	Chris Davis

8. After keying the text in Chris Davis's shape, press Esc to deactivate the text shape. Press Tab one time to move to Roy Olafsen's shape, and press Tab to move to the first shape under Roy Olafsen.

9. In the two shapes under Roy Olafsen, key the following employee information:

Events	Marketing
Ian Mahoney	Evan Johnson

10. In the first two shapes under Michele Jenkins, key the following and leave the last shape blank:

Kitchen	Purchasing
Eric Dennis	Jessie Smith

11. Notice that the organization chart again adjusted the text to a smaller size, as shown in Figure 7-16. From the View tab, in the Zoom group, click the Fit to Window button 🔲.

Figure 7-16
Organization chart
with text

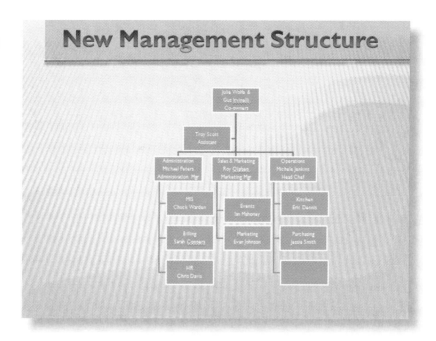

Exercise 7-13 CHANGE LAYOUT, DELETE, AND REARRANGE SHAPES

The layout of the organization chart can be changed to show subordinates in a *standard* format or a *hanging indent* format. A shape can be repositioned to a higher level by promoting (moving up) or repositioned to a lower level by demoting (moving down). An entire group of connected shapes can be moved right or left. If you have more shapes than necessary, you can delete them at any time.

1. On slide 8, select the shape for Michael Peters. From the SmartArt Tools Design tab, in the Create Graphic group, click the Layout button ⊞ and choose Standard. The subordinate shapes below Michael Peters (co-workers) are now arranged side by side instead of in a vertical, hanging arrangement.

2. Select the blank subordinate shape below Michele Jenkins and press ⌈Delete⌋.

3. Select the shape for Eric Dennis and click the Promote button ⊡. It moves up a level and the connected shape moves with it. Click the Undo button ⊡.

4. Click Roy Olafsen's shape and change the Layout to Standard. Repeat this process to change the Layout for Michele Jenkins's shape to Standard.

5. This arrangement communicates nicely the three levels of the organization as shown in Figure 7-17; however, the text is very small. The next steps will rearrange the layout so each shape can be a little larger.

PowerPoint 2007

Figure 7-17
Organization chart with standard layout

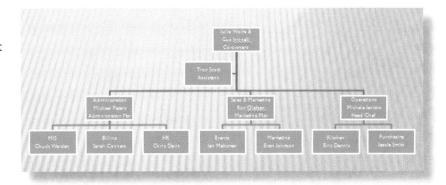

6. Select the shape for Michael Peters. From the SmartArt Tools Design tab, in the Create Graphic group, click the Layout button and choose Right Hanging. Repeat this process to apply the Right Hanging indent to the other two level 2 shapes.

7. Select the shape of Sarah Conners and click the Demote button. Now this shape is indented under Chuck Warden.

8. Select the shape for Michael Peters and click the Right to Left button and this entire branch of the chart is reordered to appear on the right, as shown in Figure 7-18.

Figure 7-18
Organization chart with hanging indent layout

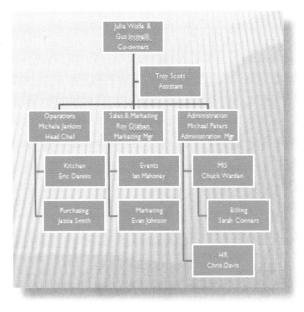

9. Update the handout footer text to **[7-13your initials]**.

10. Save the presentation as **[7-13your initials]** in your Lesson 7 folder. Leave the presentation open for the next exercise.

Exercise 7-14 CHANGE SHAPE SIZING AND STYLES

The entire SmartArt area can be made larger to accommodate charts with several levels. Selected shapes can be resized, and connected shapes repositioned so the text fits better. Text can be made larger, too.

1. On slide 8, resize the SmartArt area by dragging its border to expand it horizontally on both sides as well as vertically.

2. Select the level 1 shape and resize it horizontally to make it wider so both names fit on one line.

3. Select all three level 2 shapes and resize horizontally and vertically to allow a little more room in each shape.

4. Select all of the chart's shapes and increase the font size to 16 points in bold. Adjust the horizontal size of shapes if the text word-wraps.

5. Now spread apart the related shapes in the chart for easier reading. Select the Michael Peters shape and the related shapes below him. Press Ctrl and the right arrow about five times to move this branch to the right. The connecting lines automatically adjust.

6. Select the Michele Jenkins shape and the related shapes below her. Press Ctrl and the left arrow about five times to move this branch to the right.

7. With the SmartArt area selected, from the SmartArt Tools Design tab, in the SmartArt Styles group, click the Change Colors button and select the Colorful – Accent Colors thumbnail.

8. You can also change the color of individual shapes. Select the Assistant shape and then from the SmartArt Tools Format tab, in the Shape Styles group, choose a Shape Fill that will make the fill color a little lighter.

9. From the SmartArt Tools Design tab, in the SmartArt Styles group, examine the effect of different SmartArt Styles on the chart. Click the SmartArt Styles More button then choose the Intense Effect, as shown in Figure 7-19.

10. Update the handout footer text to **[7-14your initials]**. Save the presentation as **[7-14your initials]** in your Lesson 7 folder. Leave the presentation open for the next exercise.

Figure 7-19
Completed
organization chart

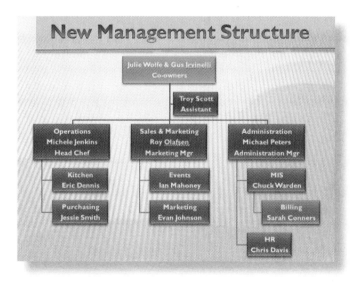

Creating Other Diagrams with SmartArt

The seven categories of PowerPoint SmartArt graphics offer many options to illustrate your thoughts in a visual way. This exercise will focus on three diagrams in the Relationship category.

Exercise 7-15 CREATE A RADIAL DIAGRAM

A *radial diagram* starts with a central circle (level 1) with four circles (level 2) connected to and surrounding the center circle. You can insert as many additional circles as you need to illustrate your message.

1. Insert a new slide after slide 8 that uses the Title and Content layout. Key the title **New Customer Philosophy**.

2. From the content placeholder click the SmartArt button [icon].

3. Choose the Relationship category, then click the Basic Radial thumbnail and click OK. A chart appears with four circle shapes that radiate from the center circle with text placeholders.

4. Click the center circle, then from the SmartArt Tools Design tab, in the Create Graphic group, click the Add Shape button [icon] and a new circle is added to the diagram. It becomes the selected circle.

5. Press Delete to remove this new shape.

6. With the center circle selected, key **Customer**.

NOTE

If PowerPoint automatically capitalizes the second and third word in each circle, change the letters to lowercase. Automatic capitalization is caused by the AutoCorrect in PowerPoint. You can turn off this feature, if you wish, by clicking the Microsoft Office button [icon], click the PowerPoint Options button [PowerPoint Options], choose Proofing, click AutoCorrection Options, deselect Capitalize first letter of sentences, then click OK.

7. Think about your positioning as though referring to the face of a round clock. Click the top outer circle (12 o'clock position) and key the information shown under "12 o'clock" in Figure 7-20. Press Enter after the individual words, so the information appears on three text lines.

8. Click the circle at the 3 o'clock position and key the corresponding text.

9. Working in a clockwise direction, key the remaining text shown in Figure 7-20 in the remaining outer circles.

Figure 7-20
Radial diagram text

12 o'clock	3 o'clock	6 o'clock	9 o'clock
Satisfy	Provide	Provide	Resolve
customer	courteous	excellent	problems
needs	service	quality	promptly

10. From the SmartArt Tools Design tab, in the SmartArt Styles group, click the Change Colors button 🔲 and choose Colored Fill – Accent 6. Then click the SmartArt Styles More button 🔳 and look at the effect of different options as you point to them. Choose the Cartoon style.

11. Drag the borders of the SmartArt area to increase the size of the diagram.

12. Choose the center shape, then from the SmartArt Tools Format tab, in the Shape Styles group, choose a darker shade of the shape fill color to emphasize the center, as shown in Figure 7-21.

13. Update the handout footer text to **[7-15your initials]**. Save the presentation as **[7-15your initials]** in your Lesson 7 folder. Leave the presentation open for the next exercise.

Figure 7-21
Radial diagram

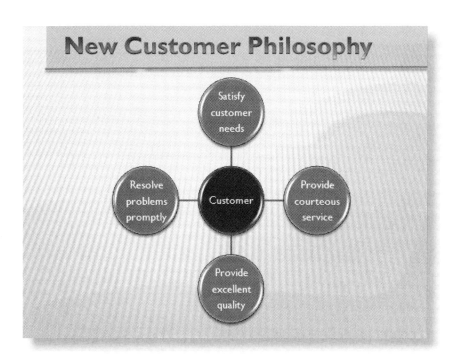

Exercise 7-16   CREATE A GEAR DIAGRAM

Gears have spokes that stick out and lock with other gears to make them turn. The turning of each gear is dependent on the other gears. Therefore, the *gear diagram* communicates interlocking ideas that are shown as shapes.

1. Insert a new slide after slide 9 that uses the Title and Content layout. Key the title Interlocking Ideas.

2. From the content placeholder click the SmartArt button 🔲.

3. Choose the Relationship category, then click the Gear thumbnail and click OK. A chart with three shapes and directional arrows appears. Key the text as shown in Figure 7-22.

4. From the SmartArt Tools Design Tab, in the SmartArt Styles group, choose the SmartArt Styles More button ⊡ and choose the 3-D Inset style.

5. Resize and reposition the SmartArt graphic attractively.

Figure 7-22
Completed Gear diagram

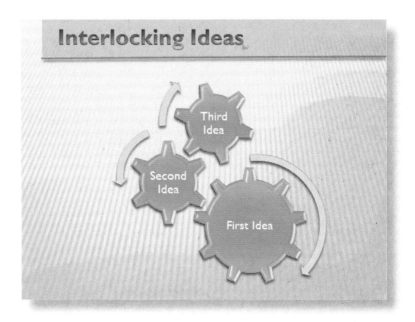

6. Update the handout footer text to **[7-16your initials]**. Save the presentation as **[7-16your initials]** in your Lesson 7 folder. Leave the presentation open for the next exercise.

Exercise 7-17   INSERT A CONTINUOUS PICTURE LIST

The *Continuous Picture List* contains round placeholders for pictures and a horizontal arrow to communicate that the items shown represent interconnected information.

1. Insert a new slide after slide 10 that uses the Title and Content layout. Key the title New Desserts.

2. From the content placeholder click the SmartArt button 🖾.

3. Choose the Relationship category, then click the Continuous Picture List thumbnail and click OK. A chart appears with three shapes that each contain a small circle with a picture placeholder.

4. Click the first picture placeholder to access the Insert Picture dialog shape. Navigate to where your student files are located, select the **cake** picture, and click Insert.

5. Repeat this process on the next two placeholders, inserting the **cookies** picture in the middle shape and the **strawberry** picture in the right shape.

6. Now key text below each of the pictures as shown in Figure 7-23 and the text will automatically resize:

Fruit Cake Holiday Delight
Oatmeal and Raisin Cookies
Cream Cake and Strawberries

7. From the SmartArt Tools Design tab, in the SmartArt Styles group, click the More button ⬇ and select the 3-D, Polished style.

8. Resize and reposition the SmartArt graphic attractively on the slide.

9. Update the handout footer text to **[7-17your initials]**. Save the presentation as **[7-17your initials]** in your Lesson 7 folder. Leave the presentation open for the next exercise.

Figure 7-23
Continuous Picture List

Changing Diagram Types and Orientation

Once a SmartArt diagram is created, the type of diagram can easily be changed by selecting a thumbnail from a different category. However, the levels of your information may not translate well into some layouts. The orientation of a diagram can be changed if an appropriate layout can be used. Shapes within the SmartArt area can also be repositioned by dragging them.

Exercise 7-18   CHANGE DIAGRAM TYPES

At any time during the development of your SmartArt diagram, you can apply a different SmartArt graphic to create a different diagram. Level 1 information and level 2 information will be reformatted to fit the new layout, so the layout you choose must have matching levels.

NOTE

Because this is a List diagram, you see those choices first. You could access all diagrams by clicking the More button ⬇.

1. Move to slide 3 and select it in the Slides and Outline pane. Press Ctrl+C to copy the slide, move to the end of your slide series, and press Ctrl+V to paste the slide after slide 11.

2. Now working on slide 12, select the SmartArt graphic, then from the SmartArt Tools Design tab,

in the Layouts group, click on several different Layout thumbnails to consider the different diagrams that are available. Notice how the level 1 and level 2 information is arranged and consider the emphasis that each level receives. The next three steps will point out specific diagrams to try and what you should notice in each one.

3. Click the Table Hierarchy thumbnail. This layout does not distinguish between the levels; level 1 information is placed above level 2, but no color or lines are used to show any connecting effect or relationship between the levels.

4. Click the Grouped List thumbnail. Now it is easy to see that certain items relate to other items because the shapes used for level 1 create a sort of container for the shapes used for level 2 information. It tends to emphasize level 2 text.

5. Click the Vertical Arrow List. This layout clearly distinguishes between the two levels and it works well for bulleted lists of information. The arrows on which level 2 information is displayed communicate that the level 2 information is an outgrowth of level 1.

6. The fill color on the arrows blends too much with the slide background to be easily visible, so change the colors and the style to make the arrows stand out more. From the SmartArt Tools Design tab, in the SmartArt Styles group, click Change Colors ▦ then choose Colorful Range – Accent Colors 5 to 6. Then click the SmartArt Style More button ▾ and choose the 3-D, Polished style.

NOTE

Although the current text fits nicely on the slide, if you need more space for level 2 bulleted text, the size of level 2 shapes could be increased and the size of the text on the level 2 shapes could be reduced.

7. Select the three arrows, then from the SmartArt Tools Format tab, in the Shape Styles group, click the Shape Fill button ▦ and choose the Orange, Accent 6, Lighter 40% color. Now the arrows still blend with the theme design, but they are easier to see, as shown in Figure 7-24.

8. Leave your presentation open for the next exercise.

Figure 7-24
Diagram with changed layout

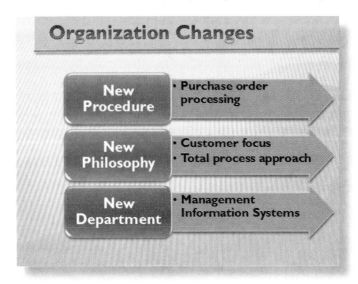

Exercise 7-19 CHANGE THE ORIENTATION OF DIAGRAMS

Because of the particular information a diagram must contain, the information may need to be displayed in a different orientation than the original SmartArt shape provides. For example, instead of a top to bottom orientation, it might need to be left to right.

1. From the Slides and Outline pane, select slide 8 and copy it. Move to the last slide in your presentation and paste the slide.

2. Now on slide 13, select the SmartArt diagram. From the SmartArt Tools Design tab, in the Layouts group, click the More button 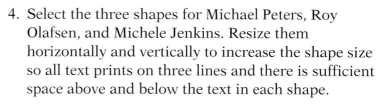 and choose the Horizontal Hierarchy layout. The shapes are now positioned horizontally as in a decision-tree diagram.

3. While the shapes are still connected, the sizes should be adjusted on some of them.

NOTE

Within the SmartArt area, shapes can be repositioned; therefore, a diagram such as the one on slide 7 could be redesigned manually to show the circles in a vertical arrangement and the shapes extending horizontally to the right.

4. Select the three shapes for Michael Peters, Roy Olafsen, and Michele Jenkins. Resize them horizontally and vertically to increase the shape size so all text prints on three lines and there is sufficient space above and below the text in each shape.

5. Select the MIS shape and all the ones below it and the Billing shape. Resize these shapes horizontally so each name fits on one text line, as shown in Figure 7-25.

6. Increase the vertical size of the Julie Wolfe & Gus Irvinelli shape.

Figure 7-25
Diagram with different orientation

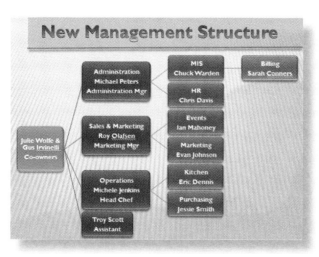

7. Update the handout footer text to **[7-19your initials]**.

8. Save the presentation as **[7-19your initials]** in your Lesson 7 folder. Print the presentation as handouts in landscape orientation with nine slides on a page.

9. Close the presentation.

Lesson 7 Summary

- SmartArt graphics are used to represent information in a visual manner.

- SmartArt graphics are arranged into seven different categories that include a wide variety of diagrams such as organization charts, radial diagrams, list diagrams, and relationship diagrams.

- The SmartArt Tools Design tab has command buttons to insert shapes and modify the predefined diagram layouts. Shapes can be added and removed.

- List diagrams provide an alternative to listing information in a bulleted list because concise text can be placed on shapes that help to communicate categories and subtopics.

- Process diagrams show a sequence of events or the progression of workflow.

- Cycle diagrams communicate a continuous or ongoing process.

- Hierarchy diagrams are used to describe a hierarchical structure, showing who reports to whom, and who is responsible for what function or task.

- Pyramid diagrams show interconnected or proportional relationships.

- Relationship diagrams contain interconnected shapes that reflect relationships in some way.

- Matrix diagrams display two axes in related quadrants that emphasize the whole or the individual parts.

- An organization chart is a type of hierarchy chart in a tree structure, branching out to multiple divisions in each lower level.

- When a chart shape is promoted, it moves up a level. When a chart shape is demoted, it moves down a level.

- A SmartArt Text pane provides a quick way to enter the text that labels diagram shapes.

- List diagrams can show both level 1 and level 2 information, but text must be concise for easy reading.

- Text entered in SmartArt shapes automatically resizes to fit the shape; if shapes increase in size, the text they contain increases in size.

- An existing bulleted list can be converted to a SmartArt graphic.

- Quick Styles provide choices for color and effect changes such as outlines, beveling, and shadows that can be applied to any selected shape.

- SmartArt Styles consist of predefined effects that work well together for diagrams.

- An illusion of depth is created with 3-D style options.

- Shapes can be repositioned within the SmartArt area.

- The Change Colors option provides many possible variations of theme colors.

- If color changes made to a SmartArt graphic are unacceptable, the colors can be reset to their original colors.
- Several layouts in the List category have placeholders for pictures.

LESSON 7		Command Summary
Feature	**Button**	**Ribbon**
Create a graphical list or diagram on a slide.		Insert, Illustrations group, Insert SmartArt Graphic
Change text from a bulleted list to a diagram		Home, Paragraph group, Convert to SmartArt Graphics
Pick from choices for shape color and effects		Home, Drawing group, Quick Styles
Rearrange diagram direction or sequencing of shapes		SmartArt Tools Design, Create Graphic group, Right to Left
Open a gallery of thumbnails showing available options		Available on many Ribbons, More
Select from variations of theme colors		SmartArt Tools Design, SmartArt Styles group, Change Colors
Change back to original formatting		SmartArt Tools Design, Reset group, Reset Graphic
Create additional shapes within a diagram		SmartArt Tools Design, Create Graphic group, Add Shape
Change organization chart layout		SmartArt Tools Design, Create Graphic group, Layout
Increase the level of a selected bulleted item or shape		SmartArt Tools Design, Create Graphic group, Promote
Decrease the level of a selected bulleted item or shape		SmartArt Tools Design, Create Graphic group, Demote
Change the color of a selected shape		SmartArt Tools Format, Shape Styles group, Shape Fill

Concepts Review

True/False Questions

Each of the following statements is either true or false. Select your choice by indicating T or F.

T F   1. SmartArt contains a wide range of diagrams organized in seven different categories.

T F   2. All the shapes in a diagram must be the same color.

T F   3. An organization chart is an example of a hierarchy diagram.

T F   4. List diagrams can show both level 1 and level 2 information as long as the text is written concisely.

T F   5. If you add too many shapes to an organization chart, you can always delete the extra shapes.

T F   6. Quick Styles provide color and effect choices for selected shapes.

T F   7. SmartArt Styles can be applied to individual shapes in a diagram.

T F   8. The Change Colors option provides choices from Standard Colors.

Short Answer Questions

Write the correct answer in the space provided.

1. How do you create a SmartArt Graphic?

2. What feature enables you to quickly key text to create a SmartArt Graphic?

3. How can you convert an existing bulleted list to a diagram?

4. If you have created a Process diagram, how can you change it to a Cycle diagram?

5. Describe how to change the size of a SmartArt shape.

6. If you have six subordinates reporting to one superior, how do you change the six shapes so they are stacked vertically in two columns?

7. Which categories of SmartArt graphics provide picture placeholders?

8. What type of diagram is used to illustrate a continuous, ongoing relationship?

Critical Thinking

Answer these questions on a separate page. There are no right or wrong answers. Support your answers with examples from your own experience, if possible.

1. When developing your presentation content and making decisions about which SmartArt graphic to use, why is it important to consider your audience's viewpoint?

2. Organization charts are by nature rather detail-oriented. Based on what you learned about designing presentations, how can you ensure that an organization chart is easy to interpret?

Skills Review

Exercise 7-20

Create a list diagram.

1. Open the file **Retail**. Insert a new slide after slide 3 that uses the Title and Content layout. Key the title **New Retail Items**. If the text moves to the top of the title placeholder, then from the Home tab, in the Slides group, click the Reset button .

2. Insert a Trapezoid List SmartArt graphic by following these steps:

    a. Click the SmartArt button 📷 in the content placeholder.

    b. From the List category, choose the Trapezoid List and click OK. A SmartArt graphic will appear with three trapezoid shapes with title and list placeholders.

    c. From the SmartArt Tools Design tab, in the Create Graphic group, click the Text pane button 🔲 to open the Text pane on the left as shown in Figure 7-26.

Figure 7-26
Trapezoid List diagram

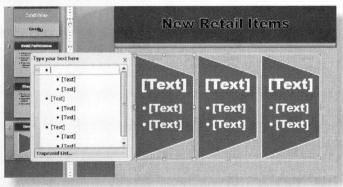

3. The first-level bullet will be the heading in each shape, and the second-level bullet will be the items listed in each shape. Two bulleted items first appear, but as you add a third and fourth item, the text will adjust its size to fit in the shape.

4. Working in the Text pane or directly on each shape, key the text to complete all three shapes as shown in Figure 7-27.

Figure 7-27
Completed
Trapezoid List
diagram

5. Close the Text pane.

6. Create a slide footer for slide 4 only including today's date and the text your name, **[7-20your initials]**.

7. Save the presentation as **[7-20your initials]** in your Lesson 7 folder. Print only slide 4 in full size. Close the presentation.

Exercise 7-21

Create a simple organization chart, change theme colors, and format shapes.

1. Open the file **Kitchen1**. Insert a new slide after slide 3 that uses the Title and Content layout. Key the title **Operations**.

2. Start an organization chart by following these steps:

   a. From the content placeholder, click the SmartArt button ⬚.

   b. In the Hierarchy category, click the Organization Chart thumbnail then click OK.

   c. In the top shape, key:

   Michele Jenkins
   Head Chef & Operations Mgr

    d. Press Esc to deactivate the shape. Click the assistant shape and press Delete.

    e. In the first shape on the second level, key:

Eric Dennis
Asst Chef & Kitchen Mgr

    f. Press Esc, press Tab to move to the next shape, and then key:

Claudia Pell
Maitre d' & Service Mgr

    g. Press Esc, press Tab to move to the right shape, then press Delete.

3. Insert subordinate shapes by following these steps:

    a. Select Eric Dennis's shape.

    b. From the SmartArt Tools Design tab, in the Create Graphic group, click the Add Shape button then choose Add Shape Below.

    c. Now the second shape is selected. To add a second shape at the same level, click the Add Shape button then choose Add Shape After.

    d. Key the following information in the two shapes:

First shape	Second shape
G. Robinson	S. Stefano
Sr. Cook	Sr. Cook, Weekends

    e. Select Claudia Pell's shape. Using the previous steps b and c, insert two shapes below Claudia Pell and key the following information:

First shape	Second shape
T. Domina	T. Conway
Banquets	Facilities & Maint

4. Change the layout:

    a. Click the shape for Eric Dennis. From the SmartArt Tools Design tab, in the Create Graphic group, click the Layout button and choose Standard to make the shapes below Eric Dennis appear beside each other.

    b. Repeat this process for the Claudia Pell shape.

5. On all shapes, make the employee names (but not their titles) bold.

6. From the SmartArt Tools Design tab, in the SmartArt Styles group,

    a. click the Change Colors button and select Primary Theme Colors of Dark 2 Outline.

    b. click the More button and choose the Intense Effect style.

7. Move the SmartArt graphic up and slightly to the left so it is balanced better on the slide, as shown in Figure 7-28.

8. Create a slide footer for only slide 4 containing today's date and the text your name, **[7-21your initials]**.

Figure 7-28
Completed slide

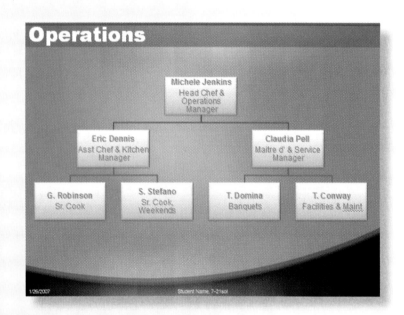

9. Move to slide 1 and save the presentation as **[7-21your initials]** in your Lesson 7 folder.

10. Print slide 4 in full size. Close the presentation.

Exercise 7-22

Create cycle and process diagrams.

1. Open the file **Health**.

2. Insert a new slide after slide 1 that uses the Title and Content layout. Key the title **Heart Smart Living**.

3. Create a cycle diagram by following these steps:

    a. Click the SmartArt button ▨ in the content placeholder.

    b. In the Cycle category, click the Block Cycle thumbnail. Click OK.

    c. With one of the shapes selected, press Delete so you have four shapes in the diagram.

4. Insert text on the diagram by following these steps:

    a. In the top shape, key the text **Get enough** Enter **sleep**.

    b. Press Esc. Click the shape at the 3 o'clock position and key **Eat right when** Enter **you're out**.

    c. Move to the text shape at the 6 o'clock position and key **Eat right** Enter **at home**.

    d. In the text shape at the 9 o'clock position, key **Exercise** Enter **regularly**.

5. Format the four text shapes. Press Ctrl while you click each of the four shapes to select them. Make the following changes:

    a. Make the text bold.

    b. Increase the font size to 20 points then stretch the shapes horizontally so the text in each shape fits on two text lines.

c. Right-click one of the shapes and from the shortcut menu choose Change Shape, then select an oval. Resize the oval shapes if necessary.

6. Insert a new slide after slide 4 that uses the Title and Content layout. Key the title **Do What's Good 4 U**.

7. Create a process diagram by following these steps:

   a. Click the SmartArt button ▣ in the content placeholder.

   b. In the Process category, click the Continuous Block Process thumbnail. Click OK.

   c. With one of the shapes selected, from the SmartArt Tools Design tab, in the Create Graphic group, click the Add Shape button ▣ and then choose Add Shape After so you have four shapes in the diagram.

8. In the first shape on the left, key **Join Our Team!!** Notice that in the small shapes of this diagram the text automatically word-wraps with one word on each line. Key the other text as follows:

   a. Second—**Eat With Us**

   b. Third—**Play With Us**

   c. Fourth—**Walk With Us**

9. Create a handout header and footer: Include the date and your name as the header, and the page number and text **[7-22your initials]** as the footer.

10. Move to slide 1 and save the presentation as **[7-22your initials]** in your Lesson 7 folder.

11. Preview, and then print the entire presentation as handouts, six slides per page, grayscale, landscape, framed. Close the presentation.

Exercise 7-23

Add, promote, demote, and rearrange shapes in an existing organizational chart.

1. Open the file **Kitchen2**. Move to slide 3 and click the organization chart to make it active.

2. Add three subordinate shapes to the G. Robinson level 2 shape, and key the information shown in Figure 7-29.

Figure 7-29
Content for organization chart

First shape	Second shape	Third shape
Pastry	Cooks	Banquets
G. Gordon	L. Tilson	T. Domina
J. Lemmer	S. Mason	J. Fulman

3. Adjust the format by following these steps:

   a. Select the level 3 Banquets shape and then from the SmartArt Tools Design tab, in the Create Graphic group, click the Promote button ⊞ to move it up to level 2.

   b. Select the level 2 Facilities shape then from the SmartArt Tools Design tab, in the Create Graphic group, click the Layout button ⊞ and choose Left Hanging.

   c. Using the sizing handles on the organization chart border, make the chart larger, as shown in Figure 7-30.

   d. Make the text on all shapes bold.

   e. Apply the Moderate Effect SmartArt Style.

   f. In all shapes, change the first text line to 14 points and the font color to Gray-80%, Text 2, Darker 25%.

Figure 7-30
Completed slide

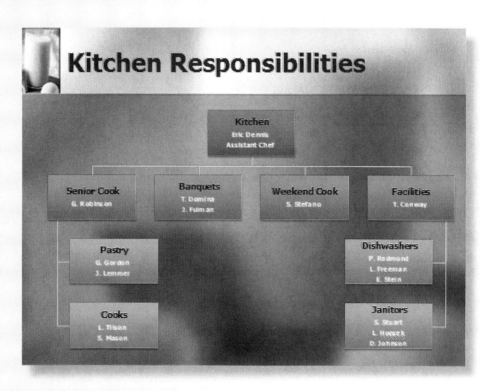

4. Create a handout header and footer: Include the date and your name as the header, and the page number and text **[7-23your initials]** as the footer.

5. Move to slide 1 and save the presentation as **[7-23your initials]** in your Lesson 7 folder.

6. Print the organization chart slide in full size. Preview, and then print the entire presentation as handouts, three slides per page, grayscale, framed. Close the presentation.

Lesson Applications

Exercise 7-24

Create a process diagram and a list diagram and apply SmartArt styles.

1. Open the file **Market1**.

2. On slide 3, select the two bulleted items. From the Home tab, in the Paragraph group, click the Convert to SmartArt Graphic button 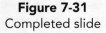. Choose More SmartArt Graphics.

3. Choose the Process category and consider which diagrams would best show these two different media categories. Click the Arrow Ribbon thumbnail and then click OK.

4. The two words are now positioned on a shape with arrows pointing in two directions.

5. Because this is such a simple shape and only two words are used, the SmartArt graphic is very large. Resize it to make the diagram smaller so it does not overpower the slide.

6. For slides 4 and 5, consider the type of diagrams that would be well suited for these lists that contain one item on level 1 and four or more items on level 2. Plan to use the same diagram on both slides.

7. On slide 4, select the bulleted list and from the Home tab, in the Paragraph group, click the Convert to SmartArt Graphic button and choose More SmartArt Graphics.

8. From the List category, choose the Pyramid list thumbnail and click OK. Now the text is positioned over a pyramid shape that can imply volume or levels of importance.

9. Repeat this process to convert the bulleted text on slide 5 to the same diagram. This time the height of the text shapes is smaller because six items are listed.

10. For slides 4 and 5, apply the SmartArt Style Metallic Scene, as shown in Figure 7-31.

Figure 7-31
Completed slide

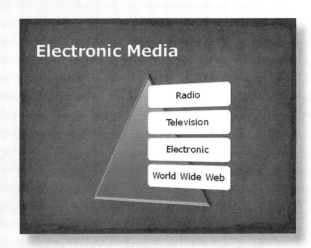

11. Create a handout header and footer: Include the date and your name as the header, and the page number and text **[7-24your initials]** as the footer.

12. Move to slide 1 and save the presentation as **[7-24your initials]** in your Lesson 7 folder.

13. Print the presentation as handouts with six slides on a page, scale to fit paper, and framed. Close the presentation.

Exercise 7-25

Create an organization chart and adjust layout.

1. Open the file **MISdept**.

2. Insert a new slide after slide 2 that uses the Title and Content layout. Key the title MIS Department Organization.

3. Create an organization chart using a horizontal hierarchy with the information shown in Figure 7-32.

Figure 7-32
Organization chart
text

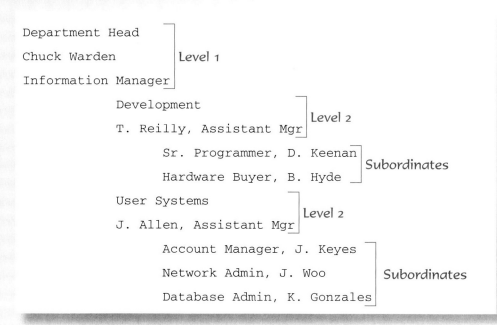

4. Change the font of all diagram text to 14 points and apply bold.

5. Adjust the shape sizing to avoid word-wrapping of the job titles, but keep the size uniform at each level.

6. Change the colors to Gradient Loop – Accent 2.

7. Adjust the position of other shapes to spread them out in the SmartArt area as shown in Figure 7-33.

Figure 7-33
Completed
organization chart

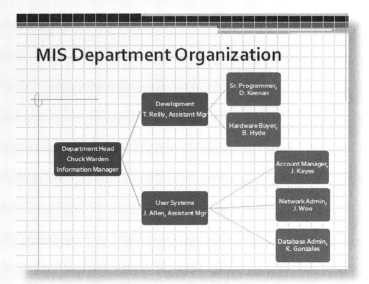

8. Create a slide footer for slide 3 containing today's date, and the text your name, **[7-25your initials]**.

9. Move to slide 1 and save the presentation as **[7-25your initials]** in your Lesson 7 folder.

10. Preview then print slide 3 in full size. Close the presentation.

Exercise 7-26

Create a radial diagram on a promotional flyer.

1. Open the file **NewYear**. Create a SmartArt graphic in the content placeholder for this single-page flyer.

2. From the Cycle category, choose the Basic Radial thumbnail.

3. Add five additional shapes (for a total of nine plus one in the center).

4. Increase the size of the SmartArt area to fill the available space.

5. Key the text Great Food in the center circle; then key the text in Figure 7-34 in the outer circles, starting with the 12 o'clock position moving in a clockwise direction.

Figure 7-34
Diagram text

```
Poached Salmon

Texan Tofu

Fresh Fruit

Pecan Pie

Peanut Soup

Veggies & Dip

Green Beans

Corn Relish

Spring Rolls
```

6. Make these design changes:

   a. Change the colors to click Colorful-Accent Colors.

   b. Apply the SmartArt Style of Polished.

   c. Change the font size for all circles to 16 points. Apply bold.

7. Make these changes to the center shape:

   a. Increase the size of the center shape and press [Shift] while you resize to keep the shape round.

   b. Change the font size for this shape to 24 points.

   c. Change the shape to a 16-point star, as shown in Figure 7-35.

Figure 7-35
Completed flyer

8. Save the presentation as **[7-26your initials]** in your Lesson 7 folder.

9. Preview, and then print the slide using color if possible. Close the presentation.

Exercise 7-27 ◆ Challenge Yourself

Convert bulleted lists to appropriate diagrams.

1. Open the file **Market3** and examine the slide content.

2. For slide 2, convert the bulleted text to an Upward Arrow SmartArt graphic from the Process category.

3. Increase the text size to 20 points and then resize the text boxes as necessary to avoid words being cut off in the middle. Change the colors to one of the colorful options and apply the Moderate Effect SmartArt Style.

4. For slides 4 and 5, convert both lists to the Multidirectional Cycle SmartArt graphic. Change the colors to one of the accent colors and apply a Moderate Effect SmartArt Style. Change the text color to black and font size to 28 points.

5. Reduce the vertical size of the SmartArt graphic on slides 4 and 5 so the diagrams are not quite so large and a little more space is allowed after the slide titles.

6. Create a handout header and footer: Include the date and your name as the header, and the page number and text **[7-27your initials]** as the footer.

7. Move to slide 1 and save the presentation as **[7-27your initials]** in your Lesson 7 folder.

8. Preview and then print the entire presentation as handouts, six slides per page, scale to fit paper, and framed. Close the presentation.

On Your Own

In these exercises you work on your own, as you would in a real-life work environment. Use the skills you've learned to accomplish the task—and be creative.

Exercise 7-28

Think of a familiar activity and create a process diagram indicating the steps in the process. For example, baking a cake, preparing for a camping trip, or paying a bill. Keep the process fairly simple—no more than 10 steps—and format it so that it is easy to understand and attractive to view. Add a title slide and one or two additional slides giving information about the process. Save the presentation as **[7-28your initials]**. Preview and then print the presentation as handouts.

Exercise 7-29

Create an organization chart of your family tree, starting with one set of great-grandparents and including all the descendants that come from that branch. If you don't want to create your own family tree, choose a famous person, a pedigreed pet, or an imaginary figure. Include a title slide for your presentation and one or two slides describing something of interest about one or more of the people (or pets) on your chart. Use your own creativity to format the presentation and the chart attractively. Save the presentation as **[7-29your initials]**. Preview and then print the presentation as handouts.

Exercise 7-30

Create a diagram to describe a relationship between several functions or departments at your school, work, or other organization. For example, a drama club might have a director, stagehands, costume designer, actors and actresses, musicians, and a playwright. Choose any of the SmartArt diagram types except the organization chart. Add a title slide and one or two other slides describing some aspect of the relationship. Save the presentation as **[7-30your initials]**. Preview and then print the diagram as a full-size slide.

Unit 2 Applications

Unit Application 2-1

Work with WordArt, work with images, group objects, and create a table.

1. Open the file **Runner1**.

2. On slide 1, key Good 4 U as the title and Proud Sponsor of the Fall Festival Marathon as the subtitle.

3. Find a clip art image of a runner and insert it into the slide. Position the clip art in the bottom right corner of the text area of the title slide.

4. Recolor the image to match one of the colors in the presentation.

5. Resize the image so it does not overlap the subtitle text.

6. Change the picture style to Drop Shadow Rectangle. Your completed slide 1 should look similar to Figure U2-1.

Figure U2-1
Completed title slide

7. Working in the Outline pane, key the text shown in Figure U2-2, inserting new slides where needed.

Figure U2-2
Presentation data

8. On slides 2 and 4, remove the bullets from the body text placeholders.

9. On slide 4, insert the **Fireworks** picture from your student data files and position it in the bottom right corner of the slide. Rotate the image so the rockets point toward the text and increase the size slightly, as shown in Figure U2-3.

Figure U2-3
Finished slide with rotated picture

10. Insert a new slide after slide 4 that uses the Blank layout. Insert a clip art image of a race. Resize the picture proportionately so it almost fills the open space on the slide. If the picture is an odd size, crop it where necessary so it is the same size and shape as the slide. Adjust the picture's brightness settings to soften the colors so WordArt will be readable when placed above the image.

11. Create a WordArt text by using Fill – Accent 2, Warm Matte Bevel. Key the following text on three lines and center this text over the image:

Award Ceremony
6 p.m.
Central Park

12. Increase the text size to 60 points and change the text color to Dark Blue, Background 1.

13. Check spelling in the presentation.

14. Create a handout header and footer: Include the date and your name as the header, and the page number and text **[U2-1your initials]** as the footer.

15. Create a Unit 2 Application folder. Move to slide 1 and save the presentation as **[U2-1your initials]** in your Unit 2 Applications folder.

16. Preview and then print the presentation as handouts, six slides per page, grayscale, framed. Close the presentation.

Unit Application 2-2

Add a table, insert a chart, create a SmartArt cycle diagram; add a shape and a text box to a chart.

1. Open the file **HeadCount**. Apply the Verve design theme and use the Trek theme color.

2. Insert a new slide after slide 3 that uses the Title and Content layout, and key the title **Current Breakdown**.

3. Create a table with five columns and four rows and key the data shown in Figure U2-4.

4. Merge two cells for "Kitchen" and two cells for "Service."

5. Adjust the column widths so that the text fits attractively, and align the text to match the figure. The overall table dimensions should be approximately 6.25 inches wide by 3 inches tall.

6. Change the Table Style to Dark Style 1 – Accent 6.

7. Vertically center all of the text in the table.

8. Position the table attractively on the slide.

Figure U2-4
Table data

	Kitchen		Service	
	F/T	P/T	F/T	P/T
Weekdays	13	8	19	9
Weekends	7	13	9	16

9. Insert a new slide after slide 4 that uses the Title and Content layout, and key the title **Past, Current, Projected**. Create a Clustered column chart by using the data shown in Figure U2-5.

Figure U2-5
Chart worksheet data

	A	B	C
1		Full-time	Part-time
2	2006	41	30
3	2007	40	35
4	2008	48	46
5	2009	38	61

10. Apply a gradient fill to each series of columns. Move the legend to the bottom.

11. Draw a text box at the top of the chart; key the text **Projecting 61 P/T, 38 F/T!**. Change the text to 24 points and make it bold. Resize the text box so the text fits all on one line.

12. Draw an arrow from the text to the top of the 2009 columns.

13. Insert a new slide after slide 5. Use the Title and Content layout, and key the title **Plan for Increasing P/T Headcount**.

14. On the new slide 6, insert a Basic Cycle SmartArt Graphic showing the five steps in Figure U2-6 starting with the top shape in the 12 o'clock position and moving clockwise.

Figure U2-6
Data for Basic Cycle SmartArt graphic

Step 1	Advertise P/T positions
Step 2	T. Scott to schedule interviews
Step 3	M. Peters to interview and hire employees
Step 4	J. Farla to train
Step 5	L. Klein to assign schedules

15. Apply the 3-D, Polished Style and make the text bold. Resize the graphic to fill the open area of the slide.

16. Apply the Wipes, Split Vertical Out transition to all of the slides.

17. View the presentation as a slide show.

18. Create a slide footer for all slides, except the title slide, containing today's date, and the text your name, **[U2-2your initials]**.

19. Create a handout header and footer: Include the date and your name as the header, and the page number and the text **[U2-2your initials]** as the footer.

20. Move to slide 1 and save the presentation as **[U2-2your initials]** in your Unit 2 Applications folder.

21. Preview and then print the entire presentation as handouts, six slides per page, grayscale, landscape, framed. Close the presentation.

Unit Application 2-3

Create a presentation with an organizational chart and a diagram.

1. Start a new presentation that uses the Solstice design theme and the Apex theme color.

2. Insert two additional slides and key the text shown in Figure U2-7. Use the Title Slide layout for the first slide, the Two Content layout for the second slide, and the Title and Content layout for the third slide.

Figure U2-7
Presentation text

Slide 1
```
Good 4 U Senior Management
      Current and Future Organization
```

Slide 2
```
Why Change What Works?
  • Current structure designed for a single-restaurant
    company
  • Management must be positioned for a national, multi-
    restaurant organization
```

Slide 3
```
Future Structure
  • Reorganization planned for 2008
  • Designed to capitalize on the individual talents of
    co-owners
  • Company will be split into two functional areas
  • Chef and Administration Managers will report to Julie
    Wolfe
  • Marketing and Information Managers will report to Gus
    Irvinelli
```

3. On slide 1, insert an appropriate clip art or picture showing managers, a business setting, etc. Recolor it to match the presentation theme color.

4. On slide 2, insert a Radial Cycle SmartArt graphic in the content placeholder.

5. Insert two more shapes on the Radial diagram, making a total of six shapes in the outer circle plus a center shape.

6. Make the diagram as large as possible without interfering with the other text on the slide.

7. Key **Good** Enter **4 U** in the center shape. For the other shapes, key the text shown in Figure U2-8, starting with "New York" in the 12 o'clock position and moving clockwise.

Figure U2-8
Data for Radial Cycle SmartArt graphic

```
New Enter York

Miami

Los Enter Angeles

San Enter Francisco

Tucson

More Enter soon
```

8. Change the SmartArt Style to 3-D, Metallic Scene and change the colors to Gradient Loop – Accent 3. Resize the bulleted text placeholder to reduce its width. Resize the diagram to make it as large as possible without overlapping the bulleted text placeholder.

9. Insert a new slide after slide 2 that uses the Title and Content layout. Give it the title **Current Organization**.

10. On slide 3, create a Hierarchy Organization Chart SmartArt graphic for the Good 4 U restaurant by using Figure U2-9. Arrange the chart boxes in an attractive and functional way.

Figure U2-9
Data for organization chart SmartArt graphic

```
Julie Wolfe, Gus Irvinelli, Co-owners ——— Level 1

    Michele Jenkins, Head Chef ————— Level 2

        Claudia Pell, Maitre d'
                                          ] Level 3
        Eric Dennis, Assistant Chef

    Roy Olafsen, Marketing Manager ——— Level 2

        Jerry Wayne, Sales
                                          ] Level 3
        Jane Kryler, Promotions

    Chuck Warden, Information Manager —— Level 2

        Tanya Reilly, Development
                                          ] Level 3
        Jerry Allen, User Systems

    Michael Peters, Administration Manager ——— Level 2

        Robert Lee, Purchasing
        Carol Lynne, Personnel            ] Level 3
        Sharon Ray, Payroll
```

11. Increase the size of the chart, making it as large as possible.

12. Choose the style 3-D, Metallic Scene. Change the colors to Colorful - Accent Colors.

13. Insert a slide after slide 4 using the Title and Content layout. Give it the title **What We Expect**. Create a table showing the positive effects that the restructuring will have on the business. See Figure U2-10 for the table data.

Figure U2-10
Table data

Positive Effects of the Restructuring
Questions/Concerns to be handled in a more timely manner
Increase in responsiveness to customers
A more focused business ready to expand into new markets
Increase in adaptability of business if turnover takes place
Empowering employees will increase job satisfaction
Tap into the skills and expertise of owners

14. Resize the table and reposition the table attractively and apply Themed Style 1 – Accent 6 to the table.

15. Review all slides, adjusting the size and position of elements where needed.

16. View the presentation as a slide show.

17. Create a slide footer for all slides containing today's date, and the text your name, **[U2-3your initials]**.

18. Create a handout header and footer: Include the date and your name as the header, and the page number and the text **[U2-3your initials]** as the footer.

19. Move to slide 1 and save the presentation as **[U2-3your initials]** in your Unit 2 Applications folder.

20. Preview and then print the entire presentation as handouts, six slides per page, grayscale, landscape, framed. Close the presentation.

Unit Application 2-4 ◆ Using the Internet

Write and design a presentation that uses graphics, numerical charts, tables, organization charts, and SmartArt graphics.

Use the Internet to research a topic of current interest that would lend itself to a presentation including graphics, numerical charts, tables, SmartArt graphics, and/or organization charts. You decide what your topic will be.

Here are a few topics to give you ideas, but you are not limited to these topics:

- The impact of increased security for air travel.

- Enrollment information at your local college or university.

- How global warming is affecting weather patterns.

- How the financial health of Hollywood is affected by the overall economy.

- The problems caused by overuse of antibiotics.

- The growth of computer use in the general population.

Illustrate the information you gathered by using a variety of graphics, charts, tables, and SmartArt graphics. Be sure to include at least five slides and format them in an attractive way. Prepare a slide listing the resources you used. When the presentation is complete check spelling.

In the slide footer, include the text **Prepared by** followed by your name. Include the slide number, but not the date, on all slides. In the handout footer, include the completed filename **[U2-4your initials]**. In the handout header, key **Presented to** and then identify to whom you would be giving this presentation. Include in the handout the date that you would be delivering the presentation.

Save the presentation as **[U2-4your initials]** in your Unit 2 Applications folder. Practice delivering the presentation. Preview and then print the presentation handouts with an appropriate number of slides per page, grayscale, framed. Close the presentation.

unit 3

VISUAL IMPACT

Lesson 8

Designing Original Illustrations

OBJECTIVES

After completing this lesson, you will be able to:

1. Change the outline color and weight.

2. Work with solid and gradient colors.

3. Work with pictures and textures.

4. Apply shape effects.

5. Adjust presentation color settings.

Estimated Time: 1½ hours

Your presentation can be greatly enhanced by applying color, pictures, shading, line styles, shape effects, and text to shapes you draw, text placeholders, and pictures. Through the addition of these effects, fills, and text, you can create original illustrations for use in your presentation.

Changing the Outline Color and Weight

There are many ways to modify the look of an outline that has been applied to a shape, picture, placeholder, or other object. The color may be changed, the line style and compound type adjusted, and transparency adjusted.

Exercise 8-1   APPLY SOLID AND GRADIENT COLORS TO OUTLINES

The fastest way to add an outline to a shape is to select the shape, and then click the Shape Outline button. *Shape Outline* refers to the type of border or outline that an object has. Options include single, double, and triple lines of varying line weights. The weight of a line is its thickness, measured in points.

To modify the Shape Outline, open the Format Shape dialog box in one of the following ways:

- Right-click the object; then choose Format Shape from the shortcut menu.

- From the Drawing Tools Format tab, in the Shape Styles group, click the Shape Outline button ☑.

1. Open the file **SanFran1** and move to slide 2.

2. Select the body text placeholder, then from the Drawing Tools Format tab, in the Shape Styles group, click the Shape Outline button ☑ and choose Dashes and then click More Lines to open the Format Shape dialog box, as shown in Figure 8-1.

Figure 8-1
Line Style options on the Format Shape dialog box

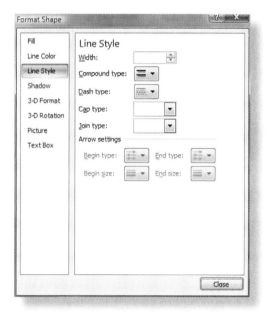

3. Click the Width spin box up arrow to change the width to 5 points.

4. Click the drop-down list box arrow beside Compound type, and choose the second option (double line). You have now applied a 5 point, double, solid color line around the body text placeholder.

5. Click on the Line Color option at the left of the Format Shape dialog box and choose Gradient Line.

6. Under the Gradient Stops heading, select Stop 1 if it is not already selected. Click the color drop-down list box and choose Indigo, Accent 1, Darker 25%; change the stop position to 24% by moving the slider or using the scroll up arrow.

7. Click Add.

8. Select Stop 2. From the Color drop-down list, choose Indigo, Accent 1, Lighter 40%. Change the Stop position to 67%, and click Add.

9. Select Stop 3 from the drop-down list, choose White, Text 1 from the Color drop-down list, change the Stop position to 100%, and click Add. You have now created a custom gradient outline using colors from the theme, as shown in Figure 8-2.

10. Click Close on the Format Shape dialog box.

Figure 8-2
Finished gradient outline

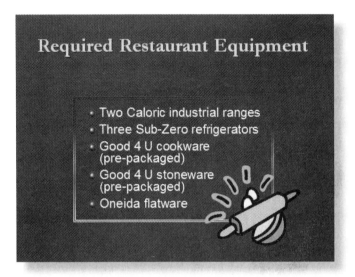

REVIEW

To change the Zoom, you can use the Zoom slider and the Fit to Window button on the Status bar or similar buttons on the View tab.

11. Deselect the text box and change the Zoom to 150% to see the double line clearly.

12. Change the Zoom setting back to Fit to Window.

13. Leave the presentation open for the next exercise.

Exercise 8-2   ADJUST LINE STYLE

PowerPoint offers a variety of dash styles to apply to outlines and borders. A *dash style* is the pattern of dashes and dots that make up an outline. Styles include solid line, square dot, dash, and combinations of dashes and dots.

When used sparingly, a dash style can add interest to a presentation. You can apply dash styles to outlines, lines, arrows, and object borders. The borders can be any color and any weight.

TIP

The outline is always present on a shape. If you do not want a contrasting color, then choose no line. If you want to emphasize the outline as a border, then choose a contrasting color that blends with your theme colors and make the line thicker, so it is easily visible on your slide.

1. Move to slide 3 and select the star object.

2. From the Drawing Tools Format tab, in the Shape Styles group, click the Shape Outline button ⬚. Choose Weight, and the select the 6-point line weight to apply it to the outline of the star. A thicker white border now surrounds the star.

Figure 8-3
Dash styles

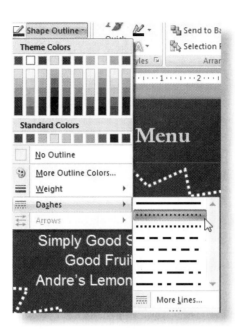

3. With the star still selected, click the Shape Outline button again, choose Dashes, and select the style titled Round Dot, as shown in Figure 8-3. A dash-style line or border can produce a dramatic effect.

4. Click the Shape Outline button again to display the line color choices.

5. Choose Periwinkle, Accent 5, Lighter 40% to change the line color.

6. Leave the presentation open for the next exercise.

Exercise 8-3   APPLY ARROWHEAD

Besides drawing block arrow shapes, you can draw lines with attached *arrowheads* by using the Arrow button found on the Insert tab in the Shapes group. You can add arrowheads to existing lines by using the Shape Outline button or the Format Shape dialog box (Line Style tab).

Arrow style options include several varieties of arrowheads, dots, and diamonds. By using the Format Shape dialog box, you can control whether to put an arrowhead on either end or on both ends of a line.

Figure 8-4
Arrow styles

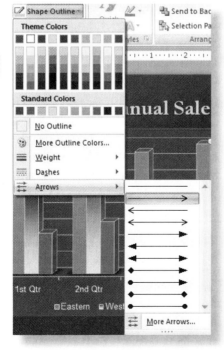

1. Move to slide 4.

2. From the Insert tab, in the Illustrations group, click the Shapes button and then click the Arrow button. Draw a line that slants down from the right, pointing toward the tallest bar on the chart.

3. From the Drawing Tools Format tab, in the Shape Styles group, click the Shape Outline button, click Weight, then choose 3-points to increase the weight of the arrow so you can see it.

4. Deselect the line. Notice the small arrowhead on the end of the line.

5. Select the arrow. From the Drawing Tools Format tab, in the Shape Styles group, click the Shape Outline button, and choose Arrows, as shown in Figure 8-4.

PowerPoint 2007

NOTE

The placement of the arrow is determined by where you started drawing the line. The left arrowhead appears at the beginning of the line, and the right arrowhead appears at the end of the line.

6. Select Arrow Style 3, a left-pointing arrow. The arrow points away from the chart.

7. Click the Shape Outline button ☑ again. Choose Arrows and Arrow Style 5, a right-pointing arrow.

8. Click the Shape Outline button ☑ again and choose Arrows and then choose More Arrows.

9. Under The End Size heading, choose Arrow R Size 9. This increases the end of the arrowhead. Click Close to close the dialog box and return to the presentation.

10. Adjust the length and angle of the arrow by dragging the sizing handle on the end of the arrow, as shown in Figure 8-5. No rotation handle is required to make lines angle on the slide.

11. Leave the presentation open for the next exercise.

Figure 8-5
Adjusting the arrow

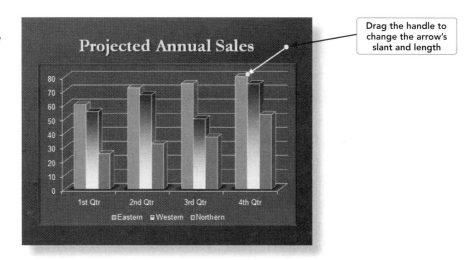

Exercise 8-4   ADJUST TRANSPARENCY AND ROTATE

When you increase the *transparency* of an outline or fill color you allow more of the background slide color to show through the selected object.

1. Still working on slide 4, select the arrow.

2. Right-click the arrow and choose Format Shape from the shortcut menu.

3. In the Format Shape dialog box, click the Line Color option at the left of the dialog box.

4. Move the Transparency slider over to 50%, as shown in Figure 8-6. Notice that the lavender background color is showing slightly through the white color.

Figure 8-6
Format Shape dialog
box with 50% line
Transparency

5. Click on the **3-D Rotation** option at the left of the dialog box.

6. Scroll the X Rotation to **60%**. Notice how the appearance of the arrow changes.

7. Click **Close** on the Format Shape dialog box.

8. Move the arrow as necessary to ensure that it is still pointing at the tallest column.

9. Create a handout header and footer: Include the date and your name as the header, and the page number and text **[8-4your initials]** as the footer.

10. Create a new folder for Lesson 8. Save the presentation as **[8-4your initials]** in the new Lesson 8 folder.

11. Print handouts with six slides per page.

12. Leave the presentation open for the next exercise.

Working with Solid and Gradient Colors

Up to this point, you have used theme colors when applying any color to objects. An infinite number of other colors are also available.

It is usually most design friendly to utilize the colors that make up the color theme, but, at times, one or two additional colors can enhance the look of a slide. Be careful when choosing extra colors because too many colors can spoil a presentation.

Extra colors are available from the Colors dialog box. This dialog box has two tabs—Standard and Custom. Standard colors are premixed colors that you choose by clicking a sample on the Standard tab. Custom colors are colors that you mix yourself on the Custom tab.

Exercise 8-5 ADD A THEME SOLID FILL COLOR TO A SHAPE

You change the fill color by using one of two options:

- Use the Shape Fill button found on the Drawing Tools Format tab in the Shape Styles group.

- Right-click on the Shape and choose **Format Shape** from the shortcut menu. The Format Shape dialog box will appear so you can use the Fill option.

If you apply a fill to a shape and later decide you don't want it, it's easy to remove. Choose the Shape Fill option and No Fill to remove the fill from the shape.

1. Move to slide 3 and right-click the star. From the shortcut menu, choose Format Shape to open the Format Shape dialog box.

2. Click the Fill option at the left of the dialog box, then click the Color drop-down list box arrow, and choose the Standard, Yellow sample color.

3. Click Close.

4. With the star still selected, from the Drawing Tools Format tab, in the Shape Styles group, click the Shape Fill button 🖫, as shown in Figure 8-7. Click the Indigo, Background 1, Darker 25% theme color.

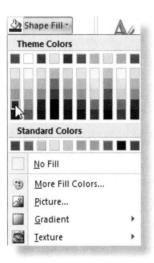

Figure 8-7
Changing an object's fill color

5. Move to slide 5 and select the large triangle shape.

6. From the Drawing Tools Format tab, in the Shape Styles group, click the Shape Fill button 🖫, and choose No Fill. The color disappears, but the line remains.

7. With the triangle still selected, click the arrow next to the Shape Outline button 🖉 and choose No Outline. The triangle's border disappears. Although it looks like the object disappeared, it is still there.

8. Click the text containing the names of cities, and then press Esc to select the object (the invisible triangle).

9. Click the Shape Fill button 🖫 again and choose the Purple, Accent 2 color. The triangle is once again visible.

10. Leave the presentation open for the next exercise.

Exercise 8-6   CHOOSE A STANDARD COLOR OR CUSTOM COLOR

You open the Colors dialog box by choosing More Fill Colors from the Shape Fill button's drop-down list or by choosing More Outline Colors from the Shape Outline button's drop-down list.

The Standard tab contains a honeycomb of preset color choices that you may apply to your presentation.

The Custom tab on the Colors dialog box enables you to create any color you desire. Drag a crosshair to choose the color you want; then use a scroll bar to choose the brightness level for the color. Remember the color terms for the RGB color model a computer uses to mix all colors that you see:

• *Hue*—the actual name of the color that you select.

• *Saturation*—the intensity of the color. Colors you select from the top of the Custom Color palette are strong colors that are highly saturated; colors at the bottom seem muted because their saturation level is low.

• *Luminance*—the brightness of the color. When you drag the pointer up on the vertical bar, you are increasing the amount of white in a color; therefore, the luminance level has increased and the color is brighter. When you drag the pointer down, you are decreasing the amount of white in the color and adding black. Therefore, the color has a lower luminance level and is less bright.

After you choose a custom color, it appears on the second line of the Shape Fill and Shape Outline buttons' drop-down lists, so you can use it again without having to re-create it.

1. With the triangle on slide 5 selected and still working on the Drawing Tools Format tab, in the Shape Styles group, click the Shape Fill button .

2. Select More Fill Colors to display the Colors dialog box.

3. Click the Standard tab. The honeycomb of colors is displayed.

4. Click a dark green/blue color in the upper left corner of the honeycomb. Notice the color sample on the right side of the dialog box, showing you the Current color and the New color you just selected, as shown in Figure 8-8.

Figure 8-8
Working with
Standard Colors

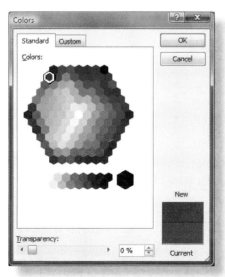

5. Click OK.

6. Still working on slide 5, select the circle on top of the triangle.

7. From the Drawing Tools Format tab, in the Shape Styles group, click the Shape Fill button and choose More Fill Colors.

8. Click the Custom tab on the Colors dialog box. This dialog box contains a color palette and a vertical bar for choosing brightness, as shown in Figure 8-9.

Figure 8-9
Working with
Custom Colors

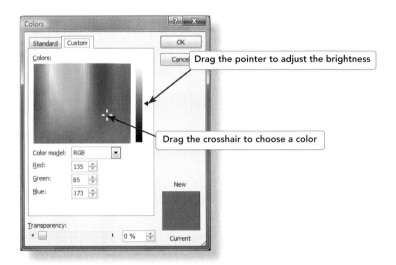

9. Drag the crosshair straight up. Notice in the sample on the lower right corner that the New color has a higher saturation level than the Current color.

10. Drag the crosshair across the top of the palette. All the colors at the top have a high saturation, and the colors change horizontally like a rainbow.

11. Drag the crosshair across the bottom of the palette. The colors are subdued due to low saturation.

12. Choose a fairly saturated color; then drag the black pointer on the vertical bar up and down to see how the color brightness changes.

13. Experiment with the color palette and the brightness bar until you find a color you like. Click OK.

14. Leave the presentation open for the next exercise.

Exercise 8-7   CHOOSE A GRADIENT FILL FOR OBJECTS

A gradient fill can add interest and dimension to PowerPoint objects including shapes, text placeholders, text boxes, and other objects. When you apply a *gradient fill*, the object contains colors that blend (or shade) into one another. A gradient fill can consist of one color blending to black, two colors that blend to each other, or a preset combination of multiple colors that are built into PowerPoint.

Besides choosing colors for gradient fills, you can specify the direction of the gradual color change, such as horizontal or diagonal.

1. Move to slide 3 ("Sample Menu") and select the star shape.

2. From the Drawing Tools Format tab, in the Shape Styles group, click the Shape Fill button ![icon]. Choose Gradient at the bottom of the menu then More Gradients. The Format Shape dialog box appears.

3. Click the Fill option at the left of the dialog box.

4. In the Fill options area, click Gradient Fill. Click the Preset colors drop-down list box arrow, which contains specially created gradient fills and choose Late Sunset. Observe the effect that this has on the star shape.

5. Click the Type drop-down list box arrow and choose Path, as shown in Figure 8-10.

Figure 8-10
Fill Effects dialog box

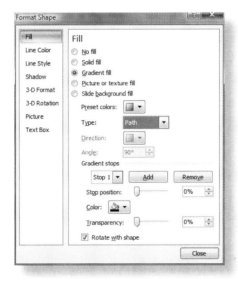

6. Click Close to view your new gradient fill.

7. Move to slide 2 and select the body text placeholder.

8. Right-click and choose Format Shape from the shortcut menu to open the Format Shape dialog box.

9. Select the Fill option at the left of the dialog box, and choose Gradient Fill.

10. Click Remove several times (until Remove is grayed out) to take out the previously set gradient stops.

11. For Gradient Stop 1, click the Color list box arrow and choose Periwinkle, Text 2, Darker 10%. Drag the Stop position slider bar to 52% and click Add.

12. For Gradient Stop 2, click the Color list box arrow and choose Indigo, Background 1, Darker 50%. Drag the Stop position slider bar to 100% and click Add.

13. Click the Type drop-down list box arrow, and choose Linear. Under Direction, choose Linear Diagonal with the darker color in the upper left corner of the sample.

14. Click Close to view your gradient-filled text placeholder.

15. Leave the presentation open for the next exercise.

Exercise 8-8   ADJUST GRADIENT COLORS

You may need to adjust gradient colors after applying an object's fill. To do this, reopen the Format Shape dialog box using either the Shape Fill button or the shortcut menu and modify only the stops you wish to change.

1. Move to slide 5 and select the circle on top of the triangle.

2. From the Drawing Tools Format tab, in the Shape Styles group, click Shape Outline and choose No Outline.

3. Still working on the Drawing Tools Format tab, in the Shape Styles group, click the Shape Fill button 🖼 and choose Gradient. The samples that are previewed under this gradient option show the current fill color combined with white or black in different arrangements of the two colors.

4. Select More Gradients to open the Format Shape dialog box and display the Fill option.

5. Choose Gradient Fill and click Remove several times to remove the previously set gradient stops.

6. Create gradient stop 1 using a light pink color (view the honeycomb of colors by clicking More Colors). Set the stop position at 27% and choose Add.

7. Add gradient stop 2, using a darker pink color, and set the stop position at 68% and choose Add.

8. Add gradient stop 3, using a very dark pink color, and set the stop position to 100% and choose Add.

9. In the Type drop-down list box, choose Path. Click Close to view your gradient. The circle now looks like a sphere with different layers of pink gradient.

10. Move to slide 3 and select the star with the gradient fill. From the Home tab, in the Clipboard group, click the Format Painter button 🖋. Move back to slide 5 and click the circle. The gradient and outline colors from the star are applied to the circle.

11. With the circle selected, click the Format Painter button again 🖋 and then click the outside edge of the triangle.

12. Change the font size to 20 points and then click at the end of the text, and press [Enter] two times to center the text in the triangle.

13. Update your handout footer to show the text **[8-8your initials]**. Save the presentation as **[8-8your initials]** in the Lesson 8 folder.

14. Print handouts with six slides per page.

Working with Pictures and Textures

Pictures and textures can be a great addition to your PowerPoint shapes. They can fill a shape to make the shape stand out on your slide. Many adjustments can be made to the picture and texture fills to modify the look of the shape.

Exercise 8-9   APPLY A PICTURE FILL

You can further customize your slides by using a picture as a shape fill. This is a creative technique that can call attention to your picture.

1. Move to slide 6. Select the last diamond on the slide.

2. From the Drawing Tools Format tab, in the Shape Styles group, click the Shape Outline button and click the More Outline Colors to change the outline color to black. Change the weight of the outline to 3 points.

3. Still working on the Drawing Tools Format tab, in the Shape Styles group, click the Shape Fill button and choose Picture.

4. Navigate to the folder where your student files are stored.

5. Select the file **Emp1** and click Insert. The diamond shape is now filled with an employee picture, as shown in Figure 8-11. This keeps the design element of the slide, but also allows content to be displayed within the shape.

Figure 8-11
Picture fill

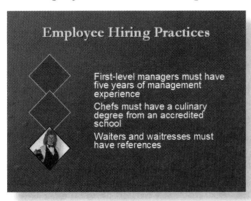

6. Click the first diamond on slide 6.

7. Click the Shape Fill button again and choose Picture.

8. Navigate to the folder where your student files are stored.

9. Select the file **Chef1** and click Insert. The diamond shape is now filled with a chef picture.

10. Select both pictures then click the Shape Outline button and choose weight. Change the weight to 3 points. Change the color to black which should now be available as a recent color sample without having to return to the Colors dialog box.

11. Leave the presentation open for the next exercise.

Exercise 8-10   APPLY A TEXTURE FILL

In addition to gradient fills and pictures, you can apply textured fill effects, such as marble and wood grain.

TIP

You are not limited to the textures shown on the Textures tab. Under Insert from, click File and you can navigate through your disk drives and network drives to choose graphics files from other sources that you can use as textures.

1. Still working on slide 6, right-click the middle diamond then choose Format Shape from the shortcut menu to open the Format Shape dialog box. Click the Fill option at the left of the dialog box.

2. In the Fill section, choose Picture or Texture Fill and click the Texture drop-down list box arrow, as shown in Figure 8-12.

3. Point to several different textures, one at a time. Notice the name of the texture appears as a ScreenTip.

Figure 8-12
Choosing a Texture fill

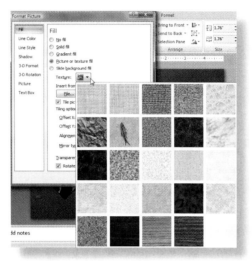

4. Choose Granite.

5. Click Close to close the Format Picture dialog box.

6. With the center diamond still selected, from the Drawing Tools Format tab, in the Shape Styles group, click the Shape Outline button ☑ and change the weight to 3 points and leave the outline color White.

7. Leave the presentation open for the next exercise.

Exercise 8-11 USE OFFSETS TO STRETCH OR REPOSITION A PICTURE

Offsets are used to scale the size of a picture within a shape or to reposition a picture within a shape. Positive numbers move the picture edge toward the center of the shape, and negative numbers move the picture edge away from the shape. Tiling options work similar to offsets but are used when a picture or texture is tiled to repeat itself.

1. Still working on slide 6, select the first diamond shape with the chef picture fill.

2. Right-click the picture of the chef and select Format Picture from the shortcut menu. Click the Title Bar of the Format Picture dialog box and drag the dialog box over so that you can view the changes to the picture as you make them.

3. In the Format Picture dialog box, click the Fill option on the left side of the dialog box.

4. Check the box Tile Picture as Texture. This allows you to adjust the position and size of the picture within the shape.

5. For Offset X, key **-7.25**.

6. For Scale X, key **44%**.

7. For Offset Y, key **-4.5**.

8. For Scale Y, key **43%** as shown in Figure 8-13.

Figure 8-13
Format Picture
dialog box

9. Click the drop-down list box arrow beside Alignment and choose several different options and note what happens to the picture within the diamond when each option is chosen. Choose Top Left.

10. Click Close to close the dialog box. Notice how the woman, who is the main focus of the picture, is more centered within the shape.

11. Right-click the picture of the server and select Format Picture from the shortcut menu.

12. Click the Fill option at the left of the dialog box, and adjust the following components under Stretch options, as shown in Figure 8-14:

Change the Left to **-4%**.
Change the Right to **0%**.
Change the Top to **3%**.
Change the Bottom to **1%**.

Figure 8-14
Format Picture
dialog box stretch
options

13. Click Close to close the dialog box. Notice how the picture looks more centered and attractive within the diamond.

14. Leave the presentation open for the next exercise.

Exercise 8-12   ADJUST TRANSPARENCY AND PICTURE ROTATION

Adjusting the transparency of an object can make the shape or picture seem to blend into the background.

1. Still working on slide 6, select the middle diamond shape that is filled with the Granite texture.

2. Right-click and choose Format Picture from the shortcut menu.

3. Working on the Fill option of the Format Picture dialog box, drag the Transparency slider to 50%. Notice the effect applied to the diamond shape on the slide.

4. Click Close to accept the transparency setting and close the Format Picture dialog box.

5. Move to slide 1. Select the picture of San Francisco.

6. From the Picture Tools Format tab, in the Arrange group, click the Rotate button and choose More Rotation options.

7. Under Size and rotate, change the Rotation box to -10%.

8. Under Scale, check the Lock aspect ratio if it is not already checked. Change the Height to 127% and change the Width to 127%, as shown in Figure 8-15.

Figure 8-15
Changing picture rotation

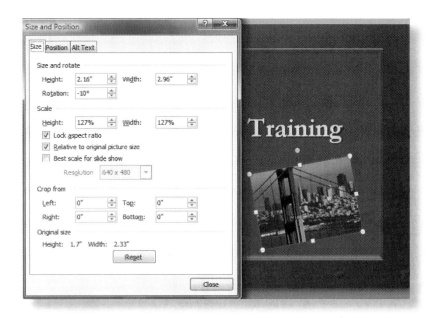

9. Click Close then notice the picture's rotation.

Exercise 8-13   USE PRECISE SIZE DIMENSIONS

Resizing stretches or shrinks the dimensions of an object such as a table, chart, graphic, equation, or other form of information. You can also resize to fit precise dimensions by using the Size and Position dialog box. *Lock aspect ratio* keeps the size relationship that the object currently has, so both vertical and horizontal dimensions will be resized to keep the same perspective.

1. Move to slide 2, and select the picture on the slide.

2. From the Picture Tools Format tab, in the Size group, click the Dialog Box Launcher.

3. Under the Size and rotate heading, decrease the Height to 2.2″. Notice that the Width changes to keep the aspect and not distort the picture, as shown in Figure 8-16.

Figure 8-16
Using precise
dimensions

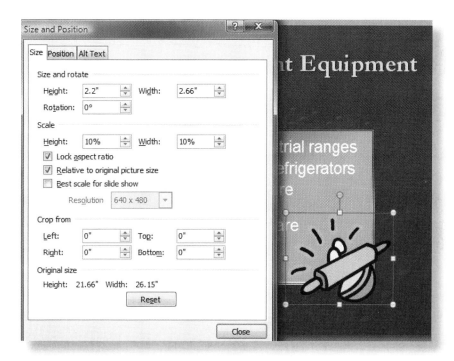

4. Click the Position tab of the dialog box.

5. Under Position on Slide, increase the Horizontal Position to 6.2″ so the clip art is positioned in the bottom right corner of the text placeholder.

6. Click Close to view the resized and repositioned clip art.

7. Update the handout footer to show the text **[8-13your initials]**.

8. Move to slide 1 and save the presentation as **[8-13your initials]** in your Lesson 8 folder.

9. Preview, and then print the presentation as handouts, six slides per page, grayscale, framed.

Applying Shape Effects

Effects can enhance the appearance of your PowerPoint objects. Effects may be applied to text, shapes, pictures, charts, tables, and more. There are many options for Shape Effects including *Shadows*, *Glow*, *Bevel Effects*, and *3-D Rotation*. Shape Effects are found on the Format tab for the corresponding object.

Exercise 8-14   ADD SHADOW AND REFLECTION

The *Shadow* and *Reflection* effects appear to create either a shadow of the selected object or a lighter transparent copy of the object appearing as a reflection.

1. Move to slide 1 and select the picture of San Francisco.

2. From the Picture Tools Format tab, in the Picture Styles group, click the Picture Effects button ⬚.

3. Choose Shadow and then select Shadow Options.

4. Working in the Format Picture dialog box under presets, choose Offset Diagonal Bottom Right.

5. Under the Color heading, click the drop-down list box arrow and choose Indigo, Background 1, Darker 50%.

6. Change the following Shadow setting options, as shown in Figure 8-17:
   Change Transparency to **69%**.
   Change Size to **103%**.
   Change Blur to **8.5 points**.
   Change Angle to **40°**.
   Change Distance to **10 points**.

Figure 8-17
Changing Shadow settings

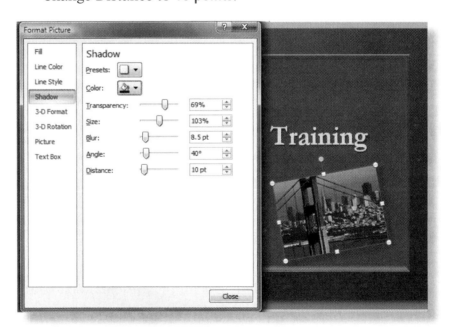

TIP

If you move your dialog box to the side of the picture, you can observe the changes that each item makes.

7. Click Close to view your shadow creation.

8. Move to slide 6 and select the middle diamond shape with the granite fill.

9. From the Drawing Tools Format tab, in the Shape Styles group, click the Shape Effects button ▣ and choose Reflection then Half Reflection, 4 point Offset.

10. Leave the presentation open for the next exercise.

Exercise 8-15 ADD GLOW AND SOFT EDGES

The *Glow* and *Soft Edges* effects appear around the entire object that is selected. The *Glow* effect applies a softened color around the object. The *Soft Edges* effect smoothes the edges of the object to make it blend into the background or just appear not as structured.

1. Move to slide 5 and select the triangle object filled with text.

TIP

If the colors displayed under the Glow option are not what you are looking for, at the bottom of the Glow option, use More Glow Colors to choose alternate colors from the theme, standard, or custom colors.

2. From the Drawing Tools Format tab, in the Shape Styles group, click the Shape Effects button ▣, as shown in Figure 8-18.

3. Choose Glow and select Accent Color 5, 18 point glow.

4. Select the circle at the top of the triangle. Click the Shape Effects button ▣ again, choose Glow, and select Accent Color 5, 18 point glow.

Figure 8-18
Applying a Glow effect

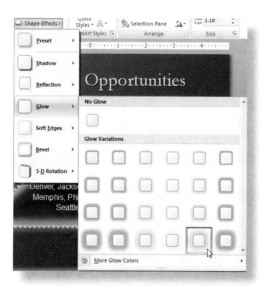

5. Move to slide 1 and select the picture of San Francisco.

6. From the Picture Tools Format tab, in the Picture Styles group, click the Picture Effects button ⊡.

7. Choose Soft Edges and 10 points. Notice the effect is applied to the picture. The picture edges are softened, but the Shadow effect is also still applied to the picture.

8. Leave the presentation open for the next exercise.

Exercise 8-16 ADD BEVEL EFFECTS

Bevel is a Shape Effect that gives an object the appearance of being three dimensional.

1. Move to slide 3 and select the star filled with text.

2. From the Drawing Tools Format tab, in the Shape Styles group, click the Shape Effects button ⊡.

3. Choose Bevel and 3-D Options.

Figure 8-19
Applying a Bevel effect

4. Under Bevel in the Top section, choose Divot and change the Width to **16 points** and the Height to **15 points**.

5. Under Contour, change the color to White, Text 1, Darker 50% and change the size to **3.5 points**.

6. Under Surface, change the material to Special Effect, Dark Edge and the Lighting to Warm, Sunrise. Change the Angle to **80°**, as shown in Figure 8-19.

7. Click Close to preview the Bevel effect you have created.

Exercise 8-17 ADJUST 3-D ROTATION

The *3-D Rotation* effect allows you to change the way your three-dimensional object is viewed.

1. Still working on slide 3 with the star selected, from the Drawing Tools Format tab, in the Shape Styles group, click the Shape Effects button ⊡.

2. Choose 3-D Rotation and 3-D Rotation Options.

3. Under Presets, in the Parallel category, choose Off Axis 1 Right.

4. Change the X Rotation to **350°** and the Z Rotation to **10°**, as shown in Figure 8-20.

5. Change the Distance to the Ground to **5 point**.

Figure 8-20
Adjust 3-D Rotation

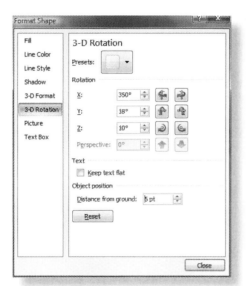

6. Click Close to preview the bevel effect you have created.

7. Update the handout footer to show the text **[8-17your initials]**.

8. Move to slide 1 and save the presentation as **[8-17your initials]** in your Lesson 8 folder.

9. Preview, and then print the presentation as handouts, six slides per page, grayscale, framed.

10. Leave the presentation open for the next exercise.

Adjusting Presentation Color Settings

Sometimes the colors of a presentation do not convert well when printing with a black printer. Using *grayscale*, slide colors are automatically converted to shades of gray. However, sometimes areas are too dark and will not reproduce well if you need to print handouts and photocopy them for your audience. In the next exercises you will try several different settings that preserve the shades of gray and readable text as much as possible. There is no one perfect solution for every situation and you will need to try out different options to see what will give you the best results. Changes made to grayscale settings do not affect the color version of your presentation.

Exercise 8-18   CHOOSE THE GRAYSCALE VERSION

The grayscale view of your presentation can be displayed in two ways:

• From the View tab, in the Color/Grayscale group, click the Grayscale button ▣.

• When the grayscale version is in view, select an object on a slide, click a button in the Change Selected Object group on the Grayscale tab to choose one of the options.

1. Move to slide 1. From the View tab, in the Color/Grayscale group, click the Grayscale button ▣. The slide changes to a grayscale view and the Grayscale tab appears, as shown in Figure 8-21.

2. Select the large rectangle on slide 1.

3. From the Grayscale tab, in the Change Selected Object group, click the Light Grayscale button ▦. The rectangle is filled with a lighter gray and the text is still easy to read. Click the Undo button ↺.

Figure 8-21
Changing grayscale settings

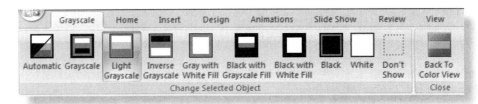

4. Move to slide 2 and select the body text placeholder. From the Grayscale tab, in the Change Selected Object group, click the Black with White Fill button ▢. This setting displays the outline in black but the white text is not visible. Click the Undo button ↺.

5. On slide 5, select the sphere on top of the triangle and click the Inverse Grayscale button ▦. Repeat this step for the triangle. Notice that this step works well for the sphere but the text on the triangle is not visible. Click the Undo button ↺ twice.

6. From the Grayscale tab, in the Close group, click the Back to Color View button ▦ to return to the normal color view.

7. Leave the presentation open for the next exercise.

Exercise 8-19 CHOOSE THE PURE BLACK-AND-WHITE VERSION

Grayscale settings may need several adjustments to lighten areas of a slide for better printing in black. The *Pure Black and White* option makes this easier and usually assures good results with text. However, pictures and other images may not convert adequately for your needs. The Pure Black and White button ▦ is on the View tab, in the Color/Grayscale group.

1. Move to slide 1. From the View tab, in the Color/Grayscale group, click the Pure Black and White button ▦. The slide changes to show only black and white and the Grayscale tab appears as in the previous exercise.

2. Move to slide 6 and notice that the pictures are not visible. Select the shape at the top and bottom that contain pictures. From the View tab, in the Change Selected Object group, click the Grayscale button ▦.

3. Click the Back to Color View button ▦ to return to the color presentation.

4. Update the handout footer to show the text **[8-19your initials]**.

5. Move to slide 1 and save the presentation as **[8-19your initials]** in your Lesson 8 folder.

6. Preview, and then print the presentation as handouts, six slides per page, grayscale, framed.

7. Close the presentation.

Lesson 8 Summary

- Many PowerPoint objects—shapes, text placeholders, text boxes, and WordArt—can be enhanced with the addition of shape outline, shape fill, and shape effects.

- Shape Outline options include solid lines, gradient lines, and dashed lines in any thickness (weight) or color you want.

- Apply Shape Outline options by using the Shape Outline button ☑. Alternatively, you can use the Format Shape dialog box.

- The Arrow button ◥ draws a line with an arrowhead on its end. You can add or remove an arrowhead from any drawn line by using the Shape Outline button ☑ and then selecting Arrows.

- The Line Style tab of the Format Shape dialog box offers additional ways to format an arrow, enabling you to choose the size and shape of the arrowhead and line formatting options.

- Shape Fill options include solid colors, gradients, textures, and pictures. In addition, solid colors and gradients can have varying degrees of transparency, enabling background objects and colors to show through.

- Remove an outline from an object by choosing the No Outline option from the Shape Outline button's drop-down list. Remove the shape fill from an object by choosing the No Fill option from the Shape Fill button's drop-down list.

- It is usually best to use the coordinating theme colors that are part of the slide design theme colors, but, occasionally, a few additional colors can enhance a presentation.

- Additional colors are available by choosing More Fill Colors from the Shape Fill button's drop-down list, More Outline Colors from the Shape Outline button's drop-down list, or More Colors from the Font Color button's drop-down list.

- The Colors dialog box enables you to choose from a honeycomb of premixed colors on the Standard tab or to mix your own colors on the Custom tab.

- You have several options when using gradient fills—the blending of colors into each other—including the direction and transparency of the effect. You may choose a preset gradient or create your own.

- PowerPoint includes several textures that you can use for fill effects. In addition, you can use graphics files containing textures from other sources that are saved on your computer or network.
- Any picture—a scanned photograph or other image—can be used to fill a shape. When using a picture, you have the choice of distorting the picture to fill the space or preserving its aspect ratio.
- Picture borders and picture effects can be modified through the Picture Tools Format tab or through the Format Picture dialog box.
- PowerPoint objects can be resized and rotated using precise dimensions for location and size.
- The Shadow and Reflection effects can be used to create a lighter transparent copy of the image either shadowed or reflected from the original shape.
- The Glow and Soft Edges effects can be used to smooth the edges of shapes and apply a soft color around shapes.
- Bevel effects create the appearance of three-dimensional shape.
- The shape in 3-D can be rotated to increase the three-dimensional perspective.
- The grayscale version and the black-and-white version of a presentation can be adjusted for clearer printing on black-and-white printers. Adjusting the grayscale settings has no effect on the color version of the presentation.

LESSON 8		Command Summary
Feature	**Button**	**Ribbon**
Format Lines and Outlines of Shapes		Drawing Tools Format, Shape Styles group, Shape Outline
Format Borders of Pictures		Picture Tools Format, Picture Styles group, Picture Border
Format Shape Fill		Drawing Tools Format, Shape Styles group, Shape Fill
Copy Formatting		Home, Clipboard group, Format Painter
Apply Shape Effects		Drawing Tools Format, Shape Styles group, Shape Effects
Apply Picture Effects		Picture Tools Format, Picture Styles group, Picture Effects
Switch from Color to Grayscale		View, Color/Grayscale group, Grayscale
Switch from Color to Pure Black and White		View, Color/Grayscale group, Pure Black and White

Concepts Review

True/False Questions

Each of the following statements is either true or false. Select your choice by indicating T or F.

T F   1. Transparency settings can only be adjusted with solid fill colors.

T F   2. Effects can be used to give shapes the appearance of being in 3-D.

T F   3. A gradient fill can only have two colors

T F   4. Shape Outlines are available in only one width.

T F   5. Granite and marble fills are examples of textures.

T F   6. Offsets can be used to reposition or stretch pictures within shapes.

T F   7. You can not create custom colors to use for Shape Fills and Outlines.

T F   8. You must be careful when making changes in Grayscale view, because they can affect the colors of your presentation.

Short Answer Questions

Write the correct answer in the space provided.

1. What dialog box can you use to change the size and shape of arrowheads?

_____

2. What button should be used to access gradient fill options?

_____

3. How do you remove a shape outline from a shape?

_____

4. Which shape effect creates the appearance of three dimensions?

_____

5. How do you apply a custom color to a Shape Outline?

_____

6. How do you create a custom gradient fill?

_____

7. How do you switch the screen display of your presentation from color to grayscale?

_____

8. How do you change grayscale settings for PowerPoint objects?

_____

Critical Thinking

Answer these questions on a separate page. There are no right or wrong answers. Support your answers with examples from your own experience, if possible.

1. Think of the way you used a gradient fill to add dimension to a simple circle. What other shapes could you change by using a gradient fill to add dimension?

2. Which shapes in a presentation are most suited to outlines or borders? What outline or border styles and colors work best against what types of backgrounds?

Skills Review

Exercise 8-20

Format outline colors and styles, and change fill colors.

1. Open the file **Funding2**.
2. Add an outline to the title text placeholder on slide 1 of the presentation by following these steps:
   a. Select the title text placeholder.
   b. From the Drawing Tools Format tab, in the Shape Styles group, click the Shape Outline button ⊡.
   c. Choose Tan, Background 1, Darker 25%.
3. Format the outline by following these steps:
   a. With the title text placeholder selected, from the Drawing Tools Format tab, in the Shape Styles group, click the Shape Outline button ⊡.
   b. Choose Weight and then 6 points.
   c. Click the Shape Outline button ⊡ again.
   d. Choose Dashes and select the Round Dot style.
   e. Apply this same outline formatting to all of the body text placeholders in the presentation.

4. Apply a fill to the title text placeholder on slide 1 by following these steps:

   a. With the title text placeholder selected, from the Drawing Tools Format tab, in the Shape Styles group, click the Shape Fill button 🖾.

   b. Select Tan, Background 1, Lighter 40%.

   c. Click the Shape Fill button 🖾 again and select More Fill Colors. On the Custom Color tab, change the transparency to 40% and click OK.

   d. Apply this same fill to all of the body text placeholders in the presentation.

5. Draw and format an arrow by following these steps:

   a. Move to slide 3, from the Insert tab, in the Illustrations group, click the Shapes button 🔲 and then click the Arrow button 🔲.

   b. Drag the crosshair pointer from the word "Specialties" in the title to the word "fat" in the first line of the body text placeholder.

6. Use the Format Shape dialog box to format the arrow by following these steps:

   a. Right-click the arrow and choose Format Shape from the shortcut menu.

   b. Click the Line Style option at the left of the dialog box.

   c. In the Width section scroll up to 6 points.

   d. In the Dash Style section, choose the solid line.

   e. In the End type drop-down list, choose Stealth Arrow.

   f. In the End size drop-down list, choose Arrow R Size 6.

   g. Click the Line Color option at the left of the dialog box.

   h. Click the Color drop-down list box arrow and choose Tan, Background 1, Darker 50%. Click Close.

7. Check spelling in the presentation.

8. Create a handout header and footer: Include the date and your name as the header, and the page number and text **[8-20your initials]** as the footer.

9. Move to slide 1 and save the presentation as **[8-20your initials]** in your Lesson 8 folder.

10. Preview, and then print the presentation as handouts, six slides per page, grayscale, framed. Close the presentation.

Exercise 8-21

Use a color from the extended color palette, apply a gradient fill, and apply a picture fill.

1. Open the file **Owners1**.

2. Apply a gradient fill to an object by following these steps:

   a. Move to slide 2 and select the body text placeholder.

   b. From the Drawing Tools Format tab, in the Shape Styles group, click the Shape Fill button 🖾 and choose Gradient and More Gradients.

c. Click the Fill option at the left of the dialog box, and then select Gradient Fill.

d. Click Remove several times to clear the previous settings.

e. Set Stop 1 to Lavender, Accent 6, Darker 50% with Stop position at 40% and Transparency at 60%. Click Add.

f. Set Stop 2 to Gray-50%, Background 2, Lighter 40% with Stop position at 100% and Transparency at 50%. Click Add.

g. Under Direction, choose Linear Diagonal with purple in the lower left and dark gray in the upper right.

h. Click Close to view your gradient fill. Notice the gradient fill applied blends nicely with the background design.

i. Apply the same effect to the two body text placeholders on slide 3 and the body text placeholder on slide 4.

TIP

PowerPoint remembers your gradient stops. If you want the same stops as the last time you created a gradient fill, proceed with creating a gradient fill on your new object and choose Stop 1 and Add, and Stop 2 and Add. This saves time by not having to adjust the numbers.

3. Add dimension to a circle by following these steps:

a. Click the top circle on slide 1.

b. From the Drawing Tools Format tab, in the Shape Styles group, click the Shape Fill button and choose Gradient and More Gradients.

c. Click the Fill option at the left of the dialog box, and then select Gradient Fill.

d. Click Remove several times to clear the previous settings.

e. Set Stop 1 to Lavender, Accent 6, Darker 50% with Stop position at 43%. Click Add.

f. Set Stop 2 to Gray-50%, Background 2, Darker 50% with Stop position at 50%. Click Add.

g. Set Stop 3 to Gray-50%, Background 2, Lighter 40% with Stop position at 70% and Transparency of 60%. Click Add.

h. Set Stop 4 to Lavender, Accent 6, Lighter 40% with Stop position at 100%. Click Add.

i. Under Type, choose Path. This makes the gradient pattern go in a circle inside your shape.

j. Click Close to view your gradient fill.

4. Use the Format Painter button to copy the formatting of the circle to the other circles following these steps:

a. Select the circle with the gradient applied.

b. From the Home tab, in the Clipboard group, double-click the Format Painter button.

c. Click each of the remaining circles in the presentation.

d. Click the Format Painter button again to turn it off.

5. Apply a custom color fill to a placeholder by following these steps:

a. Move to slide 1 and select the subtitle text placeholder.

b. From the Drawing Tools Format tab, in the Shape Styles group, click the Shape Fill button, and choose More Fill Colors.

c. In the Colors dialog box, click the Custom tab.

   d. On the Colors palette, drag the crosshair near the middle of the yellow section to create a tan color.

   e. Drag the black pointer up the vertical bar to make the color a little lighter.

   f. Add 30% transparency to the object, so you can still read the white text.

   g. Compare the Current and New colors in the sample box in the lower right corner of the dialog box. When you like the new color, click OK.

   h. Click Close to close the Colors dialog box.

6. Make the Good 4 U text two increments larger, bold, and shadowed.

7. Fill a shape with a picture by following these steps:

   a. Select the top circle on slide 1.

   b. From the Drawing Tools Format tab, in the Shape Styles group, click the Shape Fill button and choose Picture.

   c. Navigate to your student files for lesson 8 and insert **food1**.

8. Check spelling in the presentation.

9. Create a handout header and footer: Include the date and your name as the header, and the page number and text **[8-21your initials]** as the footer.

10. Move to slide 1 and save the presentation as **[8-21your initials]** in your Lesson 8 folder.

11. View the presentation as a slide show; then preview and print the presentation as handouts, four slides per page, grayscale, landscape, framed. Close the presentation.

Exercise 8-22

Apply a gradient fill, use shape effects, and change grayscale settings.

1. Open the file **Opening2**.

2. On slide 2, select the body text placeholder (banner shape) and change its Outline and Fill by following these steps:

   a. From the Drawing Tools Format tab, in the Shape Styles group, click the Shape Outline button , select No Outline.

   b. Still working on the Drawing Tools Format tab, click the Shape Fill button , and choose Gradient and More Gradients.

   c. Select Gradient Fill to activate the gradient options.

   d. Under Preset, choose Early Sunset from the Preset colors list box.

   e. Under Direction, choose the Linear Diagonal shading style with the red color in the upper right corner.

   f. Click Close.

   g. Using the Format Painter button , apply the same formatting to the subtitle placeholder on the Title slide and all of the body text placeholders in the presentation.

   h. Remove the bullet from the subtitle placeholder.

3. Apply the Soft Edges shape effect by following these steps:
   a. Move to slide 1 and select the subtitle text placeholder.
   b. From the Drawing Tools Format tab, in the Shape Styles group, click the Shape Effects button ⊡.
   c. Choose Soft Edges and 10 points.
4. From the View tab, in the Color/Grayscale group, click the Grayscale button ⊟. Scroll through the presentation.
5. Change the grayscale settings by following these steps:
   a. Select the subtitle text placeholder on slide 1.
   b. From the Grayscale tab, in the Change to Selected Object group, click the Inverse Grayscale button ⊟.
   c. Repeat this setting for the body text placeholders.
6. Scroll through all the slides to view the changes to grayscale settings.
7. From the Grayscale tab, in the Close group, click the Back to Color View button ⊟ .
8. Check spelling in the presentation.
9. Create a handout header and footer: Include the date and your name as the header, and the page number and text **[8-22your initials]** as the footer.
10. Move to slide 1 and save the presentation as **[8-22your initials]** in your Lesson 8 folder.
11. Preview, and then print the presentation as handouts, four slides per page, grayscale, landscape, framed. Close the presentation.

Exercise 8-23

Add a gradient outline, apply a gradient fill, apply shape effects, and work with grayscale settings.

1. Open the file **MiamBch1**.
2. On slide 3, apply an outline by following these steps:
   a. Select the body text placeholder on slide 3 then right-click. Choose Format Shape from the shortcut menu.
   b. Click the Line Color option at the left of the dialog box and choose Solid Line.
   c. Choose the color Orange, Accent 6, Darker 50%.
   d. Set Transparency at 25%.
   e. Click the Line Style option at the left of the dialog box and change the Width to 10 points.
   f. Under Compound type, choose the Thick Thin option of a double line with the thicker line on top and a thinner line on bottom.
   g. Click Close.

3. Use the Format Painter button  to copy the border from the placeholder on slide 3 to the picture in the lower-right corner of slide 1.

4. Apply a gradient fill to an object by following these steps:

   a. On slide 3, select the body text placeholder.

   b. From the Drawing Tools Format tab, in the Shape Styles group, click the Shape Fill button and select Gradient and More Gradients.

   c. Choose Gradient Fill.

   d. Choose Wheat from the Preset colors drop-down list.

   e. Choose one of the Linear Diagonal shading styles.

   f. Click Close.

5. Apply shape effects by following these steps:

   a. Move to slide 3 and select the first star.

   b. From the Drawing Tools Format tab, in the Shape Styles group, click the Shape Effects button and choose Bevel.

   c. Choose Relaxed Inset from the Bevel options.

   d. Use the Format Painter button to apply this shape effect and color to the other three stars on the slide, as shown in Figure 8-22.

Figure 8-22
Slide with outline, fill, and shape effects

Our Newest Location

555 South Beach Street
Tropical Breezes Center
Miami Beach, Florida

growth

6. Apply picture effects by following these steps:

   a. Move to slide 1 and select the beach picture.

   b. From the Picture Tools Format tab, in the Picture Styles group, click the Picture Effects button and choose 3-D Rotation.

   c. Choose Perspective Heroic Extreme Left from the 3-D options.

7. Adjust grayscale settings by following these steps:
   a. Move to slide 3.
   b. From the View tab, in the Color/Grayscale group, click the Grayscale button ◨.
   c. Select the first star on slide 3.
   d. From the Grayscale tab, in the Change Selected Object group, click the Light Grayscale button ◪.
   e. Apply the same settings to all of the stars on the slide.
   f. From the Grayscale tab, in the Close group, click the Back to Color View button ◪.
8. Check spelling in the presentation.
9. Create a handout header and footer: Include the date and your name as the header, and the page number and filename **[8-23your initials]** as the footer.
10. Move to slide 1 and save the presentation as **[8-23your initials]** in your Lesson 8 folder.
11. Preview, and then print the presentation as handouts, three slides per page, grayscale, framed. Close the presentation.

Lesson Applications

Exercise 8-24

Apply a custom gradient fill, apply a texture fill, and format an arrow.

1. Open the file **Recruit1** and apply the design theme Urban. Use the theme colors Trek.

2. Insert two new slides after slide 3 using the Title and Content layouts. Use the text in Figure 8-23 to create bulleted lists.

Figure 8-23
Data for slides

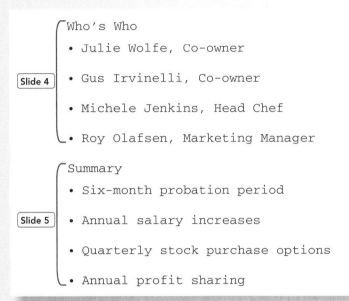

Slide 4

Who's Who
• Julie Wolfe, Co-owner
• Gus Irvinelli, Co-owner
• Michele Jenkins, Head Chef
• Roy Olafsen, Marketing Manager

Slide 5

Summary
• Six-month probation period
• Annual salary increases
• Quarterly stock purchase options
• Annual profit sharing

3. On slide 1, select the title text, and then from the Drawing Tools Format tab, in the WordArt Styles group, click the WordArt Quick Styles button. Choose Fill - Accent 6, Warm Matte Bevel.

4. Using the Format Painter button, copy the formatting of the WordArt title and paint onto the title text on the remaining slides.

5. On slide 1, select the subtitle text placeholder and create a 2 stop gradient fill using White, Background 1 with the stop position of 50% and Brown, Accent 2, Lighter 40% with a stop position of 100%. Change its direction to Linear Up.

6. Move the Good 4 U logo onto the white part of the subtitle placeholder.

7. Draw a diamond on slide 1 in the lower right corner of the slide and insert the picture **employee** from your student files. Position and size it appropriately and adjust the offsets as needed so the employee's head is not cut off.

8. On slide 5, draw a 16-point star at the bottom center of the slide. Key the text **Substantial!** inside the star. Format the star as follows:
   - Make it 1.75 inches high and 4 inches wide.
   - Change the text size to 22 points, change its color to a dark brown, and make it bold.
   - Rotate it slightly to the left.
   - Change the shape fill to the texture Cork with transparency of 25%.
   - Adjust the star's position to make a pleasing composition.

9. From the Insert tab, in the Illustrations group, click the Shapes button 🔲 then click the Arrow button 🔲, draw an arrow pointing from the star to the text "Annual profit sharing." Change the arrow's line thickness to 4.5 points and the color to Brown, Accent 4, Darker 50%.

10. Check spelling in the presentation.

11. Create a handout header and footer: Include the date and your name as the header, and the page number and text **[8-24your initials]** as the footer.

12. Move to slide 1 and save the presentation as **[8-24your initials]** in your Lesson 8 folder.

13. Preview, and then print the presentation as handouts, six slides per page, grayscale, framed. Close the presentation.

Exercise 8-25

Apply outlines and fills, use custom colors, draw an arrow, and apply shape effects.

1. Open the file **Seminar2**.

2. Key the text Good 4 U in the subtitle placeholder on slide 1.

3. Move to slide 2 and draw a rectangle slightly larger than the body text placeholder and position it on top of the placeholder. Use the Fill, Line Style, and Line Color options in the Format Shape dialog box to format the rectangle as shown in Figure 8-24 as follows:
   - Use Aqua, Accent 1 as the solid fill color then modify this color in Custom Colors and make it a little darker than the current color.
   - Change the transparency to 75%.
   - Under Line Style, change width to 6 points and change the Compound type to Triple.
   - For the Color of the line, use Gray-50%, Text 1, Darker 50%.
   - Copy the rectangle and move to slide 4 and paste it.

Figure 8-24
Slide with formatted
rectangle

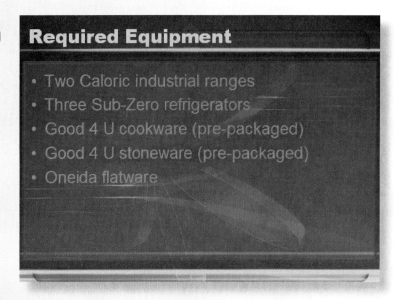

4. Search for an appropriate clip art image and position it to the right of the title and subtitle on slide 1.

5. After slide 4, insert a new slide with a blank layout. Insert WordArt with the Fill-Accent 1, Metal Bevel, Reflection and key the text **Welcome!**

6. Resize and reposition the WordArt for a pleasing appearance.

7. Move to slide 3 and draw a left block arrow from the right edge of the slide down to quarter 4. Rotate the arrow as necessary.

8. Format the arrow to include the Water droplets texture fill.

9. Apply the Glow shape effect to the arrow using the Accent color 4, 11 point glow.

10. Move to slide 1 and apply a Reflection picture effect to the picture. Choose the Half Reflection, 4 point offset.

11. View the presentation as a slide show.

12. Check spelling in the presentation.

13. Create a handout header and footer: Include the date and your name as the header, and the page number and text **[8-25your initials]** as the footer.

14. Move to slide 1 and save the presentation as **[8-25your initials]** in your Lesson 8 folder.

15. Preview, and then print the presentation as handouts, six slides per page, grayscale, framed. Close the presentation.

Exercise 8-26

Change outline colors, styles, and fills of objects; add an arrowhead; adjust grayscale settings.

1. Open the file **TrainPt3**.

2. On slide 2, recolor the dollar sign clip art image to use a green that better blends with the slide theme color.

REVIEW

To change the text box to a callout Shape, select the Shape and then from the Drawing Tools Format tab, in the Insert Shapes group, click the Edit Shape button and choose Change Shape. Select the Oval Callout shape.

3. On slide 3, insert a text box near the upper right corner of the chart with the text **Estimating over $89,000!** on two lines. Change the font to Arial bold at 20 points.

4. Add a 3-point dark green outline to the text box; then change its Shape to an Oval Callout.

5. Use the callout shape's yellow adjustment handles to make the callout line point to the tallest column on the graph.

6. On slide 4, draw a text box. In the text box, key **10% discount off the lunch menu, Monday through Thursday!**

7. Format the text box as follows to give it a blackboard effect:

   - Change the fill color to Black, Accent 4.
   - Change the text to white with the font Harlow Solid Italic at 32 points.
   - Apply a White outline at 8 points with the compound type Thin Thick on the bottom.
   - Apply the Bevel effect of Divot using Soft Edge material.

8. Resize and reposition the clip art and the text box if needed to create a pleasing composition.

9. On slide 4, change the grayscale setting for the Shape to Inverse Grayscale button ▄. Review all the slides in Grayscale view and make any other necessary adjustments.

10. Check spelling in the presentation.

11. Create a handout header and footer: Include the date and your name as the header, and the page number and text **[8-26your initials]** as the footer.

12. Move to slide 1 and save the presentation as **[8-26your initials]** in your Lesson 8 folder.

13. Preview, and then print the presentation as handouts, six slides per page, grayscale, framed. Close the presentation.

Exercise 8-27 ◆ Challenge Yourself

Apply and format fills, outlines, effects, and grayscale settings.

1. Open the file **Market3**.

2. Select the Title on slide 1 and center the text, then change the placeholder to an oval shape.

3. Apply a fill, outline, and shape effects to the selected oval with the following settings:
   - Fill: White, Background 1, Darker 35%.
   - Outline: Black, Text 2.
   - Outline Width: 6 points.
   - Dash Type: Round Dot.
   - Shadow Effect: Perspective Diagonal Upper Right.
   - Bevel Effect: Divot.

4. Apply a two-stop gradient fill to the title text placeholder on slide 2 with the following settings, as shown in Figure 8-25:
   - Stop 1: Gray-25%, Accent 5, Darker 25% with a stop position of 50%.
   - Stop 2: Gray-25%, Text 1, Lighter 60% with a stop position of 100%.
   - Direction: Linear Up.

Figure 8-25
Title placeholder
with gradient fill

5. Apply the same gradient fill to the title text placeholders on slides 3 to 5.

6. Create a line arrow on slide 5 pointing up beside the bulleted text. Format the arrow with these settings:
   - Weight: 6 points.
   - Color: Gray-25%, Text 1, Lighter 40%.
   - Stealth Arrow end type.
   - Arrow R Size 9 end size.

7. Add a Title Only slide after slide 5.

8. Key **Summary** in the title text placeholder and format the same as the other title text placeholders.

9. Draw an **Explosion 2** shape in the middle of slide 6 and format with the following settings:
   - Gradient Fill: **Chrome Preset** with **Path** type.
   - Bevel Effect: **Convex**.
   - 3-D Rotation: **Perspective Contrasting Right**.

10. Insert WordArt using Gradient **Fill-Accent 1, Outline-White** and key **Good 4 U!** Resize and rotate the WordArt to fit on the Explosion shape. Resize the shape if necessary.

11. Review the presentation in Grayscale view and make any necessary adjustments including changing several items using the Light Grayscale button ▣.

12. View the presentation as a slide show.

13. Check spelling in the presentation.

14. Create a handout header and footer: Include the date and your name as the header, and the page number and text **[8-27your initials]** as the footer.

15. Move to slide 1 and save the presentation as **[8-27your initials]** in your Lesson 8 folder.

16. Preview, and then print the presentation as handouts, six slides per page, grayscale, framed. Close the presentation.

On Your Own

In these exercises you work on your own, as you would in a real-life work environment. Use the skills you've learned to accomplish the task—and be creative.

Exercise 8-28

Plan a children's birthday party for a group of young people, church group, or an elementary school class. Prepare a presentation to help explain the event. Using a design theme with your choice of theme colors, create a title slide and separate slides listing activities or games and the rules or instructions for each one. For example, you could plan to carve pumpkins, take a hayride, and have a wiener roast, or you could plan a weekend at a hotel with an indoor water park and playground, or a trip to an aquarium with plans to eat at a fun restaurant, or a trip to your local capital city and attractions.

If you have access to a scanner or a digital camera, include digital pictures that relate to the activities. Otherwise, find clip art pictures to illustrate your presentation. Use your own creativity to format an attractive presentation that uses many of the outlines, fills, and effects presented in this lesson. Modify the grayscale settings as needed to print the presentation in grayscale. Save the presentation as **[8-28your initials]**. Preview, and then print the presentation as handouts with six slides per page.

Exercise 8-29

Imagine that you are organizing a family reunion for your extended family at a remote location where you can enjoy tourist activities (not at someone's house). For example, you could travel to South Dakota, and explore Mount Rushmore and other local attractions, or you could travel to Gatlinburg, Tennessee, and see local shows, The Great Smoky Mountains National Park, and other local attractions and shopping. Create a presentation describing the reunion, including location, who is invited, planned activities, estimated costs, and a slide encouraging family members to attend. Apply a design theme and theme color of your choice to the slides in your presentation. Format the presentation by using outline, fill, and shape effects. Add clip art and photographs. Modify the grayscale settings as needed to print the presentation in grayscale. Save the presentation as **[8-29your initials]**. Preview, and then print the presentation as handouts, four slides per page, framed.

Exercise 8-30

Open the file **SanFran1** used in this lesson. Change to a different design template and theme color of your choice. Change all the slide titles to WordArt, and apply fill effects, outlines, and shape effects to all shapes and body text placeholders in the presentation. Be careful to keep the look and style of each slide uniform throughout the presentation, and use good judgment to keep the design from looking too busy. Save the presentation as **[8-30your initials]**. Preview, and then print the presentation as handouts, six slides per page.

Lesson 9

OBJECTIVES

After completing this lesson, you will be able to:

1. Work with multiple objects.

2. Align, distribute, and flip objects.

3. Work with layers of objects.

4. Group, ungroup, and regroup objects.

5. Edit images.

Estimated Time: 1½ hours

MCAS OBJECTIVES

In this lesson:
PP07 3.5.1
PP07 3.5.2
PP07 3.5.3
PP07 3.5.4
See Appendix

Illustrations can be refined using techniques such as grouping objects, layering objects, and aligning objects. These techniques help you create more effective illustrations leading to more meaningful presentations.

Working with Multiple Objects

When you want to treat multiple objects on a slide the same way, such as making them all the same color, you can select all the objects at the same time. Several different selection techniques can be used:

- Select one object, hold down Shift, and click each additional object you want to select.

- Draw a selection rectangle around the objects you want to select by holding down your left mouse button while you drag the pointer to create a rectangle around all the objects.

- From the Home tab, in the Editing group, click the Select button ⊠ then choose from Select All, Select Objects, or Selection Pane to select objects shapes from a list.

- Press Ctrl+A to select all objects.

To deselect all items, simply click a blank area of the slide or press Esc.

Exercise 9-1 SELECT MULTIPLE OBJECTS USING THE SHIFT KEY

To select multiple objects one at a time, first click an object to select it and then add objects to the selection by pressing Shift as you click another object.

1. Open the file **Strategy**.

2. With slide 1 displayed, press Ctrl+A. Notice the multiple sets of sizing handles. Every item on slide 1 is selected as shown in Figure 9-1.

Figure 9-1
Multiple selected objects

3. Click a blank area on the slide (or press Esc) to deselect the items.

4. Click the top line of the four thin lines. Notice its sizing handles.

5. Hold down Shift and click the next line. Notice that there are sizing handles around both objects, indicating that they are both selected.

6. With the two lines selected, from the Drawing Tools Format tab, in the Shape Styles group, use the Shape Outline button ⊠ to change their color to Dark Yellow, Text 1, Darker 25%, which appears as a green color. Both selected lines change color.

7. With the two green lines selected, press ⌈Shift⌋ and click the next two lines. Now all four long thin lines are selected.

8. From the Drawing Tools Format tab, in the Shapes Styles group, click the Shape Outline button 🖉 , click Weight, then choose More Lines.

9. Follow these steps to apply a gradient fill color:

   a. From the options at the left of the Format Shape dialog box, click Line Color then choose Gradient line.

   b. For Direction, click the drop-down list box arrow and from the gallery of options choose Linear Right.

   c. Under Gradient stops, for Stop 1, click the Color button 🖉 and choose Tan, Text 2, Darker 25%. Change the Stop position by keying 50% in the spin box or by dragging the slider to the right.

   d. Under Gradient stops, click the drop-down list box arrow to select Stop 3. Click the Color button 🖉 and choose More Colors. From the Colors dialog box, click the Standard tab and select a Maroon color on the right side of the honeycomb of colors then click OK. Change the Stop position by keying 100% in the spin box or by dragging the slider to the right.

   e. Click Close to accept all these changes. Leave your presentation open for the next exercise.

Exercise 9-2   SELECT MULTIPLE OBJECTS BY DRAWING A SELECTION RECTANGLE

To draw a selection rectangle, start at a blank area of a slide, click the left mouse button and hold as you drag your pointer diagonally to create a rectangle surrounding the objects that you want to select. Only objects completely enclosed in the selection rectangle are selected.

It takes a little practice to learn where to start a selection rectangle, and it's easy to miss an object. If that happens, try drawing the selection rectangle again, or add a missed object to the selection by using the ⌈Shift⌋+click method.

1. Move to slide 2.

2. From the View tab, in the Zoom group, click the Fit to Window button 🔲 to be sure that your entire slide fits on your screen.

3. Position the pointer on the left above the first shape with text.

4. Click and hold the left mouse button while you drag your pointer diagonally to the lower right of the slide. As you drag, you will see a temporary rectangle, as shown in Figure 9-2, with a blue border and semitransparent blue fill—a selection rectangle—that shows the area you are attempting to select.

Figure 9-2
Selection rectangle

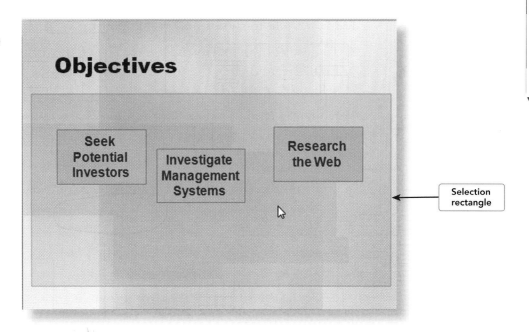

5. Release the mouse button. Notice the sizing handles surrounding each of the shapes with text.

6. If one or more of the shapes is not selected, try again, making sure that all shapes are completely inside the selection rectangle.

7. Now change to a gradient fill for all selected shapes following these steps:

   a. From the Drawing Tools Format tab, click the Shape Fill button 🔲, choose Gradient then More Gradients.

   b. From the Format Shape dialog box, click the Fill option on the left then select Gradient fill.

   c. For Preset colors, click the drop-down list box arrow and from the gallery select the Gold gradient.

   d. For Type, choose Path.

   e. Click Close.

8. With the shapes selected, click the Shape Outline button 🔲 and choose No Outline.

Exercise 9-3   REMOVE AN OBJECT FROM A GROUP OF SELECTED OBJECTS

You might want to change the composition of a group of selected object as you work. One way is to deselect all the objects by clicking a blank part of the slide. Another way is to hold down [Shift] and click a selected item to deselect it, leaving the remaining items in the group selected.

1. Move back to slide 1 and select all four lines.

2. To deselect the line at the top and leave the other three lines selected, hold ⟦Shift⟧ and click the top line. The remaining three lines are still selected.

3. Hold ⟦Shift⟧ and click the bottom line. The bottom line is deselected, leaving only the two center lines selected.

4. Now change the direction of the linear fill by following these steps:

   a. From the Drawing Tools Format tab, in the Shapes Styles group, click the Shape Outline button 🖉, click Weight, then choose More Lines.

   b. From the options at the left of the Format Shape dialog box, click Line Color then choose Gradient line.

   c. For Direction, click the drop-down list box arrow and from the gallery of options choose Linear Right.
   Left

   d. Click Close.

Exercise 9-4   CREATE A DIAGRAM WITH SHAPES AND CONNECTOR LINES

A *connector line* is a straight, curved, or angled line with special endpoints that can lock onto an object's *connection sites*—handles on an object indicating where connector lines can be attached. When you rearrange objects joined with connector lines, the lines stay attached and adjust to the new position of the shapes they connect.

Connector lines can be used in combination with shapes to create a diagram.

1. Move to slide 2 and select the shape "Seek Potential Investors."

Figure 9-3
Drawing a connector line

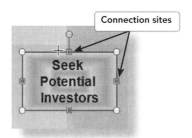

2. From the Drawing Tools Format tab, in the Insert Shapes group, choose the More button 🔽. From the Lines category click the Arrow ◥. Move the pointer over one of the shapes. Notice that a red connection site appears on each side of the shape and your pointer changes to a crosshair, as shown in Figure 9-3.

3. Click the connection site on the right side of the first shape, "Seek Potential Investors," and an arrow will appear. Click on the tip of the arrow and move it to the left connection site of the second shape, "Investigate Management Systems." When the arrow is selected, the endpoints will be red showing that it is connected to the shapes. The arrow is thin right now, but you will change the line color and thickness later.

4. Select the first shape and change its position slightly. Notice that the two shapes stay connected when you move one.

5. From the Insert Shapes gallery, click the Arrow button ⬐ then repeat step 3 to connect the middle shape to the right shape, "Research the Web."

6. Select the right shape and from the Insert Shapes gallery, click the Elbow Arrow Connector button ⬐. Connect the bottom of the third shape to the bottom of the first shape. You may need to use the yellow adjustment handle then move the shapes as needed to make sure your arrows point in the directions shown in Figure 9-4 to create a looping pattern.

Figure 9-4
Finished connector lines

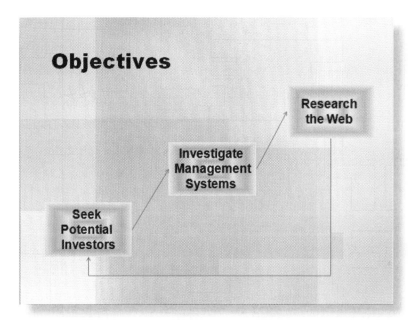

7. Select all of the arrow connectors, then from the Drawing Tools Format tab, click the Shape Outline button ☑, click Weight then choose 3 points.

8. Click the Shape Outline button ☑ again and select the Brown, Accent 6 color so the line is more visible.

9. Create a new folder for Lesson 9, and save the presentation as **[9-4your initials]** in the new folder but do not print the presentation. Leave it open for the next exercise.

Aligning, Distributing, and Flipping Shapes

PowerPoint has a number of tools that you can use to reorient objects on a slide. You can rotate and flip them, creating mirror images of the original. Selected objects can be aligned with each other, either vertically or horizontally. And you can distribute multiple objects, spacing them evenly across the slide either horizontally or vertically.

Exercise 9-5 ALIGN OBJECTS HORIZONTALLY AND VERTICALLY

When multiple objects are selected, you access the tools to accomplish alignment and distribution tasks by choosing the Home tab, in the Drawing group, the Arrange button 🔲, then Align. Table 9-1 lists the various alignment options.

TABLE 9-1 Alignment Options

Option	Purpose
Align Left	Vertically aligns the left edges of objects.
Align Center	Vertically aligns the centers of objects.
Align Right	Vertically aligns the right edges of objects.
Align Top	Horizontally aligns the top edges of objects.
Align Middle	Horizontally aligns the center points of objects.
Align Bottom	Horizontally aligns the bottom edges of objects.
Distribute Horizontally	Spaces objects evenly in a horizontal direction relative to each other.
Distribute Vertically	Spaces objects evenly in a vertical direction relative to each other.
Align to Slide	A toggle button. When selected, aligns or spaces objects relative to slide. When not selected, aligns or spaces objects relative to each other.
Align Selected Objects	A toggle button. When selected, aligns or spaces objects relative to other selected objects on the slide. When not selected, aligns or spaces objects relative to the slide.

1. On slide 2, select the three rectangles.

2. From the Home tab, in the Drawing group, click the Arrange button 🔲 and choose Align to view the Alignment options.

3. Click Align to Slide if it is not already checked.

4. From the Home tab, in the Drawing group, click the Arrange button 🔲, and choose the Align Middle option. The objects line up across the middle of the slide.

5. Deselect the objects. From the View tab, in the Show/Hide group, click the check box beside Ruler and the check box beside Gridlines.

TIP

When working with the Align or Distribute commands, be sure you pay attention to the Align to Slide option because all alignment actions will be relative to the slide, not the selected objects.

6. Drag the shape that is farthest to the right up about 1 inch; use the ruler to help you position the shape. Drag the shape that is farthest to the left down to the bottom of the slide leaving enough room to still view the connector line.

7. Draw a selection rectangle around all three shapes and their connector lines.

8. From the Home tab, in the Drawing group, click the Arrange button and choose Align. Select Align Selected Objects.

9. Access the Alignment Options again, and click the Align Bottom option. The objects align horizontally again, but this time they align with the bottom of the slide.

10. Click the Undo button several times to return the shapes to their previous position where they are evenly aligned in the middle of the slide.

11. With the three shapes still selected, from the Home tab in the Drawing group, click the Arrange button and choose Align. Click the Align Left option. The objects are all aligned at the left, but two of the shapes are hidden because they are under one shape.

Exercise 9-6 DISTRIBUTE OBJECTS HORIZONTALLY AND VERTICALLY

1. Still working on slide 2, deselect the shapes. Select only the top shape and drag it up about 1.5 inches. Select the bottom shape and drag it down about 1 inch.

2. Reselect the three rectangles and not the connector lines.

3. From the Home tab, in the Drawing group, click the Arrange button and choose Align. Click Align Selected Objects. Choose Align again and click the Distribute Vertically option. Now the shapes are evenly spaced vertically based on the positions of the highest and lowest shapes—the extra space is divided evenly between the shapes.

4. Using the gridline to keep the same height on the slide, select the top shape and move it to the right then select the bottom shape and move it to the left.

5. Select all three shapes then from the Home tab, in the Drawing group, click the Arrange button and choose the Distribute Horizontally option so the shapes are spaced evenly.

6. Adjust the arrow connectors as needed.

Exercise 9-7   FLIP AND ROTATE OBJECTS

Use the Rotate and Flip commands on a single object or a group of objects. You can rotate and flip any PowerPoint object, including text placeholders.

When you have an object selected, the Rotate and Flip options can be found from the Home tab, in the Drawing group, under the Arrange button ⊞ and by choosing Rotate.

1. Move to slide 1 and select the picture.

2. From the Home tab, in the Drawing group, click the Arrange button ⊞ and choose Rotate.

3. Choose the Flip Horizontal option as shown in Figure 9-5. The man is now pointing the bow and arrow to the right.

4. From the Home tab, in the Drawing group, click the Arrange button ⊞ and choose Rotate. Click the Rotate Right 90° option. Complete this three more times. The picture rotates around and ends up in the previous position.

Figure 9-5
Rotating an object

5. Move to slide 5, select the WordArt text "Teamwork" and the banner behind it. With the objects selected, use the ⬇ on your keyboard to move the objects down to the right above the clip art image.

6. Select all of the objects on the slide. Click the Arrange button ⊞, click Align, click Align to Slide then access the Alignment Options again to choose Align Center.

7. From the View tab, remove the checks in front of the Ruler and Gridlines to turn off these features.

8. Save the presentation as **[9-7your initials]** in your Lesson 9 folder, but do not print the presentation. Leave it open for the next exercise.

Working with Layers of Objects

Although objects appear to be drawn on one surface, each of a slide's objects actually exists as a separate layer. Imagine that the objects are drawn on individual sheets of transparent plastic stacked on top of one another. When you rearrange the sheets, different objects appear on the top, sometimes hiding parts of the objects beneath them. The most recently drawn object is added to the top of the stack.

Within a stack of objects, you can move an individual object backward and forward by using the options available from the Home tab, in the Drawing group, and the Arrange button 🖽 , as listed in Table 9-2.

TABLE 9-2 Order Options

Option	Purpose
Bring to Front	Brings an object to the top of the stack
Send to Back	Moves an object to the bottom of the stack
Bring Forward	Brings an object up one layer in the stack
Send Backward	Moves an object down one layer in the stack

Exercise 9-8 BRING OBJECTS FORWARD OR BACKWARD

If several objects are already layered on a slide and you draw a new object, it automatically becomes the top object on the stack. To change its layer, select it, and then from the Home tab, in the Drawing group, click the Arrange button 🖽 and choose from among the order options.

When you are working with layered objects, sometimes you want to change the stacking order by just one level to make one object appear on top of another object. Select the object, click the Arrange button 🖽 , then choose the Bring Forward or Send Backward commands to move the object one layer at a time. If the object is not visible, you can press Tab several times until the desired object is selected and then you can move it.

Using the Bring to Front or Send to Back commands moves a selected object to the front of all other objects or behind all other objects.

1. Move to slide 4. From the Home tab, in the Drawing group, click the Shapes button 🖽 and click the Rectangle. Press Shift while you click and drag to draw a square larger than the circle to cover it.

2. With the shape selected, from the Home tab, in the Drawing group, click the Shape Fill button ▨ to change fill color to Brown, Background 1, Lighter 40%. Choose the Shape fill button ▨ again and choose More Fill Colors then change Transparency to 25%.

3. With the shape selected, from the Home tab, in the Drawing group, click the Shape Outline button ▨ and remove the outline. Now you can see the circle faintly behind the rectangle.

4. Press Tab and notice that selection handles appear around the circle. Pressing Tab is a good technique to use when layering because it is difficult to select an object with your pointer when it is under another object.

5. From the Home tab, in the Drawing group, click the Arrange button ▨.

6. Under the Order Objects heading, click Bring Forward to move the circle on top of the square, as shown in Figure 9-6.

Figure 9-6
Rectangle and circle

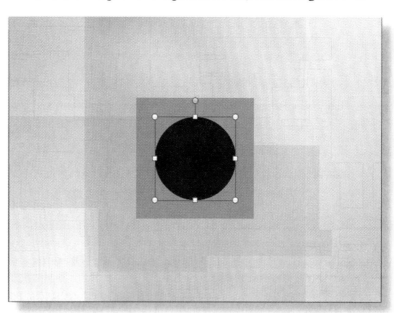

7. Still working on slide 4, deselect the circle.

8. Click the Shapes button ▨, then from the Basic Shapes category, click the Diamond. Click and drag to draw a diamond fitting inside the square then select the Shape Fill of Tan, Text 2. Choose no outline.

9. With the diamond shape selected, from the Home tab, in the Drawing group, click the Arrange button ▨ and under the Order Objects heading choose Send Backward. The diamond moves behind the circle but is in front of the square.

10. Repeat this step to make the diamond go behind the square.

11. Leave the presentation open for the next exercise.

Exercise 9-9   BRING OBJECTS TO THE FRONT OR SEND TO THE BACK

To rearrange the stacking order of an object that is located behind several other objects, you can send the top objects to the back, one at a time, until the desired object is on top.

1. Still working on slide 4, draw a square to cover the existing shapes on the slide and make the Shape Fill Brown, Background 1.

2. From the Home tab, in the Drawing group, click the Arrange button.

3. Under the Order Objects heading, choose the Send to Back option. The new square moves behind all other objects.

4. Select the diamond by clicking on one object and pressing Tab until the diamond is selected. Remember that it was sent behind the first square.

5. From the Home tab, in the Drawing group, click the Arrange button.

6. Under the Order Objects heading, choose the Bring to Front option. The diamond moves to the top of the object stack.

7. Leave the presentation open for the next exercise.

Exercise 9-10   USE THE SELECTION AND VISIBILITY PANE TO CHANGE THE STACKING ORDER

When you are planning to change the order of multiple objects, the Selection and Visibility pane can be a productivity booster. Because this pane stays open, you can change the order of all objects quickly.

Figure 9-7
The Selection and Visibility pane

1. Still working on slide 4, from the Home tab, in the Editing group, click the Select button and choose Selection Pane. The Selection and Visibility pane opens on the right side of your screen, as shown in Figure 9-7.

2. Click on Rectangle 2 in the Selection pane. Notice that the rectangle is now selected in Normal view. Click the re-order Bring Forward (points up) arrow at the bottom of the Selection pane twice. The tan transparent rectangle is now on top of the stack.

3. Click Oval 2 in the Selection pane, and click the Re-order Bring Forward up arrow twice. The circle is now back on top, as shown in Figure 9-8.

Figure 9-8
The completed
stack of objects

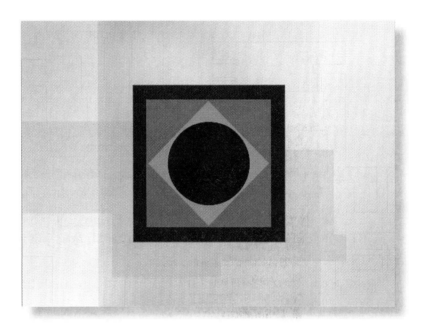

4. Click the Close button [×] on the Selection and Visibility pane.

5. Save the presentation as **[9-10your initials]** in your Lesson 9 folder but do not print it. Leave the presentation open for the next exercise.

Grouping, Ungrouping, and Regrouping Objects

When you group objects, you combine two or more objects so they behave as one. If you then move one object of the group, all the other objects move with it. Grouping assures that objects meant to stay together don't accidentally get moved individually or deleted. When you apply formatting to a group, all the objects of the group receive the same formatting.

Exercise 9-11 GROUP OBJECTS

To create a group of objects, first select the objects and then from the Home tab, in the Drawing group, click the Arrange button 🔲 and choose Group.

1. Move to slide 1, select the four lines in the middle of the slide. Notice the four sets of sizing handles.

2. From the Home tab, in the Drawing group, click the Arrange button
   and choose Group. Now there is only one set of sizing handles,
   indicating that all four lines are grouped as a single object, as shown
   in Figure 9-9.

Figure 9-9
Objects after
grouping

One set of sizing
handles

3. Drag the top resizing handle up, just below the WordArt. Notice that
   it creates more space between the lines and the top line moves up.

4. Click the Undo button , so the lines are positioned in the previous
   place.

5. Move your pointer over the box around the four lines until you get a
   four-pointed arrow .

6. Click and drag the group up. Notice that it moved the four lines to a
   new position without creating space between them.

7. Click the Undo button , so the lines are positioned in the previous
   place.

Exercise 9-12   UNGROUP AND REGROUP OBJECTS

If you want to delete an object in a group, change its position relative to the
other members, or change its size, you must first ungroup the objects. When
the objects are ungrouped, they once again become individual objects.

After working on individual objects of an ungrouped object, you can
easily regroup the objects by selecting any one of the group's original objects.
The Regroup command finds all the objects of the original group that remain
on the slide and groups them again.

1. Right-click any of the grouped lines, and then choose Group from the shortcut menu and Ungroup. Each line now has its own set of sizing handles.

2. Click a blank area of the slide to deselect all the lines.

3. Click the third line to select it (the other lines should not be selected) and then press Delete. One line is deleted from the slide.

4. Move the last line up under the second line and select all three lines by using a selection rectangle.

5. With the three lines selected, from the Home tab, in the Drawing group, click the Arrange button 🔲 and verify that Align Selected Objects is selected, then choose Distribute Vertically.

6. Select one of the remaining lines; then from the Home tab, in the Drawing group, click the Arrange button 🔲 and choose Regroup. The three remaining lines are grouped again.

Exercise 9-13 FORMAT PART OF A GROUPED OBJECT

You can easily select one object in a group of objects to make individual changes. First select the group; then click an object within the group. The group remains selected, but the object also displays selection handles, indicating that you can change its shape fill, outline, and orientation without affecting the other objects in the group.

1. Move to slide 2, and select the three shapes containing text only.

2. Group the shapes to make one object. A set of white sizing handles appears and the whole group could be moved or resized.

3. Click the edge of the middle shape. Selection handles surround the rectangle, as shown in Figure 9-10. Text can be edited in each of the grouped shapes and the shapes can still be resized or moved individually within the group even though they are contained in the group.

Figure 9-10
Selecting a single
object in a group

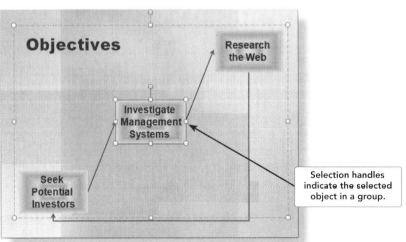

4. From the Home tab, in the Drawing group, click the Arrange button and choose Rotate and the Flip Vertical option. The selected rectangle turns upside down.

5. Repeat the previous step again to make the rectangle return to its previous position.

6. For the selected rectangle, click the Shape Fill button , click Gradient, and change the Gradient Fill Variation (direction) to Linear Left.

7. Save the presentation as **[9-13your initials]** in your Lesson 9 folder but do not print it. Leave the presentation open for the next exercise.

Editing Images

PowerPoint enables you to customize clip art and pictures in a variety of ways. Clip art can be recolored, ungrouped with parts removed, or rearranged as needed for unique illustrations. Pictures can be made more vivid or subtle, styles applied for creating framing, and compressed to reduce file sizes.

Exercise 9-14   RECOLOR CLIP ART

The *recolor* feature may be applied to clip art images or pictures to blend them with the theme colors. When the recolor feature is chosen, the whole image is changed to shades of the variation chosen.

1. Move to slide 5, and select the clip art image on the slide.

2. From the Picture Tools Format tab, in the Adjust group, click the Recolor button .

3. From the Light Variations listed choose Accent color 2, Light. Notice how the whole clip art is changed to match this variation, as shown in Figure 9-11.

Figure 9-11
Recoloring clip art

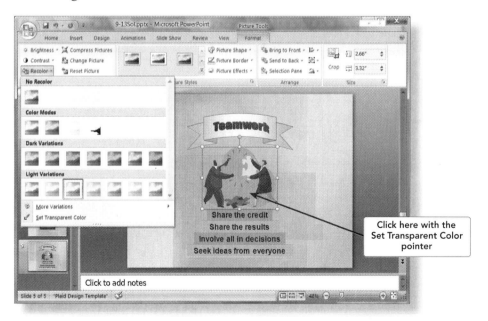

4. Select the clip art image; then from the Picture Tools Format tab, in the Adjust group, click the Recolor button 🖼 and choose No Recolor to return the image to its original colors.

5. From the Picture Tools Format tab, in the Adjust group, click the Recolor button 🖼 and choose Set Transparent Color.

6. Move your pointer over the clip art, and click in the area that is the background color of the clip art as shown in Figure 9-11 above. Only one color can be removed in this way.

Exercise 9-15   UNGROUP AND CHANGE FILL COLOR FOR PARTS OF A CLIP ART IMAGE

When you insert a Microsoft Windows Metafile (a vector graphics format used mostly as a clip art format) image, from the Clip Organizer, you can ungroup and change colors in the image to match the color theme of your presentation.

When a vector-based image is ungrouped, it is converted into a collection of PowerPoint objects that you can delete, resize, and reposition, just like any objects that you draw. You can also change the fill color and outline for parts of an image that has been converted.

1. Still working on slide 5, select the clip art picture.

2. With the picture selected, from the View tab, change the Zoom setting to 100% so you can see the details better.

3. Right-click the picture and choose Group from the shortcut menu, and Ungroup. A dialog box asks whether you want to convert this image to a Microsoft Office drawing object, as shown in Figure 9-12.

Figure 9-12
Converting a picture
to a Microsoft Office
drawing object

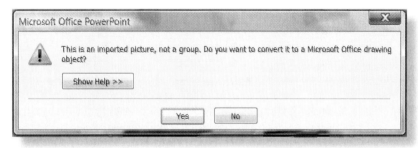

NOTE

Not all clip art images can be ungrouped. It depends on how they are made.

4. Click Yes to agree to the conversion. Notice that when you ungroup, the picture resets to the original color overriding the transparency setting that was applied in the previous activity.

Figure 9-13
Ungrouped object

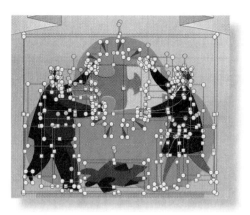

5. Right-click the image and choose Group from the shortcut menu and Ungroup. You will see many sets of selection handles, as shown in Figure 9-13. Notice that on this particular image you have two rotation handles and two corner selection handles at the top of the image. One of these sets is for the green background shape; the other is for a square behind the green shape that isn't needed. You'll remove these shapes in the next exercise.

6. Press Esc (or click any blank area of the slide) to deselect all of the pieces of the clip art.

Figure 9-14
Selecting a part of an ungrouped image

7. Select the puzzle piece that the woman is holding, as shown in Figure 9-14. From the Drawing Tools Format tab, in the Shape Styles group, click Shape Fill button, click More Fill colors, then choose maroon.

8. Hold down the Shift key while you carefully select the four small pointed shapes above and below the puzzle pieces and change their color to maroon now available from the Recent Colors category. Be careful not to select the green background shape.

Exercise 9-16 DELETE PARTS OF AN IMAGE

If you want to delete pieces of an ungrouped image, you must select them and then press Delete.

1. Select the green puzzle piece at the bottom of the image. Press Delete.

2. Select the brown puzzle piece at the bottom of the image. Press Delete.

3. Select the green shape that creates the background of the image. Because of its rounded shape, the selection handles seem far away from the image. Press Delete.

4. As mentioned in step 5 in the previous exercise, this image has a rectangle behind it that is currently the same color as the slide background. Click above the woman's head and you will see selection handles in a similar position as the shape you just removed. To confirm this, apply a different color and you can see where the rectangle is located. Press Delete.

5. Compare your picture with Figure 9-15. If too much of the picture was deleted, click the Undo button ↺ and try again.

Figure 9-15
The completed picture

6. Draw a selection rectangle around the remaining parts of the picture and group them. (Do not use the Regroup command.)

7. From the View tab, click the Fit to Window button.

8. If the ruler is displayed, hide it by clicking the View tab, in the Show/Hide group, and removing the check in the box beside Ruler.

Exercise 9-17 CREATE SOFT EDGES

Many editing features are available in PowerPoint 2007. These features can be combined to create original illustrations and refine current illustrations.

1. Move to slide 1 and select the picture.

2. From the Picture Tools Format tab, in the Size group, change the picture height to 3" and the width will change to 4.5" automatically.

3. From the Home tab, in the Drawing group, click the Shapes button and select a Rectangle shape. Draw a rectangle to cover the picture. From the Format tab, adjust its size to a height of 3.5" and a width of 5.0" so it is larger than the picture.

4. With the shape selected, use the Format tab to change its appearance by following these steps:

   a. Click the Shape Fill button then click More Fill Colors. From the Standard tab, select white and click OK.

   b. Click the Shape Outline button and choose No Outline.

c. Click the Shape Effects button ☐ and choose Soft Edges, then 10 Points.

d. From the Arrange group, choose Send to Back so the rectangle is behind the picture. This creates a soft frame around the edge to blend with the clouds in the picture.

5. Select the picture and make a similar change to soften the edges:

a. From the Picture Tools Format tab, in the Picture Styles group, select the Picture Styles More button ☐ to view the Style Gallery.

b. Choose Soft Edge Rectangle from the Style Gallery, as shown in Figure 9-16.

Figure 9-16
Changing Picture Styles

6. With the picture still selected, use the Picture Tools Format tab to make the following color changes:

a. In the Adjust group, click the Recolor button ☐ and, in the Light Variations category, choose Accent color 2 Light.

b. In the Adjust group, click the Brightness button ☐. Choose +20% from the drop-down list. Notice how the picture lightens and blends with the white rectangle.

7. Select both the picture and the rectangle and group them to make one object.

8. Save the presentation as **[9-17your initials]** in your Lesson 9 folder.

Exercise 9-18 COMPRESS PICTURES

When you use many photographic images, the file size of a presentation increases dramatically. So optimizing your pictures (clip art and photographs) can reduce your presentation's file size. However, you will only want to do this if the presentation is for viewing as a slide show or on the Web. A reduction in image quality will usually not be noticeable for on-screen viewing, but it will make a difference in printed output. You will also have the option to delete cropped areas of pictures.

To decrease the file size, use the Compress Pictures button ☐ from the Picture Tools format tab, in the Adjust group.

1. On slide 1, select the picture.

2. From the Picture Tools Format tab, in the Adjust group, click the Compress Pictures button ☐ and choose Options.

3. Be sure you have checks in front of both boxes at the top of the dialog box. Change the Target output to **Screen**, as shown in Figure 9-17. This will compress all images in the presentation, remove cropped areas, and make them at a good quality for viewing on the Web or through a projection device such as an LCD projector.

Figure 9-17
Compressing
pictures

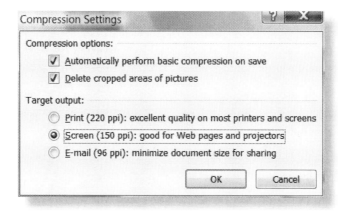

4. Click **OK** to accept these changes and click **OK** again.

5. Check spelling in the presentation.

6. View the presentation in grayscale to be sure all slides will be readable for printing. Make any changes if necessary.

7. Create a handout header and footer: Include the date and your name as the header, and the page number and text **[9-18your initials]** as the footer.

8. Save the file as **[9-18your initials]** in your Lesson 9 folder. Preview and then print the presentation as handouts, six slides per page, grayscale, framed.

9. Just to test the difference in file sizes, access the storage location where your exercise files are saved and compare the file sizes of exercise 17 with exercise 18. In this case, you may not see a reduction because of the particular picture used. However, the reduction can be dramatic depending on the type of images you are using.

TIP

In presentations where you have more photographs, especially high-resolution images, you will see a dramatic difference in file size.

Lesson 9

- Select multiple objects when you want to perform the same operation on all of them, for example, making them all the same color or moving all of them at the same time.

- Select multiple objects one at a time by holding down [Shift] while clicking each object.

- Select multiple objects all at once by drawing a selection rectangle around them (click and drag the pointer). Be sure to start dragging on a blank area of the slide.

- Add items to a selection by using the [Shift]+click method. Remove an item from a group of selected items by [Shift]+clicking it.

- Selected objects can be aligned horizontally or vertically to the whole slide or to other selected objects. They can be aligned by the top, bottom, middle, right side, left side, or center. They can be aligned relative to the edges of a slide when the Align to Slide option is selected.

- Selected objects can be evenly spaced by using the Distribute Horizontally or Distribute Vertically options. Objects can also be evenly distributed across the width or height of a slide when the Align to Slide option is turned on.

- Flipping an object creates a mirror image of it. The Rotate Left and Rotate Right options rotate objects in 90-degree increments.

- When objects overlap, use the Order options or the Selection and Visibility pane to control which object appears on the top. The most recently drawn object will be on top until you change its order.

- Grouping two or more objects combines them so they behave as if they were one object.

- After grouping objects, an individual object within the group can be selected without ungrouping all the objects. First click the group to select it; then click an object in the group. The selection handles indicate which object is selected. The selected group object can have its shape fill and outline formatted and can be flipped, but it cannot be deleted, resized, or rotated.

- To delete, resize, or rotate an individual object within a group, first ungroup the objects. After you are finished working on individual items in a group, regroup them.

- Vector-based pictures (for example, pictures with the .wmf file extension) can be converted into a group of PowerPoint objects by using the Ungroup command. Once ungrouped, the individual objects can be formatted and manipulated like any PowerPoint object.

- To reduce the file size of a presentation containing pictures, use the Compress Pictures command to reduce the resolution, remove cropped areas, and compress the pictures.

LESSON 9		Command Summary	
Feature	**Button**	**Menu**	**Keyboard**
Select all objects		Editing, Select All	Ctrl + A
Deselect all selected objects			Esc
Deselect one object from a group of selected objects			Shift + click
Add to a selection of objects			Shift + click
Align or distribute objects		Home, Drawing group, Arrange, Align	
Flip or rotate objects		Home, Drawing group, Arrange, Rotate	
Change the order of objects		Home, Drawing group, Arrange, Order Objects	
Group objects		Home, Drawing group, Arrange, Group	Ctrl + Shift + G
Ungroup objects		Home, Drawing group, Arrange, Ungroup	
Regroup objects		Home, Drawing group, Arrange, Regroup	
Display the ruler		View, Show/Hide group, Ruler	
Display the gridlines		View, Show/Hide group, Gridlines	
Recolor clip art		Picture Tools Format, Adjust group, Recolor	
Compress pictures		Picture Tools Format, Adjust group, Compress Pictures	

Concepts Review

True/False Questions

Each of the following statements is either true or false. Select your choice by indicating T or F.

T (F)   1. You cannot use selection rectangles to select multiple objects.

T (F)   2. Flipping an object makes it appear at a 45-degree angle.

(T) F   3. If you click the Rotate Left option several times while an object is selected, the object eventually returns to its original position.

(T) F   4. To select multiple objects, press [Shift] while clicking each object.

(T) F   5. You can align objects relative to other selected objects or relative to the slide.

(T) F   6. Many different 3-D Rotation options can be applied to objects and pictures.

T (F)   7. You cannot change the order of objects using the Selection and Visibility pane.

(T) F   8. The keyboard command to select all objects on a slide is [Ctrl]+[A].

Short Answer Questions

Write the correct answer in the space provided.

1. To select multiple objects with the pointer, which key do you press while clicking?

   Shift

2. What appears when you drag the pointer to select multiple objects?

   a selection rectangle

3. Which Align options are used to line up objects side-by-side along the bottom of the slide?

   Align to slide / bottom

4. Which button flips an object from left to right?

   Flip (L/R) = horizontal

5. Which Order places an object at the top of all the other objects on a slide?

   Bring to front.

6. On what layer does the most recently drawn object appear?

Top

7. What appears when you ungroup a clip art image?

selection handles / several

8. What can you do to reduce the file size of a presentation that contains clip art and photographs?

Compress - pictures

Critical Thinking

Answer these questions on a separate page. There are no right or wrong answers. Support your answers with examples from your own experience, if possible.

1. In this lesson you learned how to work with layers of objects. Which objects might you place on top of each other? When would you find it useful to overlap them?
2. Think of the way you have utilized the ability to work with multiple objects. In what other ways could you use this feature?

Skills Review

Exercise 9-19

Select multiple objects; and align, distribute, flip, rotate, and group objects.

1. Open the file **Cooking3**.
2. Change the color of multiple objects by following these steps:
   a. On slide 1, click one of the small black diamonds below the title.
   b. Press and hold Shift while clicking the remaining two diamonds.
   c. With all three diamonds selected, change the shape fill to Dark Green, Accent 2.
3. Align and distribute the selected diamonds. From the Home tab, in the Drawing group, click the Arrange button and choose Align three times making a different adjustment each time:
   a. Align Selected Objects.
   b. Align Top.
   c. Distribute Horizontally.

4. Now copy the green diamonds and paste to other slides by following these steps:

    a. Use a selection rectangle to select all three diamonds and group them into one object.

    b. Copy the diamond group and paste it on slide 2, 3, 4. Move it between the title placeholder and the body text placeholder.

5. On slide 2, select the diamond group. From the Home tab, in the Drawing group, click the Arrange button 🔳 and choose Align then Align Center.

6. Repeat step 5 for slides 3 and 4.

7. Move to slide 1. Click on one of the small red squares on the upper left. On the Drawing Tools Format tab, notice that the square has height and width .25″ dimensions.

8. Use a selection rectangle to select all of the red squares.

9. Align and distribute objects relative to the slide. From the Home tab, in the Drawing group, click the Arrange button 🔳 and choose Align three times making a different adjustment each time:

    a. Align to Slide.

    b. Align Top.

    c. Distribute Horizontally.

    d. You should have a series of evenly spaced red squares along the top edge of the slide similar to Figure 9-18. If not, click the Undo button 🔳 several times and try again.

Figure 9-18
Red squares
distributed and
aligned to slide

10. Now prepare a checkerboard pattern of squares by following these steps:

    a. Deselect the red squares. Select one red square, press Ctrl+D to duplicate it, and move the duplicated square away from the other squares.

    b. Use a selection rectangle to select all the red squares across the top of the slide and from the Drawing Tools Format tab, in the Drawing group, click the Arrange button 🔳 and choose Group.

c. With the group selected, duplicate it. Move the second group of squares down and to the left to form a checkerboard pattern. Remember that you can use Ctrl + the keyboard arrow keys to nudge an object.

d. Move the extra square into position on the right to finish the second row of squares.

e. Use a selection rectangle to select both groups and the extra square. From the Home tab, in the Drawing group, click the Arrange button ⊞, choose Group.

11. Create the same checkerboard pattern for the bottom of the slide by duplicating the grouped squares, and moving the copy to the bottom of the slide. From the Home tab, in the Drawing group, click the Arrange button ⊞ then choose Align three times making a different adjustment each time:

a. Align to Slide.

b. Align Bottom.

c. Distribute Horizontally.

d. Click the Arrange button ⊞ again, click Rotate and choose the Flip Vertical option to reverse the position of the two rows of squares. (The checkerboard pattern at the bottom of the slide now mirrors the pattern at the top of the slide.)

12. Select the top checkerboard pattern and copy it. Paste to each of the remaining slides in the presentation.

13. Create a handout header and footer: Include the date and your name as the header, and the page number and text **[9-19your initials]** as the footer.

14. Move to slide 1 and save the presentation as **[9-19your initials]** in your Lesson 9 folder.

15. Preview and then print the presentation as handouts, four slides on a page, grayscale, landscape, framed. Close the presentation.

Exercise 9-20

Align and distribute objects relative to the slide and relative to selected objects, and work with layers of objects.

1. Open the file **MiamBch2**.

2. On slide 1, draw a constrained Sun shape. Make the height and width 5 inches. Position it on top of the title and subtitle text.

3. With the shape selected, from the Drawing Tools Format tab, click the Shape Fill button ⊞, click Gradient, then choose More Gradients. Apply a two-color gradient fill to the shape with the following attributes:

a. For Type, choose Rectangular.

b. For Direction, choose From Center.

c. For Stop 1, choose the color Light Orange, Accent 1 with a stop position at 50%.

d. For Stop 2, choose the color Brown, Text 2 with a stop position at 100%.

e. If other stops are available, delete them.

f. Click Close.

4. With the sun selected, click the Shape Outline button ☑ then select No Outline.

5. Select the sun then arrange the positioning of the sun. From the Drawing Tools Format tab, in the Arrange group, click the Align button ⬛⁚ three times making a different adjustment each time:

a. Align to Slide.

b. Align Center.

c. Align Middle.

6. From the Drawing Tools Format tab, in the Arrange group, choose Send to Back.

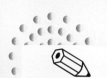

TIP

To fine-tune the sun's position, hold down Ctrl while pressing the arrow keys on your keyboard or hold down Alt and drag the sun with your mouse.

7. Copy the sun from slide 1 and paste it on slide 2.

8. Reduce the sun on slide 2 proportionately, to 1.5 inches wide. Move the sun so it covers the uppercase "G" in the title.

9. With the sun still selected, from the Drawing Tools Format tab, choose Send to Back. Fine-tune its position so that the "G" is centered inside the sun.

10. Copy the sun from slide 2 and paste it on slide 3. Position it behind the "W" in "We" using the same process as step 9.

11. On slide 3, resize the text placeholder, making it just large enough for the text to fit without word-wrapping.

12. From the Drawing Tools Format tab, in the Arrange group, click the Align button ⬛⁚ then choose Align Center.

13. From the Drawing Tools Format tab, in the Arrange group, click the Align button ⬛⁚ then choose Align Middle.

14. Check the grayscale settings and make adjustments if needed.

15. Create a handout header and footer: Include the date and your name as the header, and the page number and text **[9-20your initials]** as the footer.

16. Move to slide 1 and save the presentation as **[9-20your initials]** in your Lesson 9 folder.

17. Preview and then print the presentation as handouts, three slides per page, grayscale, scale to fit paper, framed. Close the presentation.

Exercise 9-21

Select multiple objects; align, distribute, and group objects; and work with layers.

1. Open the file **AdMedia**.

2. Move to slide 2 and select the four arrows using the Shift +click method.

3. Align and distribute the arrows. From the Home tab, in the Drawing group, click the Arrange button 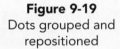, then click Align three times making a different adjustment each time:

    a. Align Selected Objects.

    b. Align Center.

    c. Distribute Vertically.

4. Key the following text inside the arrows:

    Arrow 1: **Quality**
    Arrow 2: **Frequency**
    Arrow 3: **Effectiveness**
    Arrow 4: **Cost**

5. Select all four arrows using a selection rectangle. From the Home tab, in the Drawing group, click the Arrange button and choose Group.

6. Edit the arrows by following these steps:

    a. Select the Arrow group.

    b. From the Drawing Tools Format tab, in the Shape Styles group, click the Shape Effects button and choose Bevel.

    c. From the Bevel gallery choose Cool Slant.

7. Change the order of the objects to reveal a hidden logo:

    a. Move to slide 1.

    b. Select the diamond shape.

    c. Right-click the diamond shape and choose Send to Back from the shortcut menu.

8. Move to slide 4, select the four bright red dots. Align their tops and distribute them evenly among themselves (not relative to the slide).

9. Select the four bright red dots using a selection rectangle. From the Home tab, in the Drawing group, click the Arrange button and choose Group.

10. Position the grouped red dots under the word "Steps" so they help to separate the slide title from other text on the slide, similar to Figure 9-19.

Figure 9-19
Dots grouped and
repositioned

11. Copy the grouped dots and paste them on slides 1, 2, and 3.

    a. Paste the grouped dots on slides 2 and 3 in the same position as on slide 4.

    b. Paste the grouped dots on slide 1 then reposition them to appear below the title.

12. On slide 1 select the diamond shape. From the Drawing Tools Format tab, in the Shape Styles group, click the Shape Effects button ⬛ and choose Bevel then Cool Slant.

13. On slide 2, move the grouped arrows to the right side of the slide.

14. Check the presentation in Grayscale view. If necessary, change the grayscale setting for the diamond shape on slide 1 to Light Grayscale.

15. Create a handout header and footer: Include the date and your name as the header, and the page number and text **[9-21your initials]** as the footer.

16. Move to slide 1 and save the presentation as **[9-21your initials]** in your Lesson 9 folder.

17. Preview and then print the presentation as handouts, four slides per page, grayscale, landscape, framed. Close the presentation.

Exercise 9-22

Select multiple objects, work with layers of objects, align and distribute objects, flip an object, group objects, and use image editing tools.

1. Open the file **Opening3**.

2. On slide 1, select the beach umbrella clip art and recolor parts of it by following these steps:

    a. From the Home tab, in the Drawing group, click the Arrange button ⬛ and choose Ungroup. When asked about converting to a drawing object, click Yes.

    b. With the clip art still selected, from the Home tab, in the Drawing group, click the Arrange button ⬛ and choose Ungroup again.

    c. With the clip art selected, zoom to 200%. Click off of the picture once, so the selection handles disappear.

    d. Click one of the white sections of the beach ball then change its color to bright yellow. Select each of the remaining white sections of the beach ball and change them to bright yellow. One section has two pieces to change.

    e. For the remaining alternating sections, including the circle on the ball, change their color to red.

    f. Right-click on any piece of the clip art and choose Group from the shortcut menu and choose Regroup.

    g. From the View tab, click the Fit to Window button ⬛.

3. Now resize and reposition the beach umbrella using the Drawing Tools Format tab:

   a. Temporarily move the beach umbrella to the center of the slide so you can change its height and width to 5 inches.

   b. In the Arrange group, click the Rotate button 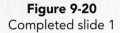 then select Flip Horizontal.

   c. In the Arrange group, click the Align button then select Align to Slide. Repeat this step to choose Align Right and Align Bottom.

4. On slide 1, select the sun and move it to the upper left of the slide with part of the sun rays extending off the edge of the slide as shown in Figure 9-20.

5. On slide 1, select the title text. Right-click and from the floating font group, change to left alignment and change the font color to dark red.

6. With the title placeholder selected, make these changes using the Drawing Tools Format tab:

   a. Click Bring to Front.

   b. Move the title text so the first letter is in the middle of the sun.

   c. Select the sun and the title text. Click the Align button and choose Align Middle

7. On slide 1, select the subtitle text. Right-click and from the floating font group, change to left alignment.

8. With the subtitle selected, make the following changes:

   a. Press [Shift] then click the title text to add it to your selection.

   b. From the Drawing Tools Format tab, in the Arrange group, click the Align button then choose Align Left.

   c. Select just the subtitle text and nudge it down below the umbrella as shown in Figure 9-20.

Figure 9-20
Completed slide 1

9. On slide 1, copy the umbrella clip art and paste it on slide 2 then make these changes using the Drawing Tools Format tab:

   a. Change the height and width to 1.5 inches.

   b. Click the Align button 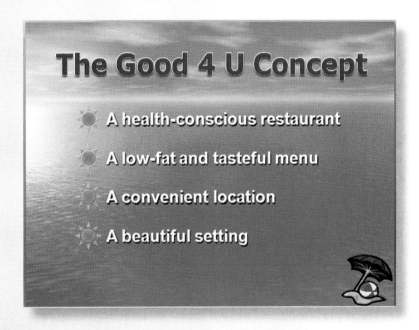 twice to choose Align Right and Align Bottom.

10. On slide 2, select the title and change the text color to dark red.

11. On slide 2, select both the small sun and the text box and make these changes using the Drawing Tools Format tab:

    a. Click the Align button then select Align Selected Objects. Repeat this step then select Align Middle.

    b. Click the Group button and choose Group.

12. Press Ctrl+D three times to duplicate the sun/text group three times.

13. Now position the lowest item by dragging down one sun/text group to position it slightly above the top of the umbrella. Drag another copy up, so it is approximately an inch below the title (use the ruler and gridlines as needed to position the objects).

14. Select all the sun/text groups being careful not to select the umbrella. Make these changes using the Drawing Tools Format tab:

    a. Click the Align button and choose Distribute Vertically.

    b. Repeat step a, but select Align Center.

    c. If the spacing doesn't look correct, move the top or bottom group up or down a small amount and then vertically redistribute the groups again.

    d. Edit the text in groups 2 through 4 as shown in Figure 9-21.

    e. Group the four sun/text groups.

Figure 9-21
Completed slide 2

The Good 4 U Concept

☀ A health-conscious restaurant

☀ A low-fat and tasteful menu

☀ A convenient location

☀ A beautiful setting

15. In the Slides and Outline pane, select slide 2 and press Ctrl+D to duplicate it then make these changes:

    a. Edit the title text by keying **A Unique Setting**.

    b. Edit the first three sun/text groups by keying:

       Beach front
       Patio juice bar
       Boardwalk

    c. Ungroup the text and delete the last sun/text group. Draw a selection rectangle around the three items and group them.

    d. From the Drawing Tools Format tab, in the Arrange group, click the Align button 🖿 and choose Align to Slide.

    e. Repeat step d, but select Align Center.

16. From the Slides and Outline pane, copy slide 1 and paste the copy after slide 3.

17. On slide 4, edit the title text by keying **Come Visit!**.

18. On slide 4, edit the subtitle text by keying **Healthy dining in the sun** and adjust the size of the text box so the text fits on two lines beside the umbrella.

19. Check spelling in the presentation.

20. Create a handout header and footer: Include the date and your name as the header, and the page number and text **[9-22your initials]** as the footer.

21. Move to slide 1 and save the presentation as **[9-22your initials]** in your Lesson 9 folder.

22. Preview and then print the presentation as handouts, four slides per page, grayscale, landscape, framed. Close the presentation.

Lesson Applications

Exercise 9-23
Select, align, and layer multiple objects; group objects.

1. Open the file **InfoPak1**.

2. On slide 1, select all the tiny diamonds and make these changes:
   a. Click Align Selected Objects, Align Top, and Distribute Horizontally.
   b. Select the third diamond from the right and the left then change their color to Tan, Text 2, Darker 25%.
   c. Select all the small diamonds and group them. Center the diamonds horizontally on the slide and move the group down slightly below the title.

3. Copy the group of diamonds and paste them on the remaining slides. Position the grouped diamonds between the title placeholders and the body text placeholders.

4. On slide 1, make these changes to the large diamond:
   a. Send the large diamond shape behind the subtitle text.
   b. Select the large diamond and the subtitle text then choose Align Middle.
   c. Center these two items horizontally by choosing Align to Slide then Align Center.

5. On slide 5, select the large diamond and make these changes:
   a. Apply an Angle Bevel shape effect.
   b. Duplicate the diamond and increase its size proportionally.
   c. Change its color to the Brown, Background 1, Lighter 40%.
   d. Send it to the back and then make any necessary adjustments so it is evenly spaced behind the first diamond.
   e. Group the text box and both diamonds, and center them horizontally on the slide. Adjust the vertical position of the group to make a pleasing composition.

6. On slide 5, for the text on the diamond make these changes:
   a. Remove the Glow text effect and then use Shadow Options to apply a dark brown shadow.
   b. Change the text color to white.

7. View the presentation in Grayscale view and make any necessary adjustments to the grayscale settings.

8. Create a handout header and footer: Include the date and your name as the header, and the page number and text **[9-23your initials]** as the footer.

9. Move to slide 1 and save the presentation as **[9-23your initials]** in your Lesson 9 folder.

10. Preview and then print the presentation as handouts, six slides per page, grayscale, framed. Close the presentation.

Exercise 9-24

Work with multiple objects; and align, distribute, and group objects.

1. Open the file **Recruit2**.

2. On slide 1, select the title placeholder, choose the WordArt Quick Style of Fill – Accent 6, Warm Matte Bevel, then change the font color to Light Blue.

3. Draw a 0.25-inch constrained four-point star in the center of the slide. Make the star Purple, Accent 6, Lighter 60%.

4. Duplicate the star you just created 15 times (without repositioning), so you have a total of 16 stars. Select all the stars; then align their tops relative to each other. Distribute the stars horizontally, relative to the slide.

5. Beginning with the second star, select every other star and make it Light Blue as shown in Figure 9-22.

6. Group the stars.

Figure 9-22
Slide with star pattern

7. Select the title placeholder, the group of stars, and the subtitle placeholder. Choose Align to Slide and then choose Distribute Vertically. This spaces the line of stars evenly between the two placeholders.

8. Copy the group of stars and paste it to the remaining slides, between the title placeholder and the body text placeholder.

9. On slide 1, for the subtitle placeholder, key **Good 4 U**, then make the text bold and change the font color to Purple, Accent 6, Darker 50%.

10. Draw a rounded rectangle over the subtitle and make the height 1 inch and width 3.5 inches. Apply the Shape Style of Subtle Effect Accent 2. Send the shape to the back so it is behind the text.

11. On slide 4, key the following text in the body text placeholder:
    - **Reinforce our message of healthy living**
    - **Describe our new franchising philosophy**
    - **Encourage fresh ideas from new employees**

12. Check spelling in the presentation.

13. Create a handout header and footer: Include the date and your name as the header, and the page number and text **[9-24your initials]** as the footer.

14. Move to slide 1 and save the presentation as **[9-24your initials]** in your Lesson 9 folder.

15. Preview and then print the presentation as handouts, four slides per page, grayscale, scaled to fit paper, framed. Close the presentation.

Exercise 9-25

Work with layers, group objects, and use image editing tools.

1. Open the file **Cooking4**.

2. Apply the Module design theme to the presentation.

3. Increase the font size for "What's Cooking" to 60 points and make it bold.

4. Ungroup and convert the carrot picture to PowerPoint objects. Then select just the orange part and change its fill color to a brighter shade of orange (create a custom color). Regroup objects that make up the carrot.

5. Increase the carrot's size proportionately, making it three inches tall, and rotate it to the right about 60 degrees. Position the carrot to the right of the title so the whole carrot is in the black area.

6. Move the apple from the upper-left corner to the middle of the carrot, hiding part of the carrot. (Bring the apple to the front.)

7. Insert a picture of a cluster of grapes (or another fruit or vegetable) that works well with the apple and carrot colors. Size and rotate the picture appropriately and place it to the left or right of the apple, whichever makes the best grouping, and send the image to the back.

8. Group the three images and position the group attractively. Copy the group and paste it on slide 2. Decrease its size proportionately, making it approximately 75% of the original size, and place it to beside the title text in the black area.

9. Copy the image and paste it on the remaining slides positioned beside each title.

10. On slide 4, increase the size of the body text placeholder and increase the font size to 32 points so it matches slide 2. Align the picture with the text.

11. Reposition the picture and the text box to create an attractive layout. Move to slide 1, and draw a constrained line right below the white line dividing the black and the gray. Change the color of the line to White, Text 1, Darker 35%.

12. Copy and paste the new line. Reposition it below the original line.

13. Recolor the second line to Black, Background 1, Lighter 35%.

14. Select the two lines and group them.

15. Review the presentation in Grayscale view and make adjustments where needed.

16. Create a handout header and footer: Include the date and your name as the header, and the page number and text **[9-25your initials]** as the footer.

17. Move to slide 1 and save the presentation as **[9-25your initials]** in your Lesson 9 folder.

18. Preview and then print the presentation as handouts, four slides per page, grayscale, landscape, framed. Close the presentation.

Exercise 9-26 ◆ Challenge Yourself

Work with multiple objects; align, rotate, and flip objects; work with layers; and use image editing tools.

1. Open the file **WhoWeAre**.

2. Change to the Urban Design Theme with the Verve theme colors.

3. On slide 1, insert a picture in the lower right corner that is appropriate to the content of the presentation. Size the image appropriately and recolor it to Accent color 2 Dark. Rotate or flip the image, if needed, to create better positioning, and adjust the contrast and brightness as necessary.

4. Change the title text to Arial at 60 points, bold.

5. On slide 2, add rectangles at the bottom following these steps:
   a. Draw a rectangle with a height of .40 inches and a width of 10 inches. Change the shape fill color to Gray 50%, text 2 with no outline. Align the rectangle on the bottom of the slide.
   b. Duplicate this rectangle and change the height to .10 inches and the fill color to Pink, Accent 2 and no outline. Align it directly above the first rectangle.

    c. Duplicate the pink rectangle and change the shape fill to Pink, Accent 2, Lighter 40%.

    d. Select the three rectangles and group them.

6. Copy the group of rectangles and paste the group on the remaining slides.

7. On slide 1, select the title placeholder and apply the WordArt Quick Style of Fill-Accent 2, Warm Matte Bevel.

8. On slide 2, resize the body text placeholder to fit the text and center the placeholder horizontally and vertically on the slide.

9. On slide 2, draw a constrained diamond shape with a height and width of 4.5 inches. Change the fill color to a light shade of gray. Remove the outline.

10. Select both the diamond and the body text placeholder and align their middles and centers relative to each other. Send the diamond behind the text.

11. Copy the diamond and paste to slide 4. Resize the text placeholder to fit the text and select both the diamond and the body text placeholder and align their middles and centers relative to each other. Send the diamond behind the text.

12. Copy the diamond and paste it to slide 3. Send the diamond to the back and then position it behind the picture of people. Align the centers and middles of the picture and diamond relative to each other; then move them slightly to the left.

13. Still working on slide 3, adjust the body text placeholder by increasing the font size to 30 points. Adjust its vertical position so it is balanced with the image.

14. Format slide 5 in the same style as slide 3 but make the diamond more narrow to better fit the picture.

15. Review the presentation in Grayscale view and make adjustments where needed.

16. View the presentation as a slide show.

17. Create a handout header and footer: Include the date and your name as the header, and the page number and text **[9-26your initials]** as the footer.

18. Move to slide 1 and save the presentation as **[9-26your initials]** in your Lesson 9 folder.

19. Preview and then print the presentation as handouts, six slides per page, grayscale, framed. Close the presentation.

On Your Own

In these exercises you work on your own, as you would in a real-life work environment. Use the skills you've learned to accomplish the task—and be creative.

Exercise 9-27

Imagine that you have invented a new product: a vacuum that runs itself, a new type of breathable waterproof fabric, a new type of golf ball, or whatever else you want. Create a persuasive presentation aimed at possible financial backers for the product. Explain the product's features and the benefits of its use. Identify its potential market. Include at least five slides in your presentation. Use the tools and features presented in this lesson and in previous lessons to create an attractive presentation. Be sure to group multiple objects together and have a combination of layered objects. Save the presentation as **[9-27your initials]**. Preview and then print the presentation as handouts.

Exercise 9-28

Create a presentation to get donations for a charity event sponsored by a community organization, such as a blood drive, an adopt-a-family project, a heart walk, or bowl for kids' sake. In your presentation, describe the organization and the event activities, including dates and times. Also include one or two slides explaining to people why they should donate. Use the tools and features presented in this lesson and in previous lessons to create an attractive presentation. Be sure to have a slide with multiple objects that you can align and distribute, or flip commands on. Save the presentation as **[9-28your initials]**. Preview and then print the presentation as handouts.

Exercise 9-29

Imagine that you are organizing a chili cook-off in your local community. Create a presentation describing the contest, rules, location, and categories. Recognize winners from the previous year. Format your presentation attractively and in keeping with the theme of your idea. Use the concepts for working with layers and multiple objects on at least one slide. Save the presentation as **[9-29your initials]**. Preview and then print the presentation as handouts.

OBJECTIVES

MCAS OBJECTIVES

In this lesson:
PowerPoint 2.3.2
PowerPoint 2.3.3
PowerPoint 2.3.4
PowerPoint 2.4.1
PowerPoint 2.4.2
PowerPoint 2.4.3
See Appendix

After completing this lesson, you will be able to:

1. Apply custom animation.

2. Modify and enhance animations.

3. Add sound effects.

4. Add movies.

5. Insert links.

Estimated Time: 1¹/₂ hours

By using PowerPoint's *Custom Animation* tools, you can create interesting visual effects for objects such as clip art, drawings, text, and movie clips. Custom animation enables you to control the timing, speed, sound, and other aspects of movement. The effects can be applied to control how an object appears, how it is emphasized on a slide, or how it leaves the slide.

Applying Custom Animation

To *animate* means to apply movement that controls how the object, text or images, behave during a slide show. For example, you can make an object:

• Fly into the center of the screen accompanied by a sound effect.

• Fade into the background when another object appears.

• Blink when you click your mouse button.

• Leave the screen in a spiral path.

When objects on a slide are selected, the Custom Animation task pane enables you to add movement and other effects as well as control their animation settings and order of appearance. If you enjoy using these tools, you will want to spend time on your own experimenting with endless possibilities for animation.

But remember, use animation carefully to enhance—not distract from—the message that your presentation needs to deliver.

Exercise 10-1 ADD AN ENTRANCE EFFECT

From the Animations tab, in the Animations group, choose the Custom Animation button to open the Custom Animation task pane.

To apply an animation to an object, select it in the Slide pane, click Add Effect at the top of the Custom Animation task pane, choose an effect type, and then choose an effect from the list that appears. The four types of effects are:

- *Entrance:* An effect applied to an object to control how it first appears on a slide.

- *Emphasis:* An effect applied to draw attention to an object that is already displayed on a slide.

- *Exit:* An effect that controls how an object leaves (or disappears from) a slide.

- *Motion Paths:* A motion path defines the line of travel that an object can follow as part of an animation effect.

After you apply an effect, an animation tag—a small, numbered box—appears on the slide next to the animated object. The number in the box correlates with the list of effects in the Custom Animation task pane and indicates the order in which the effects will play in relation to other effects on the slide. Items in this list can be reordered.

1. Open the **Motion1** file, which is the Healthy Food presentation.

2. From the Animations tab, in the Animations group, click the Custom Animation button.

3. On slide 1, select the "Healthy Food" WordArt object.

4. At the top of the Custom Animation task pane, click Add Effect. The drop-down list contains four general types of effects.

5. Choose Entrance. A list of the most recently used Entrance effects appears. Your list will be different from the one pictured in Figure 10-1.

TIP

If you did not see a preview of the animation, make sure AutoPreview is checked (at the bottom of the Custom Animation task pane) and then click Play.

Figure 10-1
Choosing an
Entrance effect

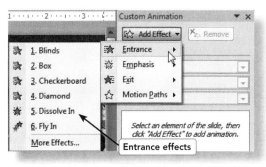

6. Choose any effect from the list. A preview of the effect is displayed in the Slide pane, and an animation tag with the number "1" appears next to the animated object.

7. Click Add Effect again, choose Entrance, and then choose the More Effects.

Figure 10-2
Choosing from more
Entrance effects

8. The Add Entrance Effect dialog box opens. Use the scroll bar to view the complete list of Entrance effects available in the categories of Basic, Subtle, Moderate, and Exciting, as shown in Figure 10-2.

9. Scroll down to the Exciting category and choose the Pinwheel effect and then click OK. A box with the number "2" appears next to the selected object. The two animation effects are listed with corresponding numbers on the Custom Animation task pane.

10. Still working on slide 1, select the text, "for the Athlete in You." Click Add Effect and choose Entrance, and then choose More Effects.

11. From the group of Basic effects, choose Dissolve In and click OK.

12. To see how the effects will appear during a show, click Slide Show at the bottom of the task pane (or click the Slide Show View button 🖳). Slide 1 appears in Slide Show view, but the WordArt that you animated is not showing. By default, the animation will appear when you click your left mouse button; therefore, click three times through all the animation effects that you applied. You will remove some of these in Exercise 10-4.

13. Press Esc to return to Normal view.

14. Leave the presentation open for the next exercise.

Exercise 10-2 ADD AN EMPHASIS AND EXIT EFFECT

In addition to Entrance animation effects, you can use interesting emphasis effects to draw your audience's attention to an object on your slide. Or you can use Exit effects to make objects leave. Effects can be combined, too. While you are learning about animation, it is fun to try different combinations. However, you ultimately want to select movements that seem logical and contribute to the audience's understanding of your information.

TIP

Make sure you see the four-pointed arrow 🕀 when you click the star, to avoid activating the text box behind it.

1. Move to slide 2 and select the small star to the right of the text "Gus Irvinelli."

2. At the top of the Custom Animation task pane, click Add Effect, click Entrance, then choose Appear. (If needed, go to the More Effects option at the bottom of the menu to find the Appear effect then click OK.)

3. With the star still selected, click Add Effect again, and point to Emphasis.

4. Choose More Effects. From the Moderate category, choose Flicker and click OK.

5. With the star still selected, click Add Effect and point to Exit.

6. Choose More Effects. From the Basic category, choose Disappear then click OK.

TIP

If you see the animation effect you want on the drop-down list, you can select it from the list. Choose More Effects only when the effect you want is not on the list.

7. With slide 2 selected, click the Slide Show button 🖵; then click to advance through the animation. When you click three times, you will see the star appear, flicker, and then disappear. Press [Esc] to end the show and return to slide 2.

8. Leave the presentation open for the next exercise.

Exercise 10-3 APPLY A MOTION PATH TO AN OBJECT

Depending on the particular effect you choose, different directions of movement are available. However, with a *Motion Path* effect, you can make an object enter a slide from any point and travel across the slide in a variety of paths, including diagonal, zigzag, or spiral paths. You can even draw your own path to customize the movement.

1. Change the zoom to a low setting, for example, 40%, so that you can see a large amount of the blank area around the slide.

2. Move to slide 1, and select the clip art runners and move them off the slide to the blank area beside the title on the left.

Figure 10-3
Choosing a preset Motion Path

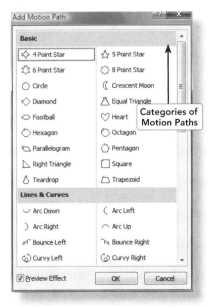

3. With the runners selected, click Add Effect on the Custom Animation task pane and point to Motion Paths. Choose More Motion Paths. The Add Motion Path dialog box offers a large number of choices, as shown in Figure 10-3. You can add motion paths to any object, including text.

4. Under Lines & Curves, scroll down to choose S Curve 2 and click OK.

5. A curving line extends from the runners to the left part of the slide with triangles at each end of the line. The green triangle indicates the start of the path, and the red triangle indicates the end, as shown in Figure 10-4.

Figure 10-4
Working with a
preset Motion Path

6. Select the Motion Path only; then drag its sizing handles to resize it, extending across the slide to the right of the title text, as shown in Figure 10-5. Use the rotation handle to adjust the angle slightly. Even if the rotation causes the green beginning triangle to move away from the runners, they will begin movement from the triangle position.

Figure 10-5
Motion Path final

7. Click Play at the bottom of the Custom Animation task pane to test these movements in Normal view. Click the Slide Show button 🔲 at the bottom of the Custom Animation task pane to test these movements in full-screen display.

8. Click Esc to return to Normal view.

9. Leave the presentation open for the next exercise.

Exercise 10-4   REMOVE CUSTOM ANIMATIONS

If you want to remove an animation effect from an object, select it in the list on the Custom Animation task pane and click Remove or press Delete. You can remove multiple items from the list in the same way that you select and delete multiple slide thumbnails.

1. Working on slide 1 in the Custom Animation task pane, click the first item for Healthy Food. A box surrounding it indicates that it is selected. Click Remove at the top of the task pane.

2. Now only three numbered items appear in the list. They are renumbered, as are the animation tags on the slide.

3. Click the Slide Show button 🔲; then click your left mouse button to see the three animations. Press Esc to end the show.

4. Create a handout header and footer: Include the date and your name as the header, and the page number and text **[10-4your initials]** as the footer.

5. Create a Lesson 10 folder. Save the presentation as **[10-4your initials]** in your new Lesson 10 folder. Keep the presentation open for the next exercise.

Exercise 10-5 ANIMATE CHART ELEMENTS

Animation effects for charts can add movement to the whole chart or make the chart appear by series or category data. Effects that work well with charts are Dissolve In, Split, Random Bars, Blinds, and Wipe.

1. On slide 3, select the chart then in the Custom Animation task pane click Add Effect and choose Entrance and More Effects. Choose the Wipe effect from the Basic category.

2. In the custom animation list, click the list box arrow for the animation "Chart 4"; then choose Effect Options.

3. Click the Chart Animation tab and then click the list box arrow for Group chart and choose By Category, as shown in Figure 10-6.

4. Clear the check box for Start animation by drawing the chart background. By turning off this option, the chart layout will appear when the slide is displayed.

Figure 10-6
Chart Animation options

5. Watch the preview of this animation, and notice how the columns come in by category.

6. In the custom animation list, click the list box arrow for the animation "Chart 4" again and then choose Effect Options.

7. Click the Chart Animation tab and then click the list box arrow for Group chart and choose By Series.

8. View the presentation as a slide show, starting with slide 3. When you get to the animated chart, click the left mouse button to make each series of columns appear, one after the other.

9. Update the handout footer to include the text **[10-5your initials]**.

10. Move to slide 1 and save the presentation as **[10-5your initials]** in your Lesson 10 folder. Leave the presentation open for the next exercise.

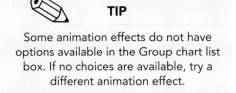

TIP

Some animation effects do not have options available in the Group chart list box. If no choices are available, try a different animation effect.

Modifying and Enhancing Animations

Animations can be modified in many ways. They can be made to appear faster or slower, dissolve or fly, be activated by a mouse click or play automatically. In addition, you can attach sound effects to them.

Exercise 10-6   MODIFY ANIMATIONS

The animations you created up to this point appear during a slide show when you click your mouse. You can modify an animation so that it appears automatically, and you can also change the speed at which the animation occurs.

TIP

When listed items move to a different position, timing and start settings sometimes need to be changed. Experimentation is often the only way to determine the best settings for the effect you want.

TIP

Choosing After Previous when there is no previous event makes the animation start as soon as the slide is displayed. The previous event is the display of the slide, before any animation occurs.

1. Working on slide 1, click anywhere on the text "for the Athlete in You." Notice the Dissolve In Entrance effect applied earlier.

2. In the Custom Animation task pane, under Modify: Dissolve In, click the drop-down arrow for the Start list box and choose After Previous. A clock icon replaces the mouse icon, indicating that the animation will start automatically after the first animation completes. The item is renumbered on the slide, indicating that it is now considered part of the first animation.

3. With this item still selected, click the drop-down arrow for the Speed list box and choose Medium.

4. Click the image of the runners. From the Start drop-down list box, choose After Previous. Change the Speed to Slow. Notice that all the animation tags on the slide now contain the number "1," indicating that this is one animation sequence.

5. Click the Slide Show button 🖳. One click will start the first animation, and then the other two will appear automatically, one after the other, without a mouse click. Press Esc to end the show.

6. Move to slide 2 and select the star. To make the star flicker more than one time, click the list box arrow for the animation item number 2 and choose Timing from the drop-down list. The Timing tab for the Flicker dialog box appears. (If the dialog box title is not Flicker, click Cancel and choose another list item.)

7. From the Repeat list box, choose 3 and click OK. The star will now flicker three times.

8. Click the down arrow next to the first item which has the Appear effect. For Start choose After Previous. Notice that the animation tag changes to 0.

9. For the second item which has the Flicker effect, change the Start to After Previous.

10. For the third item which has the Disappear effect, change the Start to After Previous. Now the star will appear, flicker, and then disappear without the need for additional mouse clicks.

11. Leave the presentation open for the next exercise.

Exercise 10-7 ADD SOUND EFFECTS TO ANIMATIONS

In this exercise you will add sound effects as part of an object's animation by using the Custom Animation task pane. Later in this lesson you will use the Insert tab, the Media Clips group, and the Sound button 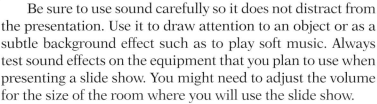 to insert sound in a different way.

TIP

If you have trouble adjusting the volume the way you want, click the speaker icon 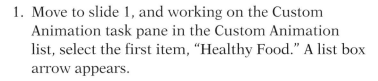 on the right side of the Windows task bar to adjust your system's sound. Some speakers have volume knobs as well.

TIP

Sounds that you have recorded can be inserted using the same dialog box.

Be sure to use sound carefully so it does not distract from the presentation. Use it to draw attention to an object or as a subtle background effect such as to play soft music. Always test sound effects on the equipment that you plan to use when presenting a slide show. You might need to adjust the volume for the size of the room where you will use the slide show.

1. Move to slide 1, and working on the Custom Animation task pane in the Custom Animation list, select the first item, "Healthy Food." A list box arrow appears.

2. Click the list box arrow and choose Effect Options. The Pinwheel dialog box opens. Each animation effect has its own dialog box. The options vary, depending on the animation.

3. Click the Sound list box arrow; then scroll down the list of sounds and select Chime.

4. Click the Speaker button to the right of the Sound list box. Move the Volume slider down, near the bottom, to lower the sound level, as shown in Figure 10-7. Click OK. The chime sound plays.

Figure 10-7
Adding a Sound effect

Volume control

5. If necessary, access Effect Options again to adjust the sound up or down as needed to create a quiet sound.

6. Use the steps outlined above to add the same chime sound to the second text animation.

7. Click Play at the bottom of the Custom Animation task pane to preview the animations and sounds.

8. Leave the presentation open for the next exercise.

Exercise 10-8 MODIFY THE ORDER OF ANIMATIONS

When animating a body text placeholder, you can control the order of how the text appears:

- All at once so text appears as one object.

- All paragraphs (or bulleted items) at the same time.

- Paragraphs (or bullet items) entering by their level.

To make an animation appear at the same time as another animation, reposition its listing in the Custom Animation list so that it is directly below the other animation, and change its Start setting to With Previous.

1. Move to slide 4 and select the text box.

2. From the Custom Animation task pane, click Add Effect and choose Entrance and More Effects. Choose the Stretch effect from the Moderate category.

3. Select the first of the three blue arrows.

4. For each arrow, apply the Entrance effect Fly In.

5. In the Start drop-down list for all three arrows, choose With Previous.

6. Click Play to preview the effect. The arrows appear after the listed text.

Figure 10-8
Moving an item in the Custom Animation list

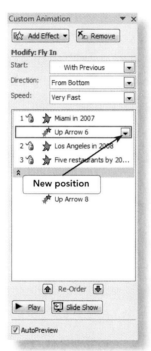

7. Click "Up arrow 6" in the Custom Animation task pane in the Custom Animation list. With "Up arrow 6" selected, click the Re-Order up arrow until it is below item 1 ("Miami in 2007"), as shown in Figure 10-8. Notice in the Slide pane that the first arrow's animation tag number changed to match the animation tag for the first text line.

8. Reorder "Up arrow 7" to move it below the animation for "Los Angeles 2008." Now the arrows will appear on click from shortest to tallest to match the sequence of years.

9. Click the Slide Show button 🖳; then click your mouse to advance through the animations on the slide. Press [Esc] to end the show.

10. Leave the presentation open for the next exercise.

Exercise 10-9   MODIFY AN ANIMATION'S TIMING

You have already seen that you can make an animation start automatically with the display of a slide, start immediately after another animation has completed, or wait until you click your mouse. You can fine-tune the timing of an animation by specifying a delay before the animation begins.

1. Move to slide 1, select the second item in the Custom Animation list ("for the Athlete"), and click its list box arrow. Choose Timing and a dialog box for this effect opens.

2. On the Timing tab, in the Delay spin box, key 2 (for two seconds). Click OK. This delays the current animation two seconds for the previous one to have time to take effect.

3. Using steps 1 and 2 as a guide, add a two-second delay to the first listed item ("Healthy Food").

4. Move to slide 2 and select the star. Select item 1, click its list box arrow, and choose Timing. Key **0.5** (for 0.5 seconds) in the Delay box. Click OK.

5. Move to slide 1 and then click the Slide Show button 🔲 at the bottom of the Custom Animation task pane to see the effect of the delayed start. When the animations complete in slides 1 and 2, press [Esc] to end the show.

6. Leave the presentation open for the next exercise.

Exercise 10-10   COPY AN ANIMATED OBJECT

Sometimes you want two or more objects to have the same animation effect. If it is an elaborate animation that takes many steps to create, as is the case with the star in the previous exercise, you can save time by copying the object to a new position on the same slide or to a new slide. The animations are copied along with the object.

1. Working on slide 2, select the star on the slide, copy it to the clipboard, and then paste it on the same slide.

2. Use your arrow keys to nudge the copied star to the right of the name "Julie Wolfe," as shown in Figure 10-9. Three more animation items appear at the bottom of the custom animation list, referring to the copied star.

Figure 10-9
Slide 2 with the completed star animation

3. Select the text box, and apply the Entrance effect Stretch. Then re-order the star effects to appear after each name in the list. Select all three star effects and use the re-order arrows to move them into position at one time.

4. Click the Slide Show button 🔲 and click your left mouse button to advance through the text animations. The flickering star appears to the right of "Gus Irvinelli" and again to the right of "Julie Wolfe." Press [Esc] to end the slide show.

5. Close the Custom Animation task pane.

6. Update the handout footer to include the text **[10-10your initials]** as the footer.

7. Save the presentation as **[10-10your initials]** in your Lesson 10 folder. Leave the presentation open for the next exercise.

Adding Sound Effects

Besides attaching sound effects to custom animations, you can add sound objects that stand on their own. Like most animations, sound objects can be set to play automatically when a slide appears or to wait for a mouse click. Like the chime sound you used with custom animation, many of the sounds are short "event" sounds, such as a door closing or glass clinking, that are small files with the extension of .wav. However, some of the sounds are music sounds with the extension of .midi. In the following exercises you will distinguish between these file types and look at the file properties.

Exercise 10-11   INSERT A SOUND FROM THE CLIP ORGANIZER

Sounds, like other effects, should be chosen carefully to make sure that they enhance—not distract from—your presentation's message. You can play a short burst of music to accompany an effect, or you can set music to play for an entire slide or an entire presentation.

1. Move to slide 1 in Normal view.

2. From the Insert tab, in the Media Clips group, click the bottom half of the Sound button ⏹ and select Sound from the Clip Organizer.

3. The Clip Art task pane opens, displaying icons for sound files. When you move the pointer over the sound thumbnail, information about the file appears. You can see the file size and the type of file. Those marked with WAV are usually short sound effects, such as a drum roll, chimes, or applause. Those marked with MID or MIDI are music files that are usually longer in length.

4. In the Search text box, key Sports.

5. Click the Results should be list box arrow and make sure Sounds is checked. Clear any other check boxes that might be selected. Click the list arrow again to close the list box; then click Go. If Microsoft media content was installed on your computer or if your computer is connected to the Internet, a list of sound files relating to sports themes appears as shown in Figure 10-10.

Figure 10-10
Sound files in the
Clip Art task pane

6. Right-click any sound file icon and choose Preview/Properties from the shortcut menu. The current sound file begins to play.

7. In the Preview/Properties dialog box, click the Next button to preview the next sound. Most (if not all) the sounds are short sound effects. Click Close to close the Preview/Properties dialog box.

8. Locate the sound file **Sports Drive** in the clip organizer and click it to insert.

9. When the dialog box asking whether you want to play the sound automatically appears, click When Clicked. A small speaker object appears in the center of the slide.

10. Working in Normal view, make sure you're on slide 1 and view the presentation as a slide show. Click the speaker object. The music starts to play. Click a blank area of the screen to turn off the music. Press Esc to end the slide show and close the Clip Art task pane.

11. Leave the presentation open because you will make some adjustments to how this music plays in the next exercise.

Exercise 10-12 CONTROL START AND PLAY EFFECT OPTIONS

By using the Custom Animation task pane, you can change a music object so that it plays automatically when a slide starts, with a mouse click, or after another animation. If the music is set to play automatically, you can hide the speaker icon in one of two ways—by checking Hide During Show on the Sound Tools Options tab or by dragging the sound icon off your slide onto the gray desktop area of the Slide pane.

Figure 10-11
Custom animation
list showing four
items

1. Return to slide 1 in Normal view. Click the speaker object.

2. From the Animations tab, in the Animations group, click the Custom Animation button to open the Custom Animation task pane. Depending on how you inserted your sound object, you might or might not see an item for the sound object in the custom animation list.

3. If your custom animation list contains items not shown in Figure 10-11, delete the extra list items.

4. Select the music object name in the Custom Animation task pane; then change the sound object's Start setting to With Previous. Use the Re-Order up arrow to move the item to the top of the custom animation list.

5. Click the list box arrow beside the sound item and choose Effect Options. The Play Sound dialog box opens, displaying the Effect tab, as shown in Figure 10-12.

Figure 10-12
Setting sound options

6. Under Start playing, choose From beginning.

7. Under Stop playing, choose After current slide.

8. On the Sound Settings tab, click the Speaker button and turn down the Sound volume.

9. Place a check in the Hide sound icon during slide show option so that the speaker icon is not visible. Click OK.

10. Select the second item in the custom animation list, "Healthy Food," and open its list box. Choose Timing. Change the Start setting to With Previous, and then reset the Delay to 2 seconds. Click OK.

11. View the presentation as a slide show, starting on slide 1; then return to slide 1 in Normal view. Leave the presentation open for the next exercise.

TIP

This change is necessary because the After Previous setting would cause this event to wait until the music stops playing. By adding the two-second delay, the animation gives the appearance of starting after the music starts.

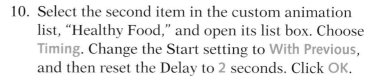

TIP

To make a sound play for the duration of an entire presentation, right-click the sound object and choose Edit Sound Object from the shortcut menu. In the Sound Options dialog box, check the box labeled Loop until stopped and click OK.

Exercise 10-13   INSERT A SOUND CLIP FROM A FILE

At times you may wish to insert your own sound files in a presentation. Acceptable sound file formats include AIFF, AU, MIDI, MP3, WAV, and WMA.

1. Move to slide 7.

2. From the Insert tab, in the Media Clips group, click the arrow on the bottom half of the Sound button and select Sound from File.

Figure 10-13
Insert sound clip
from file

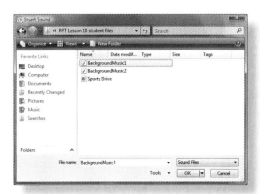

3. Select the WAV file **BackgroundMusic1** from your Lesson 10 student files and click OK, as shown in Figure 10-13.

4. When the dialog box asking whether you want to play the sound automatically appears, click Automatically.

5. Click the list box arrow beside the sound item in the Custom Animation list and choose Effect Options. On the Sound Settings tab, check the option to Hide the sound icon during slide show.

6. Click OK.

7. View slide 7 in Slide Show view, then press Esc to end the show.

8. Leave the presentation open for the next exercise.

Exercise 10-14 PLAY A CD AUDIO TRACK

Music played from a CD may have a superior quality to what you will hear with either a .wav or .midi file. Therefore, you can achieve very professional results playing music from a CD. You might want to play music before a presentation as people are entering the room, or to energize your audience after an afternoon break. Inserting a CD music track is much like inserting any other sound.

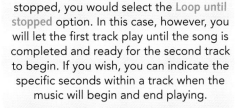

TIP

If you wanted the CD to play until stopped, you would select the Loop until stopped option. In this case, however, you will let the first track play until the song is completed and ready for the second track to begin. If you wish, you can indicate the specific seconds within a track when the music will begin and end playing.

1. Working on slide 7, place a music CD in the CD drive of your computer.

2. From the Insert tab, in the Media Clips group, click the arrow on the bottom of the Sound button 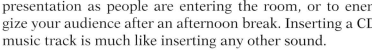 and select Play CD Audio Track. The Insert CD Audio dialog will open, as shown in Figure 10-14.

Figure 10-14
Insert CD Audio
Track

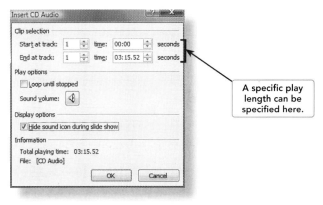

A specific play length can be specified here.

3. Under Clip Selection, the Start at track should be 1 and the time should be 00:00 seconds, then change the End at track to be 1 and the time will change to show the length of track 1.

TIP

Be sure to take the CD with you wherever you will be presenting if you choose to use this option. The CD must be in the CD drive for this option to work.

4. Click the Hide sound icon during slide show check box and click OK.

5. PowerPoint will ask how you want the sound to start in your slide show. Click Automatically to have the music start when this slide appears. Now start your slide show to make sure your CD audio track is working correctly. You should hear the background music and when it completes, your CD audio track should start.

6. Leave the presentation open for the next exercise.

Exercise 10-15   RECORD SOUND

PowerPoint also has the ability to record audio input. For example, a microphone connected to the computer may be used to record your own voice to create a sound clip. The *Record Sound* feature should be used for short sound clips and not for narrating, which is covered later in the book. You may skip the following exercise if a microphone is not available.

1. Move to slide 3, the financial growth chart.

Figure 10-15
Recording sound

2. From the Insert tab, in the Media Clips group, click the arrow on the bottom half of the Sound button and select Record Sound, as shown in Figure 10-15.

3. In the Name box, key the title for the sound recording as **Financial Growth**.

4. Click the Record button to begin your recording and then speak into the microphone "Wow! Look at the third year profit jump!" or you may provide a different comment of your own about the chart.

5. When finished, click the Stop button to stop the recording.

6. Click the Play button to review your recording. If you are satisfied, click OK to insert the recording into your slide.

7. Move the sound icon over to the right side of the slide beside the chart.

8. View the slide in Slide Show view and click the sound icon when you are ready to listen to your recording. Click [Esc] to return to Normal view.

TIP

If you are not satisfied with the recording, click Cancel and try again.

9. Update the handout footer to include the text **[10-15your initials]** as the footer.

10. Save the presentation as **[10-15your initials]** in your Lesson 10 folder. Leave the presentation open for the next exercise.

Adding Movies

In PowerPoint, the term *movie* refers to any motion file, for example, a video clip or animated clip art file. Microsoft provides many animated files (sometimes called animated GIFs) within Office 2007. Additional material is available on the Web at Microsoft Office Online. You can also insert movie files from other sources.

Exercise 10-16 INSERT A MOVIE FROM THE CLIP ORGANIZER

Inserting a movie (or animated clip art file) onto a slide is similar to inserting a sound object. Once it's on the slide, you can add animation effects to control when and how it appears.

1. Move to slide 7, from the Insert tab, in the Media Clips group, click the arrow on the bottom half of the Movie button and select Movie from Clip Organizer. A small yellow star animation icon in the lower-right corner of the thumbnails identifies movie files.

2. In the Search for box, key **Sports**.

3. In the Search in list box, check Everywhere so that the search will be performed not only on your computer but also on Microsoft Online if you are currently connected to the Internet.

4. In the Results should be list box, check Movies if it is not already checked and clear all the other check boxes.

5. Close the Custom Animation task pane and then click Go.

6. Right-click one of the thumbnails and choose Preview/Properties to preview several of the animations and then click Close. Insert one with a suitable theme and colors onto the slide. Once it's on the slide, use your judgment to resize it proportionately to fit below the gold text on the slide, as shown in Figure 10-16.

Figure 10-16
Insert a Movie

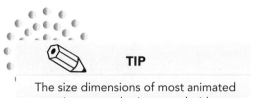

7. Redisplay the Custom Animation task pane; then click Play to see the movie. It will play as soon as the slide appears.

8. Click Stop at the bottom of the Custom Animation task pane (or press Esc).

9. Close the Clip Art task pane.

10. Leave the presentation open for the next exercise.

Exercise 10-17 INSERT A MOVIE FROM A FILE

Just as with inserting your own sound files, you can also insert your own movie files. Acceptable move file formats include ASF, AVI, MPEG, WMV, and DVR-MS (Microsoft DVR recording from Windows Media Center Edition).

1. Move to slide 6.

2. From the Insert tab, in the Media Clips group, click the arrow on the bottom half of the Movie button and select Movie from File.

Figure 10-17
Insert movie from file

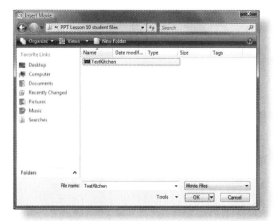

3. Select the file **TestKitchen. mpg** from your lesson 10 student files, as shown in Figure 10-17. Click OK and then allow the movie to start automatically. Resize as appropriate.

4. Preview the slide show from slide 6 to watch the movie then press Esc to end the show.

5. Update the handout footer to include the text **[10-17your initials]** as the footer.

6. Save the presentation as **[10-17your initials]** in your Lesson 10 folder. Keep the presentation open for the next exercise.

Inserting Hyperlinks

Hyperlinks are links from a particular place in your presentation to other slides, other PowerPoint presentations, other applications, or to a Web site on the Internet. Hyperlinks can be created from text, Action buttons, or objects. They provide a way to integrate outside information into a presentation.

To create a text hyperlink, select text that will become the link; then from the Insert tab, in the Links group, click the Hyperlink button. You may also press Ctrl+K to open the Insert Hyperlink dialog box.

Exercise 10-18 ADD HYPERLINKS TO SELECTED SLIDES

By default, PowerPoint shows each slide in your presentation in sequential order. Creating hyperlinks to other slides is a convenient way to move to certain slides within your presentation. For instance, if you are discussing five major points, you could create a menu with the text of each major point linked to the first slide in a series that explains each point. The menu could be used as an agenda slide or a table-of-contents slide. It could also be used for a wrap-up or summary slide at the end of a presentation.

1. Insert a new Title and Content slide between current slides 1 and 2. The new slide 2 will act as a menu linking to other slides in the presentation.

2. For the slide title, key **Discussion Points**.

3. For the first bulleted item, key **Where We Began**.

4. To create a hyperlink for the Where We Began bullet in the body text placeholder, select the text "Where We Began," right-click the selection and choose Hyperlink from the shortcut menu (or press Ctrl + K).

Figure 10-18
Inserting a hyperlink on a menu slide

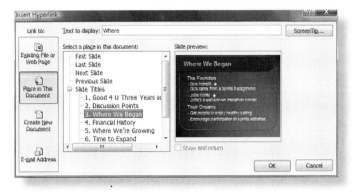

5. In the Insert Hyperlink dialog box under Link to, choose Place in this Document, as shown in Figure 10-18. In the Select a place in this document list box, choose "3. Where We Began." Click OK.

6. Create additional bullets using slide titles and hyperlinks for slides 4 through 6.

7. Leave the presentation open for the next exercise.

Exercise 10-19 CREATE ACTION BUTTONS FOR MENU OPTIONS

Setting up links on a menu slide enables you to jump to many different slides in a presentation. Usually, after you get to a linked slide, you'll want to return to the menu slide and then link to another. This requires an action button or hyperlink on the appropriate slides that takes you back to the menu slide.

Figure 10-19
Inserting an Action button

1. Move to slide 3.

2. From the Insert tab, in the Illustrations group, click the Shapes button 📋 to create an Action button to return to the menu slide.

3. Under the Action buttons category, as shown in Figure 10-19, select the button shaped like a house—with the ScreenTip Action Button: Home—and draw a small rectangle in any convenient blank area of the slide.

4. In the Action Settings dialog box that appears after you draw the Action button, click the Hyperlink to list box arrow and choose Slide.

5. In the Hyperlink to Slide dialog box, choose Slide 2, Discussion Points. Click OK. Click OK again to close the Action Settings dialog box.

6. Repeat this process for slides 4 through 6.

7. Start a slide show beginning with slide 2, Discussion Points.

8. Click Financial History. The show jumps to that slide. Click the Action Button: Home 🏠 that you created. The discussion points slide reappears. Press Esc to end the slide show.

9. Update the handout footer to include the text **[10-19your initials]** as the footer.

10. Save the presentation as **[10-19your initials]** in your Lesson 10 folder. Leave the presentation open for the next exercise.

TIP

Usually you do not use automatic slide timings when you are using a menu slide with hyperlinks.

TIP

When creating hyperlinks for a menu slide, make sure that the slide to which you link matches the text in the text box at the top of the Insert Hyperlink dialog box.

Exercise 10-20   ADD HYPERLINKS TO OTHER PRESENTATIONS

When you want to create a hyperlink to another file (for example, to another PowerPoint presentation), it is a good idea to first copy or save the file to the same directory as the presentation containing the hyperlink. If you move the presentation to another location, be sure to move the hyperlinked file as well. Otherwise, the hyperlink will no longer work after the move.

1. Working on **[10-19your initials]**, display slide 6, Time to Expand, and select the word "contests" in the first bullet under "The Plan."

2. From the Insert tab, in the Links group, choose the Hyperlink button 🔗 (or press Ctrl+K). The Insert Hyperlink dialog box opens.

3. In the Link to box on the left side, choose Existing File or Web Page.

4. In the Look in box, navigate to your Lesson 10 student files.

5. From the list of files, select **CookCon2**. Notice the PowerPoint icon to the left of the filename, indicating that the file is a PowerPoint presentation.

6. Click ScreenTip in the upper-right corner. The Set Hyperlink ScreenTip dialog box opens, as shown in Figure 10-20.

7. In the ScreenTip text box, key **Cooking Contest details**. This is the ScreenTip text that will appear when you point to the hyperlink during a slide show.

Figure 10-20
Setting the hyperlink
ScreenTip

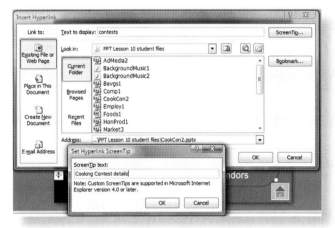

8. Click OK to close the Set Hyperlink ScreenTip dialog box; then click OK again to close the Insert Hyperlink dialog box.

9. Deselect the text "contests." The text is now in a contrasting color and underlined, indicating that it is a hyperlink.

10. Leave the presentation open for the next exercise.

Exercise 10-21   ADD HYPERLINKS TO OTHER FILES

As you learned for linking to presentation files, it is a good idea to save the file you will be linking to in the same folder as the presentation containing the hyperlink.

1. Working again on slide 6, Time to Expand, select the text "vendors" in the second bullet.

2. Press Ctrl+K to open the Insert Hyperlink dialog box.

3. Under Link to, click Existing File or Web Page.

4. Navigate to your Lesson 10 student files and select the Excel spreadsheet **VendExp** from the list of files. Notice the Excel icon to the left of the filename, indicating that this is an Excel file.

5. Click ScreenTip, and then key **Major Vendors Chart**. Click OK.

6. Click OK again to close the Insert Hyperlink dialog box.

7. Preview the slide show from slide 6 and test the hyperlinks. Press [Esc] to end the slide show. Close any additional files opened by clicking the hyperlinks.

8. Leave the presentation open for the next exercise.

Exercise 10-22 ADD HYPERLINKS TO WEB PAGES

Hyperlinks to Web pages enable you to open a Web site from within PowerPoint. A Web browser will automatically load and the page will appear.

1. The computer you are using may be connected to the Internet. If you do not already have access to the Internet, make a connection now.

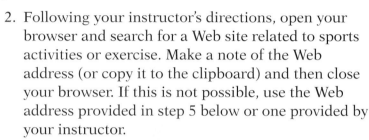

NOTE

Internet access is needed to complete this exercise. If you do not have Internet access, you can still do most of the exercise, but you will not be able to test the hyperlink.

2. Following your instructor's directions, open your browser and search for a Web site related to sports activities or exercise. Make a note of the Web address (or copy it to the clipboard) and then close your browser. If this is not possible, use the Web address provided in step 5 below or one provided by your instructor.

3. Working on slide 3, select the text "sports activities" and then press [Ctrl]+[K] to open the Insert Hyperlink dialog box.

4. Under Link to, click the Existing File or Web Page option, as shown in Figure 10-21.

5. In the Address box at the bottom of the dialog box, key the address for the Web site you found in step 2 above (or paste it from the clipboard). For example, key **http://www.fitness.gov**.

Figure 10-21
Insert Hyperlink
dialog box

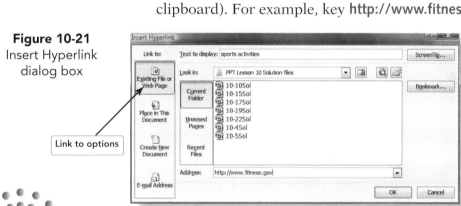

Link to options

NOTE

Web addresses often change. The Web address provided might not exist at the time that you do this exercise.

6. Click ScreenTip and key descriptive text appropriate to the Web site you are using. For example: The President's Council on Fitness and Sports. Click OK to close the Set Hyperlink ScreenTip dialog box. Click OK again to close the Insert Hyperlink dialog box.

7. View slide 3 in Slide Show view, and test the Hyperlink to the Web site. Close the browser and press [Esc] to return to Normal view.

8. If you made an Internet connection earlier in this exercise, close the connection.

9. Update the handout footer to include the text **[10-22your initials]** as the footer.

10. Save the presentation as **[10-22your initials]** in your Lesson 10 folder.

11. Preview and then print the presentation as handouts, four slides per page, grayscale, landscape, framed. Close the presentation.

Lesson 10

- Custom animation enables you to control the timing, speed, sound, and other aspects of how and when a slide's objects appear on the screen.

- To animate an object means to apply visual effects that control how an object behaves during a slide show. You can apply several animation effects, including sound, to a single object.

- All animation effects are available from the Custom Animation task pane. You can choose from entrance, emphasis, and exit effects and vary the direction, timing, speed, and other options.

- A motion path can be used to control how an object moves across the screen. PowerPoint provides a large variety of predefined paths that you can resize, rotate, and reposition to suit your needs.

- To remove an animation from a slide, select its listing in the custom animation list then click **Remove** or press [Delete].

- Sound effects can be added to individual animations. The sound effect plays when the animation occurs. Be careful with sounds, making sure that they are appropriate and play at the proper volume.

- When multiple animations are used on a slide, the order of their appearance is determined by the order they are listed on the Custom Animation task pane. You change the order in the list by selecting the item and then using the Reorder arrows to move within the list.

- As part of the timing options, you can choose to have an animation appear when you click your mouse, appear when a previous animation appears, or be delayed a number of seconds that you specify.

- An animated object can be copied to the same slide, another slide, or another presentation. All the animation settings are copied along with the object.

- Besides attaching sound effects to individual animations, you can also add sound objects that stand on their own in presentations. Sound objects can be set to play for the duration of a single slide, for an entire presentation, or until you click your mouse. Music can be played from an audio CD, too.

- Movies—animated clip art or videos—can be inserted on a slide. Once on a slide, they can be animated in the same way as any other object.
- Creating Action Buttons or hyperlinks to presentation slides makes it easy to jump to preplanned locations within your presentation.
- Another way to manage a slide show is to create a menu slide listing the titles of each slide, each with hyperlinks to the actual slide.
- Hyperlinks enable you to jump to supplemental material during a presentation. Hyperlinks can link to other slides in your slide shows, other presentations, documents created in other programs, and Web sites on the Internet.
- To use a hyperlink, start a slide show and then click the hyperlinked text. You can distinguish hyperlinked text by its contrasting color and its underline.

Lesson 10		Command Summary	
Feature	Button	Ribbon or Task Pane	Keyboard
Custom Animation		Animation, Animations group, Custom Animation	
Entrance Animation Effect	Add Effect ▾	Custom Animation task pane, Add Effect, Entrance	
Exit Animation Effect	Add Effect ▾	Custom Animation task pane, Add Effect, Emphasis	
Motion Path	Add Effect ▾	Custom Animation task pane, Add Effect, Motion Paths	
Remove Animation	Remove	Custom Animation task pane, Remove	
Modify an Effect		Custom Animation task pane, Select item, Effect Options	
Add Sound Effects		Custom Animation task pane, Select item, Effect Options	
Modify Timings		Custom Animation task pane, Select item, Timing	
Add Music		Insert, Media Clips group, Sound	
Add Movies		Insert, Media Clips group, Movie	
Hyperlink		Insert, Links group, Hyperlink	Ctrl + K
Action Button		Insert, Illustrations group, Shapes, Action Buttons	

Concepts Review

True/False Questions

Each of the following statements is either true or false. Select your choice by indicating T or F.

T (F) 1. An emphasis effect controls how an animated object first appears on a slide.

T F 2. Before adding a different animation effect to an object, you can delete its existing animations by selecting the object on the slide and pressing Delete .

T (F) 3. You add sound effects to animated objects from the Insert tab. *use animation*

(T) F 4. You can change the order of animations on a slide.

(T) F 5. You can insert movies and sounds to your presentation from the Clip Art task pane.

(T) F 6. You can set different timings for each animated object in a slide show.

(T) F 7. Sound recordings can be added to slides without animating objects.

T (F) 8. You can insert a hyperlink on a slide by pressing Ctrl + M .
K

Short Answer Questions

Write the correct answer in the space provided.

1. How do you add an animation effect?

   Select obj, then Anim tab, Cust group Add eff

2. How do you change the order in which animations occur on a slide?

   re order arrows

3. How do you copy an animated object?

   copy/paste

4. What do you call an object that, when clicked, displays another slide?

   hyperlink or action button

5. How do you set an animation effect to start automatically without a mouse click?

   start with/after prev.

6. How do you display the Action Buttons?

Insert shapes, Illustrations, then to action buttons

7. What is the purpose of a hyperlink?

More info to link other slides, pres. etc

8. What happens to hyperlink text after you click it during a slide show?

Changes Color

Critical Thinking

Answer these questions on a separate page. There are no right or wrong answers. Support your answers with examples from your own experience, if possible.

1. Which animation effects are your favorites? How do you like to use them?

2. Adding sound effects, text or object animations, and slide transitions to a slide show allows for a great deal of variety. How can you avoid distracting from the presentation's message?

Skills Review

Exercise 10-23

Add entrance, emphasis, and exit animation effects; add an animation sound effect; and change animation timing.

1. Open the file **Promo1**.
2. On slide 1, animate the hat—but not its logo—by following these steps:
   a. Select the hat and ungroup it once. Deselect the grouping.
   b. From the Animations tab, in the Animation group, click the Custom Animation button 🔳 to open the Custom Animation task pane.
   c. Select the hat (not its red logo) and in the Custom Animation task pane, click Add Effect, point to Entrance, and choose More Effects.
   d. Choose Dissolve In from the Basic category. Click OK.
3. Change the timing and speed for the animation by following these steps:
   a. Make sure the hat is still selected.
   b. On the Custom Animation task pane, click the arrow next to Start and choose With Previous from its drop-down list.
   c. Click the arrow next to Speed and choose Medium from its drop-down list.

4. Animate the hat's logo by following these steps:

   a. Select the red logo on the front of the hat.

   b. Using steps 2c and 2d as a guide, apply the Entrance effect Spiral In from the Exciting category.

   c. Using step 3 as a guide, change the logo's Start setting to After Previous and make sure its Speed setting is Fast.

5. Apply a sound effect and delay the appearance of the logo by following these steps:

   a. Make sure the red logo is still selected.

   b. In the custom animation list on the task pane, click the list box arrow for the second item, labeled Group 49.

   c. Choose Effect Options from the list.

   d. Click the Sound list box arrow and choose Wind.

   e. Click the Speaker button 🔊 and move the slider down near the bottom to lower the volume.

   f. Click the Timing tab in the dialog box.

   g. In the Delay spin box, key **1** (for 1 second). Click OK.

6. Move to slide 4 and animate the star on the T-shirt by following these steps:

   a. Select the T-shirt and zoom to 100% (so you can easily select the star).

   b. Select the star on the T-shirt's shoulder.

   c. From the Custom Animation task pane, click Add Effect, point to Emphasis, and choose More Effects.

   d. From the Basic category, choose Spin. Click OK.

7. Change effect options for the star's animation by following these steps:

   a. Make sure the star is selected. In the Custom Animation list box, click the drop-down arrow and choose Effect Options.

   b. On the Effect tab in the Settings area, click the drop-down list box for Amount and choose Half Spin.

   c. On the Timing tab, in the Start list box, choose With Previous.

   d. In the Speed list box, choose 0.5 seconds (Very Fast).

   e. In the Repeat list box, choose 3. Click OK.

8. Add a second Emphasis effect to the star by following these steps:

   a. Make sure the star is selected, then from the Custom Animation task pane, click Add Effect, point to Emphasis, and then click More Effects.

   b. Choose Complementary Color from the Subtle category. Click OK.

   c. Select the second item in the custom animation list, click its drop-down arrow and choose Timing.

   d. Set the following timing options:
      Start   With Previous
      Speed   0.5 seconds (Very Fast)
      Repeat   3

   e. Click OK.

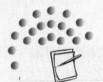

NOTE

Because this lesson addresses visual and sound effects, your instructor may have different exercise submission guidelines than for other lessons.

9. Add an Entrance and an Exit effect for the star by following these steps:

   a. Make sure the star is selected. From the Custom Animation task pane, click Add Effect, point to Entrance, and choose More Effects.

   b. Choose Dissolve In from the Basic category and click OK. Change the Speed to Very Fast if it is not already set on this.

   c. In the Custom Animation list, select the last item (the Dissolve In entrance effect) and reorder it to appear at the top of the list so that it will play first.

   d. Make sure the star is selected; then click Add Effect again. This time click Exit, and choose More Effects.

   e. Choose Dissolve Out from the Basic category and click OK.

   f. For the Exit effect (the last one on the list), change the Start setting to After Previous.

   g. From the View tab, in the Zoom group, click the Fit to Window button 🔲.

10. Create a handout header and footer: Include the date and your name as the header, and the page number and text **[10-23your initials]** as the footer.

11. Move to slide 1 and save the presentation as **[10-23your initials]** in your Lesson 10 folder.

12. Move to slide 1 and view the presentation as a slide show. Use your mouse to advance from one slide to the next. When you reach slide 4, click your mouse once to run the star animation; then click again to complete the show. Return to slide 1.

13. Preview and then print the presentation as handouts, four slides per page, grayscale, landscape, framed. Close the presentation.

Exercise 10-24

Add animation effects, animate a chart, and add music.

1. Open the file **Bevgs1**.

2. Add an Entrance effect to the slide 1 title by following these steps:

   a. Select the title text on slide 1.

   b. From the Animation tab, in the Animations group, click the Custom Animation button 🔲.

   c. Click Add Effect, point to Entrance, and choose More Effects

   d. From the Moderate category, click the Stretch effect and click OK.

   e. Click the Start list box and choose With Previous.

   f. Click the Direction list box and choose From Left.

   g. Click the Speed list box and choose Medium.

3. Using step 2 as a guide, apply an Entrance effect to the subtitle text on slide 1:

   a. Use the Faded Zoom Entrance effect, starting After Previous.

   b. Click the list box arrow beside the animation for the subtitle text in the Custom Animation list, and choose timing.

   c. Change the delay to a 3-seconds. Click OK.

4. Insert a music file that plays through the entire slide show by following these steps:

   a. From the Insert tab, in the Media Clips group, click the bottom half of the Sound button 🔊 and choose Sound from File.

   b. Select the WAV file **BackgroundMusic2** from your lesson 10 student files. Click OK. When the message box appears, click Automatically.

   c. On the Custom Animation task pane, click the list box on the sound object from the Custom Animation list and choose Effect Options.

   d. On the Sound Settings tab, click the Speaker button 🔊 and reduce the volume, then check Hide sound icon during slide show.

   e. On the Effect tab, and under Start playing, make sure that From beginning is selected.

   f. Under Stop playing, key **5** slides in the After spin box.

   g. On the Timing tab, under Start, click the drop-down list box, and choose With Previous.

   h. Check the box for Rewind when done playing.

   i. Click the Repeat list box arrow and choose Until End of Slide

   j. Click OK.

   k. In the Custom Animation task pane, reorder the sound clip item to the top of the Custom Animation list.

5. Animate the chart on slide 3 by following these steps:

   a. Select the chart and in the Custom Animation task pane, click Add Effect, point to Entrance and choose More Effects.

   b. Choose the Wipe effect in the Basic category and click OK.

   c. Change the Speed to Medium.

   d. In the Custom Animation list, click the list box arrow for chart Object 2, and choose Effect Options.

   e. On the Chart Animation tab, click the list box arrow for Group chart and choose By Category.

   f. Clear the check box for Start animation by drawing the chart background. By turning off this option, the chart layout will appear when the slide is displayed. Click OK.

6. Animate an object to appear and then disappear by following these steps:

   a. Move to slide 4, select the picture in the lower-right corner.

   b. In the Custom Animation task pane, click Add Effect, point to Entrance and choose More Effects.

   c. In the Basic category, choose the Wheel effect.

   d. Change its Start setting to After Previous.

   e. With the picture still selected, click Add Effect, point to Exit and choose More Effects.

   f. In the Basic category, choose the Wheel effect.

   g. Change its Start setting to After Previous.

    h. Click the second object in the custom animation list (the Exit effect), click its drop-down list arrow, and choose Timing.

    i. In the Delay spin box, key **3** to delay the effect's start for three seconds. Click OK.

7. Create a handout header and footer: Include the date and your name as the header, and the page number and text **[10-24your initials]** as the footer.

8. Move to slide 1 and save the presentation as **[10-24your initials]** in your Lesson 10 folder.

9. View the presentation as a slide show.

10. Preview and then print the presentation as handouts, six slides per page, grayscale, framed. Close the presentation.

Exercise 10-25

Change animation settings and create action buttons and hyperlinks.

1. Open the file **Employ1**. View the presentation as a slide show to view the existing text animation.

2. On slide 2, change the existing animation effect by following these steps:

    a. Select the second item group labeled "Rectangle 9" in the custom animation list, which is the body text.

    b. Click Change at the top of the Custom Animation task pane.

    c. Point to Entrance and choose More Effects.

    d. In the Basic category, choose the Fly In effect.

3. Modify the animation effect by following these steps:

    a. Click the list box arrow for the second item and choose Effect Options.

    b. On the Text Animation tab, change the Group text setting to By 2nd level paragraphs.

    c. On the Timing tab, change the Speed setting to 2 seconds (Medium). Click OK.

4. Add effects to the clip art image on slide 1 by following these steps:

    a. Working on the Custom Animation task pane, click Add Effect, point to Entrance, and choose More Effects.

    b. Choose the Spiral In effect from the Exciting category.

    c. Move this animation effect to the top of the Custom Animation list, so that the Spiral In effect occurs before the other text animations.

    d. Change the Start setting to With Previous and the speed to Medium.

5. Apply an Exit effect to the clip art image on slide 1 by following these steps:

    a. Working on the Custom Animation task pane, click Add Effect, point to Exit, and choose More Effects.

    b. Choose the Spiral Out effect from the Exciting category.

   c. Change the Start setting to With Previous and the speed to Medium.

   d. Click the list box arrow for the Exit effect and choose Timing. Add a 3-second delay and click OK.

   e. Close the Custom Animation task pane.

6. Create hyperlinks to other slides by following these steps:

   a. Move to slide 2.

   b. Select the second item on the agenda bullet list, Company Vision, and right-click the selection.

   c. Choose Hyperlink from the shortcut menu (or press Ctrl+K).

   d. In the Insert Hyperlink dialog box under Link to, click Place in this Document.

   e. From the list of slides in the presentation, select slide 3. Our Vision.

   f. Click OK.

7. Repeat step 6 for the remaining items on the Agenda list.

8. On slide 3, create an Action Button to return to the Agenda by following these steps:

   a. From the Insert tab, in the Illustrations group, click the Shapes button 🔲.

   b. Under the Action Buttons category, select the button shaped like a house—with the ScreenTip Action Button: Home—and draw a small rectangle in any convenient blank area of the slide.

   c. In the Action Settings dialog box, click the Hyperlink to list box arrow and choose Slide.

   d. In the Hyperlink to Slide dialog box, choose 2. Agenda. Click OK. Click OK again to close the Action Settings dialog box.

   e. Adjust the size and position of the Action Button to give it a neat and unobtrusive effect in the lower-right corner of the slide.

9. Copy the Action Button on slide 3 and paste to the remaining slides. When you copy and paste this button, it will copy the link settings also. The buttons will work without going through the process to link back to the slide 2 again.

10. Create a handout header and footer: Include the date and your name as the header, and the page number and text **[10-25your initials]** as the footer.

11. Move to slide 1 and save the presentation as **[10-25your initials]** in your Lesson 10 folder.

12. Preview and then print the presentation as handouts, six slides per page, grayscale, framed. Close the presentation.

Exercise 10-26

Insert a movie and create hyperlinks to other files.

1. Open the file **AdMedia2**.

2. Create a hyperlink to another presentation by following these steps:
   a. Open the presentations **Market3** and **Market4** from the drive and folder where your student files are stored.
   b. Without making any changes, save the files with the same names in your Lesson 10 folder. Close **Market3** and **Market4**.
   c. On slide 6, select "Marketing Strategy" and then right-click and choose Hyperlink (or press Ctrl+K).
   d. In the Insert Hyperlink dialog box under Link to, choose Existing File or Web Page.
   e. Navigate to your Lesson 10 folder; then select the presentation **Market4**.
   f. Click ScreenTip, and then key **Marketing Strategy** as the ScreenTip text. Click OK and then click OK again to close the Insert Hyperlink dialog box.
   g. Still working on slide 6, select "Marketing Our Business," and create a hyperlink to the presentation **Market3** by following steps 2c–2f. Use the ScreenTip **Employee Training**.

3. Insert a movie from the Clip Organizer on slide 2 by following these steps:
   a. Move to slide 2.
   b. From the Insert tab, in the Media Clips group, click the bottom half of the Movie button 🎬, and choose Movie from Clip Organizer.
   c. In the Search for box, key **Dollar Sign**, and click Go.
   d. Click on an appropriate movie to insert it on slide 2. Resize and reposition the movie on the right side of the slide.

4. Create a handout header and footer: Include the date and your name as the header, and the page number and text **[10-26your initials]** as the footer.

5. Move to slide 1 and save the presentation as **[10-26your initials]** in your Lesson 10 folder.

6. View the presentation as a slide show. When you come to slide 6, click each of the hyperlinks to jump to the linked presentations. Press Esc to return to the main presentation.

7. Preview and then print the presentation as handouts, six slides per page, grayscale, framed. Close the presentation.

Lesson Applications

Exercise 10-27

Animate text and objects.

1. Open the file **Comp1**.

2. Move to slide 4.

3. Apply the Wheel Entrance effect from the Basic category to the Bread clip art and have it appear after the previous effect with a one second delay.

4. Still working on the Bread clip art, apply the Wheel Exit effect from the Basic category and have it appear after the previous effect with a two second delay.

5. In the Custom Animation list, select both of the bread animation items and move them up so that they are inserted below item 1 ("Best bread").

6. Animate the plate of spaghetti and meatballs by using the same settings as for the loaf of bread. Move the spaghetti and meatball animation items up and insert them below item 2 ("Power-packed pasta").

7. Animate the soup tureen in the same manner and make it appear after the "Healthy fast foods" animation item.

8. Animate the piece of cake in the same manner and make it appear after the "Fat-free desserts" animation item.

9. Move to slide 5, apply the same animation effects to the three clip art images, making them appear with one clip art after each of the first three bullets.

10. Move to slide 1 and move the prize ribbon to the top left just off of the edge of the slide. Choose a motion path to animate it going diagonally down to the right. Adjust the position as needed and adjust the length of the motion path as needed.

11. Move to slide 3 and add an Entrance effect to make the picture of people Dissolve In. For Start, choose On Click so the picture appears after all text.

12. Run the slide show, making sure all animations are correct, and then stop it by pressing [Esc].

13. Create a handout header and footer: Include the date and your name as the header, and the page number and text **[10-27your initials]** as the footer.

14. Move to slide 1 and save the presentation as **[10-27your initials]** in your Lesson 10 folder.

15. Preview and then print the presentation as handouts, six slides per page, grayscale, framed. Close the presentation.

Exercise 10-28

Create text animations, object animations, add a movie and music, and add action buttons.

1. Open the file **SpEvent3**.

2. On slide 1, select the Scheduling Events title and apply the Split Entrance Effect from the Basic category. For the Direction, choose Vertical Out and for the Start setting, choose On Click.

3. Draw a long, thin, right-pointing block arrow shape as shown in Figure 10-22. Make the arrow the same length as the title, and position it between the title and the subtitle.

Figure 10-22
Arrow shape and placement

4. Apply the Stretch Entrance effect from the Moderate category to the arrow. Change the Direction setting to From Left and change the Speed setting to Medium. Apply the Drum Roll sound effect at an appropriate volume. Change the Start setting to With Previous and move the effect to the top of the custom animation list.

5. On slide 1, at the bottom center of the slide, insert an appropriate movie from the Clip Organizer using the Search for keyword "Gymnastics." Recolor the movie to match the theme colors.

6. Insert a sound clip of your choice on slide 2 and use the display options to hide the sound icon during the slide show. Make it play automatically for the duration of slide 2. Adjust its sound to an appropriate volume.

7. On slide 2, create an Action Button that links to slide 3. Use Action Button: Information.

8. On slide 3, create an Action Button that links back to slide 2. Use Action Button: Return.

9. Create a handout header and footer: Include the date and your name as the header, and the page number and text **[10-28your initials]** as the footer.

10. Move to slide 1 and save the presentation as **[10-28your initials]** in your Lesson 10 folder.

11. View the presentation as a slide show. On slide 2, click the Action Button to display slide 3. Use the Action Button on slide 3 to return to slide 2, and then continue viewing the slide show.

12. Preview and then print the presentation as handouts, six slides per page, grayscale, framed. Close the presentation.

Exercise 10-29

Add and modify animations and insert a hyperlink to a Word document.

1. Open the file **HonProd1**.

2. On slide 1, apply an Entrance and Exit animation effect to the title text, Natural Honey Products.

3. On slides 2 and 3, apply Entrance animation effects to the bullet lists by 1st level paragraphs.

4. On slide 3, find an appropriate clip art image to place below the text, apply animation, and include a sound effect with the animation.

5. Open the Word document **Foods1** and save it with the same name in your Lesson 10 folder. Close Word.

6. On slide 2, create a hyperlink that will display the Word file **Foods1** when you click the text "Products made with honey." Give it the ScreenTip Foods and Beverages Made with Honey.

7. Create a handout header and footer: Include the date and your name as the header, and the page number and text **[10-29your initials]** as the footer.

8. Move to slide 1 and save the presentation as **[10-29your initials]** in your Lesson 10 folder.

9. View the presentation as a slide show and click the hyperlink on slide 2.

10. Preview and then print the presentation as handouts, three slides per page, grayscale, framed. Close the presentation.

Exercise 10-30 ◆ Challenge Yourself

Apply entrance, emphasis, and exit effects to objects; animate text; add sound to animations.

1. Open the file **Stratgy2**.

2. On slide 1, ungroup the four arrows in the center of the slide and move them apart slightly. Position the Marketing Strategy subtitle in the middle.

3. Make each arrow fly in from a corner of the slide, one after the other in a clockwise direction by applying the following Entrance effects:

   - *Light blue arrow:* Fly In, From Top-Left, With Previous, Push sound effect, Fast speed.

   - *Yellow arrow:* Fly In, From Top-Right, After Previous, Push sound effect, Fast speed.

   - *Royal blue arrow:* Fly In, From Bottom-Right, After Previous, Push sound effect, Fast speed.

   - *Red arrow:* Fly In, From Bottom-Left, After Previous, Push sound effect, Fast speed.

4. On slide 2, apply a Zoom Entrance effect to the clip art, coming From Screen Center, starting with a mouse click, at medium speed.

5. In the middle of the light bulb, draw a small star Shape. Color and animate the star in such a way that it spins or blinks several times without any mouse clicks after the clip art animation is completed. Have it appear by spiraling in and disappear by spiraling out.

6. Animate the body text on slides 2 through 4 by using any effect that you like, making sure that the bullets appear one at a time with a mouse click.

7. Create a handout header and footer: Include the date and your name as the header, and the page number and text **[10-30your initials]** as the footer.

8. Move to slide 1 and save the presentation as **[10-30your initials]** in your Lesson 10 folder.

9. View as a slide show watching all the animation.

10. Preview and then print the presentation as handouts, four slides per page, grayscale, framed. Close the presentation.

On Your Own

In these exercises you work on your own, as you would in a real-life work environment. Use the skills you've learned to accomplish the task—and be creative.

Exercise 10-31

Create a presentation with at least six slides that describes your favorite movie. Identify the main characters, quotable lines, and the main idea of the movie. Animate the presentation to draw attention to key points and to help promote the movie to your audience. The slide show should advance by mouse clicks. Insert sounds, movies, and hyperlinks to create interest in your presentation. Add a slide footer with your name and the text **[10-31your initials]**. Save the presentation as **[10-31your initials]**. Preview and then print the presentation as handouts.

Exercise 10-32

Create a presentation of at least six slides that is designed to run in a kiosk in a car dealership. The presentation should promote new models and features of vehicles. It could be a new SUV, car, truck, or the like that might draw the interest of people entering the dealership. Apply eye-catching animations to the presentation, including sound, but make sure the animations do not obscure the presentation's message. Test and refine the presentation's animations as needed to make it run smoothly and professionally. Check spelling and grayscale settings. Add a slide footer with your name and the text **[10-32your initials]**. Save the presentation as **[10-32your initials]**. Preview and then print the presentation as handouts.

Exercise 10-33

Imagine that you are an artist or someone marketing the work of an artist. Choose an artistic theme and then design a four-slide presentation by using several animation sequences, making objects and text appear and disappear as you please, adding music, movies, and other sound effects. Play the animation and then fine-tune it. Be prepared to run your presentation for your instructor and your classmates. Add a slide footer with your name and the text **[10-33your initials]**. Save the presentation as **[10-33your initials]**. Preview and then print the presentation as handouts.

OBJECTIVES

MCAS OBJECTIVES

In this lesson:
PP07 1.2.1
PP07 1.2.2
PP07 1.3
PP07 2.2.1
PP07 2.2.3
PP07 2.2.7
PP07 2.3.1
PP07 2.3.2
PP07 3.4.1
See Appendix

After completing this lesson, you will be able to:

1. Customize existing themes.

2. Format background styles.

3. Work with Slide Masters to create customized design themes.

4. Apply themes and templates from Microsoft Office Online.

5. Customize handout and notes masters.

Estimated Time: 1½ hours

NOTE

The procedures outlined here will work when you are using your own computer and a new custom theme will be available to use again. However, in computer lab classrooms, the new theme may not remain on the computer when it is rebooted. Some labs use routine maintenance procedures where the computer is restored to its original state each day; therefore, changes to default settings or files that have been saved will be removed.

PowerPoint *themes* give presentations a unified appearance. Each theme provides a completely different "look" because of the built-in effects applied to backgrounds, text, tables, charts, SmartArt, and other objects.

The ability to achieve consistency is not a new feature to PowerPoint, because design templates in previous versions provided backgrounds and fonts that worked well together. However, beginning with PowerPoint 2007, the term "template" refers to a presentation that provides content to help get you started. Themes replace design templates to control backgrounds, fonts, placeholder positioning, and other graphics. *Slide Masters* with a variety of *Slide Layouts* store this information.

Themes can be customized and new themes saved for use in PowerPoint and other applications. Additional themes and templates are available at Microsoft Office Online.

Customizing an Existing Theme

In previous lessons you have selected colors and fonts from PowerPoint's existing themes. In this lesson you learn more about how these colors and fonts work and how to customize them by making your own selections to create new themes. Changes made to theme components immediately affect the active presentation.

Exercise 11-1   EXAMINE BUILT-IN COLOR THEMES

This exercise will develop your understanding of theme colors. You will create three slides with sample text and graphics so you can see how the default colors are affected when the theme colors change.

 From the Design tab, in the Themes group, the Colors button displays four colors of the current theme; the colors on the button change as you select different themes. When you click this button, you will see all theme colors listed alphabetically by the name for each group. It appears as though each theme consists of eight colors. However, you can actually change 12 different theme colors: four text and background, six accent, and two hyperlink colors.

1. Start a new blank presentation. From the Design tab, in the Themes group, click the Colors button and notice that the "Office" Theme is selected. The words "Office Theme" also appear in the Status bar on the lower left to define this particular group of colors.

2. Refer to Figure 11-1 as you complete the next steps.

Figure 11-1
Sample slides

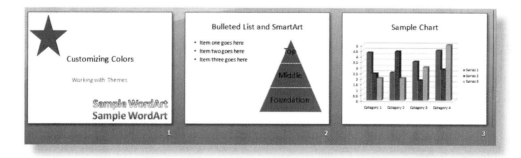

3. On slide 1, use the Title Slide layout:

   a. For the slide title, key **Customizing Colors** and for the subtitle key **Working with Themes**.

   b. Insert a star in the upper left corner.

   c. Insert WordArt and use the Quick Style Fill - White, Gradient Outline - Accent 1. Key **Sample WordArt**. Move the WordArt below the subtitle and to the right.

   d. Duplicate the WordArt and position the copy below the previous WordArt text. Change the Quick Style to Fill - Accent 2, Warm Matte Bevel.

4. Create a new slide 2 using the Two Content layout:

    a. For the slide title, key **Bulleted List and SmartArt**.

    b. For the bulleted items, key sample text for three items such as **Item one goes here**, etc.

    c. Insert a SmartArt Graphic, and from the Pyramid category click the Basic Pyramid then click OK.

    d. On the pyramid shapes, key three words with **Foundation** (on the bottom), **Middle**, and **Top**.

5. Create a new slide 3 using the Title and Content layout:

    a. For the slide title, key **Sample Chart**.

    b. Click the Insert Chart button 📊, and choose the 3-D Clustered Column chart and click OK. Excel will appear showing sample data.

    c. Close Excel to accept the sample data.

6. Now you have a short presentation with a variety of graphics so you can see how Theme Colors affect them.

7. Create a new folder for Lesson 11 and save this presentation as **[11-1your initials]** in your Lesson 11 folder. Leave the presentation open for the next exercise.

Exercise 11-2 CREATE AND SAVE CUSTOM THEME COLORS

You change *Theme Colors* by first clicking the Design tab and the Colors button 🔳 and then choosing Create New Theme Colors at the bottom of the built-in colors list. A dialog box will open where the theme colors can be changed individually.

After the dialog box is open, click the button of a color you want to change and select from other theme colors or standard colors. If you choose More Colors, you can choose colors from the Standard tab or click the Custom tab to mix your own color. The color changes will be illustrated in the Sample area on the right of the Create New Theme Colors dialog box. If you don't like the changes, you can click the Reset button 🔳. If you want to use the new colors in the future, then you can save them as new theme colors, too.

1. Expand your Slides and Outline pane so you can see color changes on all three slides at the same time.

2. From the Design tab, in the Themes group, click the Theme Colors button 🔳 then click Create New Theme Colors. Notice the Theme colors that are displayed in the Create New Theme Colors dialog box and displayed in Figure 11-2.

Figure 11-2
Create New Theme
Colors dialog box

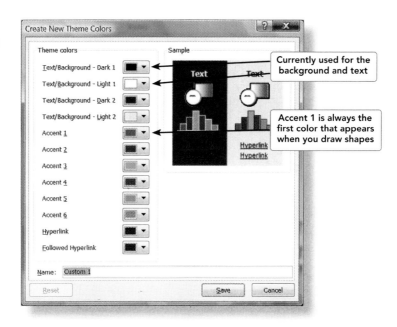

3. Position this dialog box on your screen so you can see it as well as your Slides and Outline pane. The different theme colors are shown on the left and a sample of the colors are shown on the right. Notice that you have both light and dark versions of text and background colors. Right now the presentation is using the Light 1 for the white background and Dark 1 for the text color for slide titles and other text.

4. Six accent colors are shown. Notice these applications:

   a. Accent 1 color is used on the star shape, on the ShapeArt diagram, and on the first series on the chart.

   b. Accent 2 and Accent 3 are used on the chart, too. Charts or diagrams may use more colors depending on how they are constructed.

   c. The WordArt colors are Accent 1 and Accent 2. All of the styles you see when you access the WordArt gallery are displayed in theme colors.

   d. The Hyperlink and Followed Hyperlink colors are not being used because the presentation does not include these features. The two hyperlink colors are used to control the color when a text hyperlink is first displayed and after it has been clicked during a presentation.

5. Click the Accent 1 color, and your color choices will appear in color swatches. Notice that the different theme colors span the top of this window and then variations of those colors, which represent shades (percentages) of the theme colors are below. Standard color swatches are arranged almost like a rainbow at the bottom of this window.

NOTE

From the Theme Colors gallery, you can choose More Colors then select additional colors from the Standard swatches or mix your own color from the Custom tab just as you have changed fill colors for shapes.

6. Use the Standard colors to change the first three Accent colors and notice the different colors displayed on the sample:

   a. Change Accent 1 to Yellow.

   b. Change Accent 2 to Light Blue.

   c. Change Accent 3 to Purple.

7. At the bottom of this dialog box, key **Color practice** as the name for this new theme, then click Save. Changes are immediately made to your slides, the Colors button ■ shows different colors, and this new theme name is added to your Custom Theme Colors list.

Figure 11-3
Editing a Custom Theme Color

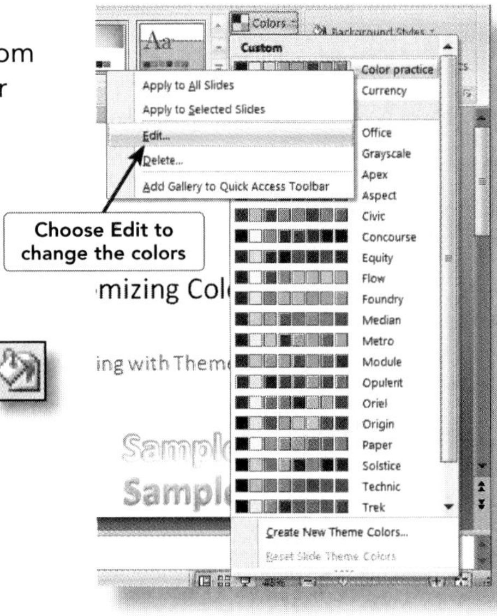

Choose Edit to change the colors

8. These colors can be edited, as shown in Figure 11-3. Click the Colors button ■, right-click the Color practice theme, then choose Edit.

9. From the dialog box, change the Accent 3 color to the Standard Color Orange. Click Save.

10. From the Design tab, click the Background Styles ▨ to select a different background color. The four variations of light and dark colors are shown across the Background Styles gallery with gradient variations for each color, as shown in Figure 11-4.

11. Click Style 11 to place the darkest area of the gradient background around the edges of the slide.

Figure 11-4
Changing the Background Style

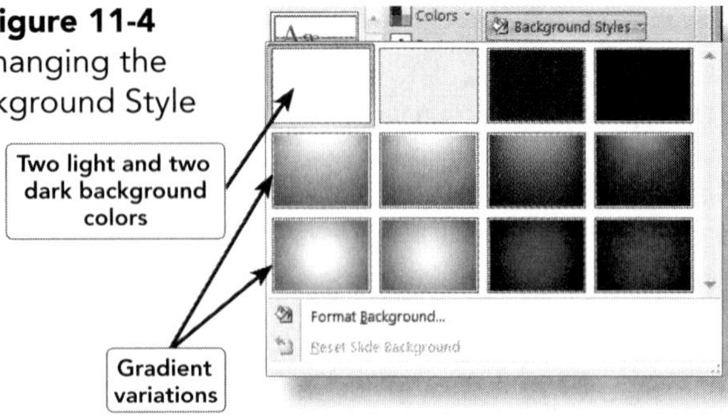

Two light and two dark background colors

Gradient variations

12. Because this style uses a dark background, the theme font color changes to white; however, this causes a problem with the yellow accent color that was earlier applied because white text does not have sufficient contrast to be readable on top of yellow.

13. Click the Theme Colors button ■ then right-click on the Color Practice theme and choose Edit. Change the yellow Accent 1 color to the Standard Color Dark Blue. Click Save to change your custom theme. Be sure you are resaving it with the same name.

14. Move to slide 1 and select the star. Even though the star was colored using the first accent color in the theme, it can be recolored individually just as you have been coloring shapes in the last several lessons. From the Home tab, click the Shape Fill button and choose the orange color that you used in the color theme for a unified look.

Exercise 11-3　CHANGE THEME FONTS AND EXAMINE BUILT-IN EFFECTS

Remember that text must be easy to read. When you change text placeholder font colors, be sure to have a high contrast between the slide background colors and the text colors. For many fonts, a bold attribute will make the text easier to read, too. Sometimes a shadow can help to define letterforms, but again, contrast is needed so that the shadow outlines the text and does not make it look blurred.

The fonts you choose will affect the tone of your presentation. Some look very formal or traditional, while others seem more modern. Some fonts seem casual and resemble handwriting. Use one or perhaps two fonts in a presentation. Be sure that slide titles are emphasized more than the text in the body of the slides.

Theme fonts in PowerPoint control the heading font and the body text font. For many of the themes, the same font is used in both places; however, some themes use two fonts.

1. From the Design tab, in the Themes group, click the Fonts button A to access the gallery of font combinations organized by a built-in theme name.

2. At the bottom of the gallery, click the Create New Theme Fonts option, as shown in Figure 11-5.

Figure 11-5
Creating New Theme
Fonts

3. Change the Heading font to Cooper Black and the Body font to Arial. Click Save.

4. Notice that the text is automatically updated to these fonts. In this font and size, the titles stand out more from other information on the slides. However, no adjustments have been made to the positions of the slide elements. The different font makes the WordArt samples larger, so you may need to adjust their position to be sure all text is on the slide.

Exercise 11-4   SAVE A CUSTOM THEME

So far in this lesson you started with a blank slide then added some sample text and shapes. You changed colors and saved and edited a Theme Color. You also saved a new Theme Font and applied a background style with a gradient effect. All of these settings can be saved in a theme that will be available for use again.

1. From the Design tab, in the Themes group, click the More button ⊡. Click Save Current Theme and a dialog box will appear. Notice that this new theme will, by default, go into your Document Themes folder, as shown in Figure 11-6.

Figure 11-6
Saving a current theme

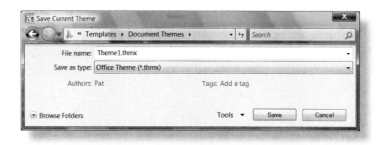

NOTE

In classroom lab situations where you use different computers, you may prefer to save your theme in a folder on a removable storage device so you can have the theme available for use on different computers.

2. For the file name, key Practice theme. The Save as type should remain Office Theme because this new theme will be available to use across Microsoft Office Applications. Click Save.

3. Save this presentation as **[11-4your initials]** in your Lesson 11 folder. Preview then print a handout copy with three slides on a page, sized to fit paper, and frame slides.

4. Now consider what happens to all of your color selections if you choose a different built-in theme. From the Design tab, in the Themes group, click the More button ⊡. Click the Median theme to apply it.

5. Notice that when the new theme is applied, placeholder positioning has changed as well as the colors and fonts for title text and bulleted lists. The WordArt samples overlap where the title and subtitle information is in this theme design.

6. Notice, also, that the star has retained its orange color because it was changed as a separate shape after the theme colors were saved.

7. When you need to control placeholder positioning, you need to adjust Slide Layouts by using the Slide Master feature that you will learn about in Objective 3 exercises. Close this presentation without saving and continue to the next exercises to learn about creating your own custom presentation backgrounds.

Formatting Background Styles

In the previous exercise you changed the appearance of the background by choosing one of the preset styles that uses theme colors. Many more changes are possible. You can change background effects for an entire presentation or for just one slide. Just as shapes can have a variety of fill types applied, backgrounds can be solid colors, gradient fills, textures, or pictures.

REVIEW

Although the process of selecting a gradient for a background is the same as when using this fill on a shape, when the gradient is filling the entire slide it sometimes looks much different than when filling a small shape. The number of Gradient stops will vary based on the type of gradient used. The gradient in Exercise 11-5 uses six stops, which control how the colors change from light to dark and dark to light in the gradual color changes that you see. For Gradient stops you can change:

- The number of stops.
- The position of the stops shown in percent from the edge of the slide.
- Each separate color that is used for the stops.
- The amount of transparency for each stop.

Exercise 11-5 APPLY SOLID FILL AND GRADIENT BACKGROUNDS

The Background dialog box lets you choose from the theme colors, other colors, or fill effects.

In this exercise you will work with a presentation that has a very simple background so you can concentrate on the impact that the backgrounds have on the slides. Later you will insert graphics and adjust the backgrounds in different ways.

1. Open the presentation **Nutrition**. This presentation has a background with a solid fill color. The placeholders for body text (subtitle and bulleted lists) have been filled in with a color that blends with the background color.

2. On slide 1, click the Design tab then in the Background group, click the Background Styles button 🔲. The current theme colors show with solid and gradient colors. On the bottom of this gallery click Format Background.

3. From the dialog box that appears, choose Solid fill and then change the color to Tan, Background 2, Darker 50% as shown in Figure 11-7. Immediately the background color changes on the slide and the title text has better color contrast on this darker color.

Figure 11-7
Format Background
dialog box

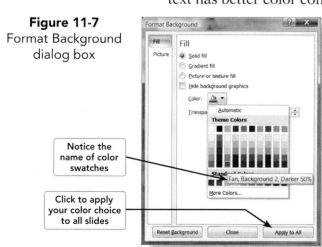

4. Click Apply to All so this color is placed on all slides in the presentation. Click Close.

5. Still working on slide 1, repeat this process but apply a gradient fill. From the Design tab, in the Background group, click the Background Styles button 🔲, and choose Format Background, then click Gradient fill. Make the following adjustments as shown in Figure 11-8.

a. For Preset colors choose Gold.

b. For Type choose Radial.

c. For Direction choose the first thumbnail on the left labeled From Corner.

d. For Stops, in this case, do not change the gradient stops.

e. Click Close to apply this gradient to the background on the title slide only.

Figure 11-8
Applying a gradient
fill to a background

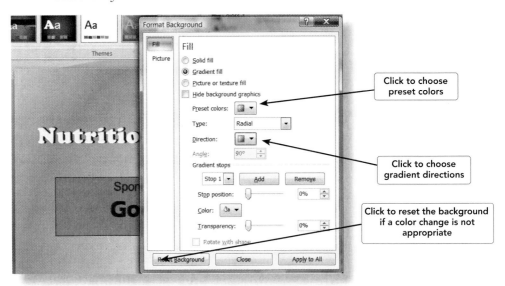

6. Leave the presentation open for the next exercise.

Exercise 11-6   APPLY TEXTURED BACKGROUNDS

In addition to solid and gradient colors, textured effects can be used for back-grounds. Choose these effects carefully so your text will remain easy to read with the colors and fonts that you are using.

1. Still working on slide 1, from the Design tab, in the Background group, click the Background Styles button [icon], then Format Background.

2. Choose Picture or texture fill. Click Texture and you will see a limited number of textures. Click the Walnut texture that looks like dark wood.

3. Click Apply to All and then click Close. Scroll through the presentation to see the dark wood on all slides. Click the Undo button [icon] to remove the walnut texture from slides 2-7.

4. Now repeat the process but search for an image to use as a texture. Still working on slide 1, from the Design tab, in the Background group, click the Background Styles button [icon], then Format Background.

5. Choose Picture or texture fill. Under Insert from: click Clip Art, and for the Search text, key **texture**. Be sure you have a check at the top of the dialog box to Include content from Office Online, then click Go.

6. Find a food-related image such as a picture of lemons. Click OK and the single image fills the entire screen.

7. To use this image as a wallpaper-like texture as shown in Figure 11-9, choose the option Tile picture as texture, and then additional Tiling options appear (to control how the image repeats). For Alignment, choose Center, and for Mirror type, choose Both.

8. Click Close to apply this texture to the title slide only.

TIP

Be careful when using a picture as a textured fill to make sure that the text is still easy to read on top of it.

Figure 11-9
Texture fill created with a tiled picture

9. Save your presentation as **[11-6your initials]**. Leave the presentation open for the next exercise.

Exercise 11-7 CREATE A PICTURE BACKGROUND FROM A FILE

Using a picture as a slide background is an interesting technique, but it provides some design challenges. Because pictures are made up of so many colors, it is difficult to select text colors and fonts that are easily readable over all areas of a picture. In this exercise you will apply a picture of vegetables and consider how the solid color of the text placeholders keeps the text easy to read.

Although background consistency is important for a unified presentation theme, at times you will want a different background for one or more slides in a presentation. For example, slide 7 in the current presentation already displays several pictures, so the background may need a different effect. From the Format Background dialog box you can adjust the transparency setting or even choose to hide the background. It is important to be sure that the colors you choose blend with the overall theme colors and the tone of the presentation.

1. On slide 1, from the Design tab, in the Background group, click the Background Styles button ▨, then Format Background.

2. For the Fill, select Picture or texture fill then under Insert from: click File. On the Insert Picture dialog box, locate your student files and choose **Vegetable1** and click Insert. The picture immediately appears on slide 1, as shown in Figure 11-10.

Figure 11-10
Background picture
fill

TIP

The picture shown in Figure 11-10 is available in Microsoft Office Online. Search for photos by using the search word "onions." It is also available with your student data files with the filename of Vegetable1.

3. Click Apply to All and the picture appears as the background for all slides. Click Close.

4. Scroll through the presentation to verify that the vegetable picture background appears on all slides. Notice that this colorful background is not appropriate for slide 7 because the pictures of vegetables are not easy to see on top of the background vegetable picture.

5. Move to slide 7 ("To Good Health!") and from the Design tab, in the Background group, click the Dialog Box Launcher button 🔲 to open the Background dialog box.

6. Click the Transparency slider and drag it to 50% (or key **50%** in the spin box). Now the picture is faded out so the vegetable pictures on top can be featured.

7. On the Format Background dialog box, practice a few more adjustments.

   a. On the left of the dialog box click Picture and then Recolor.

   b. Try several different color settings including Sepia.

   c. Try adjusting the Brightness and Contrast to look at those effects.

   d. These effects may work well for future needs, but for this presentation the first adjustment works best. So click Reset picture to return to the 50% transparency setting you chose in the previous step.

   e. Click Close.

8. On slide 7, select all five pictures. Click the Picture Tools Format tab in the Picture Styles group, click the Picture Border button ▣. Apply Brown, Accent 2, Lighter 25% and change the Weight to 3 points. Now the pictures have the same border effect as the placeholders on the other slides.

9. Reposition the pictures by aligning them as shown in Figure 11-11.

10. Save the presentation as **[11-7your initials]**. Preview and print slides 1 and 2 on a single handout page with two slides on a page.

11. Leave the presentation open for the next exercise.

Figure 11-11
Background picture fill with 50% transparency

Working with Slide Masters for a Custom Theme

Presentation themes can be used to control fonts and colors, but PowerPoint's *Slide Masters* enable you to design a custom background and position graphics to be displayed on all slides. Using Slide Masters you can adjust *Slide Layouts* to control placeholder positioning for titles, subtitles, bulleted lists, charts, SmartArt, etc., in addition to storing color and font information.

When combined, these features can create a theme so you apply design elements consistently throughout a presentation for a unified appearance. Any design element that appears on all slides should be controlled on the Slide Master.

You can create a theme from a blank presentation or from an existing theme. Themes can be customized for a topic or designed with specific needs in mind such as matching university colors or including a company logo on all slides. They can be saved, too, for future use. Also, a wide variety of themes exist at Microsoft Office Online that you can download and apply to your presentation.

Exercise 11-8 REARRANGE BACKGROUND GRAPHICS

To customize the look of a theme, you can modify or delete existing objects (lines, shapes, images) plus add your own objects suitable for your particular topic. Remember to keep the design changes you make professional and suitable for the presentation topic. These changes are made using the Slide Master.

1. On slide 1, click the View tab. From the Presentation Views group, click the Slide Master button ▣. In Slide Master View, you see all the possible predesigned slide layouts that are available to use as shown on the left in Figure 11-12. Each of these can be customized.

Figure 11-12
Slide Master View

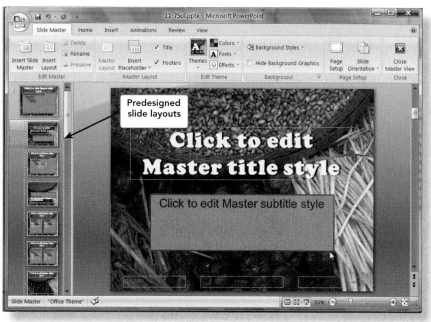

2. The first layout controls the background for all slides; other layouts can be made to look different if you wish. So begin with your changes on this layout and then change additional layouts as needed. You will not use all of the layouts, so no work is required on the ones you do not use in your presentation.

3. From the Slide Master tab, in the Edit Theme group, click the Colors button ▣ and select the Technic colors.

4. From the Slide Master tab, in the Background group, click the Background Styles button ▣ then choose Format Background. From the Format Background dialog box, click Gradient fill. From the Preset colors, choose Moss.

5. For Type choose Rectangular and for Direction choose From Corner (the first thumbnail with the darkest green in the upper left).

6. Click Apply to All. This step removes the picture that you applied in the last exercise and applies the same gradient coloring to all slides. Click Close.

7. On the first layout, add a rectangle on the left side of the slide. Click the Home tab, then from the Drawing Tools Format tab, click the Rectangle shape and draw a rectangle extending from the top to bottom with the following settings as shown in Figure 11-13.

- Size—height is 7.5 inches and width is 1.5 inches.

- Shape Fill color—click Shape Fill, Gradient, More Gradients and choose the same Preset color of Moss. Choose the Direction of Linear Down. This applies the same colors as the slide background but the light green is now on the top.

- Shape Outline—click Shape Outline and choose No Outline.

- Layer order—click Send to Back so the rectangle is behind the text placeholders on the slide.

Figure 11-13
Slide master with rectangle added

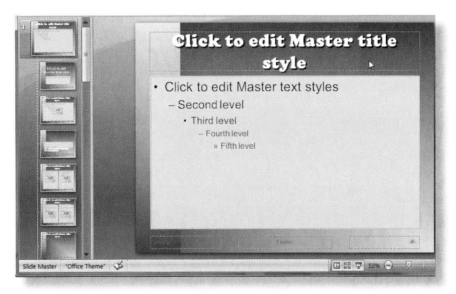

8. Select the rectangle and copy it. Move to the first layout master below the one you have just changed. This is the Title Slide master. The rectangle you positioned previously now appears here; however, it is not wide enough for this slide.

9. Paste the copied rectangle and from the Drawing Tools Format tab, increase its width to 2.5 inches. The height remains the same. Be sure to align this rectangle with the left of the slide. Click Send to Back so the rectangle is behind the text placeholders.

10. Leave the presentation open for the next exercise.

Exercise 11-9   CHANGE AND REPOSITION PLACEHOLDERS

When you change the layout of the graphics and the backgrounds of a theme, you often must reposition the theme placeholders for all objects to fit attractively on the slide. Previously the slide titles were centered, but in this exercise the added shape at the left calls for a left alignment pattern. Also, the positioning and fill of the placeholders should be changed to fit this new design. In a later exercise, you will adjust the position of other objects, too.

1. Still working in Master view, click the first master at the top left. Select the Title placeholder and, from the Home tab, in the Font group, click Left Alignment. Resize it from the left so the text starts beside the rectangle and not on it.

2. Select the body placeholder and from the Home tab, in the Drawing group, change the Shape Fill to No Fill and Shape Outline to No Outline. Resize the placeholder from the left and top to indent it more on the slide.

3. Select the placeholder text and change the text color to black. From the Drawing Tools Format tab, in the Shape Styles group, remove the text outline.

4. Click the second layout master for the Title Slide. Resize the title placeholder from the left so the text fits on three lines. Move it to the right as shown in Figure 11-14.

5. Select the subtitle placeholder and move it down and to the right. Remove the fill and outline color and change to left alignment. Be sure the text color is black and make it bold.

Figure 11-14
Placeholder positions on the Slide Master Title Slide layout

6. Save the presentation as **[11-9your initials]** in your Lesson 11 folder. Leave the presentation open for the next exercise.

Exercise 11-10   CHANGE BULLETS

Now the bullet needs to be updated. For this design, you will use a picture bullet.

1. On the first Slide Master layout, select the bulleted list placeholder and click on the first-level bulleted text. From the Home tab, in the Paragraph group, click the down arrow on the Bullets button to open the gallery and then click Bullets and Numbering.

2. From the Bullets and Numbering dialog box, click Picture. From the Picture Bullet dialog box then select a round-shaped bullet in a brown color. Click OK. Now the picture bullet will be applied to all of the bullets in this presentation because they are all level 1 bullets.

3. Leave your presentation open for the next exercise.

Exercise 11-11   INSERT AN IMAGE AND ADD WORDART

To add interest to your theme and help to establish your presentation's meaning, insert a clip art image on the Slide Master Title Slide layout. Repeat the same image in a smaller size on the Slide Master layout for all the slides in the presentation.

1. On the Title Slide layout, click the Insert tab, in the Illustrations group, then click the Clip Art button. Search for an apple clip art image as shown in Figure 11-15.

2. From the Picture Tools Format tab, in the Size group, resize it to make the height 3 inches and the width will automatically change to 3.42 inches.

TIP

One or more images can be added to Slide Masters. You can recolor these images if they are Windows Metafile pictures (filename extension .wmf) to harmonize with your theme's colors. Also, you can ungroup images, rearrange some or all parts of them, and use these modified images in your design. You can include other objects such as shapes or photograph images. The effects for your background should be rather subtle so that your audience will focus on the information each slide contains.

3. Click the More button on Picture Styles and choose Reflected Perspectve Right. Position the image at the left beside the title text.

4. From the Insert tab, in the Text group, click the WordArt button and choose the Quick Style of Fill – Accent 2, Warm Matte Bevel. Key **The Healthy Living Series**.

5. From the Home tab, in the Font group, apply bold and change the size to 28 points.

6. From the Drawing Tools Format tab, in the Arrange group, click the Rotate button and choose Rotate Left 90°. Move the rotated WordArt into position between the left edge of the slide and the image.

Figure 11-15
Completed Slide Master Title Slide layout

7. Copy the image, paste it on the first Slide Master layout, resize it to a width of 1.25 inches, and position it on top of the rectangle beside the title placeholder.

8. Save the presentation as **[11-11your initials]** in your Lesson 11 folder. Leave the presentation open for the next exercise.

Exercise 11-12 ADJUST FOOTER POSITIONING AND ADD FOOTER TEXT

By default, the objects that appear in a footer (date, footer text, and slide numbering) appear across the bottom of the slide. In this exercise you will change the position and color of the text on the Slide Master layout to better fit your background design, then add footer text so it will show on the slides.

1. On the first Slide Master layout, select the footer placeholders for the date and footer text. From the Home tab, in the Font group, change the font size to 14 points, apply bold, white text color, and left alignment.

2. Select only the date text placeholder and move it to the left and up just a little from the bottom of the slide. Move the footer text placeholder above the date placeholder and align them on the left.

3. On the Slide Master tab, click the Close Master View button ⊠ .

4. From the Insert tab, in the Text group, add a slide header with the date and a footer with the text **[11-12 Your Name].** Click Apply to All.

5. Leave the presentation open for the next exercise.

Exercise 11-13 ADJUST SLIDE ELEMENTS TO FIT THE NEW THEME

After a new theme is complete, the positioning of images and other graphics already used in the presentation may need adjusting. This presentation now has the graphic treatments at the left that require other slide content to move slightly to the right to fit nicely on the slide.

1. Move to slide 3 and select the three arrows and the three rectangles on the right. Move them slightly to the right, close to the edge of the rectangle behind them.

2. Resize the rectangle behind these shapes from the left to make it smaller.

3. Select all of these shapes and group them. Move the grouped shape to the right so it does not overlap the gradient rectangle you added to the Slide Master layout.

4. Move to slide 7 and reposition all of the pictures so they do not overlap with the gradient rectangle.

5. Update your footer text to **[11-13 Your Name]**.

6. Move to slide 1 and reposition the Good 4 U logo below "Sponsored by."

7. Save your presentation as **[11-13your initials]**. Also save this customized theme by following these steps:

   a. From the Design tab, in the Themes group, click the More button ⊞ and choose Save Current Theme.

   b. On the Save Current Theme dialog box, name the file **Green background**. Because this file is an Office Theme, it will have the file extension of .thmx and will automatically be saved in the Document Themes directory. Click Save.

   c. Notice that the new theme appears in your Themes gallery in the Custom category and can be used for other presentations.

8. Leave the presentation open for the next exercise.

Exercise 11-14   SAVE A NEW DESIGN TEMPLATE

For situations where you have customized a theme and developed presentation content that you may need to use again in another way, you might prefer to save the file as a PowerPoint template. You can save a template for future use in the default Template directory, on your student disk, in your lesson folder, or in any other place that provides convenient access.

1. Click the Microsoft Office Button 🔘, choose Save As, and then Other Formats to open the Save As dialog box.

2. In the Save as type drop-down list, choose PowerPoint Template. Automatically, the Templates folder on the computer you are using will be selected as the destination. However, you need to save this file with your other files.

3. In the Save in box, navigate to your Lesson 11 folder.

4. In the File name box, key the filename **Green gradient**. Click OK. Your template is now ready to use. You can tell it is a template file because the file extension is .potx instead of the presentation extension of .pptx.

5. Close the template.

Exercise 11-15   ADJUST A PRESENTATION THEME

At any time when you are developing a presentation, you can apply different themes to change your background, colors, and fonts. However, if you have added a shape such as a rectangle with the gradient fill from the previous exercises, that color will not change automatically. Some individual adjustments on the Slide Master layouts will be necessary.

1. Open your last solution file for **Exercise 11-13** and move to slide 1.

2. From the Design tab, click the Metro theme. A gradient black background is applied and the placeholder positioning and fonts have changed because of the layouts for this theme.

3. From the View tab, in the Presentation Views group, click the Slide Master button 🖥 to see all the layouts.

4. On the Title Slide Master, adjust the size and positioning of the title placeholder as you did in a previous exercise to place it beside the image. From the Home tab, in the Font group, change the title font size to 54 points. Click the Change Case button ⒶⱯ and choose Capitalize Each Word.

5. Resize the subtitle placeholder and move it under the title placeholder.

6. On the first layout in the Slide Master list, move the title placeholder and the bulleted list placeholder so they do not overlap the rectangle on the left.

7. Select the rectangle, then from the Home tab, use the Shape Fill to select Gradient then More Gradients. Choose the Preset Rainbow II color and a Linear type. Change the direction to the first Linear Diagonal and change the Angle to 40°. Click Close.

8. Repeat these color settings for the rectangle on the Title Slide Master, too.

9. Resize the footer placeholders and align the text with the left edge of the subtitle.

10. On the Slide Master tab, click Close Master View button ⊠ .

11. Move the Good4U logo to the left to align with other text on the slide as shown in Figure 11-16. Edit the footer text to read **[11-15your initials]**.

Figure 11-16
Completed title slide

12. On slide 3 adjust where the title appears on the slide by selecting a different slide layout. From the Home tab, in the Slides group, click the Layout button 🗔 and choose the Title and Content layout.

13. On slide 7, repeat this step to adjust the title position. Also move the picture on the lower left to the right so it is even with the picture above it.

14. Save your presentation as **[11-15your initials]** and leave it open for the next exercise.

Applying Themes and Design Templates from Microsoft Office Online

Many professionally designed themes and templates are available from Microsoft Office Online. These themes can be used as is, or you can customize them, too. Downloading these file requires ActiveX control for downloads on your computer.

Exercise 11-16   SEARCH MICROSOFT OFFICE ONLINE

From the Design tab, in the Themes group, click the More button ⬇ then click More Themes on Microsoft Office Online and a collection of themes shown as thumbnails will appear that you can download from this site.

Another place to look for templates on this site is from the menu on the left. Click Templates Home to see the main templates page. Then from the list of templates, click Design slides. The templates are arranged in different categories. Take a few moments to familiarize yourself with these designs. Some of them have simple backgrounds while others include a lot of artwork that is very specific to a particular topic. Some of these are made available for use by companies other than Microsoft; others have been submitted by people who wanted to provide a service and allow others to use their designs.

From the Templates Home page, you can click Presentations. This link contains templates organized by categories, but these templates also include suggested content to help you get started developing a presentation.

1. By default, themes and templates are downloaded to specific locations on your computer unless you specify other locations. Here are some concepts to remember:

   - Themes will download into the Document Themes folder within the Office program files on your computer.

   - If additional color or font themes are used in this design template, they will be placed in the related folders within the Document Themes folder.

   - Templates are downloaded into the Templates folder.

   - Themes and templates that you download may be saved in an earlier version of PowerPoint.

2. Using any of the methods described above, download at least three themes or design templates that you find attractive. As you download them, each will open in a new window. Close these windows.

3. You will apply one of these designs in the next exercise.

Exercise 11-17   BROWSE FOR THEMES

Once themes or design templates have been downloaded, they are available for future use.

1. Open your last solutions file from **Exercise 11-15** if it is not already open. From the Design tab, in the Themes group, click the More button ⬇. The new theme will be displayed in the Custom category.

2. To look for additional themes that may have been downloaded in a previous work session, click the More button ⬇ again and choose Browse for Themes to locate the folder where you saved them.

3. Select the theme, and click Open so it will be applied to your current presentation.

4. Adjust placeholder alignment and position as needed to fit with the existing presentation content. Make the Good4U logo smaller so it does not appear larger than the title on the first slide.

5. Update the slide footer with **[11-17your initials]**. Save the presentation as **[11-17your initials]**.

6. Close the presentation.

Customizing a Handout Master and a Notes Master

Just as the Slide Master controls the appearance of the slides in your presentation, the Notes Master and Handout Master control the overall look and formatting of notes and handouts.

Exercise 11-18   WORK WITH THE NOTES MASTER

The main purpose of a Notes page is to provide detailed information about a slide that a speaker might need as a reference when delivering a presentation. On a Notes Master, you can format, resize, and reposition the body text placeholder, the slide image placeholder, and the header and footer placeholders in the same way as you do on a Slide Master. You can also add pictures, text boxes, and other shapes. All of these options are available on the Notes Master Ribbon.

1. Reopen the file you saved as **[11-13your initials]**.

2. From the View tab, in the Presentation Views group, click the Notes Master button ▦. Note the portrait orientation of the notes master page.

3. Click the Page Setup button ▢ and select Letter Paper. Click OK.

4. Now from the Home tab, make these adjustments:

   a. Select the slide image and apply an outline in black with 3-point weight.

b. Select the notes text placeholder and increase the font size to 18 points.

c. Select the header placeholder and increase the font size to 24 points, bold. Increase the width of the header placeholder so the text that will be entered will fit on one line.

d. Select the date placeholder and reduce its width so the date still fits without scrolling.

e. Change the text alignment to bottom for both the header and date placeholders then move them down slightly as shown in Figure 11-17.

Figure 11-17
Notes Master with adjustments

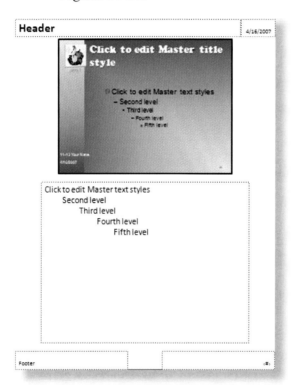

5. From the Notes Master tab, click the Close Master View button. From the View tab, click the Normal view button.

6. Add the following notes to the slides indicated. You may need to increase the size of the notes pane so you can easily key the text below each slide.

a. Slide 3: **Remind employees that they can also find directions and more information about each location on the employee Web site.**

b. Slide 5: **Remind employees that the necessary equipment will be provided or available for rent.**

7. Update the slide footer to read **[11-18 Your Name]**. For notes and handouts include a date and the same footer information. Key the header text **Nutrition Seminar sponsored by Good4U**. Click Apply to All.

8. Use Print Preview to examine these changes. Print the pages that contain the notes you added for slides 3 and 5.

9. Close Print Preview. From the View tab, click the Normal view button 🔲.

10. Leave your presentation open for the next exercise.

Exercise 11-19   WORK WITH THE HANDOUT MASTER

On a Handout Master, you can make the same kinds of changes as on the Notes Master, except that you cannot alter the size or position of the slide image placeholders. Handout Masters come with six different prearranged layouts, ranging from one to nine slides per page. When placing pictures or other objects on a Handout Master, you must be careful to size and position them so that they do not overlap the slide placeholders.

1. From slide 1, copy the Good4U logo.

2. From the View tab, in Presentation Views group, click the Handout Master button 🔳.

3. Notice the portrait orientation of this page. Click the Handout Orientation button 🔲 and choose Landscape. The slides are represented by dotted outlines.

4. Press Ctrl+V to paste the logo. Make it smaller and then move it to the lower right to be near the page number.

5. From the Home tab, make these adjustments:

   a. Use a shape tool to draw a rectangle across the top of the page. Click the Quick Styles button 🔲 and choose Intense Effect - Accent 3.

   b. Click the Arrange button 🔲 then choose Send to Back behind the header and date placeholders. Adjust the placeholder size and position as shown in Figure 11-18.

   c. Change the title placeholder text to 28 points in bold and align both placeholders in the middle.

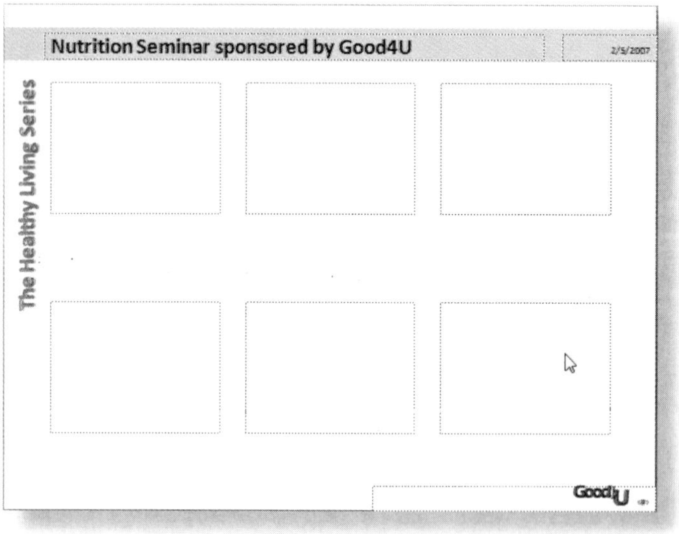

Figure 11-18
Handout Master with adjustments

6. From the View tab, in the Presentation Views group, click the Slide Master button 🔲 then click the Title Slide layout.

7. Press Ctrl+C to copy the WordArt on the left. Click the View tab then the Handout Master button 🔲. Press Ctrl+V to paste.

8. Position the WordArt on the left.

9. From the Handout Master tab, in the Placeholders group, remove the check before Footer.

10. From the Handout Master tab, in the Close group, click the Close Master View button ✖.

11. Update the slide footer and the notes and handouts footer to read **[11-19 Your Name]**.

12. Save the presentation as **[11-19your initials]** in your Lesson 11 folder.

13. Preview and then print handouts for all slides, six slides per page, landscape, grayscale, scale to fit paper, framed.

14. Close the presentation.

Lesson 11

- You can customize presentation theme colors to suit individual needs. From the Design tab, in the Themes group, click the Colors button and then choose from available themes. Click Create New Theme Colors to change individual colors and save them as a new theme. You can choose colors from the Colors dialog box using the Standard tab or create one by using the Custom tab.

- From the Design tab, in the Background group, use the Background styles button to apply a background effect to one or more slides in a presentation. Backgrounds can be solid colors, gradient fills, textures, or pictures.

- The Apply to All command on the Background dialog box applies a background effect to all slides in a presentation. The Close command applies a background effect only to slides that are currently selected.

- If graphic objects from a Slide Master interfere with the design of one or more slides, they can be hidden on those slides by selecting Hide Background Graphics on the Design tab.

- Customize a predesigned theme by rearranging graphics, changing the background, repositioning placeholders, and changing font treatments.

- Create a new design template by changing and adding elements on the slide and title masters of an existing theme or a blank presentation. Save it as a template by using the Save As dialog box and choosing PowerPoint Template in the Save as type list box.
- Notes and Handout Masters can be customized in a way similar to customizing Slide Master layouts. Slide placeholders on the Handout Master cannot be moved or resized. When printing, the size can be made slightly larger by choosing Scale to Fit Paper.
- When placing text boxes or pictures on a Handout Master, care must be taken to make sure that the objects do not conflict with the slide placeholder layouts.

LESSON 11		Command Summary
Feature	Button	Ribbon
Change background		Design tab, Background group, Background Styles, Format Background
Omit master graphics from a slide		Design, Background group, Hide Background Graphics
Customize a color theme		Design, Themes group, Colors, Create New Themes group, Colors
Change theme fonts		Design, Themes group, Fonts
Use Slide Masters		View, Presentation Views group, Slide Master
Save the current theme		Design, Themes group, More, Save Current Theme
Save a design template		Microsoft Office Button, Save As, choose Design Template from Save as type box
Customize Handout Master		View, Presentation Views group, Handout Master
Customize Notes Master		View, Presentation Views group, Notes Master

Concepts Review

True/False Questions

Each of the following statements is either true or false. Select your choice by indicating T or F.

T F   1. You can create gradient fills for slide backgrounds.

T F   2. Gradient fills are available in preset colors only.

T F   3. You can omit background graphics from individual slides.

T F   4. If you choose a picture for a background, it must be applied to only one slide.

T F   5. You can use both theme colors and standard colors in custom theme colors.

T F   6. It is possible to modify an existing theme to fit a unique presentation topic.

T F   7. You can save a design template that you create on your computer or a removable storage device.

T F   8. If you want to apply a design template from Microsoft Office Online, you must first complete the presentation before applying the design template.

Short Answer Questions

Write the correct answer in the space provided.

1. How do you change slide backgrounds?

   _____

2. What are the kinds of fill effects that you can apply to backgrounds?

   _____

3. How do you apply a background to only slide 2 in a presentation?

   _____

4. How do you create new theme colors?

   _____

5. When customizing a presentation's theme colors, what is the maximum number of accent colors that you can change?

   _____

6. How do you apply a theme that does not appear on the Design tab Themes group?

_____

7. What must you use to rearrange the graphics in a theme or template?

_____

8. How can you customize a Handout Master to compliment a presentation's design?

_____

Critical Thinking

Answer these questions on a separate page. There are no right or wrong answers. Support your answers with examples from your own experience, if possible.

1. Discuss some benefits for customizing a background for your presentation's content. What are some ways that the use of graphics can help to establish the tone of a presentation or convey the identity of a company?

2. Describe a situation where it might be more productive to create your own design theme than to modify an existing one.

Skills Review

Exercise 11-20

Change colors and fonts in an existing theme.

1. Open the file **Investors**.
2. Change the background for the entire presentation. From the Design tab,
   a. In the Themes group, click the Colors button █ and choose Origin theme colors.
   b. In the Background group, click the Background Styles button 🖾 and from the gallery that appears, click Style 11, which applies a horizontal pinstripe effect.
3. Change the background for just one slide. On slide 1, from the Design tab
   a. In the Background group, click the Dialog Box Launcher.
   b. For the Fill option, choose a solid fill and change the color to Indigo, Background 2, Darker 50%.
   c. Click Close.

4. From the Design tab, in the Themes group, click the Theme Fonts button [A] and choose the Trek theme, which applies the font Franklin Gothic Book.

5. Make these changes to slide 1:

   a. Select the title placeholder and move it up and to the left. From the Home tab, in the Font group, increase the text size to 54 points and change the case to capitalize each word. Change the font color to Ice Blue, Background 2.

   b. From the Insert tab, in the Illustrations group, search for and insert a picture of money. Resize the picture to be 5.5 inches wide. Apply a picture border in white at 6 points to blend with the other white lines shown on the slide.

   c. Adjust the positioning of the picture and title as shown in Figure 11-19.

Figure 11-19
Title slide completed

6. Create a handout header and footer: Include the date and your name as the header, and the page number and text **[11-20your initials]** as the footer.

7. Move to slide 1 and save the presentation as **[11-20your initials]** in your Lesson 11 folder.

8. Preview and then print the presentation as handouts, six slides per page, grayscale, landscape, scale to fit paper, framed. Close the presentation.

Exercise 11-21

Apply gradient and a picture fill to create a custom theme.

1. Open the presentation file **RaceParty**.

2. From the Design tab, in the Background group, click the Background Styles button [icon] and select Style 12.

3. From the View tab, in Presentation Views group, click the Slide Master button [icon]. On the Title Slide layout, delete the clip art image and the red line. From the Slide Master tab, click Close Master View.

4. On slide 1, make these changes:

   a. Select "Pre-race Party." From the Home tab, change the font to Impact, remove bold, and change the size to 54 points. Resize the placeholder so the text fits on one line and then move this text below "New York Marathon."

   b. Move the flag picture down. On the Insert tab, in the Illustrations group, click the Shapes button 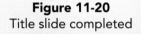 and choose the Oval tool. Draw an oval large enough to cover all the white area of the flag picture. Make the oval white with a black outline. Send it behind the flag picture and be sure that no corners of the flag picture extend beyond the edge of the oval. Group the flag and the oval. Position these grouped shapes on the right of the slide.

   c. From the Insert tab, in the Illustrations group, click the Clip Art button 🖼 then search for a picture image of runners and insert it.

   d. With the picture selected, from the Picture Format tab, in the Picture Styles group, choose the Picture Style of Beveled Oval, Black. Resize as shown in Figure 11-20.

Figure 11-20
Title slide completed

5. Create a new slide 4 with a blank layout. On slide 4, make these changes:

   a. From the Design tab, in the Background group, click the Dialog Box Launcher. On the Format Background dialog box, for the Fill, choose Picture or texture fill. For Insert From, click Clip Art. From the Select Picture dialog box, search for runners. Select the same picture that you used on slide 1. Click OK to accept the picture. Click Close to place it only on slide 4.

   b. From the Insert tab, in the Text group, click the Text box button 🅰 and key the text **On to Victory!** Right-click and from the floating font group change the font to Impact at 54 points. Apply a black fill, bold, and center alignment.

   c. From the Drawing Tools Format tab, in the WordArt Styles group, click the Quick Styles button 🄰 then from the gallery select the Fill – Accent 2, Warm Matte Bevel effect. Increase the width of the text box to 7 inches so the text is emphasized a little more by the black fill color behind it. Position this text box as shown in Figure 11-21.

Figure 11-21
Slide 4 completed

6. Create a handout header and footer: Include the date and your name as the header, and the page number and text **[11-21your initials]** as the footer.

7. Move to slide 1 and save the presentation as **[11-21your initials]** in your Lesson 11 folder.

8. Preview and then print the presentation as handouts, three slides per page, grayscale, framed.

Exercise 11-22

Use Slide Masters to create and save a new PowerPoint template.

1. Start a new blank presentation.

2. From the View tab, in the Presentation Views group, click the Slide Master button .

3. From the Design tab, in the Themes group, click the Theme Colors button and make these changes:

   a. Choose the Opulent color theme.

   b. From the Theme Colors gallery, click the Create New Theme Colors.

   c. Notice the setting for Accent 1 in the fifth column of color swatches.

   d. Change the Text/Background – Dark 2 to be a darker variation of that accent color, Accent 1, Darker 25%.

   e. Name the new Theme Color **boxes** and save it.

4. Now you will work on the Slide Master layouts to add a background color and some shapes. Select the first Slide Master layout then from the Slide Master tab, in the Background group, click the Background Styles button then choose Style 3.

5. Move to the Slide Master Title and Content layout (third layout). From the Insert tab, in the Illustrations group, click the Shapes button

and select the rectangle tool. Draw a rectangle, 2.85 inches high by 3.95 inches wide. Use the Drawing Tools Format tab to make these changes:

a. For the fill color, choose Gradient; then from the gallery click Linear Diagonal with darkest color in the upper-left corner.

b. From the Gradient gallery, click More Gradients and then set Transparency to 50%.

c. Choose No Outline.

6. Duplicate the rectangle three times (for a total of four rectangles) then make these changes:

a. Select one rectangle and align it with the upper left of the slide. Select another rectangle and align it with the lower right of the slide.

b. Select all four rectangles then from the Drawing Tools Format tab, click the Align button and be sure Align Selected Objects is checked. Use the Align button two more times to choose Distribute Horizontally and Distribute Vertically. The rectangles will be positioned evenly across the slide going from the upper-left corner to the lower-right corner.

c. Group the rectangles, and send them to the back behind the text placeholders.

7. Copy the grouped rectangles then move to the Title Slide layout and paste. (Do not send the rectangles to the back on the Title Slide Master layout yet.)

8. On the Title Slide Master layout, make these changes:

a. Ungroup the rectangles, delete the third one from the top, and make the second rectangle larger by dragging its lower-right corner down and to the right, as shown in Figure 11-22.

Figure 11-22
Slide Master title
layout

b. Group the three rectangles and send them to the back.

c. Select the title placeholder and from the Drawing Tools Format tab, click the WordArt Quick Styles button 🄰. From the gallery that appears, choose the Fill – White, Drop Shadow style.

d. From the Home tab, increase the font size to 54 points then adjust the position of the title placeholder so that it coincides with the large rectangle. Use left alignment.

e. Select the subtitle placeholder and move it below the title placeholder and slightly to the right. Make this text bold.

9. On the Title and Content layout, make the following changes to the placeholders, as shown in Figure 11-23:

a. Change the title placeholder to left alignment and choose the Fill – White, Drop Shadow WordArt Quick Style to match the treatment used on the title slide.

b. Change the bullet to a square and reduce first line of the bulleted text by one font size.

Figure 11-23
Slide Master title and content layout

10. Save the presentation as a design template in your Lesson 11 folder by following these steps:

a. Click the Microsoft Office Button ; then choose Save As then Other Formats.

b. Key the filename **Boxes** and change the Save as type to PowerPoint Template. Save this file in your Lesson 11 folder.

c. Close the presentation.

11. Open the file **Reservations** then apply the **Boxes** template that you just created following these steps:

a. From the Design tab, in the Themes group, click the More button .

b. From the gallery that appears, click Browse for Themes and locate the folder where you saved your new template.

c. Select the template **Boxes** and click Apply.

12. On the title slide, make these changes:

a. Remove the comma after "Reservations Policy" since the year now fits on the second line.

b. Reduce the size of the subtitle placeholder and move it to the right so the word "Operations" fits on the rectangle there.

13. Notice that the gradient boxes are not showing on slides 2–4. These slides were created using a different layout other than the one you have prepared. So change the layout following these steps:

    a. In the Slides and Outline pane, select slides 2–4.

    b. From the Home tab, in the Slides group, choose the Layout button 📰 then Title and Content.

14. Create a handout header and footer: Include the date and your name as the header, and the page number and text **[11-22your initials]** as the footer.

15. Move to slide 1 and save the presentation in your Lesson 11 folder with the filename **[11-22your initials]**.

16. Preview and then print the presentation as handouts, four slides per page, landscape, scale to fit paper, framed. Close the presentation.

Exercise 11-23

Apply a design template from Microsoft Office Online.

1. Open the file **Training3**.

2. From the Design tab, in the Themes group, click the More button 🔽 then choose More Themes on Microsoft Office Online.

3. From the Microsoft Office Online site, click the link for Templates Home then the link for Design slides.

4. Search in the Whimsy category for the Blue-green cave design template.

5. Click Download Now to add this template to the computer you are using. Instead of starting a new presentation, close the presentation that automatically starts.

6. A thumbnail for this design now shows in the Themes gallery. Click the thumbnail to apply this design to the current presentation.

7. Check placeholder positioning to see if all slide elements adjusted effectively.

8. On slide 3, from the Chart Tools Design tab, in the Chart Styles group, change the Chart Styles to Style 44 so the chart labeling is easier to read.

9. Create a handout header and footer: Include the date and your name as the header, and the page number and text **[11-23your initials]** as the footer.

10. Move to slide 1 and save the presentation as **[11-23your initials]** in your Lesson 11 folder.

11. Preview and then print the presentation as handouts, six slides per page, grayscale, framed.

Lesson Applications

Exercise 11-24

Change colors, fonts, and backgrounds in an existing theme.

1. Open the file **Specials**.

2. From the Design tab, make these changes:

   a. In the Themes group, click the Colors button and change to the Solstice theme.

   b. In the Background group, click the Background Styles button and choose Format Background.

   c. Choose a Gradient fill and choose the preset color of Wheat. The Type should be set to Linear and the Angle to 45°. Click Apply to All then click Close.

3. On slide 1, from the View tab, in the Presentation Views group, click the Slide Master button and make these changes to the Slide Master Title layout:

   a. For the teal-colored rectangle, increase its size vertically to 2" and send it to the back so it is behind the title text.

   b. Select the title placeholder, move it up, slightly to be centered on the rectangle.

   c. From the Home tab, change the font to Arial Black at 60 points.

   d. From the Drawing Tools Format tab, click the WordArt Quick Styles and choose Gradient Fill - Black, Outline - White, Outer Shadow. Adjust positioning if necessary so the text is centered over the rectangle.

   e. Close Master View.

4. On slide 1, delete the subtitle placeholder and move the title text up slightly then make these changes to the clip art image:

   a. Change the width to 5 inches and the height will automatically increase to 3.97 inches.

   b. Adjust its position to fit on the right of the slide. Refer to the finished slide shown in Figure 11-24.

Figure 11-24
Title slide completed

5. On slide 2, from the View tab, in the Presentation Views group, click the Slide Master button ▣ and make these changes to the Slide Master Two Content layout:

   a. Select the rectangle at the top of the slide and make it large enough to cover the title text. Send to back so it is behind the slide title placeholder.

   b. Change the title text to Arial Black at 36 points then apply the same WordArt Quick Style, Gradient Fill - Black, Outline - White, Outer Shadow. The placeholder sample text will word wrap, but when you return to your slides you will see that your text does not because each title is shorter than the sample text.

   c. Click on the first-level bulleted item on the left and apply bold. Repeat this step for the list on the right.

   d. For both bulleted lists, change the first-level bullet to a square in Aqua, Accent 1, Darker 50%.

6. Close the Slide Master view.

7. Create a handout header and footer: Include the date and your name as the header, and the page number and text **[11-24your initials]** as the footer.

8. Move to slide 1 and save the presentation as **[11-24your initials]** in your Lesson 11 folder.

9. View the presentation as a slide show. Preview and then print the presentation as handouts in landscape, four slides per page, framed. Close the presentation.

Exercise 11-25

Create a custom theme and add picture backgrounds.

1. Open the file **ThreeYears**.

2. From the Design tab, in the Themes group, choose the Opulent Theme Colors then make these custom changes:

   a. From the View tab, in the Presentation Views group, click the Slide Master button ▣ then select the first Slide Master layout.

   b. On the Slide Master tab, in the Background group, click the Dialog Box Launcher (or right-click on the slide background and choose Format Background).

   c. From Format Background dialog box, click Picture or texture fill. Click File and locate your Lesson 11 student files folder. Click the image **perspective** and click Insert. Click Apply to All then Close.

3. On the Title Slide layout, draw a rectangle to cover both the title and subtitle placeholders. Make these changes:

   a. Change the Shape fill color to Lavender, Background 2, Darker 90% then set the transparency to 30%.

    b. Remove the outline.

    c. Send this rectangle behind the placeholders.

    d. Copy the rectangle.

4. On the Title and Content layout, make these changes:

    a. Paste the rectangle then resize it to fit across the slide and from below the title placeholder to the bottom of the slide.

    b. Send this rectangle behind the content placeholder.

    c. Draw a line as an accent below the title placeholder. Use the theme color Orange, Accent 6 and make the line width 10 points.

    d. Select the title placeholder and choose the WordArt Quick Style Fill – Accent 6, Warm Matte Bevel.

    e. Select the content placeholder and move it down slightly. Make the text white.

    f. Change the first-level bullet to the same color, Accent 6.

5. On the Title Slide layout, make these changes:

    a. Select the rectangle and add the same line color and width for the Shape Outline.

    b. Select the title placeholder and apply the same WordArt Quick Style and increase the font size to 54 points.

    c. Click the subtitle placeholder and change the font color to white.

6. Close the Slide Master View.

7. When you look now at the Slides and Outline pane, you can see that your new design has been applied to the title slide but not the other slides. This is because they were prepared with a Title and Text layout.

8. Select slides 2–4 and change the layout to Title and Content. Now all of your changes appear as shown in Figure 11-25.

Figure 11-25
Custom theme slides

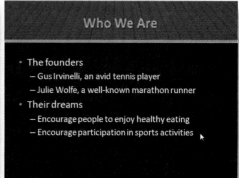

9. Create a handout header and footer: Include the date and your name as the header, and the page number and text **[11-25your initials]** as the footer.

10. Move to slide 1 and save the presentation as **[11-25your initials]** in your Lesson 11 folder.

11. View the presentation as a slide show; then preview and print the presentation as handouts, landscape, four slides per page, framed. Close the presentation.

Exercise 11-26

Apply a design template from Microsoft Online and adjust placeholders.

1. Open the file **Retreat**.

2. From the Design tab, in the Themes group, click the More button ⊡ then choose More Themes on Microsoft Office Online.

3. From the Microsoft Office Online site, click the link for Templates Home then the link for Design slides.

4. Search in the Nature category for the Botanical extract design template.

5. Click Download Now to add this template to the computer you are using. Instead of starting a new presentation, close the presentation that automatically starts but keep the Retreat presentation open.

6. A thumbnail for this design now shows in the Themes gallery. Click the thumbnail to apply this design to the current presentation.

7. This attractive background uses soft colors that work well for the background. However, the text colors are too soft for easy reading. Also, the title slide text is not as bold as the slide text. So the text appearance can be improved.

8. From the Design tab, in the Themes group, create new Theme Fonts for heading and body and use the font Segoe Print for both the heading and body to create casual appearance.

9. From the View tab, in the Presentation Views group, click the Slide Master button ⊡ .

10. On the Title Slide layout, make these changes to the text placeholders:

    a. Select both placeholders, make the text bold, and nudge them slightly to the right to better fit the background.

    b. Select the title placeholder and apply the Bevel effect of Cool Slant and apply the Shadow effect of Offset Diagonal Bottom Left.

    c. Adjust the Shadow settings to be Transparency 30%, Size 100%, Blur 4 points, Angle 135°, and Distance 3 points. Change the shadow color to Gray 50%, Background 2, Darker 50%.

    d. Increase the size of the title text to be 60 points.

11. On the first Slide Master layout, make these changes to the text placeholders:

    a. On the title placeholder, use the same text effects but make the text 44 points and top align the placeholder.

    b. On the bulleted list, make the text bold, change the color to Gray 50%, Background 2, Darker 50%.

    c. Change the first-level bullet to a check mark Pink, Text 2, Darker 50% and increase the size to 120%.

    d. Reposition the text placeholders as shown in Figure 11-26.

Figure 11-26
Customized
template

12. Close Master View.

13. Create a handout header and footer: Include the date and your name as the header, and the page number and text **[11-26your initials]** as the footer.

14. Move to slide 1 and save the presentation as **[11-26your initials]** in your Lesson 11 folder.

15. View the presentation as a slide show; then preview and print the presentation as handouts, landscape, four slides per page, framed. Close the presentation.

Exercise 11-27 ◆ Challenge Yourself

Apply a design theme then modify it for a new theme with customized handouts.

1. Open the file **EmpAward** and apply the Oriel design theme.

2. Choose the Flow Theme Colors and customize the Theme Fonts to Cooper Black for headings and Arial for the body.

3. Right-click the background and choose Format Background. Click Gradient fill then choose the Preset color of Sapphire. Change the type to Linear and the Direction to Linear Left and apply these changes to all slides.

4. Change placeholder treatments to work well on the new background. On the Slide Master Title and Content layout, make the following changes:

    a. Delete the circle on the lower right behind the slide number placeholder.

    b. Change the title placeholder text to white and 40 points. Apply a Text Effect of Circle bevel.

    c. Change the bulleted text to white and bold. Move the placeholder down and slightly to the right.

5. On the Slide Master Title Slide layout, make the following changes:

   a. Delete the circles on the left and move the slide number placeholder to the lower left.

   b. Increase the size of the title placeholder font to 54 points and move it up and slightly to the right. Apply a Text effect of Circle bevel.

   c. Increase the size of the subtitle placeholder font to 32 points and make the color white. Move it slightly to the right.

   d. Search for a clipart image using the word "achievement" and insert it to the left of the title. Apply the Picture Style of Rotated White.

6. From the View tab, in the Presentation Views group, click the Handout Master button ⊞ then make these changes:

   a. Adjust all the placeholders by reducing their height.

   b. Move the header placeholder down to the bottom of the page below the footer.

   c. Move the date down to the bottom of the page above the page number.

   d. Add a rectangle across the top of the page and apply a gradient fill to match the one used in the presentation, Sapphire. Change the direction of the gradient to Linear Down because this will work better for this shape.

   e. Add WordArt and choose a Quick Style with a white fill. Key the text **Employee Awards** and position it on top of the blue shape.

7. Close Master view.

8. Check each of the slides to be sure that slides 1 and 5 use the Title Slide layout and the other slides use the Title and Content layout.

9. On slide 4, change the color of the two ovals to Blue – Accent 1, Lighter 40% then move them up behind the words "week" and "paid."

10. On slide 6, change the colored text to Blue – Accent 1, Lighter 40% so it is easier to read.

11. Search for an appropriate picture image of a male cook and position it in the space at the right. Apply the Picture Style of Rotated White.

12. Create a handout header and footer: Include the date and your name as the header, and the page number and text **[11-27your initials]** as the footer.

13. Move to slide 1 and save the presentation as **[11-27your initials]** in your Lesson 11 folder.

14. Preview and then print the presentation as handouts, six slides per page, grayscale, framed. Close the presentation.

On Your Own

In these exercises you work on your own, as you would in a real-life work environment. Use the skills you've learned to accomplish the task—and be creative.

Exercise 11-28

Open the file **Fitness**. Change the theme and graphics. Use any tools you have learned about up to this point to create a unique design template expressing your own taste, but remember to keep a uniform look throughout that harmonizes with the presentation's subject matter. Customize the Handout Master to blend with your theme design. Save the presentation as **[11-28your initials]**. Preview and then print the presentation as handouts.

Exercise 11-29

Create a new PowerPoint template and use your own creativity to make it interesting and attractive. You could develop a design that would be suitable for a wide range of topics or you could develop a design appropriate for a specific topic depending on the graphics you choose to use. Be sure to customize the Slide Masters Title Slide layout and the Title and Content layout so you have two background variations that blend together. Save the template as **[11-29your initialsDesign]**. Create a blank presentation then apply this template. Key text on at least two slides so your placeholder positioning is evident. Customize the Handout Master to blend with your template design. Save the presentation as **[11-29your initials]**. Preview and then print the two slides as handouts with two on a page.

Exercise 11-30

Search the Web for information on your favorite music group or singer. Condense the information into major points and use these points to create a presentation of at least six slides. Using the tools you learned in this lesson and in previous lessons, create a theme and format your presentation attractively and in keeping with your topic. Save the presentation as **[11-30your initials]**. Customize the Handout Master to blend with your theme. Preview and then print the presentation as handouts.

Unit 3 Applications

Unit Application 3-1

Work with clip art; create and format WordArt objects; use gradient fills; align, rotate, and flip objects; and ungroup and group objects.

1. Open the file **FranOpt**.

2. Delete the title text placeholder. In its place, insert a WordArt title and key **Good 4 U**. Apply the following formatting:

   a. Choose the WordArt style from the fourth column, third row Gradient Fill-Accent 1.

   b. Change the font to 60-points, bold, Arial Black.

   c. Change the WordArt gradient fill to the preset color Fire, Type Linear, Direction Linear Down, and Angle 908.

   d. Change the text outline to 3-points, dark red.

   e. Add a Black –Text 1 shadow Offset Bottom with no transparency.

   f. Center the WordArt horizontally, approximately 1.5 inches from the top of the slide.

3. For the subtitle placeholder, remove the shadow.

4. Insert a new slide with the Title and Content layout. Select the Title placeholder and apply Text effects with the same settings as for the WordArt on slide 1. Reduce the font size to 40 points. Key the title **Advantages**.

5. In the Slides and Outline pane, copy slide 2 and paste to create slide 3.

6. On slide 3, key the title **Objectives**.

7. Using the text in Figure U3-1, key the subtitle text for slide 1 and the body text for slides 2 and 3.

Figure U3-1
Data for slides 1 through 3

```
Good 4 U      Restaurant Franchise Opportunities

Advantages

        •     Fast-growing market

        •     Excellent income potential

        •     Expert training and support

Objectives

        •     Help people achieve a healthy lifestyle

        •     Help you grow a healthy business
```

8. On slides 2 and 3, move the bulleted list placeholders slightly to the right and resize as necessary to keep all text on the yellow area of the slide.

9. On slide 1, ungroup and convert the picture of the knife, fork, and spoon to PowerPoint objects. Ungroup the objects again; then delete all the parts that make up the spoon. Delete the transparent rectangle that is behind the objects.

10. Manipulate the remaining knife and fork parts by performing the following:

   a. Select all of the parts of the knife and group them, and then select all the fork parts and group them as a second group.

   b. Rotate the fork to the right and the knife to the left.

   c. Align the knife and fork middles and centers relative to each other; then group them to form one object.

   d. Position the knife and fork at the bottom of the yellow shape.

   e. Increase the subtitle placeholder size so it fits on one line and move it up slightly, as shown in Figure U3-2.

Figure U3-2
Completed title slide

11. Review each slide to be sure all elements are positioned effectively.

12. Change the grayscale settings for all three WordArt objects to Light Grayscale.

13. Check spelling in the presentation.

14. Create a handout header and footer: Include the date and your name as the header, and the page number and text **[U3-1your initials]** as the footer.

15. Create a new folder for Unit 3 Applications. Save the presentation with the filename **[U3-1your initials]** in this folder.

16. View the presentation as a slide show.

17. Preview and then print the presentation as handouts, three slides per page, grayscale, scale to fit paper, framed. Close the presentation.

Unit Application 3-2

Work with WordArt and images, align and distribute objects, group objects, and apply and customize 3-D effects.

1. Open the file **Training**.

2. Duplicate the clip art image on slide 1 and move the second image to the lower-left corner.

3. Crop the original image so only the lecturer and her lectern remain. Crop the copy (in the lower-left corner) so that only the three audience members remain.

4. Duplicate the audience members and position the second image evenly spaced to the right of the first image. Duplicate two more times and move both images to the right side of the slide and line them up.

5. Select the two audience member images (six people) on the right and group them. Flip this image horizontally and move it to the right of the slide to allow a little space between the people on the left and right. Group all of the people at the bottom of the slide.

6. Reduce the size of the grouped people slightly; then center the group horizontally at the bottom of the slide. Reduce the contrast and brightness settings on the audience.

7. Horizontally center the picture of the lecturer. Refer to Figure U3-3 for the final arrangement of the slide.

Figure U3-3
Object placement guide

8. Copy the group of people and then view the Slide Master. Paste this image to the bottom of the Title and Content and Two Content slide masters.

9. On the first Slide Master layout, select the title placeholder and apply a WordArt Quick Style of Fill – Accent 2, Warm Matte Bevel. Change the text fill color to a standard blue. Make the body text bold.

10. On the Two Content layout, remove the bullet on the first line in the list. Increase the font size of the content placeholders by one increment.

11. Close Master view.

12. On slide 1, make the following changes:

   a. Apply a WordArt Quick Style of Fill – Accent 2, Warm Matte Bevel. Change the text fill color to a standard blue.

   b. Change the title placeholder to 60 points.

   c. Make the placeholder 9.25 inches wide, 3 inches tall, and center it horizontally across the top of the slide above the picture of the lecturer.

   d. From Text Effects choose Transform then apply the Deflate Bottom shape.

13. Reset the slide layout for slide 2, and then remove the bullet from the text.

14. Create a new slide after slide 2 using the Two Content layout. Key the text shown for the first slide in Figure U3-4. Right-align the text in the right-column placeholder. Resize and arrange the placeholders so the two columns of text are not so far apart. Be sure to align the tops of the column placeholders.

15. Create two more new slides after slide 3 and key the text shown in Figure U3-4 adjusting the columns in the same manner as for slide 3.

Figure U3-4
Data for slides

	Training Presentation	
	Managers	8:30 a.m.
Slide 3	Servers	10:15 a.m.
	Greeters	1:00 p.m.
	Kitchen staff	3:15 p.m.
	On-the-job Training	
	Managers	7:30 p.m.
Slide 4	Servers	5:30 p.m.
	Greeters	8:15 p.m.
	Kitchen staff	4:30 p.m.
	Food Services Training	
	Managers	January 17
Slide 5	Servers	January 18
	Greeters	January 19
	Kitchen staff	January 20

16. Check spelling in the presentation.

17. Create a handout header and footer: Include the date and your name as the header, and the page number and text **[U3-2 your initials]** as the footer.

18. Move to slide 1 and save the presentation as **[U3-2 your initials]** in your Unit 3 Applications folder.

19. Preview and then print the presentation as handouts, six slides per page, grayscale, scale to fit paper, framed. Close the presentation.

Unit Application 3-3

Customize a design template, work with bullets and tabs, add text and object animations, and customize a Handout Master.

1. Open the file **JobFair3**. Change the theme colors to Verve. Customize the theme colors by changing both the Text/Background dark colors to a standard Dark Blue. Change the Text/Background light colors to White, and the Accent 4 color to a standard Light Green.

2. On the Slide Master, increase all text in the title placeholder and the body text placeholder by one increment. Change the font for all text to Arial Narrow, and make all text bold. Select the title placeholder and use the Change Case option to Capitalize Each Word.

3. Still working on the Slide Master, change the first-level bullet to a slightly larger Wingdings 2 round bullet and make it Lime, Accent 4.

4. On the Slide Master title slide layout, increase the title placeholder text to 54 points and the subtitle placeholder text to 48 points and center the text in both title slide placeholders.

5. Close Master view.

6. On slide 1, reset the layout and then adjust the position of the logo to align with the other text. Resize the logo to make it slightly smaller.

7. After slide 2, insert a new slide with the Title Only layout. Key the title **Salary Ranges** and insert a text box to create a tabbed table using the following text:

    Wait staff `Tab` $8.00 `Tab` plus tips

    Assistant chefs `Tab` $12.50 `Tab` to start

    Experienced chefs `Tab` $17.50 `Tab` and up

8. Format the table text as 36-point bold Arial Narrow. Use a decimal tab for the wage, and a right-aligned tab for the last item. Set tab stops, and size and position the text box appropriately.

9. To the table, apply the Entrance animation effect Dissolve In at Medium speed, making it appear on click. Make sure the table appears after the slide's title.

10. On slide 1, select the "Great Jobs 4 U" text and make it 60 points. Change its outline to a 1-point Lime, Accent 4 line.

11. On slide 1, select the title and apply the Entrance animation effect Fly In and choose the direction From bottom. Change the speed to Medium. Apply the same treatment to the word "at" and the logo. Adjust the animation order, if necessary, so the logo is the last item to appear on the slide, appearing with a 1-second delay.

12. Insert a music file of your choice on slide 1. Hide the sound object by dragging it off the slide. Make it start playing at the beginning of the slide show and loop continuously for the duration of the show.

13. On slide 4, change the slide layout to Title Slide.

14. Still working on slide 4, search for a clipart picture picture of a server and insert it. Apply your choice of picture effects.

TIP

An easy way to make sound run through the end of a slide show is to insert the sound, then from the Custom Animation task pane, click the drop-down list box for the sound, and choose Effect Options. On the Effect tab, under stop playing choose after a certain number of slides, then on the Timing tab, choose Repeat Until End of Slide.

15. Move to slide 1 and copy the logo and paste it below the text on slide 4. Resize to make it smaller so it blends well with the other text.

16. Apply the Wipe Left slide transition effect to all the slides in the presentation, using Medium speed and No Sound.

17. Review the slides, making adjustments to text size and text box placement as needed to make an attractive presentation. Run the slide show; then make any changes needed to the slides' timing and animation effects.

18. Adjust grayscale settings, if necessary.

19. Customize the Handout Master by deleting the page number placeholder and keying the text **Job Fair Presentation** in the footer placeholder. Resize the footer placeholder and center it horizontally, center-align the footer text, change the font to Arial Narrow, and increase the font by one size increment. Move it up slightly. Close Master view.

20. Create a handout header and footer: Include the date and your name and the text **[U3-3your initials]** as the header. The footer text was already entered on the Master. Delete the check beside page number.

21. Move to slide 1 and save the presentation as **[U3-3your initials]** in your Unit 3 Applications folder.

22. Preview and then print the presentation as handouts, four slides per page, grayscale, scale for paper, landscape, framed. Close the presentation.

Unit Application 3-4 ◆ Using the Internet

Add an image to the Slide Master, apply custom animation, add music or sound effects, add 3-D effects, and create action buttons.

Use the Internet to research a vacation destination, for example, Orlando, Florida; San Diego, California; Billings, Montana; Williamsburg, Virginia; or other location. Gather information about places to visit, unique restaurants and places to stay, and any other information that you find interesting.

Use the information you gathered to create a presentation. Select a design theme and create a new set of theme colors that complements your material. Add a clip art or a photo that relates to the presentation to the Slide Master and apply picture effects. Include at least six slides. Include text and object animations, music, and sound effects where appropriate. Create a slide that lists the title of each slide and create action buttons to each slide. Include a "Home" action button on the Slide Master Title and Content layout so each slide will have a link back to the original slide. Check spelling and review all the slides in grayscale view, making grayscale adjustments if needed.

In the slide footer, include the text **Prepared by** followed by your name. Include the slide number on all slides but not the date. In the handout footer, include the completed filename **[U3-4your initials]**. In the handout header, key **Presented to** and then identify to whom you would be giving this presentation. Include in the handout the date you would be delivering the presentation.

Save the presentation as **[U3-4your initials]** in your Unit 3 folder. Practice delivering the presentation. Preview and then print the presentation handouts with an appropriate number of slides per page, grayscale, framed. Close the presentation.

unit 4

DEVELOPMENT AND DISTRIBUTION

PPT4.12

Lesson 12

Integrating with Other Programs

OBJECTIVES

After completing this lesson, you will be able to:

1. Use content from other sources.

2. Insert screen captures.

3. Work with multiple open presentations.

4. Collaborate with others.

5. Save objects as pictures.

MCAS OBJECTIVES

In this lesson:

PP07 1.1.4
PP07 2.3.1
PP07 2.3.2
PP07 4.1.1
PP07 4.1.2
PP07 4.3.6

See Appendix

Estimated Time: 1½ hours

The illustrations or other content you need for a presentation may have been created in other Microsoft applications; therefore, PowerPoint can integrate content from other sources such as outlines, images, slides, and worksheets. Another application window can be displayed within a presentation, too, and artwork developed in PowerPoint can be used in other applications.

Understanding techniques for working with multiple presentations is important. When you need feedback from other people, they can insert comments within your presentation file. All of the techniques explained in this lesson can help you to be more efficient and productive.

Using Content from Other Sources

When using PowerPoint to create a presentation, the user may decide to incorporate data from other locations such as from Microsoft Excel or Microsoft Word. PowerPoint is very user-friendly for integrating between applications and linking to the Web.

Exercise 12-1   IMPORT AN OUTLINE FROM WORD

When writing the text for a presentation, some people prefer to develop their outline using a word processing program, such as Microsoft Word, and then import the Word outline file into PowerPoint to create slides instead of keying directly into PowerPoint.

To import a Word outline into PowerPoint, use one of these methods:

- From the Microsoft Office Button , choose Open to open the outline file from within PowerPoint.

- From the Home tab, in the Slides group, click the down arrow on the New Slide button and choose Slides from Outline.

1. Working in PowerPoint, click the Microsoft Office Button , and choose Open.

2. Navigate to the Lesson 12 Student Data files. In the Files of type list box, choose All Files.

3. Notice that **Poster Ideas.docx** has a Word file icon near the filename. Choose the **Poster Ideas.docx** file from the list of files.

4. Click Open. PowerPoint interprets the structure of your outline and creates new slides, creating titles from the level 1 headings and body text from the level 2 and level 3 headings. All the slides use the Title and Text layout.

5. Change the layout of the new slide 1 "Poster Ideas" to the Title Slide layout.

6. Apply the design theme Civic and use the theme colors Oriel.

7. Leave the presentation open for the next exercise.

Exercise 12-2   INSERT A MICROSOFT WORD DOCUMENT

You can integrate PowerPoint with other Microsoft software. If you have created a flyer or other document in Word, you can insert it as an object into PowerPoint.

Inserting a Word document into PowerPoint can be completed using the following steps: from the Insert tab, in the Text group, click the Object button .

1. Move to slide 4.

2. From the Insert tab, in the Text group, click the Object button .

3. In the Insert Object dialog box, choose the Create from File option.

4. Click the Browse button and navigate to your student files for Lesson 12 and choose the **Fourth of July.docx** file.

5. Click OK.

Figure 12-1
Insert Object dialog
box

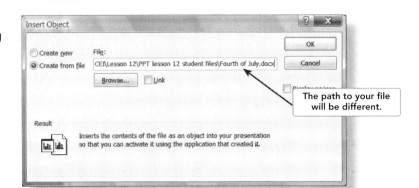

6. The Insert Object dialog box should appear as in Figure 12-1 above. Click OK to insert the document. The Fourth of July Celebration flyer is now inserted on slide 4.

7. Resize the flyer to match Figure 12-2.

Figure 12-2
Flyer displayed on a
slide

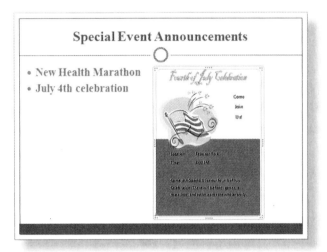

8. From the Drawing Tools Format tab, in the Shape Styles group, click the Shape Outline button ⬛ and change the Weight to 1½ points so a line appears around the edge of the flyer to distinguish it from the slide background.

9. Double-click on the flyer. Notice that a Word screen opens where you can edit the file.

10. Change the time to 4:30 PM then press Esc to return to PowerPoint.

11. Leave the presentation open for the next exercise.

Exercise 12-3 REUSE SLIDES FROM A DIFFERENT PRESENTATION

Compiling slides from multiple presentations is a common task in PowerPoint. For example, perhaps you need to reuse a particular diagram or drawing from one presentation in another.

Inserting slides from a different presentation can be completed using the following steps: from the Home tab, in the Slides group, click the down arrow on the New Slide button and choose Reuse Slides. From the Reuse Slides task pane, use Browse then Browse File to find the presentation that you wish to use.

1. Move to slide 1.

2. From the Home tab, in the Slides group, click the down arrow on the New Slide button and choose Reuse Slides.

3. The Reuse Slide task pane opens on the right side of the screen.

4. Click the Browse button and choose Browse File.

Figure 12-3
The Reuse Slides task pane

5. Navigate to your student data files for Lesson 12 and choose the file **Public Relations**.

6. Click Open. The slides that are in the Public Relations presentation are displayed in the Reuse Slides task pane as shown in Figure 12-3.

7. When you point to the slide thumbnail, the size temporarily increases so you can read the slide title. Click on the second slide in the list to insert it into the presentation after slide 1.

8. Click the Close button on the Reuse Slides task pane. Notice that the inserted slide took on the Slide Master formatting from the current presentation.

Exercise 12-4   LINK AN EXCEL WORKSHEET

Another integration technique is to *link* files from other Microsoft programs, such as Excel. When a file is *linked*, any changes that are made in the source document or the destination document are reflected in both documents.

Linking an Excel worksheet can be completed using the following steps: Open the Excel worksheet, select the range you want to link, and click the Copy button . Within PowerPoint, from the Home tab, in the Clipboard group, click the down arrow on the Paste button and choose Paste Special.

Figure 12-4
Selected range in Excel

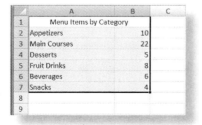

1. Open Microsoft Excel, and navigate to your student data files for Lesson 12.

2. Open the file **Menu items by category**.

3. Select cells A1:B7 by clicking on the title "Menu Items by Category" and dragging the pointer down through row 7, as shown in Figure 12-4.

4. Working in Excel, from the Home tab, in the Clipboard group, click the Copy button ▣.

5. Return to your PowerPoint file, and move to slide 3.

6. From the Home tab, in the Clipboard group, click the down arrow on the Paste button ▣ and choose Paste Special.

7. From the Paste Special dialog box, choose Paste Link and Microsoft Office Excel Worksheet Object, as shown in Figure 12-5.

Figure 12-5
Paste Special dialog box

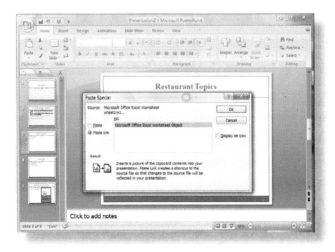

8. Click OK. PowerPoint inserts a small Excel worksheet into your presentation.

9. Double-click the worksheet in PowerPoint. Notice that you are automatically returned to Excel to edit.

TIP

Because the Excel file is read only, when you close out of the PowerPoint file and reenter, you will receive a warning of a potential security concern about accessing linked files. Click Cancel to avoid updating the links. If you were working on your own files, you would want to save changes and update the links when entering and exiting the files.

TIP

If you would like the source file to open up within the source applications, create a hyperlink to the file.

10. In Excel, click on the word "Snacks" and change to the word Salads. In the task bar, click the PowerPoint file to return to your presentation and notice that the word has also been changed in the small worksheet. This happens because of the link between PowerPoint and Excel.

11. Close Excel without saving changes.

12. In PowerPoint, select the table and from the Drawing Tools Format tab change the width to 5 inches so the text is easy to read.

13. Create a handout header and footer: Include the date and your name as the header, and the page number and text **[12-4your initials]** as the footer.

14. Create a new Lesson 12 folder. Save the presentation as **[12-4your initials]** in your Lesson 12 folder. Leave the presentation open for the next exercise.

Inserting Screen Captures

PowerPoint is often used for training purposes. During training, it may be relevent to show a *screen capture* of what a screen looks like in another application. For example, this book shows you screen captures of what your screen should look like to help you understand the concept of the task you are completing.

Exercise 12-5   CREATE AND INSERT A SCREEN CAPTURE

When you make a screen capture, a copy of whatever is displayed on your computer screen is placed in the clipboard. The copy can then be placed in any Microsoft application.

Screen captures can be made in two ways:

- Press Print Screen on your keyboard to capture the entire screen.

- Press Alt + Print Screen on your keyboard to capture the active window only.

1. Move to slide 4.

2. Open your Internet browser and perform a search for "fish hatchery." Find a Web site about this type of business.

3. With the browser open and the first page of the Web site on the screen, press Print Screen on your keyboard.

4. Move back to PowerPoint on slide 4 and from the Home tab, in the Clipboard group, click the Paste button. Notice that a full screen capture comes into PowerPoint.

5. From the Picture Tools Format tab, in the Size group, click the Crop button and crop the picture of the Web page down to only view the Web page and not the other areas of the browser window or your screen that may show.

6. Reposition the picture of the Web page to create an attractive appearance, as shown in Figure 12-6.

Figure 12-6
Screen capture of a
Web page

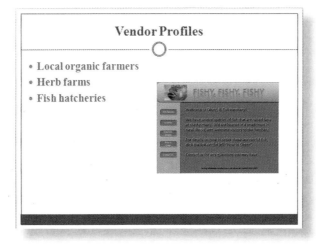

7. Right-click the picture and choose Format Picture from the shortcut menu.

8. With the Format Picture dialog box open, press [Alt]+[Print Screen] on your keyboard to capture just the active window.

9. Click Close on the dialog box. Move to slide 4 and press [Ctrl]+[V] to paste the screen capture. Note that you have a picture of only the current window, which is the Format Picture dialog box.

10. Click the Undo button to remove this screen capture.

11. Update the handout footer to include the text **[12-5your initials]**.

12. Save the presentation as **[12-5your initials]** in your Lesson 12 folder. Leave the presentation open for the next exercise.

Working with Multiple Open Presentations

PowerPoint allows you to move information from presentation to another presentation seamlessly by using the copy and paste features. The copy and paste can be used to reorganize information from existing presentations or to add selected slides to a new presentation. With two presentations open, you can layer them on your screen or you can arrange them in small sizes so you can see more than one presentation at the same time. These different views allow you to more easily work with multiple files.

Exercise 12-6 USE CASCADE TO LAYER MULTIPLE PRESENTATION WINDOWS

The *Cascade* feature allows you to display open presentations in separate windows that can be layered or resized. If you click on the window title bar you can drag a window to reposition it on your screen.

1. Still working in PowerPoint, navigate to your student data files for Lesson 12 and open the file **PR2**. You should now have two presentations open.

2. In either presentation, from the View tab, in the Window group, click the Cascade button. Notice how the two presentations are layered with the names of the presentations viewable on the title bar for both, as shown in Figure 12-7.

3. The active presentations window is on top. To switch windows, from the View tab, in the Window group, click the Switch Windows button and choose the other presentation name from the list that appears. You can switch between presentations by clicking from the task bar, too.

Figure 12-7
Presentations layered using Cascade

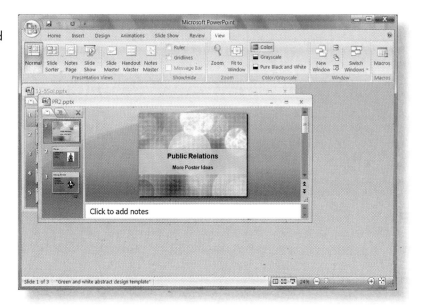

4. Leave the two presentations open for the next exercise.

Exercise 12-7 USE ARRANGE ALL TO SEE MULTIPLE PRESENTATION WINDOWS

The *Arrange All* feature allows you to view multiple files at the same time. This is an excellent feature to use when copying and pasting from one presentation to another because the separate windows for each presentation are displayed side-by-side on the screen.

1. In either presentation, from the View tab, in the Window group, click the Arrange All button 🖺.

2. The presentations are now side by side, making it easy to compare and change both presentations, as shown in Figure 12-8.

Figure 12-8
Presentations displayed using Arrange All

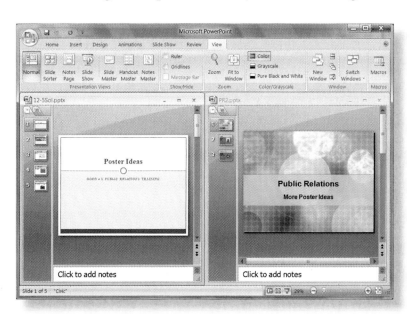

3. Leave the presentation open for the next exercise.

Exercise 12-8 COPY AND PASTE BETWEEN PRESENTATIONS

You have used the copy and paste for many of the individual presentations you have completed. In this exercise, you will copy and paste between two presentations.

1. In the file **PR2**, select slide 2 in the Slides and Outline pane.

2. From the Home tab, in the Clipboard group, click the Copy button.

3. Click anywhere on the presentation **12-5your initials** to make it active, and click after slide 5. Notice how convenient it is to work with the two presentations using the Arrange All feature.

4. From the Home tab, in the Clipboard group, click the Paste button. The slide takes on the characteristics of the design theme of the presentation that you pasted it into, as shown in Figure 12-9.

Figure 12-9
Pasted slide

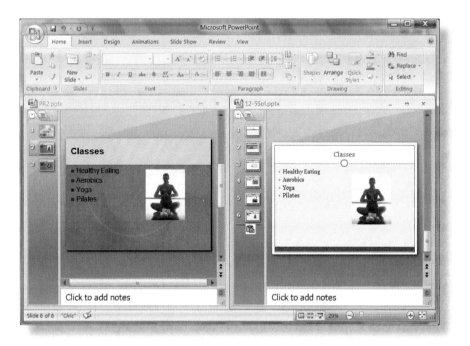

5. In the file **PR2**, select slide 3 in the Slides and Outline pane.

6. From the Home tab, in the Clipboard group, click the Copy button.

7. Return to the presentation **12-5your initials** and click after slide 6.

8. From the Home tab, in the Clipboard group, click the Paste button.

9. Leave the presentation open for the next exercise.

Exercise 12-9   USE FORMAT PAINTER TO COPY FORMATTING BETWEEN PRESENTATIONS

Format Painter can be used to copy formatting from slides in one presentation to slides in another presentation. It is easiest to complete this task if the presentations are arranged so you can see multiple presentations using Arrange All.

1. In the file **PR2**, select slide 1 in the Slides and Outline pane.

2. From the Home tab, in the Clipboard group, click the Format Painter button .

3. In the presentation **12-5your initials**, click on slide 1 in the Slides and Outline pane to make this presentation active, then click slide 1 again to apply the formatting from the other presentation.

4. In the file **PR2**, select slide 2 in the Slides and Outline pane.

5. From the Home tab, in the Clipboard group, double-click the Format Painter button so the Format Painter remains on.

6. In the presentation **12-5your initials**, click slide 2 to make the presentation active then click again to apply the formatting. Continue clicking on the remaining slides to apply the formatting from the other presentation, as shown in Figure 12-10.

7. Click the Format Painter button to turn off the Format Painter.

Figure 12-10
Using Format Painter to format slide backgrounds

8. Close the file **PR2** without saving any changes and maximize the screen for the open presentation.

9. Select each slide in the Slides and Outline pane and from the Home tab, in the Slides group, click the Reset button to change all text to black with the different font that is used in this design template.

10. On slide 3, enlarge and reposition the "Menu Items by Category Worksheet" for an attractive appearance.

11. Scroll through the presentation, and notice that the Word flyer, on slide 5, that was inserted was changed to match the theme colors. The top of the flyer now looks transparent. Make a white rectangle with no outline and send it to the back so it is behind the flyer. Adjust the width of the flyer and the rectangle to be the exact same size. Click the Slide Show button 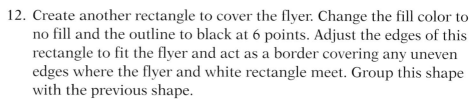 to test your alignment on the full screen. When you are satisfied that the appearance is correct, group these objects.

12. Create another rectangle to cover the flyer. Change the fill color to no fill and the outline to black at 6 points. Adjust the edges of this rectangle to fit the flyer and act as a border covering any uneven edges where the flyer and white rectangle meet. Group this shape with the previous shape.

13. On slide 6, add a border to the picture in black at 6 points to match slide 5.

14. Update the handout footer to include the text **[12-9your initials]**.

15. Save the presentation as **[12-9your initials]** in your Lesson 12 folder. Leave the presentation open for the next exercise.

Collaborating with Others

Before delivering a presentation, you might want others to review it and perhaps contribute to it. PowerPoint makes this an easy and convenient task. The reviewer can make comments on the presentations for you to view and consider. If you have access to available network space, PowerPoint can create a Document Workspace for sharing files with others. This last feature may not be possible in computer classrooms.

Exercise 12-10 INSERT AND EDIT COMMENTS IN A PRESENTATION

Comments are similar to the comments you add when working with a word processing program. When the Show Markup button 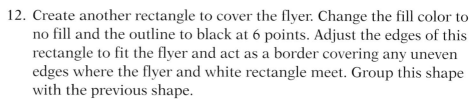 is active, comments are represented on the slide by a *comment marker*, a small colored rectangle in the upper-left corner of a slide. You might use this feature to make notes to yourself as you fine-tune a presentation. You might ask others to review the presentation and use this feature to obtain their feedback as you are developing the presentation. Comments are identified by the reviewer's initials. You can read a comment by double-clicking the comment marker, but comments will not print on the slides or display during a slide show.

1. Move to slide 1.

2. From the Review tab, in the Comments group, click the New Comment button ⬜. A colored box appears in which you can key a comment.

3. Key the following in the comment box: **We need to create a logo for the title slide.**

4. Click outside the comment box to close it. Notice the comment marker (the small colored box in the upper-left corner) with the reviewer's initials and the number "1," indicating the first comment inserted by this reviewer.

5. To edit the comment you keyed, double-click the comment marker and then key the following text at the end of the existing comment: **Maybe you can create a logo and add it to the presentation.**

6. The complete comment is shown Figure 12-11.

Figure 12-11
Inserting a comment

7. Still working on the Review tab, in the Comments group, click the Show Markup button ⬜ and notice that the comment marker disappears. This can be used so others do not see the comments in the presentation.

8. Move to slide 2 then click the New Comment button ⬜ and key the following comment: **This slide is great since many people do not understand Public Relations.**

9. Still working on slide 2, and on the Review tab, in the Comments group, click the Delete button ☒ and choose Delete All Markup on the Current Slide.

Exercise 12-11   PRINT SLIDE COMMENTS

As you saw in Exercise 10, *Show Markup* enables you to see the comments within a presentation and you can turn off this feature so the comments do not display on the slide. However, you may need a printed copy of all comments that have been made. For printing, PowerPoint organizes the comments together on a page following your last presentation slide. For example, you can print handouts showing the comment markers and a sheet listing the related slide comments.

1. Update the handout footer to include the text **[12-11your initials]**.

2. Save the presentation as **[12-11your initials]** in your Lesson 12 folder.

3. From the Microsoft Office Button ☒, choose Print to open the Print dialog box.

4. Set up the dialog box so that all slides will print as handouts, nine slides per page, grayscale, scale to fit paper, framed.

5. At the bottom of the Print dialog box, check the Print comments and ink markup check box.

TIP

If multiple people reviewed the presentation, then different initials would precede each comment.

6. Click Preview. In the Preview window, move to the second page and change the zoom to 100%. The comments appear on this separate page, identified by the slide on which they were placed and by the initials of the reviewer, as shown in Figure 12-12. In this example, only one slide is displayed; however, the same procedure would be followed if you had many comments.

Figure 12-12
Printing slide comments

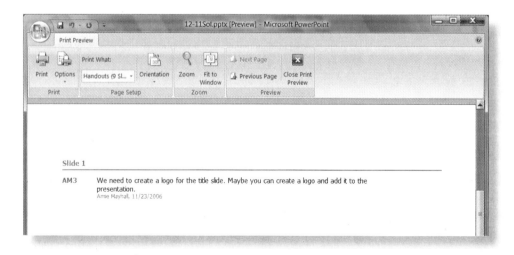

7. Click Print and then click OK.

8. Leave the presentation open for the next exercise.

Saving Objects as Pictures

PowerPoint provides many tools for creating original illustrations and enables saving these objects as pictures for use in other applications or for later use in other presentations.

While PowerPoint's illustration tools provide a wide array of ways to visually arrange your slide content, you can use PowerPoint, also, to create artwork for other applications or to create files of individual slides.

Exercise 12-12   DESIGN A LOGO AND SAVE AS A PICTURE

One example of artwork that you could create in PowerPoint for use in other programs is a logo. Logos are symbols of the organization that they stand for. Many of the presentations in this book include a Good 4 U logo. In this exercise you will create a Good 4 U logo that is a little a different by combining text with an image.

1. Move to slide 1. As you create the parts of the logo, position them randomly across the top of the slide then arrange all parts when they are complete.

2. Key the logo text using three different effects from the WordArt gallery:

   a. Click the WordArt button and choose the Fill Accent 6, Warm Matte Bevel. Key **Good**.

   b. Click the WordArt button and choose the Fill – Background1, Metal Bevel. Key **4**.

   c. Click the WordArt button and choose the Fill – Accent 4, Outer Shadow- Accent 4, Soft Edge Bevel. Key **U**. Change the Fill color to Dark Green, Accent 6, Darker 50%.

3. Insert the **Apple.jpg** picture from your student files.

4. From the Picture Tools Format tab, make these adjustments to the apple image:

   a. In the Adjust group, click the Recolor button then choose Set Transparent Color and click on the background of the apple image to remove it. Some color will remain in the upper right and in the shadow area below the apple. Too much color is removed from the top of the apple, but this problem will be disguised based on where the finished logo is positioned.

b. In the Adjust group, click the Brightness button ▣ then Picture Corrections Options. Change the Brightness to 18% and the Contrast to 11%. Click Close.

c. In the Size group, click the Crop button ▣ then crop the apple image from the top to remove the extra background color in the upper right. Crop the image from the bottom to remove most of the shadow area below the apple. Press ⌷Esc⌷ to turn off the Crop.

d. In the Size group, resize the apple to a width of 2.5 inches.

e. In the Arrange group, click the Send to Back button ▣ to put the apple behind the WordArt text.

5. Rearrange the WordArt text and the apple as shown in Figure 12-13.

Figure 12-13
Create a logo

6. Select the WordArt text "Good 4 U" and the apple, then group them to form one object.

7. Now save this grouped object three times so you can compare the results of using different graphic file types. Each different format can be used in other Microsoft applications or even in designing a Web site.

a. Right-click on this grouped object and choose Save as Picture from the shortcut menu.

b. In the Save as type list box, select the JPEG File Interchange Format.

c. Name the picture **Logo1** and save it with your solution files. It will have the file extension of .jpg.

TIP

You can also save other objects and SmartArt Graphics using this same process.

d. Repeat this process using the filename **Logo2** and the Save as type GIF Graphics Interchange Format. It will have a file extension of .gif.

e. Repeat this process using the filename **Logo3** and the Save as type PNG Portable Network Graphics Format. It will have a file extension of .png.

8. After slide 1, insert a new slide with a blank layout. From the Insert tab, in the Illustrations group, use the Picture button to insert each of these logos so you can examine the quality of each image. Position them on the slide as shown in Figure 12-14, then click the Slide Show button so you can compare them in a larger size considering these comments.

a. Logo1.jpg—this image has excellent photo quality because the JPEG file format is well suited for photographs. However, a white background has been added, so this format will work best when your slide background is white.

b. Logo2.gif—this image preserved the transparent areas of the logo, but the apple and text look "grainy" and the edges of the letters are not smooth. The .gif format works best for simple line art and drawings with solid colors. It typically does not work well for photographs.

c. Logo3.png—this image preserved the transparent areas of the logo and the image quality is similar to the .jpg image. So this image would work well when you want to create transparent areas of a photograph. The file size of this image is much larger than the other two.

9. Delete slide 2 and keep the presentation open for the next exercise.

Figure 12-14
Graphic formats
compared

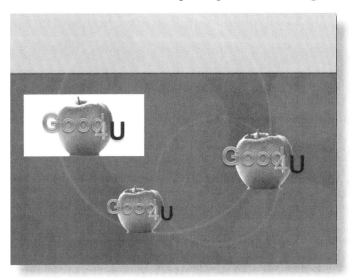

Exercise 12-13 SAVE A SLIDE AS A PICTURE

Slides can be saved as pictures and inserted into other presentations or documents. For example, you might need to reference slide content for training materials, reports, or other documents. This capability can be especially helpful if you need to use diagrams or other artwork you have created.

1. Move to slide 1.

2. Click the Microsoft Office Button 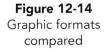, point to the arrow next to Save As, and then click Other Formats.

3. From the Save As dialog box, select your Lesson 12 folder. Name the file as **Slide1**.

4. In the Save as type list box, select the JPEG File Interchange Format.

5. In the message box that appears, as shown in Figure 12-15, click Current Slide Only. The slide is now saved as a picture that can be inserted from file.

Figure 12-15
Save current slide
only

6. To test this action of saving a slide, create a new slide with a blank layout after slide 8.

7. From the Insert tab, in the Illustrations group, click the Picture button 🖼 then locate your Lesson 12 folder and click the image **Slide1**. Click Insert. The complete slide will appear.

8. Resize the image just as you would any other illustration for a width of 5 inches. Center the image.

9. Update the handout footer to include the text **[12-13your initials]**.

10. Save the presentation as **[12-13your initials]** in your Lesson 12 folder.

11. Close this presentation.

Lesson 12 Summary

- Outlines can be created in Word and imported into PowerPoint as presentation slides by using the Slides from Outline feature.
- A flyer or other Word document can be inserted into PowerPoint as a PowerPoint Object using the Object button 🖼 found on the Insert tab.
- Slides from other presentations can be placed in a current presentation with the Reuse Slides feature.
- You can choose whether to keep the source formatting or use the current slide formatting when reusing slides.
- Files from other Microsoft applications can be linked using the Paste Special feature. When either the source document or the destination document is edited, both documents are changed.
- Screen captures can be made in two ways. Press Print Screen to capture a full screen; press Alt + Print Screen to capture the active window only. Use the Paste button 📋 or press Ctrl + V to insert a screen capture.

- The Window options available on the View tab make working with multiple open presentations more convenient because you can see more than one presentation at the same time.
- Use the Cascade button 🔲 to layer presentation windows.
- Use the Arrange All button 🔲 to view presentations side by side.
- Use Copy and Paste to share information between multiple open presentations and the Format Painter to copy formatting between presentations.
- From the Review tab, in the Comments group, use Comments to communicate with others who are reviewing your presentation and receive feedback from them. Comments can be edited, deleted, shown or hidden, and printed to make collaborating with others easy.
- Objects in PowerPoint can be saved as pictures to be inserted into other applications or used at a later date. Examples of objects that can be saved as pictures are logos, WordArt, SmartArt graphics, and slides.

LESSON 12		Command Summary	
Feature	**Button**	**Ribbon**	**Keyboard**
Import a Word Outline		Home tab, Slides group, New slide down arrow, choose Slides from Outline	
Insert a Word Document		Insert tab, Text group, Object	
Reuse Slides		Home tab, Slides group, New slide down arrow, choose Reuse Slides	
Link an Excel Worksheet		Home tab, Clipboard group, Paste down arrow, choose Paste Special	
Capture a Full Screen			Print Screen
Capture a Window			Alt + Print Screen
Insert a Screen Capture		Home tab, Clipboard group, Paste	Ctrl + V
Cascade Presentation Windows		View tab, Window group, Cascade	
Arrange Presentation Windows		View tab, Window group, Arrange All	
Switch Windows		View tab, Window group, Switch Windows	
Insert Comments		Review tab, Comments group, New comment	
Save a Slide as Picture		Microsoft Office Button, Save As, Other Format	

Concepts Review

True/False Questions

Each of the following statements is either true or false. Select your choice by indicating T or F.

T F   1. A Word outline can be imported into PowerPoint as a presentation.

T F   2. Objects in PowerPoint can be linked to other Microsoft Office files.

T F   3. PowerPoint slides cannot be reused in different presentations.

T F   4. Comments can be viewed in a presentation or hidden.

T F   5. To print reviewers' comments, choose Comments from the Print what drop-down list in the Print dialog box.

T F   6. Screen captures of Web pages or other applications can be inserted in PowerPoint.

T F   7. Arrange All makes it convenient to work with multiple open presentations.

T F   8. Original illustrations can be saved as images in several different file formats.

Short Answer Questions

Write the correct answer in the space provided.

1. How do you insert a Microsoft Word document into a presentation?

_____

2. What does it mean to link to an Excel worksheet?

_____

3. How do you capture the active window for a screen capture?

_____

4. How do you delete a comment?

_____

5. How do you print reviewer comments?

_____

6. What are the steps to save a created logo as a picture?

_____

7. How can you copy formatting from one presentation to another?

_____

8. How can you get a slide from one presentation into another?

_____

Critical Thinking

Answer these questions on a separate page. There are no right or wrong answers. Support your answers with examples from your own experience, if possible.

1. Think about the type of applications in which you could use artwork or drawings. Now that you know how to save objects as pictures, list one way you might use the Save as Picture feature.

2. Discuss ways that screen captures can be used to enhance training materials.

Skills Review

Exercise 12-14

Import an outline from Word and reuse slides.

1. Open PowerPoint and start a new, blank presentation.
2. Import an outline from Word following these steps:
   a. From the Home tab, in the Slides group, click the down arrow on the New Slide button .
   b. Choose Slides from Outline.
   c. Navigate to your student files for Lesson 12 and choose the file **Catering Outline** then click Insert.
   d. Delete the blank slide 1.
   e. Change the layout for the new slide 1 to a Title Slide.
3. Choose the Median design theme and Aspect color theme for the presentation.
4. Reuse slides from another presentation by following these steps:
   a. Click after slide 4 in the presentation.
   b. From the Home tab, in the Slides group, click the down arrow on the New Slide button .

    c. Choose Reuse Slides.

    d. From the Reuse Slides task pane, choose Browse and Browse File.

    e. Navigate to your student files for Lesson 12, and choose **Catering Services** and click Open.

    f. Click slide 2 to add it into the current presentation.

    g. Close the Reuse Slides task pane.

    h. Notice that the new slide is using a different font than the other slides. Use the Format Painter button 🗐 to copy the formatting for the title and text from slide 4 to slide 5.

5. Create a handout header and footer: Include the date and your name as the header, and the page number and text **[12-14your initials]** as the footer.

6. Save the presentation as **[12-14your initials]** in your Lesson 12 folder.

7. Print handouts with six slides per page, grayscale, scale to fit paper, and framed.

Exercise 12-15

Insert a Microsoft Word document, insert a screen capture, use Arrange All to see multiple presentation windows, copy formatting from one presentation to another.

1. Open the file **OneStop**.

2. Move to slide 5.

3. Insert a Microsoft Word document by following these steps:

    a. Delete the content placeholder on the right.

    b. From the Insert tab, in the Text group, click the Object button 🖼.

    c. Choose Create from File.

    d. Click Browse then navigate to your student files.

    e. Click **Cater Wedding** then click OK to close the Browse dialog box. Click OK to close the Insert Object dialog box.

    f. The document is inserted into the presentation. Resize it to an appropriate size and position as needed, as shown in Figure 12-16. From the Drawing Tools Format tab, click the Shape Outline button 🗐 and choose the weight of 3 points in black. This outline will define the flyer since white is used on both the flyer and the slide background.

Figure 12-16
Slide with flyer

4. Insert a slide after slide 5 using the Title and Content layout.

   a. Key the title text **Other Services**.

   b. Key the body text **Good 4 U computer operators can design a PowerPoint presentation including pictures of you and your spouse growing up through the years.**

   c. Press Esc twice to turn off the body text selection.

5. Insert a screen capture by following these steps:

   a. Open the file **SamplePresentation**.

   b. With slide 1 displayed, press Alt + Print Screen on your keyboard.

   c. Move to slide 6 in the **OneStop** presentation. From the Home tab, in the Clipboard group, click the Paste button .

   d. The image of slide 1 may be so large that you cannot see the corner sizing handles to make it smaller. Therefore, double-click the image to open the Format dialog box and set the height to 5 inches. Crop the screen capture so only the slide is showing.

   e. Position this image on the lower left of the slide.

   f. Add a black, 3-point border.

6. Working in the **OneStop** presentation, from the View tab, in the Window group, click the Arrange All button .

7. With the presentations side by side, copy the formatting from **SamplePresentation** to **OneStop** by following these steps:

   a. In the **SamplePresentation** Slides and Outline pane, select slide 1.

   b. From the Home tab, in the Clipboard group, click the Format Painter button .

   c. In the **OneStop** Slides and Outline pane, click slide 1 twice to copy the formatting.

   d. For slide 1, change the font to Calibri at 48 points in white.

   e. Close **SamplePresentation**.

8. On slide 6, select the inserted screen capture image then double-click the Format Painter button ⟨🖌⟩.

9. Now use the same border line on the pictures on slides 2, 3, and 4 by clicking the Format Painter button ⟨🖌⟩ once on each picture.

10. Check the position of objects on each slide and resize or reposition them if necessary.

11. Create a handout header and footer: Include the date and your name as the header, and the page number and text **[12-15your initials]** as the footer.

12. Save the presentation as **[12-15your initials]** in your Lesson 12 folder.

Exercise 12-16

Link an Excel worksheet, use Cascade to layer multiple presentations, copy and paste between presentations.

1. Open the file **Healthy Living**.

2. Open the file **Poster Ideas**.

3. Layer the two presentations by following these steps:

   a. Make the **Poster Ideas** file your active file.

   b. From the View tab, in the Windows group, click the Cascade button ⟨🗗⟩.

4. Copy and paste between presentations by following these steps:

   a. Still working in the **Poster Ideas** file, select slide 6 in the Slides and Outline pane.

   b. From the Home tab, in the Clipboard group, click the Copy button ⟨📋⟩.

   c. Click the title bar of the **Healthy Living** presentation to make it active.

   d. Click after slide 2 in the Slides and Outline pane, press ⟨Ctrl⟩+⟨V⟩. Notice that the whole slide is copied to the new location and changed to the destination design theme.

   e. Close the **Poster Ideas** PowerPoint presentation and maximize the **Healthy Living** window.

5. Insert a new slide after slide 3 using the title only layout. Key the title **Cost Analysis of the Classes**.

6. Link an Excel Worksheet by following these steps:

   a. Open Excel, then navigate to your student files for Lesson 12 and open the Excel file **Cost for Classes**.

   b. Select from A1:F8 by clicking in cell A1 and dragging the pointer through F8.

   c. Press ⟨Ctrl⟩+⟨C⟩ to copy.

   d. Move back to slide 4 in the **Healthy Living** presentation.

   e. From the Home tab, in the Clipboard group, click the down arrow on the Paste button ⟨📋⟩ and choose Paste Special.

   f. Choose Paste Link.

    g. Choose as Microsoft Office Excel Worksheet Object.

    h. Click OK.

    i. Enlarge and reposition the worksheet as needed to fit the slide.

    j. Double-click the worksheet to edit it. Increase the size of "Community Classes" to 18 points then check the presentation slide to be sure the change appears there, too.

    k. Close the Excel worksheet without saving.

7. Create a handout header and footer: Include the date and your name as the header, and the page number and text **[12-16your initials]** as the footer.

8. Save the presentation as **[12-16your initials]** in your Lesson 12 folder.

Exercise 12-17

Insert comments, print slide markup, and create a logo.

1. Open the file **Menu3** and select slide 1.

2. Create a logo for Good 4 U with a font size of 44 points. Key the logo text using three different effects from the WordArt gallery:

    a. Click the WordArt button and choose the Gradient fill – Accent 1, Outline White. Key **Good**.

    b. Click the WordArt button and choose the Fill – Accent 4, Outer Shadow – Accent 4, Soft Edge Bevel. Key **4**.

    c. Click the WordArt button and choose the Fill – Accent 2, Warm Matte Bevel. Key **U**.

3. Insert a shape using a 5-point star. For the Fill color, click Gradient then choose More Gradients. For the Gradient fill use the preset color Fire and for the Type use Path. Click Close.

4. Position the star behind the WordArt. Resize and reposition the WordArt and shape to appear similar to Figure 12-17. Group these objects together and position the group attractively below the subtitle.

5. Right-click the object and choose Save as Picture with the name **Logo-star** using the PNG file type.

Figure 12-17
Logo

6. On slide 3, delete the Chicken and Potato Salad entrée. Insert your own idea of a healthy entrée in its place.

7. Insert a comment on slide 3 by following these instructions:

   a. Move to slide 3.

   b. From the Review tab, in the Comments group, click anywhere in the new entrée you inserted and click the New Comment button ▢.

   c. In the colored comment box, key **I removed the Chicken and Potato Salad entree because it got poor reviews from the taste testers.**

   d. Click outside the comment box to close it.

   e. On slide 4, change "Rice Pudding" to **Julie's Cherry Jubilee Pudding.**

   f. Insert a comment explaining why you changed the name of the Rice Pudding dessert: **The rice pudding needed a jazzier name.**

8. Create a handout header and footer: Include the date and your name as the header, and the page number and text **[12-17your initials]** as the footer.

9. Save the presentation as **[12-17your initials]** in your Lesson 12 folder.

10. Print comments pages by following these steps:

    a. Open the Print dialog box.

    b. Set up the print options so that all slides will print as handouts, four slides per page, grayscale, framed.

    c. At the bottom of the Print dialog box, check the Print comments and ink markup box.

    d. Click Preview. In the Preview window, move to the second page and then zoom to 100%. The comments appear, identified by the slide on which they appear and by the initials of the reviewer.

    e. From the Print Preview tab, in the Print group, click the Print button ▢ and then click OK. Close the Preview window and close the presentation.

Lesson Applications

Exercise 12-18

Import an outline from Word, insert a Word document, and link an Excel file.

1. Start a new blank presentation.

2. Create a presentation from the Word file **Yoga** included with your student files.

3. If you have a blank slide 1, delete it. Change the layout of the new slide 1, "Yoga Classes" to a Title Slide layout.

4. Move to slide 3 and change to a Two Content layout, and cut from "Head to Knee" through "The Corpse" and paste these items in the second column. Change the font size to 28 points if necessary.

5. Change the body text size on slides 2 and 5 to 28 points.

6. On slide 1, select the title text and apply a WordArt Quick Style that will make the title easier to read.

7. Insert appropriate clip art or pictures on slides 4 and 5.

8. Apply a design theme and theme colors of your choice.

9. On slide 2, resize the text placeholder and insert the Word document **Yoga Flyer** as an object Resize and position attractively. Add an outline with a color that blends well with the other slide colors.

10. Open Excel and then the Excel file **Yoga Budget** and link the range A1: B4 to slide 5 of your presentation. Resize and position it attractively with your picture and text on the slide. See Figure 12-18 for an example.

Figure 12-18
Positioning of
objects on the slide

Equipment Needed

- A good slip-free mat
- A quiet area
- Comfortable pants and shirt

Budget for Yoga Beginners	Cost
Mat	$55
Outfit	$40
Total Investment	$95

11. Create a handout header and footer: Include the current date and your name as the header, and the text **[12-18your initials]** as the footer.

12. Save the file as **[12-18your initials]**. Print it as handouts, grayscale, framed, six slides per page.

Exercise 12-19

Insert screen captures, use Arrange All to view multiple presentations, copy and paste from another presentation.

1. Open the file **Healthy Eating**.

2. Add a slide after slide 3 using the Title and Content layout.

3. Key the information from Figure 12-19.

Figure 12-19
Slide 4

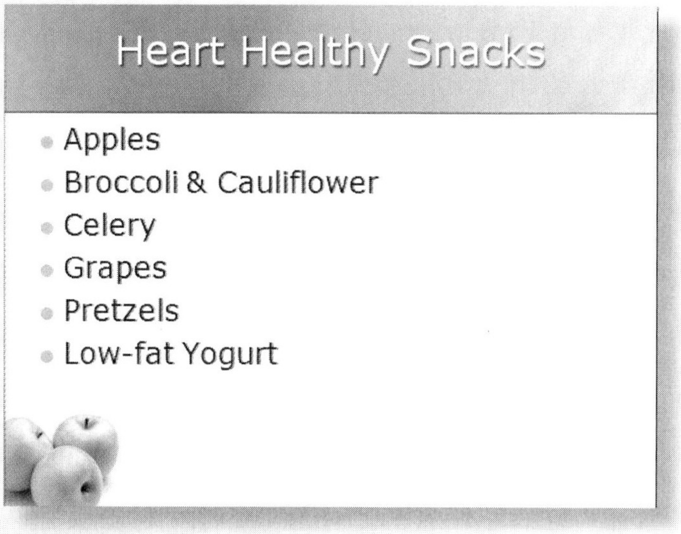

Heart Healthy Snacks

- Apples
- Broccoli & Cauliflower
- Celery
- Grapes
- Pretzels
- Low-fat Yogurt

4. Create a slide after slide 5 using the Title and Content layout. Key the title Upcoming Classes and key the text Don't miss out on our Nutrition Myth class coming up Saturday, August 19!

5. Open the presentation **Nutrition**.

6. Make a screen capture of slide 1 and paste it on slide 6 of the **Healthy Eating** presentation.

7. Crop and reposition the screen capture so that only slide 1 is showing.

8. Use the Arrange All feature to view the presentations side by side.

9. Select slide 2 and 3 out of the **Nutrition** presentation and cut them.

10. Paste them into the **Healthy Eating** presentation after slide 5.

11. Close the **Nutrition** file without saving changes and maximize the screen of the file you are working in.

12. Add slide transitions to the whole presentation.

13. Create a handout header and footer: Include the current date and your name as the header, and the text **[12-19your initials]** as the footer.

14. Save the file as **[12-19your initials]**. Print it as handouts, grayscale, framed, nine slides per page.

Exercise 12-20

Insert comments and print slide markup.

1. Open the file **JulyFun2**.

2. Correct all the spelling errors in the presentation and create a comment for each spelling correction noting that you corrected it, as shown in Figure 12-20.

Figure 12-20
Comment

3. On slide 1, move the title down a little and create a comment stating that you changed its position.

4. On slide 3, remove the comma and the words "and no seeds to spoil the fun." Create a comment stating the change that you made.

5. On slide 5, change the slide title from uppercase to capitalize each word. Create a comment describing this change.

6. Add custom animation to all objects in the presentation.

7. Add a party horn sound to slide 1 and hide the icon during the slide show.

8. Create a handout header and footer: Include the current date and your name as the header, and the text **[12-20your initials]** as the footer.

9. Save the file as **[12-20your initials]**. Print it as handouts, grayscale, framed, six slides per page, and include the comments and ink markup.

Exercise 12-21 ◆ Challenge Yourself

Import slides from an outline, create a logo and save as a picture, insert comments, print slide markup.

1. Open the presentation **Nutrition**.

2. Reuse all slides from the **Nutrition Myths** outline after slide 1 and before slide 2.

3. Select all of the slides you just inserted and apply the Title Slide layout.

4. Select all of the slides you inserted and change the font to white matching slide 1 by clicking the Reset button 📄.

5. Insert a clapping sound on slide 1 and hide the icon.

6. Create a Good 4 U logo matching the slide theme and topic, group it, and save it as a **picture2** using the PNG file type.

7. Insert the **picture2** file on the Slide Master for the Title Slide layout and the Title and Content layout in an appropriate place.

8. Adjust your text and content as needed on each slide based on how the logo is positioned.

9. Insert at least two comments into the presentation.

10. Create a handout header and footer: Include the current date and your name as the header, and the text **[12-21your initials]** as the footer.

11. Save the file as **[12-21your initials]**. Print it as handouts, grayscale, framed, six slides per page, and include the comments and ink markup pages.

On Your Own

In these exercises you work on your own, as you would in a real-life work environment. Use the skills you've learned to accomplish the task—and be creative.

Exercise 12-22

Create a PowerPoint presentation biography of your favorite sports player. Create at least six slides. Use tables, charts, and/or diagrams to show their statistics. Create an attractive and lively presentation. Write a script that you could use if presenting your presentation to an audience, and use the script to create suitable notes pages. Insert a screen capture of something you find on the Web about this player and create a references slide listing all the resources you used. Use the topics learned in this lesson to enhance your presentation.

Insert a handout header and footer: Include the current date and your name as the header, and the text **[12-22your initials]** as the footer. Save your presentation as **[12-22your initials]**. Preview it and then print as handouts.

Exercise 12-23

Imagine you are planning a class party. Create a presentation that lists and organizes tasks that need to be completed to have a successful event. Also list games and/or award items that can enhance the party. Make the slides interesting and fun to view. Use the topics learned in this chapter to include content from other sources and copy formatting from another presentation that you have completed previously. Have another student in your class evaluate the presentation and give you comments using the comment feature in PowerPoint. Based on this evaluation, make any needed corrections.

Insert a handout header and footer: Include the current date and your name as the header, and the text **[12-23your initials]** as the footer. Print the comment pages with a copy of the handouts. Save the presentation as **[12-23your initials]**.

Exercise 12-24

Imagine that you are starting your own business. Create a presentation that builds a case for why a bank should give you a loan to start the business. Create your own logo and save it as a picture. Create at least six slides describing the business, the major tasks necessary to open the business, and who will be responsible. Provide estimated earnings for the first few years of the business. Use content from other sources as necessary to build your case.

Insert a handout header and footer: Include the current date and your name as the header, and the text **[12-24your initials]** as the footer. Save the presentation as **[12-24your initials]**. Print the presentation as handouts.

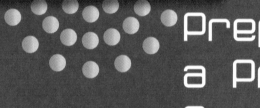

Lesson 13

Preparing a Presentation for Delivery

OBJECTIVES

MCAS OBJECTIVES

In this lesson:
PowerPoint 4.5.1
PowerPoint 4.5.2
PowerPoint 4.5.3
PowerPoint 4.5.5
See Appendix

After completing this lesson, you will be able to:

1. Control a slide show.

2. Adjust for different computer screen sizes.

3. Present with projection equipment.

4. Prepare presentations for delivery in other formats.

5. Create a menu-based kiosk presentation.

Estimated Time: 2 hours

This lesson will introduce PowerPoint features designed to help you prepare for and deliver a presentation. You can rehearse your presentation plus set timings to automate transitions. If you want to create a self-running slide show, for example, you can set slide timings so that the animations and slides advance automatically. A self-running approach would be appropriate for a show displayed continuously such as at an open house event or at a trade show *kiosk*. A menu-based approach can be used for situations where the viewer of the presentation controls how it is displayed based on menu selections. A menu-based approach would be suitable for a Web-based presentation or a presentation distributed to viewers on a CD.

When using computer projection equipment, you may need to adjust screen resolution for different screen sizes. Annotation pens allow you to mark up slides or make notes on your slides during a presentation. For situations where projection equipment is not available, different types of output are needed. With a menu-based or kiosk presentation, your PowerPoint slides must tell the complete story.

Controlling a Slide Show

Presentation slide shows can be used in different ways. By using PowerPoint's *Rehearse Timings* feature, you can practice the delivery of your presentation. You can set up a slide show to display only selected slides in your presentation. You can also make your presentation free running with automatic looping to repeat continuously.

Exercise 13-1   USE REHEARSE TIMINGS TO SET AUTOMATIC SLIDE TIMINGS

PowerPoint's *Rehearse Timings* feature offers a convenient way to set slide timings. When you start the Rehearse Timings procedure, the slide show begins with the Rehearsal toolbar displayed, as shown in Figure 13-1. You use its buttons to advance animations and slides, to pause, or to repeat a slide. Slides can be advanced, too, by using the [Spacebar] or clicking the left mouse button.

The time it takes to advance from one animation or one slide to another is automatically recorded. These times are used when the slide show is set to run automatically. During a rehearsal procedure, make sure to allow enough time for each animation so that your viewer can read and absorb the information before moving on.

1. Open the file **Ads1**.

2. From the Slide Show tab, in the Set Up group, click the Rehearse Timings button. A slide show begins, starting on slide 1. The Rehearsal toolbar appears in the upper-left corner of your screen.

3. When all the animation on slide 1 is complete, wait two or three seconds, then click the Next button on the Rehearsal toolbar to move to slide 2.

Figure 13-1
Rehearsal toolbar

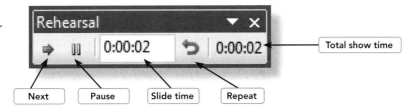

4. Wait for the title text to appear then click the Next button to make the first of two bulleted items appear and allow enough time to read the text.

5. Click the Next button again to see the second bulleted item appear and allow enough time to read the text.

6. Click the Next button to begin the animation of the pie chart and then wait for a few seconds to allow time to analyze the chart.

TIP

If you make a mistake on a slide, click the Repeat button ↺ to start the slide again. If you need to stop in the middle of a rehearsal for any reason, click the Pause button ‖ to stop the timer temporarily. Click Pause ‖ again to continue with the rehearsal.

7. Click the Next button ➡ to advance to slide 3 where a SmartArt diagram will appear. Wait for all three shapes to appear and allow enough time to read the text.

8. Continue clicking the Next button ➡ at appropriate times to advance through the nine slides in this presentation.

9. When the last slide has displayed, an information box appears, informing you of the slide show's total time, as shown in Figure 13-2. Click Yes to keep the slide timings that were recorded during the rehearsal. Slide Sorter view is displayed, showing the timings underneath each slide.

Figure 13-2
Save slide timings

10. Select slide 1 then click the Slide Show View button ▯. The show progresses automatically without any mouse clicks according to the times recorded during rehearsal.

11. When the show is complete, press Esc to return to Slide Sorter view.

12. If you need more practice with the timings, you can repeat the process to rehearse timings again. The timings are not permanently recorded until you save your presentation.

13. Leave the presentation open for the next exercise.

Exercise 13-2   SET TIMINGS MANUALLY

It is also possible to set timings manually if you can estimate how long each slide must be displayed. You can set the timing on each slide individually, or use Rehearse Timings first and then edit the time as necessary for selected slides.

1. From the Slide Sorter view, select slide 2. From the Animations tab, in the Transition to This Slide group, in the Advance Slide section, change the Automatically After number to **20** seconds.

2. Select slide 3 and change the Automatically After number to **10** seconds.

3. Select slides 4–9 and change the Automatically After number to **5** seconds.

4. Move to slide 1 and view the presentation as a slide show and notice that slide timings are set a little differently than before. Click [Esc] to return to Slide Sorter view.

5. Create a Lesson 13 folder and save the presentation as **[13-2your initials]** in your Lesson 13 folder.

6. Leave the presentation open for the next exercise.

Exercise 13-3 SET UP A SLIDE SHOW

A slide show can run in several different ways. Prior to this lesson, you viewed all slide shows as full-screen shows, advancing manually from one slide to the next. PowerPoint gives you tools to fine-tune the way you run a show. For example, you can:

- Run a show in a window or using the full screen.

- Advance slides by using the mouse and keyboard or have slides advance automatically by using preset slide timings as you did in Exercises 13-1 and 13-2.

- Run a show with or without preset animations.

- Run a show with or without prerecorded voice narration.

- Display a show on one or two monitors.

- Adjust slide show resolution for different screen sizes.

Click the Set Up Slide Show button to access the various options you can use to customize your slide show. If your slide show does not run as expected, chances are that changing a setting in the Set Up Show dialog box will fix the problem.

1. From the Slide Show tab, in the Set Up group, click the Set Up Slide Show button. Notice the many options in this dialog box as shown in Figure 13-3.

Figure 13-3
Set Up Show dialog box

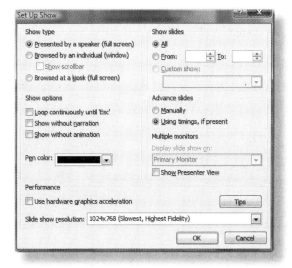

2. Under Show type, the first option is selected by default. Presented by a speaker (full screen) is what you have used throughout this text as you have viewed the presentations you have prepared. This is the most common way to use PowerPoint when giving a presentation.

3. Click the Show type Browsed at a kiosk (full screen). This option makes a show loop continuously until you press Esc to stop it.

4. Click OK. The kiosk option is useful for a presentation that is set up to run unattended in a public place.

5. Select slide 8, and then click the Slide Show View button 🖻 to start the slide show on this slide. Slide 9 will appear and then the slide show will automatically repeat. After slide 1 appears, press Esc to stop the slide show.

6. From the Slide Show tab, in the Set Up group, reopen the Set Up Show dialog box by clicking the Set Up Slide Show button 🖻. Under Show Type, choose Presented by a speaker (full screen).

7. Under Advance slides, choose Manually. This option will override any slide timings that have been set. It gives the speaker flexibility in deciding when it's time to display the next animation or the next slide. It's also the best choice if you plan to use hyperlinks during a show.

8. Click OK then view the slide show starting with slide 1 so you can see the difference of how much mouse clicking is required on slides 1–3.

9. Leave the presentation open for the next exercise.

Exercise 13-4   CREATE AND RUN CUSTOM SHOWS

A *custom show* is a presentation within a presentation. It displays only specially selected slides instead of all the slides in a show. This is convenient if you have a large presentation that deals with several different topics. You can create a custom show for each topic that includes only related slides, but the entire presentation is still available to you if you want to switch to another topic.

    You create a custom show by selecting related slides within a presentation and giving the selected group a name.

1. From the Slide Show tab, in the Start Slide Show group, click the Custom Slide Show button 🖻 then choose Custom Shows. The Custom Shows dialog box opens.

2. Click New. The Define Custom Show dialog box appears. The slide titles from the current presentation are listed in the Slides in presentation list box.

3. In the Slide show name box, key **Advertising**.

4. Using Ctrl+click, select slides 1, 2, 4, 5, 6, and 7. Click Add. The selected slides are added to the Slides in custom show list box on the right, as shown in Figure 13-4.

Figure 13-4
Define Custom Show
dialog box

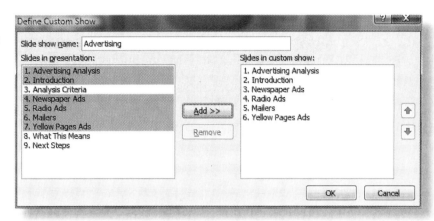

5. In the Slides in custom show list box, select slide 2, Introduction. Click Remove. Slide 2 is removed from the custom show list. Click OK. You have defined a custom show containing five slides.

6. With the Custom Shows dialog box still open, click New again to create a second show.

7. For the Slide show name, key **Planning**.

8. Select slides 3, 8, and 9. Click Add.

9. Select slide 1 from the Slides in presentation list box and click Add again. Slide 1 is added to the bottom of the Slides in custom show list, meaning that it will be the last slide displayed in the custom show.

10. Select the last slide in the Slides in custom show list and then click the Move Up button three times until it is at the top of the list, as shown in Figure 13-5.

Figure 13-5
Repositioning a slide
in the Custom Show
list

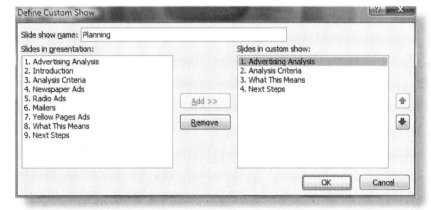

11. Click OK. The Custom Shows dialog box is once again displayed, and two shows are listed in the Custom shows list box.

12. Select "Advertising" from the list and then click Show. A slide show with five slides displays on the screen; move forward through the entire presentation.

13. When the show ends, return to Normal view. From the Slide Show tab, in the Start Slide Show group, click the Custom Slide Show button [img] and notice that both custom shows are listed.

14. Click Planning and the slide show will start automatically. Press [Esc] to end the slide show.

15. Leave the presentation open for the next exercise.

Exercise 13-5 CREATE ACTION BUTTONS FOR CUSTOM SHOWS

Using the Custom Shows dialog box to start a presentation is not very professional-looking when you are delivering your presentation. Instead, when you prepare your slide show, you can create an *action button* for each slide show—a button with a link associated with it—or a hyperlink that you can click to discreetly choose the slide show that's right for your audience.

The action buttons you create in this exercise will be placed on slide 1. Because both custom shows start on slide 1 as well, this will create a conflict unless the custom show lists are edited.

1. From the Slide Show tab, in the Start Slide Show group, click the Custom Slide Show button [img] then choose Custom shows.

2. Select "Advertising" and then click Edit. In the Slides in custom show list box on the right, select the first item, "Advertising Analysis," and click Remove. Click OK.

3. Using step 2 above as a guide, remove the first slide from the "Planning" custom show.

4. Click Close to close the Custom Shows dialog box.

5. Display slide 1 in Normal view.

6. From the Insert tab, in the Illustrations group, click the Shapes button [img], then in the Action Buttons category select the Action Button: Custom button [img], which displays as an empty box. Your pointer changes to a crosshair.

7. Use this pointer to draw a rectangle with an approximate height of 0.5 inches and width of 1.5 inches in the lower-left corner of slide 1 above the Good 4 U logo. The Action Settings dialog box automatically opens.

8. On the Mouse Click tab under Action on click, choose Hyperlink to.

9. In the Hyperlink to list box, scroll to the bottom of the list, and choose Custom Show.

Figure 13-6
Links to Custom
Shows dialog box

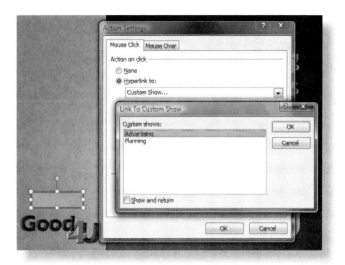

10. In the Link to Custom Show dialog box, as shown in Figure 13-6, select "Advertising" and click OK. Click OK again to close the Action Settings dialog box.

11. In the Slide pane, with the Action button shape selected, key **Advertising** to identify the button.

12. To make the button less obvious on the slide, from the Drawing Tools Format tab, in the Shape Styles group, click the Shape Styles More button ⊡ and choose Moderate Effect – Accent 6. Adjust the button size, if needed, so the text fits inside the button.

13. Duplicate the button and move the duplicate above the original but keep the two buttons close together and align them on the left.

14. Select the bottom button and change the text to **Planning**.

15. Right-click the "Planning" button (be sure you have the button selected and not just the text) and choose Edit Hyperlink from the shortcut menu. Working on the Mouse Click tab, from the Hyperlink to drop-down list box, choose Custom Show then choose "Planning." Click OK. Click OK again to close the Action Settings dialog box.

16. Move to slide 1 and view the presentation as a slide show. As soon as all the animated text placeholders and the picture appear, click one of the action buttons. The custom show you selected should run automatically. Run the show again to test the other action button.

17. On slide 1, delete Student Name and key **Your Name**.

18. Create a handout header and footer: Include the date and your name as the header and the page number and text **[13-5your initials]** as the footer.

19. Save the presentation as **[13-5your initials]** in your Lesson 13 folder.

20. Preview and then print only the first two slides of the presentation as handouts, two slides per page, scale to fit paper, framed.

21. Leave the presentation open for the next exercise.

Adjusting for Different Computer Screen Sizes

Today's computer screens come in a variety of sizes. The standard 17-inch or 19-inch computer screen has a 4:3 *aspect ratio,* which is the relationship (ratio) of width to height. This is close to the almost square appearance of television sets we have enjoyed watching for years. However, the increasingly popular wide-screen televisions use a 16:9 aspect ratio to display a more panoramic view. Wide-screen computer screens, both desktop and notebook, also use this ratio.

So understanding the particular screen ratio being used for development and for presentation is important. Designs that fit well at a 4:3 aspect ratio will look stretched out at the 16:9 ratio. Conversely, wide-screen designs will look crowded when displayed at a 4:3 ratio.

Exercise 13-6 ADJUST ON-SCREEN SHOW ASPECT RATIO

Changing the aspect ratio adjustment is very simple. This feature is available from the Design tab, in the Page Setup group, by clicking the Page Setup button ▢.

1. Move to slide 1. From the Design tab, in the Page Setup group, click the Page Setup button ▢. Notice that the Slides sized for setting displays On-screen Show (4:3) with a width of 10 inches and a height of 7.5 inches as shown in Figure 13-7.

Figure 13-7
Page Setup dialog box

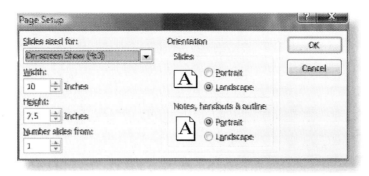

2. Open the Slides sized for list box to see additional sizes available and choose On-screen Show (16:9). The width is still 10 inches but the height changes to 5.63 inches. Click OK and the result of this change will be very apparent.

3. Click the Slide Show View button 🖵 to see how all the layouts have changed. View the entire presentation and note the adjustments that would be needed if this screen size was used. Those slides with only bulleted lists are affected the least; however, the images are stretched horizontally. The pie chart and diagram would require several adjustments to work at this screen size.

4. Click the Undo button 🔄 to return to the 4:3 aspect ratio.

5. Leave the presentation open for the next exercise.

Exercise 13-7   ADJUST SCREEN RESOLUTION

The image on your computer screen is made up of small elements, called *pixels*, that display closely spaced colors of red, green, and blue. All the colors that we see are created from a blending of those colors. Image clarity, or sharpness, is directly related to the number of pixels that are available to create the image. This sharpness is generally described as *resolution*. Pixels are arranged in horizontal lines that fill the screen; therefore, with a resolution of 1024 × 768, the horizontal axis has 1024 pixels and the vertical axis has 768 pixels. The horizontal number is always expressed first.

For the best projected image, the resolution of your computer screen should be set to the highest possible resolution. However, you may have a situation where your output device is an older data/video projector or another type of projector that cannot handle the highest resolution. Therefore, you can adjust this setting in PowerPoint.

1. From the Slide Show tab, in the Monitors group, click the Resolution list box to see your options. Click 720 x 480 (Fastest, Lowest Fidelity). You may have a different number on your computer; if you do, then select the lowest number available.

2. On slide 1, click the Slide Show View button 🖵 then advance through several slides to notice how the text looks blurred and the edges of letters look jagged.

3. Now change the Resolution to 1680 x 1050 (Slowest, Highest Fidelity). Once again, you may have a different number on your computer; if you do, then select the highest number available.

4. On slide 1, click the Slide Show View button 🖵 and notice the difference in clarity as you advance through several slides.

5. Click the Undo button 🔄 twice to return to your original resolution. Leave the presentation open for the next exercise.

Exercise 13-8   SHOW PRESENTER VIEW

PowerPoint's *Presenter View* enables you to display your presentation on the screens of two computer monitors. Therefore, this option may not be available for you to test if you are working from home or in a computer lab setting. To use two monitors, a desktop computer requires either two video cards or a dual-output video card; most notebook computers have multiple monitor capability built in.

Presenter View provides several benefits because a speaker can:

- Select slides out of sequence to create a customized show during a presentation.

- Preview text to see what is displayed on the next slide before you display it to your audience.

- View speaker notes in a large size for easy viewing.

- Blank out a screen.

NOTE

If students have one monitor and click Use Presenter View, they will receive an error message asking them to check to see if their computer can display on multiple monitors.

In Presenter View, buttons to advance through your presentation appear in a larger size that is easier to use when you are presenting. Slide numbers and the elapsed time since the start of your presentation are displayed.

First you must set up your computer to use two monitors. If you have two monitors, you can complete the following steps. If you do not, then continue to the next exercise.

1. Click the Start button, click Control Panel, then choose Personalization.

2. Click the Display Settings link to open the Display Settings dialog box. Monitor 1 should be your main monitor that will display Presenter View; Monitor 2 should display the presentation slide show. Click Identify Monitors to confirm the location of each one. Select an appropriate resolution for each monitor, too.

3. Select Monitor 2 then check Extend the desktop onto this monitor. Click OK.

4. In PowerPoint, from the Slide Show tab, in the Monitors group, click Use Presenter View.

5. Click the Slide Show View button 🖵 and the slide show will display on your Monitor 2 while Presenter View is displayed on Monitor 1. View your presentation.

6. Update the handout footer to include the text **[13-8your initials]**.

7. Save the presentation as **[13-8your initials]** in your Lesson 13 folder.

8. Leave your presentation open for the next exercise.

Presenting with Projection Equipment

When you are presenting with PowerPoint and projection equipment, set up your equipment well in advance of your presentation and test the equipment and your slide show. Be sure your equipment is arranged in an effective manner so that your computer monitor is visible to you while you are talking. It is better to glance at the monitor than to look at the projected image on a large screen while you are talking. For safety, arrange any necessary cables or electrical cords so that they will not trip you.

The following exercises will introduce you to several of PowerPoint's features that can be very helpful during your delivery of a presentation.

Exercise 13-9   USE ON-SCREEN NAVIGATION TOOLS

During a slide show, you can navigate from slide to slide or to a specific slide by using a shortcut menu.

TIP

If you're going to be presenting at a live meeting, slide timings are usually not appropriate because you'll want to be flexible with the amount of time spent on individual slides to encourage discussion. Slide timings are most appropriate for self-running presentations.

1. From the Slide Show tab, in the Set Up group, click the Set Up Slide Show button.

2. In the Set Up Show dialog box, under Show type, choose the Presented by a speaker (full screen). Under Show options, choose Show without animation. Under Advance slides, choose Manually. Click OK. This turns off any slide animations and timings that might have been set.

3. Run the presentation as a slide show, starting with slide 1. Imagine that you are presenting this at a meeting and that the group is commenting and making decisions as you move from slide to slide. You will move back and forth between the slides as your discussion progresses.

Figure 13-8
Shortcut menu for slide show navigation

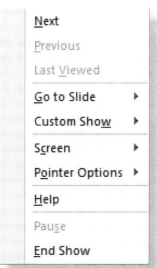

4. With slide 1 displayed, right-click anywhere on the screen to display the shortcut menu, as shown in Figure 13-8.

5. The shortcut menu provides a variety of options related to the slide show. Notice that you can click Next or Previous (when you have slides available before or after your current location in the presentation) to move forward or backward in the slide show.

6. Point to Go to Slide on the shortcut menu. Notice that slides are listed in order with their titles displayed. Click "3 Analysis Criteria" to go to slide 3.

7. Click the left mouse button twice to advance through slide 4 and slide 5 to display each slide.

8. Another way to move between your slides is with the menu options that are displayed when you mouse over them on the lower left of the slide during a slide show, as shown in Figure 13-9.

Figure 13-9
Menu options for slide show navigation

Back   Pen   Slide show menu   Forward

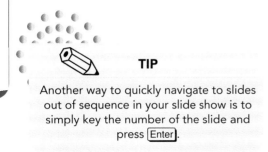

TIP

Another way to quickly navigate to slides out of sequence in your slide show is to simply key the number of the slide and press Enter.

9. Click the Slide Show menu button 🖳 then point to Go to Slide on the menu. Click slide 2.

10. Click the left mouse button one time to advance to slide 3.

11. Leave the presentation open for the next exercise.

Exercise 13-10   USE ANNOTATION PENS

During a slide show you can use your pointer to direct your audience's attention to something on your slide. Be careful when using the pointer that you don't move too quickly or display nervous mannerisms by making the pointer move too much. The *annotation pens* are useful to "draw" on your slides during a slide show with your choice of three different tools. For example, you can use the Ballpoint Pen or the Felt Tip Pen to draw a circle around an important number or underline a word. You can use the Highlighter to draw a wider mark to make something stand out on the slide.

   You could even use a pen to add a simple handwritten note to a slide. At the end of a slide show, you have the option to save annotations so anything that you draw or write can be saved with your presentation.

1. With slide 3 displayed in Slide Show view, right-click the screen; choose Pointer Options and then Ballpoint Pen from the shortcut menu, as shown in Figure 13-10. The pointer changes to a pen shape.

Figure 13-10
Using the Pen during a Slide Show

2. Using the Ballpoint Pen pointer, draw an oval around the title word "Criteria" to emphasize this word. The current pen color may vary on your computer.

3. Right-click the screen, choose Pointer Options and then Eraser from the shortcut menu. Your pointer changes to an eraser, so click on the oval to erase it. You can also press E on your keyboard to activate the eraser, then click on lines you have drawn to remove these annotations.

4. Right-click the screen, choose Pointer Options and then choose Ballpoint Pen.

5. Right-click the screen again, and choose Pointer Options, and then choose Ink Color. Choose Red for the pen color.

6. Draw an oval around the word "Criteria" and notice the different color.

TIP

You don't have to draw precisely when using the annotation pen. Pen marks remain on one slide when you advance to another. You will be given the option at the end of the slide show to retain the marks. Then you can use drawing tools to modify them or delete the ones you don't want to keep.

7. Right-click the screen again, and choose Pointer Options and then Felt Tip Pen. Draw an oval around "Effectiveness." Notice that the mark made with this pen is thicker.

8. Right-click the screen, choose Pointer Options and then Highlighter. Right-click the screen again, and choose Pointer Options, and then choose Ink Color. Choose Yellow for the highlighter color. Draw a mark through "Frequency" and "Quality," as shown in Figure 13-11.

Figure 13-11
Annotation pen sample marks

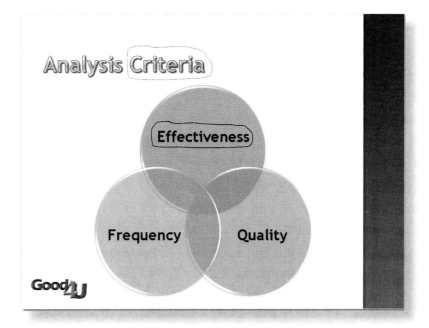

9. Open the shortcut menu again, choose Pointer Options, and then choose Arrow to restore the arrow pointer. (Or press the keyboard shortcut Ctrl + A.)

10. Advance through the last slide. When you reach the end of the presentation, click once more to exit the presentation. A message box will automatically appear, as shown in Figure 13-12.

Figure 13-12
Dialog box concerning Ink Annotations

11. Click Keep to retain the annotation pen marks.

12. Now look at the slides where you used annotation pens. You will see your drawings that can be recolored or resized with line tools. Even though you might have drawn a rectangle shape, you cannot apply fill colors.

13. Create a blank slide after slide 3 and practice with these tools a little more. The keyboard shortcut to activate the pen is Ctrl+P; press Esc to turn off the pen. During a meeting it might be very helpful to draw a quick diagram or to make a sketch about something. When you have finished practicing, delete this slide.

14. Leave the presentation open for the next exercise.

Exercise 13-11   BLANK SLIDES

During a slide show you can blank your computer screen without closing your slide show. You might want to digress from your original topic, or simply have a discussion without an image being projected. Two letters from the keyboard, B and W, will *blank slides* during a slide show. This feature works with uppercase or lowercase letters. This technique does not require any advance set up and can be used effectively to manage when your slides are displayed.

1. Move to slide 4, and view the presentation as a slide show.

2. With slide 4 displayed in Slide Show view, press B on your keyboard to blank the screen to black; press B again to return to this slide in your slide show. The transition effect when the slide comes back can be very dramatic after the screen has been black.

3. With slide 4 still displayed in Slide Show view, press W on your keyboard to blank the screen to white; press W again to return to this slide in your slide show. A white screen can be glaring, however, so blanking to white might not be the best choice to use.

4. Press Esc to return to Normal view.

5. Leave the presentation open for the next exercise.

Exercise 13-12   HIDE AND REVEAL SLIDES

You may decide to include a few extra slides in your presentation in case someone in the audience has a question about these concepts or the slides might be about supplemental content you may or may not have time to cover. You can include these slides as part of your presentation, but use the *hide slides* option and *reveal* them only if you choose to.

1. Click the Slide Sorter view button [icon] and select slide 8 with the title "What This Means."

2. With slide 8 selected, from the Slide Show tab, in the Set Up group, click the Hide Slide button [icon].

Figure 13-13
Hiding a slide

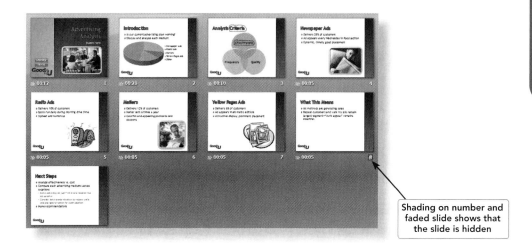

Shading on number and
faded slide shows that
the slide is hidden

3. Now the slide will not be displayed during a sequential slide show. Figure 13-13 shows the identifier for a slide that is hidden. Still in Slide Sorter view, select slide 7 and click the Slide Show View button [icon] , and then advance to the next slide. Slide 9 appears.

4. Still on slide 9 in Slide Show view, key **8** then press [Enter]. The hidden slide is then revealed. This technique of keying a number works from any slide in your presentation to immediately move to a different slide.

5. Press [Esc] to return to Slide Sorter view.

6. Update your handout footer to include the text **[13-12your initials]**.

7. Move to slide 1 in Normal view and save the presentation as **[13-12your initials]** in your Lesson 13 folder.

8. Leave the presentation open for the next exercise.

Preparing Presentations for Delivery in Other Formats

Throughout this book, you have viewed presentations on your computer screen and printed them on paper. You can also print presentations on transparency film for use with an overhead projector. You can send your presentation file (on a CD or as a file attachment through e-mail) to a service bureau where your presentation can be reproduced as *35mm slides* or full-color *overhead transparencies*. Table 13-1 lists the qualities of different delivery methods.

You have used the Page Setup dialog box to change slide orientation from landscape to portrait and to change how the slides are sized for different monitor sizes. In the same dialog box, you can resize presentation slides for letter paper, 35mm slides, overhead transparencies, or custom paper sizes.

NOTE

Remember, any animation effects that your presentation contains will be lost when preparing your slide show as 35mm slides or overhead transparencies.

TABLE 13-1 Choosing a Presentation Delivery Method

Method	Maximum Audience	Advantages
On-screen show displayed on a single computer monitor	4-20, depending on monitor size	Allows last-minute changes and use of animation
On-screen show displayed on a computer with a large-screen projector	200	Same as preceding
Slide projector	200	Quality color with high color saturation
Overhead projector	200	Simple, transparencies are inexpensive to create, and an excellent option when a computer is not available

Exercise 13-13 PREPARE A PRESENTATION IN 35MM FORMAT

When you want to deliver a presentation in a format other than an on-screen show, you need to change the slide size by using the Page Setup dialog box. For example, *35mm slides* have a different aspect ratio than on-screen slides or overhead transparencies.

1. From the Design tab, in the Page Setup group, click the Page Setup button ▢ to open the Page Setup dialog box. Notice that the slides are sized for On-screen Show (4:3 aspect ratio)—they have a 10-inch width and 7.5 inch height with a landscape orientation.

2. Click the Slides sized for list box drop-down arrow to display the available choices. Notice that there are several sizes from which to choose.

3. Choose 35mm Slides. Notice that the width has changed to 11.25 inches, but the height remains the same as for an On-screen Show, as shown in Figure 13-14.

Figure 13-14
Page Setup dialog
box

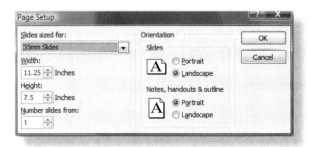

4. Click OK to close the dialog box. Notice that the 35mm format is slightly wider than the on-screen format.

5. Scroll through all the slides and observe any changes in proportions to individual objects. In this case, the body placeholders have simply become wider.

TIP

It is best to choose the output format of a presentation (on-screen, letter paper, 35mm slides, overhead, and so on) and the orientation (landscape or portrait) before creating the presentation. However, you might have to change the output format after the presentation is complete. In that case, review each slide because a change in the aspect ratio will change objects, too. You may need to change object proportions, positions, and font sizes.

6. On slide 2 resize the pie chart and reposition it a little lower.

7. Update the handout footer to include the text **[13-13your initials]** as the footer.

8. Move to slide 1 and save the presentation as **[13-13your initials]** in your Lesson 13 folder. Your presentation is now ready to be translated into 35mm slides for use with a slide projector. You can send the presentation file as an e-mail attachment to a service bureau, or use the Package for CD feature (covered in Lesson 14) to copy the presentation to a CD-R and then mail or hand-deliver it to a service bureau for 35mm slide production.

9. Preview and then print the presentation as handouts, six slides per page, grayscale, framed. Notice that the slide miniatures on this printout are slightly shorter and wider than slides formatted for an on-screen presentation.

Exercise 13-14 PREPARE A PRESENTATION FOR USE AS OVERHEAD TRANSPARENCIES

NOTE

PowerPoint's default orientation is landscape because that dimension fits computer screens and you have more horizontal space on each slide. Also, this orientation is better for audience viewing than portrait orientation where some of the information would be too low on a projection screen for an audience to see. However, you may encounter a situation where portrait orientation will work better than landscape. If you know you will need portrait orientation, it is best to change the orientation before creating any slides. Because this setting changes the slide aspect ratio, it can affect a lot of slide elements if you change orientation after your development work has been done.

You can use your printer to print *overhead transparencies* simply by inserting transparency film in your printer's paper tray. Or, you can copy paper printouts onto transparency film by using a copy machine. Several types of transparency film are available, specially formulated for laser printers, ink-jet printers, and copy machines. Make sure you use the correct film for your printer or copier. You can obtain professional-quality color overhead transparencies by sending your presentation file to a service bureau, just as you would for 35mm slides.

1. From the Design tab, in the Page Setup group, click the Page Setup button and change the Slides sized for setting to Overhead. This changes the width to 10 inches, keeping the height at 7.5 inches (the same as for an on-screen show), which works well for most overhead projectors.

2. Click OK to close the dialog box.

3. Insert a slide footer for slide 1 only, containing the slide number, your name, and the text **[13-14your initials]**.

4. Update the handout footer to include the text **[13-14your initials]**.

5. Save the presentation as **[13-14your initials]** in your Lesson 13 folder.

6. Print slide 1, framed, on transparency film if it is available.

7. Print the entire presentation as handouts, six slides per page, grayscale, framed. Compare this printout to the printout from the previous exercise. Notice the difference in the slide proportions.

8. Change Page Setup to return to an On-screen Show with a 4:3 aspect ratio.

9. Leave the presentation open for the next exercise.

TIP

It is important to understand the capabilities of your printer and the type of output it generates. If you are using a small ink-jet printer, then you might want to conserve ink and print as fast as possible. Large areas of dark or intense colors will take a long time to print and use a lot of ink. You could choose light background colors and use dark or intense colors for accent colors. For color laser printing, you do not have these limitations.

Creating a Menu-Based Kiosk Presentation

A *kiosk* presentation is a self-running slide show or one that can be controlled by a single person. This type of presentation can be used for trade shows or open house events where people might walk up to a computer and decide what portion of the slide show they want to read. A menu with *hyperlinks* to certain slides makes it easy to view portions of the presentation.

Exercise 13-15   PROVIDE NAVIGATION OPTIONS

A menu slide with a list of topics that are hyperlinked in some way, either as text or as labeled shapes, enables the person viewing the presentation to jump to the first slide that begins each topic. At the end of each topic, a hyperlink is needed to return to the menu slide. This exercise will create a menu slide using shapes made to look like actual buttons with a linking action associated with each one.

1. Move to slide 1 and delete the buttons for Advertising and Planning since you are now preparing a different type of navigation.

2. Insert a new slide with a Title Only layout. On the new slide 2, key the title **Menu**.

3. From the Insert tab, in the Illustrations group, click the Shapes button 🔲 , then select the Rounded Rectangle button 🔲 .

4. Draw a rectangle with a height of .6 inches and a width of 2.75 inches.

5. Change the Shape Fill to Gold, Accent 4, then apply a Shape Effect of Bevel, Circle. Click on the yellow adjustment handle and drag it in

to add dimension and make the shape edges more rounded like an actual button.

6. From the Home tab, in the Font group, change the font size to 28 points with left alignment and key the text **Introduction**.

7. Select the text and apply the WordArt Quick Style of Fill – White, Drop Shadow.

8. Select the shape, and then from the Insert tab, in the Links group, click the Action button [icon]. On the Action Settings dialog box, select Hyperlink to: and from the list box choose Slide .... Choose 3. Introduction. Click OK. Click OK again to close the Action Settings dialog box.

9. Now with the shape selected, press [Ctrl]+[D] twice then position the duplicated shapes below the first one.

10. Change the text on the second shape to **Options** and on the third shape to **Next Steps**.

11. Select the "Options" shape, and then from the Insert tab, in the Links group, click the Action button: Custom [icon]. Follow the procedure of step 8 but change the hyperlink to Slide 5.

12. Repeat this process for the "Next Steps" shape so it is linked to Slide 10.

13. Position the three action shapes as shown in Figure 13-15.

14. For a decorative effect, add a star on the left of the "Introduction" shape. Use a Ice Blue, Accent 1 then apply the same Shape Effect of Bevel, Circle. Rotate the star slightly as shown in Figure 13-15.

15. Duplicate the star and position the copy on the left of the "Options" shape.

16. Duplicate the star again and position the copy on the left of the "Next Steps" shape.

17. Adjust any positioning and alignment of shapes as needed and your menu slide is complete.

Figure 13-15
Menu options

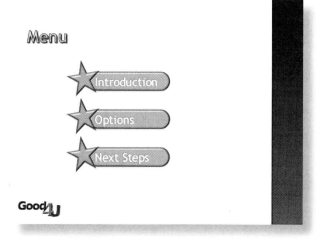

18. Move to slide 3. Draw a Right Block Arrow on the lower right of the slide using the Ice Blue, Accent 1 color. Key the text **Next**.

19. With this shape selected (not the text), from the Insert tab, in the Links group, click the Action button ![icon]. Click Hyperlink to: and then choose Next Slide. Click OK.

20. Copy this "Next" shape now that it contains the linked setting and paste it on the slides that need to advance: slides 1, 5, 6, and 7.

21. Paste the shape on slide 10, and change the shape to a left arrow and change the text to **Menu**. From the Insert tab, in the Links group, click the Action button: Custom ![icon], select Hyperlink to: and Slide... and then choose 2. Menu and click OK.

22. Copy this "Menu" shape and paste a copy on slides 4 and 8.

23. Leave the presentation open for the next exercise.

Exercise 13-16   USE SET UP SHOW TO CREATE A KIOSK PRESENTATION

For a kiosk presentation where the slides are shown in sequence, the slide show should be set up to loop continuously so the slide show automatically repeats. This exercise illustrates the steps to do this. However, because a menu is being used for navigation in this slide show, the navigation made possible by the menu and other action settings controls the movement through the slides.

1. From the Slide Show tab, in the Set Up group, click the Set Up Slide Show button ![icon].

2. In the Set Up Show dialog box, under Show type, choose Browsed at a kiosk (full screen). Under Show options, notice that Loop continuously until 'Esc' is selected and gray, which indicates that you may not deselect this option. If Show without animation is not selected, check the box.

3. For Advance slides, choose Manually if not selected, and then click OK.

4. Move to slide 1 and view your slide show using your action buttons to be sure that all slides advance or return to the menu as you planned. Click [Esc] to return to Normal view.

5. Update the handout footer to include the text **[13-16your initials]**.

6. Update the slide footer on slide 1 to include the text **[13-16your initials]**.

7. Save the presentation as **[13-16your initials]** in your Lesson 13 folder.

8. Close the presentation.

Lesson 13 Summary

- Use the Rehearse Timings feature to practice the timing of a presentation or record the timing for how long slides are displayed as you advance through a presentation. These timings can be edited and also used for a self-running slide show.

- Use the Animations tab to set transition timings for individual slides or for all slides in a presentation.

- Using the Set Up Show dialog box, slide shows can be set to run continuously with no manual intervention, to be run only on mouse clicks, or to be modified in many other ways.

- Another way to make a presentation adaptable to varying audiences is to create custom shows. Custom shows are subsets of a complete show, displaying only preselected slides.

- Creating action buttons or hyperlinks to custom shows makes it easy to manage a slide show during a presentation.

- Another way to manage a slide show is to create a menu slide listing the titles of selected slides, each with hyperlinks to the actual slide.

- Resolution can be adjusted to be the appropriate quality for the computer you are using.

- Presenter View enables you to display your presentation on two monitors while the audience can see only what is displayed on one of them.

- Use the annotation pens during a slide show to call attention to something on a slide, draw an impromptu diagram, or record audience feedback.

- During a slide show, you can blank the screen to black by pressing B; press B again to return to the slide show. To blank to a white screen, press W.

- Slides can be hidden so that they will not be displayed during a slide show. To reveal hidden slides, key the slide number and press Enter.

- The page size and orientation of presentation slides can be changed to fit your needs. Use the Page Setup dialog box to choose landscape or portrait orientation and to select standard sizes such as letter paper, 35mm slides, overheads, or to create a custom size.

- Presentations prepared for 35mm format or for overhead format can be sent to a service bureau on a CD or as an e-mail attachment to be created as 35mm color slides, color transparencies, or color prints. Overheads (also called overhead transparencies) can also be created by using transparency film in a standard printer.

LESSON 13		Command Summary	
Feature	**Button**	**Ribbon**	**Keyboard**
Rehearse Timings		Slide Show tab, Set Up group, Rehearse Timings	
Set Up Slide Show		Slide Show tab, Set Up group, Set Up Slide Show	Shift +
Set Timings Manually		Animations tab, Transitions to This Slide group, Automatically After	
Create a Custom Show		Slide Show tab, Start Slide Show group, Custom Slide Show	
Adjust Page Set Up		Design tab, Page Setup group, Page Setup	
Pointer Options		Slide Show view, shortcut menu, Pointer Options	Ctrl + P Turn off with Esc
Screen Resolution		Slide Show tab, Monitors group, Resolution	
Show Presenter View		Slide Show tab, Monitors group, Use Presenter View	
Blank Slides			B or W in slide show view
Hide Slide		Slide Show tab, Set Up group, Hide Slide	
Action Buttons		Insert tab, Illustrations group, Shapes, and Action Buttons	
Action		Insert tab, Links group, Action	

Concepts Review

True/False Questions

Each of the following statements is either true or false. Select your choice by indicating T or F.

T F   1. You can set different transition timings for each slide in a slide show.

T F   2. Only one custom show is possible in a presentation.

T F   3. Action buttons provide the ability to hyperlink within a presentation.

T F   4. The aspect ratio is determined by comparing the number of slides that are illustrated to the number that contain only text.

T F   5. Resolution is a measurement of the number of pixels on a computer screen; a smaller number of pixels helps to keep the image less cluttered and more sharp.

T F   6. The Felt Tip pen tool makes a wider mark on a slide than the Highlighter when you use it to annotate a slide.

T F   7. Files can be sent over the Internet to a service bureau for printing as 35mm slides or overhead transparencies.

T F   8. A kiosk presentation is one that is speaker independent because it will usually be designed as a self-running slide show.

Short Answer Questions

Write the correct answer in the space provided.

1. How do you display the Action Button shapes?

   _____

2. What do you call an object that, when clicked, displays another slide?

   _____

3. Without using a hyperlink, action button, or the Set Up Show dialog box, how can you run a custom show?

   _____

4. What is the most common aspect ratio for computer screens and what is the ratio for wide-screen computers.

   _____

5. When you are viewing a presentation, what is the keyboard shortcut to activate the annotation pen? How do you turn off the annotation pen?

   _____

6. When you are viewing a presentation, what is the keyboard shortcut to blank the screen?

_____

7. How can you hide a slide so it does not display during a presentation?

_____

8. Why might a presenter use a menu with action buttons?

_____

Critical Thinking

Answer these questions on a separate page. There are no right or wrong answers. Support your answers with examples from your own experience, if possible.

1. Think about when and where you might use the various presentation methods you learned about in this course. For example, which methods would be best for small groups, and which would be best for large ones? How might you prepare for a presentation if you were traveling on business?

2. Discuss ways that annotating slides during a presentation would be useful for you during a meeting to plan a future event.

Skills Review

Exercise 13-17

Rehearse timings, adjust timings manually, and set up show.

1. Open the file **WalkFood**.
2. Apply the Blinds Entrance Custom Animation effect to the objects in the presentation.
3. Apply the Dissolve transition effect to all of the slides in the presentation and modify it so it runs at a Medium speed.
4. Check the presentation for spelling errors and correct the word "Consideratons" to "Considerations" and any other spelling errors that appear.
5. Move to slide 1.
6. Use Rehearse Timings to set timings for the presentation by following these steps:
   a. From the Slide Show tab, in the Set Up group, click the Rehearse Timings button ⧉.
   b. Click the Next button ⧉ on the Rehearsal toolbar to begin making objects appear on the slides.

   c. Continue clicking the Next button ⬛ each time you are ready for another object to appear on the slide. If you need to redo a slide, press the Repeat button ⬛ and fix the timing.

   d. When you have completed the slide timings, a dialog box will appear and ask you if you want to keep the timings. Click **Yes**.

7. Change the timings manually by following these steps:

   a. Working in Slide Sorter view, click slide 1.

   b. From the Animations tab, in the Transitions to This Slide group, change the **Automatically After** time to **10** seconds for slide 1.

   c. Move to slide 5, and change the **Automatically After** time to **5** seconds.

   d. Return to Normal view and move to slide 1.

8. Set up the presentation to be browsed at a kiosk by following these steps:

   a. From the Slide Show tab, in the Set Up group, click the Set Up Slide Show button ⬛.

   b. In the Set Up Show dialog box, choose **Browsed at a Kiosk (Full Screen)**. The Show options will then automatically select Loop Continuously until 'Esc' and this option will be grayed out.

   c. Click **OK** to exit the dialog box.

9. Create a handout header and footer: Include the current date and your name as the header and the page number and the text **[13-17your initials]** as the footer.

10. View the presentation as a slide show pressing ⌨Esc at the end to exit the Slide Show view.

11. Save the presentation as **[13-17your initials]** in your Lesson 13 folder.

12. Print handouts six slides per page, grayscale, and framed.

Exercise 13-18

Change screen size, screen resolution, and use annotation tools.

1. Open the file **WalkPromotion**.

2. Change the theme colors to **Apex**.

3. Adjust the aspect ratio of the presentation to a wide-screen format by following these steps:

   a. From the Design tab, in the Page Setup group, click the Page Setup button ⬛.

   b. In the Slides sized for drop-down list, choose **On-screen Show (16:9)**.

   c. Click **OK**. Notice that the slides have changed size.

4. Move to slide 2.

5. Decrease the size of the diagram to better match the size of the tables on slides 3 and 4. Move it down slightly.

6. Move to slide 1. Resize and reposition the clip art image so it does not appear distorted.

7. Assume the computer you plan on presenting with only goes to 800 × 600 screen resolution. Modify screen resolution by following these steps:

   a. From the Slide Show tab, in the Monitors group, click the drop-down list arrow for Resolution.

   b. Choose 800 x 600 resolution.

   c. View the presentation as a slide show to ensure all objects appear clearly.

8. Use annotation tools to make annotations in the presentation by following these steps:

   a. View the presentation as a slide show.

   b. Move to slide 2.

   c. Right-click the slide and choose Pointer Options.

   d. Click Felt-Tip Pen and draw an arrow from the upper right corner of the slide to the dates of the walk.

   e. Right-click the slide again and choose Next to move to slide 3.

   f. Circle the number 6 using the Felt-Tip Pen.

   g. Right-click the slide and choose Pointer Options and select Arrow.

   h. Finish viewing the presentation and choose to Keep the annotations.

9. Create a handout header and footer: Include the current date and your name as the header and the page number and text [13-18your initials] as the footer.

10. Save the presentation as [13-18your initials] in your Lesson 13 folder.

11. Print handouts four slides per page, grayscale, and framed.

Exercise 13-19

Change to 35mm slide format and use on-screen navigation tools.

1. Open the file **LunchMenu**.

2. Format the presentation for output as 35mm slides by following these steps:

   a. From the Design tab, in the Page Setup group, click the Page Setup button ▢.

   b. In the Slides sized for drop-down list, choose 35mm Slides.

   c. Click OK. Notice that the slides have changed size.

3. Review each slide individually, and make adjustments to placeholder size and spacing so that all text is aligned correctly. Resize the picture so that it is not distorted.

4. Copy the picture from slide 1 and paste it to slide 2. Make it smaller to fit in the upper part of the slide.

5. Cut the picture from slide 2 and paste it onto the Slide Master so it appears in the upper part of the slide on all content slides.

6. View the presentation as a slide show, and use the on-screen navigation tools to move throughout the presentation.

7. Create a handout header and footer: Include the date and your name as the header and include the page number and text **[13-19your initials]** as the footer.

8. Save the presentation as **[13-19your initials]** in your Lesson 13 folder.

9. Print as handouts, four slides per page, grayscale, landscape, framed.

Lesson Applications

Exercise 13-20

Create a custom show, adjust screen resolution, and set up the show for browsing at a kiosk.

1. Open PowerPoint, start a new presentation. From the New Presentation dialog box, in the Microsoft Office Online category, click Presentations, then Health Care. Download the presentation **Food Pyramid Presentation**. If you are not connected to the Internet, open the **FoodPyramid** file from your student files from Lesson 13.

2. Apply Strips Right-Down transitions with a Chime sound to all of the slides in the presentation.

3. Create a custom show called Portions using slides 4-9 of the original presentation.

4. Create another custom show called Final Thoughts using slides 11-13 of the original presentation.

5. Create custom action buttons on slide 2 with the title of each custom show on the button and link to each custom show.

6. On slide 9 and slide 13 create a custom action button that matches the previous action buttons with the text Menu that will return the viewer to slide 2 which contains the link to the other custom show.

7. Make all of the action buttons coordinate with the slide theme and colors.

8. Test the presentation action buttons to ensure they all work correctly.

9. Set up the slide show for browsing at a kiosk.

10. Assume the kiosk that you will be using can only display a presentation up to 800×600; therefore, update the presentation resolution as 800×600.

11. Create a handout header and footer: Include the date and your name as the header and include the page number and text **[13-20your initials]** as the footer.

12. Save the presentation as **[13-20your initials]** in your Lesson 13 folder.

13. Print as handouts, nine slides per page, grayscale, landscape, framed.

Exercise 13-21

Prepare a presentation slide as a flyer in letter paper size.

1. Create a new presentation.

2. Change the orientation to Portrait and size to Letter Paper format.

3. Create a black triangle shape and a dark blue triangle shape as the background for a flyer, as shown in Figure 13-16, with about 1/2 inch of white around the edge of the page still showing. Group the objects.

Figure 13-16
Flyer background

4. Use the font Calibri for all text that you arrange in different ways as described in the next steps.

5. Create a text box with left alignment over the top of the black triangle and key:

   PowerWalk
   with
   Enter Enter
   June 21!

6. Make all of the text white with "PowerWalk" in italic at 60 points and the other text at 40 points.

7. Create a Good 4 U logo using WordArt and position it in the blank space in the text box you created in step 4.

8. Insert a picture showing someone power walking and position it on the right. Apply a border that blends with the blue triangle.

9. Create another text box with a white fill and no outline. Make the left edge of the box align with the text above as shown in Figure 13-17. Key Fitness counts . . . in 36 points, bold, left alignment.

10. Create a black oval shape with gold outline. Use center alignment and key Community in white, 18 points, bold.

Figure 13-17
Complete flyer

11. Duplicate the object three times and replace the shape text with Contribution, Promotions, and Fun.

12. Use alignment tools to align the ovals as shown in Figure 13-17 then draw a straight line to connect them. Select the four ovals and bring them to the front.

13. Save the presentation as **[13-21your initials]** in your Lesson 13 folder.

14. Print the slide to be distributed as a flyer.

Exercise 13-22 ◆ Challenge Yourself

Create a menu-based kiosk presentation using action buttons.

1. Open the file **WalkSponsor**.

2. After slide 1, insert a new slide with a Title Only layout. Key the title Menu.

3. Draw a rounded rectangle shape and change the shape style to Intense Effect-Accent 2.

4. Key **Purpose** on the rectangle.

5. Duplicate the rectangle four times and replace the text on each one as follows:

   Overview
   Advertising
   Training Seminars
   Sponsors

6. Use alignment and distribute features to position these shapes in a vertical arrangement to create a menu.

7. From the Insert menu, in the Illustrations group, click the Shapes button, and choose the Action Button: Custom 🔲 to link each button to the correct slide.

8. Insert a picture of a stop watch or timer on the left of the slide and recolor it to match the slide theme colors.

9. Move to slide 3, and draw a left arrow and key **Menu** in the bottom left corner of the presentation.

10. Change the arrow to Intense Effect-Accent 2 shape style to match the other menu items.

11. From the Insert menu, in the Illustrations group, click the Shapes button, and choose the Action button: custom 🔲 to link to the menu.

12. Copy the menu button and paste it in the same position on slides 4–7.

13. Set up the slide show to be viewed at a kiosk.

14. Check the spelling in the presentation and correct any spelling errors; Change "Clientel" to "Clientele".

15. Create a handout header and footer: Include the date and your name as the header and include the page number and text **[13-22your initials]** as the footer.

16. Save the presentation as **[13-22your initials]** in your Lesson 13 folder.

17. Print as handouts, four slides per page, grayscale, landscape, framed.

On Your Own

In these exercises you work on your own, as you would in a real-life work environment. Use the skills you've learned to accomplish the task—and be creative.

Exercise 13-23

Create a presentation describing the different type of products to be viewed at a collector's convention. Examples include: figurines, baseball gloves, bears, antiques, etc. Describe elements of a good collection of these items, inserting pictures, clip art, and diagrams as appropriate. Using rehearse timings, set transition timings allowing enough time for a viewer to read the content on each slide. Modify the timings as necessary. Create a menu-based presentation to be viewed at a kiosk and looped continuously as the collectors pass.

Insert a handout header and footer: Include the date and your name as the header and the page number and text **[13-23your initials]** as the footer. Save the presentation as **[13-23your initials]**. Preview and then print the presentation as handouts.

Exercise 13-24

Research and compare the different types of computer file storage. Compare the storage devices by price, reliability, compatibility, durability, and amount of information that they can hold.

Create a presentation summarizing your findings. Prepare the presentation sized for overhead transparencies that could be in a classroom where computer projection equipment was not available. Add appropriate graphics, and charts as necessary. As a final slide in the presentation, recommend what storage device that you believe is the best choice for students in computer classes today.

Insert a handout header and footer: Include the date and your name as the header and the page number and text **[13-24your initials]** as the footer. Save the presentation as **[13-24your initials]**. Preview and then print the presentation as handouts.

Exercise 13-25

Create a presentation describing the major tasks when purchasing and selling real estate. Create a menu-based presentation using action buttons for you to present at an upcoming meeting. Use appropriate clip art and graphics and walk the audience through the home purchasing and home selling process. Create a custom show for the purchasing process and one for the selling process. If available, set up the presentation for presenter view. After completing the presentation, view it as a slide show using on-screen tools to circle, draw, and emphasize objects in the presentation. Keep the ink annotations at the end.

Insert a handout header and footer: Include the date and your name as the header and the page number and text **[13-25your initials]** as the footer. Save the presentation as **[13-25your initials]**. Preview and then print the presentation as handouts.

Preparing for Electronic Distribution

OBJECTIVES

After completing this lesson, you will be able to:

1. Narrate a presentation.

2. Prepare and protect a presentation.

3. Prepare and publish a presentation.

4. Save in appropriate file types.

5. Convert between PowerPoint versions.

Estimated Time: 2 hours

MCAS OBJECTIVES

In this lesson:
PP07 4.2.1
PP07 4.3.1
PP07 4.3.2
PP07 4.3.3
PP07 4.3.4
PP07 4.5.4
PP07 4.5.5
See Appendix

For situations when you cannot meet in person, presentations can be distributed electronically as e-mail attachments. You might need to do this when you are working collaboratively with other people to develop the presentation or to follow up on details after a presentation you have delivered. Also, you could prepare the presentation for use as a Web page when people need to view it from different locations. If your audience needs to hear you discuss the slide content, then you can record narration so people can hear your voice for situations when you cannot meet face to face.

In this lesson you will use these features plus learn ways to make the file copy of your presentation more secure and to identify your presentation using document properties.

Narrating a Presentation

Narration can add value to a presentation designed to be shown at a kiosk or through a Web site because people watching the presentation can also hear your comments. You will need a microphone connected to your computer to record your narration.

Exercise 14-1 PLAN NARRATION FOR EACH PRESENTATION SLIDE

A narration can be recorded either before or during a presentation. Narration can be recorded on all slides or only on selected slides in a presentation. If narration is recorded and you decide you don't want to use it, you can turn off narration.

1. Open the file **Picnic**.

2. Before actually recording, spend a few minutes thinking about which slides in the presentation you will want to narrate.

3. Suggested text is provided in the Notes pane for slide 2. Add your thoughts to the Notes pane of each slide to use as a guideline when speaking to record your narration.

4. When finished, print a copy of the Notes pages to use as a script:

    a. Click the Microsoft Office Button , click Print and then click Print Preview.

    b. In the Page Setup group, click the arrow in the Print What box, and then click Notes Pages.

    c. Click Print.

5. Create a new Lesson 14 folder and save the presentation as **[14-1your initials]**. Leave the presentation open for the next exercise.

Exercise 14-2 RECORD NARRATION

When recording narration, you choose the slide to start on then begin recording your voice as you speak. You can pause if necessary. Depending on your preference, the narration can be either embedded (default) or linked to the presentation. Slide timings can be saved along with slide narration.

1. Move to slide 1 in the presentation.

2. From the Slide Show tab, in the Set Up group, click the Record Narration button .

3. From the Record Narration dialog box, shown in Figure 14-1, click the Set Microphone Level button Set Microphone Level... to set an appropriate volume for your microphone and verify that it is functioning properly.

Figure 14-1
Record Narration
dialog box

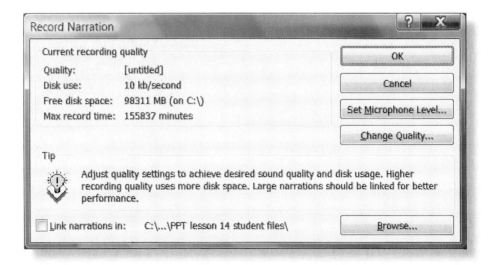

4. Accept the default option to not link the narration and click OK.

5. When prompted to Record Narration, click Current Slide to begin recording on slide 1. The screen will switch over to the Slide Show view.

6. Use the Notes pages printed in the first exercise to explain the content of the slides as you advance them.

7. If you need to pause for a moment, right-click in the Slide Show and choose Pause Narration. To continue, right-click in the Slide Show again and choose Resume Narration.

8. At the end of the slide show, choose Save to embed the narration to your presentation file and save the slide timings. Notice the sound icons that appear on each slide as a result of saving the narration.

9. View your slide show again and listen to the narration.

10. Save the presentation as **[14-2your initials]**. Close the presentation.

Preparing and Protecting a Presentation

Before you share a file copy of your presentation, you may need to check it for hidden or personal information that other people should not see. You may want to identify the presentation in some way or protect it so the presentation cannot be changed.

In the following exercises you will learn several different techniques using the **Kitchen** presentation.

Exercise 14-3   USE THE DOCUMENT INSPECTOR TO IDENTIFY HIDDEN INFORMATION

When preparing presentations, you routinely check the arrangement of all slide content and check spelling. However, when you distribute electronic versions of your presentation, you should check for hidden data that may be confidential or personal.

Electronic files contain *metadata,* which is data that describes data. It is hidden information that is placed in files automatically, such as the author's name and subject of the presentation. It can also include e-mail addresses or file information you may not want to share publicly. Microsoft's *Document Inspector* can identify and remove this hidden data or personal information.

1. Open the file **Kitchen**.

2. From the Microsoft Office Button 🔘, click Prepare, then Inspect Document. From the Document Inspector dialog box, check all of the options except Off-Slide Content, as shown in Figure 14-2.

Figure 14-2
Document Inspector

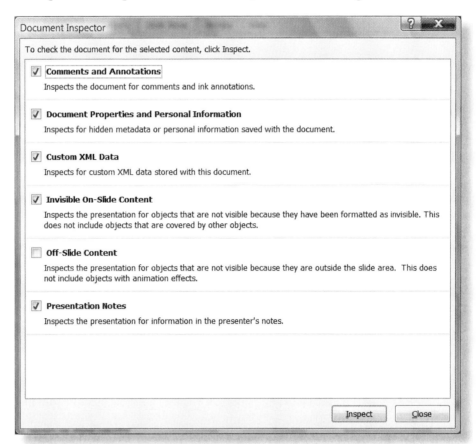

3. Click Inspect. The results are displayed with a check before each of the options where nothing is found. For Document Properties and Personal Information, information was found.

4. Click Close.

NOTE

At this point you could remove all properties of the document, in this case, a presentation. However, you will modify document properties in the next exercise.

Exercise 14-4   EDIT PRESENTATION PROPERTIES

Document Properties records metadata about the presentation file. The information is stored automatically and can be customized.

1. From the Microsoft Office Button 🔘, click Prepare, then Properties. A Document Information Panel opens between the Ribbon and

the slide area. It shows the title and other information about the presentation that needs to change.

2. Key the following information as shown in Figure 14-3.

Author:	**Your Name**
Title:	**Kitchen Planning Seminar**
Subject:	**Kitchen Planning**
Keywords:	**Training, Kitchen**
Category:	**Community Service Event**
Status:	**In progress**
Comments:	**This training event will be held as needed based on community interest.**

Figure 14-3
Document Properties

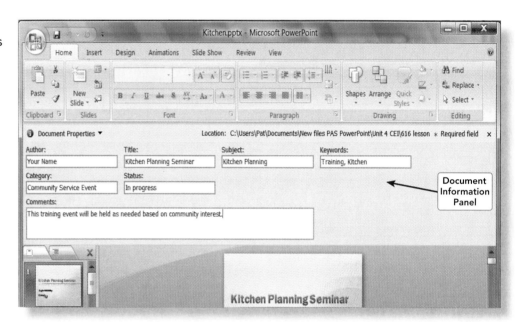

3. At the top of this area, click Document Properties and select Advanced Properties. From the dialog box that appears, click the tabs at the top and notice the type of information that appears in each tab, as shown in Figure 14-4.

General	The type of file, location of storage, file size, and file dates.
Summary	The information you entered will appear here and can be edited.
Statistics	File dates, revisions, editing time, and statistics.
Contents	Fonts, themes, and slide titles.
Custom	Name options, type, and value that can be added or deleted.

Figure 14-4
Advanced Document
Properties

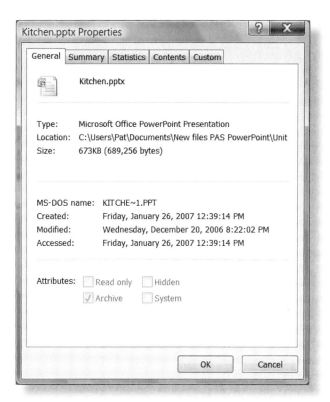

4. No changes are necessary now, so click OK. On the Document Information Panel, click the Close button.

5. Save the presentation as **[14-4your initials]** in your Lesson 14 folder. You will use this file again in Exercise 14-8.

Exercise 14-5   ADD A DIGITAL SIGNATURE

A *Digital Signature* can help to verify a document's integrity. However, Microsoft does not warrant the legality of this signature because laws affecting evidence vary. To use a digital signature, you must create your own *digital ID* or purchase one from a certificate authority. A digital ID is necessary because it provides a means to authenticate digital information. Once a presentation has been digitally signed, it becomes read-only to prevent modifications.

1. A presentation cannot be resaved once a signature has been added because any changes to the presentation invalidate the signature. Therefore, save the Kitchen Planning Seminar presentation now as **[14-5your initials]** in your Lesson 14 folder.

2. From the Microsoft Office Button click Prepare, then Add a Digital Signature. A warning box appears that briefly explains Microsoft's position, as shown in Figure 14-5.

Figure 14-5
Digital Signature
Legality Statement

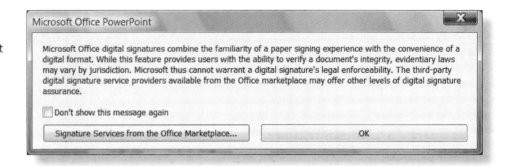

3. Click OK.

4. On the Get a Digital ID dialog box, click Create your own digital ID and notice the statement about how you will be able to authenticate your digital signature only on the computer you are using.

5. Click OK.

6. On the Create a Digital ID dialog box, key your personal information for Name, E-mail address, Organization, and Location.

7. Click Create.

8. On the Sign dialog box, for the Purpose for signing this document key **Presentation security**, as shown in Figure 14-6.

Figure 14-6
Sign dialog box

9. Click Sign. You will receive a Signature Confirmation message.

10. Click OK. A Signature task pane, as shown in Figure 14-7, appears on the right of your window showing that the document is signed and a Signature button appears in the Status Bar. Any edits to the document will invalidate the signature.

Figure 14-7
Signature task pane
and Signature button

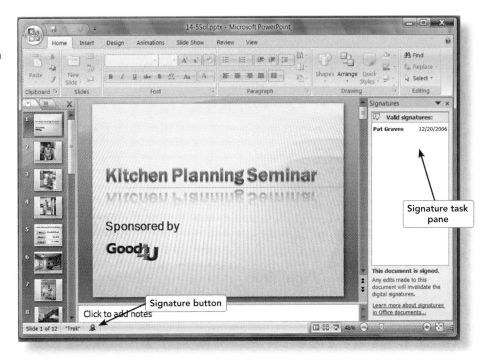

11. Close the Signatures task pane. Close the presentation.

Exercise 14-6 GRANT ACCESS BUT RESTRICT PERMISSION WITH PASSWORDS

Another important aspect of collaborating electronically in today's workplace is making sure that only the people authorized to receive information are the ones that can view the files, thereby protecting sensitive information. Through *Information Rights Management (IRM)*, Microsoft has provided a way to control access and restrict usage no matter where the information is because the permission is stored in the document file itself. However, you must sign up for this service from Microsoft; therefore, this exercise will help you understand this service but you will not be able to complete the exercise if you are using a computer in a computer classroom.

IRM was designed to help individuals protect personal and private information as well as to help organizations enforce policies about the control and distribution of their information. The level of permission can vary from very limited to full control:

- Read—users can read a presentation but cannot edit, copy, or print.

- Change—users can read, edit, and save a presentation, but they cannot print.

- Full control—users have full authoring privileges to modify the presentation and also set expiration dates or give others permission.

Different permission levels can be assigned to multiple people allowed to access the presentation. However, after a permission expires, the presentation can be opened only by the author or by users with full control.

1. Open the presentation **[14-4your initials]** from your Lesson 14 folder. (You need to use this file and not the one from the previous exercise because **14-5your initials** has a signature.)

2. From the Microsoft Office Button 🔘, click Prepare, Restrict Permission, then choose Restricted Access.

3. As you can see from the information on the Service Sign-Up dialog box in Figure 14-8, you must use a Windows Live ID to use this service.

Figure 14-8
Information Rights Management Service Sign-Up

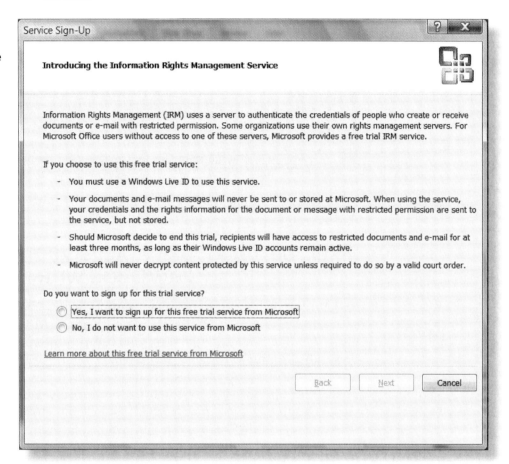

Service Sign-Up

Introducing the Information Rights Management Service

Information Rights Management (IRM) uses a server to authenticate the credentials of people who create or receive documents or e-mail with restricted permission. Some organizations use their own rights management servers. For Microsoft Office users without access to one of these servers, Microsoft provides a free trial IRM service.

If you choose to use this free trial service:

- You must use a Windows Live ID to use this service.

- Your documents and e-mail messages will never be sent to or stored at Microsoft. When using the service, your credentials and the rights information for the document or message with restricted permission are sent to the service, but not stored.

- Should Microsoft decide to end this trial, recipients will have access to restricted documents and e-mail for at least three months, as long as their Windows Live ID accounts remain active.

- Microsoft will never decrypt content protected by this service unless required to do so by a valid court order.

Do you want to sign up for this trial service?

- ◯ Yes, I want to sign up for this free trial service from Microsoft
- ◯ No, I do not want to use this service from Microsoft

Learn more about this free trial service from Microsoft

[Back] [Next] [Cancel]

4. If you have your own computer and want to participate in this service, select Yes and click Next. If you are using a computer in a computer classroom, click Cancel.

5. Leave the presentation open for the next session.

Exercise 14-7 MARK THE PRESENTATION AS FINAL

To prevent changes to a presentation when you distribute an electronic copy to other people, you can use the *Mark as Final* command to create a read-only file. This action helps to communicate that the presentation is complete, and it prevents inadvertent or intentional changes from being made.

However, this command is not considered a security feature because the Mark as Final status can be removed by people receiving the file.

1. Because the process of marking the presentation as final saves the presentation, you need to save your presentation now as **[14-7your initials]** in your Lesson 14 folder.

2. From the Microsoft Office Button , click Prepare, and then choose Mark as Final.

3. A confirmation message appears and a Mark as Final button is now displayed in the status bar as shown in Figure 14-9. Click OK.

Figure 14-9
Mark as Final message and button in Status Bar

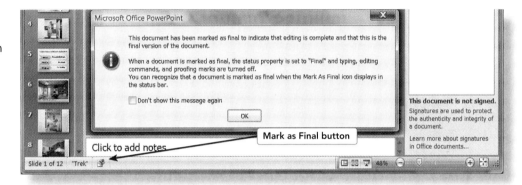

4. Click Close to close the presentation file so it will remain marked as final.

Preparing and Publishing a Presentation

Package for CD conveniently saves your presentation file and any linked files to a CD or to a folder that you designate to contain the files. This is especially helpful when you need to present with a computer that is not the one used to develop your presentation. You can include a viewer program that makes it possible to display the slide show without PowerPoint.

When you deliver your presentation using a different computer from the one you used to develop the presentation, the same fonts may not be available. Fortunately, you can embed, or save, the fonts used in your presentation so that they will be available wherever your presentation is displayed.

Exercise 14-8 SAVE EMBEDDED FONTS IN A PRESENTATION

You can *embed* almost any TrueType font included with the Microsoft Office installation. A TrueType font is one that can be sized to any size and that prints exactly the same as it appears on your screen.

1. Open **[14-4your initials]** before signatures or other restrictions were added to the file.

NOTE

If fonts have an icon that looks like a printer, they are available for use only on the currently selected printer for your computer.

2. Select some text on slide 2. From the Home tab, in the Font group, click to open the Font drop-down list. Notice that the font used in this presentation, Franklin Gothic Book, is a TrueType font. Most of the fonts available on your computer are likely to be TrueType fonts, indicated by the TrueType logo 🔤 to the left of the font name, as shown in Figure 14-10.

3. Press Esc to close the drop-down list.

Figure 14-10
Font types

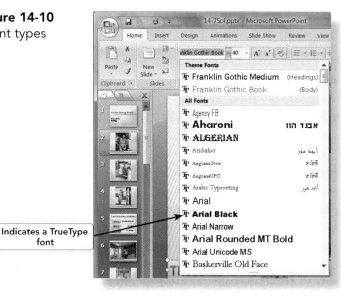

Indicates a TrueType font

4. From the Microsoft Office Button 🔘, choose Save As.

5. At the bottom of the Microsoft Office menu, click the PowerPoint Options button 🔘 PowerPoint Options.

6. From the PowerPoint Options dialog box, click the Save option on the left, as shown in Figure 14-11. Check the option Embed fonts in the file and then select the option Embed all characters (best for editing by other people).

Figure 14-11
Embedding fonts in the presentation file

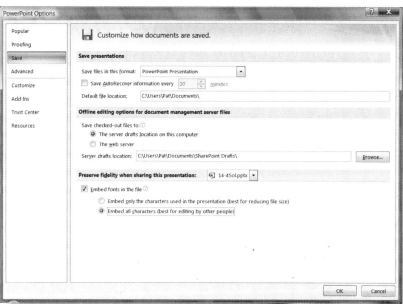

TIP

If you are concerned about file size and disk space, don't embed TrueType fonts unless necessary. Embedding fonts increases the size of your presentation files.

7. Click OK to close the PowerPoint Options dialog box.

8. Save the presentation as **[14-8your initials]** in your Lesson 14 folder. The presentation is now saved with the embedded TrueType font Franklin Gothic Book (the only font used in this presentation).

Exercise 14-9   SAVE WITH PACKAGE FOR CD TO MAINTAIN MEDIA LINKS

The *Package for CD* feature allows you to copy your presentation to a CD, a folder on the hard drive of your computer, or a network location. This feature also copies any linked files, such as movies and sounds, too, which is very important when you are using media files and presenting with a computer different from the one on which you developed the presentation. You may include a PowerPoint Viewer so people who do not have PowerPoint 2007 installed on their computers can still view your presentation.

Before using the Package for CD feature, decide how you want to store your presentation. You can copy to a blank recordable CD (CD-R) or a blank rewritable CD (CD-RW). If you do not have a CD available, you can save the presentation to a folder on your hard drive. If you save it to a hard drive folder, you can later copy the contents of the folder to the type of removable media you are using such as a flash drive or a CD-R, a CD-RW, or even a DVD-R.

In this exercise, you will save a presentation to a CD-R disk or to a different location that your instructor specifies. Make sure you have a blank CD-R disk on hand before beginning.

1. With the file **[14-8your initials]** open, move to slide 1. Resave the presentation as **[14-9your initials]**.

2. From the Insert tab, in the Media Clips group, click the Sound button then choose Sound from Clip Organizer so you can search for a music file from the Clip Art task pane that opens. In the Search for box key **song** and in the Results should be box check only Sounds. Click Go.

3. Choose the midi file **Maple Leaf Rag**, which is a brief music clip. Set it to play automatically as the slide show starts.

4. Close the ClipArt task pane.

5. From the Sound Tools Options tab, in the Sound Options group, click Hide During Show so the speaker icon will not be displayed.

6. From the Animations tab, in the animations group, click the Custom Animation button . From the Custom Animation task pane, set Play to Start With Previous.

7. On the midi file name in the list, click the list box down arrow and choose Effect Options.

8. On the Play Sound dialog box Effect tab, for Stop Playing select After then key **12** slides so the music will end with the last slide. Click OK.

TIP

If this file doesn't show up when you search for it, you can insert the file from your student data files.

NOTE

You may need to adjust these timings for your computer so all 12 slides are displayed while the music plays twice.

9. Click the Slide Sorter button 🖩 and select slide 1. Click the Transition More button ⊟ then from the gallery of transitions choose Wipe Right. Change the speed to Medium. Remove the check for On Mouse Click and check Automatically After and key **00:03** for 3 seconds. Click Apply To All.

10. For slides 1 and 5, increase the advance time to 6 seconds.

11. From the Slide Show tab, in the Set Up group, click the Set Up Slide Show button 🖳. For Show type click Presented by a speaker (full screen) and for Show options click Loop continuously until 'Esc' then click OK.

12. Move to slide 1 and view the presentation as a slide show to test the timings and music. If necessary, adjust the timings so the slide show is complete when the music ends for the second time.

13. Click the Microsoft Office Button 🔘, click Publish, and choose Package for CD. The Package for CD dialog box appears, as shown in Figure 14-12.

Figure 14-12
Package for CD dialog box

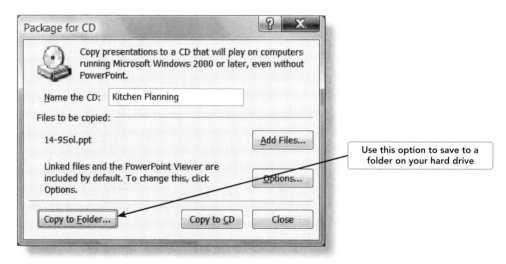

14. Give the CD a name that will identify its content; in the Name the CD box, key **Kitchen Planning**.

15. Click the Options button Options ▾ ; then on the Options window, notice that Viewer Package is already selected as the Package type. This selection will cause all of the PowerPoint Viewer files to be copied to your destination folder.

TIP

If you want to package a presentation that's not currently open, choose Add Files and select one or more files on your computer or network.

16. Check both Linked files and Embedded TrueType fonts, as shown in Figure 14-13. As you learned in the previous exercise, embedding fonts will save the fonts you used with your presentation. Saving linked files will copy the necessary files and maintain all the links to sound or movie files you may have used.

Figure 14-13
Options dialog box

17. Click OK to close this dialog box.

18. Click the Copy to CD button [Copy to CD] and the tray for the default CD burner will open if you have not already inserted a CD.

19. Insert the blank CD-R disk then press the eject button on your computer's drive to retract the CD. It will be detected automatically by PowerPoint and CD burning will begin. If you do not have a CD available, then you can click the Copy to Folder button [Copy to Folder...] and create a folder to hold the files.

[Copy to Folder...]

20. When the Package for CD process is complete, your presentation file plus linked files and PowerPoint Viewer files are saved in the location you specified.

21. Close the presentation without saving it, and then remove your CD-R disk and label it appropriately.

Exercise 14-10   USE A PACKAGE FOR CD FILE

With PowerPoint loaded, using a Package for CD file is easy because it loads just like any other PowerPoint file. The difference is that the presentation file and any linked files have been saved to the folder that you specified.

Figure 14-14
Run a PowerPoint presentation

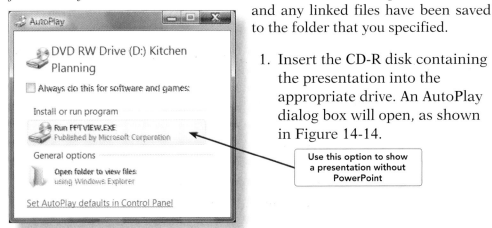

1. Insert the CD-R disk containing the presentation into the appropriate drive. An AutoPlay dialog box will open, as shown in Figure 14-14.

Use this option to show a presentation without PowerPoint

2. Click Run PPTVIEW.EXE to open PowerPoint Viewer and run the presentation automatically without PowerPoint being loaded. Close the presentation.

3. To display the presentation using PowerPoint, click Open folder to view files. The CD contents will automatically display (or if you saved to a folder, navigate to the Kitchen Planning folder in your Lesson 14 folder).

4. Click Views then Details to see all the files in this folder. You started with only the **[14-9your initials]** PowerPoint file and the MIDI sequence file for your music. All the other files were added so the presentation can play automatically without PowerPoint.

5. Double-click the presentation file to load it and test to be sure the music file plays appropriately.

6. Close the presentation and remove the CD-R disk.

Saving in Appropriate File Types

Now you will explore options available when you publish a presentation for viewing on the Web. Publishing a presentation means saving a copy in an HTML format (Hypertext Markup Language) that can be made available on a Web server or a shared folder.

The following are some of the options you can set when you publish a presentation to the Web:

- The title for the Web page. This title appears in the browser's title bar. If you do not specify a title, the title on slide 1 is used.

- What slides you want to publish. You can publish an entire presentation or just a part of it.

- Whether to display the presentation's animations in the browser. (Animations do not always run smoothly in a browser.)

- Whether to display notes pages. They will be displayed in a Notes pane similar to the way they look in Normal view.

- Which browser or browsers to use. If you don't know what browser viewers will use, you can specify multiple browsers. (This creates a larger file.)

Additional Web options are available by clicking Web Options on the Publish as Web Page dialog box.

Exercise 14-11   SAVING AS A WEB PAGE

When you choose the Web Page type from the Save As dialog box, several different adjustments can be made for how a presentation displays through a Web browser.

1. Start PowerPoint if necessary and open the file **Picnic**.

2. Click the Microsoft Office Button , choose Save As then PowerPoint Presentation.

3. From the Save As dialog box, change the Save as type: to Single File Web Page. The Save As dialog box changes and it now has additional options, as shown in Figure 14-15.

4. On the left, select your Lesson 14 folder then create a new folder called **Picnic-web**, as shown in Figure 14-15.

5. In the Save in box, navigate to your Lesson 14 folder. In the File name box, key Picnic.

Figure 14-15
Saving a presentation as a Web Page

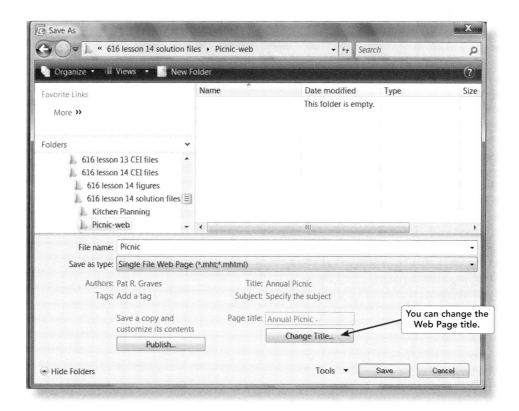

6. Click Change Title. In the Set Page Title dialog box, key **Good 4 U Annual Picnic**. Click OK. This text will appear on the title bar of your browser when you view the Web page.

7. Click Publish to display the Publish as Web Page dialog box, as shown in Figure 14-16.

8. In the Publish what? section, choose Complete presentation and deselect the Display speaker notes check box.

9. In the Browser support section, choose All browsers listed above. This option will enable your Web page to be viewed on browsers compatible with either Microsoft Internet Explorer or Netscape Navigator in the versions listed.

10. At the bottom of the dialog box, check Open published Web page in browser as shown in Figure 14-16. Checking this box will cause your presentation to automatically display in your browser after it is saved.

Figure 14-16
Publish as Web Page
dialog box

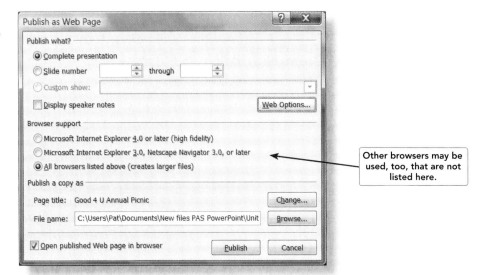

Other browsers may be used, too, that are not listed here.

NOTE

This exercise takes you through saving a presentation in HTML format so that it can be viewed on the Web with a suitable browser. To be viewed over the Internet or an Intranet, your presentation must be saved in a folder on a file server that is accessible over the Internet. If you have publishing privileges at an Internet or Intranet Web site, you can key the site's address (also known as its URL) in the File name text box in the Publish as Web Page dialog box. See your system administrator for more information about available Web sites.

11. Click Web Options (near the upper-right corner of the dialog box). In the Web Options dialog box, click the General tab, as shown in Figure 14-17. Here you can choose options for how the presentation will appear in a browser window. Make sure the following options are set:

- Select Add slide navigation controls.

- In the Colors list box, choose Presentation colors (text color).

- Do not select Show slide animation while browsing.

- Select Resize graphics to fit browser window.

Figure 14-17
Web Options dialog
box

12. Click the Files tab. Under File names and locations, make sure Organize supporting files in a folder is checked. This option collects the many files that publishing a Web page creates in a separate folder that you have created.

13. Click each of the other tabs in the Web Options dialog box and look at the options available for customizing your Web pages. No other changes are required. When you are finished, click OK to close the Web Options dialog box.

14. Click Publish to save the Web page and to close the Publish as Web Page dialog box. After a short period, your browser window will appear and display your presentation as a Web page, as shown in Figure 14-18. If you receive a protection message at the top of your browser window, click to display options and allow blocked content.

Figure 14-18
Presentation displayed in a browser

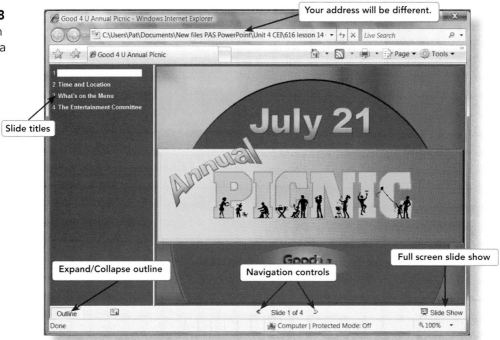

15. Leave the presentation open in the browser window for the next exercise.

Exercise 14-12 PREVIEW A PRESENTATION IN A BROWSER

As long as your computer has a browser installed on it, you can preview your presentation. You do not have to actually be online, because your browser is reading the file from its location on your computer.

1. Notice how the slide titles are displayed at the left. You can click on the titles to display each slide on the larger right area. At the bottom of the Outline pane, you can click the Outline button to expand the outline, and bulleted text will be displayed below the slide titles.

2. Browse the presentation by clicking the navigation controls for Next slide and Previous slide.

3. Click the Slide Show button 🖵 to see the presentation on the full screen. Use the [Spacebar] or left-click to advance forward. Once you have advanced the slides during the full-screen slide show, you can use the [Backspace] key to go back one slide at a time. Your navigation controls are not quite as smooth as when you are using PowerPoint.

4. When you are finished, close the browser window.

5. Close the presentation without saving it. (You already saved it as a Web page.) Close PowerPoint.

6. Right-click the Start button, choose Explore, then use the Navigation pane to locate your Lesson 14 folder.

TIP

To complete this exercise you have worked with these files on your local computer. However, all of these files would have to be on a file server for this presentation to be viewable as a Web Page over the Internet.

7. Open the Picnic-web folder. Notice the file **Picnic** that is an HTML document and the folder **Picnic_files** that were created. Both the file and the folder (containing supporting files) are needed to display a Web page.

8. Double click the **Picnic_files** folder to see the files that were created and scroll through the list, as shown in Figure 14-19.

Figure 14-19
List of created files

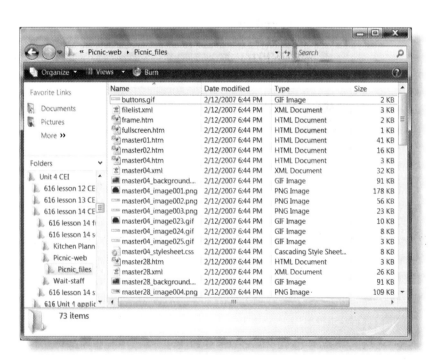

9. Close this window.

Exercise 14-13 LEARN ABOUT ADD-INS TO PUBLISH AS PDF OR XPS FILES

Add-Ins are supplemental programs that extend the functionality of Microsoft Office. Custom buttons and controls are added to the Ribbon when these programs are available. While this capability can be very useful for individuals, adding such customized features are rarely available to users in computer classroom situations where controls are likely placed on computers to assure consistency of features for instructional purposes. Microsoft provides protection through its Trust Center to test if an add-in is considered safe to install.

PowerPoint Options are used to install and manage add-ins. In this exercise, you will examine the add-ins that are installed on your computer.

NOTE

If you are working in a computer lab and this feature is not available on your computer, simply read through this exercise to gain familiarity with this capability.

1. Start a blank presentation.

2. From the Microsoft Office Button , click the PowerPoint Options button [PowerPoint Options], then choose Add-Ins. Your screen will look similar to Figure 14-20.

Figure 14-20
Active Application
Add-ins

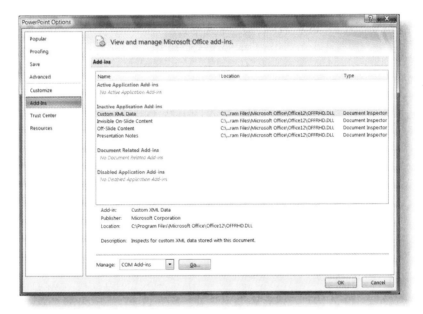

3. Add-Ins are listed in four categories:

- Active Application Add-ins—currently running in your Office program.

- Inactive Application Add-ins—available on your computer but not currently loaded.

- Document Related Add-ins—template files referenced by open documents.

- Disabled Application Add-ins—files that caused an Office program to crash.

4. Although not part of this exercise, if you had downloaded a PowerPoint add-in, the Manage list at the bottom of this dialog box would be used to install the add-in.

5. No changes are required now, so click OK.

6. Microsoft provides two popular add-ins that are designed to save files in a fixed-layout format that is easy to share and print but difficult to modify. These are:

   - Portable Document Format (PDF)—preserves document formatting for viewing online or printing as originally designed. This format is useful for commercial printing, too.

   - XML Paper Specification (XPS)—preserves document formatting for viewing online or printing as originally designed.

NOTE

Once this Add-in has been installed this finding option is no longer listed in the menu.

7. From the Microsoft Office Button , click Save As, then choose Find add-ins for other file formats.

8. This step will open a PowerPoint Help page where you can read about how to install and use the Publish as PDF or XPS add-in from Microsoft.

9. If you are using your own computer or have permission to install the Add-in, then click the link from this page to go to Microsoft's Download Center. Follow the instructions to download the 2007 Microsoft Save as PDF or XPS Add-in.

10. Close your presentation without saving and continue to the next exercise.

Converting Between PowerPoint Versions

Opening a presentation in PowerPoint 2007 that was saved in PowerPoint 97-2003, which represents several earlier versions, is very simple because the file will open automatically. You can preserve this version when you resave the file or upgrade it to 2007. However, a PowerPoint 2007 presentation cannot automatically be opened in an earlier version.

A PowerPoint 2007 presentation can be saved in a format for viewing with a previous version of PowerPoint; however, some of the graphics and visual effects may be displayed differently or not at all in an earlier version. The exercises in this section will guide you through the processes of converting between PowerPoint versions and help you understand what features of PowerPoint 2007 are not supported with PowerPoint 97-2003. These concepts can be very important for you to understand if you are collaborating with other people who have not yet upgraded to the current software version.

Exercise 14-14 CONVERT FROM A PREVIOUS POWERPOINT VERSION

Presentations created in earlier versions of PowerPoint have a file extension of .ppt. When you open one of these presentations, you can work on it in *Compatibility Mode* in case you need to open it again in the earlier PowerPoint version. If you want to upgrade the presentation to use 2007 capabilities, then you can resave it as a PowerPoint presentation which will give it a file extension of .pptx.

NOTE

If you are using a computer that has both PowerPoint 2003 and PowerPoint 2007, then be sure to launch PowerPoint 2007 and then open the file to operate in compatibility mode. If you attempt to open the file from a Windows Explorer or My Computer list, it will automatically open in PowerPoint 2003 instead.

1. Open the file **NewMenu1.ppt**.

2. Notice in the title bar the words "Compatibility Mode" follow the file name. This indicates that you are using a file from a previous version of PowerPoint.

3. Click the Microsoft Office Button , choose Save As then PowerPoint Presentation. Save the presentation as **[14-14your initials]** so you can use effects available in the current software.

4. From the Design tab, in the Themes group, change the design theme to Solstice.

5. On slide 1, delete the lower rectangle that now has the green border.

6. From the View tab, in the Presentation Views group, click Slide Master. On the left, scroll up to the top of the Slide Master layouts and delete all of the layouts with the gray background that are no longer being used.

7. On the first Slide Master layout, delete the rectangle that has the green border.

8. Change the Theme fonts to the Trek combination of Franklin Gothic.

9. Select the title placeholder and apply the Text Effects of Bevel, Circle, and Glow, Accent Color 1, 5 pt Glow. Add a Reflection effect of Tight Reflection, Touching.

10. Select the bulleted list placeholder, make it bold, and resize it down slightly from the top.

11. From the Slide Master tab, click Close Master View.

12. On slide 1, change the font size for the title to 66 points; reposition and move the title placeholder up toward the top of the slide.

13. On slide 1, search for a photograph of food that would be appropriate for this presentation. Position this image on the right and add a picture style of Reflected Bevel, Black. Now both the title and the picture have a reflection effect.

14. Resize the subtitle placeholder and reposition the text below the picture, as shown in Figure 14-21.

Figure 14-21
Completed title slide

15. On slide 2, delete the bulleted text and the bulleted text placeholder. Insert a SmartArt graphic. From the Cycle category choose the Multidirectional Cycle and click OK. Now key abbreviated text in the diagram shapes that will replace the bulleted list text.

    • Top shape   **Patron ordering habits monitored**

    • Lower left shape   **Patron survey conducted**

    • Lower right shape   **Weekly entrée orders tallied**

16. Increase the size of the SmartArt area and adjust the size of the shapes so the text size increases. Choose a Primary Theme Color of Dark Fill 2 and the Polished style, as shown in Figure 14-22.

Figure 14-22
Completed SmartArt graphic

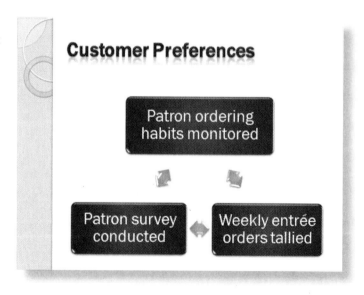

17. After slide 3, insert a new slide with the title "Number of Menu Items." Click the Table button 🔲 to insert a four-column, three-row table. Enter the text shown in Figure 14-23.

18. Reformat the table to blend with other effects used in the presentation.

   • Use the Medium Style 2, Accent 5.

   • Apply a Cell Bevel, Circle effect.

   • Add a Reflection, Half Reflection, 4 pt Offset.

   • Change the font to 32 points, bold.

   • Change number cell alignment to right.

Figure 14-23
Completed table

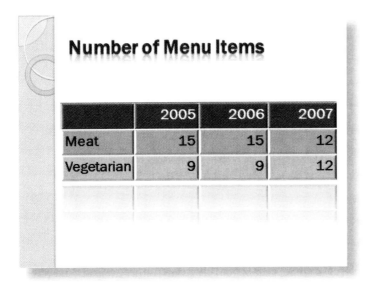

	2005	2006	2007
Meat	15	15	12
Vegetarian	9	9	12

Number of Menu Items

19. Save the presentation again as a PowerPoint 2007 file named **[14-14your initials]** and leave the presentation open for the next exercise.

Exercise 14-15 IDENTIFY FEATURES NOT SUPPORTED BY PREVIOUS POWERPOINT VERSIONS

If you know that you will need to save your presentation in an earlier version of PowerPoint, then you can run the *Compatibility Checker* to see what features used are not supported in earlier versions. While PowerPoint 2007 files can be saved to be compatible with PowerPoint 97-2003 versions, some of the features will change when the presentation is opened in an earlier version. The following list is not all-inclusive, but will give you an idea of the type of changes that will be made:

   • Charts—converted to OLE (Object Linking and Embedding) objects that can be edited; however, they may appear differently.

   • Drop shadows—soft shadows will be converted to hard shadows that can be edited.

- New PowerPoint 2007 effects—the objects where new effects are applied are converted to uneditable pictures.

- SmartArt graphics—the graphics are converted to uneditable pictures.

Once you understand these limitations, you could choose not to use those particular effects when you develop a presentation using PowerPoint 2007 when it must be displayed using the PowerPoint 97-2003 version.

1. From the Microsoft Office Button 🔘, click Prepare, then choose Run Compatibility Checker.

2. A dialog box will appear similar to the one shown in Figure 14-24 indicating the features used in this presentation that may be lost or degraded when you save.

Figure 14-24
Compatibility
Checker dialog box

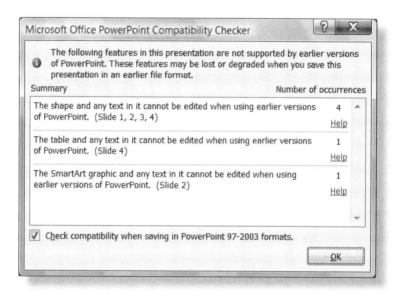

3. Click OK to indicate that you are aware of these features.

Exercise 14-16   SAVE AS COMPATIBLE WITH POWERPOINT 97-2003

When you work in compatibility mode, some of the PowerPoint 2007 features will not be available to you. The Compatibility Checker runs automatically when you save your presentation. While the list that is generated will give you a good indication of what will change, you should still open your file in the earlier version of PowerPoint that you will be using to test the impact of these changes. The results could be minor changes or you may need to redo some of the slides.

1. From the Microsoft Office Button 🔘, click Save As, then choose PowerPoint 97-2003 Presentation. Save the presentation as **[14-16 your initials]**. When the Compatibility Checker list appears showing the features that are not supported, click Continue.

2. If an earlier version of PowerPoint is available, open this file and test it to see how the slides have changed. They will look similar to the slides shown in Figure 14-25.

Figure 14-25
Slides after saving in the PowerPoint 97-2003 version

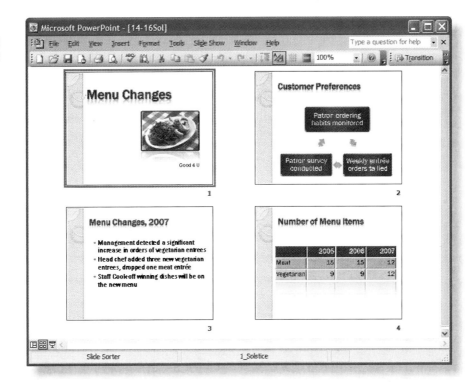

3. The slides look very similar in PowerPoint 2003, but the SmartArt graphic and table are now images that cannot be edited.

4. Close your presentation.

Lesson 14 Summary

- Narrating allows you to save the audio portion of a presentation using a microphone attached to your computer.
- You can record narration on all slides in a presentation or only on selected slides.
- Presentation Properties contain file metadata.
- The Document Inspector can remove hidden data or personal data that is stored as metadata with a file.
- A Digital Signature can help to verify a document's integrity through the use of a digital ID to authenticate the signature.
- Information Rights Management is a service provided by Microsoft so subscribers can control file access and restrict usage to protect personal and private information. The necessary permission is stored in the file itself.

- The Mark as Final command creates a read-only file that prevents changes in files distributed electronically.
- When preparing presentations that will be displayed on other computers, you should embed the fonts you use. Your presentation will be displayed with the fonts you used to create it.
- The Package for CD saves a presentation with all of its linked files on a CD or other removable medium for use on another computer. When using Package for CD, you have the option of embedding fonts.
- The PowerPoint Viewer can be included when you use the Package for CD feature and it enables your presentation to be run on a computer that does not have PowerPoint installed.
- Publishing a presentation to the Web means saving a presentation as an HTML file in a shared folder or on a Web server. You publish it by choosing Web Page in the Save as type drop-down list in the Save As dialog box. It is only viewable over the Internet if the folder in which it is saved is accessible over the Internet.
- To access a presentation that was saved as a Web page, open your browser and key the address in the Address box. Alternatively, use My Computer or Windows Explorer to navigate to the location where it is saved; then double-click its file name.
- Presentation files created in previous versions of PowerPoint will open in PowerPoint 2007 in compatibility mode. You can continue to work with these files in compatibility mode or upgrade the file to the 2007 version so all of PowerPoint's new features can be used.
- Before saving a PowerPoint 2007 file in a PowerPoint 97-2003 version, it is a good idea to check compatibility to identify the features used that are not supported by the older software.
- When a file is converted from PowerPoint 2007 to a PowerPoint 97-2003 version, some content will remain editable while other content will not. For example, text in bulleted lists will still be editable while text used in SmartArt graphics or tables will not. Graphics made possible only in the newer software will be converted to images that cannot be edited.

LESSON 14		Command Summary
Feature	**Button**	**Ribbon**
Print Notes Pages		Microsoft Office Button, Print, Print Preview, Print What, Notes Pages
Record Narration		Slide Show tab, Set Up group, Record Narration
Inspect Document		Microsoft Office Button, Prepare, Inspect Document
View Document Properties		Microsoft Office Button, Prepare, Properties

continues

LESSON 14	Command Summary *continued*	
Feature	**Button**	**Ribbon**
Add Digital Signature		Microsoft Office Button, Prepare, Add Digital Signature
Restrict Permission		Microsoft Office Button, Prepare, Restrict Permission
Mark as Final		Microsoft Office Button, Prepare, Mark as Final
Embed Fonts	PowerPoint Options	Microsoft Office Button, PowerPoint Options, Save option, Embed fonts in the file
Package for CD		Microsoft Office Button, Publish, Package for CD
Check for Compatibility		Microsoft Office Button, Prepare, Run Compatibility Checker
Publish a presentation to the Web		Microsoft Office Button, Save as Presentation, Save as type, Web Page
Change PowerPoint Options	PowerPoint Options	Microsoft Office Button, PowerPoint Options
Install Add-Ins		Microsoft Office Button, PowerPoint Options, Add-Ins

True/False Questions

Each of the following statements is either true or false. Select your choice by indicating T or F.

T F   1. Narration can be included with all slides in a presentation or on only some slides.

T F   2. Information saved in the Document Information Panel is there for security reasons and cannot be changed.

T F   3. A digital signature can help to verify a document's integrity.

T F   4. A read-only file is created when you use the Mark as Final command.

T F   5. The Package for CD feature will work with CD-R disks only.

T F   6. The Package for CD feature can be used to maintain links to media files.

T F   7. When working on a presentation that will be saved as a Web page, you can preview the presentation in a browser.

T F   8. PowerPoint 2007 presentations cannot be viewed in earlier versions of PowerPoint.

Short Answer Questions

Write the correct answer in the space provided.

1. How can you use Record Narration to also set slide timings?

2. Can a presentation Marked as Final be changed? If so, how?

3. How do you embed a font in a presentation?

4. Why is it important to use the Package for CD feature when you will be presenting using a computer different from the one you used to develop your presentation?

5. For a presentation saved as a Web page, where does the presentation title appear?

_____

6. How can you preview a presentation saved as a Web page if it is not accessible over the Internet?

_____

7. What happens to features unique to PowerPoint 2007, such as SmartArt and reflection effects, when you save a presentation as a PowerPoint 97-2003 version?

_____

Critical Thinking

Answer these questions on a separate page. There are no right or wrong answers. Support your answers with examples from your own experience, if possible.

1. Discuss techniques for getting organized before recording narration. How might a slide show that includes audio be useful where you work, for organizations to which you belong, or for your volunteer activities?

2. Describe why an individual might need to add a digital signature to a presentation distributed electronically.

Skills Review

Exercise 14-17

Record narration in a presentation.

1. Open the file **Beverage**.
2. Notice information provided in the Notes pane for four of the five slides.
3. To make recording easier, make a copy of this text by either printing notes pages or copying the text and pasting it into a Word document so it will fit on one page.
4. If you wish, revise the wording slightly.
5. On slide 3, make plans to point out that soft drinks and fruit juice account for the largest number of sales.
6. Move to slide 1. From the Slide Show tab, in the Set Up group, click the Record Narration button 🎙 and check the microphone level. Click OK then begin recording the information for this slide.
7. Advance through all five slides and record the appropriate text for each slide.

8. At the end of the slide show, choose Save to embed the narration in your presentation file and save slide timings.

9. Save the presentation as **[14-17your initials]** in your Lesson 14 folder. Close the presentation.

Exercise 14-18

Use the Document Inspector, edit Presentation Properties, and Mark as Final.

1. Open the file **Event**.

2. From the Microsoft Office Button ⓢ, click Prepare, then Inspect Document. Choose all selected content to inspect except Off-Slide Content. Click Inspect.

3. Document Properties and Personal Information is found. Click Remove All and click Close.

4. From the Microsoft Office Button ⓢ, click Prepare, then Properties. In the Document Information Panel, key the following information:

Author:	Your Name
Title:	Special Event Revenue
Subject:	Financial Analysis
Keywords:	New York
Category:	Income
Status:	Year-end summary report
Comments:	This summary represents New York only; additional reports will be made for other locations.

5. Close the Document Information Panel.

6. From the Microsoft Office Button ⓢ, click Prepare, and then choose Mark as Final. On the message box that appears, click OK. The Mark as Final button ⓢ should be displayed in the status bar.

7. Save the presentation as **[14-18your initials]** in your Lesson 14 folder. Close the presentation.

Exercise 14-19

Embed fonts using the Package for CD option and save to a folder.

1. Open the file **Apply**.

2. From the Microsoft Office Button ⓢ, click Publish, and then choose Package for CD. On the message box that opens, click OK.

3. Name the CD Apply Wait Staff.

4. Click the Options button [Options ▾] and check Embedded TrueType fonts. Click OK.

5. Click the Copy to Folder button [Copy to Folder...] and create a folder with in Lesson 14 folder on your hard drive or other storage location to hold the presentation called **Wait-staff**.

6. Click OK. On the message box that appears, click Yes.

7. From the Package for CD dialog box, click Close.

8. Test the presentation to be sure it runs using PowerPoint Viewer. Close the presentation.

Lesson Applications

Exercise 14-20

Convert a presentation from a PowerPoint 2003 version, apply chart styles, and record narration.

1. Open the file **Apparel.ppt**.

2. From the Microsoft Office Button , click Convert, then from the message box click OK. Save the persentation as **[14-20your initials]** in your lesson 14 folder.

3. For the pie chart on slide 4, change the chart style to Style 26.

4. For the column chart on slide 5, also change the chart style to Style 26.

5. Print the notes pages to use as a script while narrating the presentation or copy the text and paste it on a single page using Word.

6. Move to slide 1 and go through the presentation to rehearse how you will say the information for each slide. When you have practiced, then begin your recording.

7. At the end of the presentation, choose Save to embed the narration in your presentation file and save slide timings.

8. Save and close the presentation.

Exercise 14-21

Save a presentation as a Web page.

1. Open the file **InfoPak.**

2. Add transition effects of your choice.

3. From the Microsoft Office Button , click Save As, then choose PowerPoint Presentation.

4. From the Save As dialog box, create a new folder called **Franchise-info** in your Lesson 14 folder.

5. Name the file **[14-21your initials]**. For Save as type choose Single File Web Page.

6. Click Change Title and key Franchise Information Package and click OK.

7. Click Publish. In the Publish what? section, choose Complete presentation and deselect Display speaker notes.

8. In the Browser support section, choose All browsers listed above. Check Open published Web page in browser.

9. Click Web Options and on the General tab choose appropriate options.

10. In the Files tab, check Organize supporting files in a folder and click OK.

11. Click Publish to save the Web page.

12. Test your Web page presentation in a browser to be sure that it loads correctly.

Exercise 14-22

Identify effects not supported in earlier PowerPoint versions and save as a PowerPoint 97-2003 presentation.

1. Open the file **WaitStaff**.

2. From the Microsoft Office Button ⊚, click Prepare, then choose Run Compatibility Checker to see what features will not be supported in earlier versions of PowerPoint. The SmartArt graphics on slides 2 and 3 will be identified.

3. Click OK.

4. From the Microsoft Office Button ⊚, click Save As, then PowerPoint 97-2003 Presentation. Name the file **[14-22your initials]** in your Lesson 14 folder.

5. If an earlier version of PowerPoint is available, open the presentation to see if all slides display correctly. The SmartArt graphics will appear as images and the text will not be editable.

On Your Own

In these exercises you work on your own, as you would in a real-life work environment. Use the skills you've learned to accomplish the task—and be creative.

Exercise 14-23

What will you do in an emergency such as a severe storm or burglary? Assume you are a restaurant manager and you are faced with this question. Identify three different scenarios that would be dangerous to the patrons of your business. Develop a presentation for shift managers and wait staff at your restaurant with discussion points and guidelines for emergency preparedness to promote safety for your employees and patrons. Create a unique background design by customizing a design theme. Use Package for CD to make a copy of the presentation for each employee to review at home. Save the presentation as **[14-23your initials]**.

Exercise 14-24

Assume you are a member of the National Restaurant Association and you want to make employees in restaurants such as Good 4 U aware of services the organization provides for the restaurant and food service industry. Review the two sites for the association and its foundation, www.restaurant. org and www.nraef.org, to learn about what is available, then develop a presentation based on the concepts you think would be most helpful.

Customize a design theme for this topic. Mark the presentation a final and use the Package for CD feature to copy it to a CD that can be distributed to restaurants when you speak about the association. Save the presentation as **[14-24your initials].** Preview and then print the presentation as handouts.

Exercise 14-25

Prepare a presentation to promote family-oriented events and seasonal activities for your restaurant. You might plan a frightful Halloween dinner with special entrées, breakfast with Santa, or a New Year's Eve extravaganza. Prepare a presentation to announce and explain this event, then save it as a Web page. Assume that you would place the finished Web presentation on your restaurant's Web site in an area where you feature these seasonal events. Create a custom design theme for your topic. Save the presentation as **[14-25your initials]** then save it again as a Web page. Preview it in a browser and print the first slide through your browser.

Unit 4 Applications

Unit Application 4-1

Insert slides from another presentation, work with multiple open presentations, copy formatting from one presentation to another, use navigation tools, blank a slide, and copy and paste from another presentation.

1. Open the file **Fish1** and apply the Flow design theme.

2. After slide 2, insert slides 2 through 5 from the file **Fish2** using the Reuse Slides command.

3. View the changes to the presentation.

4. Open **Fish2**.

5. With both presentations open, use the Arrange All feature to see both presentations at once.

6. Copy the formatting from **Fish2** to **Fish1** for all of the slides.

7. Copy the rectangle on slide 1 of **Fish2** to slide 1 of **Fish1**. Send the rectangle to the back so it is behind the title and subtitle.

8. Close the **Fish2** file.

9. Working in the Slide Sorter, rearrange slides 3 through 6 so that they are in the following order:

Slide number	Title
3	Saltwater Fish
4	Freshwater Fish
5	Shellfish
6	Specialties

10. Return to Normal view; cut and paste the following text to a different slide:

Text to move	From	To
Catfish	slide 3	slide 4, first bullet position
Swordfish	slide 4	slide 3, second bullet position
Trout	slide 6	slide 4, second bullet position
Bass	slide 6	slide 4, third bullet position
Sushi	slide 4	slide 6, first bullet position
Sashimi	slide 4	slide 6, second bullet position

11. On slide 5 "Shellfish," promote all the bulleted text one level to first-level bullets.

12. Create a logo for Good 4 U with a seafood theme including clip art and colors to match the design theme as shown in Figure U4-1. Group the logo and save as **picture1** using the PNG file format to your Unit 4 folder. Insert the picture on the Slide Master by copying and pasting so that the logo is in the bottom center of all slides.

13. Copy the formatting from the text in the body text placeholder and the title text placeholder on slide 3 to slide 2.

14. Add clip art or pictures to liven up the presentation and apply appropriate picture effects and/or styles to the pictures to make them look professional.

15. Add animation and transitions to the objects and slides of the presentation.

Figure U4-1
Title slide with logo

16. Create a handout header and footer: Include the date and your name as the header, and the page number and text **[U4-1your initials]** as the footer.

17. Move to slide 1 and in the subtitle placeholder make "Server Training" appear on the second line. Save the presentation as **[U4-1your initials]** in your Unit 4 Applications folder.

18. View the presentation as a slide show using the navigation tools and blank a slide.

19. Preview and then print the presentation as handouts, six slides per page, grayscale, framed. Close the presentation.

Unit Application 4-2

Create slides from a Word outline, add speaker's notes, create an Excel chart screen capture, link an Excel worksheet, and save the presentation as a Web page.

1. Create a new presentation from the Word outline file **PwrWalk4** using the Slides from Outline command. You should have five slides. If you have more, delete the blank slides.

2. Apply the design theme Solstice with the Civic theme color.

3. Apply the Title Slide layout to slide 1.

4. On slide 2, promote the third-level bullets under "Healthy diet" to second-level bullets.

5. Reverse the positions of slide 4 and slide 5.

6. On slide 1, delete the word "Restaurant" and add the following speaker's note to slide 1: **Read first paragraph from mayor's press release on power walk event.**

7. On slide 2, change the case of the body text placeholder to sentence case.

8. Insert two new slides after slide 5 with the Title only layout.

9. Open the Excel file **Calories1** and save it in your Unit 4 Applications folder.

10. Make a screen capture of chart 1 and paste it on slide 6. Crop to only show the chart.

11. At the bottom of the Excel file, click on Sheet 1 and copy from A1:H12 and create a link to the Excel Worksheet on slide 7. Resize the pasted link as necessary for an attractive appearance.

12. Key **Why Walk?** as the title of slide 6 and slide 7.

13. Create a text box on the lower part of slide 5. Key the text **We hope to see you here!** Make the text Verdana, 28 points, bold, and italic. Rotate the text box slightly.

14. Create a handout header and footer: Include the date and your name as the header, and the page number and text **[U4-2your initials]** as the footer.

15. Move to slide 1 and save the presentation with the filename **[U4-2your initials]** in your Unit 4 Applications folder. Save it again as a Web page.

16. If possible, view your presentation as a Web page. If not, view it as a slide show.

17. Preview and print the presentation as handouts, four slides per page, grayscale, framed. Print the notes page for slide 1. Close the presentation.

Unit Application 4-3

Insert comments, print slide markup, use the annotation pen, set timings, adjust screen resolution, and mark the presentation as final.

1. Open **Summertime**.

2. Insert a slide with the Title Only layout after slide 1 and key **Timeline for Roll-Out of New Products** as the title.

3. Draw a timeline using constrained lines, text boxes for the months, and callout boxes labeling each major event as shown in Figure U4-2.

Figure U4-2
Completed timeline

4. Insert a comment on slide 4 about the Tex-Mex Tofu and key, **The Tex-Mex Tofu was a hit, but the crowd overwhelmingly chose the Swordfish as number 1. This could be a great start for next summer!**

5. Insert a comment on slide 5 about the Grilled Bananas and Peaches and key, **The combination of bananas and peaches was not favored.**

6. Add slide transitions to the presentation, and apply appropriate animations to the text and objects.

7. Insert appropriate clip art or pictures.

8. Create a handout header and footer: Include the date and your name as the header, and the page number and text **[U4-3your initials]** as the footer.

9. Move to slide 1 and save the presentation with the filename **[U4-3your initials]** in your Unit 4 Applications folder.

10. Set timings for the presentation using rehearse timings as you read the items on the slide.

11. View the presentation as a slide show and use the annotation pen to write **WOW!** on slide 6, finish the presentation, and choose to Keep the annotations.

12. For Document Properties, key your name and add an appropriate title.

13. Preview and print the presentation as handouts, six slides per page, grayscale, framed. Print the slide markup.

14. Mark the presentation as final and close the presentation.

Unit Application 4-4 ◆ Using the Internet

Create a presentation, prepare speaker's notes, record narration, and package for CD.

Use the Internet to research the most prevalent types of manufacturing industries in the state where you live or go to school.

Create a presentation with at least six slides describing these industries, including historical information and what the future holds for them. Include at least one chart or diagram and at least one table.

Add visual interest to your presentation by choosing an appropriate design theme and color theme. Customize the theme as you see fit and add graphic elements to enhance it.

Compose a script for your presentation and use the script to create suitable notes pages for each slide.

In the slide footer, include the text **Prepared by** followed by your name. Include the slide number on all slides but not the date. In the handout footer, include the completed filename **[U4-4your initials]**. In the handout header, key **Presented to** and then identify to whom you would be giving this presentation. Include in the handout the date you would be delivering the presentation and the page number.

Preview and then print your presentation as handouts; then print the notes pages for each slide. You will read these pages as narration for your presentation.

As you record your narration, read the notes pages that you printed earlier. Make sure that the microphone is turned on and correctly recording before starting.

Use the Package for CD feature to save this presentation in a folder within your Unit 4 folder with the filename **[U4-4your initials]**.

PowerPoint 2007 MCAS Objectives

Unit 1—Basic Skills	MS Objectives

Lesson 1: Getting Started in PowerPoint

1 Exploring PowerPoint
1-1 Identify Parts of the PowerPoint Window
1-2 Use the Quick Access Toolbar
1-3 Open an Existing Presentation
1-4 Work with Ribbons, Tabs, Groups, and Command Buttons
1-5 Use Microsoft Office PowerPoint Help

2 Viewing a Presentation
1-6 Use Normal and Slide Sorter Views
1-7 Use the Slides and Outline Pane
1-8 Move from Slide to Slide
1-9 Use the Zoom and Fit to Window
1-10 Run a Slide Show
1-11 Observe Animation Effects

3 Adding Text Using Placeholders
1-12 Key Placeholder Text
1-13 Change and Reset Placeholder Layout

4 Naming and Saving a Presentation
1-14 Create a Folder for Saving Your Files   4.3.6
1-15 Name and Save a Presentation

5 Preparing Presentation Supplements
1-16 Preview a Presentation
1-17 Print a Slide, Notes Page, Outline, and Handout   4.4.2
1-18 Choose Print Options

6 Ending Your Work Session
1-19 Close a Presentation and Exit PowerPoint

Summary of Lesson 1 MCAS Objectives	PP07 4.3.6
	PP07 4.4.2

Lesson 2: Developing Presentation Text

1 Creating a New Blank Presentation
2-1 Start a New Blank Presentation   1.1.1
2-2 Add New Slides and Use Slide Layouts   1.5

2 Using the Font Group Commands
2-3 Change the Font Face and Font Size   2.2.3
2-4 Apply Bold, Italic, Color, and Shadow   2.2.3
2-5 Change the Case of Selected Text
2-6 Change Line Spacing within Paragraphs   2.2.6
2-7 Change Line Spacing between Paragraphs   2.2.6
2-8 Use the Font Dialog Box to Make Multiple Changes

Unit 1—Basic Skills	MS Objectives
3 Adjusting Text Placeholders	
2-9 Select a Text Placeholder	
2-10 Change Text Horizontal Alignment	2.1.4
2-11 Resize a Placeholder	2.1.2
2-12 Move a Placeholder	
4 Working with Bullets and Numbering	
2-13 Remove Bullets	2.2.5
2-14 Promote and Demote Bulleted Text	2.2.5
2-15 Change the Color and Shape of a Bullet	2.2.5
2-16 Create a Bullet from a Picture	2.2.5
2-17 Create Numbered Paragraphs	2.2.5
2-18 Use the Ruler to Adjust Paragraph Indents	
5 Working with Text Boxes	
2-19 Create a Text Box	2.1.1, 2.1.2
2-20 Change the Font and Font Color	2.1.3
2-21 Rotate and Change Text Direction	2.1.4
2-22 Wrap Text and Change Alignment	2.1.4
Summary of Lesson 2 MCAS Objectives	PP07 1.1.1
	PP07 1.5
	PP07 2.1.1
	PP07 2.1.2
	PP07 2.1.3
	PP07 2.1.4
	PP07 2.2.3
	PP07 2.2.5
	PP07 2.2.6
Lesson 3: Revising Presentation Text	
1 Selecting, Rearranging and Deleting Slides	
3-1 Select Multiple Slides	1.5
3-2 Rearrange Slide Order	1.5
3-3 Delete Slides	1.5
2 Using the Clipboard	
3-4 Use Cut, Copy, and Paste to Rearrange Slides	2.2.1
3-5 Use Cut, Copy, and Paste to Rearrange Text	2.2.1, 2.3.2
3-6 Clear the Clipboard Task Pane	2.2.1
3-7 Use Undo and Redo	
3-8 Use Format Painter	2.2.4
3 Checking Spelling and Word Usage	
3-9 Check Spelling	
3-10 Use Research	
3-11 Use the Thesaurus	
3-12 Use Find and Replace	
4 Inserting Headers and Footers	
3-13 Add Slide Date, Page Number, and Footer	1.3
3-14 Add Handout Date, Page Number, and Header	

Unit 1—Basic Skills	MS Objectives
5 Applying a Consistent Background and Color Scheme	
3-15 Select a Design Theme	1.2.1
3-16 Change Theme Colors	
3-17 Change Theme Fonts	
3-18 Change Theme Effects	
3-19 Create New Theme Fonts	
6 Adding Movement Effects	
3-20 Apply Slide Transitions	1.4.2
3-21 Adjust Sounds and Speeds	
Summary of Lesson 3 MCAS Objectives	PP07 1.2.1
	PP07 1.3
	PP07 1.4.2
	PP07 1.5
	PP07 2.2.1
	PP07 2.2.4
	PP07 2.3.2

Unit 2—Presentation Illustration	MS Objectives
Lesson 4: Working with Graphics	
1 Working with Shapes	
4-1 Draw Shapes—Rectangles, Ovals, and Lines	3.3.2
4-2 Draw Horizontal Constrained Lines	
4-3 Add Connector Lines	
4-4 Create Squares and Circles	
4-5 Resize and Move Shapes	
4-6 Use Adjustment Handles to Modify Shapes	
4-7 Place Text in a Shape and Rotate	3.3.4, 3.5.1
2 Inserting Clip Art Images	
4-8 Find Clip Art then Modify a Search	3.3.3
4-9 Preview and Insert Clip Art Images	3.3.3
4-10 Rearrange, Delete, Copy, Paste, and Duplicate Clip Art Images	3.5.2
4-11 Group and Ungroup Images and Text	3.5.3
3 Inserting and Enhancing a Picture	
4-12 Insert Stock Photography	
4-13 Crop a Picture	
4-14 Recolor a Picture then Reset Colors	3.4.2
4-15 Apply a Picture Style	3.3.1, 3.4.1
4-16 Insert a Picture from File	
4-17 Adjust Contrast and Brightness	3.4.2
4-18 Change a Picture Shape	
4-19 Add a Border to a Picture	
4-20 Apply Picture Effects	
4 Creating WordArt	
4-21 Create and Modify WordArt Text	2.2.2, 2.2.7
4-22 Apply WordArt Effects	2.2.7
4-23 Edit WordArt Text Fill and Text Outline Colors	2.2.7

Unit 2—Presentation Illustration	MS Objectives

Lesson 6: Creating Charts

1 Creating a Chart
6-1 Choose a Slide Layout for a Chart   3.6.1
6-2 Edit the Data Source
6-3 Switch Rows/Column Data

2 Formatting a Column Chart
6-4 Explore Parts of a Chart
6-5 Change Chart Styles
6-6 Format the Vertical (Value) and Horizontal (Category) Axes
6-7 Apply Different Chart Layouts
6-8 Change or Remove the Legend   3.6.4
6-9 Apply or Remove Gridlines

3 Using Different Chart Types
6-10 Switch to Other Chart Types   3.6.2
6-11 Add a Secondary Chart Axis
6-12 Combine Chart Types
6-13 Format a Primary and Secondary Axis

4 Working with Pie Charts
6-14 Create a Pie Chart
6-15 Add Pie Slice Labels
6-16 Apply 3-D Rotation

5 Enhancing Chart Elements
6-17 Adding Shapes for Emphasis
6-18 Change Colors in Chart Areas   3.6.3
6-19 Add a Picture Fill Behind Chart

Summary of Lesson 6 MCAS Objectives	PP07 3.6.1
	PP07 3.6.2
	PP07 3.6.3
	PP07 3.6.4

Lesson 7: Creating Diagrams with SmartArt Graphics

1 Choosing SmartArt Graphics
7-1 Use Diagrams for Communication Purposes
7-2 Use Lists to Show Groups of Information   3.1.1, 3.2.1
7-3 Use Process Diagrams to Show Sequential Workflow Steps   3.1.1, 3.2.1
7-4 Use Cycle Diagrams to Show a Continuing Sequence   3.1.1, 3.1.2, 3.2.1

2 Enhancing the Diagrams
7-5 Apply Shape Quick Styles   3.2.3
7-6 Adjust 3-D Format and Rotation
7-7 Adjust the Overall Size and Layout of the Diagram   3.2.4
7-8 Add Shapes
7-9 Change Colors and Reset the Graphic   3.2.2

3 Preparing an Organization Chart
7-10 Create an Organization Chart
7-11 Insert Subordinate Shapes   3.2.6
7-12 Add Assistant and Coworker Shapes   3.2.6
7-13 Change Layout, Delete, and Rearrange Shapes   3.2.6
7-14 Change Shape Sizing and Styles

Unit 2—Presentation Illustration	MS Objectives
4 Creating Other SmartArt Diagrams	
7-15 Create a Radial Diagram	
7-16 Create a Gear Diagram	
7-17 Insert a Continuous Picture List	
5 Change Diagram Types and Orientation	
7-18 Change Diagram Types	3.2.7
7-19 Change the Orientation of Diagrams	3.2.5
Summary of Lesson 7 MCAS Objectives	PP07 3.1.1
	PP07 3.1.2
	PP07 3.2.1
	PP07 3.2.2
	PP07 3.2.3
	PP07 3.2.4
	PP07 3.2.5
	PP07 3.2.6
	PP07 3.2.7

Unit 3—Visual Impact	MS Objectives
Lesson 8: Designing Original Illustrations	
1 Changing the Outline Color and Weight	
8-1 Apply Solid and Gradient Colors to Outlines	
8-2 Adjust Line Style	
8-3 Apply Arrowhead	
8-4 Adjust Transparency and Rotate	3.4.1, 3.5.1
2 Working with Solid and Gradient Colors	
8-5 Add a Theme Solid Fill Color to a Shape	3.4.1
8-6 Choose a Standard Color or Custom Color	
8-7 Choose a Gradient Fill for Objects	
8-8 Adjust Gradient Colors	
2 Working with Pictures and Textures	
8-9 Apply a Picture Fill	3.4.1
8-10 Apply a Texture Fill	3.4.1
8-11 Use Offsets to Stretch or Reposition a Picture	
8-12 Adjust Transparency and Picture Rotation	3.4.2, 3.5.1
8-13 Use Precise Size Dimensions	3.5.1
4 Applying Shape Effects	
8-14 Add Shadow and Reflection	3.4.1
8-15 Add Glow and Soft Edges	
8-16 Add Bevel Effects	
8-17 Adjust 3-D Rotation	
5 Adjusting Presentation Color Settings	
8-18 Choose the Grayscale Version	
8-19 Choose the Pure Black-and-White Version	
Summary of Lesson 8 MCAS Objectives	PP07 3.4.1
	PP07 3.4.2
	PP07 3.5.1

Unit 3—Visual Impact	MS Objectives
Lesson 9: Refining Original Illustrations	

1 Working with Multiple Objects	
9-1 Select Multiple Objects Using the Shift Key	
9-2 Select Multiple Objects by Drawing a Selection Rectangle	
9-3 Remove an Object from a Group of Selected Objects	
9-4 Create a Diagram with Shapes and Connector Lines	

2 Aligning, Distributing, and Flipping Shapes	
9-5 Align Objects Horizontally and Vertically	3.5.1, 3.5.4
9-6 Distribute Objects Horizontally and Vertically	3.5.1, 3.5.4
9-7 Flip and Rotate Objects	3.5.1, 3.5.4

3 Working with Layers of Objects	
9-8 Bring Objects Forward or Backward	3.5.2
9-9 Bring Objects to the Front or Send to the Back	3.5.2
9-10 Use the Selection and Visibility Pane to Change Stacking Order	

4 Grouping, Ungrouping, and Regrouping Objects	
9-11 Group Objects	3.5.3
9-12 Ungroup and Regroup Objects	3.5.3
9-13 Format Part of a Grouped Object	

5 Editing Images	
9-14 Recolor Clip Art	
9-15 Ungroup and Change Fill Color for Parts of a Clip Art Image	
9-16 Delete Parts of an Image	
9-17 Create Soft Edges	
9-18 Compress Pictures	4.3.5

Summary of Lesson 9 MCAS Objectives	PP07 3.5.1
	PP07 3.5.2
	PP07 3.5.3
	PP07 3.5.4
	PP07 4.3.5

Lesson 10: Animating and Using Multimedia Effects	

1 Applying Animation	
10-1 Add an Entrance Effect	2.4.1, 2.4.3
10-2 Add an Emphasis and Exit Effect	2.4.3
10-3 Apply a Motion Path to an Object	2.4.3
10-4 Remove Custom Animations	2.4.2
10-5 Animate Chart Elements	

2 Modifying and Enhancing Animations	
10-6 Modify Animations	2.4.2
10-7 Add Sound Effects to Animations	
10-8 Modify the Order of Animations	
10-9 Modify an Animation's Timing	
10-10 Copy an Animated Object	2.3.2

Unit 3—Visual Impact	MS Objectives
3 Adding Sound Effects	
10-11 Insert a Sound from the Clip Organizer	2.3.4
10-12 Control Start and Play Effect Options	2.3.4
10-13 Insert a Sound Clip from a File	2.3.4
10-14 Play a CD Audio Track	
10-15 Record Sound	
4 Adding Movies	
10-16 Insert a Movie from the Clip Organizer	2.3.4
10-17 Insert a Movie from a File	2.3.4
5 Inserting Hyperlinks	
10-18 Add Hyperlinks to Selected Slides	2.3.3
10-19 Create Action Buttons for Menu Options	2.3.3, 2.3.4
10-20 Add Hyperlinks to Other Presentations	2.3.3
10-21 Add Hyperlinks to Other Files	2.3.3
10-22 Add Hyperlinks to Web Pages	2.3.3
Summary of Lesson 10 MCAS Objectives	PP07 2.3.2
	PP07 2.3.3
	PP07 2.3.4
	PP07 2.4.1
	PP07 2.4.2
	PP07 2.4.3
Lesson 11: Customizing Themes and Master Slides	
1 Customizing an Existing Theme	
11-1 Examine Built-In Color Themes	1.2.1
11-2 Create and Save Custom Theme Colors	
11-3 Change Theme Fonts and Examine Built-In Effects	
11-4 Save a Custom Theme	
2 Formatting Background Styles	
11-5 Apply Solid Fill and Gradient Backgrounds	1.2.2
11-6 Apply Textured Backgrounds	
11-7 Create a Picture Background from a File	
3 Working with Slide Masters for a Custom Design Template	
11-8 Rearrange Background Graphics	2.3.2
11-9 Change and Reposition Placeholders	2.2.3
11-10 Change Bullets	
11-11 Insert an Image and Add WordArt	1.3, 2.2.2, 2.2.7, 2.3.2
11-12 Adjust Footer Positioning and Add Footer Text	1.3
11-13 Adjust Slide Elements to Fit the New Theme	1.3
11-14 Save a New Design Template	
11-15 Adjust a Presentation Theme	
4 Applying Themes and Design Templates from Microsoft Office Online	
11-16 Search Microsoft Office Online	2.3.1
11-17 Browse for Themes	
5 Customizing a Handout Master and a Notes Master	
11-18 Work with the Notes Master	
11-19 Work with the Handout Master	4.4.1

Unit 3—Visual Impact	MS Objectives
Summary of Lesson 11 MCAS Objectives	PP07 1.2.1
	PP07 1.2.2
	PP07 1.3
	PP07 2.2.2
	PP07 2.2.3
	PP07 2.2.7
	PP07 2.3.1
	PP07 2.3.2
	PP07 4.4.1

Unit 4—Development and Distribution	MS Objectives

Lesson 12: Integrating with Other Programs

1 Using Content from Other Sources

12-1 Import an Outline from Word	1.1.4
12-2 Insert a Microsoft Word Document	
12-3 Reuse Slides from a Different Presentation	2.3.1
12-4 Link an Excel Worksheet	

2 Inserting Screen Captures

12-5 Create and Insert a Screen Capture	

3 Working with Multiple Open Presentations

12-6 Use Cascade to Layer Multiple Presentation Windows	
12-7 Use Arrange All to See Multiple Presentation Windows	
12-8 Copy and Paste between Presentations	2.3.2
12-9 Use Format Painter to Copy Formatting between Presentations	

4 Collaborating with Others

12-10 Insert and Edit Comments in a Presentation	4.1.1, 4.1.2
12-11 Print Slide Comments	

5 Saving Objects as Pictures

12-12 Design a Logo and Save as a Picture	
12-13 Save a Slide as a Picture	4.3.6

Summary of Lesson 12 MCAS Objectives	PP07 1.1.4
	PP07 2.3.1
	PP07 2.3.2
	PP07 4.1.1
	PP07 4.1.2
	PP07 4.3.6

Lesson 13: Preparing a Presentation for Delivery

1 Controlling a Slide Show

13-1 Use Rehearse Timings to Set Automatic Slide Timings	4.5.2
13-2 Set Timings Manually	
13-3 Set Up a Slide Show	
13-4 Create and Run Custom Shows	4.5.1, 4.5.5
13-5 Create Action Buttons for Custom Shows	

2 Adjusting for Different Computer Screen Sizes

13-6 Adjust On-screen Show Aspect Ratio	
13-7 Adjust Screen Resolution	
13-8 Show Presenter View	

Unit 4—Development and Distribution	MS Objectives
3 Presenting with Projection Equipment	
13-9 Use On-Screen Navigation Tools	4.5.3
13-10 Use Annotation Pens	4.5.3
13-11 Blank Slides	4.5.3
13-12 Hide and Reveal Slides	4.5.1
4 Preparing Presentations for Delivery in Other Formats	
13-13 Prepare a Presentation in 35mm Format	
13-14 Prepare a Presentation for Use as Overhead Transparencies	
5 Creating a Menu-Based Kiosk Presentation	
13-15 Provide Navigation Options	4.5.1
13-16 Use Set Up Show to Create a Kiosk Presentation	
Summary of Lesson 13 MCAS Objectives	PP07 4.5.1
	PP07 4.5.2
	PP07 4.5.3
	PP07 4.5.5
Lesson 14: Preparing for Electronic Distribution	
1 Narrating a Presentation	
14-1 Plan Narration for Each Presentation Slide	
14-2 Record Narration	4.5.5
2 Preparing and Protecting a Presentation	
14-3 Use the Document Inspector to Identify Hidden Information	4.3.2
14-4 Edit Presentation Properties	
14-5 Add a Digital Signature	4.2.1
14-6 Grant Access but Restrict Permission with Passwords	4.3.3
14-7 Mark the Presentation as Final	4.3.4
3 Preparing and Publishing a Presentation	
14-8 Save Embedded Fonts in a Presentation	
14-9 Save with Package for CD to Maintain Media Links	4.5.4
14-10 Use a Package for CD File	4.5.4
4 Saving in Appropriate File Types	
14-11 Saving as a Web Page	
14-12 Preview a Presentation in a Browser	
14-13 Learn About Add-Ins to Publish as PDF or XPS Files	
5 Converting Between PowerPoint Versions	
14-14 Convert from a Previous PowerPoint Version	
14-15 Identify Features Not Supported by Previous PowerPoint Versions	4.3.1
14-16 Save as Compatible with PowerPoint 97-2003	4.3.1
Summary of Lesson 14 MCAS Objectives	PP07 4.2.1
	PP07 4.3.1
	PP07 4.3.2
	PP07 4.3.3
	PP07 4.3.4
	PP07 4.5.4
	PP07 4.5.5

Microsoft Objective/Domain		Covered in Lesson Number
Creating and Formatting Presentations		
1.1	Create new presentations	See Below
1.1.1	Create presentations from blank presentations	Lesson 2
1.1.2	Create presentations from templates	Lesson 11
1.1.3	Create presentations from existing presentations	Lesson 12
1.1.4	Create presentations from Microsoft Office Word 2007 outlines	Lesson 12
1.2	Customize slide masters	See Below
1.2.1	Apply themes to slide masters	Lesson 3, Lesson 11
1.2.2	Format slide master backgrounds • Add background graphics to slide masters • Apply Quick Styles to backgrounds • Change font theme	Lesson 11
1.3	Add elements to slide masters • Add slide numbers • Add footers • Add headers • Add placeholders • Add graphic elements • Add date and time • Set date and time to update automatically	Lesson 3, Lesson 11
1.4	Create and change presentation automatically	See Below
1.4.1	Change presentation orientation	Lesson 3
1.4.2	Add, change and remove transitions between slides at the presentation level	Lesson 3
1.4.3	Set slide size	Lesson 3
1.5	Arrange slides • Insert or delete slides • Use the slide sorter to organize slides • Arrange slides by cutting, pasting, and dragging in normal view	Lesson 2, Lesson 3
Creating and Formatting Slide Content		
2.1	Insert and format text boxes	See Below
2.1.1	Insert and remove text boxes	Lesson 2
2.1.2	Size text boxes	Lesson 2
2.1.3	Format text boxes • Select fill • Select border • Select effects	Lesson 2
2.1.4	Select text orientation and alignment • Set text direction • Set text alignment	Lesson 2

Microsoft Objective/Domain		Covered in Lesson Number
2.1.5	Set margins	Lesson 2
2.1.6	Create columns in text boxes	Lesson 5
2.2	Manipulate text	See Below
2.2.1	Cut, copy, and paste text • Move text using drag and drop • Copy and paste text • Cut and paste text • Cut and paste special	Lesson 3, Lesson 11
2.2.2	Apply Quick Styles from the Style Gallery	Lesson 4
2.2.3	Format font attributes • Change text size • Change text font • Change text color • Apply text such as bold, italic, underline, and shadow	Lesson 2, Lesson 11
2.2.4	Use the Format Painter to format text	Lesson 3
2.2.5	Create and format bulleted and numbered lists • Add bullets • Add numbered lists • Format bullets • Format numbered lists • Promote and demote bullets and numbering	Lesson 2
2.2.6	Format paragraphs • Align text • Change line spacing • Change indentation	Lesson 2
2.2.7	Insert and modify WordArt • Create and format WordArt • Apply Quick Styles to WordArt • Change WordArt shape	Lesson 4, Lesson 11
2.3	Add and link existing content to presentations	See Below
2.3.1	Reuse slides from an existing presentation • Apply current slide masters to content	Lesson 11, Lesson 12
2.3.2	Copy elements from one slide to another • Copy elements within presentations • Copy elements between presentations	Lesson 3, Lesson 10, Lesson 11, Lesson 12
2.3.3	Insert hyperlinks	Lesson 10
2.3.4	Insert media clips • Movies • Sounds	Lesson 10
2.4	Apply, customize, modify, and remove animations	See Below
2.4.1	Apply built-in animations	Lesson 10

Microsoft Objective/Domain		Covered in Lesson Number
2.4.2	Modify animations • Remove animations • Change animations	Lesson 10
2.4.3	Create custom animations • Insert entrance effects • Insert emphasis effects • Insert exit effects • Change effect speeds • Change start settings	Lesson 10
Working with Visual Content		
3.1	Create SmartArt diagrams	See Below
3.1.1	Create a SmartArt diagram • Relationship • Workflow • Cycle • Hierarchy	Lesson 7
3.1.2	Create SmartArt diagrams from bullet points	Lesson 7
3.2	Modify SmartArt diagrams	See Below
3.2.1	Add text to SmartArt diagrams	Lesson 7
3.2.2	Change theme colors	Lesson 7
3.2.3	Add effects using Quick Styles	Lesson 7
3.2.4	Change the layout of diagrams	Lesson 7
3.2.5	Change the orientation of charts	Lesson 7
3.2.6	Add or remove shapes within SmartArt	Lesson 7
3.2.7	Change diagram types	Lesson 7
3.3	Insert illustrations and shapes	See Below
3.3.1	Insert pictures from file	Lesson 4
3.3.2	Insert shapes • Line • Polygon • Arrow	Lesson 4
3.3.3	Insert clip art	Lesson 4
3.3.4	Add text to shapes	Lesson 4
3.4	Modify illustrations	See Below
3.4.1	Apply Quick Styles to shapes and pictures • Apply fill to shapes • Remove borders from shapes	Lesson 8, Lesson 11
3.4.2	Add, change, and remove illustration effects • Remove background (transparencies) • Modify brightness and contrast	Lesson 4, Lesson 8

Microsoft Objective/Domain		Covered in Lesson Number
3.5	Arrange illustrations and other content	See Below
3.5.1	Size, scale, and rotate illustrations and other content • Adjust size • Adjust scale • Adjust rotation	Lesson 4, Lesson 8, Lesson 9
3.5.2	Order illustrations and other content • Bring to front and send to back	Lesson 4, Lesson 9
3.5.3	Group and align illustrations and other content	Lesson 4, Lesson 9
3.5.4	Use gridlines and guides to arrange illustrations and other content	Lesson 9
3.6	Insert and modify charts	Lesson 6
3.6.1	Insert charts	Lesson 6
3.6.2	Change chart types	Lesson 6
3.6.3	Format fill and other effects	Lesson 6
3.6.4	Add chart elements • Legend • Title	Lesson 6
3.7	Insert and modify tables	Lesson 5
3.7.1	Insert tables in a slide	Lesson 5
3.7.2	Apply Quick Styles to tables	Lesson 5
3.7.3	Change alignment and orientation of table text	Lesson 5
3.7.4	Add images to tables	Lesson 5
Collaborating on and Delivering Presentations		
4.1	Review presentations	See Below
4.1.1	Insert, delete, and modify comments	Lesson 12
4.1.2	Show and hide markup	Lesson 12
4.2	Protect presentations	See Below
4.2.1	Add digital signatures to presentations • Add a digital signature • Set passwords on presentations	Lesson 14
4.3	Secure and share presentations	See Below
4.3.1	Identify presentation features not supported by previous versions	Lesson 14
4.3.2	Remove inappropriate information using Document Inspector	Lesson 14
4.3.3	Restrict permissions to a document using Information Rights Management (IRM)	Lesson 14

Microsoft Objective/Domain		Covered in Lesson Number
4.3.4	Mark presentations as final	Lesson 14
4.3.5	Compress images	Lesson 9
4.3.6	Save presentations as appropriate file types • Save files in .pps format so they open as a slide show • Save presentations for Web viewing (.html format) • Save slides as images (.jpg, .gif, .tif, etc.)	Lesson 1, Lesson 12
4.4	Prepare printed materials	See Below
4.4.1	Customize handout masters • Add headers, footers, and page numbers • Apply Quick Styles to handout masters	Lesson 11
4.4.2	Print a presentation in various formats • Slides • Handouts • Outlines • Notes	Lesson 1
4.5	Prepare for and rehearse presentation delivery	See Below
4.5.1	Show only specific slides in presentations • Hide specific slides • Create custom slide shows	Lesson 13
4.5.2	Rehearse and time the delivery of a presentation	Lesson 13
4.5.3	Use presentation tools • Use a pen and highlighter, add annotations, etc. • Navigate to specific slides	Lesson 13
4.5.4	Package presentations for a CD	Lesson 14
4.5.5	Set slide show options • Set presentations to loop continuously • Show presentation with or without narration • Select presentation resolution	Lesson 13, Lesson 14

35mm slides An output format that creates individual, 35 millimeter slides from each slide in a presentation. These slides are usually prepared by a service bureau and then arranged in a slide carousel tray to project with a 35mm projector. Excellent color is possible but room illumination must usually be reduced. (13)

3-D rotation Effect that enables the picture to be displayed in a variety of dimensional treatments. (4, 8)

Action button Button you draw on a slide that has a link associated with it. Although you generally use special shapes for action buttons, any shape or other object that you place on a slide can be set up to act as an action button. Action buttons serve the same purpose as hyperlinks. (10, 13)

Activate To select a placeholder by clicking it. An activated text placeholder can accept text that you key or it can be moved or resized. (1)

Add-ins Supplemental programs that extend the functionality of Microsoft Office. (14)

Adjustment handle Yellow diamond-shaped handle found on many shapes that is used to change a prominent feature of a shape. For example, you can change the size of an arrowhead relative to the body of the arrow, or you can change the tilt of a triangle. (4)

Album layout Used to change the layout of slides created with the Photo Album feature. (4)

Alignment In text placeholders, the left, center, right, or justify attribute for text positioning. Also refers to how objects are positioned on a slide in relation to other objects. (9)

Animate To apply movement effects for objects on a slide. (10)

Animation effects Special visual or sound effects used when objects are displayed on the screen or removed from view. (1)

Annotation pen Pointer that you can use to "draw" on the screen during a slide show presentation. Annotation pen marks can be in any color and can be saved with the presentation as drawn objects. (13)

Arrange all A feature that allows you to view multiple files at the same time. (12)

Arrowheads Shape of the tip on the end of a line. Arrowheads come in several varieties, including dots and diamonds. They can be placed on either end of a drawn line or on both ends. (8)

Aspect ratio The relationship of width to height of an object. (13)

Assistant shape Shape in an organization chart that is usually placed below a superior shape and above subordinate shapes. Usually, an assistant shape has no subordinates. (7)

AutoCorrect Feature that automatically corrects common spelling errors and typos as you key text. It can be turned on or off, and you can customize so it will find errors that you frequently make. (2)

Autofit options Contains options for fitting text into placeholders. (2)

Axis Line that borders one side of the chart plot area. A vertical (value) axis displays a range of numbers, and a horizontal (category) axis displays category names. (6)

Backward Used to adjust object stacking order and move a selected object behind another object. (9)

Bar chart A chart that compares one data element with another data element using horizontal bars. (6)

Bevel Effect that makes a picture look dimensional with several different options available. (4, 8)

Bitmap pictures Made up of tiny colored dots. The more you enlarge a bitmap, the more blurred it becomes. You can crop bitmaps and easily change the contrast and brightness. Other changes can be made only by using a paint-type graphics program. Examples of bitmaps are pictures created in a paint program, photographs and other images that come from a scanner, and images that come from a digital camera. (4)

Blank presentation One way to start a new presentation with no design elements displayed. (2)

Blank slides During a slide show the display screen can blank to black by pressing B or it can blank to white by pressing W. Pressing the same key will redisplay the current slide. (13)

Body text Text in the body of a slide or other document. On a PowerPoint slide, body text is usually placed in a body text placeholder and can be displayed as bulleted text. (1)

Brightness Adjusts the overall lightness of the colors in a picture. (4)

Bring to front Used to adjust object stacking order and move a selected object in front of all other objects. (9)

Bullet A small dot, square, or other symbol placed at the left of each item in a list or series of paragraphs. Bullets are often used in presentations and outlines. (1)

Cascade A feature that layers open presentations in separate windows that can be resized and layered. (12)

Case text Capitalization treatment: uppercase (all capital letters), lowercase (all small letters), sentence case (first letter only capitalized), title case (first letter of all words capitalized). (2)

Cell Rectangle formed by the intersection of a row and a column in a table or a worksheet. (5, 6)

Cell bevel effect A dimensional effect that can be applied to cells to give the appearance of a raised, rounded, or pressed in look. (5)

Cell margin Space between the text in a cell and its borders. (5)

Cell pointer Pointer in the shape of a white cross used to select cells in a Microsoft Excel worksheet or Microsoft Graph datasheet. (6)

Chart Diagram that displays numbers in pictorial format, such as slices of a pie shape, or rows of columns of varying height. Charts are sometimes called graphs. (6)

Chart layouts Control the position in which different chart elements appear on the chart. (6)

Chart styles Preset styles that can be applied to a chart to enhance the appearance through colors matching the document theme colors. (6)

Clip art Ready-to-use graphic images that you can insert in a presentation. (4)

Clipboard Temporary storage place for cut and copied items. Holds up to 24 items at a time. (3)

Clipboard options Allows the control of settings on the Clipboard task pane. (3)

Collate To print all the pages of a document before starting to print the first page of the next copy. When pages are not collated, all the copies of page 1 are printed first, then all the copies of page 2, etc. (1)

Column chart A chart that compares one data element with another data element using vertical bars. (6)

Columns Individual cells aligned vertically down the table or worksheet. (5)

Command buttons Buttons designed to perform a function or display a gallery of options. (1)

Comment marker Small rectangle appearing on a slide that indicates the presence of a reviewer comment. You read a comment by pointing to the comment marker. (12)

Comments Information inserted during a review of a presentation. (12)

Compatibility Checker Checks the current presentation to see if it is compatible with other versions and produces a list of items that will not be modifiable. (14)

Compatibility Mode Permits working on a presentation in a PowerPoint 97-2003 version. (14)

Compress picture An optimization feature for reducing file sizes that can be applied to one or all pictures in a presentation. It reduces a picture's resolution and discards cropped areas of a picture. (9)

Connection sites Red squares that appear on a shape, clip art, or text box object when the connector tool is active or when a connector is selected. Connection sites indicate places where a connector can be attached to an object. (4)

Connector line Straight, curved, or angled line with special endpoints that can lock onto connection sites on a shape or other PowerPoint object. (4, 9)

Connector sites Handles on an object indicating where connector lines can be attached. (9)

Constrain Used to draw objects in precise increments or proportions. For example, a line will be straight or angled in precise amounts, a rectangle will be square, and an oval will be round. When resizing an object, the correct size ratio is maintained. (2, 4)

Contiguous slides Slides that follow one after another. For example, slides numbered 2, 3, and 4 are contiguous. See "Noncontiguous slides." (3)

Continuous picture list Diagram that contains placeholders for pictures and a horizontal arrow to communicate that the items shown represent interconnected information. (7)

Contrast Adjusts the intensity of the colors in a picture by adjusting the difference between the lightest and darkest areas. (4)

Copy To copy a selected object or text from a presentation and store it on the clipboard without removing the selection from its original place. (3)

Coworker shape Shape in an organization chart that is connected to the same superior shape as another shape. (7)

Crop To trim the vertical or horizontal edges of a picture. (4)

Cropping handles Short black markers on the sides and corners of a picture selected for cropping. When you drag one of these handles with the cropping tool, an edge of the picture is cut away (trimmed). (4)

Crosshair pointer The shape of your pointer when drawing objects. (4)

Custom animation Visual effects that you create to control how text, pictures, movies, and other objects move on a slide during a slide show. May include sound. (10)

Custom animation list List on the Custom Animation task pane of all the animation effects applied to objects on the current slide. Items are listed in the order that they will occur during a slide show. (10)

Custom color Color that you mix on the Custom tab of the Colors dialog box. (8)

Custom show Presentation within a presentation. It displays only specially selected slides instead of all the slides in a slide show. (13)

Cut To remove a selected object or text from a presentation and store it on the clipboard. (3)

Cycle diagram Diagram used to illustrate a process that is continuous. (7)

Dash style Pattern of dashes and dots that make up a line. Styles include solid line, round dot, square dot, dash dot, dash, and combinations of dashes and dots. Dash styles can be applied to object outlines, borders, lines, and arrows. (8)

Data series Group of data that relates to a common object or category such as product, geographic area, or year. A single chart may display more than one data series. (6)

Datasheet Table that is part of Microsoft Graph and in which you enter numbers and labels that are used to create a chart if you do not have Microsoft Excel installed on your computer. When you start a new chart, the datasheet appears automatically, containing sample data that you can delete or overwrite. (6)

Demote To move selected text to the next-lower outline or heading level by increasing the indent level. (2)

Design template   Available online and used to add a uniform color theme and design background to each slide in a presentation. (2)

Design theme   Predesigned background graphics, theme colors, theme fonts, theme effects, and other formatting options that can be applied to presentations for a consistent presentation appearance. These can be customized for a particular topic or unique design. (3)

Destination   When working with clipboard objects, the presentation or other document in which the objects are pasted. (3)

Diagram   A visual representation of information. (7)

Digital ID   Can be created or purchased from a certificate authority and is necessary to provide a means to authenticate digital information. (14)

Digital Signature   Used to verify a document's integrity. (14)

Distribute   To evenly space selected objects, either in relation to one another or across the length or width of a slide. Objects can be distributed either horizontally or vertically. (9)

Distribute Columns   Adjusts columns to be the same width. (5)

Distribute Rows   Adjusts rows to be the same height. (5)

Document Inspector   Used to identify and remove metadata from files. (14)

Document Properties   Records metadata about the presentation file. (14)

Drag   Selecting an object then holding down the left mouse button while moving the pointer to position the object in a different location. (1)

Duplicate   To make a second copy of a selected object on the same slide. (4)

Embedded object   Object, such as an Excel chart or a Word table, that is placed in and becomes part of a PowerPoint slide. An embedded object is saved as part of the file in which it is placed. When you change an embedded object, it does not affect the original file (the source) from which it came. (14)

Emphasis effect   Animation effect applied to draw attention to an object that is already showing on a slide. (10)

Entrance effect   Animation effect applied to text or an object to control how it first appears on a slide. (10)

Eraser   Used to delete table cell borders. (5)

Exit effect   Animation effect applied to control how an object leaves (or disappears from) a slide. (10)

Explode   To move a pie slice away from other slices in a pie chart to add emphasis. (6)

Filename   Unique name given to a PowerPoint presentation file, a Word document file, or files created by other applications. (1)

Fill color   Color of a shape. Shapes can be filled with a solid color, a gradient, a texture, a picture, or have no fill at all. (8)

Find   Locates specified text in a presentation. (3)

First-line indent   Indent where the first line of the paragraph is indented farther to the right than the other lines in the paragraph. (2)

Fit to Window   Changes from the current zoom settings so the slide will fit in the window that is open. (1)

Flip   To reverse an object either horizontally or vertically, creating a mirror image of the original object. (9)

Font   A set of characters A–Z, in uppercase and lowercase, and related symbols in a specific design. (2)

Font face   Names of a set of characters with a specific design such as Times New Roman or Arial. (2)

Font size   Describes the size of a font and is measured in points. (2)

Footer   Text that appears at the bottom of each slide, notes page, or handouts page. (3)

Format Painter   Used to copy formatting from one object to another. (3)

Forward   Used to adjust object stacking order and move a selected object in front of another object. (9)

Four-pointed arrow   Used to move placeholders and other objects without resizing them. Can also select text in a bulleted list by clicking the bullet. (2)

Gallery   A collection of thumbnails displaying different effect options you can choose. (1)

Gear diagram   Diagram that illustrates interlocking ideas. (7)

Glow   Effect that adds a soft color around the object edges that makes the object stand out from the background. (4, 8)

Go to slide   A feature available using the right-click menu during a slide show that allows you to skip forward or backward in a presentation to a certain slide. (13)

Gradient fill   Shape fill effect in which one color blends or fades into one or more colors. (8)

Graph   See "Chart." (6)

Grayscale   Displays slides in shades of gray for printing on a black-and-white printer. (1)

Grid   A set of intersecting lines used to align objects that you can show or hide. (4)

Gridlines   The background lines on a chart that aid interpretation of data quantities. (6)

Group   To combine selected objects so that they behave as one object. (4, 9)

Groups   Command buttons are broken into logical groups by type of task. (1)

Guides   Horizontal and vertical lines used to align objects. Guides do not display in Slide Show view or when printed. (4)

Handout   Printout that contains one, two, three, four, six, or nine PowerPoint slides on a page. (1)

Handout master   Used to control how objects are positioned on each printed handout page. Often includes header or footer text, date, and page numbers; graphic elements such as a company logo can be included, also. (11)

Hanging indent   Indent where the first line extends farther to the left than the rest of the paragraph. Also can be used to describe a format of displaying an organization chart where each shape is displayed hanging under their superior and coworker shapes. (2, 7)

Header   Text that appears at the top of each slide, notes page, or handouts page. (3)

Help   A reference tool for getting assistance with PowerPoint. (1)

Hide slides   Slides can remain in a presentation file but be hidden when you run a presentation. This feature is available from the Slide Show tab. (13)

Hierarchy diagram   Diagram that illustrates reporting relationships or lines of authority between employees in a company. (7)

HTML   Acronym for Hypertext Markup Language. See "Hypertext Markup Language." (14)

Hue   The name of a color that you select. (8)

Hyperlink   Text or graphic object you click to move to another slide, another application, or a location on the Internet. Text hyperlinks are displayed with an underline. (10, 13)

Hypertext Markup Language   File format used to make a file readable when using a browser on the Internet or on an intranet. (14)

I-beam   Pointer that has the shape of an uppercase "I." The I-beam pointer is used to select text or mark the location where you can insert text. (1)

Indent markers   Two small triangles and one small rectangle that appear on the ruler to control the indents. (2)

Information Rights Management   A method to control access and restrict usage. (14)

Insertion point   Vertical flashing bar indicating the position where text that you key will be inserted. Clicking an I-beam pointer is one way to place an insertion point. (1)

Keyword   Word or words that describe the subject matter of your clip art search. (4)

Kiosk   A continuously running presentation to be viewed by an individual who is controlling the slide show. (13)

Landscape   A horizontal orientation for slides or printed pages; the opposite of Portrait. (1)

Layer   When several objects are inserted in the same area, layers occur. You can change the stacking order of the layers. (9)

Legend   Box showing the colors and formatting assigned to the data series or categories in a chart. (6)

Level   In organization charts, the position in the hierarchy of the organization being diagrammed. (7)

Line spacing   The spacing between lines of text within and between paragraphs. (2)

Line weight   Thickness of a line measured in points. (4)

Linked object   Object, such as an Excel chart or Word table, that is displayed within a document (the destination) created by a different program. A linked object is a pointer to an external file (the source) that contains the data. Only the pointer is saved with the document in which it is placed. When changes are made to a linked object, you are making changes to the actual file that was used to create the object. (12)

List diagram   Diagram that provides an alternative to listing text in bulleted lists. (7)

Live Preview   A feature that allows you to see exactly what your changes will look like before selecting an effect. (1)

Lock drawing mode   Enables drawing the same shape multiple times without having to reactivate the shape tool. (4)

Locked aspect ratio   Keeps the aspect that the object currently has, so both sides will be resized in perspective. (8)

Logo   A symbol of an organization; usually includes text and images. (12)

Luminance   The brightness of a color. (8)

Mark as final   Changes the presentation to a read-only file. (14)

Matrix diagram   Diagram that allows placement of concepts along two axes or in related quadrants. (7)

Merge cells   To combine two or more table cells into one larger cell. (5)

Metadata   Electronic data that describes presentation data including personal information about the author or the presentation that you may not want to share. (14)

Microsoft Office Button   Button that provides access to opening, saving, printing, and sharing your PowerPoint file with others. (1)

Microsoft Windows Metafile   A vector graphics format used mostly for clip art. (9)

Motion paths   Paths that an object follows as part of an animation effect. (10)

Movie   Any motion file such as an animated clip art file or a video file. Movies can be inserted on slides in the same way as clip art. These are also called movie clips and they play during a slide show. (10)

Narration   Audio comments that can be recorded before or during a presentation. (14)

Noncontiguous slides   Slides that do not follow one after another. For example, slides numbered 1, 4, 5, and 7 are noncontiguous. See "Contiguous slides." (3)

Normal indent   Indent where all lines are indented the same amount from the left margin. (2)

Normal view   This view provides one place for viewing the different parts of your presentation and displays the Slides and Outline pane, Slide pane, and Notes pane. (1)

Notes master Used to control how objects are positioned on each printed notes page. Often includes header or footer text, date, and page numbers; graphic elements such as a company logo can be included, also. (11)

Notes pane Area where you can add presentation notes for either the presenter or the audience. The Notes pane is located below the Slide pane. (1)

Nudge To move an object in very small increments by using the arrow keys. (2, 4)

Offsets Used to determine how much to scale a picture to fit a shape. (8)

Organization chart Diagram used to show the relationships and reporting structure of the people in an organization in a hierarchical format. (7)

Overhead transparencies An output format that creates individual transparency sheets for projecting with an overhead projector when computer projection is not available. Transparencies can be prepared with an inkjet printer, a laser printing, or a photocopier. (13)

Package for CD Saves a presentation and all the files that link to it for display on a different computer. A viewer can be included so the presentation will display without PowerPoint being loaded. (14)

Paste To insert an item stored on the clipboard at the current location. (3)

Paste options A button appears near a pasted item when the source formatting is different from the formatting of the destination presentation. (3)

Pencil pointer Used to draw and recolor table borders and cells. (5)

Photo album Creates a presentation consisting mostly of pictures that can be formatted to create electronic scrapbooks or photo albums. (4)

Picture border The line that surrounds pictures. (4)

Picture effects Many customizable special effects are available to apply to pictures such as shadows, glow, bevel effects, and soft edges. (4)

Picture shape Used to change the shape of a picture to any of the shapes in the Shapes gallery. (4)

Picture style A selection of preset treatments that can be applied to pictures to enhance the appearance of pictures. (4)

Pie chart A chart that shows the proportions of individual components compared to the whole. (6)

Pixels Small elements that make up the image displayed on your computer screen. In general, the higher the number, the clearer the image. (13)

Placeholder Box that can contain title text, body text, pictures, or other objects. Most slide layouts contain placeholders. A placeholder's formatting, size, and position is set on a master slide and can be customized. (1)

Plot area The area of a chart that displays the shapes such as bars or pie slices that represent the data. (6)

Points The measurement unit of font size; one inch has 72 points. (2)

Portable Document Format (PDF) Preserves document formatting for viewing online or printing as originally designed. This format is useful for commercial printing. (14)

Portrait A vertical orientation for slides or printed pages where the slide or page is taller than it is wide; the opposite of landscape. (1)

Presenter view Enables the display of a presentation on two computer screens including one for the audience view and one for the presenter. (13)

Print preview Feature that enables you to see what your printed pages will look like before you actually print them. You can view preview pages in black and white, grayscale, or color. (1)

Process diagram Reflects concepts or events that occur sequentially. (7)

Promote To move selected text to the next-higher outline or heading level by decreasing the indent. (2)

Proofreaders' marks Special notation used to mark up a printed draft with changes to be made before final printing. Some proofreaders' marks might be confusing if you are unfamiliar with them. For example, a handwritten "=" indicates that a hyphen is to be inserted. (1)

Proportions Relationship between the height and width of an object. When an object is resized, its proportions will be preserved if both the height and width of the object change at the same rate or percentage. An object that is out of proportion is either too tall and skinny, or too short and wide. (4)

Pure Black and White Print option that converts all colors to either black or white, eliminating shades of gray. (1)

Pyramid diagram Diagram that illustrates relationships based on a foundation. (7)

Quick Access toolbar Toolbar that is located at the top of the PowerPoint window by default and provides access to commands that are used frequently. (1)

Quick Styles A gallery of preset effects used to change the appearance of shapes. (7)

Radial diagram Diagram that illustrates relationships focused on or directed from a central element. (7)

Recolor Used to change to different color modes or change to light and dark variations of the presentation's theme colors. (4, 9)

Redo Reverses a previous action such as an editing change. Up to 20 actions can be reversed if the save feature has not been used. (3)

Reflection An effect that gives the illusion that the object is reflecting off water by displaying a lighter transparent copy of the object. (4, 5, 8)

Regroup Recombine objects that were at one time part of the same group. (4, 9)

Rehearse timings A PowerPoint feature used to record the amount of time you spent on each slide as you practice a presentation. It could also be used to control the speed of advancing slides when audio is recorded to support a self-running presentation. (13)

Relationship diagram   Diagram that shows interconnected, hierarchical, proportional, or overlapping relationships. Some of these diagrams also appear in other categories. (7)

Replace   Locates specified text in a presentation and replaces it with different text that you specify. (3)

Research   Searches reference materials such as dictionaries, encyclopedias, and translation services to find information you need. (3)

Reset picture   Used to return a picture to its original state after its colors have been changed. (4)

Resolution   The image clarity or sharpness that is directly related to the number of pixels available to create the image. (13)

Reuse slides   Brings in slides from alternate locations and reuses them in the current presentation. (12)

Reveal slides   Used to display slides that are marked as hidden in a presentation. This feature is available from the Slide Show tab. (13)

Ribbon   Consists of task-oriented tabs that each contain commands organized in logical groups. (1)

Rotate   To change the positioning of an object determined in degree increments or freely turn it using the rotation handle. (2, 9)

Rotation handle   Green handle that appears above a selected object. You change the rotation of an object by dragging the rotation handle. (4)

Rows   Individual cells arranged across the table or worksheet horizontally. (5)

Saturation   The intensity of a color. (8)

Scale   Specifies the range of values on a chart's value axis and the interval between values. (6)

Screen capture   A picture of the screen at any given moment. Can be displayed on slides and printed documents. (12)

ScreenTip   Box that identifies the name of an on-screen object when you point to the object. (1)

Scroll bars   Used in several areas of the application window to move what you see right or left, and up or down. You can also use the vertical scroll bar to move from slide to slide. (1)

Selection rectangle   The shape that you draw by dragging the pointer to select objects on a slide. All objects contained inside the shape are selected. (4)

Send to back   Used to adjust object stacking order and move a selected object behind all other objects. (9)

Service bureau   Business that translates computer files into high-quality output in various media, such as slide transparencies, high-resolution full-color prints, and large-format prints. (13)

Shadow   An effect that gives the illusion that there is light shining on an object producing a shadow. (4, 5, 8)

Shape   One of a group of predefined shapes that are easy to draw. Available shapes include rectangles, circles, arrows, flowchart symbols, stars, banners, callouts, lines, and connectors. (4)

Shape outline   The line that goes around the edge of a shape that can be modified by changing the weight, the color, or the dash style of the line. (8)

Show markup   Feature that can be turned on or off and enables you to see the comments in a presentation. (12)

Sizing handles   Small circles and squares around placeholders and other objects used to resize them. (2)

Slide layouts   Contain placeholders for slide content such as titles, bulleted lists, charts, and shapes. (2, 11)

Slide master   Used to control colors, fonts, placeholders, and background graphics for slides created with the layout and will carry those changes throughout the presentation. (11)

Slide pane   Area where you create, edit, and display presentation slides. (1)

Slide show   The view that displays slides sequentially in full-screen size. Slides can advance manually or automatically with slide timings using a variety of transition effects. Slide shows can display movies and animated elements. (1)

Slide Sorter view   Displays several thumbnails of slides making it easy to reorder, add, delete, or duplicate slides and set transition effects. (1, 3)

Slide thumbnail   Miniature version of a graphic image. In PowerPoint, a miniature version of a slide is often referred to as a "thumbnail." (1)

Slide transition   Visual effect that you can apply to enhance the way the screen changes during a slide show as you move from one slide to another. For example, the current slide could fade to a black screen before the next slide appears. (3)

Slides and Outline pane   Area that can display either an outline of the presentation's text or thumbnails of the presentation's slides. You choose either Outline or Slides by clicking the appropriate tab. (1)

SmartArt graphic   Categorized in seven major types of diagrams that produce a professional-looking visual representation of information. (7)

Snap to grid   Feature that causes objects to align on the grid that may or may not be visible when working on a slide. (4)

Soft edges   Effect that changes a picture's normal hard edges to a soft, feathered appearance that gradually fades into the background color. (4, 8)

Sound files   These files can be inserted on a slide or associated with a custom animation. (10)

Source   When working with clipboard objects, the presentation or other document from which the objects were cut or copied. (3)

Source formatting   The formatting of text and other elements that appear in the document from which the objects were cut or copied. (3)

Spell checker   Feature that corrects spelling by comparing words to an internal dictionary file. (3)

Split cells   To divide a table cell into two smaller cells. (5)

Standard   A format of displaying an organization chart where each shape is displayed in a hierarchy format. (7)

Standard color   Premixed color on the Standard tab of the Colors dialog box. (8)

Status bar   Displays information about the presentation you're working on. It is located at the bottom of the PowerPoint window. (1)

Stock photography   Microsoft's online collection of photo images that can be searched by keyword. (4)

Subordinate shape   Shape in an organization chart that is connected to a superior shape reflecting a higher level. (7)

Table   Organized arrangement of information in rows and columns. (5)

Table borders   The lines forming the edges of cells, columns, rows, and the outside border of the table. (5)

Table style   Combination of formatting options, including color combinations based on theme colors. (5)

Tabs   Designed to be task oriented and contain groups of commands. Also, tabs can be used to align and indent text on a slide. Tab stops appear on the horizontal ruler. (1, 5)

Task pane   Area that appears at appropriate times on the right side of the PowerPoint window, displaying a list of commands that are relevant to certain tasks on which you are currently working. (3)

Text box   A free-form text object used to add text to slides. (2)

Text fill   Fill of WordArt and other text that can be a solid color, gradient fill, or other fill. (4)

Text outline   Outline of WordArt and other text that can be modified in color and thickness. (4)

Theme colors   Preset groups of colors for text, background, accent, and hyperlink colors. (2, 3, 11)

Theme effects   Selection of built-in effects that are applied to a presentation. (3)

Theme fonts   Selection of fonts that can be applied to a presentation. (3)

Themes   Provide attractive backgrounds to ensure that the look of the presentation is kept consistent. (11)

Thesaurus   Finds words with similar meanings. (3)

Tick marks   Small measurement marks, similar to the marks on a ruler, that cross a chart value or category axis. (6)

Title text   Text that usually appears at the top of a PowerPoint slide. Title text is usually placed in a title text placeholder. (1)

Toggle button   Switches between on and off when clicked. (2)

Transform   Effect that changes your text into different shapes. (4)

Transition effects   Visual or sound effects used when changing between slides. (1)

Transition, Slide   See "Slide transition." (3)

Transparency   Allows the color behind an object to show through. (8)

TrueType font   Font faces that are available universally on computers. (2)

Undo   Reverses the last action such as an editing change. PowerPoint can undo up to 20 actions if the Save feature has not been used. (3)

Ungroup   To separate a group of objects. When an object is ungrouped, each of its parts behaves as an individual object. (4, 9)

Vector drawing   Picture made up of an arrangement of line segments and shapes that can be scaled to any size or aspect ratio without blurring. Vector drawings can be modified in PowerPoint by recoloring and by adding, removing, and rearranging individual elements. A shape is an example of a simple vector drawing. (4)

View buttons   Three buttons located on the lower-right corner of the PowerPoint window. You use these buttons to switch between Normal view (the default), Slide Sorter view, and Slide Show view. (1)

Weight   Thickness of a line measured in points. (8)

Word wrap   Text wraps to the next line when you reach the end of a placeholder or text box. (2)

WordArt   Text objects you create with special shading, shapes, and 3-D effects. (4)

Worksheet   Area in Microsoft Excel in which you enter numbers and labels that are used to create a chart. When you create a new chart, the worksheet in Microsoft Excel appears automatically, containing sample data that you can delete or overwrite. (6)

XML Paper Specification (XPS)   Preserves document formatting for viewing online or printing as originally designed. (14)

Zoom   Used in several areas of the application window to change the size at which you view that area. (1)